International Dispute Settlement

The Library of Essays in International Law

General Editor: Robert McCorquodale

Titles in the Series

International Human Rights Law, Volumes I and II
Michael Addo

International Law and Indigenous Peoples
S. James Anaya

Law of the Sea
Hugo Caminos

Humanitarian Law
Judith Gardam

International Economic Regulation
Jane Kelsey

Sources of International Law
Martti Koskenniemi

Self-Determination in International Law
Robert McCorquodale

International Dispute Settlement
Mary Ellen O'Connell

International Crimes
Nikos Passas

International Environmental Law, Volumes I and II
Paula M. Pevato

State Responsibility in International Law
René Provost

Jurisdiction in International Law
Michael Reisman

Title to Territory
Malcolm Shaw

The Nature of International Law
Gerry Simpson

Collective Security Law
Nigel D. White

International Dispute Settlement

Edited by

Mary Ellen O'Connell

Michael E. Moritz College of Law, The Ohio State University, USA

ASHGATE
DARTMOUTH

Published by
Ashgate Publishing Limited
Wey Court East
Union Road
Farnham
Surrey, GU9 7PT
England

Ashgate Publishing Company
110 Cherry Street
Suite 3-1
Burlington
VT 05401-3818
USA

Ashgate website: http://www.ashgate.com

British Library Cataloguing in Publication Data
International dispute settlement. – (The library of essays in
  international law)
  1. Pacific settlement of international disputes
  I. O'Connell, Mary Ellen, 1958–
  341.5

Library of Congress Cataloging-in-Publication Data
International dispute settlement / edited by Mary Ellen O'Connell.
      p. cm.
  Includes bibliographical references.
  ISBN 978-0-7546-2236-9
      1. Pacific settlement of international disputes. 2. Diplomatic negotiations in
  international disputes. I. O'Connell, Mary Ellen, 1958–

  JZ6010 .I575 2002
  327.1'7—dc21

2002019416

ISBN 978-0-7546-2236-9

Transfered to Digital Printing in 2010

 MIX
Paper from
responsible sources
FSC
www.fsc.org   FSC® C013985

Printed in the United Kingdom by Henry Ling Limited,
at the Dorset Press, Dorchester, DT1 1HD

International Dispute Settlement

Edited by

Mary Ellen O'Connell

Michael E. Moritz College of Law, The Ohio State University, USA

ASHGATE
DARTMOUTH

Published by
Ashgate Publishing Limited
Wey Court East
Union Road
Farnham
Surrey, GU9 7PT
England

Ashgate Publishing Company
110 Cherry Street
Suite 3-1
Burlington
VT 05401-3818
USA

Ashgate website: http://www.ashgate.com

British Library Cataloguing in Publication Data
International dispute settlement. – (The library of essays in
   international law)
   1. Pacific settlement of international disputes
   I. O'Connell, Mary Ellen, 1958–
   341.5

Library of Congress Cataloging-in-Publication Data
International dispute settlement / edited by Mary Ellen O'Connell.
      p. cm.
   Includes bibliographical references.
   ISBN 978-0-7546-2236-9
      1. Pacific settlement of international disputes. 2. Diplomatic negotiations in
   international disputes. I. O'Connell, Mary Ellen, 1958–

   JZ6010 .I575 2002
   327.1'7—dc21

                                                                    2002019416

ISBN 978-0-7546-2236-9

Transfered to Digital Printing in 2010

Printed in the United Kingdom by Henry Ling Limited,
at the Dorset Press, Dorchester, DT1 1HD

Contents

Acknowledgements

The editor and publishers wish to thank the following for permission to use copyright material.

American Society of International Law for the essays: B.G. Ramcharan (1982), 'The Good Offices of the United Nations Secretary-General in the Field of Human Rights', *American Journal of International Law*, **76**, pp. 130–41. Copyright © 1982 American Society of International Law; Lori Fisler Damrosch (1980), 'Retaliation or Arbitration – or Both? The 1978 United States-France Aviation Dispute', *American Journal of International Law*, **74**, pp. 785–807. Copyright © 1980 American Society of International Law; David D. Caron (1990), 'The Nature of the Iran–United States Claims Tribunal and the Evolving Structure of International Dispute Resolution', *American Journal of International Law*, **84**, pp. 104–56. Copyright © 1990 American Society of International Law; Robert Y. Jennings (1995), 'The Proliferation of Adjudicatory Bodies: Dangers and Possible Answers', *American Society of International Law Bulletin*, **9**, pp. 2–7. Copyright © American Society of International Law; Rosalyn Higgins (1970), 'The Place of International Law in the Settlement of Disputes by the Security Council', *American Journal of International Law*, **64**, pp. 1–18. Copyright © 1970 American Society of International Law. Reprinted with permission.

Blackwell Publishing Ltd for the essay: Ernst-Ulrich Petersmann (1988), 'Strengthening GATT Procedures for Settling Trade Disputes', *World Economy*, **11**, pp. 55–89.

Emory International Law Review for the essay: Richard B. Bilder (1986), 'An Overview of International Dispute Settlement', *Journal of International Dispute Resolution*, **1**, pp. 1–32.

Hart Publishing Ltd for the essay: Christine Chinkin (1998), 'Alternative Dispute Resolution under International Law', in Malcolm Evans (ed.), *Remedies in International Law: The Institutional Dilemma*, Oxford: Hart Publishing, pp. 123–40.

Indiana International & Comparative Law Review for the essay: M. Cherif Bassiouni (1991), 'The Time Has Come for an International Criminal Court', *Indiana International and Comparative Law Review*, **1**, pp. 1–43.

Kluwer Academic/Plenum Publishers for the essay: Thomas Princen (1987), 'International Mediation – The View from the Vatican: Lessons from Mediating the Beagle Channel Dispute', *Negotiation Journal*, **3**, pp. 347–66. Copyright © 1987 Plenum Publishing Corporation.

MIT Press Journals for the essay: Robert O. Keohane, Andrew Moravcsik and Anne-Marie Slaughter (2000), 'Legalized Dispute Resolution: Interstate and Transnational', *International Organization*, **54**, pp. 457–88. Copyright © 2000 IO Foundation and the Massachusetts Institute of Technology.

Oxford University Press for the essay: Hazel Fox (1988), 'States and the Undertaking to Arbitrate', *International and Comparative Law Quarterly*, **37**, pp. 1–29.

Royal Institute of International Affairs for the essays: Charles Cheney Hyde (1929), 'The Place of Commissions of Inquiry and Conciliation Treaties in the Peaceful Settlement of International Disputes', *British Yearbook of International Law*, **10**, pp. 96–110; C.H.M. Waldock (1957), 'Decline of the Optional Clause', *British Yearbook of International Law*, **32**, pp. 244–87.

San Diego Law Review for the essay: Louis B. Sohn (1975), 'Settlement of Disputes Arising Out of the Law of the Sea Convention', *San Diego Law Review*, **12**, pp. 495–517. Copyright © 1975 San Diego Law Review. Reprinted with the permission of the San Diego Law Review.

University of Cincinnati for the essay: Richard B. Lillich (1985), 'Invoking International Human Rights Law in Domestic Courts', *University of Cincinnati Law Review*, **54**, pp. 367–415.

US Naval War College for the essay: Richard Ned Lebow (1978), 'Accidents and Crises: The Dogger Bank Affair', *Naval War College Review*, **31**, pp. 66–75.

Every effort has been made to trace all the copyright holders, but if any have been inadvertently overlooked the publishers will be pleased to make the necessary arrangement at the first opportunity.

Personal Acknowledgement

I wish to thank my secretary, Michele Whetzel-Newton, for her assistance.

Series Preface

Open a newspaper, listen to the radio or watch television any day of the week and you will read or hear of some matter concerning international law. The range of matters include the extent to which issues of trade and human rights should be linked, concerns about refugees and labour conditions, negotiations of treaties and the settlement of disputes, and decisions by the United Nations Security Council concerning actions to ensure compliance with international law. International legal issues have impact on governments, corporations, organisations and people around the world and the process of globalisation has increased this impact. In the global legal environment, knowledge of international law is an indispensable tool for all scholars, legal practitioners, decision-makers and citizens of the 21st century.

The Library of Essays in International Law is designed to provide the essential elements for the development of this knowledge. Each volume contains essays of central importance in the development of international law in a subject area. The proliferation of legal and other specialist journals, the increase in international materials and the use of the internet, has meant that it is increasingly difficult for legal scholars to have access to all the relevant articles on international law and many valuable older articles are now unable to be obtained readily. These problems are addressed by this series, which makes available an extensive range of materials in a manner that is of immeasurable value for both teaching and research at all levels.

Each volume is written by a leading authority in the subject area who selects the articles and provides an informative introduction, which analyses the context of the articles and comments on their significance within the developments in that area. The volumes complement each other to give a clear view of the burgeoning area of international law. It is not an easy task to select, order and place in context essays from the enormous quantity of academic legal writing prublished in journals – in many languages – throughout the world. This task requires professional scholarly judgment and difficult choices. The editors in this series have done an excellent job, for which I thank and congratulate them. It has been a pleasure working with them.

ROBERT McCORQUODALE
General Series Editor
School of Law
University of Nottingham

Introduction

Law's purpose is to settle 'by authority of the group various types of questions of concern to the group' (O'Connell, 1999, p. 336, quoting Hart and Sacks, 1994, p. lxxxiii). International law, like national law, uses both substantive rules as well as procedures to settle international society's questions. Procedures are central to any legal system's ability to accomplish the basic purpose of settlement. Procedures perform two functions. First, they provide the means to interpret, apply and enforce the substantive rules of law and, in addition, they can be used to settle society's questions in areas where the existing substantive rules prove vague or inadequate. While, in many important respects, the procedures of international dispute settlement are remarkably similar to those of national legal systems, they also have important differences. The essays in this volume analyse the procedures of international law for settling international society's questions. After some further comments regarding the goals of international dispute settlement, this Introduction describes generally what those procedures are, the principles that govern them, and how they developed.

The Goals of International Dispute Settlement

In international society, the failure to settle disputed questions has, at times, resulted in widespread conflict and war. Providing effective alternatives to war for the settlement of disputes is the ultimate goal of this branch of international law. In addition, international dispute settlement has the intermediate goals of implementing the law and otherwise promoting international society's interests. Thus, according to Sohn:

> The need to provide adequate means for the settlement of international disputes is related to two fundamental problems of international law – the necessity to prevent escalation of conflicts between states into breaches of the peace, and the requirement of providing proper procedures for the interpretation and application of rules of international law, both customary and conventional. (Sohn, 1983, p. 1121)

Supporting legal rules through interpretation and application of law also serves the goal of preserving the peace, in ways more indirect than preventing a conflict from escalating. In either respect, the means of dispute settlement in international law serve to preserve the peace. In this aim, international law is not unlike national law. There, too, a primary purpose, if not *the* primary purpose, in resolving or settling questions is to prevent unresolved issues from turning into disputes, especially disputes that parties might attempt to resolve through violence. National law seeks to prevent interpersonal violence; international law seeks to prevent violence at the interstate level.

Collier and Lowe express a somewhat different view of dispute settlement. While they agree that: '[t]here is a widespread assumption that in a successful legal system disputes should be avoided, or a least resolved quickly and peacefully', they suggest: 'It is assumed that disputes – or, more strictly, the conflicts from which disputes emerge – are not wholly undesirable but have certain valuable characteristics, and that the proper function of law is to manage, rather than to suppress or resolve, conflict' (Collier and Lowe, 1999, p. 1). While it is true that conflict cannot be wholly eliminated, nor, as the writers say, would that necessarily be entirely good for society, on the other hand, successful legal systems should be able to help resolve disputes when parties positively seek resolution. More importantly, all legal systems should surely aim at preventing the violence that can result when disputes are not resolved. Dispute settlement systems should be able to resolve these disputes quickly and peacefully. They need more than management, and it is clear from the history of international dispute settlement that scholars and activists have consistently sought more – they have sought the means to preserve peace.

Yet, with so much war and violence in the world, it might be concluded that international procedures for peaceful settlement have failed in the pursuit of the ultimate goal of war avoidance. Of course we can find many important examples of failure, but the essays in this volume provide many examples of success, too. The story of international dispute settlement that follows is not one of cynicism or pessimism. Rather, it is a story of continuing efforts to improve and expand the means of peaceful settlement. It is a positive story full of evidence of ever better, more effective, procedures in the pursuit of peace.

The Principles and Procedures of International Dispute Settlement

The phrase 'international dispute settlement' is used synonymously with the phrases 'international dispute resolution' and 'peaceful settlement of disputes'. All three phrases refer to ending disagreements on the international plane without resort to violence. The study of international dispute settlement is the study of international disputes, disputants, the substantive obligations requiring peaceful resolution and, most of all, the means developed under international law for resolving disputes without force or coercion.

Overview

The volume's first essay by Richard Bilder, 'An Overview of International Dispute Settlement' (Chapter 1) provides a comprehensive look at the principles of dispute settlement and the means of settlement. It also discusses the meaning of basic terms such as 'dispute' within the field of dispute settlement. Not all international disagreements come within the scope of international dispute settlement. The Permanent Court of International Justice defined a dispute as a 'disagreement on a point of law or fact, a conflict of legal views or of interests between two persons'.[1] According to Merrills (1991, p. 1), 'A dispute may be defined as a specific disagreement concerning a matter of fact, law or policy in which a claim or assertion of one party is met with refusal, counter-claim or denial by another' (see also Chinkin and Sadurska, 1991). The International Court of Justice (ICJ) emphasized in the *Headquarters Agreement Case*[2] that the meaning of 'dispute' is important because the obligations in the area of international dispute settlement revolve around disputes, rather than lesser or greater sorts of issues between states. Thus, the United Nations Charter, Article 2(3), requires that '[a]ll members shall settle their international *disputes* by peaceful means in such a manner that international peace and security, and justice, are not endangered'.[3] Disputes must be resolved peacefully, but states may use armed force in self-defence if faced with an armed attack. At the opposite extreme, a mere difference of opinion, as opposed to a dispute, will not trigger binding commitments to enter into consultations, arbitration or adjudication.

One of the oldest discussions among international lawyers working in the area of dispute resolution concerns whether all disputes are amenable to settlement through dispute resolution mechanisms. Early in the twentieth century, lawyers held the firm belief that some disputes must be excluded from the jurisdiction of courts and tribunals as non-justiciable.[4] So, should we leave some disputes out of the discussion because they are not 'justiciable' owing to their political, normative or aesthetic nature (Collier and Lowe, 1999, pp. 10–16)? This approach is reflected in Article 36(2) of the Statute of the International Court of Justice (ICJ), which sets out the Court's jurisdiction enumerating the disputes it could consider, including:

> All legal disputes concerning: a. the interpretation of a treaty; b. any questions of international law; c. the existence of any fact which, if established, would constitute a breach of an international obligation; d. the nature or extent of the reparation to be made for the breach of an international obligation.

In 1984 the United States urged that a decision by the ICJ in a case brought against it by Nicaragua would violate an international law 'political question' doctrine.[5] The Court ruled that there was no such doctrine in international law. Today, courts and tribunals take on disputes of every conceivable category, as long as they can be characterized as involving a question of law or fact. The mechanisms of negotiation, mediation and conciliation are not even that limited. Nevertheless, some important dispute settlement agreements still deliberately omit dispute settlement mechanisms or make exceptions for certain categories of disputes. Those exceptions, however, tend to indicate where states remain unready to submit to dispute settlement, rather than any *a priori* understanding that the certain disputes are not susceptible of settlement through dispute settlement procedures.[6]

An international dispute can involve states (including quasi-states and state-like entities), intergovernmental organizations, and natural and juridical persons, including, most importantly, non-governmental organizations (NGOs) and multinational corporations. To some extent, the procedures for peaceful settlement can accommodate any combination of disputants and have done so since Hugo Grotius, credited by many scholars with founding modern international law, wrote his seminal work, *De Jure Belli Ac Pacis*, in 1623–24.[7] Centuries before Grotius, law prohibited piracy by individuals, and the courts of the day could interpret, apply and enforce this law. Evidence also exists of arbitration between the Greek city states from as early as 600 BC (Verzijl, 1976, p. 72). Commercial interests, too, made claims on states, which were regularly resolved by claims commissions, like those provided for in the Jay Treaty of 1794 between the United States and Britain (Simpson and Fox, 1959, pp. 1–4). As early as 1804, with the establishment of the first international organizations, those entities, too, were subject to international law and could participate in international dispute settlement procedures (Riggs and Plato, 1994, p. 3). Today states still continue to have the most complete set of rights and obligations on the international plane, including the widest access and responsibility regarding dispute settlement. Nevertheless, the study of international dispute settlement includes the study of a wide group of disputants in many possible combinations, when the dispute involves rights or duties under international law or when the disputants have chosen a procedure for peaceful settlement established under international law.

Article 33 of the United Nations Charter sets out the classic procedures available under international law for disputants to resolve their disputes. It also refers to several of the general principles of dispute settlement. Article 33 provides:

> (1) The parties to any dispute, the continuance of which is likely to endanger the maintenance of international peace and security, shall, first of all, seek a solution by negotiation, enquiry, mediation, conciliation, arbitration, judicial settlement, resort to regional agencies or arrangements, or other peaceful means of their own choice. (2) The Security Council shall, when it deems necessary, call upon the parties to settle their disputes by such means.

The reference in Article 33 to judicial settlement may encompass resort to international, as well as national, courts.[8] Traditionally, the study of dispute settlement in international law is organized around these classic procedures referred to in Article 33 (see Merrills, 1999; Collier and Lowe, 1999), often divided between the diplomatic or non-binding methods (negotiation, mediation, inquiry and conciliation) and the legal or binding methods (arbitration or judicial settlement). Article 33 does not mandate that states choose any particular means for settling disputes, nor that they actually settle or even attempt to settle disputes. The Charter only requires that if states do attempt to resolve a dispute, they reject the use of violence. Article 33 supports the free choice of means by parties, and even the simultaneous use of several means. The International Court of Justice supported this general principle in the *Aegean Sea Case* when it decided that negotiations could continue even while adjudication was underway, because the 'fact that negotiations are being actively pursued during the present proceedings, is not, legally, any obstacle to the exercise by the Court of its judicial function'.[9] The United Nations General Assembly has reiterated and reaffirmed these principles on several occasions.[10]

In addition to these general principles, dispute settlement in international law is characterized by its consensual nature in contrast to domestic legal dispute settlement. Sovereign states generally must have given their consent at some point before they are obliged to negotiate, arbitrate or litigate. On the other hand, a number of important multilateral conventions require parties, when joining, to agree to some form of compulsory dispute settlement. This means that states are finding themselves before international courts and tribunals without giving consent in a specific case on an increasingly frequent basis. Moreover, all subjects of international law are finding themselves compelled to answer for violations of international law in domestic courts as these courts systematically remove the barriers to jurisdiction. Richard Lillich's essay, 'Invoking International Human Rights Law in Domestic Courts' (Chapter 14), describes the well-known case of *Filartiga* v. *Pena-Irala*,[11] which is the *locus classicus* of the contemporary movement towards the interpretation, application and enforcement of international law in national courts. As a result of these developments, the principle of consent is no longer the central, defining principle of dispute settlement it once was. On the other hand, with the growing use of dispute settlement mechanisms in international law, new principles are emerging, the most important of which is arguably the general principle that participation in any attempt to settle disputes must be undertaken in good faith. Good faith, as defined by O'Connor (1991, p. 121) is 'directly related to honesty, fairness and reasonableness . . . and it is determined at any particular time by the compelling standards of honesty, fairness and reasonableness prevailing in the international community at that time'.

This conclusion regarding the requirement of good faith is not based on the explicit statements of any single authority, although it is found throughout dispute settlement agreements and has been applied as a dispute settlement principle by the ICJ. The Vienna Convention on the Law of Treaties, for example, provides that: 'Every treaty in force is binding upon the parties to it and must be performed by them in good faith.' [12] Thus, to the extent that a dispute settlement obligation is a treaty-based obligation, states must perform in good faith. The World Trade Organization (WTO) Dispute Settlement Understanding provides explicitly that 'If a request for consultations is made pursuant to a covered agreement, the Member to which the request is made shall, . . . reply to the request within 10 days after the date of its receipt and shall enter into consultations in good faith. . . .'[13] The Iran–US Claims Tribunal decided in 1987, in *Case No. A21*, that for the United States to fulfil its good faith obligation, it had to provide for enforcement of Tribunal decisions against US nationals in US courts.[14] In the *Fisheries Jurisdiction Case*, the ICJ found that Iceland, Germany and Britain had a customary law-based obligation to negotiate and to conduct the negotiations in good faith.[15] Finally, the proper functioning of any dispute settlement mechanism depends on participants acting in good faith. This fact alone qualifies good faith as a general principle of dispute settlement (Bin Cheng, 1953).

Negotiation and Consultation

International dispute settlement is characterized by a wide array of possible disputes and disputants and several important general principles. The core of the subject, however, is the procedures: from negotiation to judicial settlement. To some extent, negotiation is the antithesis of a legal procedure. At one time it was a matter of debate whether a means such as negotiation should be considered a legal topic at all because of its informality. In fact, negotiation is categorized as a 'diplomatic' means, along with good offices, mediation, inquiry and conciliation, in contrast to the 'legal means' of arbitration and judicial settlement (Merrills, 1999, p. ix). Nevertheless, despite the labels, all the 'diplomatic' means, including negotiation, are subject to legal rules.

The real basis of the distinction between the legal and diplomatic means is not that the diplomatic means are 'lawless' – that is, without rules for guiding their use or having no role in resolving questions of law – but, rather, that the outcomes are generally non-binding, unlike those achieved by the legal means. Rules exist for the use of all the diplomatic means, even simple negotiation, which is merely face to face communication to settle a dispute without the aid of third parties. Once a state or other international actor consents to be part of an international dispute settlement procedure it is, at the very least, bound by the obligation to proceed in good faith. The essay by Charles Fombad, 'Consultation and Negotiation in the Pacific Settlement of International Disputes' (Chapter 2) explains the obligation on states in international law to engage sometimes in negotiation or its close relative, consultation, and the obligation to negotiate or consult in good faith. The essay by Manfred Lachs, 'International Law, Mediation, and Negotiation' (Chapter 3), also emphasizes that international law is relevant to the practice of negotiation, despite its informal nature. He points to rules from international law that condition negotiation, from obligations to negotiate in the first place to the limits on the proper subjects of negotiation. International law, for example, clearly limits a state's right to form agreements that violate *jus cogens* principles, such as the prohibition on genocide or slavery. International law also limits the right of two states to modify multilateral agreements without the consent of some or all other parties to the agreement.

Good Offices and Mediation

Good offices and mediation are defined as variations on negotiation. With these methods, instead of direct communication between the parties, a third party will lend assistance. Good offices refer to the most minimal role an outside party can play: simply bringing the parties together. It is not mentioned in Article 33 of the UN Charter but, as discussed in the essay by B.G. Ramcharan, 'The Good Offices of the United Nations Secretary-General in the Field of Human Rights' (Chapter 4), it is uniformly considered a standard method.

Good offices differ only subtly from mediation. In mediation, the third party will play a more active role, making suggestions and bargaining with the parties. Thomas Princen's essay, 'International Mediation – The View from the Vatican' (Chapter 5), describes one of the most famous mediations of all time, the Vatican's mediation of the Beagle Channel dispute. Chile and Argentina had tried to settle a disputed section of their boundary by arbitration. When Argentina rejected the arbitral award, both states began to mobilize their armed forces. Pope John Paul II sent his emissary, Cardinal Samoré, to prevent the war and mediate the dispute. Samoré's efforts led to eventual success in both missions.

It may be right to say that good offices and mediation are the least 'regulated' of all the dispute settlement mechanisms. Good faith nevertheless applies to the extent it does for all dispute settlement procedures. However, there are some counterindications in the case of mediation. The WTO Dispute Settlement Understanding (DSU), for example, provides in Article 4 for consultations and explicitly mentions the obligation of good faith, but Article 5 of the DSU, providing for mediation, does not mention good faith. [11] Neither of the essays included in Part III mention good faith or other procedural rules, and this omission supplies further evidence that good offices and mediation have few, if any, rules associated with them. More definitive conclusions, however, must await further study. We have yet to subject good offices and mediation to the same systematic legal analysis carried out for the other mechanisms under Article 33 of the UN Charter.

Inquiry and Conciliation

As to this last point on the degree of regulation, there is a marked contrast between good offices and mediation on the one hand, and inquiry and conciliation on the other. Like good offices and mediation, inquiry and conciliation also involve third parties, usually formal commissions, that provide non-binding reports on questions of law or fact (Fox, 1972). When confined to fact-finding, the commission is usually called a 'fact-finding commission'. Unlike good offices and mediation, dozens of treaties are devoted to the subject of these commissions. Also, lawyers have written numerous books and articles on when and how inquiry and conciliation should or must be used.

From the Second World War until very recently, commissions whether for fact-finding, inquiry or conciliation fell out of fashion. Today they are being used again and are once again a topic of scholarly interest. The essay by Charles Hyde, 'The Place of Commissions of Inquiry and Conciliation Treaties in the Peaceful Settlement of International Disputes' (Chapter 6), was written in 1929 when these methods were of greatest interest. He describes the many treaties providing for inquiry and conciliation and the elaborate sets of principles devised to guide their use. These developments followed the highly successful use of inquiry in the Dogger

Bank Affair of 1904, described in the essay by Richard Lebow, 'Accidents and Crises: The Dogger Bank Affair' (Chapter 7). Lebow's essay, like that of Princen on mediation, does not discuss legal principles, but the Dogger Bank Affair itself demonstrated such a successful use of peaceful settlement that the story has been retold by international lawyers ever since, relying, in recent years, on the version provided by Lebow.

Arbitration

This new interest in commissions (discussed further below) is eclipsed by the current interest in the binding means of dispute settlement, especially through judicial settlement. International law scholars involved in dispute settlement have always had as their great hope and aim the achievement of binding, compulsory procedures for dispute settlement – procedures as close as possible to the compulsory, binding mechanisms available for settling disputes in national societies. Interest in these mechanisms has probably never been greater.

Binding settlement can be achieved through both arbitration and judicial settlement. Arbitration is the older form and is less formal than judicial settlement. Hazel Fox's essay, 'States and the Undertaking to Arbitrate' (Chapter 8), provides a taxonomy of arbitration types and basic principles of arbitration. Fox describes the relative decline in interstate arbitration compared with the tremendous growth in international commercial arbitration, including international commercial arbitration between states and private parties. The success of commercial arbitration, she suggests, is due in large measure to the fact that, through the New York Convention on the Recognition and Enforcement of Foreign Arbitral Awards,[17] states have finally resolved the problem of how to enforce binding arbitral awards. However, the failure to develop similar methods of enforcement for pure interstate arbitration may partly account for its relative decline. The essay by Lori Fisler Damrosch, 'Retaliation or Arbitration – or Both? The 1978 United States-France Aviation Dispute' (Chapter 9), discusses the use of countermeasures to induce a state into complying with an arbitral award or the agreement to arbitrate in the first place. Her essay describes the Air Services Arbitration between the US and France and the US threat to suspend France's treaty rights in response to a prior denial of US rights under the same treaty. The case is highly significant for explaining how any rule of international law may be enforced in a system that has both eliminated the right to use armed force but has not replaced it with a compulsory system of binding dispute resolution. States may resort to self-help, short of armed force, in the form of proportional countermeasures. Plainly, however, countermeasures are inferior to the national court-based system for enforcement devised under the New York Convention.

Nevertheless, countermeasures are often the only means of coercion and can be effective. The United States took countermeasures in the form of freezing substantial assets of the state of Iran when Iranian students in 1979–80 took several dozen Americans hostage in the US embassy in Tehran. As a result of controlling these assets, the United States, through the mediation assistance of Algeria, persuaded Iran to free the hostages and to take part in a claims tribunal to resolve the many claims US citizens had on the government of Iran. The Iran–US Claims Tribunal is one of the most successful dispute settlement mechanisms ever formed. David Caron's essay, 'The Nature of the Iran–United States Claims Tribunal and the Evolving Structure of International Dispute Resolution' (Chapter 10), describes the tribunal's design, a key to its success, and the procedure it follows.

Another highly successful dispute settlement mechanism is the World Trade Organization Dispute Settlement Body (DSB) established in 1995 (see Hudec, 1999). The DSB's origins are described in Ernst-Ulrich Petersmann's essay, 'Strengthening GATT Procedures for Settling Trade Disputes' (Chapter 11). Interestingly, the DSB has much in common with the Iran–US Claims Tribunal. Both mechanisms were originally conceived as arbitral tribunals but actually have much in common with judicial settlement. In existence for more than 20 years, the Iran–US Claims Tribunal is quasi-permanent. It follows its own past decisions, develops its own procedural rules, and performs in other ways like a court. The WTO Dispute Settlement Body is permanent. Its secretariat forms panels as needed, from lists of panellists, but its appellate body members serve a term, just like judges. Petersmann explains the needs that drove the development of the Dispute Settlement Body and the hybrid form it took on, combining the forms of the arbitral tribunals and courts.

Judicial Settlement

Projects for general adjudication like the Permanent Court of Arbitration, the Permanent Court of International Justice, and, its successor, the International Court of Justice, have always been, in a sense, the 'higher' topics of dispute settlement.[18] Within the topic of international courts, the question of compulsory jurisdiction has received most attention. The essay by Humphrey Waldock, 'Decline of the Optional Clause' (Chapter 12), describes the failure to get many states to commit, even on the basis of reciprocity, to the compulsory jurisdiction of the ICJ. Yet, despite that failure, the ICJ has enjoyed great success since the end of the Cold War and, indeed, has inspired the creation of new courts: Louis Sohn's essay, 'Settlement of Disputes Arising Out of the Law of the Sea Convention' (Chapter 13), describes the development of one of these, the International Tribunal for the Law of the Sea. Since then, several international criminal courts have been formed, inspired not only by the ICJ but also by the example of the Nuremberg Tribunal established after the Second World War and the more contemporary cases in national courts against persons accused of the most serious violations of international law. The essay by Richard Lillich, 'Invoking International Human Rights Law in Domestic Courts' (Chapter 14), championed such national trials and, in turn, inspired many more. Cherif Bassiouni's essay, 'The Time Has Come for an International Criminal Court' (Chapter 15), provides both the rationale and the design that influenced worldwide agreement for the International Criminal Court in Rome in 1998.[19]

These many new developments in international adjudication, however, may raise problems for the system of international law. According to Judge Sir Robert Jennings in 'The Proliferation of Adjudicatory Bodies: Dangers and Possible Answers' (Chapter 16), increased decision-making on questions of international law can lead to the development of conflicting principles. Although the ICJ is not yet perceived as a 'supreme court' or 'privy council' for resolving conflicting decisions, Jennings finds that, given the proliferation of international courts and international decisions, such a role would be welcome for the system of international law.

Agencies

The United Nations Security Council and the United Nations Secretary-General are the most important agencies for the settlement of the world's most dangerous disputes. Rosalyn Higgins in 'The Place of International Law in the Settlement of Disputes by the Security Council' (Chapter 17), describes the extent to which international law is relevant to the work of the Council. Ramacharan (in Chapter 4) takes up a similar theme regarding the Secretary-General.

Regional dispute settlement, such as that provided for in the treaties of the European Union or the North America Free Trade Agreement (Folsom *et al.*, 1998; Brown and Kennedy, 2000), is plainly an important topic that cannot be wholly segregated from international dispute settlement. Similarly, private international law – the law governing private, usually commercial, concerns active in more than one state – and private international dispute resolution, such as private commercial arbitration, are adding to the knowledge and sophistication of public international law procedures. The essays in this volume do not particularly focus on regional and private international dispute settlement, although Fox's essay in Part V is helpful in pointing out the congruencies and distinctions in public and private international arbitration.

The essay by Robert Keohane, Andrew Moravcsik and Anne-Marie Slaughter, 'Legalized Dispute Resolution: Interstate and Transnational' (Chapter 18), discusses the breakdown in the once firm categories of international, domestic and regional dispute resolution. These authors' insights argue for including more essays in this volume on the private, regional and transnational mechanisms – mechanisms that bridge national and international law.

Although barriers are breaking down, however, it is also true that, today, more activity than ever before can be identified as public, as opposed to private, and international, as opposed to regional. While we need to be aware that the categories are less neat than previously, they nevertheless still exist and are perhaps even more useful than in the past for organizing the ever-expanding study of international dispute settlement.

The Future of International Dispute Settlement

The final two essays in the volume look to the future of international dispute settlement and are at the forefront of the current dialogue among international lawyers regarding the next phase of dispute settlement studies. Interestingly, the basic dispute settlement procedures are likely to continue for the foreseeable future, but they are being used more often by a greater variety of disputants, to solve a wider array of disputes. As a result, nowadays the topics in this field can range from the obligation to negotiate investment disputes in good faith between states and multinationals to individuals bringing civil suits in national courts against those who they accuse of violating international human rights law.

As the final two essays in the volume suggest, international dispute settlement is closely associated with two related streams of scholarship: the study of dispute settlement in international relations and the study of negotiation, mediation and arbitration within national legal systems. The essays suggest that all three streams are converging although they plainly come from distinct sources. In international relations, dispute resolution studies are known as the study of conflict prevention or conflict resolution. Conflict prevention scholarship focuses on effectiveness, rather than rules, as in international law. Scholars tend to ask such questions as whether a particular conflict is 'ripe' for negotiation or mediation. They ask whether a particular mediator has the trust of two disputing parties to effectively resolve a dispute, or why parties comply with binding dispute resolution outcomes (Zartman, 1989; Zartman and Rasmussen, 1997; Bercovitch, 1996; Bercovitch and Rubin, 1992). The essay by Princen (Chapter 5) on the Vatican's mediation of the Beagle Channel dispute and Lebow's description of the Dogger Bank inquiry (Chapter 7) are classic examples of conflict prevention scholarship.

International lawyers, by contrast, tend to focus on whether parties have an obligation to obey the outcome of a dispute resolution process or to follow particular conduct mandated by procedural rules. International law and international relations have always had some overlap and mutual interest; the overlap has grown along with the prominence of dispute resolution in the study of international relations. The essay by Robert Keohane, Andrew Moravcsik and Anne-Marie Slaughter, 'Legalized Dispute Resolution: Interstate and Transnational' (Chapter 18) reflects the interdisciplinary approach being taken by some international law and international relations scholars into international dispute settlement. They ask, among other questions, why dispute settlement is increasingly moving from the non-binding, diplomatic approaches to the more legalized, binding methods of adjudication.

Despite the present synergies, international law and international relations developed and remained largely distinct from one another for most of the twentieth century. One of the classic works in the field of international dispute resolution is an interdisciplinary study of conflict resolution looking at both the procedures available in international law and case studies of actual attempts at conflict prevention. The study appears, however, in two separate volumes, one edited by international relations scholars (Donelan and Grieve, 1971) and one by an international law scholar (Waldock, 1972), with little or no connection between them. Other works from international relations tend to include one chapter or essay on the international law approach to dispute settlement (for example, Bilder, 1997). However, as ever more work is done on the same international social phenomena by international lawyers and international relations specialists, the integration of the two fields is bound to increase.

Interestingly, American Alternative Dispute Resolution (ADR) has long combined both a rules approach and an effectiveness approach. Fisher and Ury's *Getting to Yes* (1981) is a staple of the American law school curriculum on negotiation. It is a manual teaching, in enumerated steps, how to negotiate, rather than examining what the law requires. Although it is a standard in conflict prevention courses in places like the Johns Hopkins University Nitze School of Advanced International Studies, it finds only brief mention in classic treatments of international dispute settlement in international law, like Merrills (1999) or Lowe and Collier (1999). Courses on ADR in law schools are including the growing number of judicial decisions and statutes on alternative dispute resolution,[20] but the American study of negotiation, mediation or arbitration is still heavily weighted towards training. It is also focused on the effectiveness of international relations, presenting statistical studies about the circumstances surrounding successful outcomes.

These substantive differences between ADR and international dispute settlement can be partly accounted for by the fact that international dispute settlement as a subfield of international law existed long before the modern movement of psychology and its connections with training people in how to prevent or resolve disputes. Arbitration, as will be discussed further below, pre-dates international law's emergence in the seventeenth century. Certainly the practice of diplomacy was studied, but modern ADR follows developments in social psychology in the 1960s in how to influence the outcome of negotiations or disputes among people. By then, the approach to the study of international dispute settlement was established.

Nevertheless, the future of dispute settlement will be influenced not only by globalization and the development of transnational mechanisms, but also by the robust practice of negotiation, mediation, and arbitration in the United States. The essay by Christine Chinkin, 'Alternative Dispute Resolution under International Law' (Chapter 19), discusses these alternatives to litigation found in national societies and describes how national practices are influencing the international scene. Chinkin describes a future in which international dispute settlement takes on more of the trappings of domestic, particularly American, dispute resolution, rather than integrating more closely with the study of conflict prevention in international relations. The force and dynamism of American legal culture has meant that topics such as arbitration, once developed wholly within international law, are plainly being influenced today by developments in American arbitration (Reed and Sutcliffe, 2001). Generally, that means a move towards more formal, legalized procedures.

The History of International Dispute Settlement

The trend towards more formal, legalized procedures, which American ADR may accelerate, really got underway for international law in 1899, the year in which states adopted the Hague Convention on the Pacific Settlement of Disputes.[21] The Convention aimed at developing alternatives to, and mitigating the use of, armed force. The 1899 conference was both a culmination of the work and aims of international lawyers since the founding of international law, as well as the beginning of a new period of endeavour in the formal study and promotion of means for the peaceful settlement of disputes. Between 1899 and 1928 all the means of peaceful settlement mentioned in Article 33 of the Charter had been developed and committed to formal, multilateral agreement (Merrills, 1999, p. 62). The last of the major techniques to be committed to treaty was conciliation. According to Merrills, the first conciliation treaty was concluded between Sweden and Chile in 1920. Conciliation was included in the multilateral General Act for the Pacific Settlement of Disputes in 1928.[22]

The achievements of 1899–1928 grew out of centuries-long efforts. Of the contemporary dispute settlement procedures, the more informal ones – negotiation, good offices, and mediation – have, in one version or another, always been with us. Arbitration, on the other hand, is easier to trace to its starting point in international relations and international law. It was the first procedure to develop a sophisticated set of procedural rules under international law (Verzijl, 1976, p. 52). The Peace of Westphalia itself was produced, in part, through mediation: 'Among the most famous instances of mediation I cite that of Venice and the Pope between France and the Empire . . . and of Denmark between the Empire and Sweden . . . prior to and during the Congress of Westphalia of 1648' (Verzijl, 1976, p. 52). Vattel, and others, refer to arbitration in relation to legal settlement of disputes in the seventeenth century (see Gray and Kingsbury, 1992). In the Jay Treaty of 1794 between the United States and Britain, the parties included arbitration as a peaceful means of resolving any future disputes. In 1804, European states formed the first permanent institutions for the joint regulation of shared resources with the authority to adjudicate and resolve differences (Teclaff, 1991, p. 97). It was, however, the use of arbitration under the Jay Treaty, in particular in the Alabama Claims Arbitration of 1871–72, that really launched international dispute settlement as both a subject and a cause of international law (Caron, 2000, p. 9).

By the late nineteenth century the growing mechanization of war and its associated horrors encouraged the rise of peace movements, which lobbied governments for alternatives to war, like arbitration (Caron, 2000, pp. 7–9). The 1898 Spanish–American War – a bloody conflict in which Spain lost most of its remaining overseas colonies to the United States – became a prominent example for the peace movements. The popular view of the day was that the war began due to a mistaken belief that Spanish agents had sunk a US naval vessel, the *Maine*, in the Port of Havana (Caron, 2000, p. 7). The Russian tsar responded to the peace movements – as well as to Russia's declining ability to afford the new technology of war – by calling for an international conference to find means of peaceful settlement and provide some controls on the use of arms (Sadat, 1999, p. 97, n. 1, citing Hull, 1908).

In the First Hague Peace Conference of 1899, delegates from 26 states drafted a convention defining and setting out rules and procedures for good offices, mediation, inquiry and arbitration. The use of inquiry in 1906, to resolve the Dogger Bank dispute between Russia and Britain, is another classic case in international dispute settlement. The incident encouraged the further development of dispute settlement procedures, with the result that, in the Second Hague Peace Conference in 1907, more rules were added for inquiry and the arbitration rules were modified and improved.

Already in 1899, the British delegation had formally proposed an international court for the settlement of disputes. That did not come about, nor did a real, as opposed to a titular, permanent arbitral body. Instead the delegates formed the Permanent Court of Arbitration (PCA) constituting only a list of available arbitrators, a set of arbitration rules and a small secretariat in the Hague[23] and to which no state was bound to have resort. However, the United States delegation, in particular, was inspired by the British proposals and, with others, made diligent efforts to bring about a permanent international court at the Second Hague Peace Conference of 1907. These efforts failed, but the delegates in 1907 did agree to the first multilateral treaty, the Convention Respecting the Limitation of the Employment of Force for the Recovery of Contract Debts 1907,[24] which outlawed the use of force for this particular class of dispute. The delegates also agreed to form a permanent prize court, although, in the event, that court was never established (Schlochauer, 1981).

Nevertheless, US Secretary of State, Elihu Root, left The Hague even more committed to the idea of judicial settlement of disputes. Subsequently, he promoted the idea in Central America where governments succeeded in establishing the Central American Court of Justice in 1911 (Jessup, 1937, p. 50)[25] – the first permanent court for the settlement of interstate disputes (Hill, 1981, pp. 41–44). This court existed for ten years and might have gone on longer had the United States taken a greater interest in promoting its survival. In addition to the Central American Court, Root also oversaw the establishment of the International Joint Commission (IJC) with Canada. Founded as a permanent institution for the regulation of joint resources and the resolution of boundary-related disputes, the IJC continues to this day, playing a role in the general consensus that disputes between the United States and Canada can be settled as easily as any among the American states or the Canadian provinces. The United States also promoted the commitment to binding dispute resolution through bilateral agreements with South American and European states.

Unfortunately, neither Root nor any of the other Americans long involved in promoting peace through law, were part of the American delegation to the Paris peace talks after the First World War (Jessup, 1937, p. 380; Dunne, 1988, pp. 20–21). Jessup, in his two-volume biography of Root, attributes this to President Woodrow Wilson's dislike of lawyers and his desire to exclude prominent Republicans from the delegation. More significantly, Root's vision for the post-war order differed from Wilson's. Root did not support Wilson's idea that the collective use of force be made available to enforce the peaceful settlement of disputes. He felt strongly that the United States could not support what emerged as Article 10 of the League Covenant – the commitment 'to respect and preserve as against external aggression the territorial integrity and existing political independence of all members of the League'. In Root's opinion, Wilson was promoting this and other ideas with his own legacy in mind, as opposed to what would actually work and what the American people could accept.

In the end, Root was right. The United States did not join the League nor did the mechanisms for peace in the Covenant prevent the Second World War. Nevertheless, they worked to some extent and provided a foundation for post-war improvement. At the heart of the plan to ensure peace through the League was Article 12 of the Covenant:

> The Members of the League agree that if there should arise between them any dispute likely to lead to a rupture they will submit the matter either to arbitration or to inquiry by the Council, and they agree in no case to resort to war until three months after the award by the arbitrators or the report by the Council.[26]

Article 13 of the Covenant prohibited resort to war against any state that complied with a judicial or arbitral award or a report of the Council. But war could be used to force a settlement. Brownlie (1963, p. 57) suggests that the Covenant created a 'distinction between legal and illegal wars based upon the formal criterion of compliance or non-compliance with obligations to use procedures for pacific settlement of disputes'. The United States tried to demonstrate its commitment to peace despite rejecting the league by promoting the Kellogg–Briand Pact of 1928 (Brownlie, 1963, p. 63). The parties to the Pact renounced war and committed themselves to seeking the peaceful settlement of disputes, but the Pact itself did not eliminate the right to use force in self-defence, nor was it ever clear whether it was meant to prohibit the use of force for the enforcement of legal rights. In Brownlie's opinion, the Pact rendered war illegal except in self-defence or under the authority of an international organization (1963, p. 89).

In addition to these prohibitions on war, statesmen worked to improve the existing methods available as alternatives to war. In 1920, ten distinguished international jurists drafted the Statute of the Permanent Court of International Justice, the first permanent, international court for the peaceful settlement of international disputes. Two main obstacles had prevented the organization of an international court open to all states prior to 1920: how judges would be selected and the jurisdiction of the court, including whether it would have compulsory jurisdiction. Elihu Root and his British colleague Lord Philimore were responsible for the breakthrough in selecting judges. At the time of the 1907 Hague Conference, all states wanted to have a judge on the court. In 1920, the Root–Philimore plan guaranteed that the great powers would always have judges and all other states could fill openings on a rotating basis. ICJ judges today are selected on substantially the same method: the five permanent members of the Security Council always have a judge of their nationality on the Court and ten other places are filled on a rotating basis from the main regions of the world. If a state or states party to a case do not have a judge of their nationality on the Court, and the other party does, an ad hoc judge may be appointed. Article 31 of the Statute of the International Court of Justice provides:

> (1) Judges of the nationality of each of the parties shall retain their right to sit in the case before the Court. (2) If the Court includes upon the Bench a judge of the nationality of one of the parties, any other party may choose a person to sit as judge.

Elihu Root also played a key role in determining the PCIJ's jurisdiction. He always felt strongly that, when states seek out judicial or arbitral settlement, they want an outcome based on law, not on the personal views of the judges as to a just or workable outcome (Kelsen, 1949, p. 421). Consequently, the PCIJ decided cases on the basis of international law.

The Hague delegates had another breakthrough in the idea of the optional clause. Some of the delegates passionately supported a court with compulsory jurisdiction; others were adamant that states would not accept such a court. Waldock, in Chapter 12 of this volume, describes how the Brazilian delegate, Fernandez, proposed the possibility of states accepting compulsory jurisdiction at their option, on the basis of reciprocity with other states that accepted the same obligation. Many states did accept compulsory jurisdiction on the basis of reciprocity, while many others brought cases by special agreement. Hence the PCIJ was able to compile an impressive record, deciding 21 contentious cases and 26 advisory opinions in a period of less than 20 years (Schlochauer, 1981, p. 167).

Conciliation also originated at the beginning of the twentieth century. After a number of bilateral agreements for conciliation, including the Locarno Agreements of 1925, conciliation was included in a general multilateral treaty, the General Act for the Peaceful Settlement of Disputes of September 26, 1928.[27]

Thus, by the outbreak of the Second World War, the international society had a variety of means to settle disputes. Their failure to prevent war challenged international lawyers to strengthen the core obligation of peaceful settlement and the general prohibition on the use of armed force to settle disputes in the United Nations Charter. Interest in dispute settlement continued to grow during the years following the adoption of the Charter. A number of important international treaties contained binding dispute settlement clauses – often commitments to settle any disputes at the PCIJ's successor, the ICJ. Added to negotiation and mediation was the hybrid of those two procedures that emerged in multinational conference negotiation. Several key conference chairs, such as Tommy Koh at the United Nations Conference on the Law of the Sea and Maurice Strong at the United Nations Conferences on the Human Environment and Environment and Development, developed a form of mediation to lead hundreds of delegates to the successful conclusion of long and complex negotiations (see, for example, Antrim and Sebenius, 1992, p. 97). Furthermore, the United Nations Secretary-General practised the art of good offices to good effect, as described in Ramcharan's essay (Chapter 4).

New courts and tribunals, patterned after the models forged in the earlier part of the century were formed: human rights courts in Europe and the Americas; a court to settle ocean law disputes; and the semi-permanent arbitral tribunal to resolve the issues between the United States and Iran emerging from the Iranian Revolution. Other procedures languished, however. Inquiry and conciliation practically faded from the scene. The ICJ saw some years with no new cases on its docket. The Permanent Court of Arbitration experienced decades with no activity. Disappointment with the whole experiment in binding, compulsory dispute resolution during the Cold War is evident in Waldock's essay on the decline of the optional clause (Chapter 12).

By the late 1980s and early 1990s, however, with the Cold War obstacles to cooperation among international actors fading, the pressing demands of globalization became a driving force for the establishment of new courts, new commitments to arbitrate, new procedures for dispute resolution, and new uses of national courts for the resolution of international disputes (O'Connell, 2000, p. 100). Post-Cold War international commercial disputes among states and multinational corporations are now regularly resolved in arbitration, either under the terms of the Convention for the Settlement of Investment Disputes,[28] or in ad hoc arbitration. Judges of the International Court of Justice now complain of their heavy workload. As Waldock foreshadowed, the ICJ's current cases come not so often through optional clause jurisdiction as through compromissory clauses in treaties and by special agreement. A statute for an international criminal court has been adopted. The Law of the Sea Tribunal and the WTO Dispute Settlement Body have already been mentioned. Judge Sir Robert Jennings launched a new scholarly concern with his short essay on the proliferation of international courts (Chapter 16). In stark contrast to the beginning of the last century, the new century begins with the concern that international law will develop inconsistently or even contradictorily, through the development of new sources of authoritative decision-making (Charney, 1998). This is a problem that could scarcely have occurred to Elihu Root or Lord Philimore.

Inquiry and conciliation, too, are back on the scene with prominent commissions of inquiry investigating, for example, the violence accompanying East Timor's independence referendum,[29] NATO's bombing of Yugoslavia,[30] and the outbreak of violence in the Middle East.[31] Israel and Egypt tried conciliation in the Taba dispute. The peace agreement between Egypt and Israel called for a boundary commission to attempt to demarcate the boundary. When the attempt failed, the parties then went to arbitration.[32] In 2000, Ethiopia and Eritrea at first considered conciliation of their boundary dispute, agreeing that 'a neutral Boundary Commission composed of five members [two non-nationals/non-residents per state and a mutually agreed president] shall be established with a mandate to delimit and demarcate the colonial treaty border [between Ethiopia and Eritrea] based on pertinent colonial treaties (1900, 1902 and 1908) and applicable international law'. The Commission sat in The Hague and did 'not have the powers to make decisions *ex aequo et bono*'.[33] Subsequently, the parties chose arbitration to settle the dispute.

States party to the Montreal Protocol and the Long-Range Transboundary Air Pollution Treaty are trying a variation on conciliation commissions with panels organized to help parties comply with obligations under the conventions.[34] At Dayton, Ambassador Richard Holbrooke also practised conciliation – although it has not been labelled as such – to press a solution to the Bosnian conflict in 1995:

> His was not the role of a neutral or disinterested mediator who was there simply to facilitate the talks. The United States wanted an agreement, one that was acceptable to all the parties, but one that also could be enforced through a peacekeeping implementation force on terms acceptable to the United States and NATO. (Greenberg and McGuiness, 2000, p. 35)

In addition, the Organization for Security and Cooperation in Europe has formed a permanent court of conciliation and arbitration, and the WTO Dispute Settlement Understanding incorporates conciliation among the dispute settlement options open to members, as does the United Nations Convention on the Law of the Sea.

Some variations on the traditional procedures are also being tried – Cambodia and Sierra Leone have developed combination national/international courts for the trials of persons accused of serious human rights abuse.[35] Other traditional topics, such as the use of claims commissions, continue to concern scholars. The Iran–US Claims Tribunal and the United Nations Iraqi Claims Commission are both much-studied examples of successful, contemporary dispute settlement procedures. Prominent attempts at mediation have abounded in the post-Cold War era, including Norway's efforts in Sri Lanka,[36] the United States' efforts in the Middle East, and those of the

European Union and NATO in Macedonia (Kaminski, 2001). However, the United States opposition to the International Criminal Court is a backward step for international dispute settlement.[37]

International dispute settlement is one of the fastest-growing, most dynamic fields in international law at the beginning of the twenty-first century. The essays gathered in this volume played an important role in the thinking of those charged with designing the dispute settlement systems of the post-Cold War era. They reflect the international law tradition of peace through law, which continues in the era of globalization as the prime hope and motivation of all in the field.

Conclusion

A legal system cannot settle social issues by means of substantive rules alone. Procedures are necessary to interpret, apply and enforce the rules and to handle those questions for which the rules are inadequate. The role of legal procedures in the international legal system may be even more important than in national systems. As international law has no legislature for the development of substantive rules, gaps are more likely to exist and, with the accelerated pace of international life, are increasingly likely. The procedures of negotiation, good offices, mediation, inquiry, conciliation, arbitration and judicial settlement have grown up to meet the dispute settlement needs of international society. All these procedures are experiencing a renaissance since the end of the Cold War both in response to globalization and as a result of the end of Cold War obstacles to cooperation in solving international society's issues. Each procedure is continually being put to new uses and being further developed to meet new needs.

The open question remains, however, as to whether the traditional mechanisms will keep pace with international society's future needs. Will they prove adequate to deal with questions over boundaries, ensuring free and fair trade, regulating use of the Internet, protecting the environment, promoting respect for human rights and so on? Or will they need thorough modification or complete revision to handle these issues and, most importantly, disputes that can threaten the peace? In an age of weapons of mass destruction, the work of international lawyers in the field of peaceful settlement of disputes is as compelling as in any previous era. It continues to be their challenge to design dispute settlement mechanisms of the future that will preserve the peace.

Notes

1   *Mavrommatis Palestine Concessions* (*Greece* v. *U.K.*), 1924 PCIJ. ser. A No. 2, at 11.
2   *Headquarters Agreement Case*, 1988 ICJ 12 (Advisory Opinion).
3   UN Charter, 59 Stat. 1031, TS No. 993, 3 Bevans 1153, *amended* 24 UST 2225, TIAS 7739 (emphasis added).
4   59 Stat. 1055, TS No. 993, 3 Bevans 1179 (June 26, 1945).
5   *Case Concerning Military and Paramilitary Activities in and against Nicaragua,* (*Nicaragua* v. *U.S.*), 1984 ICJ 392, 429, para. 84.
6   See, for example, United Nations Convention on the Law of the Sea 1982, Part XV, Arts 297 and 298, UN Doc. A/CONF.62/122. Exceptions from the requirement of compulsory dispute resolution are made for disputes involving certain coastal state rights, military activities, and law enforcement.

7   Quoted in Henkin *et al.* (1993, p. xxiv). Until the nineteenth century, one found references to the phrase 'law of nations' but not to the term 'international law', which was introduced by Jeremy Bentham. See Janis (1999, pp. 1–2). The law of nations may not be strictly equivalent to international law but, in respect to arbitration and other aspects of dispute resolution, the line of development is unbroken.

8   Article 33 also refers to 'regional agencies' for dispute settlement. To limit the subject under review, regional agencies will not be included in the following study in preference to international means. Two international agencies are included, however – the United Nations Secretary-General and the Security Council.

9   *Aegean Sea Continental Shelf (Greece* v. *Turkey),* 1978 ICJ 3, 12. See also Merrills (1999, p. 21).

10 See the Declaration Principles of International Law Concerning Friendly Relations and Cooperation Among States in Accordance with the Charter of the United Nations, GA/RES/ 2625 (XXV), Annex, and the Manila Declaration on the Peaceful Settlement of International Disputes, GA/RES/37/10, Annex.

11 *Filartiga* v. *Pena-Irala,* 630 F.2d 876, 2nd Cir. (1980).

12 Vienna Convention on the Law of Treaties, May 23, 1969, 1155 UNTS 331, Art. 26.

13 Final Act Embodying the Uruguay Round of Multilateral Trade Negotiations 1994, 33 ILM 1143; Understanding on Rules and Procedures Governing the Settlement of Disputes 1994, Art. 4, WTO Agreement, Annex 2, art. 4 idem, 33 ILM 1224, 1228 (1994).

14 *The Islamic Republic of Iran* v. *The United States of America,* DEC 62-A21-FT, reprinted in 14 *Iran–U.S. Claims Tribunal Reports,* 324, 330 (4 May 1987).

15 *Fisheries Jurisdiction Case (U.K.* v. *Iceland)* (Merits), 1974 ICJ 3, paras. 75 and 78.

16 See note 13 *supra.*

17 New York Convention on the Recognition and Enforcement of Foreign Arbitral Awards, 1958, 21 UST 2517, 330 UNTS 38.

18 As a result, this much-studied topic has a very large literature associated with it. A few general treatments include Eyffinger (1997); Lowe and Fitzmaurice (1996); and Damrosch (1987).

19 Rome Statute of the International Criminal Court 1998, Art. 103, 37 ILM 999 (1998). See also *Report of the Preparatory Committee on the Establishment of an International Criminal Court,* UN Doc. A/CONF.183/2/Add. 1 (14 April 1998).

20 One of the standards in the field is Goldberg *et al.* (1999).

21 See The Final Act of the Peace Conference of 1899, July 29, 1899 in Scott (1909, p. 61); 'Symposium: The Hague Peace Conferences', *American Journal of International Law,* **94** (2000), p. 1.

22 General Act for the Pacific Settlement of Disputes 1928, 93 LNTS 343.

23 See the website of the Permanent Court of Arbitration: http://www.pca-cpa.org; also Hamilton *et al.* (1999).

24 Convention Respecting the Limitation of the Employment of Force for the Recovery of Contract Debts 1907, Stat. 36: 2241, *Malloy's T.S.* 2: 2248.

25 See also www.nobel.se/peace/laureates/1912/root-bio.html.

26 League of Nations Covenant, reprinted in Hudson (1931, pp. 7–8).

27 General Act for the Peaceful Settlement of Disputes, 93 LNTS 343.

28 Convention for the Settlement of Investment Disputes 1965, 17 UST 1270, 575, 159.

29 'UN Investigator Names Indonesia Army Officers in Violence Probe', *Agence Fr.-Presse,* (20 April 2001), 2001 WL 2388525.

30 See IICK (2000); also Final Report to the Prosecutor by the Committee Established to Review the NATO Bombing Campaign Against the Federal Republic of Yugoslavia, available at http://www.un.org/icty/pressreal/nato061300.htm.

31 Sharm El-Sheikh Fact-Finding Committee (Mitchell Panel Report), available at http://usinfo.state.gov/regional/nea/mitchell.htm.

32 *Agreement to Arbitrate the Boundary Dispute Concerning the Taba Beachfront, Egypt-Israel* (1986), 26 ILM 1 (1987).

33 Peace Agreement between Ethiopia and Eritrea, 12 December 2000, 40 *ILM* (2001), p. 260. See also 'Ethiopia Reportedly Names Boundary Dispute Commissioners', *World News Connection,* 30 January 2001), 2001 WL 12257182; 'Eritrea, Ethiopia Recommit to Peace Agreement', *Mealey's International Arbitration Reports,* **16,** (2001), p. 16.

34   Montreal Protocol on Substances that Deplete the Ozone Layer 1987, 26 ILM 1541 (1987) (Decision IV/5, Non-Compliance Procedure, in Report of the 4th Meeting of the Parties, UN Doc. UNEP/OzL.Pro.4/15 (1992)); Convention on Long-Range Transboundary Air Pollution, Geneva 1979, 18 ILM 1442 (1979) (15th Session of the Executive Body, Decision 1997/2 concerning the Implementation Committee, its Structure and Functions and Procedures for Review of Compliance).

35   UN Doc. S/RES/1315 (2002); 'U.N. to Create Genocide Tribunal', *Washington Post*, 15 August 2000, p. A6 (Sierra Leone); Lynch (2000).

36   'Norway Steps Up Sri Lanka Peace Effort as Troops, Rebels Clash', *Agence Français-Presse*, 6 June 2001.

37   See also 'President Bush's Order on the Trial of Terrorists by Military Commission', *New York Times*, 14 November 2001, p. B8.

References

Antrim, Lance N. and Sebenius, James K. (1992), 'Formal Individual Mediation and the Negotiators' Dilemma: Tommy Koh at the Law of the Sea Conference', in Jacob Bercovitch and Jeffrey Z. Rubin (eds), *Mediation in International Relations: Multiple Approaches to Conflict Management*, New York: St Martin's Press, pp. 97–130.

Bercovitch, Jacob (ed.) (1996), *Resolving International Conflicts: The Theory and Practice of Mediation*, Boulder, CO: Lynne Rienner Publishers.

Bercovitch, Jacob and Rubin, Jeffrey Z. (eds) (1992), *Mediation in International Relations: Multiple Approaches to Conflict Management*, New York: St Martin's Press.

Bernhardt, Rudolf (ed.) (1992), *Encyclopedia of Public International Law*, Vol. 2, Amsterdam: Elsevier North-Holland.

Bilder, Richard (1997), 'Adjudication: International Arbitral Tribunals and Courts', in I. William Zartman and J. Lewis Rasmussen (eds) (1997), *Peacemaking in International Conflict: Methods and Techniques*, Washington, DC: United States Institute of Peace Press.

Bin Cheng (1953), *General Principles of Law as Applied by International Courts and Tribunals. Part II: Good Faith*, London: Stevens.

Brown, L. Neville and Kennedy, Tom (2000), *The Court of Justice of the European Communities*, London: Sweet & Maxwell.

Brownlie, Ian (1963), *International Law and the Use of Force by States*, Oxford: Clarendon Press.

Caron, David (2000), 'War and International Adjudication: Reflections on the 1899 Peace Conference', *American Journal of International Law*, **94**, pp. 4–30.

Charney, Jonathan I. (1998), 'Is International Law Threatened by Multiple International Tribunals?', *Recueil des Cours*, **271**, pp. 103–382.

Chinkin, Christine and Sadurska, Romana (1991), 'The Anatomy of International Dispute Resolution', *Journal of Dispute Resolution*, 7, pp. 45–53.

Collier, John and Lowe, Vaughan (1999), *The Settlement of Disputes in International Law: Institutions and Procedures*, New York: Oxford University Press.

Damrosch, Lori F. (ed.) (1987), *The International Court of Justice at a Crossroads*, Dobbs Ferry, NY: Transnational Publishers.

Donelan, M.D. and Grieve, M.J. (1971), *International Disputes: The Political Aspects*, London: Europa Publishers.

Dunne, Michael (1988), *The United States and the World Court, 1920–1935*, London: Pinter Publications.

Eyffinger, Arthur (1997), *The International Court of Justice 1946–1996 (with contributions by Arthur Witteveen)*, Boston, MA: Kluwer.

Fisher, Roger *et al.* (1991), *Getting to Yes: Negotiating Agreement Without Giving In*, New York: Penguin Books.

Folsom, Ralph H. *et al.* (1998), *Handbook of NAFTA Dispute Settlement*, Ardsley, NY: Transnational Publications.

Fox, Hazel (1972), 'Conciliation in International Disputes', in C.M.H. Waldock (ed.), *International Disputes: The Legal Aspects*, London: Europa Publishers.

Goldberg, Stephan B. *et al.* (1999), *Dispute Resolution: Negotiation, Mediation and Other Processes*, Gaithersburg, MD: Aspen Law & Business.

Gray, Christine and Kingsbury, Benedict (1992), 'Developments in Dispute Settlement: Inter-State Arbitration Since 1945', *British Yearbook of International Law*, **63**, pp. 97–134.

Greenberg, Melanie C. and McGuiness, Margaret E. (2000), 'From Lisbon to Dayton: International Mediation and the Bosnia Crisis', in Melanie Greenberg *et al.* (eds), *Words Over War: Mediation and Arbitration to Prevent Deadly Conflict*, Lanham, MD: Rowman and Littlefield Publishers.

Hamilton, P. *et al.* (1999), *The Permanent Court of Arbitration: International Arbitration and Dispute. Summaries of Awards Settlement Agreements and Reports*, New York: Dodd, Mead & Co.

Hart, Henry M. Jr and Sacks, Albert M. (1994), *The Legal Process: Basic Problems in the Making and Application of Law*, in W.N. Eskridge and P.P. Frickey (eds), Westbury, New York: Foundation.

Henkin, Louis *et al.* (1993), *International Law*, Boston, MA: Martinus Nijhoff Publishers.

Hill, Humphrey M. (1992), 'The Central American Court of Justice', in Rudolf Bernhardt (ed.), *Encyclopedia of Public International Law*, Amsterdam: Elsevier North-Holland, pp. 41–44.

Hudec, Robert E. (1999), 'The New WTO Dispute Settlement Procedure: An Overview of the First Three Years', *Minnesota Journal of Global Trade*, **8**, pp. 1–53.

Hudson, M. (1931), *International Legislation*, Vol. I, Washington DC: Carnegie Endowment for International Peace.

Hull, William I. (1908), *The Two Hague Conferences and their Contributions to International Law*, Boston: For the International School for Peace, Ginn.

Independent Commission on Kosovo (IICK) (2000), *The Kosovo Report: Conflict, International Response, Lessons Learned*, Oxford: Oxford University Press.

Janis, Mark W. (1999), *An Introduction to International Law*, Gaithersburg, MD: Aspen Law & Business.

Jessup, Philip C. (1937), *Elihu Root*, Hamden, CT: Archon Books.

Kaminski, Matthew (2001), 'Fighting in Macedonia Puts Pressure on NATO: EU to Consider Political-Mediation Steps', *Wall Street Journal Europe*, 19 March.

Kelsen, Hans (1949), *General Theory of Law and State*, Cambridge, MA: Harvard University Press.

Lowe, Vaughan and Fitzmaurice, Malgosia (eds) (1996), *Fifty Years of the International Court of Justice*, New York: Cambridge University Press.

Lynch, Colum (2000), 'U.N., Cambodia Agree on Court for Khmer Rouge Trials', *Washington Post*, 25 May, p. A31.

Merrills, J.G. (1999), *International Dispute Settlement*, New York: Cambridge University Press.

O'Connell, Mary Ellen (1999), 'New International Legal Process', *American Journal of International Law*, **93**, pp. 334–49.

O'Connell, Mary Ellen (2000), 'The Role of Soft Law in a Global Order', in Dinah Shelton (ed.), *Commitment and Compliance: The Role of Non-Binding Norms in the International Legal System*, Oxford: Oxford University Press, pp. 100–114.

O'Connor, J.F. (1991), *Good Faith in International Law*, Brookfield, VT: Dartmouth.

Reed, Lucy and Sutcliffe, Jonathan (2001), 'The "Americanization" of International Arbitration?', *Mealey's International Arbitration Reports*, **16**, pp. 37–47.

Riggs, Robert E. and Plato, Jack C. (1994), *The United Nations, International Organization and World Politics*, Belmont, CA: Wadsworth Publishing.

Sadat, Leila Nadya (1999), 'The Establishment of the International Criminal Court: From The Hague to Rome and Back Again', *Journal of International Law and Practice*, **8**, pp. 97–118.

Schlochauer, Hans-Jürgen (1981), 'Permanent Court of International Justice', in Rudolf Bernhardt (ed.), *Encyclopedia of Public International Law*, Vol. I, Amsterdam: Elsevier North-Holland, pp. 163–64.

Scott, James Brown (1909), *The Hague Peace Conferences 1899 and 1907*, Baltimore: Johns Hopkins University Press.

Simpson, J.L. and Fox, Hazel (1959), *International Arbitration, Law and Practice*, New York: Praeger.

Sohn, Louis (1983), 'The Future of Dispute Resolution', in R. St J. MacDonald and Douglas M. Johnston (eds), *The Structure and Process of International Law: Essays in Legal Philosophy, Doctrine and Theory*, Boston, MA: Martinus Nijhoff Publishers, pp. 1121–1146.

Teclaff, Ludwik A. (1991), 'Fiat or Custom? The Checkered Development of International Water Law', *Natural Resources Journal*, **31**, pp. 50–56.

Verzijl, J.H.W. (1976), *International Law in Historical Perspective: Inter-state Disputes and Their Settlement*, Vol. VII, Leyden, The Netherlands: A.W. Sijthoff.

Zartman, I. William (1989), *Ripe for Resolution: Conflict and Intervention in Africa*, New York: Oxford University Press.

Zartman, I. William and Rasmussen, J. Lewis (eds) (1997), *Peacemaking in International Conflict: Methods and Techniques*, Washington DC: United States Institute of Peace Press.

Part I
Overview

[1]

AN OVERVIEW OF INTERNATIONAL DISPUTE SETTLEMENT

by
Richard B. Bilder*

Article 2, paragraph 3 of the U.N. Charter requires that: "All Members shall settle their international disputes by peaceful means in such a manner that international peace and security, and justice, are not endangered." The U.N. General Assembly, in adopting its 1982 Manila Declaration on the Peaceful Settlement of Disputes,[1] emphasized "the need to exert utmost efforts in order to settle any conflicts and disputes between States exclusively by peaceful means" and that "the question of the peaceful settlement of disputes should represent one of the central concerns for States and for the United Nations." In an age of nuclear weapons, the importance of the principle of peaceful settlement of international disputes is apparent.

Every discipline concerned with international relations and diplomacy necessarily has an important stake in the task of crafting practical and acceptable ways of more effectively dealing with international conflicts and disputes. But international lawyers, as professional specialists in dispute resolution, have a special responsibility and can make a unique contribution in this respect. Consequently, it may be useful to suggest, from a lawyer's perspective, a

---

* Burrus-Bascom Professor of Law, University of Wisconsin-Madison. B.A. Williams College 1949, J.D. Harvard Law School 1956.

This paper was part of one of a number of studies prepared by members of the American Society of International Law's Special Panel on International Adjudication and the Jurisdiction of the International Court of Justice, and has appeared as Part I of Disputes Processing Research Program Working Paper 7:8, "International Dispute Settlement and the Role of Adjudication" (May 1986), distributed by the University of Wisconsin Law School Institute of Legal Studies. Another part of the study will appear in THE INTERNATIONAL COURT OF JUSTICE AT A CROSSROADS (L. Damrosch ed. 1987)(hereinafter cited as "Damrosch").

[1] U.N. General Assembly Resolution 37/10, 51 U.N. GAOR Supp. 261 U.N. GAOR Supp. 261, U.N. Doc. A/37/51 (Nov. 15, 1982) (hereinafter cited as "Manila Declaration").

2   JOURNAL OF INTERNATIONAL DISPUTE RESOLUTION   [Vol. 1

framework for thinking about international dispute settlement.

Unfortunately, we do not know as much as we would like to about disputes and dispute settlement, either within or among nations. While sophisticated empirical and theoretical research is beginning to be done concerning dispute processing within domestic societies,[2] our study of international disputes and the way they are dealt with is less developed, and our knowledge is still to a considerable extent intuitive and anecdotal. Consequently, this overview necessarily includes a number of questions for which we do not yet have satisfactory answers.[3]

---

[2] *See, e.g.*, materials collected and cited in Special Issue on *Dispute Processing and Civil Litigation*, 15 LAW AND SOC. REV. 389-928 (1980-81); DISPUTE RESOLUTION, (S. Goldberg, E. Green and F. Sander eds. 1985); DISPUTING IN AMERICA: THE CHANGING ROLE OF LAWYERS, (E. Green, J. Marks, F. Sander eds. (1985) (all with extensive bibliographies). *See also* Sander, *Varieties of Dispute Processing*, 70 F.R.D. 111 (1976); and Galanter, *Reading the Landscape of Disputes: What We Know And Don't Know (And Think We Know) About Our Allegedly Contentious and Litigious Society*, 31 UCLA LAW REV. 4 (1983).

On the growing interest in non-judicial or "alternative" dispute resolution, see references above and, e.g., L. KONOWITZ, ALTERNATIVE DISPUTE RESOLUTION: CASES AND MATERIALS (1985) (with extensive bibliography).

For interesting discussions of disputes and dispute processing from a broader cross-cultural and anthropological perspective, *see, e.g.*, Abel, *A Comparative Theory of Dispute Institutions in Society*, 8 LAW AND SOC. REV. 217 (1973); S. ROBERTS, ORDER AND DISPUTES (1979); P. Gulliver, DISPUTES AND NEGOTIATIONS: A CROSS-CULTURAL PERSPECTIVE (1979); THE DISPUTING PROCESS—LAW IN TEN SOCIETIES, (L. Nader and H. Todd eds. 1978).

[3] This may be due more to inherent difficulties of empirical research in the area of international dispute settlement than to any lack of will or imagination. There has, of course, been a great deal of very good more traditional research and writing in this area. For excellent overviews, *see, e.g.*, J.G. MERRILLS, INTERNATIONAL DISPUTE SETTLEMENT (1984) (hereinafter cited as "MERRILLS"); INTERNATIONAL DISPUTES: THE LEGAL ASPECTS, A Report of a Study Group of David Davies Memorial Institute (H. Waldock ed. 1972) (with supporting individual studies) (hereinafter cited as "WALDOCK"); F. NORTHEDGE and M. DONELAN, INTERNATIONAL DISPUTES: THE POLITICAL ASPECTS (David Davies Memorial Institute 1971) (hereinafter cited as "NORTHEDGE AND DONELAN"); O. Schachter, *International Law in Theory and Practice*, 178 RECUEIL DES COURS 10, esp. chs. III, X, XI (hereinafter cited as "Schachter"); Sohn, *The Future of Dispute Settlement* in R. St. J., THE STRUCTURE AND PROCESS OF INTERNATIONAL LAW: ESSAYS IN LEGAL PHILOSOPHY, DOCTRINES AND THEORY 1121 (MacDonald and D.M. Johnson eds. 1983) (hereinafter cited as "Sohn"); Book IV C. DE VISSCHER, THEORY AND REALITY IN INTERNATIONAL LAW (Trans. by Corbett 1968); INTERNATIONAL LAW: CASES AND MATERIALS Ch. 13 (L. Henkin, R. Pugh, O. Schachter, and H. Smit eds. 1980) (hereinafter cited as "Henkin et al."); H. LAUTERPACHT, THE FUNCTION OF LAW IN THE INTERNATIONAL COMMUNITY (1933); DISPUTE SETTLEMENT THROUGH THE UNITED NATIONS (K. Raman ed. 1977) (hereinafter cited as "Raman"); and references cited in notes, *infra*, particularly notes 30-37. *See also*, on dispute settlement in particular fields, *e.g.*, Sohn, *Settlement of Disputes Arising Out of the Law of the Sea Convention*, 12 SAN DIEGO L. REV.

I. WHAT IS AN INTERNATIONAL DISPUTE?

In the *Mavromattis* case, the Permanent Court of International Justice defined a dispute as "a disagreement on a point of law or fact, a conflict of legal views or interests between two persons."[4] More specifically, J.G. Merrills suggests that:

> A dispute may be defined as a specific disagreement concerning a matter of fact, law or policy in which a claim or assertion of one party is met with refusal, counter-claim or denial by another. In the broadest sense, an international dispute can be said to exist whenever such a disagreement involves governments, institutions, juristic persons (corporations) or private individuals in different parts of the world. However, the disputes with which the present work is primarily concerned are those in which the parties are two or more of the one hundred and sixty or so sovereign states into which the world is currently divided.[5]

---

495 (1975); Bilder, *The Settlement of Disputes in the Field of the International Law of the Environment*, 1 RECUEIL DES COURS 139 (1975).

Among recent empirical or otherwise less-traditional studies, *see, e.g.*, Bailey, *Peaceful Settlement of International Disputes* in Raman, *supra* note 2; T. FRANCK, THE STRUCTURE OF IMPARTIALITY (1968); J. GAMBLE and D. FISCHER, THE INTERNATIONAL COURT OF JUSTICE: AN ANALYSIS OF A FAILURE (1976); G. RAYMOND, CONFLICT RESOLUTION AND THE STRUCTURE OF THE STATE SYSTEM: AN ANALYSIS OF ARBITRATIVE SETTLEMENTS (1980); A. STUYT, SURVEY OF INTERNATIONAL ARBITRATIONS 1794-1970 (1972); F. NORTHEDGE AND GRIEVE, INTERNATIONAL DISPUTES: CASE HISTORIES 1945-70 (1973); Coplin and Rochester, *The Permanent Court of International Justice, The International Court of Justice, The League of Nations and the United Nations: A Comparative Empirical Survey*, 66 AM. POL. SCI. REV. 529 (1972); and L. PROTT, THE LATENT POWER OF CULTURE AND THE INTERNATIONAL JUDGE (1979).

[4] *Mavromattis Palestine Concessions* (Greece v. U.K.), 1924 P.C.I.J. ser. A No. 2, at 11 (Judgment of Aug. 13).

[5] Merrills, *supra* note 3, at 1. *See also* discussion Darwin, *General Introduction*, in Waldock, *supra* note 3, at 57-58.

For other definitions of "dispute," *see, e.g.*, Miller and Sarat, *Grievances, Claims and Disputes: Assessing the Adversary Culture*, 15 LAW AND SOC'Y REV. 525, 527 (1980-81) ("[a] dispute exists when a claim based on a grievance is rejected in whole or in part"); Mather and Yngvesson, *Language, Audience and the Transformation of Disputes*, 15 LAW AND SOC'Y REV. 775, 776 (1980-81) (a "dispute" refers to "a conflict between two parties (individuals or groups) [that] is asserted publicly—that is, before a third party"); Gulliver, *supra* note 2, at 75-76 (a dispute occurs when the parties are unable to resolve their disagreement and one of them decides to take it into the public domain); Nader and Todd, *supra* note 2, at 15 (a dispute results when a personal conflict escalates and is made public).

I will use Merrills' meaning in this article and will generally refer to the nations involved in a particular disagreement as "parties" to the dispute.

The significant elements of the concept of "dispute" are that:

1.   The disagreement must be *specific*. That is, it must have a reasonably well-defined subject-matter, so that one can say what the dispute, at least nominally, is "about."

2.   The disagreement must involve *conflicting claims or assertions*. That is, one party must actually assert or manifest what it wants or believes itself entitled to with respect to the other, and the other party must manifest its refusal or its conflicting claim. Such a manifestation may be through statements, diplomatic notes, specific actions or otherwise.

Thus, a "dispute" is something more than general attitudes of mutual dislike or hostility. Two nations may have general feelings of antagonism towards each other, yet not have any *specific* or *particular* disagreement one can identify as a dispute; conversely, two nations may be on friendly terms, yet have a particular disagreement which can be considered a dispute. Moreover, a "dispute" means something more than a situation in which one nation feels a sense of injury or grievance towards another; until that sense of grievance is formulated into a specific claim or assertion which is resisted by the other, there is no "dispute" between them.

The concept of "dispute" is useful for several reasons. First, it serves to distinguish a disagreement which has reached a level of active assertion and intensity potentially threatening the relations between the parties or the social order more generally, from lower-level and less threatening types of complaints, grievances or disagreements. Second, it serves as a way of indicating that a disagreement has reached a point of sufficient definition and concreteness where the use of certain established methods of dispute resolution may be appropriate. That is, from the perspective of the international legal system, an international dispute can be viewed as a disagreement between or among nations which international dispute-settlement techniques, such as adjudication, may be useful in resolving.[6] Indeed, the jurisdiction of international judicial institutions, such as the International Court of Justice, typically extends only to cases involving international "disputes."[7]

II. Do We Need to Settle International Disputes?

Disputes are inevitable in any society; at any moment there are certainly millions of disputes occurring at different levels of social interaction all over the world—within families, between social groups or business enterprises, and among nations. Obviously, each nation pursues its own interests, objectives and values. But when nations coexist and interact in a common social framework, some of these interests, objectives or values may come into conflict. Each will then seek ways of making its own interests prevail.

In this event, the more powerful nation may, of course, seek simply to impose its views or interests on the other party through coercion or force. More typically, however, a nation—particularly if it is less powerful than the other party—will also try to exert moral influence on its opponent by asserting that its claim is justified, legitimate or right. Framing a demand in moral or legal terms probably serves not only as a way of bringing moral pressure on the other party to accede to the demand, but also as a way of mobilizing support for the demand within the nation making it and of appealing for support of the claim by other nations and the inter-

---

[6] Of course, a grievant may deliberately seek to escalate a particular complaint into a dispute in the hope of focusing public attention on it and bringing international dispute settlement norms and procedures into play. Some terrorist groups appear to have adopted this strategy.

[7] *See* Mavromattis case, *supra* note 4, at 11-12; Schachter, *supra* note 3, p. 202; I.C.J. Statute, Arts. 36, 38; RESTATEMENT OF THE LAW, FOREIGN RELATIONS LAW OF THE UNITED STATES (Revised) (hereinafter cited as "RESTATEMENT"), (Tent. Draft No. 5 Apr. 5, 1984), § 902, Rept's Note 7, pp. 178-79 (*Existence of a dispute as prerequisite to certain dispute settlement procedures.* Before resorting to an international remedy, the injured state is obliged to prove the existence of an 'international dispute'. . .") In some cases, an international tribunal has rejected a claim on the ground that the claimant did not establish the existence of a dispute. *See, e.g.,* Electricity Company of Sofia (Belgium v. Bulgaria) 1939 P.C.I.J., Ser. A/B, No. 77, at 64, 83 (Judgment of April 14).

For discussions of whether negotiation is a precondition to establishing the existence of, and in particular invoking third party settlement of, disputes, *see, e.g.,* MERRILLS, *supra* note 3, at 15-18; Schachter, *supra* note 3, at 201-07; RESTATEMENT, *supra*, Tent. Draft No. 5 § 902, Rept's Note 6, at 177-78.

national community. Whatever its basis, a feeling that demands or claims must be justified or legitimized by reference to normative principles has become deeply engrained in international (and other types of) social behavior and interaction.

As indicated, disputes are a by-product of energetic social interaction and not in themselves necessarily a "bad thing."[8] Certainly, they need not imply a failure or breakdown of social order; indeed, a society without disputes would likely be a static society, without change and development. And, in practice, most disputes do not pose significant social problems and can be left to work themselves out, either (as is usually the case) through informal and routine low-level negotiations between the parties, by fading away over time, or otherwise. Disputes become a social problem only when and to the extent they disrupt, or threaten to disrupt, useful social relations or the more general social order—that is, when they may lead to conflict or when their social costs become excessive.

Thus, every political system must find ways to identify and try to deal with disputes that *do* pose significant social risks. In most domestic legal orders, complex and sophisticated techniques have been developed for identifying and resolving disputes that are considered to warrant or require public attention or intervention. Typically, either party acting on its own may seek state intervention, or the state under certain circumstances may intervene at its own discretion; and there are few kinds of disputes in which the state cannot if it wishes so intervene. In international society, on the other hand, the discretion of the international community or third parties to intervene in disputes is much more limited. In most cases, third-party or community intervention is considered appropriate or permissible only when *both or all* parties to the dispute have consented, or where the dispute has escalated to a point threatening general international peace and security.

It is worth noting that there may be some cases where even a significant dispute is best left unresolved. Thus, if any conceivable settlement or even attempt of settlement is likely only to exacer-

---

[8] *See generally, e.g.,* S. ROBERTS, ORDER AND DISPUTES (1979); L. COSER, THE FUNCTIONS OF SOCIAL CONFLICT (1956).

bate the sense of grievance of one or another party and increase tensions, it may be wisest simply to leave the dispute to simmer, hoping that someday, somehow, it will go away. The success of the Antarctic Treaty System, for example, is based largely on the parties' decision to bypass or "freeze" the very difficult and potentially troublesome issue of disputed claims to territory in Antarctica.[9]

The timing of dispute settlement efforts may also be crucial; such efforts, or the use of a particular technique, may be helpful at one stage of a dispute but not at another. Diplomats and international lawyers need to learn more about *when*, as well as *how*, to try to settle international disputes.

III. Do States Have an Obligation to Settle Their Disputes Peacefully?

The prevailing view is that, in the absence of special agreement, states are under no international legal obligation to settle, or even try to settle, their disputes.[10] It is well established in particular that, absent special agreement, they have no obligation to submit their disputes to third parties for impartial settlement.[11]

---

[9] *See, e.g.*, R. Bilder, Managing the Risks of International Agreement (1981), at 40. The relevant provision is Article IV of the Antarctic Treaty of 1959, 54 Am. J. Int'l L. 476 (1960), which in effect provides that neither anything in the treaty nor acts or activities taking place while the treaty is in force will affect any of the parties' positions regarding the issue of claims. For a similar "bypassing" solution, *see* the 1972 U.S.-Brazilian Shrimp Conservation Agreement, May 9, 1972, 11 I.L.M. 453 (1973) (bypassing the issue of resource jurisdiction).

[10] *See* Henkin *et al.*, *supra* note 3, at 910 ("As long as a State does not resort to force, there has been no disposition to find a violation of law in failure to settle disputes peacefully, as by leaving them unsettled.").

[11] *See* Restatement, *supra* note 7, Tent. Draft No. 5, § 902, comment (e) at 168: "It is well established in international law that no State can, without its consent, be compelled to submit its disputes with other states either to mediation or to arbitration, or to any other kind of pacific settlement." Eastern Carelia (Finland v. Russia), 1923 P.C.I.J., ser. B, No. 5 at 27 (Advisory Opinion of July 23). Consequently, international claims "cannot, in the present state of the law as to international jurisdiction, be submitted to a tribunal, except with the consent of the States concerned." Reparation for Injuries, 1949 I.C.J. Rep. 177-78 (Advisory Opinion of April 11).
As to arbitration, *see also* Ambatielos, (Greece v. U.K.) 19537 I.C.J. 10, 19 (Judgment of

However, those states that are parties to the U.N. Charter (which means, in effect, almost all of the world's nations) have assumed at least certain broad treaty obligations in this respect. Article 1(1) of the Charter provides that the first of the purposes of the United Nations organization shall be:

> to maintain international peace and security, and to that end:
> . . . to bring about by peaceful means, and in conformity with the principles of justice and international law, adjustment or settlement of international disputes or situations which might lead to a breach of the peace.

Article 2(3) of the Charter provides:

> All Members shall settle their international disputes by peaceful means in such a manner that international peace and security, and justice, are not endangered.

Article 33 of the Charter provides:

> 1. The parties to any dispute, the continuance of which is likely to endanger the maintenance of international peace and security, shall, first of all, seek a solution by negotiation, enquiry, mediation, conciliation, arbitration, judicial settlement, resort to regional agencies or arrangements, or other peaceful means of their own choice.
> 2. The Security Council shall, when it deems necessary, call upon the parties to settle their dispute by such means.

It may be noted that, while Article 2(3) establishes an essentially negative obligation—that Member nations *not* settle disputes by means that might endanger international peace, Article 33 affirmatively requires that Member nations actively seek to settle by peaceful means any dispute the continuance of which is likely to endanger international peace. It is well established that Article 33 does not purport to establish an exclusive list of such peaceful means or any particular order in which they should be used.[12]

Chapter VI (Articles 33-37) of the Charter, entitled "Pacific Set-

---

May 19) ("a State may not be compelled to submit its disputes to arbitration without its consent").

[12] *See, e.g.*, MERRILLS, *supra* note 3, at 1-2 and 18.

tlement of Disputes" establishes further obligations of the parties and various dispute settlement powers of the Security Council. Under Article 35, any state may bring any dispute to the attention of the Security Council or General Assembly. Under Article 36, the Security Council may, at any stage of a dispute the continuance of which is likely to endanger the maintenance of international peace or security, recommend appropriate procedures or methods of adjustment; in doing so, the Council should take into consideration that legal disputes should as a general rule be referred by the parties to the International Court of Justice. Article 37 provides that, should the parties to a dispute of the nature referred to in Article 33 fail to settle it by the means indicated in Article 33, they shall refer it to the Security Council which, if it deems that the continuance of the dispute is in fact likely to endanger the maintenance of international peace and security, shall decide whether to take action under Article 36 or to recommend such terms of settlement as it may consider appropriate. Article 38 provides that:

> Without prejudice to the provisions of Article 33 to 37, the Security Council may, if all the parties to any dispute so request, make recommendations to the parties with a view to a pacific settlement of the dispute.

Other articles of the Charter authorize the General Assembly and Secretary General to make recommendations or take certain action with respect to disputes, and encourage the development of pacific settlement through regional arrangements.[13]

It is apparent that the U.N. Charter establishes international obligations of the parties and interventionary powers of the Organization principally with respect to a particular category of disputes—those whose continuation "is likely to endanger the maintenance of international peace and security." It is less clear whether Member nations are also under an obligation to seek to settle *all* disputes — even those which are *not* likely to threaten international peace and security. Perhaps Article 2(3) could be read as establishing such a broader duty,[14] as might also the rele-

---

[13] *See, e.g.*, U.N. Charter, Arts. 10, 11, 12, 14, 52(2), 99.
[14] *See* Waldock, *supra* note 3, "The Report," at 8-14.

vant sections of the General Assembly's authoritative 1970 Declaration of Principles regarding Friendly Relations[15] and the 1982 Manila Declaration on the Peaceful Settlement of International Disputes.[16] Such an interpretation would place the emphasis on the word "settle" in Article 2(3), rather than on "peaceful means"; certainly, this reading would have been strengthened had there been a comma after the word "disputes." However, Articles 1(1), 33, and 38 seem more persuasively to suggest a narrower construction, under which the Charter's obligation to seek to settle disputes does *not* apply to those disputes *not* likely to threaten international peace and security. Certainly, Article 38 makes clear that, absent consent of all parties to the dispute, the Organization has no general authority to intervene to bring about a settlement of international disputes which do not involve either coercion or a threat to international peace and security.

The obligation that any settlement of disputes must be accomplished peacefully is, of course, buttressed by the prohibition on the use of force contained in Article 2(4) of the Charter and by the authority of the Security Council under Chapter VII of the Charter to intervene when it determines that any situation or dispute involves a "threat to the peace, breach of the peace, or act of aggression." It is an interesting question whether the Security Council's authority to "decide what measures shall be taken in accordance with Articles 41 and 42, to maintain or restore international peace and security" (which "decisions" are binding on all Members under Article 25 of the Charter) could include a "decision" requiring the parties to a dispute to adopt particular peaceful settlement procedures; arguably, such authority might be included by implication in the Council's far more drastic authority to employ economic or even military coercion under Articles 41 and 42.

The characterization of the dispute, and thus the potential ap-

---

[15] Declaration on Principles of International Law Concerning Friendly Relations and Cooperation Among States in Accordance with the Charter of the United Nations, G.A. Res. 2625 (XXV) of Oct. 24, 1970, U.N.G.A. Off. Rec. 25th Sess., Supp. No. 28 (A/8028), p. 121, especially the "[p]rinciple that states shall settle their international disputes by peaceful means."

[16] Manila Declaration, *supra* note 1.

plication of these obligations, is presumably a matter upon which the Security Council may appropriately reach its own judgment, rather than one solely within the judgment of one or all of the disputing states themselves. Thus, Article 34 expressly authorizes the Council to investigate any dispute, or any situation which might lead to international friction or give rise to a dispute, in order to determine whether the continuance of the dispute or situation is likely to endanger the maintenance of international peace and security.

The obligations of Articles 2(3) and 33 to seek to settle disputes peacefully, at least if their continuance is likely to threaten international peace and security, is probably now customary international law, binding even on any nations not parties to the Charter.[17] This has generally been accepted as the case with respect to the analogous obligations of Article 2(4) of the Charter.[18]

It is debatable whether contemporary customary international law is moving towards carrying the obligation to seek to settle disputes somewhat further than the Charter requires.[19] It is difficult to argue that customary law requires states to try to settle or actually settle *all* of their disputes. Each nation may have many disputes with other nations, most of which are probably minor and some of which may perhaps best be left unresolved; to require

---

[17] *See, e.g.,* Waldock, *supra* note 3, at 9-10 (noting the recognition and proclamation of the principle in many other international instruments such as the Pact of the Arab League, Inter-American Treaties, Charter of the Organization of African Unity, the Warsaw Pact, the Bandung and Belgrade Declarations and the European Convention for the Peaceful Settlement of Disputes).

[18] *See* Henkin *et al., supra* note 3, at 910 ("It is commonly accepted that in substance Article 2(4) has become a principle of international law binding on all states").

As Professor Sohn has pointed out there is a close relation between the obligations of Article 2(3) and 2(4) since:

Any attempt to impose a rule that states 'must refrain in their international relations from the threat or use of force against other states' must be accompanied by making available to states alternative processes for solving problems and changing inequitable situations. Otherwise, continuous disputes put a strain on relations between the states concerned and sooner or later may explode into a breach of the peace.

Sohn, *supra* note 3, at 1121.

[19] I have drawn on some suggestions of Professor Oscar Schachter in my discussion of this point.

states to actively pursue the settlement of *all* of these would be unreasonable, burdensome and unnecessary. Moreover, there does not seem to be any practical way in which the international legal order could implement or enforce such a broad requirement. There is some evidence, however, that a principle of customary law is gradually emerging requiring parties to at least *significant* disputes to negotiate in good faith respecting settlement, if not to actually reach a settlement. This principle finds support in provisions to this effect in many bilateral and multilateral treaties, the Declaration on Friendly Relations, a variety of other resolutions of international organizations, and various international judicial decisions such as the International Court's opinion in the *Fisheries* case.[20] Certainly, a state which deliberately refuses to take part in good faith negotiations to settle a significant dispute incurs the risk that the international community may not only condemn its unwillingness to seek peaceful settlement but will draw adverse inferences as to the merits of its position with respect to the dispute.

It is, of course, open to nations to enter into international agreements with each other which include "compromissory clauses" or other obligations to settle their disputes peacefully, and a great number of such agreements are in effect.[21] Frequently, such agree-

---

[20] Fisheries Jurisdiction (U.K. v. Iceland), 1974 I.C.J. 3 (Judgment of July 25) (Governments of Iceland and the U.K. are under mutual obligations to undertake negotiations in good faith for the equitable solution of their differences concerning their respective fisheries rights in the areas specified). *See also* North Sea Continental Shelf cases (Fed. Rep. Ger. v. Denmark, Fed. Rep. Ger. v. Neth.), 1969 I.C.J. 47-48 ("the parties are under an obligation to enter into negotiations with a view to arriving at agreement" and this obligation is "a principle which underlies all international relations"), citing with approval a similar statement in Railway Traffic Between Lithuania and Poland (Lithuania v. Poland), 1931 P.C.I.J. ser. A/ B, No. 42, at 116. And *see, supra*, references, notes 14 and 15.

[21] There are some 250 agreements, bilateral and multilateral, conferring on the International Court of Justice jurisdiction over disputes as to the interpretation or application of the agreements. *See* 1983-84 I.C.J.Y.B. 51-56, 92-108 (1984). Of these, the U.S. is a party to about 75. *See* Sen. Comm. on For. Rels., International Convention for the Prevention and Punishment of the Crime of Genocide, S. Exec. Rep. No. 50, 98th Cong., 2d Sess., at 37-41. *See generally*, Sohn, *Settlement of Disputes Relating to the Interpretation and Application of Treaties*, 150 RECUEIL DES COURS 195 (1976) (Hague Academy); and Morrison, *Treaties as a Source of Jurisdiction for the International Court of Justice* in Damrosch, *supra*. There are many additional agreements containing provisions for dispute settlement by means other than reference to the World Court. *See, e.g.*, Sohn, *supra* note 3, and United Nations, A SURVEY OF TREATY PROVISIONS FOR THE PACIFIC SETTLEMENT OF INTERNATIONAL

ments will not only include general obligations of peaceful settlement, but will require, recommend, or provide procedures for the use of specific dispute settlement techniques, such as negotiation, conciliation, arbitration or adjudication.

IV. What Kinds of International Disputes Are There?

We know generally that there are a great many international disputes between many different nations involving many different types of claims. But, so far as I am aware, we have little hard empirical data on how frequently different kinds of disputes arise, between or among what states, and what kinds of claims they involve. Nor, to my knowledge, has there been much research seeking to analyze the causes of disputes or to explain differences in their frequency or nature.

Since different kinds of disputes may call for the use of different kinds of dispute settlement techniques, an attempt to draw at least some distinctions among them may be useful.

Disputes can be roughly classified in several ways:

1. *Subject matter of the dispute.* In terms of traditional areas of international law, the dispute may raise issues involving territorial claims, jurisdiction, diplomatic protection, treaty obligations, the law of the sea, or so on. More specifically, it may involve a particular subject matter such as taxation, taking of property, fishing rights, interference with aircraft, pollution, and so forth.

2. *Character of the dispute.* It is often useful to distinguish among disputes which principally involve disagreements as to: (a) the facts (what happened); (b) what the law is (the particular normative or legal principles claimed to be applicable); (c) what the law *should* be (the reasonableness and justness of existing law, and whether and how it should be changed); (d) simply the terms of some particular arrangement or allocation (e.g., the way some existing "pie," such as quotas under a commodity agreement or fisheries agreement, should be apportioned); or (e) who should decide

DISPUTES 1949-62 (1966).

any of the above questions, and by what procedures.

It is not always easy to say what a dispute is really "about." Indeed, one of the most important tasks of a negotiator, mediator or arbitrator may be to discover—and to help the parties discover—where disagreement really lies. It may sometimes be easier to help the parties settle the problem they really have than the one they think, or at least say, they are arguing about—and, of course, sometimes *vice versa*.

3. *The nature of the relations between or among the parties.* It will often make a difference whether the dispute is between parties who have continuing long term relations with each other or between parties who only occasionally interact. Recent research suggests that dealings and dispute handling between parties who are "repeat-players" in a long term continuing relationship (marriage, continuing business relations and so forth) are of a very different character from dealings between parties who only rarely have to cooperate.[22] For example, the parties to long term relationships may be particularly reluctant to "take their partner to court" as a way of settling disputes, for fear of disrupting an otherwise advantageous continuing relationship. It is arguable, of course, that relations between nations, which must necessarily be continuing, tend inherently to be of this character. Indeed, it is interesting to note that when a long-continuing international relationship is suddenly disrupted by the emergence of a new revolutionary regime in one of the parties, disputes having a particularly intractable character may sometimes arise; this, for example, has been the recent experience with respect to U.S. relations with new governments in Cuba and Nicaragua.

---

[22] *See, e.g.,* Macaulay, *Non-Contractual Relations in Business: A Preliminary Study,* 28 AM. SOC. REV. 55 (1963); and, *generally,* Symposium issue on *Law, Private Governance and Continuing Relationships,* 1985 WIS. L. REV., No. 3. The phrase "repeat players" is taken from Galanter, *Why the Haves Come Out Ahead: Speculation on the Limits of Legal Change,* 9 LAW AND SOC. REV. 95 (1974). For a related discussion, in the context of game theory and "prisoner's dilemma" research, of the concept of "iterated games" and of the influence of "the shadow of the future" on cooperative behavior, *see, e.g.,* R. AXELROD, THE EVOLUTION OF COOPERATION (1984).

4. *Importance of the dispute to the parties.* It will obviously make a difference whether one or both parties considers the dispute important to its national interests (a matter of "vital concern") or considers it relatively unimportant, or at least one which that party can afford to compromise or lose.

5. *Effect of the dispute on other nations or the international community.* It will make a difference whether the dispute is likely to affect other nations. If so, they will obviously have a particular interest in constraining or promoting settlement of the dispute. As we have seen, the U.N. Charter draws a distinction between disputes which are likely to affect international peace and security and those which are not.

6. *Presumed appropriateness of judicial settlement.* A distinction is sometimes drawn between so-called "legal" or "justiciable" disputes, and "political," "non-legal" or "non-justiciable" disputes.[23] The implication is that some disputes have inherent characteristics that make them either particularly appropriate or inappropriate for the use of adjudication as a dispute settlement technique. For example, it has been suggested that adjudication is not an appropriate or useful way of trying to resolve disputes where national "honor" or national security or other "vital" interests are involved; disputes which are essentially about what the law "should be" rather than what the law "is"; disputes which involve types of national decisions which international law arguably leaves largely to national discretion; disputes which political organs of international organizations such as the U.N. or the Organization of American States (O.A.S.) are currently attempting to resolve; or disputes involving issues, such as the use of force, which the parties arguably have agreed to settle exclusively through political means, such as the U.N. Security Council, rather than by adjudication.[24]

---

[23] For discussions, *see, e.g.,* Schachter, *supra* note 3, 211-15 and Schachter, *Compulsory Jurisdiction in Cases Involving the Use of Force* in Damrosch, *supra*; Henkin *et al., supra* note 3, 829-31; Darwin, *General Introduction* in Waldock, *supra* note 3, at 6-13; RESTATEMENT, *supra* note 4, Tent. Draft No. 6, Vol. 1 (Apr. 12, 1985), § 903, Rept.'s Note 7; Gamble and Fischer, *supra* note 3, at 20.

[24] *See, e.g.,* the U.S. State Department's *Statement on the U.S. Withdrawal from the Proceedings Initiated by Nicaragua in the International Court of Justice,* January 18, 1985, *reprinted in* 85 DEP'T ST. BULL., March 1985 at 64 and 24 I.L.M. 246, stating the U.S.

It is true that nations may typically be less willing to agree to adjudication of some kinds of dispute than others; for example, they may be particularly reluctant to submit to courts those disputes they consider to involve their national security or other "vital interests"—unless, of course, they are a relatively weak nation which sees adjudication as its best or only hope. It is also probably true that judicial settlement is not necessarily the "best" or most useful technique for dealing with certain kinds of disputes.[25]

However, since international law is at least in theory a complete system, it is difficult to argue that particular types of dispute are *inherently* beyond the jurisdiction or capacity of a court or arbitral tribunal to decide, even if the parties desire and have given their consent to that court doing so. For example, the Iraq-Iran war is clearly a matter of great "vital interest" to the parties, involving a variety of highly emotional political and religious issues as well as grievances arising from long-disputed boundaries. But clearly, there are legal rules—in the U.N. Charter, treaties between the parties and customary law—which a court *could* apply in attempting to reach a principled decision on the dispute. Consequently, if Iran and Iraq both decided that they wished to submit their dispute to the International Court for settlement—that far too many of their people were being killed and that adjudication by the court was a far preferable way of settling the matter—I do not believe

---

position, *inter alia*, that:

> The conflict in Central America, therefore, is not a narrow legal dispute; it is an inherently political problem that is not appropriate for judicial resolution. The conflict will be solved only by political and diplomatic means—not through a judicial tribunal. The International Court of Justice was never intended to resolve issues of collective security and self-defense and it is patently unsuited for such a role.

and that:

> The [I.C.J.] decision of November 26 represents an overreaching of the Court's limits, a departure from its tradition of judicial restraint, and a risky venture into treacherous political waters.

For general discussions of the suggestion that there may be inherent limits on the appropriateness of adjudication, based on the nature of courts and the adjudicative process, see, e.g., Fuller, *The Forms and Limits of Adjudication* 92 HARV. L. REV. 353 (1979) and Council on the Role of Courts THE ROLE OF COURTS IN AMERICAN SOCIETY (J. Lieberman ed. 1984).

[25] I will discuss the role of international adjudication, and some of its advantages and disadvantages as a dispute settlement technique, in an article which will appear in the next issue of this *Journal*.

that the Court either would or could appropriately decline jurisdiction.

Thus, at least in theory, all international disputes seem to be "justiciable."[26] Indeed, as Professor Schachter points out, the International Court has never yet rejected a case on the grounds that it involved non-legal issues or that it could more appropriately be resolved by a political organ of the United Nations.[27]

V. Do Disputes Follow a Typical Pattern?

We don't know much about the "life cycle" of disputes, or indeed whether they tend to follow a common pattern of birth, development, maturity, and resolution or gradual disappearance. Perhaps if diplomats and international lawyers did know more, they could do a better job of avoiding or settling disputes. Some of the questions we might want to ask are the following:[28]

1. *How do international disputes arise?* What particular kinds of situations or international relationships tend to breed disputes? What causes some experiences or differences, but not others, to be perceived as grievances, and what is the process by which such grievances become gradually articulated into claims and then disputes? Presumably, a nation must (1) perceive itself to be injured; (2) decide some other nation is responsible; (3) form a sense of entitlement to some kind of redress; and (4) formulate a specific claim which is rejected by the other nation. (Of course, on occasion a nation which has a grievance may seek a remedy by direct action or "self-help" without formulating an express claim; in that case, it will be the other party which actually asserts a claim—namely, a claim that the grievant's "self-help" actions are wrongful.) But

---

[26] *See* Henkin *et al.*, *supra* note 3, at 829.

[27] Schachter, *supra* note 3, at 214; *see also* RESTATEMENT, *supra* note 4, Tent. Draft No. 6, § 903. Rept's Note 7, at 640.

[28] I have drawn heavily in this section on work presented in the Symposium on *Dispute Processing* in 15 LAW AND SOC. REV. 389-928 (1980-81), especially D. Coates and S. Penrod, *Social Psychology and the Emergence of Disputes*, at 655; W. Felstiner, R. Abe and A. Sarat, *The Emergence and Transformation of Disputes: Naming, Blaming, Claiming. . .*, at 631; and J. Fitzgerald and R. Dickens, *Disputing in Legal and Non-Legal Contexts: Some Questions of Sociologists of Law*, at 681.

what triggers the various stages of this process? How do norms shape the parties' perceptions? Are some nations more contentious or "dispute-prone" than others? Are there fads and fashions in disputes?

2. *What happens after a dispute arises?* Are there typical strategies and patterns of claim and response which each nation party to a dispute is likely to pursue? What leads nations to try one kind of technique rather than another in their efforts to prevail or to resolve the dispute? Why do they invoke norms to try to legitimate their positions? Are the parties' perceptions of the dispute likely to be transformed during the period of negotiation or attempted settlement, and, if so, in ways more likely to help or hurt chances of settlement?[29] What is the effect of internal public opinion or pressure groups on the flexibility of government officials in compromising or settling disputes? Are there strategies which nations ought to pursue in dispute situations, either in their own or the broader international community interest? Do particular nations, or a particular group of nations, tend to evolve special dispute management systems—that is, a unique set of practices, procedures, techniques and institutions to deal with their particular quarrels?[30]

3. *What is the effect of third parties on the dispute resolution process?* Under what circumstances are third parties likely to be-

---

[29] Professor Louis Sohn has pointed out that this may be particularly likely to occur if the parties have exchanged briefs and discovered the strength (or weakness) of the other party's arguments, or when a preliminary question, such as jurisdiction, has been resolved. *See, e.g.,* Nationality Decrees in Tunis and Morocco (France v. G.B.), 1923 P.C.I.J. ser. B, No. 4 (Advisory Opinion of Feb. 7); 1 M. Hudson, WORLD COURT REPORTS, 144 (1934) ("the opinion of the Court enabled the French and British Governments to reach an agreement, effected by an exchange of notes on May 24, 1923.").

[30] Every bilateral or other international relationship has its own unique character or environment which shapes both the kinds of disputes that arise and how the nations involved tend to deal with them. Some factors which may affect this "dispute-processing environment" between or among nations are: (1) the extent and diversity of the interaction and interdependence of the countries involved, and, in particular, whether they are "repeat players" in a continuing relationship with each other; (2) their relative population, power and ability to exert influence on each other; (3) their geographical and political relationship to each other and to third countries; (4) the similarities or differences in their wealth, culture, language, religion, race, ethnic character, or political and economic ideology; (5) the history of their relationship and how they each have resolved conflicts and disputes in the past; (6) their respective governmental structures and political systems; and (7) their respective com-

come involved in the dispute either as an audience, as supporters of one or the other party, as intervenors, or simply as neutral helpers in seeking resolution of the dispute? Under what circumstances will the parties be concerned with the views or action of third parties? What affects third party perceptions of the persuasiveness or legitimacy of the respective positions of the parties? Do third parties tend to defuse or to escalate a dispute, and, if so, under what conditions? For example, are General Assembly or Security Council resolutions favoring one party to a dispute in practice effective in putting pressure on the other party to engage in dispute resolution efforts or to be more conciliatory, or can they in some circumstances "raise the stakes" or reinforce a party's intransigence and thus make concessions and eventual settlement more difficult? In general, when and how can third parties help, and when are they likely to make matters worse?

4. *What is the range of outcomes for different kinds of disputes?* Who is likely to come out ahead and why? What happens after the dispute is settled, with respect to both the problem that was the particular subject of the dispute and the more general relations of the parties? What are the precedential effects of different kinds of outcomes? Are certain kinds of settlements likely to encourage similar claims by other grievants against a party that has made concessions or similarly situated other states? Do they tend to lead to similar settlements in similar or analogous disputes? Do they tend to lead to efforts by the parties or other states to avoid similar kinds of disputes in the future?

VI. What Techniques Are Available for Settling International Disputes?

Disputes can be disposed of in various ways. While international lawyers are primarily concerned with certain traditional techniques

---

mitments to international law and institutions and the principle of peaceful settlement of disputes.

For a survey and discussion of a particular bilateral dispute processing-system, *see* my current 1986-87 Claude T. Bissell Lectures at the University of Toronto entitled "When Neighbors Quarrel: Canada-U.S. Dispute-Settlement Experience," which will be submitted for publication to the University of Toronto Press.

of peaceful settlement, it is worth at least briefly noting some other ways in which disputes can be resolved:

1. *Coercion.* The use of force or other forms of coercion as a means of securing a favorable outcome of a dispute is as old as history and, unfortunately, still an all-too-frequent occurrence in contemporary international affairs. As has been suggested, since coercive settlement poses a threat to social order, every legal system, including the international legal system, seeks to induce or in some cases require the parties to resolve their disputes through peaceful means rather than coercion.[31] However, it is not always easy or perhaps realistic to eliminate the element of power entirely from the dispute settlement process; it may reemerge under the guise of "bargaining power" in negotiations or "practical considerations" in a judicial decision. Arguably, a "settlement" which ignores the realities of power may prove unstable over the long run and the dispute may bubble to the surface again in some other shape or form.[32]

2. *Voluntary relinquishment.* A party might decide voluntarily to relinquish its claim because, for example, the circumstances or particular perceptions giving rise to its sense of grievance change or disappear, because the other party succeeds in persuading it that

---

[31] The U.N., since its founding, has of course been continually involved in a great number and wide variety of situations in which it has attempted to persuade the parties to settle their disputes peacefully rather than by violence. And *see, e.g.,* the refusal of the U.N. to accept coerced "settlements" in the 1946 Iran-USSR dispute, *see* G. Snyder and P. Dieseng, Conflict Among Nations at 556-59 (1977), and in the 1948 Hyderabad dispute, discussed in L. Sohn, Cases on United Nations Law 393-45 (1967).

[32] But Professor Louis Sohn has pointed to instances in which judicial decisions have been effective in resolving disputes despite great disparities of power. *See, e.g.,* Free Zones (Switzerland v. France), 1930 P.C.I.J., ser. A, No. 24, in which the Court's decision in favor of Switzerland surprised the "experts," as did France's subsequent execution of the judgment. *See also* Norwegian Shipowners (Norway v. U.S.), (1922), 1 Rep. Intl. Arb. Awds. 344 (UN 1948) in which the U.S. satisfied the $12 million judgment against it, despite its strong objection to the decision, Secretary of State Hughes stating that "by this action the Government of the United States gives tangible proof of its desire to respect arbitral awards" and that it "again acknowledges devotion to the principles of arbitral settlements even in the face of a decision proclaiming certain theories of international law which it cannot accept." Cited in L. Sohn, The Need to Improve the U.S. Declaration, n.4, a paper presented at a workshop sponsored by the Center for Law and National Security at the University of Virginia, Aug. 16-17, 1985.

the claim has no merit, or because it becomes discouraged or bored with the futility of continuing to pursue its claim over a long period and decides to simply give up or "lump it."

3. *Chance.* Minor private differences are often resolved by the laws of chance—a flip of the coin. But since chance is not considered a "principled" method of dispute resolution, most legal systems reject it as a legitimate technique of settlement. However, at least with respect to some minor international disputes in which the equities are evenly balanced, chance may in some situations be as "rational" a technique as any other. Indeed, in cases where the law is uncertain, the equities are evenly balanced, and the judges attitudes and biases unknown, any confident prediction of how third-parties are likely to decide the dispute may be impossible and resort to adjudication in practice simply a gamble.

4. *Voting.* In democratic societies, the members of the community or their representatives may decide certain disputes—at least those involving broad issues of social policy, in contrast to disputes between particular individuals—by majority vote. Since the representative organs of international organizations, such as the U.N. General Assembly, do not normally have legislative powers, there is little direct use of such techniques in the international social order. However analogies may perhaps be found in a few cases such as the 1947 General Assembly resolution on the partition of Palestine, and U.N.-administered plebiscites such as those in the trust territories of Togoland and the Cameroons.[33]

The more usual and accepted methods of peaceful settlement of international disputes are those listed in Article 33 of the U.N. Charter—negotiation, inquiry, mediation, conciliation, arbitration, judicial settlement, resort to regional agencies or arrangements and resort to the U.N. or other international organization dispute settlement procedures. In essence, this list of methods reflects a spectrum of techniques ranging from so-called "diplomatic means,"

---

[33] For the Palestine partition plan, *see* General Assembly Resolution 181(II), at 135 (1947), and *generally,* Sohn, *supra* note 31, at 131-51; and on Togoland and the Cameroons, *see* P. JACOB, A. ATHERTON and A. WALLENSTEIN, THE DYNAMICS OF INTERNATIONAL ORGANIZATION 514-15 (1972). For a later phase of the Cameroons problem, *see* Northern Cameroons (Cameroun v. U.K.), 1963 I.C.J. 15.

which give control of the outcome primarily to the parties themselves, to so-called "legal means" which give control of the outcome primarily to a third party or parties. That is, the principal difference among these techniques is in the extent to which third parties can legitimately participate in helping to bring about or determining the settlement and, conversely, the extent to which the parties can reject a settlement proposed by the third party. In practice, distinctions between these techniques may be more theoretical than real, and a particular process of dispute settlement may combine elements of various techniques. For example, international arbitration or adjudication may often embody compromises reflecting strong elements of negotiation or mediation among the arbitrators or judges, at least some of whom may see their role as safeguarding the interests or representing the point of view of one or the other party.

The more traditional methods of peaceful settlement, and their distinctive characteristics, are briefly as follows:[34]

1. *Negotiation.*[35] Negotiation is a process whereby the parties directly communicate and bargain with each other in an attempt to agree on a settlement of the issue. By choosing to use this technique, the parties retain maximum control of the process and outcome.

Negotiation is clearly the predominant, usual and preferred method of resolving international disputes.[36] Except in cases where

---

[34] For excellent general discussions of each of these dispute settlement procedures, *see* MERRILLS, *supra* note 3; Waldock, *supra* note 3; and Sohn, *supra* note 3; all citing other references.

[35] *See, e.g.,* MERRILLS, *supra* note 3, at ch. 1; Darwin, *Negotiation,* in Waldock, *supra* note 3, at 77; DE WAART, THE ELEMENT OF NEGOTIATION IN THE PACIFIC SETTLEMENT OF DISPUTES BETWEEN STATES (1974); and, on process, A. LALL, MODERN INTERNATIONAL NEGOTIATION: PRINCIPLES AND PRACTICES (1966); and F. IKLE, HOW NATIONS NEGOTIATE (1964).

Professor Sohn points out that "it is an axiom of international diplomacy that the most efficient method of settling international disputes is through negotiations between the two governments concerned, without any meddling of third parties, other states or international organizations" and that "in most instances negotiations lead to a solution." Sohn, *supra* note 3, at 1122.

[36] Some of the reasons why nations usually prefer negotiation to other methods of dispute resolution involving third parties include:

(1) negotiation is the least risky way of trying to deal with disputes. Each coun-

the dispute is submitted directly to settlement by binding adjudi-

try has maximum control over both the dispute settlement process and outcome, since it always has the option of simply walking away from the negotiation and *not* agreeing. In contrast, any type of third-party involvement carries a risk of reducing a country's flexibility and freedom to do what it wants, and of somehow trapping it into an undesirable outcome.

(2) Negotiation places responsibility for resolving the dispute on the parties themselves, who are in the best position to develop a sensible, workable and acceptable solution. Sometimes, the adage "too many cooks may spoil the broth" is applicable to international dispute resolution.

(3) Since any settlement reached by negotiation is presumed to be freely agreed to by the parties to the dispute, rather than imposed on them by third parties, it is likely to have maximum acceptability and stability.

(4) Negotiation favors compromise and accommodation between the parties—a "give-and-take" rather than "all-or-nothing" solution—which is most likely to preserve good long term cooperative relations.

(5) Negotiation is generally simpler and less costly than alternative dispute settlement methods and it can more easily be carried on secretly or without publicity. Moreover, the process of negotiation can develop attitudes, procedures and relationships which foster cooperation and dispute management between or among the parties more generally.

But negotiation also has some disadvantages and limitations, including the following:

(1) Negotiation cannot assure settlement of a dispute. If the parties' positions are too far apart and neither is willing to compromise, negotiations may break down and reach an impasse. Without some kind of third party involvement or intervention to help the parties reach a compromise, or to decide the matter for them, resolution of the dispute may be impossible.

(2) A negotiated settlement may reflect only the parties' relative negotiating power, rather than the legal or equitable merits or inherent justice of their respective positions. Thus, if one party believes its bargaining position is weak, it may prefer if possible to use other dispute settlement techniques, such as conciliation or adjudication, which can lend to its position third party support or support from neutral legal principles.

(3) Negotiations are inherently political and are often subject to a variety of pressures from special interest groups. Sometimes such special pressures may complicate, delay or obstruct negotiations or even make it politically impracticable for the government of one or another party to reach compromises or accommodations it otherwise considers sensible and in its national interest. Where this is the case, the involvement of third parties, or even submission of the dispute to third-party decision, may relieve the government of direct responsibility and accountability for a compromise—allow it to "pass the buck" to the third party—and thus make settlement possible.

(4) A party may not be willing to negotiate and compromise what it considers an issue of "principle".

(5) The parties' negotiating procedures and resources may not be adequate to develop mutually agreed facts or data instrumental for a potential solution of the dispute. Particularly where special expertise in technically complex facts is involved, third parties may be helpful in this respect.

cation or conciliation, or where settlement is otherwise imposed by a third party, negotiation is normally an essential component of any dispute settlement process. Indeed, the use of other techniques, including adjudication, is usually preceded, accompanied by and arranged through some kind of negotiation process.

2. *Good offices and mediation.*[37] Good offices and mediation are techniques in which the parties, unable to resolve a dispute by negotiation, request or agree to limited intervention by a third party to help them break the impasse. In the case of good offices, the role of the third party is usually limited to simply bringing the parties into communication and facilitating their negotiations. In the case of mediation, the mediator usually plays a more active part in facilitating communications and negotiations between the parties, and is sometimes permitted or expected to advance informal and nonbinding proposals of his or her own.

3. *Fact-finding, inquiry and conciliation.*[38] These are methods of settlement in which the parties request or agree to the intervention of a third party, usually on a more formal basis, for the purpose of determining particular facts or otherwise conducting an impartial examination of the dispute and, if the parties so agree, attempting to suggest or define the terms of a mutually acceptable settlement. Like mediation, the report of a fact-finding body or conciliation commission is normally non-binding, although the third party finding or recommendation may, of course exercise an important influence on the settlement.

4. *Arbitration.*[39] This method involves the reference of a dispute or series of disputes, by the agreement of the parties, to an *ad hoc*

---

[37] *See, e.g.,* MERRILLS, *supra* note 3, at ch. 1; Darwin, *Mediation and Good Offices,* in Waldock, *supra* note 3, at 83; Raman, *supra* note 3, at ch. 3; and, *generally,* O. YOUNG, THE INTERMEDIARIES: THIRD PARTIES IN INTERNATIONAL CRISES (1967).

[38] *See, e.g.,* MERRILLS, *supra* note 3, at chs. 3 and 4; Fox, *Conciliation,* in Waldock, *supra* note 3, at 93; Darwin, *Fact-Finding and Commissions of Inquiry,* in Waldock, *supra* note 3, at 159; BAR-YAACOV, THE HANDLING OF INTERNATIONAL DISPUTES BY MEANS OF INQUIRY (1974); COT, INTERNATIONAL CONCILIATION (1972); Firmage, *Fact-Finding in the Resolution of International Disputes: From the Hague Peace Conference to the United Nations,* 1971 UTAH L. REV. 421.

[39] *See, e.g.,* MERRILLS, *supra* note 3, at ch. 5; Fox, *Arbitration,* in Waldock, *supra* note 3, at 101; WETTER, THE INTERNATIONAL ARBITRAL PROCESS PUBLIC AND PRIVATE (1979); Simp-

tribunal for binding decision, usually on the basis of international law. The parties by agreement establish the issue to be arbitrated and the machinery and procedure of the tribunal, including the method of selection of the arbitrator or arbitrators. While arbitration is normally binding, it is open to the parties to provide that the tribunal's opinion will be only advisory.

5. *Judicial Settlement.*[40] This method involves the reference of the dispute, by the agreement or consent of the parties, to the International Court of Justice or some other standing and permanent judicial body for binding decision, usually on the basis of international law. Again, if the rules establishing the court so allow, the parties may agree to an advisory or nonbinding opinion rather than a binding decision, or to a declaratory judgment specifying the principles which the parties should apply in the settlement of their dispute, as the parties did in the *North Sea Continental Shelf* case[41] and *Continental Shelf Tunisia/Libyan Arab Jamahiriya)* case.[42]

6. *Settlement through the United Nations or other global or regional international organizations or agencies.*[43] In some circumstances, the parties may request the assistance of the U.N., a regional organization, or another international organization in

---

son and Fox, INTERNATIONAL ARBITRATION (1959); Sohn, *The Function of International Arbitration Today,* 1 RECUEIL DES COURS 108 (1963); CARLSTON, THE PROCESS OF INTERNATIONAL ARBITRATION (1946).

[40] *See, e.g.,* MERRILLS, *supra* note 3, at ch. 6; Allott, *The International Court of Justice,* in Waldock, *supra* note 3, at 128; S. ROSENNE, THE WORLD COURT (3d ed. 1973); S. Rosenne, THE LAW AND PRACTICE OF THE INTERNATIONAL COURT (1965); JENKS, THE PROSPECTS OF INTERNATIONAL ADJUDICATION (1964); and the excellent collection of articles in THE FUTURE OF THE INTERNATIONAL COURT OF JUSTICE (L. Gross ed., 2 vols., 1976) (hereinafter cited as "Gross"); and JUDICIAL SETTLEMENT OF INTERNATIONAL DISPUTES (H. Mosler & R. Bernhardt eds. 1979); Schachter, *supra* note 3; and Sohn, *supra* note 3;

For a listing and brief description of the various present international courts, *see* Sohn, *supra* note 3, at 1127-30.

[41] North Sea Continental Shelf (Fed. Rep. of Germany v. Denmark; Fed. Rep. of Germany v. Netherlands), 1969 I.C.J. 10 (Judgment of Feb. 20).

[42] Continental Shelf (Tunisia v. Libyan Arab Jamahiriya), 1982 I.C.J. Rep. 18 (Judgment of Feb. 24).

[43] *See* MERRILLS, *supra* note 3, at chs. 8 and 9; Bowett, *The United Nations and Peaceful Settlement,* in Waldock, *supra,* at 179; Raman, *supra* note 3.

Some international agreements empower the organizations established by them to render a binding decision. *See* RESTATEMENT, *supra* note 7, Tent. Draft No. 5, § 902, Rept's Note 6, 176. *See also* Sohn, note 19, *supra* note 3.

settling their dispute, or the U.N. or another organization (for example, a regional organization) may on its own motion legitimately intervene in the dispute, at least for the purposes of trying to bring about a peaceful settlement. Sometimes a third party may ask for the organization's intervention.[44] This assistance may, *inter alia*, take the form of good offices, mediation, fact-finding or conciliation. The role of the U.N. in dispute settlement, particularly under Chapter VI of the Charter, has been previously noted.[45] The rights and obligations of the parties and authority of each organization in these respects are in each case set out in their respective Charters and other constitutive instruments, as well as developed through their practice.

A great deal more could be said about the characteristics, advantages and disadvantages of each of these various techniques; each has been the subject of a great deal of study, and the relevant literature is very extensive.[46] I will not discuss particular techniques further here.[47] But it may be useful to emphasize several broad points concerning international dispute settlement techniques in general:

1. As indicated, with the important exception of U.N. intervention under Chapters VI or VII of the Charter, all of these dispute settlement techniques are consensual, although a nation's consent to the use of a particular technique may be, and often is, given by agreement in advance.

2. Clearly, different kinds of disputes may call for different methods of settlement. Indeed, sometimes it may be better to deal with problems as they arise, on a pragmatic and *ad hoc* basis; in other situations, it may make more sense to develop highly structured arrangements in advance and have them in place and ready for use should need arise. The craft of effective dispute settlement to a considerable extent involves judging what method or combina-

---

[44] *See, e.g.*, Australia and India's request for U.N. intervention in the 1947 Netherlands-Indonesia dispute, discussed in Sohn, *supra* note 28, at 353-4.

[45] *See* Sec. I(C), *supra*.

[46] *See supra* references in notes 3 and 31 to 39.

[47] As indicated, the role, and *pros* and *cons*, of adjudication will be a subject of the next issue of this *Journal*.

tion of methods may be most useful in helping to resolve the particular dispute and how and when such techniques can best be employed. Indeed, under the U.N. Charter's Chapter VI procedures, the role of the Security Council is primarily to act as a "traffic director," channeling each dispute into the most appropriate procedure.[48]

3. As indicated, the various techniques are not mutually exclusive, nor are the boundaries between them rigidly drawn. A number of them can be, and usually are, employed either *seriatim* (although in no fixed order) or in combination to supplement or complement each other. The recent 1982 U.N. Convention on the Law of the Sea, which deploys a variety of techniques to deal with diverse types of disputes that may arise, shows how these possibilities can be exploited in an innovative and imaginative way.[49] As Professor Schachter points out:

> Flexibility and adaptability to the particular circumstances are the essential characteristics of these various procedures. There is little to be gained by seeking to give them precise legal limits or procedural rules as a general matter.[50]

4. These techniques do not exhaust the possibilities. It is open to the parties to agree to modify them as they wish (except in the

---

[48] I have drawn on a suggestion of Professor Louis Sohn for this point.

[49] *See* Convention on the Law of the Sea, U.N. Doc. A/Conf. 62/122 (1982), Part XV and Annexes V-VIII, *reprinted in* 21 I.L.M. 1245 (1982), MERRILLS, *supra* note 3, Ch. 7; A. Adede, *The Basic Structure of the Dispute Settlement Part of the Law of the Sea Convention*, 11 OCEAN DEV. AND INT'L L. 125 (1982); Sohn, *Settlement of Disputes Arising Out of the Law of the Sea Convention*, 12 SAN DIEGO L. REV. 495 (1975).

[50] Schachter, *supra* note 3, at 205.

See also the comments of Judge Lachs in his individual opinion in the Aegean Sea Continental Shelf case (Greece v. Turkey), 1978 I.C.J. 52 (19 Dec. 1978).

"There are obviously some disputes which can be resolved only by negotiations, because there is no alternative in view of the character of the subject-matter involved and the measures envisaged. But there are many other disputes in which a combination of methods would facilitate their resolution. The frequently unorthodox nature of the problems facing States today requires as many tools to be used and as many avenues to be opened as possible, in order to resolve the intricate and frequently multi-dimensional issues involved. It is sometimes desirable to apply several methods at the same time or successively. Thus, no incompatibility should be seen between the various instruments and fora to which States may resort, for all are mutually complementary."

case of judicial settlement by an existing court with established rules), or to creatively develop such additional methods as their needs and ingenuity suggest.

5. Finally, even the best dispute settlement techniques or institutions cannot substitute for general attitudes of cooperativeness, accomodation and good neighborliness between or among the nations involved, or for their will to settle problems by peaceful means and in good faith.

VII.   WHEN IS A DISPUTE SETTLED?

As a legal matter, a dispute is settled when either (1) the parties formally agree to a particular settlement, either on their own or by accepting the proposal of a mediator or a conciliation commission, or (2) an international arbitral or judicial tribunal, with jurisdiction over the parties and the dispute, delivers a legally binding judgment respecting it.

As a practical matter, of course, the question is more complex. Presumably, a dispute is *really* settled only when each of the parties ceases to have a continuing sense of grievance, or at least ceases to continue actively to assert its claim. That is, a settlement, whether reached through negotiated agreement or third-party decision, must be subjectively accepted by both parties as a fair and legitimate resolution of the matter if the dispute is really to be ended and put to rest.[51]

Certainly, one element in the acceptability of a settlement will be each party's sense of the inherent fairness of the settlement, in terms of the parties respective claims and interests. Thus, a settlement which contains elements of compromise, giving something to each of the parties (but also taking something from each), is in many cases more likely to be regarded as acceptable and complied with than an all-or-nothing outcome. Another element will be the parties' sense of the fairness and legitimacy of the procedures through which the settlement was reached. Perhaps a third ele-

---

[51] *See, e.g.*, discussion in Darwin, *General Introduction*, in Waldock, *supra* note 3, at 66.

ment may be the parties' sense of the extent to which the settlement bears some relation to the practical realities of their relative power with respect to the dispute—what each nation thinks it could have obtained if it had *not* agreed to peaceful settlement of the dispute. A nation may be willing to give up something, but could be very unhappy at having lost all, by resorting to peaceful settlement. Recent research by social psychologists in the field of "equity theory" may offer useful and interesting insights into the kinds of factors that affect the parties perceptions of the fairness of a particular settlement.[52]

Certainly, one thing it would be useful to know more about is what happens after a dispute has legally been settled by agreement or adjudication—whether such settlements are real solutions which are in fact carried out and complied with by the parties and leave both parties satisfied.

VIII. How Can Disputes Be Avoided?

While dispute avoidance is conceptually different from dispute settlement, the role and importance of dispute avoidance techniques is highly relevant and worth briefly noting. There are, of course, a variety of ways in which nations can seek to forestall disagreements and keep disputes from occurring. These include prior agreement on clear rules to deal with problems which might give rise to disagreements or disputes; a practice of prior notification and consultation before taking unilateral action which could cause disputes;[53] the establishment of *ad hoc* or permanent consultative

---

[52] *See, e.g.*, D. Coates and S. Penrod, *Social Psychology and the Emergence of Disputes*, 15 LAW AND SOC'Y REV. 655, 656-9 (1980-81); Walster, Berscheid and Walster, *New Directions in Equity Research*, in ADVANCES IN EXPERIMENTAL SOCIAL PSYCHOLOGY (L. Bukavitz ed. 1976).

[53] *See, e.g.*, R. KIRGIS, PRIOR CONSULTATION IN INTERNATIONAL LAW: A STUDY OF STATE PRACTICE (1983).

Prior notification and consultation is one of the most useful techniques nations can use to avoid or manage disputes. This is a process in which a nation which is considering adopting a policy or taking an action which might adversely affect another nation, tells the other nation what it is thinking of doing and discusses the matter beforehand with the other nation in an effort to avoid frictions and problems.

Some advantages of prior notification and consultation are that:

   (1) Consultation permits nations to identify and try to resolve potential frictions

bodies or joint commissions to resolve grievances, complaints or
disagreements at an early stage;[54] and, in general, a genuine at-

---

and problems at an early stage, before positions become fixed and polarized
and differences become more serious and intractable.

(2) Consultation may give the nation proposing action a better understanding of
how its proposed policy may adversely affect the other nation, perhaps leading it to abandon the policy, or to vary it so as to avoid or limit harm to the
other nation.

(3) Even if consultation does not result in a change of the acting nation's policy,
it may provide opportunity for the nation affected to take measures of its
own to avoid or reduce the harm.

(4) Consultation shows an attitude of good will, good faith and good neighborliness, thus helping to establish a climate favorable to dispute settlement and
cooperation more generally.

But prior notification and consultation also has certain drawbacks and limitations. For
example:

(1) Prior notification and consultation assume that the nation considering taking
action *cares* about not harming the other nation which might be affected.
But if the two nations are enemies, or indifferent to each other's concerns or
interests, this may not be the case.

(2) Prior consultation implies that a nation is willing and able to change its proposed policy or action. But if that nation is already irrevocably committed to
a particular policy or course of action—and nothing the other nation can say
will have the remotest chance of changing its mind—then nothing can be
gained by consultation. Indeed, a useless consultation held under these circumstances, may expose a nation to charges of bad faith or hypocrisy.

(3) Prior notification and consultation may result in delay or publicity, diminish-
ing the usefulness of a proposed policy or action which may be particularly
dependent on urgency or secrecy for its effectiveness.

(4) Prior notification and consultation may permit the other potentially affected
nation to take steps to obstruct, complicate, or prevent adoption or implementation of the proposed policy or action—for example, by mobilizing domestic or international political pressure in opposition to the policy or action,
or by taking or threatening to take protective or retaliatory measures to frustrate it.

Prior notification and consultation has been a very significant feature of Canada-U.S. dis-
pute-management practice in recent years. *See, e.g.,* KIRGIS, *supra* note 53, and my Bissell
lectures, *supra* note 30. *See also, e.g.,* the exchange of letters between the International
Joint Commission Canada-U.S., and the U.S. and Canadian Governments, dated February
13 and July 12, 1976 respectively, concerning the Commission's suggestion for a broader and
more systematic use by the two governments of prior notification and consultation with
respect to water and air pollution questions having effects along the common frontier, *reprinted in The Annual Report 1976 of the International Joint Commission Canada-U.S.*
(1977), Appendix 4, at 39-43.

[54] *See, e.g.,* the work of the International Joint Commission, U.S.-Canada, well-de-
scribed in Cohen, 146 RECUEIL DES COURS 219 (1975), and in *Controlling Great Lakes Pollution: A Study in United States-Canadian Environmental Cooperation*, 70 MICH. L. REV.
469 (1972); and the work of the Standing Consultative Commission established under sev-

tempt by every nation to recognize, understand, and take into account other nations' legitimate interests, views and concerns. The "Golden Rule" and the concept that one should always try to "imagine yourself in the other person's shoes" remain valid, sensible and moral principles of behavior for nations as well as individuals.

It may be impossible or too costly to prevent *all* international disputes. But certainly, one good way of trying to deal with disputes is to forestall as many as possible from ever arising, or at least try to find ways to solve them quickly before the dispute becomes exacerbated and the parties' positions harden.

IX. WHAT IS THE RELEVANCE OF LAW TO DISPUTE SETTLEMENT?

The international legal order is relevant to dispute settlement in many ways. First, the international legal system, explicitly and implicitly, establishes the general principle that international disputes should be settled peacefully, crystallizing each state's national interest in the maintenance of international order.

Second, the legal system more specifically establishes norms, procedures and a variety of formal and informal institutions which can facilitate both the avoidance and resolution of international disputes. In particular, international law provides salient rules and principles which generally shape the parties perceptions of legitimacy and guide their efforts to reach agreement. To the extent rules and relevant expectations are clear, nations are less likely to behave in ways which give rise to disputes and, should disputes nevertheless arise, will be able to settle them more easily on the basis of the relevant rules. Even when, as is usually the case, the parties to a dispute seek to achieve their own negotiated settlement without the intervention of third parties or international courts, they will still typically bargain "in the shadow of the law."

Finally, international agreements provide a technique through which nations can both commit themselves to the principle of

---

eral U.S.-Soviet Arms Control agreements, described in D. Caldwell, *The Standing Consultative Commission: Past Performance and Future Possibilities,* in VERIFICATION AND ARMS CONTROL (W. Potter ed. 1985).

peaceful settlement and establish specific methods for resolving their disputes, including the reaching of legally-binding settlement agreements.

Part II
Negotiation and Consultation

[2]

CONSULTATION AND NEGOTIATION IN THE PACIFIC SETTLEMENT OF INTERNATIONAL DISPUTES

CHARLES MANGA FOMBAD*

INTRODUCTION

Disputes between states are as old as international society and have throughout remained one of the fundamental preoccupations of International law. Amongst the various methods of pacific settlement of international disputes, consultations and negotiations are usually set out as the first, and in practice constitute the principle technique by virtue of its frequent use as compared with all the other methods combined.

The vital role of consultations and negotiations in the dispute settlement process is not only due to the fact that it is often the first method tried but also because it operates as an important and essential technique for resolving as well as preventing or avoiding disputes. Recent developments in many areas of International law indicate how this method of pacific settlement of disputes if well understood and boldly applied could play an even more significant role sometimes concurrently with other methods. Of particular importance is the distinctive yet complementary role of consultations operating separately or in combination with negotiations and their extended application through the mechanism of "Judicial Negotiation" and conference or parliamentary diplomacy.-

I – THE NATURE OF THE OBLIGATION TO CONSULT AND NEGOTIATE[1]

The Concepts of Consultation and Negotiation

The terms "negotiations" and "consultations" are often used

* Lic. en Dt (Yaoundé); LL.M, Ph.D (London)
* Lecturer in Law, University of Yaoundé, Cameroon.

[1] See in general, De Waart, *The Element of Negotiation in the Pacific Settlement of Disputes between states. An analysis of provisions made or applied since 1918 in the field of the Pacific Settlement of International disputes.* The Hague, Martinus Nijhoff (1973)
Falk and Black (eds.) *The Future of the International legal order vol. I Trends and Patterns.* New Jersey, Princeton University Press (1969)
Gebrehana T. *Duty to Negotiate. An element of International Law.* Uppsala, Svenska Institut for Internationell Ratt (1978)
Gulliver P. H., "Negotiations as a mode of dispute settlement", 7. *Law and Society Review* (1973) pp. 667–691

708   *Charles Manga Fombad*

interchangeably.[2] This usage is correct in many instances where these two concepts constitute part of a unified process. There however exist a distinction between the two concepts which is of great practical importance, especially with regards to their role in the pacific settlement of international disputes.

"Negotiation" is a broad complex notion which at first sight appears easy to define and understand but on detail analysis will reveal its multiple dimensions.[3] For our purposes and in the context of pacific settlement of international disputes, the most satisfactory definition is that stated in the dissenting opinion of Judge MOORE in the *Mavrommatis Palestine Concessions* case, where he said:

> ". . . in the international sphere and in the sense of International Law, negotiation is the legal and orderly administrative process by which Governments, in the exercice of their unquestionable powers conduct their relations with another and discuss, adjust and settle their differences."[4]

This definition brings out three important features of negotiation;

(i) It makes it clear that negotiations are a legal process and as such must operate and function within the general framework of International law.

(ii) From the broad formulation, it covers both "ad hoc" and permanent or institutional negotiations, as well as bilateral and multilateral negotiations, and

(iii) The fact that negotiations provide a medium both for general discussions and affecting adjustments which help towards both preventing or avoiding potential disputes and resolving actual disputes that have arisen.

The effectiveness of negotiations in any particular dispute will therefore depend on the interaction of these three factors. But, negotiation, defined in these broad terms, also covers and incorporates the notion of "consultation".

"Consultation" per se is a rather complex legal notion that eludes a precise definition. It could however be described as consisting of the

---

[2] See,Bin Cheng, "Dispute Settlement in bilateral air transport agreements", in Böckstiegel k (ed.) *Settlement of Space Law disputes. The present state of the Law and Perspectives of further development*. Proceedings of an International Colloquium, Munich 13 and 14 September 1979. Bonn, Carl Heymanns Verlag (1980), at p. 106
Kozhevnikow (ed.) Denis Ogden (tr.) *International Law. A textbook for use in law schools*. Moscow Foreign languages Publishing House (1961), at p. 378
Judo Umarto Kusamouidagdo, *Consultation Clauses — As a means of providing for treaty obedience. A study in the law of treaties*. Stockholm, Almqvist & Wiksell International (1981), at p. 56

[3] See Grigoire Geamânu, "Théorie et pratique des négociations," *Hague Recueil* (1980), p. 401 *et seq.*

[4] The *Mavrommatis Palestine Concessions* case (Judgement) PCIJ series A. No. 2 (1924); pp. 62–63

Consultation and Negotiation in International Disputes 709

formal or informal, "ad hoc" or permanent, bilateral or multilateral discussions and conversations between states aimed at resolving their differences although it is more often to avoid or prevent potential rather than actual disputes. Consultation as such, unlike negotiation *stricto sensu*, relates more to situations and issues of potential controversy rather than actual disputes.

But the distinction between these two concepts, whilst widely recognized and accepted[5] need not be stretched too far, inasmuch as there is no clear-cut and well marked borderline which separates the two. Not only are the two terms often correctly used interchangeably, but may even have the same legal effect. Thus where a consultation clause is designed to or operates to facilitate the settlement of an actual dispute that has arisen, then it becomes indistinguishable from the operation of a negotiation clause.[6] Even when this is not so, the consultation and negotiation process could be operated concurrently, with the former gradually merging into the latter where the discussions and conversations expose underlying differences of view between the parties. Perhaps the fundamental point here is that the existence of a dispute is not a condition *sine qua non*, nor an essential for the invocation of the consultation process generally, as it is for the negotiation process.

The legal Nature of the Obligation to Consult and Negotiate

It is generally agreed that where there is an express stipulation or where it could be reasonably inferred from the dispute settlement clause that forms the basis of jurisdiction, that preliminary negotiations are a condition. Then an international tribunal seized is bound to satisfy itself that this obligation had been fulfilled.[7]

A controversy has for sometime persisted over the legal nature of the obligation to negotiate in the absence of an express or implied stipulation to that effect. To one school of thought, the obligation to undertake preliminary negotiations in respect of all international disputes is

[5]See, Paul Guggenheim, *Traité de droit International Public.* Tome II, Génève, Libraire de l'Université, George & Cie (1954), at p. 197

Pauterpacht H., (ed.) *Oppenheim's International Law. Vol;. II Disputes, War and Neutrality.* 7th ed. London Longman & Co (1952), at p. 8

Serensen M., (ed.) *Manual of Public International Law.* London, Macmillan & Co (1968), at p. 679 but also

See, Gould W., who in, *An Introduction to International Law.* New York, Harper Brothers Publishers (1957) at p. 541 expresses the interesting view that the differences between the two are determined by the number of parties involved.

[6]See, Paul Guggenheim, *ibid;* Lauterpacht H., *ibid*; and Serensen M., *ibid.*

[7] See, Shabtai Rosenne, *The Law and Practice of the International Court.* 2 Vols. Leyden. A. W. Sijthoff (1965), at p. 512 and

Jacques Soubreyrol, "La négociation diplomatique élément du contentieux international," 68 *RGDIP* (1964), at p. 324

710   *Charles Manga Fombad*

considered to be a well established rule of Customary International Law or may even arise as a general principle of International Law to be complied with before any international tribunal can de seized.[8] This view is strongly opposed by others who argue that there is neither a principle nor a rule of International Law which justifies the concept of compulsory preliminary negotiations in the absence of an express or implied stipulation to that effect.[9] This latter view is more consistent with International Jurisprudence and the unfettered freedom of states to specifically define the method of dispute settlement procedures they will pursue when a dispute arises.

A rather broad formulation was adopted by the Permanent Court in the *Mavrommatis Palestine concessions* case, where it stated:

> The court realizes to the full the importance of the rule laying down that only disputes which cannot be settled by negotiation should be brought before it. It recognizes in fact that before a dispute can be made the subject of an action of law, its subject matter should have been clearly defined by means of diplomatic negotiation.[10]

Although this judgement has frequently been relied upon by proponents of the view that there is a binding international obligation to undertake preliminary negotiations prior to the commencement of proceedings before an international tribunal. It would seem that the court rather than attempting to state a general principle, was referring specifically to the precise wordings of the clauses in the mandate on which its jurisdiction was founded. Nevertheless, subsequent decisions have been more unequivocal.

In the *interpretation of Judgements N°s 7 and 8 (the Chorzow* Factory Case)[11] the court pointed out that although it would no doubt be desirable that a state before proceeding to take as serious a step as summoning another state to appear before it, should have attempted to settle the matter through negotiations. It however reaffirmed the views it had expressed in the *German interests in Polish Upper Silesia* case[12] that, in the

---

[8] Proponents of this view include;

Mehdi Madjdi Ahi, *Les négociations diplomatiques préalable à la soumission d'un différend à une instance internationale*. (Thèse.) Génève (1957) discussed in Jacques Soubreyrol, *loc. cit.* in footnotes 7 at p. 322

Kaasik N., "La clause de négociation diplomatique dans le droit international positif et dans le jurisprudence de la Cour Permanente de Justice Internationale", 14 *RDILC* (1933), p. 65 *et seq.*

[9] See, Manley O. Hudson, *The Permanent Court of International Justice 1920–1942*, New York, Macmillan & Co (1942), at p. 413

Shabtai Rosenne, *loc. cit.* in footnotes 7, at p. 513

Simpson and Fox, *International Arbiration. Law and Practice*. London, Stevens & Sons (1959), ar p. 126

Jacques Soubreyrol, *loc. cit.* in footnote 7, p. 323 *et seq.*

Humphrey Waldock, "The decline of the optional clause," 32 *BYIL* (1955), pp. 254–266.

[10] The *Mavrommatis Palestine Concessions* case *supra* at p. 15

[11] The *interpretation of Judgments Nos. 7 and 8 (The Chorzow Factory)* case. PCIJ series A. No. 13 (1927), pp. 10–11

[12] The *German interests in Polish Upper Silesia* case (Jurisdiction) PCIJ series A. No. 6 (1925), p. 14

Consultation and Negotiation in International Disputes 711

absence of specific stipulations in the jurisdictional clause rendering diplomatic negotiations a condition precedent, its jurisdiction could not be ousted on that ground.

It also follows that there is no general duty in International Law to consult in the absence of an express or implied provision in the relevant agreement or dispute settlement clause to this effect.

II – THE OPERATION OF CONSULTATIONS AND NEGOTIATIONS IN THE DISPUTE SETTLEMENT PROCESS

As pointed out earlier, it is important to distinguish between the operation of consultations prior to dispute *stricto sensu* and negotiations after the concretisation of all the elements of a dispute have arisen.

The Role of Consultations Prior to a Dispute

As a Mechanism for Preventing or Avoiding Disputes

Where there exists a duty on the parties to an agreement to consult, this may operate at three different levels depending on the nature of the issues involved.[13]

This may firstly, consist of a general obligation on the parties to undertake frequent and regular consultations. The main objective is usually to provide a regulatory framework to enable a continuous assessment and supervision of the implementations of the agreement and as such relates to issues of potential controversy.

The second stage may involve consultations relating to specific issues which have arisen, and operates where the possibility of an actual dispute arising has become particularly acute. The aim at this stage is both to resolve such issues as well as to avoid a confrontation. These first two stages, relating as it were, to situations of potential disputes rather than actual disputes *stricto sensu*, are usually and more appropriately referred to as consultations and not negotiations.

The third and final stage will often deal with those circumstances where inspite of the previous efforts under the consultation process, a dispute has in fact arisen. The objective here is really to attempt an amicable settlement and in effect, negotiate.

As noted earlier, and it must be emphasized, this distinction, whilst functionally and operationally correct, should not be stretched too far. The

---

[13] See in general, Bin Cheng, *loc. cit.* in footnote 2 and Bin Cheng, "The role of consultation in bilateral international air services agreements, as exemplified by Bermuda I and II," 19 *Columbia Journal of Translation Law* (1981), pp. 183–195 and
Fombad Charles Manga, *The settlement of disputes under Itnernational air transport agreements*. (thesis) Un. of London (1986) chapter 3. pp. 122–183

712   *Charles Manga Fombad*

process of consultations and negotiations are seldom straightforward, going clearly from one stage to the next. It will ultimately depend in many instances on the complexity of the issues that have arisen and the urgency of settlement.

Consultations in International Practice

Consultation in its strict sense operates in an all-pervasive manner, as an on-going process prior to, and independently of the existence of a dispute and aims primarily at avoiding or preventing disputes as well as identifying areas of possible divergence.

The evidence of state practice under many international agreements covering many areas of international co-operation indicates not only a wide adoption of consultation clauses but also an increasing shift in emphasis on dispute avoidance or prevention. It can be suggested that a principle of dispute avoidance or prevention is thus gradually emerging under many such agreements, even if not generally, at least with regards to specific issues covered by such clauses. This trend is particularly remarkable in the many areas of International Law.

Under international air transport agreements, consultation clauses have become a common feature and co-exist with the more specific duty to negotiate whenever a dispute arises.[14] The best example of this is found in the Bermuda 2, air transport agreement between the United Kingdom and the United States.[15] This agreement introduced a self-executory consultation procedure which isolates and concentrates on the frequently contentious issues of tariffs and capacity and provides a permanent continuing tariff working group to back the former. Its special feature is a sophisticated built-in check, which ensures that all adjustments to tariffs and capacity are adequately discussed before approval is sought and thus reduces any possibility of disputes arising or that when they do arise, they will not interfere with the smooth operation of air services between the two states.

Developments in the field of International Environmental Law also show a similar principle of dispute avoidance emerging. States contemplating or actually carrying out any activity which may threaten other states' environmental interests now accept the need not only to give timely notice and information to the states likely to be affected but often engage in consultations through which they seek in good faith to reach a compromise capable of avoiding or minimizing any possible harmful effects.[16] The obligation to consult has always been a key feature of the Agreements of the International Monetary Fund and the General

---

[14] See, Fombad Charles Manga *ibid.*

[15] *Ibid* pp. 142–146

[16] See in général, Richard B. Bilder, "The settlement of disputes in the field of the international law of the environment", *Hague Recueil* (1975), pp. 139–240

Consultation and Negotiation in International Disputes 713

Agreements on Tariffs and Trade.[17] Similarly, co-basin states have recognized the importance of regular and frequent consultations as a means of preventing or avoiding problems arising between them.[18]

In spite of these development in the role of consultations, it cannot at this stage be said that International Law imposes any general obligation on states to avoid disputes or even more specifically, to employ any particular methods to achieve this end. It may nevertheless indicate some evidence amongst member states of the United Nations to act in accordance with the spirit of the declaration on principles of International Law concerning friendly relations and co-operation amongst states in accordance with the charter which requires states to seek in "early and just settlement of their international disputes".[19]

But whatever form consultations might take, whether institutional, as in the case of Bermuda 2 or "ad hoc" as is more often the case, and whether bilateral or multilateral as in the case under the GATT, it is clear that where a divergence of views on a specific or several issues emerge and constitute elements of a dispute *stricto sensu* take shape. It becomes futile to continue. Infact, it is often at this point when clear differences of opinion have become pronounce that the consultation and negotiation processes might merge and become indistinguishable. There might still nevertheless be a more formal process of negotiations which usually has its own special features and objectives.

The Role of Negotiation after a Dispute has Arisen

Negotiations commenced after a dispute has arisen may take effect either as a condition or a first step before recourse to other methods of settlement or may even operate as the only and final method of dispute settlement contemplated by the parties under the agreement.

Negotiations as a Condition or First Step in the Dispute Settlement Process

Where negotiations are specifically provided for by the parties or this could reasonably be implied, then an international tribunal seized is obliged to ascertain that such negotiations as a matter of fact, actually took place and

---

[17] See in general, Wilfred Jenks, *The Common Law of Mankind*. London, Stevens & Sons (1958), pp. 226, 277–288 and
F. L. Kirgis, *Prior consultation in International Law. A study of state practice*. Charlottesville. University of Virginia (1983)

[18] See, C. B. Bourne, "Procedure in the development of International drainage basins: The duty to consult and to negotiate." 10 *CanYIL* (1972), pp. 212–233

[19] See in general, Šahović M., (ed.) *Principles of International Law concerning friendly relations and co-operation*. New York, Oceana Publications (1972)

714   *Charles Manga Fombad*

failed to settle the dispute. The International Court has even gone further to consider it inherent in the exercise of its judicial functions to facilitate and even where necessary, encourage such negotiations.[20]

The difficulties that have often arisen here usually relate, as we shall see below, to the form such preliminary negotiations should take.

Negotiations as the Only Method of Dispute Settlement

Negotiations as the only and final means of resolving international disputes is a common feature of agreement entered into by socialist states particularly the Soviet Union and China and is a general reflection on their distrust of third party procedures.[21] Although it has to be noted here that the fact that a particular agreement only envisages negotiations in its disputes settlement clauses does not necessarily exclude third party procedures inasmuch as the parties could subsequently agree on such other methods of settlement as they deem necessary.

Nevertheless, the exclusion of third party procedures by socialist states finds strong theoretical and ideological justification in soviet doctrine and diplomatic practice. They have consistently maintained that the right to interpret treaties is vested exclusively on the parties to such a treaty.[22] As such, any third party procedures are considered a derogation of national sovereignty and independence and hence a relic which has no place in the modern international community. The rationale for this attitude is pungently summed up in the famous axiom of Maxim Litvinov, that "only an angel would be capable of the necessary impartiality" when dealing with a dispute in which the Soviet Union is a party.[23]

It could be argued that the absence of an alternative method of dispute settlement may provide an incentive on both parties to be more accommodating and flexible during negotiations. But a major limitation is the danger of one party resorting to obstructionist or other delay tactics, secure in the knowledge that it will not be reproached in any subsequent independent proceedings. The success of negotiations in such circumstances will depend entirely on the goodwill of the parties and perhaps the issues at stake. On balance, negotiations as the only and final method of dispute settlement is not an entirely satisfactory way of ensuring

---

[20] See, Fombad Charles Manga *loc. cit.* in footnote 13, at pp. 129–130
[21] See, *ibid* pp. 151–153 and in general,
Roulin H., "Les pays de l'Est et le règlement pacifique des différends internationaux", 1 *Revue Belge de droit international* (1965), pp. 376–391
[22] See, Kazimierz Grzybowski, *Soviet Public International Law. Doctrine and diplomatique practice.* Leyden, A. W. Sijthoff 1970, at p. 464
[23] See, P. J. Allott, "The International Court of Justice," in Northedge and Donelan (eds.) *International disputes: The political Aspects.* Report of a study Group. London. Europa Publications (1972) at p. 131 and
Kazimierz Grzybowski, *loc. cit.* in footnote 22 at p. 413

an expeditious and conclusive solution to an international dispute. Particularly where one party is in a strong position, even if its legal position is less plausible.

III – THE CONDUCT OF CONSULTATIONS AND NEGOTIATIONS

The Role of Law

It has sometimes been debated whether the processes of consultations and negotiations should be subject to any strictly defined legal principles.[24] Although the very rationale of this method of dispute settlement as contrasted with arbitral and judicial procedures could be undermined by any rigid adherence to laid down rules and procedures. Nevertheless compliance with and conformity with well established principles of International Law in the conduct of consultations and negotiations is an important factor which determines the durability and effectiveness of any settlement reached by the parties.

Perhaps the most fundamental principle that regulates the whole process is that of good faith. And as Bin Cheng points out;

> The law of treaties is closely bound with the principle of good faith, if indeed not based on it, for this principle governs treaties from the time of their formation to the time of their extinction.[25]

And in the *Nuclear Test* cases, the International Court noted;

> One of the basic principles governing the creation and performance of legal obligations, whatever their source, is the principle of good faith. Trust and confidence are inherent in international co-operation, in particular in an age when this co-operation in many fields is becoming increasingly essential.[26]

Good faith in this respect is a rather vague legal principle with no *a priori* precise legal definition and is often left to illustration and description.[27] In the context of consultation and negotiation, a state would be in breach of the requisite good faith if it is guilty of "an unjustified breaking off of discussions, abnormal delays, disregard of agreed procedures, or systematic refusals to take into consideration adverse proposals or interests."[28] A recent illustration of this occurred during the futile efforts of

---

[24] See, Grigoire Geamănu, *loc. cit.* in footnote 3 pp. 411–425 and James Irvin, "The role of law in the negotiated settlement of International disputes", 3 *Vanderbilt International* (1969), pp. 58–73

[25] Bin Cheng, *General Principles of law as applied by International Courts and Tribunals*. London, Stevens & Sons (1953), at p. 106

[26] The *Nuclear Test* cases, ICJ Reports (1974), p. 253 at p. 268

[27] See, C. B. Bourne, *loc. cit* in footnote 18, p. 223 *et seq.* and Bin Cheng, *loc. cit.* in footnote 25, p. 106 *et seq.*

[28] The *Lake Lanoux Arbitration*. 24 ILR (1959), at p. 128.

716   *Charles Manga Fombad*

the United Nations to negotiate with the United States over their dispute over the interpretation of Sect. 21 of the United Nations Headquarters agreements of 1947 prior to the proceedings before the International Court. Here, it is submitted that the US was in breach of its duty of good faith, when it deliberately refused to engage in consultations and negotiations as contemplated by the dispute settlement procedure under Art 21 of the Headquarters Agreement, preferring to restrict itself to informal contacts and consultations outside the dispute settlement procedure.[29] For good faith not only applies to the conduct but also the invocation of, and implementation of solutions reached, during the consultation and negotiation process.

A breach of good faith, like the breach of any other international obligation involves international responsibility on the guilty party. Since it amounts to a failure to apply the agreement, a state may claim damages for any losses suffered as a result of abnormal delays caused by a systematic and deliberate refusal to implement or conduct consultations and negotiations in good faith as long as such damages are not too remote.[30]

Compliance with the Obligation to Consult and Negotiate

Substantive Aspect

There is no laid down general rule governing the actual nature of complying with the obligation to consult and negotiate. Its very flexibility and informality militates against stringent procedural requirements. But it remains a matter of fact to be determined objectively by an international tribunal seised whether there have been adequate consultations and negotiations to justify the conclusion that this precondition has been fulfilled. In doing so, it has often been emphasized that it is not so much the form that such consultations and negotiations may have taken, as the attitude and views of the parties concerned on the substantive issues involved.[31]

Generally, international consultations and negotiations frequently commence with the actors directly involved in the dispute before the issue is taken up at a higher level between the protecting states when no solution is reached. There is an obvious advantage in attempting to resolve issues at their lowest possible level and with the least possible publicity. Such lower-

[29] The *Applicability of the obligation to arbitrate under Sect. 21 of the UN Headquarters Agreement* case. ICJ Reports (1988), p. 12
[30] See in general, Elizabeth Zoller, *La Bonne foi en droit international public.* Paris, Edition A Pedone (1977) and
Georg Schwarzenberger and E. D. Brown, *A Manual of International Law* 6th ed. Abingdon, Oxon, Professional Books (1976), p. 128
[31] The *South West Africa Cases (Ethiopia v South Africa; Liberia v South Africa) (Preliminary objections)* ICJ Reports (1962), p. 319 et p. 346

level solution tend to be simpler, quicker and cheaper and in general, keep a controversy from being enmeshed in broader political issues or engaging national sensitivities.[32] Subsequent discussions at state level will merely proceed at the point where the previous discussions left off, as it may well happen that the nature of the earlier talks will render superfluous a renewal of all the opposing contentions from which the dispute originated.[33]

This same principle would also apply and make it unnecessary for a state intervening under Arts. 62 and 63 of the statute of the international court[34] to go through the formality of negotiations and re-open discussions which had already taken place and on which it seeks to rely. This is however subject to two qualifications examined below with regard to parliamentary or conference diplomacy.

Compliance with the mandatory obligation to engage in preliminary negotiations does not necessarily require prolonged and extensive discussions. In the *Mavrommatis Palestine Concessions* case,[35] Britain had argued that there was no dispute which could not "be settled by negotiations" under the terms of the mandate. The very small number and brevity of the communications with the idea of negotiation *stricto sensu*. In rejecting this argument, the Permanent Court stated:

Negotiations do not always of necessity presuppose a more or less lengthy series of notes and despatches; it may suffice that a discussion should have been, and this discussion may have been very short; this will be the case if a deadlock is reached, or if finally a point is reached at which one of the parties definitely declares himself unable, or refuses, to give way and there can therefore be no doubt that the dispute cannot be settled by diplomatic negotiation . . .[36]

The court also considered the question whether negotiations stood any chance of success or were deadlock, a relative one which could not be determined without regard to, amongst other considerations, the views of the states concerned, who are usually in the best position to judge as to the political or other reasons which could prevent a negotiated settlement.[37]

Even where the dispute settlement clauses provide a specified duration for consultations and negotiations, probably as a safeguard against obstructionist tactics, an international tribunal would not allow a recalcitrant party to exploit this in urgent cases to delay a prompt settlement. Thus, although such a time limit may not have expired, a tribunal would in appropriate case in accepting jurisdiction hold that a

---

[32] See, Richard B. Bilder *loc. cit.* in footnote 16, at p. 224
[33] The *Mavromatis Palestine Concession* case *supra* at p. 13
[34] See, Fombad Charles Manga, *loc. cit.* in footnote 13, pp. 133, 339–344
[35] The *Mavromtis Palestine Concession* case, *supra*
[36] *ibid.* at p. 13
[37] *ibid.* at p. 15

718   *Charles Manga Fombad*

deadlock had been reached and any further delays within such a time limit would only cause unnecessary hardship.

An important objective of consultations and negotiations being that it enables the parties to express their views and for the issues in dispute to be clearly defined and agreed upon, it goes without saying that only such issues previously raised and discussed can form the subject of subsequent proceedings before an international tribunal. The mere fact that a party threatened to invoke the legal procedure provided for in the dispute settlement clause does not render such an issue one that could not be resolved through negotiations. And as Judge CHENG put it in the *Phosphates in Morocco* case:

> . . . warning is not the same thing as negotiation. It is the essence of negotiations to discuss some question with a view to settling it, whereas warning is merely the intimation of a will to do certain things (. . .) on certain contingencies.[38]

This injunction has often been applied to issues that were never mentioned during consultations and negotiations, to which the principle that they were not issues that could not be settled through negotiations applies with full force. Thus in *Electricity company of Sofia and Bulgaria* case,[39] one of the complaints raised by Belgium in its application was rejected as being an entirely fresh issue over which there was no evidence that it had been the subject of the prior diplomatic negotiations between the parties.

On the other hand, where the issue raised is closely and intricately linked with matters that had formed the subject of previous consultations and negotiations, then the general injunction may not apply. In the *France/US Air Transport Arbitration* of 1978[40] one of the preliminary jurisdictional objections raised by the US was the fact that the issue concerning the application of Part 213 Order of the CAB Economic Regulations, unlike the dispute over the change of guage, had not been raised during its preliminary negotiations with France. The tribunal in rejecting this argument pointed out that even if the discussions on the particular issue had not been specific or extensive, the two issues were in fact closely interrelated.

An important question also raised in the above arbitration is the legitimacy threatening or actually using retaliatory measures as a means to expedite the recourse to the consultations and negotiations procedures and ultimately other third party procedures provided under the dispute settlement clause. The tribunal took the view that retaliatory measures

[38] The *Phosphates in Morocco case (Preliminary objection)* PCIJ series A/B No. 74 (1938) p. 10 at p. 39
[39] The *Electricity Company of Sofia and Bulgaria case (Preliminary objections)* PCIJ Series A/B No. 77 (1939), p. 64
[40] The *France/US Air Transport Arbitration Award* of 1978 54 ILR (1979), p. 303

were neither prohibited under the general principles of International Law nor inconsistent with the US' obligations under the relevant air transport agreement inasmuch as they were accompanied by an offer for an accelerated procedure for resolving the dispute. This, it is submitted is an unsatisfactory authority for the view that retaliatory measures could be legitimate when used in a genuine effort towards speeding up a negotiated settlement of a dispute.[41] Obviously, a policy of negotiation under the threat of retaliation is the antithesis of the good faith and mutual understanding that should prevail prior to, during and after consultations and negotiations. And besides an obligation to consult and negotiate does not imply any obligation on the parties to reach a settlement of their differences.[42] Nevertheless, good faith requires the parties at least to make a determined effort towards reaching an amicable compromise and not merely to reduce the whole process into a meaningless formality.[43]

Two other forms of consultation and negotiation are of sufficient interest to merit separate consideration here in view of their potential significance to the general process of pacific settlement of disputes.

Conference or Parliamentary Diplomacy

Conference or parliamentary diplomacy is a legal concept of relatively recent birth developed since 1945 within the proceedings of the General Assembly of the United Nations.[44] As an extension of traditional consultations and negotiations, it could in appropriate instances constitute a substitute or an alternative to the latter not only within the framework of the United Nations but also within other international forums.

The issue whether the discussion of an issue within an international organization such as the United Nations could be considered a sufficient compliance with the requirement of direct consultations and negotiations was raised in the *South west Africa* cases.[45] South Africa had raised as one of its preliminary objection to the court's jurisdiction, the argument that there had been no direct negotiation between itself and either Liberia or Ethiopia as was envisaged under the terms of the mandate. The court in rejecting this, held it was irrelevant that the negotiations that had taken place had not been directly between South Africa and the two applicants. It went further to expound the concept of conference or parliamentary diplomacy which is considered applicable to the case thus;

[41] See further criticisms in Fombad Charles Manga, *loc. cit.* in footnote 13, pp. 154–158
[42] The *Railway Traffic between Lithuania and Poland* case. PCIJ Series A/B No. 42 (1931); at p. 116
[43] The *North Sea Continental Shelf cases.* ICJ Reports (1969) p. 3 at p. 47.
[44] See in general, Philip Jessup, "Parliamentary diplomacy — An examination of the legal quality of the rules of procedure or organization of the United Nations," I *Hague Recueil* and Dean Rusk, "Parliamentary diplomacy: Debate v Negotiation," 26 *World Affairs Interpreter* (1955), pp. 121–156
[45] The *South West Africa Cases. supra*

720   *Charles Manga Fombad*

In cases where the disputed questions are of common interest to a group of states on one side or the other in an organized body, parliamentary or conference diplomacy has often been found to be the most practical form of negotiation . . . If it is one of mutual interest to many states, whether in an organized body or not, there is no reason why each of them should go through the formality and pretence of direct negotiations with the common adversary state after they have already fully participated in the collective negotiations with the samw state in opposition.[46]

But whatever its merits, this concept is not without its critics. Infact, Judges Spender and Fitzmaurice in a joint dissenting opinion expressed the views that discussions at an international organization could never be regarded as a substitute for direct negotiations nor justify the conclusion that attempts had been made at settlement at the statal or diplomatic level.[47] Judge Fitzmaurice was to repeat his views in the *Northern Cameroons* case[48] when he observed that "negotiations" did not mean "a couple of states arguing with each other across the floor of an international assembly, or circulating statements of their complaints or contentions to its member states." This he declared was "disputation, not negotiation."[49]

Although the concept of conference or parliamentary diplomacy is now fairly well established and provides a very important technique particularly suitable for resolving certain types of disputes which concerns a multitude of states. Certain checks seem necessary for such a collective process to be assimilated to or even substitute direct consultations and negotiations. Two conditions are essential, and these conditions will also apply in cases of intervention under the statute of the International Court as pointed out above.

(i)   The issues raised in the proceedings before the tribunal or in the application to intervene must be substantially the same as those previously discussed, such as to render further direct negotiations superfluous.

(ii)   The tribunal must be satisfied that there is no reasonable chance that further direct negotiation between the parties would lead to a settlement or substantially narrow down the issues raised.

Subject to such control, the concept of conference or parliamentary diplomacy offers an attractive means through which attempts could be made to resolve certain types of disputes before ultimate recourse to international litigation. International Law is not so rich in methods for pacific settlement of disputes that it can afford to ignore some of the obvious advantages that such a procedure can offer especially within the

[46] Ibid. at p. 346.
[47] *Ibid.* at p. 562
[48] The *Northern Cameroons case (Judgment)* ICJ Reports (1963), p. 15
[49] *Ibid.* at p. 123

framework of an international organization like the United Nations or any of the other specialized agencies. Whilst its exact scope and potential is still uncertain, it is perhaps too early to draw any definite conclusions.

The Concept of "Judicial Negotaition"[50]

Another dimension to the art of consultation and negotiation appears to have been added in what may appropriately be referred to as "judicial negotiation". This concept, applicable under the ICAO Council Rules for the Settlement of Differences[51] requires the council to initiate, and encourage or actively direct a negotiated settlement between the disputants, as an integral but complimentary part of its essentially adjudicatory role under chapter XVIII of the Chicago Convention of 1944.[52] It is only a discretionary function subject to the consent of the parties to dispute and may be undertaken at any stage of the proceedings but prior to the meeting at which the final decision is to be rendered. As such, it is not an independent, distinct, or autonomous method of resolving such disputes but remains incidental to adjudication. Although used only once since its formulation, it breaks new frontiers in the approach to international adjudication and the role of consultation and negotiation can still play at that stage.

The concept of judicial negotiation has more wider application even within the strict confines of traditional adjudication. Some ramifications of this can be seen in the practice of the International Court. In the *Aegean Sea Continental Shelf* case,[53] the court rejected any suggestion that the existence of active negotiations constituted a legal impediment to the exercise of jurisdiction. Referring to earlier jurisprudence on this point, it observed however that whilst negotiations and judicial proceedings could be pursued *pari passu*, the latter may be discontinued if the negotiations succeeded.

In general, both the present court and its predecessor have always stressed the fact that their judicial role is simply an alternative to direct and friendly settlement through negotiations. They have on various occasions tried to facilitate such direct and friendly settlements as far as it was compatible with their statute[54] in the *Fisheries Jurisdiction (UK v Iceland)* case,[55] the International Court after observing that the obligation to negotiation flows from the very nature of the respective rights of the

[50] See in general, Fombad Charles Manga, *loc. cit.* in footnote 13, pp. 351–355, 445–447

[51] Rules for the Settlement of Differences. 2nd ed. ICAO Doc. 7782/2 (1975)

[52] The Convention on International Civil Aviation, Chicago, 7 December 1944 in United States, Department of State, *Proceedings of the International Civil Aviation Conference.* Chicago, Illinois 1944, Publication No. 2820, 2 volumes, Washington (1948)

[53] The *Aegean Sea Continental Shelf* case. ICJ Reports (1978), p. 3 and in particular Judge Nagendra Singh at p. 48

[54] The *Pakistan Prisoners of War case* ICJ Reports (1973), p. 347

[55] The *Fisheries Jurisdiction (United Kingdom v Iceland) case* ICJ Reports (1974), p. 3 at p. 13

722   *Charles Manga Fombad*

parties, considered that to direct them to negotiate was a proper exercice of its judicial functions in the circumstances.

Judicial negotiation in this respect is a promising legal development which might go some way towards encouraging recourse to the International Court if its procedures are clearly defined.

IV – PROSPECTS OF CONSULTATIONS AND NEGOTIATIONS IN THE PACIFIC SETTLEMENT OF INTERNATIONAL DISPUTES.

An analysis of the dispute settlement clauses of most International agreements shows that consultation and negotiation clauses occupy a prominent place[56] and in practice this method of disputed settlement has proven to be the most frequently used and effective means for both preventing and resolving disputes. Even in the most intractable disputes, the operation of this method had often helped to narrow the issues to more manageable proportions. The prospects of consultations and negotiations in the pacific settlement of international disputes had to be appreciated in the light of their most important limitations and advantages.

Limitations of Consultations and Negotiations

These limitations are well summarized in the 1966 Report of the Special Committee on Principles of International Law concerning friendly relations and co-operation among states.[57] It notes that direct negotiations do not always allow the facts to be established objectively and impartially, and often do not enable third parties to exercice a moderating influence. The putting forward of exaggerated claims which might aggravate a dispute cannot be prevented. Nor can fair and just terms be ensured since one of the parties is usually in a weaker position.

Furthermore, consultations and negotiations could drag on for years, a situation that will favour the recalcitrant party. Dependent as it is on the good will of the parties, the outcome is impredictable. Where a compromise is reached, it may still be precarious. In fact since the legal positions of the parties are hardly ever clarified this is usually a poor guide for future conduct and is no guarantee that similar issues will not arise in the future.

---

[56] See in general, Fombad Charles Manga, *loc. cit.* in footnote 13, pp. 47–78 and in particular, *handbook on Administrative Clauses in Bilateral Air Transport Agreement.* ICAO Cirular 62-AT/6 (1962), pp. 72–83 and
Survey of Treaty Provisions for the Pacific Settlement of International disputes 1949–1962. New York, UN (1966)

[57] *Report of the 1966 Special Committee on Principles of International Law concerning friendly relations and co-operation among states.* UN. Doc. A/6230, pp. 93–98

Advantages of Consultations and Negotiations

Generally, the requirement of preliminary consultations and negotiations is not a mere technicality or formality. This will in many instances protect the parties from the expense and trouble of international litigation which may eventually prove to be unnecessary, premature and inadequately motivated.[58] Being very flexible, relatively simple and inexpensive, it could be brought into operation at short notice to sort our urgent and pressing issues that have suddenly arisen.

Consultations and negotiations are particularly appropriate in many international disputes which more often than not are a reflection of differences over accommodating or adjusting the interests and aspirations of the parties to changing circumstances rather than strict issues of law. In such situations, a strict legal decision by an international tribunal might well determine but not really settle the dispute in any conclusive and satisfactory manner.

Frequent and regular consultations, combined with direct negotiations should provide a favourable climate for mutual co-operation and understanding which ensures peaceful co-existence. Whilst a recourse to legal proceedings may in some situations be regarded as an unfriendly act and breed suspicion and ill-will.

CONCLUSION

The continuous relevance and effectiveness of consultations and negotiations in the pacific settlement of international disputes will depend on how current trends in state practice can be fully appreciated and some attempt made at formulating coherent and comprehensive guidelines. Of particular importance is the need for some sort of an institutional consultative framework in areas of recurrent problems or situations where frequent problems are likely to arise. This could be either bilateral or multilateral and operate at regular intervals or as and when the need arises and the emphasis should be on dispute avoidance or prevention. Although examples of these in state practice are still too few[59] the results achieved do indicate that such procedures should be encouraged. Another step in this direction could be the extention of the concept of judicial negotiation to the proceedings of the International Court. As a way of overcoming the general reluctance by states to resort to litigation, the court could be allowed the discretion in appropriate circumstances during its judicial proceedings to actively encourage or even direct a negotiated settlement. This is not to minimize the practical difficulties involved but there are sufficient advantages to warrent some thought in this direction.

[58] The *South West Africa case supra.* dissenting opinions of Judges Spender and Fitzmaurice at p. 563

[59] See in general, Fombad Charles Manga *loc. cit.* in footnote 13, pp. 141–149 and J. G. Merrills, *International dispute settlement.* London, Sweet & Maxwell (1984), pp. 6–8

724　*Charles Manga Fombad*

RÉSUMÉ

La consultation et la négociation dans le règlement pacifique des conflits internationaux

Les concepts de consultations et négociations, même si souvent inter-changeables, sont cependant fonctionnellement différents dans plusieurs situations de règlement pacifique de conflits internationaux. Consultation dans son sens strict opère indépendamment de l'éxistance d'une dispute et vise en premier lieu d'éviter et prévenir les conflits aussi bien qu'identifier les domaines de divergence possible. Les négociations d'autre part entrent en jeu lorsqu'un conflit réel est né et ont pour but de le résoudre.

En dépit de la controverse entourant cette question, il semble maintenant bien établi que l'obligation de consulter et négocier naîte d'une stipulation expresse ou tacite faite par les parties, plutôt que d'une règle de droit international coutumier ou même d'un principe général de droit international public.

Il y a eu deux développements importants au niveau du rôle des consultations et des négociations dans le règlement pacifique des conflits internationaux ces dernières années. D'une part, la conférence ou diplomatie parlementaire, un concept d'origine relativement récente, comme extention de la consultation et de la négociation traditionnelles, pourrait dans des exemples appropriés fournir un substitut ou une alternative convenable à ces dernières, notamment dans le cadre d'une organisation internationale. Ceci est également vrai du nouveau concept de "négociation judiciaire", qui fournit une formule à travers laquelle un corps essentiellement judiciaire pourrait néamoins commencer, encourager ou diriger activement un règlement négocié entre les plaideurs, ceci faisant partie de ses fonctions arbitrales.

Un second trait encore plus remarquable est le changement général d'accent vers la prévention des litiges ou les mesures de prévention avec les exemples particuliers de l'adoption dans certain cas de mécanismes de consultation institutionnelle dans les domaines de problèmes périodiques ou de situations où de fréquents problèmes risquent de se poser. Même s'il est trop tôt de conclure qu'un principe général d'éviter et prévenir les litiges a émergé, un tel principe semble prendre forme dans plusieurs domaines en développement du droit international, tels que le droit international de l'environnement, le droit international du transport par air et le droit économique international. Même si ces développements semblent très prometteurs, leur portée et leur potentiel restent incertains à cause de la timidité de leur réception.

[3]

International Law, Mediation, and Negotiation

Manfred Lachs

The theme of my reflections is the relationship between international law and negotiations. The relationship is dominated by the fact that international law creates a framework for state activities in international relations, and within this system of relationships, which knows various situations and developments, negotiations play a special role. In fact, the word for this role is multi-colored, and it has gone through various and interesting stages in the course of history. From the very day when two states came into being, problems arose that called for them to establish certain relations. Thus, relationships were a necessary consequence of their existence. This goal could be achieved only by negotiations. The original and basic institution charged with the function of negotiations was diplomacy; thus, it was the oldest and the most fundamental of all functions related to international law. The dictionary describes these functions as follows: "The management of international relations by negotiations, the methods by which these relations are adjusted and managed by ambassadors and envoys; the business or art of the diplomatist."[1]

Thus, diplomacy has constituted, and still constitutes, a special chapter of international law and, also, of negotiations. It is an instrument of foreign policy and there is an interdependence between the political activities of the state and its diplomacy: an interdependence that could be described as a relationship between strategy and tactics.[2]

In fact, diplomacy has been shaped by the historical transformation of the state, reflecting its changing status in international relations. There was the diplomacy of the days of Dante, Boccaccio, and Machiavelli; the traveling missions of Ivan the Terrible; and messengers sent out by the Kings of Poland, who at first employed foreigners only and later came to the conclusion that missions at foreign courts could be entrusted only to Polish nobility.

As to the tools of diplomacy, they were also described in various ways and in different forms at different stages of history. Suffice it to recall that Talley-rand-Périgord, in his last speech delivered at the French Academy in 1838, disclaimed that diplomacy was an art of duplicity and untruth. On another occasion, he is alleged to have said: "To lie is a good thing, but one should not abuse it."

Turning to a more serious analysis of the situation, negotiations aim at the establishment of conditions of permanent relations among states (by treaty or otherwise), serve their maintenance, and solve problems that arise through-out the existence of those relations. They serve as basic instruments for settle-ment of disputes. Today, when states have so many mutual contacts and rela-tions are spread over so many fields, negotiations have a special function to perform: They enter many fields and cover almost all the spheres of the ac-tivities concerning the state as such and, also, its physical and juridical persons.

The element of negotiation is today much more in the foreground than ever before. The wealth of problems that states face in their economic, polit-ical, scientific, and other relations imposes upon them the obligation, I would say the necessity, to negotiate in a wide sense. Thus, the instruments of ne-gotiation have multiplied, and negotiations have acquired a new and impor-tant dimension.

Approaching the subject of negotiation in its wider dimensions, we are bound to define its place within international law and its relations to it. First, there is the object of the function itself. The greater rapprochement of states and the growth of daily contacts between them has created not only a closer relationship between them but has brought into the open a host of problems that require regulation. In order to create the basis of such regulation, negotia-tions are necessary to establish conditions for mutual relations of a perma-nent character through treaties or by the establishment of international organ-izations, in a wider sense of the word, or any other instruments that would resolve specific problems among states in their relationships, at least for a certain period of time. The second object of negotiations is the settlement of disputes. That is the resolution of confrontation and different views, dif-ferent approaches, of states on a specific issue or on a series of issues. The function of the negotiator in both cases is of essential importance as he is called upon to produce agreement, and this agreement is linked with law be-cause it must correspond to the requirements of international law.

Turning to the process of negotiation itself, two points should be recalled: (1) the relationship of the parties, and (2) the relationship of their mutual in-terests. As to the relationship of the parties, there is a basic premise that dis-tinguishes negotiations from dictates, or the imposition of the will by one party upon the other or others. The very essence of negotiation is agreement, agreement freely arrived at. History offers a whole host of illustrations in which, under the guise of negotiation, decisions were reached that were the result of pressure exercised by one party upon the other. Some examples are the treaty on Japan's protectorate over Korea (1905), the treaties between Japan and China concluded prior to World War I, and a large number of colonial relationships that dominated the international scene for centuries. To this list, other treaties of recent origin may be added such as the Munich Agreement of 1938. Have these methods disappeared? Pressure in a more subtle way has remained one of the instruments used by states in their mutual relations. It might be in the guise of economic, political, or even military measures. In most cases, it is almost unnoticeable. The outcome may be an instrument that has all the form and shape of a document corresponding to the freely expressed will of the parties, but, in fact, it is the result of one yielding to the other, not due to conviction or persuasion. It is well known that the charter has proclaimed "the sovereign equality of States," that every state has one vote in international relations. The weight of the vote and the substantive value of equality remain valid. It is only through a common effort of the international community and through the intervention of all involved that this equality can become a reality in all its manifestations. It should—and here the intervention of law is very essential—guarantee the possibility of free expression of will at all stages of negotiations and bar parties from exercising an influence that is undue and that may be tantamount to pressure. The recognition of equality is a constructive element in reaching agreement. In the long run, it is in the interest of both the strong and the weak that this equality be protected. For it is in it that the guarantee of the value of the instrument, its observance, its durability rests. In the process of negotiations, as in the instrument itself, military, political, and economic coercion though resolved should not be used. In fact, they are barred by contemporary international law in regard to treaties.[3] This equally applies to all stages of the relationship between states leading to the conclusion of a treaty. Even more important is the effect of an error, of fraud, or the corruption of a representative of a state in the process of negotiations. The coercion of a representative of a state, the threat or use of force, may be invoked as invalidating consent, deprive it of legal effect, or make it void.

The second important element in the process of negotiations is that concerning the interests of the parties in the conclusion of an instrument or the resolution of a dispute. As to the first, the parties may have unequal interests: one may be more concerned with the conclusion of an instrument, be it a treaty or an agreement, while the other considers it useful but not essential; a treaty may also come into existence when negotiations are embarked upon because of the difference of the interests of the parties. A simple illustration is given by negotiations in which one party is the buyer and the other party is the seller of goods. It is only in view of this relationship that a treaty or an agreement would come into existence. In other situations, treaties come into operation due to identical interests of the parties, vis-à-vis other states, or their common effort to achieve a common goal. This objective of the treaty must be reflected in the process of negotiations, and the negotiations themselves will therefore be a mirror of the concerns, interests, and status of the parties participating in them. At each stage of the negotiation, the legal aspect is present, even if invisible. It is present because the parties discuss; agree or disagree; try to draft a formula that is to become part of a wider consensus that contains legal aspects; and, as I indicated earlier, the mere relationship between them in this process has a legal aspect. This leads me to the substance of negotiations, that is, the consideration of all the circumstances and the setting in which negotiations take place.

The background of the parties is the world of facts: geography, history, social and economic relations, political considerations. All of them constitute a point of departure and continue to be companions of the parties negotiating throughout the process of the negotiations. In many domains, the position of the parties may be more or less on the same level; equality leaves no room for doubt. In others, their relationship may be uneven, though from a declaratory point of view, it remains equal. At any rate, we have to bear in mind that this relationship in the process of negotiations is a developing phenomenon with various stages succeeding one another. The background is the reality of the world of today even if reduced to the reality of the status of those states that take part in the negotiation. In brief, negotiations constitute a dialogue between contemporaries—even if they concern matters of the past or intend to project their interests into the future. To be successful, this dialogue cannot be one between yesterday and today, or of yesterday and tomorrow, but must take into account, and it does take into account, consciously or unconsciously, the realities of the moment at which it takes place. Part of these realities is law. Here we find another of the basic premises of an objective character in the process of negotiations. Apart from bringing a dynamic into the relationship between the parties, the realities also add a background that is relevant, that is the world of today: the development of relations between other states and the general situation in a particular field or the general political and legal situation. Thus, there are various settings in which negotiations take place. Recently, a frequent type of negotiations has concerned the granting of independence to former colonial and other dependent peoples.[4] The reality was, of course, the relationship between the metropolitan power and the representatives of the liberation movements. Here the question of the equality of the parties was certainly one of crucial importance for it was necessary to assure those who were striving for the establishment of their independence that they would be given all the facilities to present their views and that the outcome would not be only a formal but a real mission of independence. This required a special setting that was secured by the United Nations: a series of resolutions determining not only the principles but also conditions and a timetable. In many cases the process has taken place outside the United Nations, and in several cases, it still continues. These negotiations then rely on the relationship between the colonial power and the liberation movements supported by those states that have been liberated only recently. Here again a de facto multilateral setting appears, though the problem in itself is a bilateral one. The legal aspects of it are of a particular interest for the colonial power, or the state that controls the territories also has allies that may be invisible in the registration itself but may support its case.

Thus, through negotiations, a series of principles acquired a certain legal status and became a guide for the future development of the law. Among them are some specific aspects of self-determination. Though, as is well known, the relevant decisions of the United Nations are mere resolutions, it has been held that they constitute a further important stage in the law-making and law-application process.

A further interesting factor in this sphere of the relationship between newly established states and former metropolitan powers or other developed states is the question of sovereignty over natural resources. Here, again, the new law has been the result of negotiations and settlement of disputes that have arisen in this area. It has been confirmed by UN resolutions: the principle of sovereignty of a state over its natural resources.[5] Another important issue in which negotiations have played a very important role (mentioned only in passing) is compensation for nationalized property.[6]

I have referred to only two domains that are in the forefront of problems dividing old and new states in the world of today. They, like many others, may be resolved by negotiations leading (as indicated) to the development of a new law. The phenomenon of negotiations is of no lesser importance in the shaping of the relationships between states of different systems. For a long time, special attention has been devoted to this aspect of international relations, and it was claimed that the ideological gap or differences of philosophical outlook make negotiations impossible and, hence, agreements unattainable. It was even claimed that the maximum one might hope for was an armistice. This, of course, is an untenable position for history reports no period in which all states were of an identical or even similar system. From their very birth, international relations were developing between different philosophical or religious beliefs, and this pluralism of systems has been a permanent factor on the international scene throughout history. Thus, the very roots of international relations lie in the recognition of these differences. Moreover, it is interesting to note that to negotiate and reach agreement, one must assume that there are differences of an important nature between the parties, and they very frequently arise between states belonging to the same system. Here again, law gives an indication of these differences by recognizing the "coexistence of States of different systems" and the coexistence of interests legally protected of various states.

In classifying negotiation further, all sorts of settings may be visualized:

negotiations between neighboring states and those removed from one another; states with conflicting interests on their territories or beyond their territories; states seeking the resolution of conflicts concerning them alone but also differences that concern other states. Thus, negotiations may be required in many areas and on many levels. They touch almost all problems of international relations and, in doing so, touch on questions of law; they are bound to remain within the bounds of law or, without violating it, help its further development.

So far, I have been dealing with what I would call the physical aspects of negotiations as a background prior to approaching the very essence of the process itself. Before completing this chapter on my reflections, one more aspect should be taken into account, that is, the number of the parties. Traditionally and historically, the oldest negotiations were of a bilateral character: Two states were usually engaged in settling their disputes or differences, working together for the elaboration of a treaty. With the growth in the number of states and the links that have been established in many areas, diplomacy has acquired a new multilateral pattern. This has obviously had its impact on the process of negotiation as a method for settling multilateral relations and the impact of law on them. Here again, different forms are possible. Negotiations may have a coalition character: representatives of two groups of states belonging to two different alliances or organizations of a regional or political character face one another, speaking on behalf of their respective allies. Formally negotiations remain bilateral, but in substance, they usually reflect more than two points of view and interests of more than two states. The legal basis of each of the parties seems to be clearly defined, but, not infrequently, one or two of the allies do not support the common position. Ever more frequently, negotiations themselves become multilateral, that is, a number of states sit at the negotiating table. They reflect a multitude of conflicting interests that are not organized nor set in an institutional form. Though they may be members of no more than two organizations, their interests within the framework of these organizations differ, and each of them sits at the negotiation table as an independent entity. As to the legal aspects of this type of relationship, the consent of all of them is necessary to reach an agreement unless it is a partial agreement with some of the parties refusing to adhere to it and remaining at odds on issues on which they refuse to subscribe to the views of the others. We have, for instance, as an illustration the North-South dialogue in which groups of states (each of which has certain common interests binding it together) confront one another as groups of states, but they do not necessarily represent identical interest, and views within each group may differ. Thus, you have the interesting illustration of a situation in which, for some, agreements may be reached in a limited sphere concerning only some issues. Speaking in legal terms, full success of the North-South dialogue would amount to the establishment of a new international economic order, something based on a multilateral treaty including all the members of the United Nations. It is, however, possible and likely that, in the interim, agreement may be reached between groups of states such as those in need and those more amenable to the claims of the poorer countries and more ready to bear their share to improve their situation.

Finally, we have the possibility of negotiations that directly concern five or six states but may affect humanity as a whole. What I obviously have in mind are negotiations between the big powers, the relationship between which is of basic importance and paramount influence on the relationship of all states, for peace and peaceful relations in global dimensions. The number may be reduced even to two in the question of nuclear weapons and the limitation of nuclear arsenals; here the two big powers are involved in negotiation that may be decisive for others. Thus, other states not taking part in the negotiations have a vital interest in an agreement being reached between the two. Here you have an illustration of two actors engaged in negotiations representing, in law, their own interests but, in fact, representing the interests of humanity as a whole. Strictly speaking, there are three stages involved. There are two powers negotiating the limitation on the manufacturing and the stationing of nuclear weapons; there are the alliances to which they are connected; and there are other states that are not members of the alliances — the neutral or nonaligned states that constitute the great majority of mankind. There are two actors only, but their decisions and their agreement or disagreement have a legal impact on the alliances and beyond them. In view of the interrelationship between members of the alliances, the armaments controlled by the big powers are not only placed on their own territories but also on the territories of other states. Therefore, should one of the two disagree on certain disarmament measures and, due to this disagreement, refuse to accept the limitation of armaments, the armament race will not stop. The legal basis for it is that the alliances constitute legal entities and, by their stipulations, provide common measures for defense. Thus, law intervenes by prompting decisions of a collective character to bring about the limitation of armaments.

On the other hand, should an agreement be reached as to the reduction of armaments, this would affect not only the two powers that dispose of the largest military potential in the world but all their allies, again by the operation of the treaties that are in force; this would also reduce their armaments, and, thus, a chain reaction would be produced. Indirectly, this may also affect the situation in the nonaligned countries, some of which are increasing their armaments not only in view of their relationship with their neighboring countries but also in view of the increase of armaments within the framework of the two big alliances dominating the world picture—their impact creeping into areas beyond their membership. Disarmament agreements are lawmaking treaties in a domain vital to humanity. Due to the specific structure of the international community, decisions taken by a very few may in this domain affect all. Thus, it is so important that the great majority of states, particularly the nonaligned states and peoples, exercise some influence in the shaping of the will—hence, the decision making—of these few. History shows that this is not an easy process; however, in the long run, it may produce practical results. It may also have a legal effect on the will and decisions of the alliance.

Finally, there is the framework within which the negotiations take place. They may proceed within an ad hoc setting for the solution of an ad hoc problem. They may have a continuous character and, therefore, build in a system of a legal nature, which is permanent: a typical illustration of the latter is an international organization or an organization that has been established for the solution of certain problems. In this respect, the United Nations is a very interesting illustration. It is a body within which negotiations permanently take place. From a legal point of view, debates in the United Nations have the character of negotiations. Its constitution provides for various subjects to be dealt with by various organs within various time limits and on a specific basis. The intention of the drafters of the charter was not to make it a forum of confrontation and decision making by fluctuating majorities but an instrument of coordination and cooperation through negotiations. Discussion in the Security Council is a form of negotiation. Draft resolutions submitted are proposals, and resolutions are often legal instruments binding upon the parties in accordance with Articles 24 and 25 of the charter. Unfortunately, these debates have degenerated into confrontations; in most cases, instead of negotiations, one faces a series of inflexible statements; the principle of unanimity intended to lead to agreements has become known as the veto (Art. 27, para. 3). In the course of time, the General Assembly, one of the principal organs of the United Nations intended "to consider the general principles of cooperation," has become a forum for raising grievances, conflicts, and confrontations existing in the world of today. Yet it should have become an instrument of a forum for negotiation and, thus, for lawmaking. Fortunately enough, in some respects, it has retained this character. Committees of the General Assembly are fora in which not only ad hoc problems are solved but also treaties are worked out, and these are obviously the product of negotiations. Both have a legal character and may have far-reaching legal consequences. Treaties such as those concerning the status of women and children, the protection of human rights, and the elaboration of details in many spheres of international cooperation are the result of negotiations held within the United Nations. It may be worth recalling that one of the first treaties elaborated by the United Nations was the Convention on the Prevention and Punishment of the Crime of Genocide in 1948. The two Covenants on Human Rights, which had their origin in the famous Universal Declaration of Human Rights of 10 December 1948, were also elaborated within the United Nations. Here the process is one of perhaps a specific nature; it takes a two-stage approach. The first stage is a resolution of the General Assembly. By the provisions of the charter and the clear will of the founders of the organization, decisions of the General Assembly, with some exceptions only, are mere recommendations; they are therefore not binding on states and do not create law, but they contribute to the creation of law. However, there are some resolutions, again as the result of negotiation, that do create law and the link between the resolution and the lawmaking process is very close. But usually, a General Assembly resolution is the first stage toward the lawmaking process. The second stage is the conclusion of an instrument of a treaty character (as was, for instance, the case with human rights just mentioned).

Similar is the situation in other international organizations such as the International Labour Organization (which has a very special provision on the subject), the World Health Organization, and the family of specialized agencies and other organizations outside their ambit.

All this shows how rich is the agenda of negotiations and how widely spread the network that, through negotiations, leads to lawmaking: the creation of binding rules in relations between states. We face a great variety of formal aspects of negotiations. They may appear minor but are frequently of major importance because the setting may in some circumstances be decisive for the result and the final success of the operation itself. It may be decisive in reaching an agreement or in dragging on the differences; so that an agreement becomes ever more remote, or the parties to it do not come closer to each other. I would conclude this part of my reflections by stating that negotiations, as a whole, are the basic instrument in interstate relations and that the rules of international law rely on negotiations: they are born through negotiations and are shaped by them.

However, the freedom of states to negotiate is not unlimited. States that have negotiated a treaty cannot abolish it without the participation of all those who were parties to it. Moreover, international law has developed a new notion that prohibits the conclusion of an instrument that, at the time of its negotiation, "conflicts with the peremptory norms of general international law" (Art. 53 of the Convention on the Law of Treaties, Vienna, 1969). (As is well-known, "a peremptory norm of general international law is a norm accepted and recognized by the international community of states as a whole as a norm from which no derogation is permitted and which can be modified only by a subsequent norm of general international law having the same character" [loc. cit.].) Existing law has not defined or specifically indicated which of its rules could be regarded as "peremptory," yet one could assume that some are obviously in this category. I would suggest that in regard to genocide, being a crime against humanity, its prevention is a peremptory rule of law. The same is true in regard to slavery or to war crimes; but, as to these, the right of negotiations of the parties is clearly very limited or even excluded. No state could negotiate with another state the establishment of a bilateral system of slavery even without any other state taking part in it. They could not legalize slavery in view of the fact that it has been outlawed by the international community. Nor could one admit the right of two states to commit an act of aggression against a third state; or to divide part or whole of its territory. It is here that the freedom of action of states is limited. They cannot negotiate and enter into agreement to institute practices or establish relations on principles that are contrary to generally binding principles of law. Nor can they negotiate, as earlier indicated, treaties that are contrary to other existing treaties; for instance, the Charter of the United Nations. However, at the same time, this limitation of the sphere of negotiations, or what one may call the freedom of negotiation, stresses the wide area of possibilities existing in this domain. For, as I indicated earlier, negotiations serve two purposes: (1) the establishment of peaceful relations between states and (2) the resolution of disputes existing between them. In regard to both areas, the freedom of action of states is limited only by the existence of certain peremptory rules of law. They cannot resolve a dispute by reaching an agreement that would impose obligations, or imply the right to conduct hostilities, against a third state or deprive its people of freedom or independence.

In the sphere of the settlement of disputes, negotiations have a paramount role to perform and are, again, closely linked with law. Each dispute touches upon issues of law for there is hardly any that would not have some legal aspects: the application, maintenance, or termination of, or compliance with, a legal relationship. Disputes arising out of these call for resolutions. Thus, directly or indirectly, negotiations of disputes lead to the modification of the existing relationships or the establishment of a new legal relationship. The resolution of any conflict enriches law every time by adding a new chapter to the existing body of rules and their interpretation. It helps the solution of a problem, perhaps of more than one, in existence and may assist the solution of those that may arise in the future. However, one should be aware of the risk that a particular outcome of negotiations may create more problems or make the resolution of other disputes more difficult. The growing interdependence of events and states calls for careful consideration of all implications of a decision before it is taken. It may be overexacting to require states, while solving their conflicts, to bear in mind potential or existing disputes between other states or to consider their value as precedents. However, even if they limit themselves to reflections on their own interests, they are bound to visualize themselves in a reverse situation and, thus, be mindful of the risks involved.

Here, then, lies the close relationship between negotiations and international law. The continuously expanding body of international law covers almost all areas of international relations, and, therefore, each negotiation in its legal implications cannot be viewed in isolation. All possible means should be used to arrive at a mutual and adaptable solution. The orthodox methods of negotiation need not be followed. For example, the dispute may be divided into several parts, and the solution of each of them enshrined in a separate instrument. Though it is difficult to visualize all possible situations in which the parties may find themselves in the future, a series of further comments may be worth adding in this respect. One concerns the time factor, which has both political and legal aspects. One of the parties may be interested in a speedy solution, the other in delaying the decision. Thus, a meeting of minds on the date by which a decision is to be reached is of primary importance. Here a balance must be struck between the advantages flowing from short negotiations and those of a protracted character. Sometimes, blinded by success in the battlefield or through diplomatic action, statesmen delay decisions hoping for an even greater advantage. Yet this need not necessarily follow—it may produce the opposite effect. A precarious advantage gained may dictate an immediate termination of a conflict with the consequences flowing from it, rather than its continuation into an uncertain future.

The time factor has also another aspect. It may be a purely legal dispute yet of a political character; or, as a result of protracted negotiations, a legal dispute may become politicized, arousing public opinion and the resentment of an important part of the population. More developments may threaten the government in power, provoke questions in parliament, and transform the whole issue into one of heated public debate in which the political element begins to dominate. Thus, the relationship between the political and legal may not only be the result of the substance of the dispute itself but of the conditions in which it arises and the time at which it matures and the negotiations begin. Here, therefore, care should be taken to negotiate at the moment that is not inconvenient to either of the parties because, in many circumstances, though they are independent states, they may not be free agents—being dependent on many factors (e.g., public opinion) that they cannot easily control.

Finally, negotiations in today's world, because of the great interdependence of states and events, should not be used to press the other party to the wall. Some leeway must be left. Relations between total winners and total losers at the negotiation table are rarely successful, or, if successful, do not augur a lasting result. After all, two or more states, whether neighbors are not, are bound to maintain mutual, lasting peaceful relations. Obviously, the victim of an unprovoked attack, of an economic or other pressure, is bound to seek compensation for damage suffered and guarantees against similar events occurring in the future. But the penalty should not be so high as to provoke ill feeling that may leave a painful heritage and prevent the development of future friendly relations. Even more so, a similar situation arises when disputes are of a less acute character. If one of the parties has really suffered a disadvantage, it should not overreact and try to use the situation to impose upon the other party a burden that will be too painful to carry for a long period of time. Here, again, law is helpful by offering all sorts of devices that parties may use in assuring their interests and regulating their relationship. Once agreement is reached and in order to avoid future disputes or difficulties, a permanent organ may be created to watch the implementation of the agreement. Should smaller difficulties arise and should the parties disagree on the interpretation of the agreement, a special body may be created and called upon to assist them in the solution of difficulties that may arise in the future. This may be a conciliation or mediation commission, or a similar organ, that would settle differences without affecting the validity of the agreement or creating a situation of confrontation between the parties.

But negotiations, as such, may in some circumstances become impossible because of the tense situation between the parties and the impossibility of bringing them to the negotiating table. In such a situation, perhaps, the intervention of a third party, the good offices of a personality playing a specific role, may be of great importance. This legal device (provided by Art. 33 of the Charter of the United Nations) should be used as soon as possible in order to avoid the deterioration of the relationship between the parties. Such an action may speed the rapprochement between the parties and, thus, the possibility of direct negotiations. This third-party factor may be limited to bringing two states to the negotiation table and to presiding at the first meeting, leaving them alone for subsequent meetings.

Finally, in order to avoid endless negotiations as a result of disagreements on substance, it may be advisable to fix a time limit after which states may resort to third-party intervention on a permanent basis. This, while advisable, is not always possible. There is one domain in which the intervention of a single third party would not be acceptable, that is, the vital domain of disarmament; there, no assistance of a third state is likely to be helpful. What could be of assistance is the pressure of world opinion and of a considerable number of states, not beneficiaries but possible victims of the arms race. In these and similar negotiations, a two- or three-stage approach may be advisable. Failure or deadlock at a lower level may encourage a meeting at a higher one and, finally, at the summit. It is well known that the reverse approach is also advocated: Summit meetings are suggested only if agreement is reached at a lower level, to avoid what some claim may become a confrontation between the leaders. The function of the summit is seen as sealing an agreement reached at a lower level. However, I feel that both approaches are acceptable. Past summit meetings have in many cases been successful; (the Congresses of Vienna, Paris, and Berlin produced lasting results). The practice, as is well known, was continued during World War I (in 1916) and after World War II. Some of them were successful, others less so. The Munich meeting that preceded World War II was certainly a calamity. On the other hand, some held during the last few decades have produced certain results: their outcomes were treaties of major importance. There is of course no ready-made recipe for the stages and instruments of negotiations. The general principle that should be applied in this respect is certainly the principle of the means serving the end. All methods should be used in order to achieve a result that is desired by the parties concerned; ingenuity and inventiveness should remain permanent companions of policy planners.

In this brief survey, I have tried to show how wide a range negotiations cover in the world of the international relations of today. I have tried to stress the close relationship between negotiations and international law. Relying on law, negotiations are intended to maintain the rule of law and possibly create new rules of law. No separation between law and negotiations is possible. Of course, negotiation may be predominantly of a political nature and dominated by political considerations, but, even so, legal elements will always be present. The basic principles are that peaceful relations among states must be maintained and protected and that the great achievements of international law, as reflected in the Charter of the United Nations and the many instruments that followed it, should not only be maintained but further enhanced. This is the way to respect the principles of peaceful settlement of disputes, of self-determination, and the abolition of confrontation whatever its source may be.

In all these domains there are legal premises that should be followed, developed, and enriched. It is through negotiation that this can be done, and the goodwill of states must manifest itself at the negotiating table so that disaster may be avoided and better relations among states of East and West and North and South be assured.

NOTES

1. *Shorter Oxford Dictionary*, 3rd ed., vol. 1 (Oxford: Oxford University Press, 1950), 514; cf., in particular, the earlier important work by Sir Ernest Satow, *Guide to Diplomatic Practice*, 2nd ed., (London: Longmans, Green & Co., 1922), 1, in which diplomatic activity is defined and practical indications are given as to its conduct.

2. Sir Victor Wellesley, *Diplomacy in Fetters*, (London, Hutchinson & Co., 1943), 30.

3. "Declaration on the Prohibition of Military, Political or Economic Coercion in the Conclusion of Treaties," adopted by the UN Conference on the Law of Treaties, Vienna, May 22, 1969.

4. "Declaration on the Granting of Independence to Colonial Countries and Peoples," GA Res. 1514 (XX), Dec. 14, 1960, and its evaluation in the advisory opinion of the International Court of Justice on Namibia, *I. C. J. Reports 1971*, 31, para. 52.

5. "Declaration of Permanent Sovereignty over Natural Resources," GA Res. 1803 (XVII), Dec. 14, 1962.

6. "Declaration on the Establishment of a New International Economic Order," GA Res. 3201 (S-VI), May 1, 1974; "Charter of Economic Rights and Duties of States," GA Res. 3281 (XXIX), Dec. 12, 1974.

Part III
Good Offices and Mediation

[4]

THE GOOD OFFICES OF THE UNITED NATIONS SECRETARY-GENERAL IN THE FIELD OF HUMAN RIGHTS

B. G. RAMCHARAN

INTRODUCTION

At the end of his term of office, the late Secretary-General U Thant lamented "the great humanitarian emergencies which the United Nations is still not equipped to meet" and underlined the principle that "the Secretary-General's obligations under the Charter must include any humanitarian action that he can take to save the lives of large numbers of human beings."[1] Similarly, in his first annual report to the General Assembly, in 1972, Secretary-General Waldheim asserted that "the unwritten moral responsibility which every Secretary-General bears does not allow him to turn a blind eye when innocent civilian lives are placed in jeopardy on a large scale."[2] He amplified this principle in his annual report of 1980, where he stated that "I have always regarded it as my duty to exercise my good offices in human rights matters and I shall continue to assist in any way I can."[3]

One of the major weaknesses in the arrangements of the United Nations for promoting and protecting human rights is the lack of adequate methods for dealing with urgent situations of violations of human rights. Consequently, the international community invariably looks to the Secretary-General of the United Nations to fill the breach by interceding discreetly on a humanitarian basis. Often, such intercession by the Secretary-General is the only form of response available and acceptable.

In customary international law, "humanitarian intercession" indicated a friendly interposition by a government or other international actor aimed at inducing another government or authority to treat persons under its jurisdiction with respect for the principles of humanity. As opposed to "diplomatic intercession of a humanitarian nature on behalf of certain foreign nationals," Sohn and Buergenthal distinguish "forcible intervention by States to protect their own nationals" and "forcible intervention to protect the nationals of the State against which the intervention has been launched." State practice shows that humanitarian intercession and good offices were intertwined. Thus, Sohn and Buergenthal cite as evidence of the practice of humanitarian intercession U.S. diplomatic correspondence involving requests to the President of the United States "to exercise his good offices in behalf of the oppressed people of Armenia."[4]

In contemporary practice the term "good offices" is usually employed to refer

---

[1] U Thant, *The Role of the Secretary-General, infra* note 11, at 185. *See also* U THANT, VIEW FROM THE UNITED NATIONS 27 (1978).

[2] UN Doc. A/8701/Add.1, section IX (1972).

[3] UN Doc. A/35/1, section IX (1980).

[4] L. SOHN & T. BUERGENTHAL, INTERNATIONAL PROTECTION OF HUMAN RIGHTS 179, 182 (1973). *See also* R. LILLICH & F. NEWMAN, INTERNATIONAL HUMAN RIGHTS: PROBLEMS OF LAW AND POLICY 485–544 (1979); O. Strauss, *Humanitarian Diplomacy of the United States*, 6 ASIL, PROC. 45–54 (1912).

to humanitarian intercessions by the Secretary-General. But good offices traditionally developed in the area of the settlement of international disputes, and the extension of the term to the humanitarian field has not been without challenge. Thus, at the 35th session of the United Nations General Assembly, in 1980, when a wide-ranging debate took place on good offices in the field of human rights, it was contended that good offices were properly used by the Secretary-General "only when his action had a bearing on international peace and security" and that "good offices constituted a means for the settlement of disputes and presupposed at least two parties agreeing to their use."

On the other hand, it was pointed out that in the field of human rights the good offices role of the Secretary-General had generally been recognized for a long time, and reference was made to a UN press release issued on April 29, 1967 announcing that the Permanent Representatives of Poland and Czechoslovakia, on behalf of a group of socialist countries, had requested that the Secretary-General use his "good offices" with a view to ending persecutions in Greece and to preventing the possible execution of political leaders who had been detained.[5] This debate took place over a draft resolution submitted by the delegation of Canada, which was aimed at developing the full potential of the good offices role of the Secretary-General to enable the United Nations system to cope more adequately with situations of mass and flagrant violations of human rights.[6] Eventually, the Third Committee of the General Assembly decided, on a procedural motion, not to vote on the draft resolution. The general view in the committee was that the Secretary-General should be left free to decide on the manner and modalities of the exercise of good offices in the field of human rights and that the function should not be restricted or regulated in any way.[7]

In view of this reluctance of some states to "legislate" on the subject, it follows necessarily that the nature and characteristics of the concept of good offices in the field of human rights must be determined by reference to the relevant international practice and to such rules or principles of international customary law as may have emerged from that practice. An examination of the relevant rules and practice will be attempted in the following pages. It will be submitted that the exercise by the Secretary-General of good offices in the field of human rights has become part of international customary law.

I. THE NATURE OF GOOD OFFICES REGARDING HUMAN RIGHTS

In their traditional meaning, good offices "consist in a third party—Government, international organization, individual—attempting to bring conflicting parties to a negotiating table without interfering in the negotiation themselves."[8]

---

[5] *See* UN Press Release SG/SM/699, April 29, 1967.

[6] UN Doc. A/C.3/35/L.78 (1980).

[7] For the records of the discussion, see UN Doc. A/C.3/35/SR.56–62 (1980).

[8] V. PECHOTA, THE QUIET APPROACH: A STUDY OF THE GOOD OFFICES EXERCISED BY THE SECRETARY-GENERAL IN THE CAUSE OF PEACE 13 (UNITAR 1972). *See* similarly Darwin, *Mediation and Good Offices*, in INTERNATIONAL DISPUTES: THE LEGAL ASPECTS 83 (Report of a Study Group of the David Davies Memorial Institute of International Studies, 1972). *Cf.* ch. III (Good offices), Art. 10(1), of the Second Report on the Peaceful Settlement of International Disputes, in INTERNATIONAL LAW ASSOCIATION, REPORT OF THE 56TH CONFERENCE 43, 48 (1974).

Good offices as a means of settling international disputes have a long history among the instruments of diplomacy. In more recent times the concept may be traced to Articles 2 and 3 of the Hague Conventions of 1899 and 1907 on the Pacific Settlement of Disputes.

As a method for furthering peaceful solutions of international disputes, the good offices of the Secretary-General have been defined by Pechota as "the informal contacts and friendly suggestions made as far as circumstances allow by the Secretary-General, which are designed to facilitate the settlement of a dispute between two or several of the Organization's Member States."[9] The same writer classifies the good offices of the Secretary-General into: (1) forms of diplomatic assistance such as informal contacts and consultations with parties to a dispute; (2) diplomatic action designed to express international concern, to induce the parties into talks before a favorable atmosphere fades away or before they reach a point of no return, and to assist them in finding a suitable framework for settlement; (3) mediation, conciliation, and coordination; and (4) inquiries, fact-finding, the supervision of plebiscites, elections, or referenda, and the determination of legal rights and duties in a specific situation. Within the third category, namely mediation, conciliation, and coordination, the author includes "various activities aimed at assisting the parties in alleviating human sufferings or easing other burdens such as refugee problems entailed in certain conflicts" but adds that "such activities can hardly be described as good offices in the usual meaning of the term."[10] Perhaps he meant the "traditional" rather than the "usual" meaning of the term, for he himself acknowledges among the categories of involvement by the Secretary-General in the exercise of good offices, "humanitarian problems," including the situation of minorities within some states.[11]

In the League of Nations system for the international protection of minorities, resolutions of the League Council provided for the handling of "exceptional and extremely urgent cases,"[12] and stipulated that in such cases the Secretary-General of the League should simultaneously inform the state concerned and the members of the Council of the matter. Minorities Committees, for their part, made it their practice to try to settle questions raised in communications by means of informal negotiations with the state concerned.[13]

The exercise of good offices with respect to human rights or humanitarian matters is quite extensive in present-day international organizations, such as

---

[9] V. PECHOTA, *supra* note 8, at 2. [10] *Id.* at 17.

[11] *Ibid.* On the good offices of the Secretary-General generally, see Simmonds, *Good Offices and the Secretary-General*, 29 NORDISK TIDSSKRIFT FOR INTERNATIONAL RET OG JUS GENTIUM 330 (1959); U Thant, *A Quiet United Nation's Road to Accord*, UN MONTHLY CHRONICLE, No. 7, July 1970, at 122; U Thant, *The United Nations and some problems of public understanding, id.*, No. 1, Jan. 1971, at 98; U Thant, *The Role of the Secretary-General, id.*, No. 9, Oct. 1971, at 178.

[12] *See* especially Council resolution of June 27, 1921, referred to in The International Protection of Minorities, note 13 *infra*, at 27.

[13] *See* The International Protection of Minorities under the League of Nations 27–32, UN Doc. E/CN.4/Sub.2/6 '(1947). *See also* P. DE AZCARATE, LEAGUE OF NATIONS AND NATIONAL MINORITIES: AN EXPERIMENT (1945); J. BARROS, OFFICE WITHOUT POWER: SECRETARY-GENERAL SIR ERIC DRUMMOND, 1919–1933, at 97–98 (1979).

the United Nations, the United Nations High Commissioner for Refugees (UNHCR), the International Labour Organisation (ILO), the United Nations Educational, Scientific and Cultural Organization (UNESCO), and the International Committee of the Red Cross (ICRC). In many of these organizations, good offices with respect to human rights or humanitarian matters are exercised at various levels: by the head or by other members of the secretariat; by organs, as well as by their presidents, chairmen, or members. In some instances there are express mandates to exercise such good offices, while in others they are based on the concept of inherent or implied competence.

In the ILO, good offices are exercised by the Director-General and, under his direction, by members of the International Labour Office. There are elements of good offices in the procedure of direct contacts introduced in 1968 for the purpose of permitting a representative of the ILO Director-General to examine directly with the competent government services, practical or legal difficulties encountered in the application of a ratified convention.[14]

In UNESCO, Decision 104/EX3.3, adopted by the Executive Board in 1978, consolidated the role of the Director-General in respect of intercessions on humanitarian grounds and representations of a conciliatory nature. In the Office of the United Nations High Commissioner for Refugees, a recent High Commissioner expressed the view that good offices "remain as useful as ever for contingencies and situations on the fringe of the normal activities of the High Commissioner's Office."[15]

The International Committee of the Red Cross exercises various kinds of good offices or related functions. Article 4 of the Statutes of the ICRC states that "the ICRC may also take any humanitarian initiative which comes within its role as a specifically neutral and independent institution and consider any question requiring examination by such an institution."[16]

With respect to international or regional instruments on human rights, reference may be made to Article 28 of the European Convention on Human Rights (friendly settlement of complaints); Article 48(1) of the American Convention on Human Rights (friendly settlement of complaints); and Article 41(e) of the International Covenant on Civil and Political Rights (good offices).

The foregoing review shows the broad scope and variety of types of good offices exercised in the human rights and humanitarian field. In essence they can all be grounded in a basic rationale: Is there a humanitarian need and how can it be addressed? The practice of good offices in the field of human rights within organizations such as the League of Nations, the United Nations, the UNHCR, the ILO, UNESCO, the ICRC, the Council of Europe, and the

---

[14] *See* ILO Doc. GB/205/21/7: past practice concerning special inquiries with particular reference to human rights questions, paras. 27–29.

[15] S. Aga Khan, *Legal Problems Relating to Refugees and Displaced Persons*, 149 RECUEIL DES COURS 287, 349 (1976 I).

[16] D. TANSLEY, FINAL REPORT: AN AGENDA FOR THE RED CROSS: RE-APPRAISAL OF THE ROLE OF THE RED CROSS 72 (1975). *See also* D. P. FORSYTHE, PRESENT ROLE OF THE RED CROSS IN PROTECTION 30–48 (Background Paper No. 1 of the Joint Committee for the Re-appraisal of the Role of the Red Cross, 1975).

OAS shows that among the purposes for which such good offices have been exercised are:

(1) To promote human rights generally, including the ratification of human rights treaties.

(2) To facilitate the establishment or restoration of an attitude of respect for human rights.

(3) To alleviate situations of gross violations of human rights.

(4) To ease tensions and facilitate the movement of refugees.

(5) To initiate consultations to help reach solutions to human rights problems.

(6) To assist individuals or groups.

(7) To assist in the drafting of legislation or the establishment of national or local institutions for the promotion and protection of human rights.

(8) To resolve practical or legal difficulties encountered in the application of a human rights convention.

(9) To provide for contingencies, cases, or situations outside regular mandates or to provide ad hoc protection where there is a lack of specific authorization.

(10) To support the activities of human rights organs through discreet facilitative action behind the scenes.

(11) To fill gaps left by human rights organs, particularly in responding to urgent situations.

(12) To bring about friendly settlements to complaints.

(13) To provide equitable relief in cases where the strict application of rules might result in lack of justice.

(14) To engage in fact-finding, diplomatic, mediatory, or conciliatory activities.

(15) To respond to human needs generally, particularly in situations of emergencies or entailing human suffering.

Good offices, in most organizations, have been tackled in a flexible manner and little attempts have been made to regulate the function.

II. Legal Bases

For the United Nations Secretary-General to exercise good offices in the field of human rights, there may be several bases. He may be exercising a power conferred upon him by the Charter, the General Assembly, the Security Council, or some other authoritative organ such as the Economic and Social Council or, under its authority, the Commission on Human Rights. Good offices may be exercised at the request of the government concerned; in other instances they may be exercised without an invitation by, or even against the wishes of, the government concerned. In practice, whatever the legal basis, the methods and modalities do not vary greatly.

In the following section, there will be set out some of the legal bases which may be invoked either separately or cumulatively, depending on the case or situation in question, to support the exercise of good offices in the field of human rights. In the first place, the Secretariat, as a principal organ of the United Nations, is enjoined in the Charter to foster international cooperation for the promotion and encouragement of respect for human rights. Secondly, the good offices functions of the Secretary-General in the field of human rights could also be based on Article 97 of the Charter, which makes the Secretary-General the chief administrative officer of the Organization. Administration may be perceived in both procedural and substantive terms. Procedurally, it is to service the Organization and to implement the resolutions and decisions of United Nations organs. Substantively, however, the Secretary-General, as chief administrative officer, is also under a duty to promote the implementation of the purposes and principles of the Organization. If, therefore, it happens— as is constantly the case—that none of the relevant human rights organs is in session and that they have no arrangements for intersessional activity, would it not be appropriate for the Secretary-General to intercede provisionally, in order to seek to provide interim relief until one of the organs concerned becomes seized of the matter? Such an "emergency response" has developed in practice as an acknowledged and essential function of the administrative heads of the European and Inter-American Commissions on Human Rights (their respective Secretaries). The concept of interim measures or provisional measures is also one that is well known in international jurisprudence.

Thirdly, good offices may be exercised in the context of the novel powers of the Secretary-General under Article 99 of the Charter, which states that the Secretary-General of the United Nations may bring to the attention of the Security Council any matter which, in his opinion, may threaten the mainte-nance of international peace and security. Professor Hersch Lauterpacht was of the view "that Article 99 presents considerable potentialities for bringing to the Security Council's attention violations of human rights so grave that they threaten the maintenance of international peace and security." Moreover, he felt, "[t]he clause of domestic jurisdiction of Article 2, paragraph 7, presents no impediment in the way of the exercise of this particular function of the Secretary-General. The matters referred to in Article 99 are not, by definition, essentially within the domestic jurisdiction of any State."[17]

In a recent instance, the question was raised whether the Secretary-General should invoke Article 99 of the Charter in situations involving serious violations of human rights. On April 8, 1979, Martin Ennals, Secretary-General of Am-nesty International, addressed a telegram to the United Nations Secretary-General requesting that he use his authority under Article 99 to convene a meeting of the Security Council to consider urgent measures to stop current

---

[17] H. LAUTERPACHT, INTERNATIONAL LAW AND HUMAN RIGHTS 187 (1950). *See also* L. GOOD-RICH, E. HAMBRO, & P. SIMONS, THE CHARTER OF THE UNITED NATIONS (1969); Schwebel, *The Origins and Development of Article 99 of the Charter*, 28 BRIT. Y.B. INT'L L. 371 (1952).

waves of political executions and murders across the world. On April 10, 1979, the Secretary-General replied that despite the seriousness of the problem and his distress at the increased number of executions, "invocation of Article 99 is not the most appropriate way to deal with the problem since that article deals explicitly and exclusively with matters involving international peace and security."

It has long been recognized in international law that serious violations of human rights could involve threats to the maintenance of international peace and security. They could therefore be proper grounds for the invocation of Article 99 by the Secretary-General; whether the violations do actually give rise to a threat to international peace and security is a matter of fact to be determined in each case. For present purposes, however, it is submitted that in the context of exercising his competence under Article 99, the Secretary-General could engage in exercises akin to good offices with respect to situations of massive and flagrant violations of human rights.

Fourthly, the doctrine of inherent or implied powers has frequently been invoked as a basis for the exercise of good offices. Indeed, the practice is so extensive that it may be said that the competence of the Secretary-General to exercise good offices has concretized into a rule of customary law within the United Nations. It could be argued that the Secretary-General has powers inherent in his office to undertake all kinds of conceivable good offices. Secretary-General Hammarskjöld felt that action on his part, without any mandate from an organ of the United Nations, was justified "should this appear to him necessary in order to help in filling any vacuum that may appear in the systems which the Charter and traditional diplomacy provide for the safeguard of peace and security."[18]

An inherent or implied competence of the Secretary-General is supported by the practice of many policy-making organs, including the General Assembly, the Economic and Social Council, and the Commission on Human Rights. Thus, United Nations human rights organs have expressly recognized and appreciated the good offices of the Secretary-General in the field of human rights (see Resolution 1979/36 of the Economic and Social Council, Resolution 34/175 of the General Assembly, and Resolution 27 (XXXVI) of the Commission on Human Rights). The latter resolution, for example, "requested the Secretary-General to continue and intensify the good offices envisaged in the Charter of the United Nations in the field of human rights." The above-mentioned resolutions, together with the related practice, lend strong support to the doctrine of implied powers as well as to the view that the competence of the Secretary-General to exercise good offices in the field of human rights is now a part of international customary law. The relevant practice will now be reviewed.

III. THE PRACTICE

Pechota reported that "the requests pouring into the Secretary-General's office include many in the field of human rights," and he added that "the

[18] 12 UN GAOR (690th plen. mtg.), paras. 72–73 (1957).

Secretary-General cannot shun such issues, especially if some expectation of assistance had been encouraged by the United Nations' resolute stands on the principles involved. There is reason to expect that discreet facilitative action in the area may soon become one of the major fields in which good offices are exercised."[19]

All four Secretaries-General of the United Nations, so far, have engaged in good offices in human rights or humanitarian matters.[20] Trygve Lie disclosed in his memoirs some of the efforts that he had undertaken on behalf of the Greek children taken to Communist countries during the guerrilla war in Greece. He reported that he had discussed the matter during visits to Marshal Tito of Yugoslavia,[21] Foreign Minister Siroky of Czechoslovakia,[22] and Marshal Stalin of the USSR.[23] He also reported on the conversations he had had with Marshal Tito concerning Bishop Aloysius Stepinac.[24]

Dag Hammarskjöld's general approach was that the Secretary-General should not be expected to exercise his good offices unless guidance could be found either in the Charter or in a decision of a major organ. He normally undertook good offices missions only at the request of governments, and he refused to take initiatives if he believed that either his right to do so or his chances of success were seriously in doubt. Pursuant to a decision of the Security Council, he addressed the human rights problems in South Africa during meetings with South African leaders in 1961, and sought to find arrangements for safeguarding human rights in accordance with United Nations principles.[25]

In his memoirs, *View From the United Nations*, U Thant gave a glimpse into some of the human rights good offices in which he had engaged:

> Regarding the problem of Soviet Jews, Mr. Tekoah[26] had been in touch with me, on a personal and confidential basis, since the middle of 1969. . . . I . . . decided that I would utilize the good offices of my two Russian aides . . . as channels of communication between myself and Moscow. Whenever I received petitions from Mr. Tekoah, I passed them on to one of them for transmission to Moscow. Even my closest colleagues did not know the procedure I was employing, since I felt that complete discretion alone would bear results.[27]

These efforts, he said, had met with much success.

[19] V. PECHOTA, *supra* note 8.

[20] Secretaries-General of the League of Nations also made intercessions on humanitarian matters. *See, e.g.*, on the humanitarian efforts of Secretary-General Drummond, J. BARROS, *supra* note 13, at 105–06.

[21] T. LIE, IN THE CAUSE OF PEACE 243 (1954).

[22] *Id.* at 289.   [23] *Id.* at 304.

[24] *Id.* at 242–43.

[25] B. URQUHART, HAMMARSKJÖLD 496–97 (1972). *See also*, on Hammarskjöld's exercise of good offices in general, pp. 308–14.

[26] The Israeli Ambassador.

[27] U THANT, *supra* note 1, at 351–52. In the UN relief operations to Bangladesh (1971), Secretary-General U Thant, relying upon the purposes of the Charter, invoked his responsibility to ensure that human well-being was protected and humanitarian principles upheld. *See* Morse, *Practice Norms and Reform of International Rescue Operations*, 157 RECUEIL DES COURS 121, 150 (1977 IV).

U Thant reported that he applied

> [s]ome general rules . . . to any exercise of good offices. Obviously efforts of this kind must be fully in accordance with the general principles of the United Nations Charter. Then the Secretary-General must reach a considered judgement as to whether his intervention is likely to be helpful, or whether, on the contrary, it will be ineffective, or even positively harmful. On this basis he must himself decide whether or not to accede to a request to take an initiative to exercise his good offices in a particular situation.

He added that "[o]nce the Secretary-General has decided to act, some other general rules apply. . . . [C]onfidence, mutual respect and absolute discretion are vital to success, and the less publicity there is, the better."[28]

In his annual reports on the work of the Organization between 1972 and 1981, Secretary-General Waldheim has consistently referred to his good offices in the field of human rights.[29] He summarized his approach in a book published in 1978:

> [J]e dispose d'une certaine marge de manoeuvre me permettant d'exercer mon influence dans la défense des droits de l'homme. Pour cela, je me conforme à un critère fondamental: le bien-être de la personne ou des personnes concernées. Le plus souvent, j'offre mes bons offices, à titre officieux, en me plaçant sur un terrain purement humanitaire. J'intercède pour assurer la vie sauve à un condamné à mort, pour favoriser la réunion de familles, pour obtenir des "clarifications" sur les conditions de détention de prisonniers ou sur le traitement réservé à une minorité nationale. J'assure toujours le gouvernement concerné de mon souci de ne pas m'ingérer dans ses affaires intérieures, tout en lui faisant valoir qu'un geste positif de sa part ne manquerait pas de relever son prestige dans l'opinion mondiale. Toute publicité à ma démarche risquerait de faire avorter l'entreprise. Aucun Etat, en effet, ne tient à donner l'impression qu'il a cédé à une quelconque sollicitation étrangère.
>
> Cependant, j'ai aussi recours aux interventions publiques quand j'estime que celles-ci sont nécessaires. Ainsi ai-je lancé, par exemple, un appel public au gouvernement ougandais pour lui demander d'autoriser une enquête impartiale sur les circonstances de la mort de l'archevêque Janani Luwum et de deux ministres. Cela ne m'a pas empêché de poursuivre des contacts confidentiels dans cette affaire.[30]

A review of the policy of Secretary-General Waldheim discloses that in dealing with individual cases in the context of the exercise of good offices, he uses his personal judgment as to whether an intercession on his part would be appropriate or useful. In this regard, he is guided mainly by the welfare of the persons concerned and acts mainly on humanitarian grounds, mindful, as a general rule, of the injunction against intervention in internal affairs. He takes into account the circumstances and responsibilities of the government(s) concerned and normally acts confidentially and discreetly, although, on occasions, he may speak out publicly when necessary. He may occasionally send a rep-

---

[28] U Thant, *A Quiet Road, supra* note 11, at 124–25.

[29] *See*, in particular, UN Docs. A/8701/Add.1, section IX (1972); A/9601/Add.1, at 8 (1974); A/31/1/Add.1, at 9 (1976); A/32/1, at 6–7 (1977); A/33/1 (1978); A/34/1 (1979); A/35/1, section IX (1980); OPI/622, at 16–17 (1978); UN Press Release SG/SM/321, at 6 (1977).

[30] K. WALDHEIM, UN MÉTIER UNIQUE AU MONDE 102 (1978).

resentative to consult with the government concerned. *Ratione materiae*, he may intercede in cases involving: danger of loss of life; torture or other serious abuses against the physical or mental integrity of persons; prisoners of conscience, where there are special reasons for acting; cases arousing widespread concern at the international level; and cases where there are other, strong humanitarian grounds for acting.

To qualify for action by the Secretary-General, certain elements should usually be present, such as a denial of justice (for example, a deliberate bypassing of the regular judicial processes or political subversion of these processes). In other words, the Secretary-General should not normally be expected to act where, for example, someone has been sentenced to death after having been found guilty through fair process of law, although he has done so on occasions, such as when former President Bhutto of Pakistan faced sentence of death. Usually, also, the Secretary-General should have enough evidence to demonstrate cause for legitimate concern on his part.

Among the types of action taken by the Secretary-General are the following. Where there is evidence giving cause for concern but the facts are not sufficiently clear, the Secretary-General may indicate his concern by asking for information as to the well-being of the person(s) concerned. In appropriate cases he may ask the government to take measures to guarantee the safety or well-being of the person concerned. In other types of cases he may ask for a stay of execution pending further review of the case. In some cases, where he has enough facts and there are reasons for doing so, he may ask the government to exercise clemency or to grant a pardon. In appropriate cases he may ask the government to consider allowing a person to leave instead of executing him.

The role of the Secretary-General in dealing with situations of gross violations of human rights has not been developed as much as his good offices role in dealing with individual cases. The objectives of the Secretary-General in discharging a role in this field seem to be:

(1) to ascertain the facts in a situation of gross violations of human rights;

(2) to maintain communications and contacts with the government concerned;

(3) to try to influence the government concerned to adopt measures that could lead to a cessation of violations and the restoration of human rights, and, in this regard, to utilize whatever possibilities of assistance available in the United Nations, such as technical assistance and advisory services;

(4) to express, if necessary, the conscience of the international community regarding the situation in question, particularly in the face of an uncooperative or recalcitrant government.

In seeking to realize the above-mentioned objectives, the Secretary-General has so far adopted the following approaches, *inter alia*: he may establish contacts with the governments concerned; he may send a representative for discussion with the government concerned; he may personally make a visit on the spot; he may designate a special representative to deal with the situation; he may seek to provide international humanitarian assistance, particularly through the office of the United Nations High Commissioner for Refugees; he may offer

United Nations technical assistance; he may convene an international conference to consider the situation; he may establish an inquiry into the situation; and he may, if he considers it necessary, comment on the situation publicly or express his concern about it.

An example of the approach of the Secretary-General to the handling of situations of gross violations of human rights was that of Chile in 1975. In its Resolution 3219 (XXIX), adopted in 1974, the General Assembly requested that the President of its 29th session and the Secretary-General assist in any way they might deem appropriate in the reestablishment of basic human rights and fundamental freedoms in Chile. The actions taken by the Secretary-General under this resolution were described in a report that he submitted to the 30th session of the General Assembly.[31] The Secretary-General and the Under-Secretary-General for Political and General Assembly Affairs held frequent meetings with the Permanent Representative of Chile to the United Nations. The Secretary-General also met with the Minister for External Relations of Chile, and the Under-Secretary-General visited Chile between February 23 and 28, 1975. On a subsequent occasion, the United Nations Legal Counsel also visted Chile.

An examination of the methods recently employed by the Secretary-General in the case of the American hostages in Iran shows that they included: definition of the issues; consultations, contacts, and representations; a visit on the spot; the making of proposals; the conduct of negotiations; and the establishment of a commission of inquiry.[32]

CONCLUSIONS

The following concluding observations may be offered.

(1) The good offices of the United Nations Secretary-General in the field of human rights have become a fully established part of, to use the words of Hammarskjöld, the "common law of organized international co-operation," and therefore of international customary law.

(2) Good offices in the field of human rights have certain characteristics that distinguish them from traditional good offices or that may not even exist in contemporary good offices in the settlement of international disputes generally. Among these the following may be mentioned:

(a) There may be only one government involved.

(b) The matter may be internal to a state (though not within its exclusive domain).

(c) The consent of the state concerned is not necessarily a prerequisite to the good offices initiative, though its cooperation will be essential to success.

(d) Good offices may be exercised with respect to situations involving gross violations as well as with respect to individual cases.

---

[31] UN Doc. A/10295 (1975).

[32] *See* para. 43 of the ICJ Judgment in the Case Concerning United States Diplomatic and Consular Staff in Tehran (USA v. Iran), [1980] ICJ REP. 3, *reproduced in* UN Doc. S/13989 (1980), 74 AJIL 746 (1980).

(3) Good offices initiatives must be in accordance with the general principles of the United Nations Charter. However, the requirements of the International Bill of Human Rights must also be taken into account. Good offices should be carried out in a spirit of mutual respect and with discretion.

(4) The exercise of good offices by the United Nations Secretary-General is always discretionary. No element of compulsion or automaticity can or should be injected into this function.

(5) In the practice of Secretary-General Waldheim on individual cases in which he exercises good offices, he acts on the following principles, *inter alia*:

> (a) He uses his personal judgment as to whether an intercession on his part would be appropriate or helpful.

> (b) He is guided mainly by the welfare of the persons concerned.

> (c) He acts mainly on humanitarian grounds, mindful as a general rule of the injunction against intervention in internal affairs.

> (d) He takes into account the circumstances and responsibilities of the government(s) concerned.

> (e) He normally acts confidentially and discreetly, but on occasions he may speak out publicly when necessary.

> (f) He may on occasion send a representative to consult with the government concerned.

(6) In dealing with situations of gross violations of human rights Secretary-General Waldheim has adopted the following approaches, *inter alia*:

> (a) He may establish contacts with the governments concerned.

> (b) He may send a representative for discussion with the government concerned.

> (c) He may personally make a visit on the spot.

> (d) He may designate a special representative to deal with the situation.

> (e) He may seek to provide international humanitarian assistance, particularly through the Office of the United Nations High Commissioner for Refugees.

> (f) He may offer United Nations technical assistance.

> (g) He may convene an international conference to consider the situation.

> (h) He may establish an inquiry into the situation.

> (i) He may, if he considers it necessary, comment on the situation publicly or express his concern about it.

B. G. RAMCHARAN*

* Special Assistant to the Director, UN Division of Human Rights, Geneva. All views expressed are those of the author in his purely personal capacity.

[5]

International Mediation—
The View from the Vatican
Lessons from Mediating the Beagle Channel Dispute

Thomas Princen

This article will examine the Vatican's mediation of a century-old border dispute between Argentina and Chile. To the observer, particularly the mediation expert, the Vatican's approach will likely appear inadequate and confused. But by first exploring the mediation from the Vatican's view and then focusing on the most significant consequence of the mediation—assuring a peace—I will argue that the Vatican's mediation effort was, in fact, a noteworthy success. While some lessons from this analysis may be peculiar to this case, I will focus on those that appear to be more broadly applicable. The last part of the analysis will be exploratory and intentionally provocative. My goal is to raise important questions regarding mediator effectiveness. A secondary aim is to illustrate through the case and the analysis, the formidable and often little recognized difficulties mediators face bringing two parties to an agreement.

History of the Beagle Channel Dispute

In late 1978, Argentina and Chile were on the verge of war. At issue were three barren, windswept islands in the Beagle Channel, a narrow passageway at the tip of South America.

An 1881 boundary treaty had not clearly specified the islands' rightful owner and, for nearly a century, the two countries had squabbled, occasionally negotiated, but for the most part, ignored the matter. By the early-1970s, however, both countries seemed more inclined to settle the matter due to changes in international law, increased hopes for resource exploitation in the region, and domestic upheavals. But diplomacy proved inadequate, and in 1971 the dispute was submitted to arbitration by a panel of International Court jurists appointed by the Queen of England. The result, in which Chile was awarded the islands, was rejected by Argentina. The two countries then set up a formal negotiation process, but that collapsed in late 1978. With tensions mounting and troops and ships being deployed to the south, war looked imminent. At the last minute, Pope John Paul II announced he was sending his personal representative, Cardinal Antonio Samoré, a career Vatican diplomat, to both Argentina and Chile. The escalation stopped, and after two weeks of shuttle diplomacy by the papal envoy, the two countries agreed to submit the matter to mediation at the Vatican under the auspices of the Pope.

The Pope, the official mediator, appointed a special mediation team headed

Thomas Princen is a member of the Harvard Negotiation Roundtable and teaches a tutorial on negotiation in the Economics Department, Harvard University. He is currently completing a Ph.D. dissertation in Political Economy at the Kennedy School of Government, Harvard University, Cambridge, Mass. 02138.

by Cardinal Samoré to conduct the day-to-day mediation of the Beagle Channel dispute. Beginning in May, 1979, this team spent six months gathering information and hearing out both sides' positions. In September, the Pope received the Argentine and Chilean delegations and put forth his conception of how the negotiation should proceed. After reminding them of their commitment not to resort to force during the course of the mediation, he suggested they start with those issues they had previously agreed upon and then explore a wide range of issues both inside and outside those of the Beagle Channel dispute. Finally, he requested that all statements regarding the progress of the mediation be issued jointly and through the mediation team, and he called upon the press to use prudence in its coverage.

For the next few months, the mediation team met separately with the two delegations, building an agenda, requesting position papers, and working on points of previous agreement. Only in mid-1980 did they turn their full attention to the central issues in dispute—the demarcation of territorial and maritime boundaries in the Beagle Channel. Draft solutions from each side were requested and received but as they were so far apart, the Pope delivered his own proposal for a solution in December, 1980. Granting the three islands to Chile and certain maritime concessions to Argentina, not to mention a common zone for the joint exploitation of natural resources, the papal proposal was accepted by Chile but never accepted—nor rejected—by Argentina. Due to Argentina's lack of response, the negotiations were at a standstill for much of 1981, even though the mediation team persisted in its attempts to resolve the impasse. In addition, renewed tensions between the two countries due to the detention of citizens along their border sidetracked the Vatican mediation.

Negotiations resumed in 1982, but soon stalled again: first when Argentina renounced a 1972 dispute settlement treaty with Chile, and then when war broke out between Argentina and Great Britain over the Falklands/Malvinas Islands. Even so, the Pope and his mediation team persisted in their efforts. While little progress was made on the Beagle Channel issues, by the end of the year the Pope did get the two sides to agree to an extension of the 1972 treaty and to accept, at least implicitly, the Pope's proposal as a basis for discussion.

As a result, active negotiations resumed in late 1982 and continued into 1983. But with the death of Cardinal Samoré in February, 1983, and Argentina's preparations to return to democratic rule, negotiations once again lapsed into impasse. During this time, several diplomats from the two sides began to meet informally outside the Vatican. These "parallel negotiations," plus continued efforts in Rome, paved the way for renewed negotiations, the signing of a final treaty in 1984, and ratification in 1985. In the end, Chile received the three islands, Argentina retained most of the maritime rights in the region, the common zone idea was abandoned, and several issues outside the Beagle Channel were settled.[1]

Vatican's View of International Mediation

Special Role of the Church

The Vatican[2] attributed its success in the peaceful resolution of the Beagle Channel dispute largely to the Pope's moral authority, particularly as that authority applies to the peoples of these two Catholic nations. From the official perspective of the Roman Catholic Church, the Church is the spiritual sovereign of Catholics everywhere. And since peace is seen as being as much a spiritual matter as a political one, the Church believed it had the right—as well as the obligation—to intervene in this dispute. As the Pope told the two delegations in September 1979, "To carry out these tasks [of mediation] seemed indispensable for one who considers that peace is one of the greatest human values and its pursuit and realization a desire, nay more, a mandate of the Son of God made Man, the Prince of Peace, whose vicar Providence has made me among men."[3]

The Pope's success can also be seen to derive from the special political role the government of the Church, the Holy See, plays in international affairs. The current Vatican Secretary of State, the second highest official in the Church hierarchy, Agostino Cardinal Casaroli, said in 1984 that

> ... the Holy See, in some ways, holds a privileged position. Not having any political, territorial or military interests of its own to defend, it is in a position to see with greater objectivity the reality and implications of the problems that arise on the international scene. At the same time, however, it has to be careful of the temptation to judge and evaluate concrete situations, which are sometimes very complex, from a point of view that is too theoretical or which oversimplifies things. The Holy See must also endeavour to maintain complete independence and the greatest balance of judgment, even when its *rapport* with the various parties involved is not always of the same quality.... It must be ready to examine and evaluate with equal objectivity the motives and behaviour of one and the other side ... (Hebblethwaite, 1986, p. 70)

While this statement was made in reference to the Church and East-West relations, it is indicative of the Church's modern view of papal diplomacy. It suggests that the Vatican viewed its special political position of disinterestedness and objectivivity—resulting from its lack of temporal power—as an asset in conducting an international mediation.

Besides moral authority and the special political role of the Church, a third feature of the Vatican's mediation was the fact that it was conducted entirely by members of the clergy. This, from the Vatican's perspective, carried special significance. The entire effort, from the hundreds of small private meetings to the occasional audiences with the Pope, was led by individuals who were trained to listen, to be understanding, to be patient, to try to reconcile differences. Cardinal Samoré in particular was known for his exceptional patience, his slow, methodical approach, and the extreme care he exercised to be impartial. The first six months of the mediation were, in fact, devoted largely to just hearing each side's position.

For the negotiators, however, his patience, combined with perseverance, sometimes proved exasperating. When he got it in his mind that progress could be made, that one side could concede just enough to make the difference, he would persevere, pushing day after day, sometimes for months, to get movement. Still, Cardinal Samoré's devotion to a peaceful resolution of the dispute was never in doubt. When hospitalized in late 1982, for example, he continued meetings with both sides at his bedside.

In sum, the Vatican viewed its role as an international mediator in both religious and political terms. This view in turn informed the Vatican's approach in mediating the Beagle Channel case and the procedures it employed.

The Function of a Mediator

Throughout the Beagle Channel mediation, the Vatican described the process primarily in terms consistent with international law. Mediation was seen as distinct from direct negotiations, as more than simply offering "good offices," yet not as a tribunal. But it was also a process that requires looking beyond strict legal strictures to find a fair and comprehensive solution.

According to the Vatican, such a quasi-legal process requires that the parties place a good deal of trust in the mediator. The Pope, in a 1979 speech to the delegates of the two countries, explained the relation between the need for parties' trust in the mediator and the peculiar function of a mediator to only give advice and make suggestions:

> [Trust] is a necessary premise in order that the mediator may feel more secure in his efforts which are of the very essence of mediation, which does not conclude with decisions, but is unfolded by means of advice. Relying on this trust, the mediator, after having asked God for enlightenment, presents suggestions to the Parties with the purpose of carrying out his work of rapprochment, aimed at safeguarding the fundamental interests of both, the supreme good of peace.[4]

In short, while the Vatican describes mediation primarily in legal terms—that it is not "good offices," nor an arbitral or adjudicatory proceeding—it sees effective mediation as depending largely on the parties' ability to trust the mediator. This trust is essential for mediator effectiveness because parties must be willing to accept the mediator's advice and suggestions and know they will be made with the parties' best interests in mind. This requisite trust factor, then, gives additional justification for the Vatican's conviction that the Pope and, presumably, religious leaders in general, can serve effectively in mediating roles.

Approach to Beagle Channel Case

While the special spiritual and political characteristics of the Church played a major role in the Vatican's successful mediation of the Beagle Channel case, what may have been equally important was the Vatican's ability to demonstrate impartiality. In many international conflicts; mediator impartiality may not be important (see, for example, Touval and Zartman, 1986), but in the Beagle Channel case it seems it was. At first, Argentina was reluctant to involve any third party, preferring to settle the matter directly. When this approach failed, Argentina took the position that it would accept third party mediation only if it could be shown there would be no bias in favor of Chile. Similarly, Chile had to be assured that a mediator would not ignore the legal grounds on which it based its entire case, and bow to pressure from Argentina. In 1978, when the two countries' foreign ministers decided that a mediator should be sought, the United States and various European countries were ruled out. Spain, the cultural patriarch of both nations, had initially appeared to be an acceptable candidate—until King Juan Carlos snubbed Chile by not visiting Santiago on a 1978 tour of South America.

To get acceptance from both Argentina and Chile, therefore, the Vatican had to demonstrate its impartially. It could do this in part because it clearly had no interest in the particular outcome of the negotiations—that is, who got the islands. Even more important, the Church could point to its own institutional needs to act impartially. Because of its perceived spiritual authority over the peoples of both countries, the unique political position the Vatican holds in international affairs, and the religious tradition of seeking understanding and the fair resolution of differences, the Church had its own reasons to demonstrate impartiality, reasons that were apparent to both sides.

Mediation Procedures

The Vatican's ability to exert moral suasion and its demonstrable impartiality may have accounted for the parties' initial acceptance of mediation[5] and, perhaps, for the fact that neither side withdrew during the six-year process. But these factors do little to explain why it took six years to come to agreement. Thus, another factor contributing to the success—and possibly the delay—of the mediation process was the specific techniques employed by the Pope and his mediation team.

Separate Meetings

From the beginning of the mediation effort, the mediation team kept the parties separate. They feared that, given the low levels of trust between the delegations and the fact that certain terms were sensitive, direct discussions would risk allowing the slightest misstatement by one side to ignite hostile responses from the other. For example, for Argentina, use of the term "*laudo*," the name for the arbitration award that favored Chile and was rejected by Argentina in 1978, smacked of prejudgment and discrimination by the international community. Similarly, for Chile, Argentina's insistence on the "bioceanic principle"—Argentina in the Atlantic, Chile in the Pacific—was viewed as a strategem for extending Argentine sovereignty at Chile's expense. In general, the mediation team felt it should encourage the parties to be patient, to avoid reacting impetuously to the ideas of the other side or of the mediator, and never to say that resolution was impossible. Separate, confidential meetings fostered this kind of atmosphere and allowed the mediator, if necessary, to deflect or absorb some of the negative emotions of the negotiators.

Joint meetings were occasionally held, nevertheless. In the early stages these were rare, specifically task-oriented, and highly controlled by the mediation team. For example, when in separate meetings it appeared there was general agreement on a list of agenda items, the mediation team would bring the two sides together to agree face-to-face on the list, but not to negotiate directly over the items themselves. Later in the mediation, the heads of the delegations would meet informally. This was initially only tolerated by the mediation team, but was eventually encouraged as it proved useful in increasing understanding.

Confidentiality

The mediation team deemed confidentiality of the proceedings and of the mediation's progress to be of utmost importance. Confidentiality would not only ensure frank disclosure of information and interests but would enable both parties to develop trust in the mediation team. That is, if the public was apprised of every move, every stalemate, every step forward and backward, the impression could easily develop that the mediation was not going well. As a result, the mediation team reasoned, the countries could be inclined to resort prematurely to other means, such as the International Court or the use of force. Thus, if this information was to be aired, exchanged, and used as the basis for agreement, it was essential that it be entrusted to the mediator.

But, one can argue, for the Vatican, confidentiality had more than a process rationale. With no history of being a democratic institution (the Holy See officially describes itself as a monarchy; see Papafava, 1984) and secrecy being the norm, confidentiality is virtually a standard operating procedure. Except for behind-the-scenes mediation such as that practiced by private diplomats, it is this capacity for confidentiality, probably more than anything else, that distinguishes Vatican mediation from other international interventions. In the Beagle Channel case, the Vatican's low need for public disclosure and public accountability, plus the separate meetings, not only cushioned the negotiators from outside criticism but also enabled the mediation team to exercise a high level of control over the proceedings.

Positions and Interests

The mediation team employed a number of procedures to probe each side's positions and interests and to stimulate movement toward agreement. To get the process started, the mediation team asked for position statements in writing from the two negotiating delegations. This was done to determine where the parties stood and to get a feel for the distance between them.

The mediation team then sought tentative agreement on the "easy" issues, and followed with steps to urge movement on the remaining issues. So, for example, in the early stages, the mediation team asked the negotiators to look at a 1978 agreement in which the two countries had agreed to cooperate on matters of economic integration, resource exploitation, and exploration of Antarctica. The mediation team's reasoning was that, once the two sides agreed on these relatively easy issues, they would more clearly see what they had to lose should they not come to a final agreement. As it turned out, in terms of movement toward agreement, little was achieved with this method. But in the process, the mediation team did thoroughly learn the positions of the two sides.

The mediation team concluded that the delay in settling, aside from the two countries' domestic affairs, was due to a difficulty in defining issues and getting the parties to reveal their true bottom lines. With no previous experience, the mediation team learned how to mediate as the process went along. A major lesson for the Vatican was that distinguishing primary, non-negotiable issues such as sovereignty and national pride from secondary, tradable issues such as resource accessibility is critical to a successful mediation effort. Making this distinction allows the mediator to lower outcome expectations regarding fundamental issues since some compromise on initial positions is usually necessary. At the same time, however, the mediator can raise parties' expectations on the secondary issues since flexibility and presumably trades can provide parties with more value than they expect.

For example, from Argentina's perspective, the "bioceanic" principle in part defined Argentina as a nation. The mediator could not expect a compromise on the principle per se, but could search for ways of drawing the line between the two oceans to preserve the principle without compromising Chile's claims. Such a line need not separate total jurisdiction but could, for example, signify separation on shipping rights but not overflight rights.

The Vatican mediation team realized, therefore, that a mediator must discover these "immovable" issues, find creative ways of getting around their strictly conflicting features, and fashion mutually beneficial solutions out of the more flexible issues. Doing so requires a clear identification of exactly what is immovable and what is not. The mediation team found it exasperating, however, to discover the two sides' true bottom line only at the very end. If the mediation team had known these positions earlier, it reasoned, a solution could have been more forthcoming.

But what the mediation team may not have fully appreciated is that, for either cognitive or representational reasons, the parties themselves may not have fully known their own bottom lines. What is more, those bottom lines may have changed over time with changing governments and new negotiators. In addition, in most negotiations there are valid strategic reasons for not revealing bottom lines, or reservation values (see, for example, Raiffa, 1982; Lax and Sebenius, 1986). And last, were it not for the momentum toward agreement generated at the very end, the bottom lines may never have emerged. Thus, while the mediation team ideally would have wanted to know the parties' reservation values—that is, to know the bargaining range—it is not likely such information would have emerged directly in the Vatican mediation. In general, it seems, a mediator must infer the bargaining range in a rough way and then take steps to push the parties toward agreement, never really knowing until agreement is achieved whether a point in the range has been found nor whether that point is somehow "fair."

Getting Agreement

In the Beagle Channel mediation, the Pope made it clear from the outset he would see the effort through to its finish. He would set no deadlines nor, even in the bleakest of times, ever back out. This, Vatican officials explained, was a necessary condition for an international mediation in which the parties' likely alternative to negotiation was hostilities. The Pope took this position, however, in early 1979 when most observers expected the mediation to be concluded in six months. Little did anyone realize that it would, in fact, take six years. Thus, the Vatican found itself in the uncomfortable position of urging movement toward agreement when it had no ability to compel either party to make a decision, a common dilemma faced by mediators.

One method the Vatican used for overcoming intransigence and encouraging movement was to exhort the parties both privately and publicly, reminding them of their commitment to abide by the terms of their original request for Vatican mediation. This commitment included the promise to consider seriously any ideas proposed by the Pope, to return gradually to the nonbelligerent military situation that existed at the beginning of 1977, and to abstain from adopting disruptive measures.

Events, of course, can often overcome such commitments. For example, the border incidents in 1981, which raised tensions to the point where hostilities looked imminent, made it impossible for the negotiators in Rome to deal effectively with the Beagle Channel issues while these new issues were being debated back home. As a result, the mediation team found itself mediating this new dispute, what became the so-called *pequeño* (small) *mediación*. It was only when the Pope sent a personal message, shortly after he was nearly assassinated in St. Peter's Square, that the two countries released prisoners and returned to the status quo. In short, the Vatican's preconditions for conducting an effective mediation were often frustrated by events outside the control of the mediator and, for that matter, of the negotiators.

A second means of inducing movement toward agreement was to seek creative solutions. For example, Chile was adamant in its position that the island of Cape Horn could not serve as a boundary since it was south of the Beagle Channel and the treaty of 1881 clearly stated that all such islands were Chilean. The mediation team proposed, however, that Cape Horn serve not as a territorial boundary but rather as an overflight boundary. Chile was eventually able to accept this concept.

The proper timing of proposals was the third technique used in moving parties toward agreement. From the Vatican's view, this timing depended on two factors. First, the dispute itself had to be "mature"—that is, the Pope could not present a proposal for a solution until both countries saw the opportunity and they themselves pressed for it. Thus, the Pope delivered his 1980 proposal only after some 18 months of active mediation and after an understanding that the two countries needed a face-saving means of making concessions. The second factor critical to timing was the internal situation of the two countries. For example, during the Falklands/Malvinas war, the mediation team determined that little progress could be made. But in the war's aftermath, the mediation team saw an opportunity to capitalize on Argentina's domestic uncertainty—as well as its need for legitimacy in the international community—and to push toward agreement.

Managing the Negotiator-Constituent Tension

In the course of the mediation, the Vatican learned that it was one thing to work effectively with the negotiators, the two nations' representatives, and quite another to convince their constituencies, the government and influential members of the public. In fact, a major source of frustration for the Vatican was to work hard with committed and talented negotiatiors only to have everyone's labors nullified by the decisions of the negotiators' superiors or by a turn of events back home.

One way the mediation team dealt with the division between negotiators and constituencies was to limit press coverage of the mediation, to admonish the press to be patient, and to encourage the press neither to raise hopes nor to be unduly pessimistic about the mediation's progress. Moreover, the Vatican urged the press not to dwell on the divisive issues—for example, the arbitration award—which could reactivate sensitivities that at one time nearly led to war. Rather, the Vatican asked the press to make its contribution by orienting "public opinion about the character of the mediation and fostering trust in the August Mediator."[6]

But handling the relationship between negotiators and constituencies required more than just guarding against the inflammatory effects of unfavorable press coverage. The Vatican found that one of its major functions in the mediation was to legitimize a negotiator's actions before that negotiator's government leaders and public. For example, in a 1980 speech, the Pope admonished the people of the two nations to accept their governments' work:

> ...I think that no one—now or in the future—should feel authorized to reproach them [the countries' authorities] with negligence or incompetence in the defense of legitimate national interests, despite the fact that acceptance of my suggestions and advice may involve a modification of the positions they maintained.[7]

While such public pronouncements may have helped the negotiators, behind-the-scenes lobbying may well have constituted a more important means of influencing constituencies. Through its diplomatic representatives, the local church hierarchy, and the parishes, the Vatican had its own built-in network to transmit information and solicit public support. In fact, it appears that at key junctures—as when tensions rose in 1981 over border incidents, or when the final treaty had to be ratified in Argentina in a public referendum—the local church played a significant role. In addition to its communication network, the Vatican—unlike many mediators—had a direct and separate channel to the two nations' leaders through its diplomatic representation.

Mediator Effectiveness in the Beagle Channel Dispute

The previous discussion of the Vatican mediation effort raises a number of questions about mediator effectiveness. For example, to what extent did the methods employed by the mediation team facilitate resolution and to what extent did they hinder it? How did the timing of the various "interventions" (for example, a speech by the Pope or a proposal by Cardinal Samoré) affect the process? How did domestic events in the two countries affect the mediator's work? How did the training, world perspective, and personality of the mediation team affect the process? Why did the mediation take so long when all the facts were essentially on the table from the beginning?

Answers to these questions are clearly needed to provide a full explanation of the Vatican's mediation effort, its success in the eventual agreement, and the difficulties it encountered over six trying years. I will frame the analysis of the Vatican mediation in terms of one overriding question: How did the Vatican influence the parties and urge them towards agreement? This question has two underlying theoretical assumptions. The first is that mediators who are committed to achieving a durable, just agreement and an agreement for which each party feels ownership, must balance their desire to achieve agreement with their desire to promote each party's sense of self-determination. In other words, the tactics a mediator employs simply to get agreement must be weighed against those employed to achieve objectives more important to parties in the long run such as fairness, durability, and efficiency.

A second, and related assumption concerns the difficulty mediators face in getting movement. A central dilemma for mediators is how to impose a negotiating structure on disputants and influence them to move from their positions when the mediators define themselves as being neutral and lacking decision-making authority. Thus, the following analysis will attempt to show how in the Beagle Channel case the mediator (both the mediation team and the Pope) tried to garner influence over the parties (both the negotiators and their constituencies); why this was deemed necessary by the mediator; and how it contributed to both progress and delay. Finally, I will conclude with several conjectural propositions about mediator effectiveness.

Mediator Actions

Each step a mediator takes, each suggestion, each proposal, contributes to the parties' perception of mediator effectiveness and to their expectation of reaching an acceptable solution. To enhance those perceptions and expectations, a mediator must be concerned with convincing each side that the mediator is capable, that the mediator is in charge, that if the other side demands too much or acts strategically, the mediator can effectively moderate such demands or quell misleading statements. Ultimately, the mediator must demonstrate the ability to protect each side's interests. To do this, the mediator must:

- structure a negotiation process that favors neither side and may, in fact, disfavor both;
- set appropriate expectations and in so doing risk challenging long-held interests;
- stay removed from the parties' positions on issues yet decide at some point what positions are inviolable and which require flexibility; and
- act solely as a purveyor of process but then be prepared to call attention to the parties' alternatives and even act to change perceived alternatives.

In short, a mediator must walk a thin line between being a neutral catalyst to a process and being an agent of change. And to the extent change is necessary—change in knowledge, perceptions, or firmly held positions and interests—the mediator must engage in an influence process.

For mediators such as the Vatican, that influence can come from two sources. One is institutional, which derives from the norms and procedures of the organization. The second source is operational necessity, the result of conducting a mediation process. As will be evident, the first, institutional, deals with factors mostly peculiar to this case and so I will only treat them briefly. The second, operational, has more generalizable implications and will involve a more extensive analysis.

1. *Influence: Institutional Imperative.* In the Beagle Channel case, the mediator's need to have control over the process and to influence the parties can in part be understood from the historical, spiritual, and organizational position of the Vatican. As noted earlier, the Church views itself as the spiritual sovereign of all Catholic peoples. Since peacemaking is seen as being as much a spiritual matter as a temporal one, the Vatican could justify its initial intervention in the Beagle Channel dispute—as well as subsequent steps throughout the mediation—as being part of its mandate to protect and guide its subjects, those individuals of the Catholic faith. In so doing, it could make demands on the parties that another third party could not. For example, the Pope often couched his urgings for reconciliation in religious terms: "God, the Father of all, drove me to make a gesture of peace."[8] Or the Vatican would call upon its local parishes to pray for peace or, for example, to garner support for Argentina's national referendum on the final treaty. From a political perspective, soliciting public support through the local parish can be seen as an effort to "bring out the vote." The difference here was that the deliverer of votes was an arm of the mediator, the Vatican, which sees itself and is seen by many Catholics as having sovereignty separate from that of the two nations.

The very structure of the Church hierarchy and the organizational routines of the Holy See lent themselves to exercising tight control over the mediation process. The Holy See, the central government of the Roman Catholic Church, is organized as a monarchy with the Pope at the top, and with the Roman Curia—the administrative apparatus of the government—acting as a papal secretariat. The Church as a whole is highly decentralized but the Curia is small and tightly run from above, especially from the Secretariat of State. In the Vatican, little of significance happens without Curia insiders knowing about it. At the same time, what does happen is often guarded as secret, even when that information seems insignificant. As a small, tradition-bound institution, the Holy See is, therefore, accustomed to keeping things under wraps.

This tradition affected, among other things, the Vatican's approach to the press in the Beagle Channel mediation. From the very beginning, the Vatican required that all press announcements be made jointly and through the mediation team. The ostensible reason was to avoid unduly arousing the two parties' respective publics, to avoid unreasonable expectations, and to head off any maneuvering on either side that could be justified by misleading press reports. Ultimately, the Vatican argued, strict control of the press was needed to build "trust in the mediator."

While control over the press is understandable from the Vatican's perspective and would certainly be the envy of other mediators, this approach to the press can be interpreted equally well, and perhaps more plausibly, as a means of building mediator influence over the parties. This interpretation has two aspects. First, controlling public announcements removes from the parties the opportunity to employ the familiar negotiating tactic of using the press to make commitments binding. That is, if in a negotiation one party must convince the other side (and, for that matter, the mediator) that it cannot budge from a stated position, a public announcement of its position makes it more difficult to find a face-saving means for moving from that position. Secondly, freeing the parties from the burden of constantly answering to the press makes it easier for the mediator to make demands of the parties. For example, the mediator can claim that a concession on a given point is not significant if it is only temporary and conditional upon a settlement on all points. Since the party's constituency need never know about such a conditional concession—and the mediator can guarantee confidentiality—it is a low-risk move.

In fact, the Vatican mediation team repeatedly used this tactic throughout the process to encourage flexibility. There is some evidence that the mediation team was able to secure tentative concessions in private that eventually found their way into the final treaty. The general point, however, is that, from the mediator's perspective, by controlling public pronouncements, the mediator can reduce parties' risk aversion and encourage creative exploration, both of which are essential conditions for overcoming obstacles and finding joint gains.

2. Influence: Operational Imperative. The Vatican's need for influence in the mediation process and its inclination to build such influence derive not only from a historical and organizational tradition, but from the very difficulty of conducting a mediation process. The Pope spoke many times of the great "risks" entailed in trying to reconcile differences between two temporal powers, differences that had eluded solution for a century. In interviews in 1986, Vatican officials likewise spoke of the great risks, but when pressed to explain them, they could say little more than that the Pope faced the risk of failure. By searching for an explanation for this perceived risk, I hope to illuminate the Vatican's need to build influence in order to help the parties reach an agreement.

The Pope's sense of risk in the mediation derived from the expected consequences of failing to reach agreement and of allowing the two sides to revert to hostilities under his auspices. This fear was enhanced by the high likelihood of an outbreak of hostilities, as evidenced by the near war in late 1978 and the continued strains between the two countries thereafter. The effect of a failed mediation would have been to allow the Church to be seen as even weaker and more ineffectual in world affairs than it is often portrayed to be. As the most prominent moral leader in the free world, the Pope, therefore, could hardly let two Catholic countries slip away and commence hostilities. If peace is as much a spiritual as a political matter, the world's most celebrated moral spokesman could lose big, even on such a relatively minor affair. Concerned about his official and public standing, the Pope had to treat every move in the mediation process as one that would affect his future ability to have an effect on other world affairs. For example, at this time, Church relations with the liberation theologists, especially in Latin America, and with the Eastern bloc countries, especially his native Poland, were high on his diplomatic agenda.

Thus, the Pope and his mediation team constantly had to be aware of the possibility of losing control, of letting the process slip out of the mediator's hands, of one party taking unilateral action, whether belligerent or legal, that would preclude the successful completion of the process under the Vatican's auspices. This would suggest, then, that many of the Vatican's actions in the Beagle Channel case can be understood in terms of the mediator's attempts to ensure firm control—that is, that above all else the Vatican had to have a positive outcome or, at least, that it had to avoid a negative one. I will examine this proposition by analyzing four prominent features of the Vatican's actions: its stated position of seeing the process through to the finish; the manner in which it controlled information; the way it handled the parties' positions and interests; and the attempts to alter the parties' alternatives to a mediated agreement.

No mediation deadline. The mediator's repeated statements that it would never abandon the mediation put the burden on the parties to withdraw. If at any time one party decided to give up, that party would suffer the opprobrium of sacrificing a peace effort for some uncertain, probably contentious, process. And given that the two sides could agree on virtually nothing on their own, it was not likely they would agree jointly to abandon the mediation. Thus, with the mediator committed to staying indefinitely, unilateral withdrawal could easily have been condemned by the other side, by the Vatican itself, or by other third parties. The cost in terms of international standing could have been high.

Interestingly, while this no-withdrawal stance of the Vatican may have contributed to the parties' reluctance to withdraw unilaterally and hence to the enhancement of the mediator's relative influence over the parties, it may have been double-edged. That is, since the parties knew the mediator would never cease its efforts, their certainty also could have undercut the Vatican's occasional threats to cut off the mediation if movement was not forthcoming. One can surmise that they were convinced of this by their appreciation of the mediator's costs of failure.

Information management. A second example of the Vatican's attempt to build influence in order to avoid failure can be found in its practice of keeping parties separate and strictly controlling the flow of information. Assuming the principle that information is power, the effect was to enhance the mediator's influence. What is important with respect to mediation, however, is how such tight information control either furthers or hinders the mediation process.

One effect of controlling the information flow in a negotiation is to allow the mediator to learn the issues and the parties' interests in a manner unencumbered by strategic play between parties. This was the reason given by the Vatican. Parties are more likely to reveal information and less likely to protect their positions or be tempted to act strategically vis-à-vis each other if they are not facing each other in the same room.

A second effect of information control is to influence the interactions between a party and the mediator. In the Beagle Channel mediation, Chile's case rested largely on standards of international law and propriety, and so its strategy in Rome was to convince the mediator that everything it did was consistent with the notion of playing by the rules. In turn, since controlling information facilitated the mediator's ability to act as a "rules manipulator," the mediator could use Chile's stance to encourage strict adherence to the rules of the mediation as written in the original agreement to request papal mediation, and as later interpreted by the Vatican. The result, one can surmise, was not only a willingness on Chile's part to be forthcoming in providing information and revealing its positions, but also to pursue imaginative paths for a solution. For example, it did accept the Pope's concept of a "common zone," a jointly administered region for the cooperative exploitation of natural resources.

Argentina, on the other hand, was looking for a concession from Chile. It seems clear that given the political turmoil in the country throughout the period of the mediation, and the risks of deviating from a hardline view, no Argentine negotiator could return home without major concessions from Chile.[9] Thus, the Argentine strategy in Rome was to give little but get the mediator to extract a lot from Chile.

Dealing with this stance was certainly more problematic for the mediator than dealing with Chile's. Even if the mediation team could extract a concesssion from Chile, it felt compelled to balance it with one from Argentina. Attempting to do this, nevertheless, required control over the process. For example, to seek concessions, the mediator would naturally feel compelled to work separately with each party, knowing that each party would never on its own be the first to move. And once movement was detected, the mediator would have to guard that information carefully so as not to jeopardize securing the concession.

While the mediation team appeared to pursue such a strategy, in time it seemed to realize that simply squeezing out concessions did not necessarily lead to agreement. In fact, such concessions may have inhibited progress if any concession on the part of an Argentine negotiator put that negotiator in an even more precarious position back home. This would make that negotiator all the more cautious about any subsequent move, whether concessionary or integrative. This interpretation of the effect of urging concessions seems to suggest that an incremental approach to achieving a settlement—especially with a focus on concessions—may, under some circumstances, be counterproductive. It suggests that negative dynamics such as increasing cautiousness can develop, and then feed back on each other to make resolution more difficult to achieve.

Once the mediation team came to realize the dilemma of the Argentine negotiator, the strategic response of the mediator seems to have been to protect the negotiator. One means, as noted, was to restrict press coverage. Another was to make direct public appeals to the negotiator's leadership and the public. Still a third method was to do all possible publicly to appear absolutely fair and impartial, thus enabling the negotiator to argue that a settlement package involved a balanced process of making concessions. All these methods, once again, required a degree of control over the process.

In sum, the above examples of a mediator's control over process direct attention toward the importance of the interaction between the mediator and each party. A party's strategy on the issues or on its role vis-à-vis its constituency in part determines its strategy with the mediator. And a mediator's strategy is in part a product of the nature of the dispute and in part—perhaps a greater part—a product of the different strategies parties bring to the table to influence the mediator. If this conclusion is correct, it suggests that a mediator's job involves more than exploring interests and crafting mutually beneficial solutions. Rather, a mediator also must be concerned about its strategic interaction with the parties if for no other reason than to enable the mediator to help the parties obtain the benefits of a successfully mediated agreement.

Positions versus interests. A third example of the mediator's attempt to build influence in order to avoid failure can be found in the Vatican's otherwise inexplicable stress on positions. It appears the mediation team dwelled on the parties' positions to such an extent that the search for underlying interests was greatly inhibited. This process started at the very beginning of the mediation with the mediation team's request for written statements from both sides. It continued throughout much of the mediation when the mediation team asked for position statements on major issue areas and when it asked for draft solutions. All this had a legitimate purpose for the mediator, of course, namely to acquire information and see how far apart were the two sides. But as others have argued, acquiring information in this way invites rigidity and an unwillingness to explore creative options (see, for example, Fisher and Ury, 1981; Raiffa, 1982; Pruitt and Rubin, 1986).

Why would the mediation team have taken such an approach? One reason could have been that, lacking any experience in mediation and with essentially nothing to serve as a guide, the mediation team simply did what seemed logical. Cardinal Samoré did do some reading on the matter and it is possible that, with so little written on actual procedures of international mediation, he may have adopted what appears to be a labor model of mediation: start with each side's last bid, determine how far each can go, and then press both sides to converge to a midpoint.

Taking a more institutional approach, another reason could have been that this is how the Holy See tends to operate. When disputes arise within the Church, say a difference between a bishop's local practices and the official doctrine of the Church, the Holy See tends to adopt an adjudicatory role rather than a neutral intermediary role. In the adjudicatory approach, those charged with resolving the dispute collect information and make a decision, a decision that presumably meets everyone's interests. The Vatican view of mediation initially could have been similar; its role was to collect information and make a *suggestion* that met both sides' interests. Since in the beginning the mediation team had every reason to believe that the two sides would accept the Pope's proposed solution, especially given the mediator's demonstrated efforts to be fair, equitable, and impartial, the only difference in procedure was a decision versus a suggestion. To the Vatican, that difference may not have appeared to be much. But as the mediator was soon to find out, when Argentina did not accept the Pope's proposed solution, the *Propuesta*, a difference in decision-making authority—between making a decision and a suggestion—can have profound affects.

A third possible reason for the focus on positions comes from the mediator's need to maintain control over the process. Given the risks to the Vatican of losing control, the mediation team's inexperience as a mediator, and, at least for Argentina, a lack of support back home, any attempt by the mediator to engage the two countries in a seemingly open-ended process of exploring underlying interests and searching for joint gains could have jeopardized the parties' faith in the Vatican's ability to effect a settlement. The mediation team often stated that it took such measures as restricting press coverage and holding separate meetings to "build trust in the mediator." While this enigmatic phrase can be taken at face value, it can also be interpreted as indicative of more strategic concerns of the Vatican.

That is, the mediation team entered into this process with a sense of considerable uncertainty and risk: the team members had never conducted such a process; the dispute had eluded solution for a century; an unexpected twist of events in South America could have easily upset the mediation team's best efforts; and failure to reach a settlement could have made war likely and could have impeded the Pope's ability to conduct foreign affairs on other fronts. Thrown into such a situation, it is not surprising that members of the mediation team would adopt a risk averse approach, an approach that would strive to give the appearance of being in charge, one that would avoid direct confrontations between parties, and one that would put control of process as much as possible into the hands of the mediation team. What is more, given the intitial positions of the two sides—Chile wanted a juridically sound solution and Argentina concessions on land—it is reasonable to conclude that, in the beginning, the two negotiating teams themselves would have balked at anything but a very formal, highly structured process.

The fact that the mediation team continued to demand written positions when such a process achieved little in terms of movement appears to confirm this interpretation of mediator control. If the mediation team only had been seeking factual and positional information by requesting written position statements (something, by the way, that could have been achieved in other ways), once it had such information it would have moved on to exploring interests and crafting solutions. The mediation team did, of course, do these things but it also regularly reverted back to a process of requesting statements on new positions, each time hoping one side or the other would move enough to provide the basis for agreement. Assuming the mediation team did learn over these six long years that requests for position statements rigidifies positions and inhibits creative problem solving, the best explanation seems to be that this was the only conceivable means of maintaining some control given external events.

Stressing alternatives. The previous three examples primarily involve the mediator's efforts to control procedures. A fourth example of control involved attempts to influence the parties' themselves, in particular, their alternatives to a mediated agreement or their perceptions of feasible agreements.

When, after a year of effort, the mediation team realized progress toward agreement was not forthcoming, Cardinal Samoré raised some unpleasant alternatives. He suggested that if the parties did not significantly change their positions, the Pope could either suspend the mediation or offer them a take-it-or-leave-it solution. When this produced no movement, the Vatican considered sending a papal representative to each country's president or simply calling in each country's foreign minister for talks. Finally, the two sides were given an audience with the Pope in which John Paul underscored the seriousness of the great distance still existing between the two sides.

All these moves can be seen as attempts to change the parties' perceived alternatives to a mediated agreement. That is, if the parties originally were convinced that the Pope would never abandon the mediation, the best alternative to "agreement now" was continued mediation. Suggesting that the pope might reverse his promise was an attempt—albeit an ineffectual one—to change that perceived alternative.

Another example of stressing alternatives occurred at the very end of the mediation, when a solution was in sight and the mediation team insisted that posturing could no longer be tolerated. First, the mediation team stressed the point and said that their positions, their truly inflexible ones and their flexible ones, had to be revealed truthfully, "as if in confession." Then, when the last objectionable feature of the Pope's *Propuesta* was excised and the mediation team determined there was nothing else that could be done to improve the proposal for either side (presumably without simultaneously hurting the other side), the mediation team said this was the final proposal: To reject it would be to terminate the mediation effort. This threat to cease the mediation may have been more credible this time because it was clear to all that the mediation team could do no better and was tired and frustrated with the entire ordeal. What is more, in Argentina in 1984, with the return of democratic rule, there existed the most favorable climate ever for resolution, and in Chile there was an increasing urgency to settle the matter and claim a foreign success. And, finally, the mediation team made its take-it-or-leave-it offer public. Conditionally imposing upon itself the public image cost of retracting such a pledge, this time the Vatican appeared to make a true commitment.

In summation, it does appear that the desire for control can explain much of the Vatican's approach to conducting an international mediation. I should emphasize that by identifying control as a major concern of the Vatican, I am not ascribing motives any less noble than working for peace. It is just that it appears the Vatican viewed strict control as a necessary means to achieving a peaceful resolution. This interpretation of mediator control also suggests that, in the tradeoff between ensuring party self-determination and ensuring mediator control over process, the Vatican mediation team opted more for mediator control. The question that naturally arises, then, is under what conditions can (or should) a mediator stress self-determination? A complete answer must await the comparative analysis of other mediation cases in a variety of settings, but several tentative thoughts in the form of propositions are offered here:

· In choosing between mediator control and party self-determination, conditions of high uncertainty and high risk for the mediator will drive the mediator to choose control.

· The training of mediator personnel and their accustomed operating procedures will, in part, determine the method they choose.

· A mediator will be inclined to emphasize party self-determination when the mediator's reputation *as a mediator* is paramount; that is, to the extent a mediator's reputation is based on previous mediation efforts and the parties' sense of having determined outcomes, the mediator will eschew strict control if the mediator hopes to continue to mediate.

Explaining Delay

One final, outstanding question remains regarding outcomes: Why did the Beagle Channel mediation take so long? If mediation is a process of identifying issues and interests, finding a suitable bargaining range, and helping parties move to agreement, then why did the Beagle Channel mediation take six years, and not six months as expected? Certainly the facts were on the table—for the most part, they had been since the arbitration of the early 1970s—and it appears the negotiators from both Argentina and Chile were experienced, competent individuals.

Part of the explanation seems to relate to the mediation team's inexperience with the process, which, I would guess, is a common occurrence in international mediation. The mediation team was searching for a method and had little guidance in procedure. The procedures they did use were developed ad hoc. In addition, it appears that Cardinal Samoré's slow methodical approach, where no stone could be left unturned, where each party was given ample opportunity to explain everything, where each nuance was carefully explored, contributed to the delay. If either party had reason to delay—and Argentina evidently did at several points—Samoré's style was well suited to allow for it.

A second factor was the apparent distributive view both sides took of the negotiation: Both saw their primary objective as getting islands and as much of the sea as possible. This is how the dispute was viewed from the beginning and there is little evidence that it changed during the mediation. Although the mediation team sincerely tried to unbundle issues and to add new issues to find integrative solutions, it appears they were not successful. In part this was probably due to the very nature of the dispute—it was primarily distributive as long as high value interests such as territorial integrity and national sovereignty were attached to the otherwise straightfoward issues of territorial and maritime delimitation. Also, as noted, the publics of each side were not expected to see beyond the question of who won and who lost. And, finally, the mediation team's methods, such as requesting position statements, tended to focus the negotiation on the distributive aspects.

A third factor, and unquestionably the most important for final settlement, was the effect of domestic events on the negotiators' ability to agree. This was particularly pronounced for Argentina. As in any negotiation with representatives, an agent-principal division occured. Here that division seems to have been a major source of frustration for the Vatican mediation team. All the painstaking work of mastering the facts and exploring interests, crafting a solution that seemed to meet those interests, and winning the negotiators' acceptance, was repeatedly defeated either intentionally by decisionmakers or inadvertently as a result of tumultuous domestic events. As for the Argentine negotiators, they were regularly receiving conflicting demands from different sectors within the military governments of this period. Furthermore, during the mediation period, Argentina had five presidents and five Vatican delegation chiefs. All told, it is little wonder that an Argentine delegation chief could ever feel confident enough to dare recommend agreement. This would have been the case no matter how reasonable the proposed solution, no matter how balanced the process and how fair the results, no matter how much creative problem solving took place, no matter how many joint gains were extracted.

Conclusion

So were the Vatican's efforts ultimately for nought? Was the mediation team playing the wrong game, engaging in details in Rome when the real problem was in South America? These are the kinds of questions any mediator must ask when a dispute appears unresolvable, when a serious division exists between negotiating representatives and constituents. A preliminary answer seems to be that if maintaining a peace is the foremost objective of any mediation effort—whether for instrumental or intrinsic reasons—the Vatican's efforts contributed to six years of such peace. This was no mean feat given the tensions between the countries at the time of the Pope's intervention and the military's propensity to seek an external success to compensate for its internal failures (witness Argentina's renewed provocations against Chile in 1981, and then the invasion of the Falklands/Malvinas islands in 1982). On this count alone, it seems the Vatican mediation can be considered a success. It was not just that a settlement was reached, but that a peace was maintained through some very rough times.

This conclusion does, however, raise an interesting question. Suppose the Vatican could have foreseen the course of events, the intransigence of the parties, the domestic upheavals. Would it have acted differently? Should it have? Accepting the above conclusion that a peace was maintained, the answer would have to be no. But then that suggests that the mediator's true task is not so much to move parties towards agreement, but rather to keep the parties busy. And since sophisticated negotiators cannot put up with busyness, even on expense accounts, they must do at least what *appears* to be the work of negotiation under the guidance of a mediator.

Thus, an alternative interpretation of the seemingly endless meetings typical of many assisted negotiations is that such meetings serve primarily to keep the parties at the table and not at each other's throats. But in order to keep them there, the mediator must convince them that they are doing something worthwhile. The most convincing activity is, naturally, "negotiating." But, in fact, they are doing nothing of the kind—they are just biding time. This, of course, is a rather ungenerous view of what mediators do. But, at least in the Beagle Channel mediation, it may partly explain why the mediation team plodded along, day after day, year after year, continuing to request position statements, sound out variations on old themes, and look for new angles.

Even if this view is close to the mark—that is, if it helps explain much of the day-to-day activity of the Vatican mediation—it does not deny the value of the fruits of those labors. Continuing to work on details when agreement on a package was impossible set the stage for an expeditious settlement when domestic conditions changed. The Pope and the mediation team seemed to realize this and never let up, even in the worst of times (for example, during and after the Malvinas/Falklands fiasco). As a result, when Argentina was ready for a solution in the Beagle Channel dispute—the time of which, by the way, no one could have ever predicted more than a few months in advance—so was a settlement package. This being the case, the day-to-day activities are indeed more important than just biding time. But contrary to popular conceptions, such activities may actually do little to bring parties closer to an agreement. The paradox, once again, is that a mediator still must convince the parties that what they are doing is what they are supposed to be doing—getting an agreement. If this conception of what a mediator actually does in the day-to-day activities of a mediation is true, it highlights in yet another way the difficulty of mediating, the contradiction and ambivalence such a role demands.

Two prescriptions for mediators follow from this line of reasoning. First, while getting agreement may appear to be one's mandate, achieving a temporary peace is in many circumstances no small matter and is a worthy achievement in its own right. Doing so may well be the necessary precursor to a more comprehensive solution. It is worth noting that even in the final solution of the Beagle Channel case, a comprehensive solution was not achieved. This was left to a "binational commission" that, since 1985, has been working out agreements on matters of "regional integration."

Second, in the course of a mediation, a mediator must continually ask him or herself whether or not to continue. It would be tempting to quit when it appears the success of the mediation (defined as getting agreement) is out of the control of the negotiators and that everything depends on constituencies and external events. The proper decision, however, pertains to the alternatives the mediator and the parties face. If abandoning the mediation is likely to lead to hostilities, continuation, even if it appears futile (in the sense of reaching an agreement) makes sense.

Another way of saying this is that for continuing the mediation, the relevant calculation is at the margin: If the cost of continuing one more time period is less than the expected value of discontinuing (where all the possible consequences including hostilities are factored in with their respective estimated probabilities), the mediator should continue. Notice, by the way, this calculation by the mediator can be thought of in either a strictly altruistic sense (What are the *parties'* expected costs?) or in a self-interested sense (What are the costs to the *mediator* if the parties incur these costs?). Thus, this is the proper calculation whether the mediator claims to be operating strictly in the interests of the parties or whether the mediator sees its own interests as paramount.

NOTES

The author would like to thank Tom Angelo, Jim Arthur, Eileen Babbitt, and Howard Raiffa for their very useful comments on drafts of this paper.

1. For a more detailed account of the entire Beagle Channel case with analysis, see Thomas Princen, Ph.D. dissertation, Harvard University, expected completion, January, 1988.

2. While, technically speaking, the term "Vatican" refers only to the tiny city-state in Italy, I use it here in the everyday sense to refer to the central authority of the Roman Catholic Church, which is headed both spirtually and administratively by the Pope. Properly speaking, the Holy See is the central government of the Church. Also, references to the Vatican's view do not necessarily indicate official positions. Rather, they reflect a composite of statements and opinions obtained both from confidential interviews I held in 1986 and from public Vatican documents.

3. *L'Osservatore Romano.* 12 November 1979, p. 14. Weekly English Edition.

4. Ibid.

5. The question of entry and the relevant decision problems for both the Vatican and the two countries will not be discussed here. It should be noted however, that, contrary to the opinion of many participants and observers in this case, the entry question for the Pope was by no means a simple one. A number of factors had to be weighed, and timing was critical.

6. Press release, Radio Vaticana, UISS, 16 May 1980

7. *L'Osservatore Romano.* 29 December 1980, p. 2. Weekly English Edition.

8. Ibid.

9. I should clarify that while this discussion is couched in terms of concessions—something both parties tended to do in interviews—it is not meant to suggest that either the mediation team or the parties did not see the potential of more creative, more integrative solutions. In terms of domestic consumption, however, especially in Argentina at this time, it is likely that both public and official reaction to any plan brought home by the negotiators would be couched in such terms. If there is a lesson here, it seems to be that even if negotiators can appreciate the potential of integrative solutions, publics tend to evaluate outcomes in simple, win-lose, distributive terms. This tendency will be exaggerated as the intensity of the conflict, domestic uncertainty, lack of political unity, economic decline, and so forth, increase.

REFERENCES

Fisher, R. and Ury, W. (1981). *Getting to YES.* Boston: Houghton Mifflin.

Hebblethwaite, P. (1986). *In the Vatican.* Bethesda, Md.: Adler & Adler.

Lax, D. and Sebenius, J. (1986). *The manager as negotiator.* New York: The Free Press.

Papafava, F. (1984). *The Vatican.* Florence, Italy: SCALA.

Pruitt, D. G. and Rubin, J. Z. (1986). *Social conflict.* New York: Random House.

Raiffa, H. (1982). *The art and science of negotiation.* Cambridge, Mass.: Harvard University Press.

Touval, S. and Zartman, I.W. (1985). *International mediation in theory and practice.* Boulder, Colo.: Westview Press.

Part IV
Inquiry and Conciliation

[6]

THE PLACE OF COMMISSIONS OF INQUIRY AND CONCILIATION TREATIES IN THE PEACEFUL SETTLEMENT OF INTERNATIONAL DISPUTES[1]

By CHARLES CHENEY HYDE, A.M., LL.D.,

Hamilton Fish Professor of International Law and Diplomacy, Columbia University, New York; Associate of the Institute of International Law.

WHAT follows is a technical discussion of certain modes of adjusting international controversies.

The obvious function of a commission of inquiry is to investigate and report. Anything may be investigated; questions of fact over which controversy has arisen, or questions of law on which there is also disagreement.[2] As a fact-finding body, a commission of inquiry, a majority of its members being nationals of outside states, should be competent to ascertain the truth regardless of the gravity of the issue, and to make a report worthy of respect. Its conclusions on any of the factual aspects of a dispute touching, for example, the causes of events, or the authorship of acts, or the consequences of acts committed or contemplated, may be of first importance, as a means of enabling the states at variance to reach accord.[3]

If, however, the function of a commission of inquiry be to report findings on the law and thereby to fix responsibility, if any, for conduct the propriety of which is challenged, the value of the service must depend in part upon the competence in law and the judicial temperament of the persons comprising the commission.[4]

---

[1] An address delivered before the American Society of International Law, at Washington, April 26, 1929.

[2] While the elucidation of facts was the objective of the Commissions of Inquiry contemplated by the Hague Conventions of 1899, and 1907, the problem before the commission in the *Dogger Bank* case was to report on a matter of law, "particularly on the question as to where the responsibility lies and the degree of blame attaching to the subjects of the two High Contracting Parties or to the subjects of other countries in the event of their responsibility being established by the inquiry." (Protocol of July 29, 1899, *Am. J.* II, 929; also *Report of Commission*, id., 931.)

Compare matter for investigation in the *Tavignano, Camouna,* and *Gaulois* cases, under agreement between France and Italy, May 20, 1912, J. B. Scott, *Hague Court Reports*, 417, and Report of Commission, id., 413. See also Report of the Commission of Inquiry in the *Tubantia* case, under convention between Germany and the Netherlands, of March 30, 1921, *Am. J.* XVI, 485.

[3] It is not believed that a commission of inquiry as a purely fact-finding body could do substantial injury to the states at variance through the exercise of its function.

[4] It will be recalled that in the *Dogger Bank Case* the commission of inquiry was com-

COMMISSIONS OF INQUIRY, ETC. IN DISPUTES   97

That the report, whether on facts or law, does not embrace recommendations or give expression to an affirmative endeavour to effect accord between the states at variance is a distinctive feature of the service rendered.[1] From the report of the commission those states remain free to draw their own conclusions as to the course thereafter to be followed. To this circumstance may perhaps be attributed the readiness of numerous states to conclude with the United States bi-lateral conventions providing for the use of the plan of inquiry set forth in the treaties concluded by Secretary Bryan in 1913 and 1914, for the Advancement of Peace.[2] That plan is based on the principle that any phase of any controversy may reasonably be subjected to impartial investigation, during the course of which the states at variance may wisely pause and refrain from conflict, provided the report of the investigators be not the medium of a preachment or recommendation, and provided also that those states retain entire freedom to disregard it.[3] The strength of the arrangement lies in the fact that it is designed to enable the states at variance, in consequence of the report of the commission, to work out themselves a solution of their controversy. It is seen also in the care taken not to jeopardize

posed of five naval officers of high rank, in pursuance of Article I of the agreement of July 29, 1899.

[1] In this respect the function of a commission of inquiry differs from that of a commission of conciliation. The distinction appears to be acknowledged in Article II of the General Convention of Inter-American Conciliation of January 5, 1929, which announces that: "The Commission of Inquiry to be established pursuant to the provisions of Article IV of the Treaty signed in Santiago de Chile on May 3, 1923, shall likewise have the character of Commission of Conciliation." See also McNair's 4th ed. of *Oppenheim*, II, § 11a.

[2] On March 29, 1929, the United States was a party to twenty-three treaties providing for commissions of inquiry, of which nineteen (those with Bolivia, Brazil, Chile, China, Denmark, Ecuador, France, Great Britain, Italy, The Netherlands, Norway, Paraguay, Peru, Portugal, Russia, Spain, Sweden, Uruguay, and Venezuela) were signed in 1913 and 1914, and of which four (those with Albania, Austria, Finland, and Germany) were signed in 1928. In addition thereto treaties had been signed in behalf of the United States, in 1928 and 1929 with nine other states (Belgium, Bulgaria, Czecho-Slovakia, Ethiopia, Hungary, Lithuania, Poland, Rumania, and the Serb-Croat-Slovene State). Negotiations for similar treaties were then in progress with ten other states. Three treaties, being those with Costa Rica (signed February 13, 1914), with Guatemala (signed September 20, 1913), and with Honduras (signed November 3, 1913), were superseded by the Convention for the establishment of International Commissions of Inquiry between the United States and the Central American Republics of February 7, 1923, *U.S. Treaty Series, No. 717.*

[3] See in this connexion, Treaties for the Advancement of Peace (between the United States and other Powers negotiated by the Honourable William J. Bryan, Secretary of State of the United States), with introduction by J. B. Scott, and Comment by George A. Finch, New York, 1920. Also Philip Marshall Brown, *La Conciliation internationale*, Paris, 1925, 75–90.

the accomplishment of that task by recommendations which might weaken the influence of the commission's report. The Bryan plan is practical because it takes shrewd cognizance of the susceptibilities of opposing states in seasons of conflict, and opens a welcome door to direct negotiation under fresh conditions which may produce accord. Again, it minimizes and substantially eliminates dangers to either of the opposing states from a report adverse to its interests, not only because those states are not bound to accept the report, but also because neither of them finds itself opposed by an affirmative endeavour to effect accord which it might prove embarrassing to disregard. The Bryan plan is believed still to offer a sound means of facilitating the amicable adjustment of international differences.

In recent years it has been perceived that a commission authorized to make impartial investigation of the facts productive of controversy, may be competent also to exercise an additional function—namely, to endeavour by recommendation or other affirmative effort to effect agreement between the opposing states. It seems to be widely acknowledged that such an endeavour, if made under reasonable conditions by an appropriate body, may be highly desirable, provided the opposing states retain freedom to disregard the effort to bring about accord.[1] Arrangement for the exercise of such a function by a permanent body was effected by the treaty between the United States and Great Britain of January 11, 1909, concerning the boundary waters between the United States and Canada. By the terms of Article XI, provision was made for the International Joint Commission (established pursuant to the treaty) not only "to examine into and report upon the facts and circumstances of the particular questions and matters referred" to it, but also to accompany its report with "such conclusions and recommendations as may be appropriate."[2] The reports were not to partake of the character of arbitral awards.[3] The same idea

---

[1] Declared Dr. Van Hamel, Director of the Legal Section of the League of Nations, on February 1, 1926: "In principle, a treaty of conciliation establishes, as between the parties, an obligation to submit disputes which may arise between them to a Conciliation Commission or Commissioner. The essential difference between treaties of conciliation and arbitration treaties is that under the former the parties are obliged, in the first instance, to have recourse to the procedure for conciliation, but they are not necessarily obliged to abide by its result. The proposals of a conciliation commission must be, from their nature, optional; whereas the decisions of arbiters are binding." (Arbitration and Security, *Publications of the League of Nations*, V. *Legal*. 1926, V. 14.)

[2] *U.S. Treaty*, Vol. III, 2607, 2612.

[3] *Id.* See in this connexion "The International Joint Commission between the United States and Canada", by R. A. MacKay, *Am. J.* XXII, 292, 308.

COMMISSIONS OF INQUIRY, ETC. IN DISPUTES   99

found expression in identical language in the proposed arbitration treaties between the United States and France, and the United States and Great Britain, signed during the Taft Administration, August 3, 1911, but which failed to be consummated.[1]

Numerous bi-lateral and multi-lateral treaties have since manifested the readiness of states to confide such powers to international commissions. Those yielded to the Council and Assembly of the League of Nations under Article XV of the Covenant are well known and present a distinctive feature of the polity of that organization.[2] The efforts of Norway and of Sweden in 1920 to secure the annexation to the Covenant of a draft designed to establish commissions of conciliation and arbitration have been widely scrutinized;[3] also the Resolution of the Third Assembly of the League, of September 22, 1922, encouraging the use of commissions of conciliation in harmony with the provisions of Articles XV and XVII of the Covenant.[4]

The several treaties have much in common. They confer upon commissions authority to do much more than to investigate and report, without, however, yielding the power to decide or adjudicate. They contemplate an affirmative effort on the part of commissioners to bring the opposing states together. Thus, for example, by the convention between the United States and the Central American Republics, for the "Establishment of International Commissions of Inquiry", concluded February 7, 1923,

[1] See Charles's Treaties (Senate Doc. 1063, 62 Cong., 3 Sess.) 380 and 385, respectively.

[2] For the text of Article XV see *U.S. Treaty*, Vol. III, 3340.

[3] See proposals of the Norwegian and Swedish Governments concerning commissions of arbitration and conciliation, *League of Nations, First Assembly, First Committee Minutes*, 75 and 83 respectively. See also Swedish explanatory statement, *id.*, 82.

[4] *League of Nations, Records of the Third Assembly, Plenary Meetings*, 1922, 199–200. See also report of M. Adatci, *Rapporteur* of the First Committee, *id.*, 196.

See in this connexion McNair's 4th ed. of *Oppenheim*, II, § 11 d; also "*La Procédure de Conciliation devant la Société des Nations*", by Charles de Visscher, *Rev. Droit Int.*, 3rd Series, IV, 21; A. J. Toynbee, *Survey of International Affairs*, 1924, London, 1926, 64–73.

See also historical statement by Dr. Arroyo Parejo, of Venezuela, on Dec. 17, 1928, before the Commission of Conciliation of the International Conference of American States on Conciliation and Arbitration. Dr. Parejo declares that "the original idea of the conciliatory method had its origin in America". He adverts to Article III of the treaty between Greater Colombia and Peru, of July 6, 1822 (William R. Manning, *Arbitration Treaties Among the American States*, 1924, 1), and also to Article XVI of the Treaty of Perpetual Union, Alliance and Confederation signed at the Panama Conference on July 15, 1926 (*International American Conference, Reports of Committees and Discussions thereon, Historical Appendix* IV, Washington, 1890, 187). It is believed, however, that the idea of conciliation found expression in the treaty of truce between Denmark and Sweden, of April 23, 1512 (Rydberg, *Sverges Traktater*, III, 570, referred to in C. E. Hill's *Danish Sound Dues*, 1926, p. 44.

the commission is given the "right to recommend any solutions or adjustments which in its opinion, may be pertinent, just, and advisable".[1] In the treaty of conciliation and judicial settlement between Italy and Switzerland of September 20, 1924, the task of the Permanent Conciliation Commission is "to further the settlement of disputes by an impartial and conscientious examination of the facts and by formulating proposals with a view to settling the case".[2]

By the terms of the Locarno Conventions of 1925,[3] and also by those of the model bi-lateral conciliation conventions submitted by Mr. Politis to the Assembly of the League of Nations in September 1928,[4] the task embraces the duty "to endeavour to bring the parties to an agreement". According to the General Convention of Inter-American Conciliation of January 5, 1929, the function of the commission is "to procure the conciliation of the differences subject to its examination by endeavouring to effect a settlement between the parties".[5]

The commission is oftentimes allowed to offer its services spontaneously on its own initiative;[6] and it may even be authorized to restrict the conduct of the states at variance during the period of reference, as by devising provisional measures applicable to them,[7] or by fixing their status.[8]

---

[1] Article V, *U.S. Treaty Series*, No. 717.

[2] Article V, treaty of conciliation and judicial settlement between Italy and Switzerland, September 20, 1924, *League of Nations Treaty Series*, No. 834; Article XIV, conciliation convention between Norway and Sweden, June 27, 1924, id., No. 717.

[3] Article VIII, arbitration convention between Germany and Belgium, initialled October 16, 1925, being Annex B of Final Protocol of the Locarno Conference, 1925, *Am. J.* XX, official documents, 25, 27.

[4] Article XVIII of Bi-lateral Conciliation Convention (Convention c), Annex 2, to Report of the Third Committee to the Assembly (*Rapporteur*: N. Politis), on Pacific Settlement of International Disputes, Non-aggression and Mutual Assistance, *Publications of League of Nations, IX. Disarmament*, 1928, IX. 12.

[5] Article VI, General Convention of Inter-American Conciliation, The International Conference of American States on Conciliation and Arbitration, Washington, December 10, 1928–January 5, 1929, Government Printing Office, Washington, 1929, p. 12.

[6] Article VI, conciliation convention between Chile and Sweden, March 26, 1920, *League of Nations Treaty Series*, No. 111; Article III, treaty for the establishment of a peace commission between Great Britain and Chile, March 28, 1919, *Brit. and For. St. Pap.*, CXII, 717, 718. See also Article III, General Convention of Inter-American Conciliation, January 5, 1929.

[7] Article XVIII, treaty of arbitration and conciliation between the Swiss Confederation and the German Reich, December 3, 1921, *League of Nations Treaty Series*, No. 320; also Article XIX, arbitration convention between Germany and Belgium, initialled at Locarno, October 16, 1925, being Annex B, to Final Protocol of the Locarno Conference, 1925, *Am. J.* XX, official documents, 21, 30.

[8] Article XIII, Convention between the United States and Central American Repub-

COMMISSIONS OF INQUIRY, ETC. IN DISPUTES 101

A commission of conciliation is ordinarily composed of an uneven number of persons, embracing not only nationals of the states at variance, but also nationals of third states, so that the control of recommendations or proposals is lodged in a person or persons neutral to the controversy.[1] A joint commission composed of an equal number of representatives or nationals of the opposing states may, however, be utilized for a like purpose. As has been noted, such was the case in the convention between the United States and Great Britain concerning the boundary waters between the United States and Canada, concluded January 11, 1909.[2] Again, the work of conciliation may be entrusted to a single commissioner possessed of a nationality other than that of either of the opposing states, as is the case in the treaty of conciliation and arbitration between Hungary and Switzerland, of June 18, 1924.[3]

The treaties prior to 1929 present one distinctive feature which is reflected in provisions varying in fullness of detail. All seemingly contemplate that the task of endeavouring to bring about accord, through appropriate recommendation or otherwise, shall be the consequence of investigation. In numerous conventions care is taken that the commissioners shall not lapse into the easy ways of mediators. According to some, provision is made for a procedure designed to give the opposing states the right to be heard, and to apprise the commission fully as to their respective pretensions before it shall essay to make recommendations. Thus, according to the language of the Locarno conventions of 1925,

lics for the Establishment of International Commissions of Inquiry, February 7, 1923, *Treaty Series*, No. 717.

[1] Thus, it is provided in Article III of the convention between Norway and Sweden concerning the establishment of a conciliation commission, June 27, 1924: "The Commission shall be composed of five members. Each Party shall appoint two members, one of which may be a national of the appointing state. The fifth member, who shall act as chairman of the Commission, shall be a national of a state not otherwise represented on the Commission. He shall be appointed jointly by the Parties. Should the Parties be unable to agree, the chairman shall, at the request of one of the Parties, be appointed by the President of the Permanent Court of International Justice, or, should the latter be a national of one of the Contracting States, by the Vice-President of the Court.

"The Commission shall be appointed within six months after the ratifications of the present Convention have been exchanged." *League of Nations Treaty Series*, No. 717.

See also Article IV, of Treaty to Avoid or Prevent Conflicts between the American States, of May 3, 1923, *Treaty Series*, No. 752; also Article VII of League of Nations Model Bi-lateral Conciliation Convention of 1928.

[2] Article IX, *U.S. Treaty*, Vol. III, 2612.

[3] Article III, *League of Nations Treaty Series*, No. 887. It was also provided that the commissioner should not be domiciled within the territory, or employed in the service of either contracting party.

102   YEAR BOOK OF INTERNATIONAL LAW

duplicated in the text of the model bi-lateral conventions submitted to the Assembly of the League in 1928:

"The task of the Permanent Conciliation Commission shall be to elucidate questions in dispute, to collect with that object all necessary information by means of enquiry or otherwise, and to endeavour to bring the Parties to an agreement. It may, after the case has been examined, inform the Parties of the terms of settlement which seem suitable to it, and lay down a period within which they are to make their decision."[1]

It also provided that:

"The Parties shall be represented before the Permanent Conciliation Commission by agents, whose duty it shall be to act as intermediary between them and the Commission; they may, moreover, be assisted by counsel and experts appointed by them for that purpose, and request that all persons whose evidence appears to them useful should be heard.

"The Commission, on its side, shall be entitled to request oral explanations from the agents, counsel and experts of the two Parties, as well as from all persons it may think useful to summon with the consent of their Government."[2]

The foregoing provisions are self-explanatory. They reveal the fact that according to European opinion what renders the recommendations or other endeavours of conciliators worthy of respect is the circumstance that they are the result of impartial and full investigation of all the facts, developed in the light of all of the contentions of every kind advanced by the states at variance. European states have accordingly, thus far exhibited no inclination to agree to have recourse to permanent commissions of conciliation, composed chiefly of nationals of third states, free to press their recommendations before being apprised of all the relevant facts, or before being made fully aware of the precise theories and contentions of the opposing countries.

The Treaty to Avoid or Prevent Conflicts between the American States, signed at Santiago de Chile, May 3, 1923,[3] together with the supplementary and amendatory provisions of the General Convention of Inter-American Conciliation signed at Washington,

---

[1] Article VIII of arbitration convention between Germany and Belgium, initialled October 16, 1925, *Am. J.* XX, documents, 27. See in this connexion, A. Pearce Higgins, *Studies in International Law and Relations*, Chap. VII, "The Locarno Treaties", Cambridge: 1928.

[2] Article XII, *Am. J.* XX, documents, 28. According to Article IX: "Failing any special provision to the contrary, the Permanent Conciliation Commission shall lay down its own procedure, which in any case must provide for both parties being heard. In regard to enquiries the commission, unless it decides unanimously to the contrary, shall act in accordance with the provisions of Chapter III (International Commissions of Enquiry) of the Hague Convention of the 18th October, 1907, for the Pacific Settlement of International Disputes."

[3] *United States Treaty Series*, No. 752.

COMMISSIONS OF INQUIRY, ETC. IN DISPUTES 103

January 5, 1929, deserves attention. They reflect in part a different theory. The former of these conventions known as the Gondra Treaty, in honour of the memory of its author, the distinguished Paraguayan statesman, Dr. Manuel Gondra, was a multi-lateral arrangement for the use of commissions of inquiry. Moreover, there were reserved from its operation "questions affecting constitutional provisions". The Gondra Treaty, having rather slowly won the approval of a large number of American Republics was deemed to offer a solid foundation for the new and broader plan set forth in the Convention of 1929.

"To the procedure of conciliation" are to be submitted all controversies of any kind without reservation, which have arisen or may arise between the contracting parties and which it may not have been possible to settle through diplomatic channels.[1] This "procedure" once under way may be interrupted—and "interrupted only" by a direct settlement between the parties or by their agreement to accept absolutely the decision *ex aequo et bono* of an American Chief of State or to submit the controversy to arbitration or to an international court.[2] The commission of inquiry provided for by the Gondra Treaty is transformed into one of conciliation.[3] It is to be composed of five members, all nationals of American states. Each Government appoints two members at the time of convocation "only one of whom may be a national of its country". The fifth is to be chosen by common accord by those already appointed and performs the duties of President.[4]

[1] Article I. See also Article XV.

[2] Article XIII.

[3] Article II. Declared Dr. Arroyo Parejo, of Venezuela, on December 17, 1928, before the Commission on Conciliation of the International Conference of American States on Conciliation and Arbitration: "The Gondra Treaty does not contain a real conciliatory method, since the commissions which it creates are not authorized to propose to the parties in discord the terms of a settlement."

[4] Article IV of Convention of May 3, 1923. According to that Article: "The fifth shall be chosen by common accord by those already appointed and shall perform the duties of President. However, a citizen of a nation already represented on the Commission may not be elected. Any of the Governments may refuse to accept the elected member, for reasons which it may reserve to itself, and in such event a substitute shall be appointed, with the mutual consent of the Parties, within thirty days following the notification of this refusal. In the failure of such agreement, the designation shall be made by the President of an American Republic not interested in the dispute, who shall be selected by lot by the Commissioners already appointed, from a list of not more than six American Presidents to be formed as follows: each Government party to the controversy, or if there are more than two Governments directly interested in the dispute, the Government or Governments on each side of the controversy, shall designate three Presidents of American States which maintain the same friendly relations with all the Parties to the dispute."

104   YEAR BOOK OF INTERNATIONAL LAW

The function of the commission is to examine, to report with recommendations, and to effect a settlement. At any stage of its labours the endeavour to bring the parties together is made appropriate. The commission may begin its work with an effort to conciliate[1] or it may do so at any time which it regards favourable therefor in the course of the investigation,[2] or within a specified period after it has made its report and recommendations to the states at variance.[3] Thus throughout its life the commission is burdened with this special task. Unless its labours to effect accord have been successful, and under conditions that are specified, the commission is obliged to undertake a conscientious and impartial investigation of the questions which are the subject of the controversy, to set forth in a report the results of its proceedings, and to propose to the parties the bases of a settlement for the equitable solution of the controversy.[4] "Once the period of time fixed by the commission for the parties to make their decisions has expired", that body is to set forth in a final act the decision of the parties, and, if conciliation has been effected, the terms of the settlement.[5] The report and recommendations of the commission, in so far as it acts as an organ of conciliation, do not have the character of a decision or of an arbitral award, and are not binding on the parties "either as regards the exposition or interpretation of the facts or as regards questions of law".[6]

Declared Dr. Varela, the distinguished Uruguayan diplomat, as Reporting Delegate for the Committee responsible for the convention:

"As a general rule, and whenever this is proper, investigation precedes conciliation and the commissions organized in accord with Article 4 of the Gondra Treaty are first and foremost commissions of investigation. It is well understood that this does not preclude the commissions making use of the right to try conciliation which is authoritatively conferred upon them by paragraphs 1 and

---

[1] Article IV of General Convention of Inter-American Conciliation, January 5, 1929.
[2] *Id.*   [3] *Id.*   [4] Article VI.   [5] Article XI.
[6] Article IX. It is provided in Article VIII that the Commission of Conciliation shall "establish its rules of procedure", and that "in the absence of agreement to the contrary, the procedure indicated in Article IV of the Treaty of Santiago de Chile of May 3, 1923, shall be followed." That Article declares that the Commission "shall itself establish its rules of procedure". There is recommended for incorporation therein the provisions contained in Articles IX, X, XI, XII, and XIII of the convention between the United States and the Central American Republics of February 7, 1923 (*U.S. Treaty Series*, No. 717). Article X provides that "during the investigation the Parties shall be heard and may have the right to be represented by one or more agents and counsel". Article XII provides in part that "the Inquiry shall be conducted so that both Parties must be heard", and that "consequently, the Commission shall notify each Party of the statements of fact submitted by the other, and shall fix periods of time in which to receive evidence."

COMMISSIONS OF INQUIRY, ETC. IN DISPUTES 105

2 of Article 4 of the draft convention, but, we again repeat, the process of pacific settlement normally begins with investigation and is continued with conciliation."

He added:

"In regard to the commissions provided for in Articles 2 and 15, the draft endeavours to give to their conciliatory action the greatest amplitude and effectiveness possible by authorizing them to proceed, as organs of conciliation, at any moment after their organization, that is to say, before investigation, during it, or finally after the investigating procedure has been closed. In the first and second cases, the intervention of the commission will be purely optional and will depend on the opinion which is formed regarding the opportunity offered by a given moment for realizing the trial of conciliation.

"Neither does it fix rules of procedure for these cases."[1]

Declared Mr. Hughes, the delegate of the United States on the same Committee:

"In Article 4 we said precisely that the commission which would be created under Article 2, to wit, the Gondra Treaty commission, should be at liberty to begin its work with conciliation without waiting for the inquiry. We also stated in the second paragraph of Article 4 that during its inquiry it could at any time endeavour to bring the parties into accord by conciliatory measures. And then we stated in the third paragraph of Article 4 that at a certain time, if the process contemplated by the Gondra Treaty had reached the end, they should be bound to see if they could not bring the parties into accord. All that is in the interest of peaceful settlement. In trying to create a friendly accord there are really no technicalities involved whatever. But if either party wished to have a full inquiry into the facts, that is the privilege of the party, and that inquiry will be had."[2]

Accordingly, either party, by rejecting the efforts of the commission to bring about accord prior to investigation, may decline to consider any conciliatory endeavours until they prove to be in fact the product of fullest investigation. Nevertheless, neither party can ward off, or prevent itself from being subjected to proposals for settlement recommended by the commission at any stage of its work.

Another feature of the convention deserves attention. Under the Gondra Treaty, two commissions, to be designated as permanent, were to be established at Washington and at Montevideo, and were to be composed of the three American diplomatic agents longest accredited in those Capitals.[3] Their functions were to be "limited to receiving from the interested Parties the request for a convocation of the Commission of Inquiry" (for which provision

---

[1] Statement made on January 3, 1929, before the Commission on Conciliation, of the International Conference of American States on Conciliation and Arbitration.

[2] Statement made before the same Committee of the Conference on January 3, 1929.

[3] *U.S. Treaty Series*, No. 752.

106   YEAR BOOK OF INTERNATIONAL LAW

was made in an earlier article) and "to notifying the other Party thereof immediately". By the convention of January 5, 1929, these permanent commissions are clothed with new and important powers. By the terms of Article III, "they shall be bound to exercise conciliatory functions, either on their own motion when it appears that there is a prospect of disturbance of peaceful relations, or at the request of a party to the dispute, until the Commission referred to in the preceding article is organized."

In explanation of the plan Mr. Hughes declared: .

"We desire to have some permanent organization that could do, perhaps, what this Conference has endeavoured to do in connexion with an existing incident, namely, to bring the parties into accord. In order to achieve that result and not to disturb the Gondra Treaty or to embarrass our relations by multiplying machinery without actually producing a helpful result, we thought we would give the permanent commissions conciliatory authority, pending the organization of the commission of inquiry.

"Then we thought that as neither party might ask under the Gondra Treaty for the creation of a commission of inquiry, we should at least have some conciliatory process available. Therefore we recommended that the permanent commissions established under the Gondra Treaty could of their own motion endeavour to effect conciliation. If that is followed by the institution of the proceedings suggested by the Gondra Treaty, well and good; then there will be machinery for investigation and conciliation. But in any event, if there is an exigent case, when there is a chance of a disturbance—a prospect of a disturbance of peaceful relations—there should be in existence some machinery of conciliation."[1]

The American states, parties to the convention of January 5, 1929, thus appear to contemplate under the contingencies there specified, the exercise of good offices by a diplomatic body on which the states at variance are not necessarily represented as the normal preliminary to the use of a commission of conciliation. In fact it is only when one of the diplomatic commissions fails to bring about accord within the brief period before the commission of conciliation is organized, that the latter shall have an oppor-

---

[1] Statement made on January 3, 1929, before the Commission on Conciliation of the International Conference of American states on Conciliation and Arbitration. Mr. Hughes also said: "Must investigation always precede conciliation? In our subcommittee we thought not. Of course, very often, perhaps most of the time, investigation would precede conciliation, but it may happen that the parties could be brought to an accord without the long and expensive inquiry which would be necessary in following out to ultimate conclusion the procedure of the Gondra Treaty. There is no reason why, if the parties can be brought to a settlement, it should not be done. There is no reason why we should not have machinery for that purpose, in the interest of peace, or why we should have a long inquiry, perhaps into a very complicated problem, before conciliation can be begun."

See also statements before the same Committee of Dr. Varela of Uruguay, of Dr. Gutiérrez of Cuba, and of Dr. Alfaro of Panama.

COMMISSIONS OF INQUIRY, ETC. IN DISPUTES　107

tunity to function. The brevity of that period may, however, serve to give to the permanent diplomatic commissions small opportunity for service.

Two American states have recently agreed to have recourse to conciliation as one of the means of adjusting a grave conflict between them. By a protocol of January 3, 1929, Bolivia and Paraguay, accepting the good offices of the International Conference of American States on Conciliation and Arbitration, agreed that a commission of investigation and conciliation should "establish the facts" productive of the conflicts which have unfortunately occurred between them.[1] The function of the Commission is "to investigate, by hearing both sides, what has taken place, taking into consideration the allegations set forth by both parties, and determining in the end, which of the parties has brought about a change in the peaceful relations between the two countries".[2] Once the investigation has been "carried out", the commission is to submit proposals and endeavour to settle the incident amicably under conditions satisfactory to both parties.[3] If this proves to be impossible, the commission is to render its report setting forth the result of its investigation and the efforts made to settle the incident.[4] Moreover, the commission is empowered, in case it is unable to effect conciliation, to "establish both the truth of the matter investigated and the responsibilities which, in accordance with international law" may appear as a result of the investigation.[5] The commission is further authorized, "to advise the parties concerning measures designed to prevent a recurrence of hostilities".[6]

A significant feature of the convention is the arrangement that the exercise of the conciliatory function in the submission of proposals for settlement shall follow, rather than precede, or be simultaneous with, the work of investigation. Again, as has been noted, the successful exercise of that function precludes the necessity of a report by the commission and the establishment by it of facts and conclusions of law which might prove embarrassing to one or both of the states concerned. In another respect the convention is of special interest. It marks the willingness of the

[1] The International Conference of American States on Conciliation and Arbitration (Washington, December 10, 1928–January 5, 1929), 90.

[2] Second stipulation.　　　　[3] Fifth stipulation.

[4] *Id.*　　　　[5] Sixth stipulation.

[6] Eighth stipulation. By this stipulation the parties "bind themselves to suspend all hostilities and to stop all concentration of troops at the points of contact of the military outposts of both countries, until the commission renders its findings".

108   YEAR BOOK OF INTERNATIONAL LAW

contracting parties not only to have recourse to a commission of inquiry and conciliation, but also to permit that body, under a specified contingency, if its conciliatory endeavours shall have failed, to act in a quasi-judicial capacity. The convention thus registers agreement to submit to inquiry and conciliation, and if need be, to something akin to arbitration, all before a single body whose members are described as "delegates" of the states appointing them, and respecting whose competence in the law no requirement is laid down.

Treaties of conciliation are designed primarily for use in situations where statesmen are reluctant to have recourse to judicial tribunals of any kind. That reluctance may slowly sink into a much-desired desuetude. Before it does, however, foreign offices are burdened with the task of determining how the recommendations of conciliators may be most wisely utilized. Already, as has been noted, there appears to be a cleavage of opinion.

According to that which prevails in Europe, the recommendations of a commission of conciliation should be the product of an investigation elucidating questions at issue, and observing a procedure calculated to develop and disclose the contentions of the opposing states. Conversely, a state should not be exposed or subjected to the recommendations of such a body until such an investigation under such conditions has been completed. In point of procedure, conciliation should follow close in the wake of arbitration. According to opinion in America, as reflected by the General Convention of Inter-American Conciliation, a commission of conciliation should be encouraged to investigate everything; but it should not be obliged to do so before pressing its recommendations. Moreover, its labours for accord may, under certain conditions, well be supplemented or rather preceded by the unfettered endeavours of a body of diplomats. In a word, conciliation should be permitted oftentimes to follow in the wake of mediation. Europe would safeguard a state against a mere weight of conciliatory opinion dealing harshly with its pretensions by minimizing the danger of recommendations having a political rather than a factual or legal basis. America, on the other hand, would seemingly welcome any recommendations serving in fact to produce accord. It would minimize the likelihood of unfair or unreasonable proposals, as well as the actual dangers derivable from those of such a character, relying upon the freedom of the aggrieved state to disregard or ward off recommendations contemptuous of its equities as a sufficient safeguard therefor. It

COMMISSIONS OF INQUIRY, ETC. IN DISPUTES   109

remains to be seen which of the two theories is to make the stronger appeal to the nations of the world.

In another respect, conciliation deserves attention. The readiness of particular states to agree through bi-lateral treaties to have recourse to this procedure for the solution of grave differences which, howsoever described, they are reluctant to submit to arbitration, may depend in part upon the nature (in point of nationality) of the individuals in whom is lodged the conciliatory function. When a commission of conciliation takes the form of a joint commission comprised exclusively of nationals of two opposing states, confidence in its recommendations may be greatly enhanced. Moreover, if such a body be a permanent one, those states may become disposed and even alert to utilize it as a consultative agency to pass upon the probable effect of prospective conduct of the one party upon the interests as well as rights of the other. They may, in a word, willingly invoke its aid to safeguard themselves against actual harm to be anticipated from conduct not forbidden by international law, yet none the less provocative of conflict. If there be, for example, a Mexican-American interest, or a Canadian-American interest deemed worthy of conservation and development, permanent joint commissions of conciliation may offer a practical means of checking acts which, however lawful, are none the less contemptuous of such interest, and may do it grievous harm. Both at Montreal in September, 1923, and at Havana in February, 1928, the distinguished President of the American Society of International Law called attention to this unique service which it lies within the power of essentially joint commissions of conciliation to render in behalf of particular states.[1] The potentialities of conciliation are not exhausted until statesmen become reluctant to entrust the pretensions of their own countries to their own countrymen.

By way of summary it may be said:

First. In cases where a trustworthy investigation and report are calculated to suffice to enable opposing states to work out themselves a solution of their differences, commissions of inquiry as contemplated by the Bryan treaties for the Advancement of Peace

---

[1] See "The Pathway of Peace", an address delivered by Charles E. Hughes before the Canadian Bar Association, at Montreal, September 4, 1923, published in volume of addresses by that author entitled *The Pathway of Peace*, New York, 1925, 3, 16–17; also observations of Mr. Hughes on arbitration and conciliation at the Sixth International Conference of American States, *Report of the Delegates of the United States of America to the Sixth International Conference of American States* (held at Havana, Cuba, January 16 to February 20, 1928), Washington, 1928, 22–5.

110   YEAR BOOK OF INTERNATIONAL LAW

offer a practical instrumentality for amicable adjustment. The absence of recommendations as well as the freedom of the parties to disregard the reports of commissioners may be expected to strengthen the appeal of such bodies.

Secondly. If amicable adjustments be sought through conciliation rather than through a commission of inquiry on the one hand, or a judicial tribunal on the other, every reason demands that the recommendations of conciliators embody the most equitable and enlightened proposal for a final settlement of the controversy, and hence one not lightly to be rejected by either party thereto. The probability that a proposal will attain such a character must depend in large degree upon the terms of the treaty confiding authority to the conciliators. Are they to exercise their good offices with the freedom and in the spirit of mediators, or are their endeavours to be the fruit of prescribed investigations? The question calls for the impartial conclusions of those responsible for the treaty policies of interested states.

Thirdly. As between two states having a special community of interest which may be seriously impaired by the unrestricted yet not unlawful action of either, conciliation exercised through the agency of an essentially joint commission representative of both states may prove to be a useful means of safeguarding that interest and of averting conflict.

[7]

States may see accidents as deliberate provocation and some provocations may be explained as accidents but true accidents seldom lead to international crises. One which did, the most serious of this century, came about when the Russian Fleet bombarded British fishing trawlers in the North Sea in 1905. The case is examined for "rules" governing the accident-crisis nexus.

ACCIDENTS AND CRISES:

THE DOGGER BANK AFFAIR

by

Richard Ned Lebow

On 24 January 1978 a crippled Soviet satellite carrying a nuclear reactor reentered the earth's atmosphere over northwestern Canada and scattered radioactive debris over a wide area. The spacecraft was a naval reconnaissance satellite of the type that the Soviet Union has used for 10 years to spy on the movements of the U.S. Fleet. Its disintegration in the vicinity of a major population center could conceivably have been calamitous as its reactor is reported to have contained 100 pounds of uranium 235. Fearful of the repercussions of such an incident, the Soviets provided the technical information requested by the United States once it had determined that the satellite's orbit had begun to decay. According to a White House official: "The real significance of this episode is that this was the first nuclear related crisis in space, and

it brought forth Soviet cooperation and informal preparations to deal with a potentially serious situation."[1]

The disintegration of the Soviet satellite was at least the third such incident of its kind and satellites are by no means the only possible source of accidents with grave international implications.[2] The close proximity of Soviet and American Fleets around the world and their frequent harassment of each other carries an even greater potential for a serious mishap. Nor can one altogether ignore the possibility of a nuclear disaster caused by the accidental or unauthorized launching of a missile or other delivery vehicle. The chance, however remote, that any of these might come to pass compels us to consider carefully the political ramifications of serious accidents. What kinds of accidents are likely to lead to an acute confrontation? What kinds of accidents are likely to be resolved by quiet diplomacy? Can we learn anything about accidents that will enable us to reduce the risks to peace associated with them? This article will explore the question in a case study of the Dogger Bank incident, the most serious international crisis triggered by an accident in modern times.

Before proceeding with the study it is necessary to acknowledge that the meaning and operational significance of accidents are highly subjective and depend almost entirely upon the context in which accidents occur. Accidents can be treated as deliberate provocations or, *vice versa*, by any of the parties involved. The interpretation policymakers choose will generally depend upon their desire to avoid or precipitate conflict.

In extreme circumstances, the party who has been injured may choose to exploit an accident as a *casus belli*. To do so he will attempt to portray the incident as a premeditated provocation on the part of his adversary. The American response to the destruction of the battleship *Maine* in Havana harbor in February 1898 is a case in point. The initial opinion of many naval officers was that the explosion was accidental; they attributed it to fire in a coal bunker adjacent to a magazine, thus absolving Spain of any responsibility. But the accident occurred at a time when Spanish-American relations were severely strained because of the festering rebellion in Cuba. An influential segment of the American press, intent on war, portrayed the explosion as an act of sabotage by Spain. The subsequent naval court of inquiry held that the explosion was externally caused. President McKinley exploited the aroused state of public opinion to impress upon the Spanish Government the certainty of American intervention in Cuba unless a satisfactory settlement was reached in the very near future. As Spain proved unable to make the kinds of concessions necessary to mollify American public opinion, McKinley was forced to go to war.[3]

Policymakers who wish to avoid a confrontation may choose to describe as an accident what they know to be a deliberate provocation. This ploy may permit them to sidestep a challenge without losing face or damaging their country's bargaining reputation. To succeed, it usually requires the tacit collusion of the protagonist's leaders who for reasons of their own also prefer to treat the incident as an accident. The *Panay* incident—the sinking of an American gunboat on the Yangtze in December 1937 by Japanese fighter planes—offers an illustration of this phenomenon. Both American and Japanese leaders suspected that the Japanese military had deliberately attacked *Panay* in order to provoke a confrontation between the two countries. As both Governments wished to avoid a confrontation at that time they agreed to treat the attack as an accident.[4]

As the *Panay* incident suggests, the nation responsible for a provocation may attempt to dismiss it as an accident. This is usually done to minimize the extent of the challenge conveyed by the provocation and is a customary means of explaining away such provocations as overflights conducted for purposes of spying. It can also be used to disavow more serious challenges as was the case in the Sussex and Corfu crises. The Sussex crisis developed in response to the sinking by a German submarine of a French channel steamer with American passengers aboard on 24 March 1916. The "accident" occurred because the German Navy, infuriated by their Government's policy of restricting naval operations so as not to give offense to neutrals, had failed to implement precautions designed to prevent attacks on unarmed passenger vessels and had actually encouraged recklessness on the part of submarine captains. The German Government avoided a

68   NAVAL WAR COLLEGE REVIEW

break in relations with the United States by portraying the attack as an unfortunate accident and by agreeing to make her U-boats adhere to stricter rules of engagement.[5]

The Corfu crisis was triggered by an even more purposeful provocation, mines placed by Albania in the Corfu Channel to discourage maritime traffic in waters she claimed to be within her jurisdiction. In October 1946 these mines severely damaged destroyers *Saumarez* and *Volage,* part of a large British force sent through the Channel to contest Albania's claim. Having swept the Channel and found it free of mines on two earlier occasions, Britain accused Yugoslavia and Albania of having subsequently layed captured German mines. Both countries denied this charge and anxious to back away from a confrontation with Britain, suggested that the destroyers had struck German laid mines which the Royal Navy had failed to locate on earlier sweeps. Albania agreed to refer the dispute to the International Court of Justice which upheld the British claim and ordered Albania to pay compensation.[6]

True accidents rarely cause crises. Of the many serious international accidents recorded in this century only the Russian Fleet's bombardment of British fishing trawlers in the North Sea in 1905 brought the nations involved to the brink of war. The failure of most accidents to spark crises is probably a function of their origins; they are rarely seen to convey a challenge to which the aggrieved state must respond. Nor do they usually establish damaging precedents. Accidents are generally perceived as nonrepeating incidents which establish no right or expectation on the part of the responsible party to carry out similar provocations in the future.

Because most accidents neither convey challenges nor establish precedents their significance is most often determined by the actual damage they cause and the political context in which they

occur. Before the nuclear age, the damage potential of accidents was sufficiently limited for them to be resolved by a simple formula. The responsible state rendered a public apology, disclaimed any intent of provoking an incident, and offered to pay compensation for loss of life or damage to property. The apology, in effect a public affirmation that the perpetrator of the accident had no right or claim to carry out such an action, protected the interests and bargaining reputation of the injured state. An apology and offer of compensation was also usually sufficient to protect that country's leaders from political recrimination. For the party responsible for the accident the formula resolved an awkward state of affairs without undue loss of face. By acknowledging the accidental nature of the incident he backed down from a challenge he never claimed to have issued.

Most accidents are still resolved according to this formula. Complications do sometimes arise, most frequently the result of the responsible state's concern to preserve what he sees as his legal or political prerogatives. While acknowledging the accidental nature of a provocation, a government may be unwilling to apologize or pay compensation because this could be interpreted as an admission that its behavior was unjustifiable. Germany, for example, was unwilling to tender a formal apology to the United States for her sinking of the *Lusitania* because she claimed with some justification that the ship, which carried contraband cargo, was an "auxiliary cruiser" according to international law and thus a legitimate target for her submarines. The German Government ultimately satisfied the United States by issuing a statement regretting the loss of neutral life and agreeing to refer the question of compensation to a postwar tribunal.[7] A similar controversy developed in response to the bombing by the United

States of Soviet merchant ships in Haiphong harbor during the Vietnam war. Claiming the right to bomb the harbor installations the United States rejected a Soviet demand for an apology, asserting that all maritime nations had been warned that ships entered the harbor at their own risk.[8] The destruction of a Libyan airliner over the Sinai by the Israeli air force in 1972 is another instance where an apology was seen to prejudice a nation's important interests. Israel admitted that her pilots, suspecting an act of terrorism, might have been overzealous in shooting down the plane but insisted that the airliner had ignored instructions to land. Fearing that an offer of compensation would be interpreted as an admission of guilt, the Israeli Government offered instead to give money to the families of the dead passengers for humanitarian reasons. The offer was coupled with a renewed assertion of Israel's right to deal with aerial intruders.[9]

The Dogger Bank Affair. Russian expansion into Manchuria in the latter part of the 19th century brought her into conflict with Japan. Russian penetration of Korea, which directly challenged Japan's economic and political primacy in that country, brought the conflict to a head. St. Petersburg's intransigence made a mockery of negotiations and Japan broke relations with Russia on 8 February 1904.[10]

That very morning Japanese torpedo boats and destroyers launched a daring surprise attack against the Russian Pacific Squadron in its moorings at Port Arthur. The attack was followed up the next day by a long-range naval bombardment of the Russian anchorage. When the smoke had cleared the Japanese Navy was supreme in the Far East. They inflicted a further defeat upon the Russians at Chemulpo in August. On land, the Japanese were equally successful. Their army moved into Manchuria

and forced the Russians to retreat down the Liaotung Peninsula. By 14 May they had invested Port Arthur.

The relief of Port Arthur became Moscow's most urgent objective. General Kuropatkin, the Russian Commander-in-Chief, ordered the navy to ready its idle Baltic Fleet for service in the Pacific. Departure of the armada awaited completion of four new battleships, during which time the Baltic Fleet, considered to be the least seaworthy component of the navy, received special training. The deteriorating military situation in the Far East forced Admiral Rozhestvensky to cut his training exercises short and on 14 October 1904 the 42 ships of the hastily assembled Second Pacific Squadron departed the Baltic port of Libau for the 10,000 mile journey to Port Arthur.[11]

As the fleet steamed through the Baltic it was warned to be on the lookout for Japanese torpedo boats disguised as trawlers which were planning an ambush somewhere between The Skaw and English Channel. This far-fetched notion had gained credence in St. Petersburg because of the reports of a Captain Hartling, sent to Copenhagen sometime earlier to organize a Russian counterintelligence network. Hartling's agents, anxious to justify their expense, had reported the existence of suspicious vessels in isolated Danish and Norwegian harbors. Rumors of a Japanese "suicide squadron" had also been picked up by the European press which speculated about the effect of Britain's assumed collusion with her Japanese ally upon Anglo-Russian relations.[12]

According to all reports the prospect of a torpedo attack reduced Admiral Rozhestvensky, a man with no command experience, to a state of extreme anxiety. He doubled all watches, arranged to have searchlights sweep the surrounding sea at night and instructed guncrews to remain by their stations around the clock. The admiral ordered

70   NAVAL WAR COLLEGE REVIEW

that "No vessel of any sort whatsoever must be allowed to get in amongst the fleet." Approaching merchantmen were warned away, often by a shot across their bows. Tension rose on the evening of 20 October, following receipt of a warning that unidentified torpedo boats had departed from secret bases in Norway. Later that night, *Navarin* reported sighting enemy reconnaissance balloons.[13]

The expected attack failed to materialize and as morning broke the fleet steamed into the North Sea, ominously shrouded by fog. More alarming intelligence came in during the day warning of floating mines and trawlers with torpedo tubes preparing to attack the fleet. At dusk, the cruiser *Kamchatka*, which had become separated from the main body of the fleet, reported that it was under attack by eight torpedo boats and was returning fire. Ninety minutes later action stations were sounded aboard the flagship *Suvorov* in response to two flares sighted from the bridge. Shortly thereafter the order to engage the enemy was flashed down the line as searchlights revealed ships barely a half mile away. Battleships and cruisers opened fire and kept up an intensive barrage for 20 minutes until the admiral could discern only a few battered trawlers bobbing hopelessly in the water. The fleet steamed off concluding that the torpedo boats had fled from the scene.[14]

The "enemy" engaged by Russian gunners was the Gamecock fleet of fishing boats which had left Hull for the Dogger Bank 2 days before and was then 200 miles northeast of the Spurn. They were identifiable as trawlers by their sails and red, white and green lights. These lights were probably the flares sighted on the bridge of *Suvorov*. When the firing began, one of the deckhands, illuminated by the searchlights, held up a plaice while his mate displayed a large haddock in the hope of signaling their peaceful intent. Their

efforts were unsuccessful and when the barrage finally ceased one trawler had been sent to the bottom and five damaged. Two seamen were dead and six seriously wounded. Fortunately for the fishermen Russian gunnery had proven extremely inaccurate.[15]

News of the incident reached London on Monday, 23 October. The next day the M.P. from Hull brought a deputation of fishermen to the Foreign Office where they produced shell splinters to substantiate their story. The Wednesday morning papers carried a more detailed account of the incident and public opinion was so incensed that the Russian Ambassador needed a police escort to leave his Embassy. Trafalgar Square was filled with protesters and the evening papers demanded strong action. The *Standard* raised the question that was on everybody's mind: was the "wretched Baltic fleet with its inefficient commanders, its drafts of raw landsmen, its blundering navigators and incompetent engineers" to be permitted to continue on its journey?[16] The czarist regime was unpopular in England and as more details were released to the press public sentiment was adamant in favor of going after the Russian Fleet. Valentine Chirol, foreign editor of *The Times*, warned the foreign office that "the feeling in this country is such that no government can trifle with it."[17]

The Balfour government, about to face an election, was particularly susceptible to popular pressure. However, the Cabinet did not act solely in response to public opinion. The majority were hostile to Russia and quite prepared to retaliate against her fleet. The Earl of Selbourne, First Lord of the Admiralty, was the most bellicose but Walter Long and Gerald Balfour, neither of whom normally displayed any interest in foreign affairs, also urged military action unless the Russians put into port and removed the officers responsible for the outrage.[18] Admiral Fisher, who had recently been promoted to First Sea

Lord, thought it a superb opportunity to destroy the Russian Fleet. It "is ours," he informed Selbourne, "whenever we like to take it."[19] The King himself referred to the incident as "a most dastardly outrage" and urged a military response although he later moderated his position, fearing that war with Russia would only be in Germany's interest.[20]

Lord Lansdowne, the Foreign Secretary, would have had support for any action against Russia he proposed. But he was an advocate of détente with Russia and was intent on resolving the incident peaceably. Lansdowne was nevertheless as outraged as his colleagues and thought Rozhestvensky's failure to stop and search for survivors particularly reprehensible. He was not convinced of the accidental nature of the incident, attributing it instead to the Russian propensity to "shoot first and ask questions later." In his opinion this trigger happy policy made a mockery of maritime law which Britain more than any other nation was dependent upon for her survival. Lansdowne believed that such incidents were likely to recur unless Russia was compelled to adhere to the established rules and customs that governed maritime behavior. Like other members of the Cabinet he also believed that Britain's reputation as a great power was at stake.[21]

In broaching the matter to the Russians, Lansdowne cabled Sir Charles Hardinge, British Minister in St. Petersburg, telling him to stress to Count Lamsdorff, the Foreign Minister, "that it is impossible to exaggerate the indignation that has been provoked." Hardinge was further instructed to demand an apology, complete and prompt reparation and "security against the reoccurrence of such intolerable incidents."[22] Lansdowne did not elaborate on the nature of the guarantees Britain sought and had probably decided to await the return of Prime Minister Balfour from

Scotland before formulating more specific demands.

Replying to the British démarche, Lamsdorff pointed out that London's version of events rested entirely on the word of some agitated fishermen and that he awaited a report from Admiral Rozhestvensky. The following day, 25 October, brought no word from Rozhestvensky. However, the Czar cabled his regrets and the Russian Foreign Office informed Lansdowne that full reparation would be forthcoming if the British information was correct.[23]

Balfour arrived in London shortly after the Czar's cable was received and was immediately briefed by Lansdowne. They surmised that the Russians were stalling in the hope that Rozhestvensky would steam out of reach of the Royal Navy before the British were prepared to resort to military action. Unwilling to let the hostage fleet escape the prime minister and foreign secretary agreed that Russia must be sent an ultimatum demanding that Rozhestvensky call at the Spanish port of Vigo and put ashore the officers responsible for the incident along with witnesses. The Russians were also to give satisfaction that the investigation of the incident would be complete and impartial.[24]

Balfour and Lansdowne agreed that the ultimatum should carry with it a time limit. Balfour had a longstanding speaking engagement in Southampton on 28 October where he would be compelled to comment on the crisis. The Russians were to be informed that war would be difficult to avoid unless the Prime Minister could announce that the crisis had been resolved satisfactorily. The following morning, 26 October, Balfour informed the Cabinet that Count Benckendorff, the Russian Ambassador, would be told that he the Prime Minister could report one of two things in his speech:

either that all our demands have been accepted, or . . . to hint—politely but not obscurely—that

72   NAVAL WAR COLLEGE REVIEW

we cannot allow the criminals to vanish into the Far East without immediate trial. We must not, however, disguise from ourselves that such words falling from the lips of a Prime Minister sound very like a declaration of war and bring the country perilously near to overt hostilities.

The cabinet readily gave its assent and Count Benckendorff was handed the ultimatum that afternoon. Balfour estimated the probability of war to be about 50 percent.[25]

The Royal Navy had already begun preparations for a showdown. Six battleships of the Home Fleet had been ordered to Gibraltar and the reserve fleet of six battleships was being readied for action. Cruisers were sent to shadow the Russian Fleet, Gibraltar was put on a war footing, and the powerful Mediterranean Fleet was hurriedly recalled from the Austrian and Italian ports it was visiting. By the evening of 26 October, 28 battleships, 44 cruisers and their supporting vessels stood poised off Gibraltar ready to intercept the Russian Fleet which in the graphic words of First Sea Lord Fisher had become the "ham of a strategic sandwich."[26]

On 27 October, Lamsdorff called on Hardinge to warn that "he considered the general purport [of the ultimatum] to be humiliating and unacceptable to a Great Power."[27] Lansdowne and Balfour, in receipt of Hardinge's report that afternoon, were pessimistic about the chances for peace. Their hopes plummeted in response to a second cable from St. Petersburg containing Rozhestvensky's account of the incident. The Russian admiral claimed that his fleet had been set upon by two torpedo boats but that he had tried to avoid firing on the trawlers even though they were in apparent complicity with the torpedo boats. Lansdowne told the Russian Ambassador that the admiral's version "seemed to bristle with

improbabilities" and did not alter the situation.[28]

Lansdowne and Benckendorff conferred at length exploring possible ways out of the crisis. Paul Cambon, the French Ambassador, also participated in these talks. As the representative of France, Russia's ally, and the architect of the Anglo-French Entente, Cambon shared the trust of both sides. He acted as translator, as Benckendorff spoke Russian and French but Lansdowne knew only English, and attempted to bridge the gap between the two men created by their uncomplementary personalities. "Benckendorff is too vague, Lansdowne too reserved," he confided to his son, "and when I am not between them, they inhabit different planets."[29]

The main impediment to a solution was the British demand for an inquiry in which British officers would participate. This was seen as humiliating by the Russians. Cambon nevertheless urged acceptance as did the French Foreign Minister in Paris.[30] On the 27th, the three men agreed that an inquiry conducted by some august international body might be more palatable to the Czar as he had urged the creation of boards of arbitration at the Hague Conference. The suggestion, attributed by Benckendorff to Cambon, was cabled to Lamsdorff who cleverly presented it to the Czar as his own idea in order to secure the autocrat's approval.[31]

No word had been received from St. Petersburg when it came time for Balfour to depart for Southampton on the morning of the 28th. The mood at the Foreign Office was gloomy and remained so until a cable arrived from Hardinge reporting that the Czar approved of an international court of inquiry. A second cable contained the welcome news that Rozhestvensky had received orders to send the ships involved in the attack on the fishing boats to Vigo, that the guilty parties, as determined by the international board of inquiry, would be punished by

Russian courts and that measures would be implemented to prevent further incidents. In return Lamsdorff requested that Balfour give credit to Russia in his speech for having expressed its prompt regrets and offering to pay proper compensation.[32]

Upon his arrival at Southampton Balfour was handed a telegram reporting the Russian capitulation. Much relieved, the Prime Minister deleted those parts of his speech which were the equivalent to a declaration of war and told the good news to the cheering crowd.[33] The Royal Navy remained on a war footing until her cruisers had "escorted" Rozhestvensky's fleet half way down the coast of Africa.

The Dogger Bank crisis is suggestive of several hypotheses with respect to the origins of accident crises. The first of these pertains to the intensity of the provocation. It would be reasonable to expect that the political pressures on policymakers to demand satisfaction would be directly proportional to the loss of life or damage to property caused by the accident. However, the magnitude of an accident appears to be a poor predictor of crisis. The Japanese attack on *Panay*, the Israeli attack on *Liberty* and the Israeli strafing of the Indian contingent of UNEF in 1967 all resulted in considerable loss of life but did not trigger serious crises. The Russian bombardment of British trawlers in the Dogger Bank killed two men and wounded six but led to such a crisis. It is conceivable, of course, that a nuclear accident could cause so much damage that it would lead to a serious crisis independent of other considerations. The movie *Fail Safe* was based, not unrealistically, on this premise.

A more important indicator of crisis seems to be the injured party's perception that the provocation is likely to be repeated. Accidents are usually seen as one shot affairs. But if an accident is believed to have arisen because of careless operating procedures or insufficient

concern to avoid it the injured party may conclude that an apology is no guarantee against repetition. That nation may demand, as did Britain in the Dogger Bank crisis and the United States in the Sussex crisis, that their protagonist implement procedures designed to prevent a recurrence of the incident and punish those responsible. Policymakers in the country responsible for the accident may find either demand to be politically unacceptable. In such circumstances a serious crisis can easily develop.

Judging from Dogger Bank another important determinant of accident crises is the effect of the incident upon the perceived vital interests of the injured state. To the extent that an important interest or commitment is threatened, policymakers are more likely to treat the accident as a challenge than would otherwise be the case. Thus Lansdowne and Balfour perceived Rozhestvensky's behavior as indicative of Russia's lack of concern for maritime laws and customs, the enforcement of which they believed to be essential to the commercial interests of the British Empire. They were also infuriated by Rozhestvensky's assertion that Britain and British fishing vessels had actually participated in an attack on the Russian Fleet, a charge Lansdowne could not let stand unchallenged without compromising Britain's international position.

A final consideration, and one noted in the introduction, is the preexisting state of relations between the states affected by the accident. Accidents are not likely to trigger crises between friends. It is difficult to conceive of an accident that could produce an acute crisis between Canada and the United States, for instance. Where relations are cordial, policymakers and public opinion will probably perceive accidents as unfortunate and embarrassing incidents to be forgotten as quickly as possible. Where relations have been

74 NAVAL WAR COLLEGE REVIEW

characterized by hostility there may be more suspicion that the provocation was intentional and more pressure from public opinion to take a confrontatory stand. In such situations policymakers are also likely to ponder the possible negative repercussions of a low key response upon their bargaining reputation. They may perceive a greater need to display toughness as a result. This was certainly true of the British at Dogger Bank and the Americans in the Sussex crisis. Both sets of policymakers believed that a weak response on their part would only encourage further transgressions against their interests.

All of the preceding observations point to the conclusion that the meaning of accidents is both highly subjective and quite malleable. The interest of the injured state will determine in the first place whether a given incident is interpreted as an accident or a deliberate provocation. Our examples suggest that either interpretation can be made to stick in almost any instance. If an

incident is perceived as accidental, its origins and the underlying state of relations between the countries involved will then determine whether or not it precipitates a crisis. Accidents, therefore, are not events which compel particular responses but embarrassments or opportunities which policymakers may seek to ignore or exploit in keeping with their interests.

BIOGRAPHIC SUMMARY

Richard Ned Lebow is Professor of Political Science in the City University of New York. He holds degrees from the University of Chicago and Yale University and received his Ph.D. from CUNY. His areas of interest include Ireland, international crises, and terrorism—on all of which he has written widely. His latest book, forthcoming, is *Between Peace and War: The Anatomy of International Crisis.*

NOTES

1. *The New York Times*, 25 January 1978, pp. 1 and 11.

2. Both mishaps were American. The first mishap occurred on 21 April 1964, during an attempt to orbit a Navy satellite, SNAP 9-A, powered by a plutonium source. The booster failed before orbit was achieved and the vehicle disintegrated over Madagascar upon its reentry into the atmosphere. The second incident was a byproduct of the explosion that turned the Apollo 13 mission into a near disaster. As the astronauts approached the earth they jettisoned their unused lunar module. The module, which carried a plutonium powered generator, went into orbit around the earth but plunged into the atmosphere on 11 April 1970. Those parts which survived reentry plunged into the Tonga Trench in the southwest Pacific.

3. For this crisis, see Ernest R. May, *Imperial Democracy: The Emergence of America as a Great Power* (New York: Harcourt, Brace & World, 1961); Walter Millis, *The Martial Spirit: A Study of Our War With Spain* (Boston: Houghton Mifflin, 1931), pp. 102-145; John Edward Weems, *The Fate of the Maine* (New York: Henry Holt, 1958), chaps. 8-9.

4. The best treatment of the incident is Darby Perry, *The Panay Incident: Prelude to Pearl Harbor* (New York: Macmillan, 1969).

5. For the Sussex crisis see Karl E. Birnbaum, *Peace Moves and U-boat Warfare* (Stockholm: Almquist & Wiksell, 1958), pp. 70-130; Arthur S. Link, *Woodrow Wilson: Confusion and Crises, 1915-1916* (Princeton: Princeton University Press, 1964), pp. 222-255; Ernest R. May, *The World War and American Isolation, 1914-1917* (Harvard: Harvard University Press, 1959), pp. 197-288; Arno Spindler, *Der handelskrieg mit U-booten* (Berlin: E.S. Multer & Sohn, 1932-34), v. III, pp. 105-153.

6. For Corfu see Leslie Gardiner, *The Eagle Spreads His Claws: A History of the Corfu Channel Dispute and of Albania's Relations with the West, 1945-65* (Edinburgh and London: William Blackwood & Sons, 1966); Eric Legget, *The Corfu Incident* (London: Purnell Book Services, 1974); and Il-yong Chong, *Legal Problems Involved in the Corfu Channel Incident* (Geneva: Librairie E. Droz, 1959), for resolution of the incident by the International Court of Justice.

7. For the *Lusitania*, see Birnbaum, pp. 86-102; Arthur S. Link, *Woodrow Wilson: The Struggle for Neutrality, 1914-1915* (Princeton: Princeton University Press, 1960), pp. 368-409; May, *The World War and American Isolation, 1914-1917*, pp. 113-180; Spindler, v. II, pp. 86-102.

8. *The New York Times*, 2, 9, 10, 18 May 1972, p. 1.

9. *Ibid.*, 23 February 1973, p. 1.

10. There are several firsthand accounts of the expedition, the best being by A. Novikoff-Priboy, *Tsushima*, trans. Eden and Cedar Paul (London: Allen & Unwin, 1936), pp. 44-51 describing the events leading up to the attack on the British trawlers. See also Vladimir Semenoff, *Rasplata (The Reckoning)* (London: John Murray, 1909) and Eugene S. Politovsky, *From Libau to Tsushima*, trans. F.R. Godfrey (London: John Murray, 1906). The best secondary account is Richard Hough, *The Fleet that Had to Die* (London: Hamish Hamilton, 1958). David Walder, *The Short Victorious War: The Russo-Japanese Conflict, 1904-5* (London: Hutchinson, 1973) is a useful account of the war as a whole.

11. Hough, pp. 42-61.

12. *Ibid.*, p. 45.

13. *Ibid.*, pp. 47-54.

14. Within the vicinity of the Russian Fleet that night were 30 steam trawlers of the Gamecock Fleet and 12 of the Leyman Company, 2 mission hospital steamers and 3 Gamecock "carriers," used to transport fish to the London market. Vision was somewhat limited by reason of an occasional "Scotch mist" but all the ships were marked with the appropriate lights and every trawler had at least one sail set. *Inquiry into the Circumstances Connected with North Sea Incident; Reports by the Commissioners Appointed by the Board of Trade* (London: HMSO, 1905).

15. *Ibid.*, pp. x-xiv.

16. *Standard*, 25 October 1904, p. 4.

17. Valentine Chirol to Charles Hardinge, 1 November 1904, *Hardinge Collection*, v. VII. Cited in G.W. Monger, *The End of Isolation; British Foreign Policy, 1900-1907* (London: T. Nelson, 1963), p. 172.

18. Monger, p. 173.

19. Admiral Fisher to Lord Selbourne, 6 November 1904. Arthur J. Marder, ed., *Fear God and Dread Nought: the Correspondence of Admiral of the Fleet, Lord Fisher of Kelverstone* (London: Jonathan Cape, 1952), v. I, pp. 47-48.

20. Valentine Chirol to Charles Hardinge, 15 November 1904, *Hardinge Collection*, v. VII; Charles Hardinge to Lord Bertie, 27 October 1904, *Bertie Collection*, Series A, no. 174. Cited in Monger, p. 174.

21. Marquess of Lansdowne to Charles Hardinge, 24 October 1904. G.P. Gooch and Harold Temperley, eds., *British Documents on the Origins of the War* (London: HMSO, 1926-32), v. IV, no. 6, p. 6.

22. *Ibid.*

23. Charles Hardinge to Marquess of Lansdowne, 24 October 1904; Lansdowne to Hardinge, 24 October 1904; Hardinge to Lansdowne, 24 October 1904. *British Documents on the Origins of the War*, v. IV, nos. 7, 8, 10, 11, pp. 7-9.

24. Lansdowne to Hardinge, 26 October 1904. *British Documents on the Origins of the War*, v. IV, no. 13, pp. 11-12.

25. Blanche E. Dugdale, *Arthur James Balfour* (London: Hutchinson, 1936), v. I, pp. 384-85; Lansdowne to Hardinge, 26 October 1904. *British Documents on the Origins of the War*, v. IV, no. 13, pp. 11-12.

26. Admiralty to Foreign Office, 28 October 1904 (Enclosures containing instructions to the commanders of the Mediterranean and Channel Fleets, 25 and 27 October respectively). *British Documents on the Origins of the War*, v. IV, no. 19, pp. 18-19.

27. Hardinge to Lansdowne, 27 October 1904. *British Documents on the Origins of the War*, v. IV, no. 15, p. 15.

28. Lansdowne to Hardinge, 27 October 1904. *British Documents on the Origins of the War*, v. IV, no. 16, p. 16.

29. Paul Cambon, *Correspondence, 1870-1924* (Paris: Grasset, 1940), v. II, p. 168.

30. *Ibid.*, p. 167; Lansdowne to Edmund Monson, 28 October 1904. *British Documents on the Origins of the War*, v. IV, no. 21, p. 22.

31. Cambon, pp. 168-69.

32. Dugdale, v. I, p. 385; Hardinge to Lansdowne, 28 October 1904. *British Documents on the Origins of the War*, v. IV, nos. 18 and 20, pp. 17, 19-22.

33. Lansdowne to Hardinge, 29 October 1904. *British Documents on the Origins of the War*, v. IV, no. 23, pp. 23-24.

Part V
Arbitration

[8]

STATES AND THE UNDERTAKING TO ARBITRATE

Hazel Fox*

I. INTRODUCTION

THE institution of arbitration, on one view, derives its force from the agreement of the parties; on another view, from the State as supervisor and enforcer of the legal process. The contractual obligation of both parties enables the settlement process to override national differences in law and procedural obstacles which exist in local courts. On the other hand, a State's jurisdiction over its territory and nationals provides an independent supervision of the settlement process and effective enforcement of decisions made according to law: usually this exercise of jurisdiction is direct through the State's own courts, but in arbitration it is carried out through the alternative process of reference to an arbitrator and recognition and execution of the arbitral award.[1]

These two bases, the autonomy of the parties and the judicial supervision of the State as sources of the authority of arbitration are given varying weight in national legal systems in relation to domestic arbitrations.[2] The great expansion of international commercial arbitration

* Director of the British Institute of International and Comparative Law, formerly Fellow of Somerville College, Oxford. This paper is based on the Freshfields lecture given, at the invitation of Professor R. M. Goode, Director, Centre for Commercial Law Studies, at Queen Mary College London on 8 June 1987. I am grateful to Professor Bin Cheng and Lawrence Collins for their comments on an early draft.

1. René David, *Arbitrage dans le commerce international* (1982, Eng. translation 1985), pp.78, 81. "Arbitration and the justice of the courts should not be regarded as competitors doomed to be enemies, but rather as two institutions whose purpose is to co-operate for the sake of better justice: a satisfactory regime for arbitration cannot be imagined without some degree of co-operation with the courts, which are called to give assistance to, and also to exercise control over arbitration . . . It is not clear in the case of international disputes as to which national courts will be called to settle any dispute which may arise. This factor may well justify the desire to be free from the particular constraints of national laws and lead us to analyse the award as being a product of the free will of the parties."
   For inter-State arbitration, J. H. Ralston, *Law and Procedure of International Tribunals* (1926); K. S. Carlston, *The Process of International Arbitration* (1946); J. L. Simpson and H. Fox, *International Arbitration, Law and Practice* (1959). For international commercial arbitration, A. Jan van den Berg, *The New York Arbitration Convention of 1958* (1981); Craig, Park and Paulsson, *International Chamber of Commerce Arbitration* (1984); Redfern and Hunter, *Law and Practice of International Commercial Arbitration* (1986). See also Mustill and Boyd, *The Law and Practice of Commercial Arbitration in England* (1982).
2. The Italian *arbitrato irrituale* is an extreme example of the autonomy of the parties; it is a contractual institution not subject to any of the formalities of the Italian Code of Civil Procedure and enforcement cannot be effected by an award but only on the basis of an action on the contract to arbitrate: A. Kiss, *Problèmes de Base de l'Arbitrage*, Vol.I,

(1988) 37 I.C.L.Q.

2   *International and Comparative Law Quarterly*   [Vol. 37

in the last ten years[3] is attributabie to the successful harnessing of these
two bases in the relatively simple machinery provided in the New York
Convention on Recognition and Enforcement of Foreign Arbitral
Awards of 1958.[4] By this Convention the agreement of the parties to
arbitrate is given effect and the resulting award executed in an increasing number of countries by the legal systems of the States parties to that
Convention. The two bases, however, continue to create uncertainty as
to the ultimate foundation and source of authority and have produced
tensions which are still in process of being resolved.

The theoretical dispute as to the legal possibility of a floating supranational arbitral award, in no way dependent on any local forum or
law,[5] is one area of tension; another arises from conflicts between local
courts and the arbitral tribunal as to jurisdiction and the applicable law
to determine the capacity of the parties to agree to arbitrate and the validity of the arbitration agreement.[6] Further conflicts arise in relation to
powers of revision, annulment or appeal exercised by local courts over
the arbitral award.[7] The extent to which the assistance of local courts is
available, prior to the making of the award, to preserve assets for the
subsequent performance of the award, is a further reflection of these
tensions; in this situation, on the one hand, autonomy of the parties is
asserted by prohibiting any application to a local court by either party to

Arbitrage juridictionnel et arbitrage contractuel (1987). The statutory arbitration which is
conducted before a tribunal whose jurisdiction derives not from the consent of the parties
but the statute under which the dispute has arisen is an extreme example of the process
totally subject to the judicial supervision of the State: Mustill and Boyd, *idem*, p.2.

3. From its foundation in 1919 to April 1987, of the 5,930 requests for arbitration filed
with the International Chamber of Commerce, half were filed in the last 11 years. The current annual rate is about 300 cases a year with 659 pending as at January 1987. The London Court of Arbitration currently has about 60 cases a year, all being of an international
character with at least one party being a non-UK national.

4. (1959) U.N.T.S. No.4739, p.38. As of 31 Dec. 1986 71 States are signatories to the
New York Convention.

5. F. A. Mann, "Lex Facit Arbitrum in International Arbitration", in *Liber Amicorum for Martin Domke* (1967), p.157; W. W. Park (1983) 32 I.C.L.Q. 21; P. Lalive
(1976) Rev. de l'Arbitrage 155; J. Paulsson (1981) 30 I.C.L.Q. 358, (1983) 32 I.C.L.Q. 53;
W. L. Craig (1985) 1 Arbitration Int. 49; K. H. Bockstiegel (1984) 1 Jo. of Int. Arb. 223.
See Donaldson MR in *Deutsche Schachtbau und Tiefbohrgesellschaft mbH* v. *Ras al Khai-
mah National Oil Co.* [1987] 2 All E.R. 769 upholding the arbitrators' choice of "internationally accepted principles of law governing contractual relations" as the proper law.

6. H. M. Holtzmann, "Arbitration in the Courts: Partners in a System of International
Justice" (1978) Rev. de l'Arbitrage 253; B. Goldmann in *ICC Court of Arbitration 60th
Anniversary: A Look at the Future* (1984), p.257. The power of the arbitrator to rectify the
arbitration agreement is also a controversial area, *Ashville Investments Ltd.* v. *Elmer Con-
tractors* (1987) *The Times*, 29 May 1987, distinguishing *Crane* v. *Hegemann Harris Co. Inc.*
[1939] 4 All E.R. 68.

7. Recent legislation in the UK, France and Belgium has restricted recourse to local
courts from international commercial arbitrations held in those countries. Schlosser,
"L'Arbitrage et les voies de recours" (1980) Rev. de L'Arbitrage 286; Stein and Wolman,
"International Commercial Arbitration in the 1980s: A Comparison of the Major Arbitral
Systems" (1983) 38 Int. Lawyer 1685.

the arbitration for pre-award attachment measures (as is the case in an arbitration conducted under the ICSID Convention rules),[8] on the other, the enforcement powers of the State are made available through its courts to back up the effectiveness of the arbitration process (as the English court did in the *Rena K*).[9]

I propose to look at the working of these two sources of authority for arbitration as they apply to a State as party to inter-State arbitration and to international commercial arbitration with a private party. These problems are frequently addressed by a definition of the State so as to exclude State-trading entities and render the latter subject to the full rigours of private law. Another method is to distinguish activities of the State in the exercise of sovereign power, *de jure imperii*, from those of a commercial nature, performed in the market place, *de jure gestionis*. I propose, however, to address the problem in a broader, different way. I want to examine what obligations are invoked in the undertaking to arbitrate and to see if the content of these obligations is the same for the State as party to international arbitration (whether inter-State or commercial) as for the private party to commercial arbitration. For the purposes of the discussion the term State is limited to the State as a direct party and excludes separately incorporated State-trading entities. Even without them the position is complicated by the fact that today the State may itself or through its departments of State be a party to commercial arbitration and that a private party may, by means of mixed claims commissions—and the Iran–US Claims Tribunal is the latest version—have its private claims taken up by the State and presented through an inter-State arbitration.

To illustrate the difference in a State's undertaking to arbitrate from that of a private party, two specific areas of law will be examined: first, the State's attitude to enforcement of the award and the relationship of its consent to arbitration to its consent to proceedings in local courts. Second, the extent to which a State's consent to arbitrate has binding effect on claims of its nationals submitted by the State to inter-State arbitration.

First, however, it is useful to consider in a general way the expectations of States concerning arbitration based on their use of the process over the last 50 years.

---

8. Washington Convention on the Settlement of Investment Disputes between States and Nationals of other States 1965 (ICSID Convention) 575 U.N.T.S. 160, Art.26; *Guinea v. Maritime International Nominees (MINE)* (1985) 24 I.L.M. 1639 (Belgian court held no jurisdiction, because ICSID's jurisdiction was exclusive and lifted attachment order on Guinea's assets); also (1987) 26 I.L.M. 382 (Geneva Surveillance Authority on appeal similarly lifted attachment order against Guinea's assets); but cf. *Guinea and Soguipeche v. Atlantic Tritan Co.* (1987) 26 I.L.M. 373 where French Court of Cassation reversed Court of Appeal of Rennes and allowed provisional measures in the form of attachment.

9. [1979] Q.B. 377.

It is not possible in the space available to support the argument by examination of the various types of arbitration to which a State is party. One area relates to arbitration cases with a private party concerning settlement of oil and other concessions and investment disputes such as the *ARAMCO, BP, TOPCO* and *LLIAMCo* cases against Libya, *Kuwait* v. *Aminoil, Framatome* and *Elf Aquitaine*[10] and arbitrations held under the ICSID Convention.[11] Another relates to *ad hoc* inter-State arbitrations on boundary disputes in cases like *The Rann of Kutch*,[12] the *Argentine–Chile Frontier Award*,[13] or under dispute settlement clauses relating to the interpretation of treaties as the *French US Air Services Arbitrations*[14] or the *Young Loans Arbitration* in respect of German external debts after the Second World War.[15] However important and distinct in legal character these arbitrations may be, they do not contradict the general point to be made. They are relatively few, always of an optional consensual character and dependent on the continuing co-operation of the State in the arbitration proceedings if an effective award is to be achieved. There are also, of course, institutionalised methods of State arbitration for specific types of disputes, as for example human rights under the European Convention. In so far as these institutionalised methods involve automatic participation of the State, they constitute an exception and thereby a contrast to the general position now to be considered.

The expectations of States differ very considerably from those of private parties who resort to commercial arbitration. Here it may be as well to remember that, unlike the situation of the private party who chooses flexibility of the arbitral process as an escape from the strict requirements of litigation, arbitration in any form is for the State a loss of liberty, an acceptance of constraints from which it is otherwise free. All

10. *Saudi Arabia* v. *Aramco* (1963) 27 I.L.R. 117; *BP Exploration Company (Libya) Ltd* v. *The Government of the Libyan Arab Republic* (1973) 53 I.L.R. 297; *Texaco Overseas Petroleum Co. (TOPCO) and Californian Asiatic Oil Co.* v. *The Government of the Libyan Arab Republic* (1977) 53 I.L.R. 389; *Libyan American Oil Company (Lliamco)* v. *The Government of the Libyan Arab Republic* (1977) 62 I.L.R. 146; *Government of Kuwait* v. *Aminoil* 66 I.L.R. 519; *Framatome et al.* v. *Atomic Energy Organisation of Iran* published in French in Clunet. (1984) Jo. du D.I. 58 and in English under the title *Company Z and others (Republic of Zanadu)* v. *State Organisation ABC (Republic of Utopia)* (1983) VIII Y.B. Comm. Arb. 94; *Elf Acquitaine* v. *National Iranian Oil Co.* (1986) XI Y.B. Comm. Arb. 97.

11. For up-to-date account see (1987) 4 ICSID News.

12. The *Rann of Kutch Arbitration* (India and Pakistan) (1976) 50 I.L.R. 1.

13. Award of HM Queen Elizabeth II for the Arbitration of a Controversy between the Argentine Republic and the Republic of Chile 24 Nov. 1966, HMSO 59–162 (1969); 16 U.N.R.I.A.A. 109.

14. Case concerning the interpretation of the Air Transport Services Agreement between USA and France (1969) 16 U.N.R.I.A.A. 5; Case concerning the Air Service Agreement of 27 March 1946 (*US* v. *France*) (1979) 54 I.L.R. 304.

15. *Young Loans Arbitration* (1980) 59 I.L.R. 494. See generally A. M. Stuyt, *Survey of International Arbitrations 1794–1970*.

international proceedings are instituted by some form of arbitration clause. There is not today and never has been any general method of compulsory adjudication at the international level. The absence of a court with international competence over States was remedied by the establishment of the Permanent Court in 1921 after the First World War, now replaced by the International Court of Justice set up after the Second World War. But as is well known the jurisdiction of that Court was and still is dependent on the consent of the parties. (The complaint of the United States in the recent judgment on the merits in the case of the *Military and Paramilitary activities against Nicaragua* brought by Nicaragua against the United States was precisely on the ground that no consent by the parties to the Court's jurisdiction had been proved to exist; Nicaragua had never completed the process of ratification necessary to its acceptance of the compulsory jurisdiction of the ICJ, it forgot to send the necessary telegram and in any event the United States had expressly revoked its acceptance of the Court's jurisdiction as it was (or so it maintained) free to do three days before the Nicaraguan application was filed. The International Court found against the United States on both grounds; it held that there was sufficient evidence of Nicaragua's consent and the purported revocation of US consent was ineffective.)[16]

The Optional clause, Article 36(2) of the Statute of the Court, introduced a form of compromissory clause; unilaterally a State might in advance confer by declaration some general or limited jurisdiction on the International Court which, if matched with a similar undertaking of another State, generated jurisdiction. The practice of attaching reservations to a State's acceptance of the Court's jurisdiction and the requirement of reciprocity of commitment have considerably reduced the effectiveness of the Optional clause as a basis for compulsory adjudication. The construction of the terms of States' acceptance of the Court's jurisdiction has led to a great increase in preliminary objections relating to the jurisdiction of the Court. Of the 71 cases before the Court from 22 May 1947 to 31 July 1985, 46 judgments and 18 advisory opinions have been given. In 27 of those preliminary objections were taken as to jurisdiction or admissibility. Nor has the number of States willing to accept in advance the Court's jurisdiction increased. As at 31 July 1985 only 46 States out of a possible 160 or so had accepted the compulsory jurisdiction of the ICJ and many of these attached reservations as to subject matter and duration. The United States has since withdrawn its acceptance.[17]

16. *Nicaragua/US Military and Paramilitary Activities* (Jurisdiction and Admissibility) [1984] I.C.J. Rep. 392.
    17. (1985–6) I.C.J.Y.B. 60.

In many respects, therefore, the Permanent Court was—and its successor, the International Court, even more so, remains—an institutionalised arbitration tribunal rather than a court. It has the attributes of a court in that it is a permanent institution staffed by judges drawn from countries other than those of the parties and has a statute and rules of procedure which the parties take no part in drafting. But it resembles an arbitration in that the parties initiate the proceedings by consent, are entitled each to have a judge of their own nationality, and in the absence of international machinery—the recourse to the Security Council under Article 94 of the UN Charter is too political a measure to be of much legal assistance—the execution of the judgment very much depends on the parties' good faith. A recent revision of the rules appears to increase the control of the parties; it is now possible for a dispute to be heard in a chamber of the Court, the members of which are appointed by the Court after the President has ascertained the views of the parties as to its "composition".[18]

II. OBLIGATIONS CONTAINED IN THE UNDERTAKING TO ARBITRATE

So much then for States' general attitude towards arbitration of inter-State disputes: let us now examine more closely the content of the undertaking to arbitrate and the extent to which it depends on the two sources of authority, the autonomy of the parties and judicial supervision of the State. The undertaking to arbitrate in arbitrations between private parties involves three major commitments:

1. an immediate irrevocable obligation to refer the dispute to arbitration;
2. an obligation to settle the dispute by means of arbitration in preference and prior to resort to any other type of legal proceedings;
3. an obligation to honour the award of the arbitrator.[19]

A. Between Private Parties

In arbitration between private parties their good faith and voluntary commitment supports these obligations but, should one party disregard them, domestic courts provide procedures of varying effectiveness to enforce these obligations. A party who cannot get the other side willingly to arbitrate may when sued on the dispute seek the court's aid to direct the parties back to the arbitration. So far as English law is concerned, where the English court is satisfied that the agreement to arbi-

18. 1978 Rules of the ICJ, Art.17(2).
19. David, *op. cit. supra* n.1, at p.209; Mustill and Boyd, *op. cit. supra* n.1, at p.73.

trate is valid according to its proper law it will give effect by staying local proceedings. Such a stay is mandatory where the agreement is not a domestic arbitration agreement within the meaning of section 1 of the Arbitration Act 1975. The same remedy is available to enforce the second undertaking where a party in disregard of the arbitration agreement seeks to commence legal proceedings in relation to the arbitrable issues and the court, by declarations as to the status of the agreement to arbitrate or as to the jurisdiction of the arbitrator and by supervision of the appointment and conduct of the arbitrator, will support the arbitrator in the carrying out of the arbitration. Finally, when the award is made a limited right of appeal is available and the court will by summary procedure or by action on the third undertaking, the promise to honour the award, convert the arbitral award into a judgment so that a party may obtain its recognition and proceed to enforce it by all measures available for execution of judgments of the English court.[20]

B. Between States

The position with regard to the three commitments in the undertaking to arbitrate is rather different in international arbitrations between States. As has been seen there is not today and never has been any general method of compulsory adjudication at the international level. A State which makes the undertaking to enter into an arbitration knows that nothing but good faith and the general principle, *pacta sunt servanda*, holds it to the arbitration. There is generally no external authority which can make an order compelling the State to submit to the arbitration. Even where a jurisdiction clause is construed by the International Court to confer jurisdiction upon it, a State which disagrees may flout the order of the Court, as the United States has done in the *Nicaragua* case. No legal sanction follows under international or municipal law. The sole deterrent is the disapproval of world opinion.[21] Similarly, there is no method by which a State can be restrained from resorting to legal methods of settling a dispute other than the agreed arbitration. Indeed the second commitment to settle the dispute exclus-

20. Mustill and Boyd, *idem*, as to remedies for the first undertaking p.9 and Chap.30, for second undertaking p.21 and Chap.32 and for the third undertaking p.30 and Chap.28.
21. Schwarzenberger, *International law as applied by International Courts and Tribunals*, Vol.IV, *International Judicial Law* (1986), pp.724–726. Rosenne, *The International Court of Justice* (1957), p.82. The unilateral withdrawal of a State from continued participation in arbitration after consenting to the setting up of the arbitration tribunal, as in the *Hungarian Optants* case and the *Buraimi Oasis* arbitration terminates the arbitration and the arbitrator's powers; these truncated arbitrations present a serious challenge to the immutability of the arbitration and have led to a distinction between use of arbitration as a method of diplomacy and as a judicial process: 1955 U.N.Y.B. 339–340, (1953) 1 I.L.C.Y.B. 51–52; Schwebel, *International Arbitration: Three Salient Problems* (1987), Chap.3.

ively by arbitration may not be one recognised in international arbitration. The International Court of Justice, anxious to encourage parties to settle their disputes by whatever means they choose, has held parties to be free, whilst engaging in proceedings before the Court, at the same time to refer the dispute to the Security Council (*US Diplomatic and Consular Staff in Tehran* case),[22] to a regional process of settlement (the Contadora process in the *Nicaragua–US Military and Paramilitary* case)[23] and to bilateral discussion (*Aegean Sea Continental Shelf* case).[24] These are bilateral solutions pursued as an alternative to arbitration. But international law also countenances unilateral acts, however unfriendly, to persuade another State to yield in a dispute, always provided they do not amount to threat or use of force or illegal reprisals.[25]

Finally, the content of the third commitment to honour the award appears to differ from that in the private party's undertaking. Whenever the latter is required to comply with the award in good faith by his own efforts, a passive role is also envisaged, should he default, of subjection to local courts' powers so far as necessary to enforce the award. In an arbitration between two States there is no question of submission to a third authority; each State undertakes to exercise its own powers to execute the award and should it lose to accept the exercise of the other party's State powers for the performance of the award. Whilst the Covenant of the League of Nations imposed a general obligation "to carry out in full good faith any award that may be rendered"[26] it is usual for most arbitration agreements to contain a specific article under which the contracting States agree to accept the award as final and binding and also undertake "to take such measures as may be requisite to carry out the arbitral award".[27] In mixed claims commissions it is usual to set out detailed provisions for the time, date and manner of payment of money claims. The Mexican–US Claims Commission of 1923, for instance, requires the Commissioners to determine the value of any property for

---

22. [1980] I.C.J. Rep. 3, 21–24.

23. See also *Merits* [1986] I.C.J. Rep. 14.

24. [1978] I.C.J. Rep. 3, 12.

25. *US French Air Services Arbitration* (1979) 54 I.L.R. 304; Zoller, *Peacetime Unilateral Remedies: An Analysis of Countermeasures* (1984).

26. Art.13(4).

27. *Aguilar Amory and Royal Bank of Canada* claims, Convention between Great Britain and Costa Rica 12 Jan. 1922, 1 U.N.R.I.A.A. 371; *Trail Smelter* case (Canada/US), Convention for Settlement of Difficulties of 15 Apr. 1935, Art.XII: "The Governments undertake to take such action as may be necessary in order to ensure due performance of the obligations undertaken hereunder, in compliance with the decision of the Tribunal" 162 L.N.T.S. 73. Indo–Pakistan Location Boundary Case (Rann of Kutch) Arbitration Agreement of 30 June 1965, Art.3(iv): "Both Governments undertake to implement the findings of the Tribunal in full as quickly as possible" 548 U.N.T.S. 277. See Witenberg, *L'Organisation judiciaire; la procédure et la sentence internationale* (1937).

which a restitution order is made and gives the respondent State an option, to be exercised within 30 days of the award, to pay the value rather than restore the property.[28] On occasions States seek a declaration of the legal position in the first instance from the arbitrator, leaving the parties themselves to agree the method of carrying out the award. For instance, in boundary arbitrations it is usual for the parties to provide for a technical commission to carry out the demarcation of the boundary in accordance with the award.[29] Whilst a State is possibly under obligation to give effect through its national laws and courts to an award to which it is party, the cases to date have revealed obstacles of incorporation into national law and of political allocation of resources.[30] The practice has been to leave to the government of the State itself as a matter of discretion the decision as to the means of performing the award.[31]

In this connection the security account established at a third State's central bank under the Algiers Accords in January 1981 between Iran and the United States which effected the release of the US Iran hostages in Tehran provides possibly a unique precedent. In that case the security account was initially funded in advance of the arbitration of claims between the States by $1 billion of Iranian assets frozen in the United States: awards have been paid out of that security account which, in accordance with the provisions of the claims settlement agreement between the two States, Iran has replenished on two or three occasions

28. In the General Claims Commission between Mexico and USA set up by Convention signed at Washington, 8 Sept. 1923, the contracting States undertook "to give full effect" to the decisions of the Commission, that the result of the proceedings of the Commission were to be a "full, perfect and final settlement of any such claim upon either government", and as regards their nationals every such claim to be treated "as fully settled, barred and henceforth inadmissible, provided the claim filed has been heard and decided" (Art. VIII). Article IX provided that a balance between the total amounts awarded to the nationals of each State having been struck, a lump sum in gold coin or its equivalent was to be paid at Washington or the City of Mexico to the government of the country in favour of whose citizens the greater amount might be awarded: A. H. Feller, *The Mexican Claims Commission 1923–1934* (1935).

29. In the Agreement for Arbitration of 22 July 1971 between Argentina and Chile for the Beagle Channel dispute Art. XII(1) provided that when the proceedings before the Court of Arbitration have been completed, it should transmit its decision to Her Britannic Majesty's Government which should include the drawing of the boundary line on a chart, and Art. XV provided "The Court of Arbitration shall not be *functus officio* until it has notified Her Britannic Majesty's Government that in the opinion of the Court of Arbitration the Award has been materially and fully executed": Cmnd. 4781 Misc.23 (1971).

30. Simpson and Fox, *op. cit. supra* n.1, at p.259; *Socobelge* v. *The Hellenic State* (Belgium, Tribunal Civil de Bruxelles, 1951) 18 I.L.R. 3; *Société Européenne d'Etudes et d'Enterprises* v. *World Bank, Republic of Yugoslavia and Republic of France* (1982) J.D.I. 931; *Waltham Press* v. *Union of Soviet Socialist Republics* (1982) 20 Can. Y.I.L. 282.

31. In the debate on the State Immunity Bill Elwyn Jones LC said "it is generally accepted that States do not take coercive action against each other or their property" 388 *Hansard*, H.L. Debs, 17 Jan. 1978, col.76.

when the account has fallen below \$0.5 billion: to date that replenishment has been out of actual interest.[32]

It is, therefore, plain that an undertaking to arbitrate may have different connotations for a State when engaging in inter-State arbitration than for a private party to commercial arbitration. Which of these connotations applies when the State itself becomes a party to international commercial arbitration? This question is particularly relevant when the scope of the undertaking is considered as regards proceedings in local courts.

III. EXTENSION OF UNDERTAKING TO ARBITRATE TO COVER LOCAL COURT PROCEEDINGS

A private party's undertaking to arbitrate is an exception to the general compulsory jurisdiction which some local court is entitled to exercise over him. As demonstrated, this is not the position for the State. A State's undertaking to arbitrate is a restriction on freedom. Is the State's undertaking when given as a party to commercial arbitration confined, therefore, to consent to comply with the arbitration process or does it extend to acceptance of the jurisdiction of local courts to support the arbitration? Once again the basis of arbitration is exposed. Clearly if the undertaking to arbitrate rests solely on consent of the parties and that consent is interpreted in the same way as a State's undertaking to arbitrate in inter-State arbitrations, it deprives the proceedings, the arbitrator and the award of the support and enforcement procedures of local courts.

A. State Immunity

Do these supervisory and enforcement powers of the local court apply when a State is party to a commercial arbitration? The obstacle to an immediate answer is the doctrine of State immunity. Until recently there was widespread observance of a rule of absolute immunity.[33] There could be no local proceedings or enforcement measures against a State without its consent and that consent had to be expressed and given

---

32. Declaration of the Government of the Democratic and Popular Republic of Algeria of 19 Jan. 1981 (General Declaration), paras.6–7, reprinted in (1981) 20 I.L.M. 223; Lillich (Ed.), *The Iran–US Claims Tribunal 1981–83* (1984), p.5. In January 1986 the balance in the security account fell below US\$500 million due to the payment of awards in favour of US claimants. It was replenished (and again in October 1986) by transfer of interest earned by the security account and held in a separate account by the Depositary Bank (1987) XII Y.B. Com.Arb. 230.

33. *The Christina* [1938] A.C. 485; *Berizzi Bros. v. S.S. Pesaro* 271 U.S. 562 (1926); Lauterpacht (1951) 28 B.Y.B.I.L. 220.

before and after judgment. For the adjudication stage English law required express consent by an authorised agent of the State to be given direct to the court after proceedings had begun—in other words an express submission.[34] After judgment a further express consent to execution was required.[35] Under such an absolute rule the consent to refer a dispute to commercial arbitration, even though made in writing and confined to an existing dispute, was insufficient to constitute consent to the local court's jurisdiction or waiver of the State's immunity.

The rule of absolute immunity has been modified in the last ten years, extensively as to the adjudication stage, less dramatically for the enforcement stage.[36] The broad justification for the modification has been that a State expresses its consent to local jurisdiction by engaging in trade, entering into transactions with close connections with a particular country, and that it is artificially narrow to require the consent to be express, in the face of the court and only to be given at a time after proceedings have been commenced in respect of the particular dispute. On the basis of this philosophy legislation of the United States, Great Britain, Canada, South Africa, Singapore, Pakistan and Australia has restricted the immunity before national courts in two ways. These laws have redefined the conditions of waiver and submission sufficient to constitute consent of the foreign State in the eyes of the local courts. Second, they have identified a number of transactions in respect of which the plea of immunity may not be raised. The commercial transaction is the best known non-immune exception, but for present purposes the exception which makes commercial arbitration non-immune and subject to proceedings in local courts in respect of the arbitration is the most relevant.

B.   *Section 9 of the State Immunity Act 1978*

Provisions relating to waiver of immunity are to be found in all of the national legislation and the extent to which they render non-immune proceedings relating to arbitration agreements depends on their word-

---

34. *Kahan* v. *Federation of Pakistan* [1951] 2 K.B. 1003.

35. *Duff Development Co.* v. *Kelantan Government* [1924] A.C. 797.

36. European Convention on State Immunity 16 May 1972, U.K.T.S. (1979) No.74 (Cmnd.7742), (1972) 11 I.L.M. 470. US Foreign Sovereign Immunities Act 1976, UK State Immunity Act 1978, Singapore State Immunity Act 1979, Pakistan State Immunity Ordinance 1981, South Africa Foreign States Immunity Act 1981, Australian Foreign States Immunities Act 1985. Draft articles on Jurisdictional Immunities of States and their Properties (1987) 26 I.L.M. 625; State practice is collected in Materials on Jurisdictional Immunities of States and their Property UN St.Leg.Ser B/20 as updated in the Special Rapporteur's Reports, 4th Report (1982) Y.B.I.L.C. Vol.II, pt.1, p.199; 5th Report (1983) Y.B.I.L.C. Vol.II, pt.1, p.25; 6th Report (1984) Y.B.I.L.C., Vol.II, pt.1, p.5 and 7th Report U.N.G.A. doc. A/CN4/388. See also Sinclair (1980–II) 167 Hag. Rec. 121; Badr, *State Immunity, An Analytical and Prognostic view* (1984).

12   *International and Comparative Law Quarterly*   [VOL. 37

ing which differs.[37] Section 9 of the United Kingdom State Immunity Act 1978, however, specifically deals with the effect a State's agreement to arbitrate may have on immunity.[38] By that section, "where a State has agreed in writing to submit a dispute which has arisen or which may arise in arbitration the State is not immune as respects proceedings in the courts of the United Kingdom which relate to the arbitration".

This section appears to effect a massive imputed extension of a State's consent to local proceedings. On the widest construction of the section, the agreement to arbitrate removes State immunity from proceedings in respect not only of commercial but of non-commercial matters, in respect of foreign awards as well as English and from proceedings to enforce the award. Such a construction produces the paradoxical result that a State by express consent to arbitration renders itself more subject to the adjudicative and enforcement powers of the local courts than when it expressly submits by written agreement under section 2 of the 1978 Act to the jurisdiction of the English court itself. It would further appear to defeat the function of the arbitral process as a different and alternative method of dispute settlement to litigation and to disregard the intention of the State which consents to arbitration precisely on the basis that it is not itself and does not wish the dispute in which it is involved to be subject to local courts' jurisdiction.

Such a wide construction highlights sharply the tension in the two bases of arbitration which I have been discussing. On one view, a State as party to an arbitration consents solely to the first base, the consensual obligation to comply with the award. The widely observed immunity of the State from enforcement proceedings in the local courts prevents the second base, the judicial supervision of the arbitration process, having any operation in an arbitration to which a State is a party. A State carries over into private law arbitration the characteristics of inter-State arbitration and its status as a litigant in local courts—that is, no enforcement except by the State itself or, at least, with its consent.[39]

On a second view, however, commercial arbitration is seen as the modern novel process; it provides a process of worldwide enforcement of commercial obligations. Just as foreign courts enforce against a pri-

37. FSIA 1976, s.1605(a)(1) and s.1610(a)(1); UK State Immunity Act 1978, s.2; Canadian State Immunity Act 1982, s.4; Australian Foreign States Immunities Act 1985, s.10.

38. The Singapore State Immunity Act 1979, s.11, the South Africa Foreign States Immunities Act 1981, s.10, and the Pakistan State Immunity Ordinance 1981, s.10, have a similar provision to that in the UK Act but it is omitted in the Canadian Act; for Australia see text at *infra* n.51.

39. This view accepts that State immunity is a relevant plea only in respect of proceedings in local courts and that it is a well-established principle that State immunity cannot be raised as a plea to jurisdiction or a defence to the merits in an arbitration to which a State is party: J. Gillis Wetter (1985) 2 Jo. of Int. Arb. 7 and cases there cited. Where however the assistance of the local courts is required for the arbitration or to enforce the arbitral award, under the rule of absolute immunity a plea of State immunity may be raised.

vate party an arbitral award more readily than a judgment obtained in his home court, so by the State's consent to arbitration foreign courts are enabled to enforce awards in circumstances where they would by reason of immunity refuse or be unable to enforce judgments obtained in their courts.[40] In the light of the tension between these two approaches it is now necessary to examine more closely the detailed arguments for and against a wide construction of section 9 of the UK Act.

First, the section contains no express limitation to proceedings relating to arbitration of commercial matters. Had section 9 followed Article 12 of the European Convention on State Immunity 1972—and one of its purposes was to enable HMG to ratify that Convention[41]—it would have restricted the proceedings to those relating to "commercial or civil matters". By omitting to do so, it theoretically covers all arbitration, domestic and international, relating to non-commercial matters.[42] For States the distinction has great importance; many disputes with private parties arise by reason of the exercise of governmental power, or involve mixed issues of commercial law and public law. It is in this sensitive area that a State may consent to settlement by arbitration where it would adamantly oppose reference to a local court. To impute automatically submission to the local court by reason of the consent to the agreement to arbitrate is to endanger States' willingness to consent to any third party process of settlement. The 1958 New York Convention on Reciprocal Enforcement of Arbitral Awards recognises the significance of the distinction between commercial and non-commercial matters by allowing States to limit the obligation of their courts to give effect to foreign awards "only to differences . . . which are considered as commercial under the national law of the State making the declaration".[43]

40. This approach is supported by Delaume (1983) 38 Arb. Jo. 34, (1981) 75 A.J.I.L. 786; and Lord Denning in a case decided prior to the State Immunity Act 1978, *Thai Europe Tapioca Services Ltd* v. *Government of Pakistan* [1975] 1 W.L.R. 1485.

41. 388 *Hansard*, H.L. Debs, cols. 52–55, 17 Jan. 1978. Article 12 of the European Convention on State Immunity provides:

> (1) Where a Contracting State has agreed in writing to submit to arbitration a dispute which has arisen or may arise out of a civil or commercial matter, that State may not claim immunity from the jurisdiction of a court of another Contracting State on the territory or according to the law of which the arbitration has taken or will take place in respect of proceedings relating to
> (a) the validity or interpretation of the arbitration agreement;
> (b) the arbitration procedure;
> (c) the setting aside of the award,
> unless the arbitration agreement otherwise provides.
> (2) Paragraph 1 shall not apply to an arbitration agreement between States.

42. The section does not apply to arbitration agreements between States, s.9(2).

43. Art.1(3).

Despite the application of section 9 to non-commercial matters, are there other inherent limitations which reduce its scope? The second omission appears to be any limitation of the section to English arbitration. Is an undertaking by a State to refer a future dispute to arbitration outside the United Kingdom, and for which the proper law is a foreign law, within the section so as to constitute consent to proceedings in the English court? Dr Mann considers the section extends to foreign awards.[44] Although, as far as I know, the point has not appeared in any English reported case, this disregards the additional requirement that the English court will require a jurisdictional connection between itself and the arbitration agreement, such as England being the place of arbitration, which would rule out such extreme situations.[45] Certainly in the United States, where, under the FSIA 1976, section 1605(a)(1) permits waiver "either expressly or by implication", the case law after some hesitation has emphasised the need for territorial links with the US courts and refused to construe a waiver of immunity in respect of one jurisdiction as waiver to all jurisdictions.[46] On this analogy consent to arbitration in England may constitute consent to proceedings in English courts but consent to arbitration elsewhere will not. Section 9 of the UK Act should, therefore, be interpreted as removing immunity only in respect of agreements to arbitrate in England. Even if restricted to English arbitrations, it is necessary to know for what type of proceedings relating to the arbitration immunity of the State party to the arbitration agreement is removed. Does the section permit proceedings in the English court to enforce the award without the consent of the State? Had section 9 once again followed the wording of Article 12 of the European Convention there would have been no ambiguity. Article 12 expressly limits the local court proceedings to those relating to the validity or interpretation of the arbitration agreement, arbitration procedure and the setting aside of the award. When the Bill was first presented to the House of Lords the relevant clause contained an additional sentence stating that the section did not apply to proceedings for the enforcement of the award. Such a limitation would seem to have been in conformity with the general approach which was to separate off enforcement measures and to require a separate express consent by the State to their application. The section in its final version, however, omitted the additional sentence.[47] Does this mean that section 9 removes immunity

44. F. A. Mann (1979) 50 B.Y.I.L. 43, 58.

45. RSC, Ord.11; 949 *Hansard*, H. C. Debs, col.409.

46. *Verlinden Bv* v. *Central Bank of Nigeria* 488 F. Supp. 1 284 (S.D.N.Y. 1980), affirmed on other grounds 647 F 2d 320 (2d Cir. 1981) reversed 103 S.Ct. 1962 (1983); *Maritime International Nominees Establishment (MINE)* v. *Republic of Guinea* 693 F 2d 1095 (2nd Circ. 1981). See Kahale (1981) 14 N.Y.U. Jo. of In. & Pol. 29; Sullivan (1983) 18 Tex. Int. L.J. 329; Oparil (1986) 3 Jo. Int. Arb. 61.

47. 389 *Hansard*, H.L. Debs, col.76, 17 Jan. 1978.

for proceedings relating to arbitration not only to matters arising before or during the arbitration but also to the recognition and enforcement of the award? On one view, the omission of the words does not alter the limitation of proceedings relating to the arbitration to the pre-award phase. The Act, it is argued, maintains the distinction between the adjudicative and enforcement stage of proceedings: section 9 and the removal of immunity by agreement to arbitrate relate to the adjudicative stage. Section 13 deals with the enforcement stage and subject to the exceptions in subsections (3) and (4) expressly prohibits the court from giving effect to the award or the property of a State being subject to any process for the enforcement of an arbitral award. Only written consent under subsection (3) is sufficient to waive the immunity from enforcement. Accordingly, on this view the implied consent of section 9 is limited in its effect to proceedings relating to matters before or during the arbitration.

On another view, a more restricted view of section 13(2)(b) is taken, namely that it is concerned with the prohibition of attachment of State property to enforce an arbitration award except by written consent or in respect of property for the time being in use or intended for use for commercial purposes. On this view, section 13 provides no bar to enforcement of arbitration awards, merely a limitation as to the property which may be attached. Certainly Lord Wilberforce, in the committee stage, argued against the inclusion of the bar: a State's entry into an arbitration clause should constitute implied waiver from execution unless express reservation to the contrary was made.[48] The net result on this view is that English courts may recognise arbitral awards and enforce them but only in respect of property of the State in commercial use. This is certainly the view of Dr Mann.[49] Professor Crawford, who advised the Australian government in the preparation of its legislation on State immunity, considered the construction of the UK section not free from doubt. He recommended that the Australian Act should make the matter plain.[50] That Act accordingly contains a wide provision clarifying most of the ambiguities in the English statute—by section 17(1) a State which is party to an arbitration agreement is not immune from the recognition and enforcement of an award made pursuant to the arbitration, wherever the award was made.[51] The Australian Act also limits sec-

---

48. 389 *Hansard*, H.L. Comm., col.1524.
49. (1979) 50 B.Y.I.L. 43, 58.
50. Australian Law Commission Report No.24 Foreign State Immunity (1984) 62. See also Triggs (1982) 9 Monash Univ. L.R. 104.
51. Section 17 provides:

(1) Where a foreign State is a party to an agreement to submit a dispute to arbitration, then, subject to any inconsistent provision in the agreement, the foreign State is not

tion 17 to non-immune matters so presumably it excludes non-commercial matters. Under this provision a State which consents to arbitration consents to proceedings being brought against it to enforce the award in local courts anywhere in the world. The second basis of arbitration is imputed from consent to the first basis, agreement of the parties to arbitrate.

It is important not to lose sight of the principle of the matter in the legislative history and points of statutory construction. Unilateral legislation of single States expanding the meaning of consent and non-immune situations, as the Australian section and the widest construction of section 9 of the 1978 Act purport to effect, cannot alone alter the international rule of immunity.[52] A foreign State may disregard such unilateral provisions if contrary to international law. There is some support for a more limited rule in the draft convention on jurisdictional immunities which the International Law Commission has been preparing for the past seven years and which had its first reading in 1986. The draft article adopted by the Commission contains the three limitations initially set out in Article 12 of the European Convention; immunity is removed only in respect of civil or commercial matters and only in respect of proceedings in local courts which have a sufficient jurisdictional nexus with the arbitration (the arbitration either being held on the territory within the local court's jurisdiction or subject to its law). Finally, consent to arbitration is not construed as removing immunity from the enforcement stage of the arbitral award.[53] This reinstatement

immune in a proceeding for the exercise of the supervisory jurisdiction of a court in respect of the arbitration including a proceeding:
  (a) by way of a case stated for the opinion of the court;
  (b) to determine a question as to the validity and operation of the agreement or as to the arbitration procedure; or
  (c) to set aside the award.
(2) Where—
  (a) apart from the operation of subpara.11(2)(a)(ii), subsec.12(4) or subsec.16(2) a foreign State would not be immune in a proceeding concerning a transaction or event; and
  (b) the foreign State is a party to an agreement to submit to arbitration about the transaction or event, then subject to any inconsistent provision in the agreement, the foreign State is not immune in a proceeding concerning the recognition as binding for any purpose or for the enforcement of an award made pursuant to the arbitration, wherever the award was made.

52. "If one State chooses to lay down by enactment certain limits, that is by itself no evidence that those limits are generally accepted by States" *I Congreso del Partido* [1983] A.C. 244, 260, *per* Lord Wilberforce.
53. Art.19 of the draft articles provides:

Effect of an arbitration agreement. If a State enters into an agreement in writing with a foreign natural or juridical person to submit to arbitration differences relating to a [commercial contract] [civil or commercial matter], that State cannot invoke

by the International Law Commission of a treaty rule adopted in 1972 provides fairly strong evidence that the international law in this area is more restricted than the provisions contained in the UK and Australian legislation.

In the absence of a clear statement at international law of the rule, it will only be when a majority of States comply with national legislation such as the Australian and UK provisions that one can say with certainty that there is sufficient State practice to show that the international rule is accurately expressed in the terms of the national legislation. A moderate assumption of the supervisory function over both the adjudicative and enforcement stage of an arbitration with territorial connections with the local jurisdiction is the rule most likely to obtain the approval of States. It gives, after all, some weight to the second basis of arbitration, the judicial supervision of the arbitral process, yet preserves the widely observed immunity of the State from enforcement in local courts. It would be wrong to allow a party to a commercial arbitration, just because it is a State, to disregard that second basis altogether which, as discussed, is part of the inherent nature of the arbitral process and upon which much of the effectiveness of modern arbitration depends. A compromise solution has to be sought by which the first basis of arbitration, autonomy of the parties, is employed to identify and give independent force to a limited and agreed version of the second basis. It is here that jurisdictional links to one particular system of local courts and the commercial nature of the arbitration are all-important. If in the arbitration agreement the State consents to the applicable law as English law, or to the arbitration being held in England and identifies the arbitration as relating to commercial matters, it is a small extension of that express consent to hold it subject to the supervision of the English courts for the purposes of the arbitration proceedings whether before or during the award.

Such moderate assumption should not, in my view, extend to attachment of State assets before or after the award. At the present stage of the development of commercial arbitration and States' growing co-operation I would not extend that judicial supervision beyond recognition of the award. To dismantle State immunity from enforcement in respect of

> immunity from jurisdiction before a court of another State which is otherwise competent in a proceeding which relates to:
> (a) the validity or interpretation of the arbitration agreement,
> (b) the arbitration procedure,
> (c) the setting aside of the award
> unless the arbitration agreement otherwise provides.

U.N.G.A. Official Records, 41st Session, Supp. No.10(A/41/10), Chap.II, pp.5–23, reprinted (1987) 26 I.L.M. 625. See also Art.III(g) of the draft Resolutions on jurisdictional immunities of the Institute of International Law, prepared by Professor I. Brownlie (1987) 62 Inst.I.L.Ann. 98, 101.

arbitral awards whilst preserving it for proceedings in local courts would unduly strain the legal system and forfeit States' co-operation. I would prefer courts to require an express acceptance of such liability to attachment in the arbitration agreement by the State or at any rate an acknowledgement that the arbitration relates to commercial matters. In the meantime, until the position is clarified, private parties in drafting arbitration clauses with States are well advised to include express waiver of immunity by the State both to adjudication and enforcement proceedings in the local court.

IV. MIXED CLAIMS COMMISSIONS AND ARBITRAL CLAIMS TRIBUNALS

THE second illustration of the working of the two bases of arbitration is drawn from one institutional form of international settlement which has a long history and recent developments suggest it may have particular relevance for commercial arbitration. That institution is the mixed claims commissions of the nineteenth century which in time led to the mixed arbitral tribunals set up under the peace treaties of the First World War. The earliest commissions are to be found under the Jay Treaty of 1794 between Great Britain and the United States to settle the boundary and war claims outstanding after the War of Independence. Although the commissions were interrupted by disagreements between the English and American commissioners, their enquiries into the facts and elucidation of principle aided the final settlement, the United States paying £600,000 in three annual instalments for the "confiscated debts" owed to the British, and Great Britain £2,330,000 in respect of 533 separate awards made to US nationals for loss of vessels and cargoes.[54] Further mixed commissions were set up by States, in particular to settle claims of their nationals for loss arising out of war or civil disturbance; this procedure was used against France after the Napoleonic wars, for US and British claims against Mexico (1838 and 1868), Chile (1883 and 1886), Venezuela (1869 and 1903), Peru (1904), in settlements involving Germany after the First World War, and again in claims of the United States against Mexico (1923 and 1924).[55] The most recent example is the Iran–US Claims Tribunal which, in addition to dealing with direct claims between the two States and disputes as to interpretation of the two declarations contained in the 1981 Accords of Algiers, confers juris-

54. 52 Consolidated T.S. 243; Moore, *International Adjudications*, Vols.1–4; A. de la Pradelle and N. Politis, *Recueil des Arbitrages internationaux* (2nd ed.), Vol.1, pp.1–28.
55. Verzijl, *International Law in Historical Perspective Pt.VIII* (1976), Chap.IX; Simpson and Fox, *op. cit. supra* n.1, at Chaps.1–4; Dolzer, "Mixed Claims Commissions" 1 Encyclopaedia of Public Int. L. 146; Ralston, *op. cit. supra* n.1; Feller, *op. cit. supra* n.28; Recueil des decisions des Tribunaux arbitraux mixtes institutes par les Traites de Paris, Vols.1–10 (1922–1930).

diction on the Tribunal to decide claims (including counterclaims arising out of the same transaction) of nationals of the United States against Iran and claims of nationals of Iran against the United States.[56] Terminology is not always exact. The institution has developed over the years with the inclusion of neutral members in the composition of the commission either at a second stage or throughout; in this form the institution is usually described as an arbitral claims tribunal. There has also been an extension to individual claimants of some right of participation in the proceedings.[57]

In all these commissions and arbitral claims tribunals some common features are observable. In all proceedings the claim of injured nationals is espoused by the State which enters into a treaty to settle the dispute with another State. The treaty between the States is more in the form of a submission than a compromissory clause—the subject matter, the tribunal, the law applicable are all agreed.

The subject matter of the dispute is broadly identified, though its precise scope often remains a fruitful source of argument in cases coming before the commission. US Secretary of State Pickering complained that the Jay Treaty "in effect made the United States the debtor for all the outstanding debts due to British subjects and contracted before the treaty of peace".[58]

The composition and procedure of the tribunal is agreed, though again some flexibility is left to the tribunal which may by administrative decisions taken early on in the proceedings lay down general guidelines as to the disposition of the claims.[59]

The law applicable is international law supplemented in some instances by special rules on which the parties agreed—as did Great Britain and the USA in the Washington Rules on the duties of neutrality for the Alabama Claims.[60] The origin of the treaty for settlement by a mixed claims commission or arbitral tribunal is the inadequacy of local law to compensate for the loss suffered (no, or inadequate, provision for damage from war, civil disturbance, or act of State is usually to be found in local laws) and the recognition by the contracting States that a standard external to local laws is required to provide compensation. It is a well-established principle that diplomatic protection of aggrieved

---

56. Claims Settlement Declaration, 19 Jan. 1981, reprinted (1981) 20 I.L.M. 230.

57. Simpson and Fox, *op. cit. supra* n.1, at pp.10–12, 34–41; Burchard (1927) 21 A.J.I.L. 472.

58. Secretary of State Pickering to Minister of US in London, 5 Feb. 1799, Moore, *op. cit. supra* n.54, Vol.3, at p.170.

59. Mixed Claims Commission US and Germany, Administrative Decisions and Opinions to 30 June 1925 (1925); Borchard (1925) 19 A.J.I.L. 133.

60. Treaty of Washington, 8 May 1871, Art.VI, 143 Consolidated T.S. 146, 149; Moore, *op. cit. supra* n.54, Vol.1 (1898); p.550.

nationals is precluded as long as the remedies available under domestic law have not been exhausted by the private party.[61]

The relationship of the jurisdiction of the commission or claims tribunal to that of local courts is a variable one.

Some treaties specifically exclude the role requiring exhaustion of local remedies, others define the circumstances in which it shall be applicable. The Algiers Accords setting up the Iran–US Claims Tribunal contain both types of provision. Claims arising under a binding contract for exclusive sole jurisdiction of the competent Iranian courts are excluded (Article II.1), whilst claims referred to the Arbitral Tribunal are treated as transferred with the consequent effect that they are "to be considered excluded from the courts of Iran or of the United States or of any other court" (Article VII.2).

Other treaties provide a right of appeal to the arbitral tribunal (as in the London Agreement on German External Debts 1953, from the mixed commission to the arbitral tribunal)[62] or a right to obtain a ruling on the interpretation of the treaty rules from the arbitral tribunal (as domestic courts of the contracting States might do under the Austro–German Property Treaty 1957).[63]

A.   The Position of the Individual Claimant

A common feature to all these procedures is that the States are the parties. Although in the commissions under the Jay Treaty and subsequent nineteenth-century mixed commissions the individual was permitted to file his claim and the sums awarded were qualified by reference to that claim, ultimate control throughout was retained by the State. Cases were conducted by agents appointed by the two States and it was rare until after the First World War for individuals to present memorials to the commission, participate in oral proceedings, appear as witnesses or be represented by counsel.[64] Claims by individuals were directly presented in the mixed arbitral tribunals set up under the peace treaties after the First World War but only after they had been subjected to a clearing system of national offices of the countries concerned. Although the Franco–German Tribunal dealt with 20,000 cases and the Anglo–German and German–Italian Tribunals with some 10,000 cases each, these represent only a fraction of the claims settled through the national

---

61. *Panevezys* v. *Saldutiskis Rly.* case P.C.I.J. Ser.A/B No.76 (1939); *Interhandel* case [1959] I.C.J., Rep.6; 18 *Halsbury's Laws* (4th ed.), Foreign Relations Law 909, para.1751.
62. London Agreement on German External Debts, 27 Feb. 1953, Arts.28(4), 31(7), 333 U.N.T.S. 2. Simpson and Fox, *op. cit. supra* n.1, at pp.35–40.
63. German Bundesgesetzblatt 1958 II 129.
64. Simpson and Fox, *op. cit. supra* n.1, at pp.99–102.

clearing system.[65] After the Second World War the London Agreement on German External Debts set up a complicated three-tier system of appeals to which individuals had somewhat limited rights.[66] Claims of less than £250,000 in the Iran–US Claims Tribunal are to be presented by the government of the national concerned; claims in excess may be presented by individual claimants but the agents of the two States are present throughout the hearing with a right of audience.[67]

It is unwise to refer to the Iran–US Claims Tribunal as a modern illustration of claims commissions without at the same time noting its novel features which distinguish it from previous inter-State arbitrations.[68] Reference has already been made to the parties' establishment in advance of a security account out of which private parties' claims could be paid. The General Principles in the first declaration for the Algiers Accords of 17 January 1981 between Iran and the United States (which effected the release of the hostages) also emphasised the intention to achieve a settlement of outstanding private law claims as well as public international law claims against either State. Principle B stated that "it was the purpose of both parties . . . to terminate all litigation as between the government of each party and the nationals of the other and to bring about the settlement and termination of all such claims through binding arbitration". To this end the terms of reference of the Tribunal included claims of US nationals against Iran and of Iranian nationals against the United States for debts, contracts (including transactions which are the subject of letters of credit and bank guarantee), expropriation and other measures affecting property rights. The applicable law provision also does not disregard the private law aspect of the arbitration, the Tribunal being directed in Article V to decide "all cases on the basis of respect for law, applying such choice of law rules and principles of commercial and international law rules as the Tribunal determines to be applicable".

The settlement of claims through the Iran–US Claims Tribunal provides an example of the fusion of State and private party claims in one procedure. An increase in demand for such a procedure is to be expected if States deliberately use their private law either by suspension of local remedies or change of substantive rules as a response to perceived illegal action on the international plane by another State. Any solution of the international dispute will then necessarily require a settlement of private claims which have been generated in the course of the dispute.

65. Wuhler, "Arbitral Tribunals" 1 Encyclopaedia Public Int. L. 146.
66. See reference at *supra* n.62.
67. Claims Settlement Declaration, *supra*. n.56, Arts.III(3), VI(2).
68. See D. Lloyd-Jones, "The Iran–US Claims Tribunal: Private Rights and State Responsibility", in Lillich (Ed.), *op. cit. supra* n.32, at p.51.

22   *International and Comparative Law Quarterly*   [Vol. 37

This increasing fusion of State and private party claims in one procedure before an arbitral claims tribunal leads back to a consideration of the basis of arbitration and the scope of the undertaking to arbitrate.

B. Relationship of Arbitral Claims Tribunals to Local Courts

It will be important to clarify the relationship between such claims tribunals and local courts if private law claims are increasingly to be referred to them. Is the authority of such an arbitral claims tribunal based on consent of the parties or the judicial authority of the State? Is it the agreement of the two States which gives legal force to the decisions of the tribunal or the combination of the judicial powers of two States? So far as the first base is concerned, does the consent of the State bind its national in all circumstances in respect of any claim that it may seek to bring in local courts whether within the State or a third State? As regards the second base, whilst international law permits and third States must recognise the exercise of judicial authority of a State within its territory or over its nationals, does international law require similar recognition by a third State of a settlement by bilateral treaty between two States of the claims of their nationals? If it does, in the absence of a treaty with the third State or implementing legislation, how are the courts of the third State to be satisfied of the validity of the awards and jurisdiction of the arbitral claims tribunal? Even if so satisfied, may those courts still reject the decisions of such tribunals, as they do in respect of foreign judgments, on grounds of fraud or by reason of the award being contrary to public policy or opposed to natural justice?

It may be helpful to illustrate these questions by an example. At the time of the US air strike on Libya the United States government froze Libyan assets in the United States. Suppose a US national tries in England to recover a loan owed to him by a Libyan State-owned bank and suppose, subsequently, the United States and Libya agree to refer all claims to arbitration, must the English court discontinue the action?

Now I appreciate that I am posing the question in such general terms that no answer is possible. The terms of the US freezing order, whether its ambit includes the loan arrangement between the US and Libyan nationals, the proper law of the transaction, whether the US national has exhausted local remedies in Libya, are all issues which require elucidation. But in broad terms you can see the underlying interests involved.[69]

There is first the situation of the individual whose claim is the subject

---

69. For a recent case involving some of the considerations raised in the hypothetical example in the text, see *Libyan Arab Foreign Bank* v. *Bankers Trust Co.*, 2 Sept. 1987, Staughton J.

of political settlement between States. If he refers his claim to the arbitral claims tribunal set up by the two States, then arguably he has personally submitted to its jurisdiction and any award will bind him finally.[70] But supposing he does not do so but wishes to continue with his action in the English court? Suppose, indeed, aware of the uneasy relations between their governments, the parties expressly chose to make the contract of loan subject to the jurisdiction and law of England. To what extent is the US national affected by the treaty of settlement between the United States and Libya? Is the arbitration treaty anything more than an agreement *inter alios*? The private party is not a direct party to the treaty and the espousal of his claim by means of the treaty enabling it to be brought before the tribunal is a matter of discretion for the State and not of right on the part of the national claimant. Certainly English law provides no remedy to such a claimant whereby he can force the UK government to take up and present his claim against another State or any remedy to enforce the payment over to him for any sum awarded or recovered by the UK government in respect of his claim under such an arbitration agreement.[71]

Has the US national a right to exhaust local remedies in Libya or to continue with his English suit and to oppose the conversion of his claim to local proceedings into an arbitration claim?

The original claim may either be grounded in private law on the contract or, if the Libyan court can be shown also to have jurisdiction, in international law on a denial of justice from the Libyan courts for failure on Libya's part to observe minimum standards in the treatment of aliens. It is generally the latter type of claim which States refer to arbitral claims tribunals although the root cause of dissatisfaction often arises from some breach of contract due to disruption of normal business relations between the countries. From the point of view of the private litigant either type of claim derives from the laws of one or other of the States parties to the arbitration. States are free to change such laws. Is the reference to arbitration equivalent to such legislative action so as to defeat any continuance or initiation of proceedings in the local court to give effect to the national's claim? This raises a nice question whether either applicant or respondent State is free to dispense with the requirement of exhaustion of local remedies when the private party concerned still wishes to pursue them. It seems probable that provided the claim is between nationals of the States concerned and is wholly grounded in the territory of one or the other, whether based on private law or public

---

70. As the court found in respect of the plaintiff in *Dallal* v. *Bank Mellat*, see text *infra* n.72; Dicey and Morris, *Conflict of Laws* (11th ed., 1987), p.563.

71. *Civilian War Claimants Association Ltd* v. *R.* [1932] A.C. 14; *Tito* v. *Waddell (No.2)* [1977] Ch. 106; 18 *Halsbury's Laws* (4th ed.), Foreign Relations Law 728, paras.1419, 1768; F. A. Mann, *Foreign Affairs in English Courts* (1986), p.77.

international law, it can be terminated by the States' reference of it to arbitration. The constitutional law, however, of a particular State may require enabling legislation to direct its courts to stay or discontinue proceedings. Here, reference to the second basis of arbitration, the judicial authority of the State, seems necessary to extend the arbitration agreement beyond the direct parties to persons outside the agreement. Is this second basis, judicial authority of a State, available and sufficient to extend the jurisdiction of the arbitral claims tribunal to the courts of a third State and over claims that may be grounded on the laws of third States? Will the second basis give primacy to the tribunal's jurisdiction? Will it bring to a halt proceedings in local courts in respect of the same claims, render null any order by such courts to attach assets in respect of the claims and require the local courts of a third State to recognise and give effect to the awards of the tribunal?

Whether such reference by treaty and legislation would effectively defeat causes of action grounded on a third State's laws with sufficient jurisdictional connection to entitle the courts of that third State to take jurisdiction is a more difficult question. It also raises the extent to which a third State and its courts are bound to give effect to a bilateral treaty to which the third State is not a party.

C.   Dallal *v.* Bank Mellat

It was precisely these problems which Hobhouse J had to consider in the recent decision of *Dallal* v. *Bank Mellat.*[72] The claimant in that case had personally submitted to the jurisdiction of the Iran–US Claims Tribunal and his claim had no independent basis in English law or jurisdictional links with the English court. But the reasoning of the judgment suggests that the English court has an inherent power to give effect to an arbitration award grounded in international law even though there was no treaty between Great Britain and the States setting up the arbitration tribunal and no implementing English legislation.

A US national in that case had a claim for two cheques dishonoured by an Iranian bank. The Iran–US Claims Tribunal had dismissed the claim by a majority award, with the American arbitrator dissenting, on

---

72. [1986] 2 W.L.R. 745. The relationship between local courts and the Iran–US Tribunal has also arisen in West German and French courts. The exercise of concurrent jurisdiction by a West German court (Frankfurt am Main District Ct., Feb. 1980) by attachment of Iranian assets to enforce US companies' claims, suspended in US courts, led Iran to file a complaint before the Iran–US Tribunal, Case No. A/5. The French Cour de Cassation has refused to annul an award obtained in an ICC arbitration against the Iranian Air Force which the applicant is seeking to enforce by filing a claim before the Iran–US Claims Tribunal and in proceedings before West German courts: *Commandement des Forces Aeriennes de la République Islamique d'Iran c. Bendone—De Rossi* International, 1st Ch. Civ. Cour de Cassation, Arrêt No.449, 5 May 1987, (July 1987) I.F.L.R. 44.

the ground that the applicant had failed to discharge the burden of proof that the transaction was not illegal as contrary to the Iranian foreign exchange law, and held that the US applicant should not be allowed to amend his claim to a plea of unjust enrichment. The applicant subsequently brought an action on the cheques in the English court and the defendant, relying on the award of the Iran–US Claims Tribunal, applied to strike out the action as an abuse of the process of the court. Hobhouse J, in considering the validity of the arbitration and the award, tested it by reference to the two bases of arbitration, consensual autonomy of the parties and the power of the State to enforce the legal process. He first approached the problem as one of recognition of a valid arbitration agreement either under the New York Convention or by English conflict of laws rules. By reason of the arbitration being held at The Hague it was argued the proper law of the arbitration agreement was Dutch.[73] Here a well-known obstacle, the legal requirement for a formal submission of the parties, is encountered. Article 623 of the Dutch Civil Code required such a formal submission and its absence rendered any agreement a nullity. Consequently there could be no recognition by the English court of the proceedings and award of the Claims Tribunal "from the application of the ordinary principle applicable to consensual arbitration".

It was suggested by the plaintiff that if Dutch law was not the proper law, international law might be. Hobhouse J was emphatic that private parties had no consensual autonomy to choose international law:

> But what I am concerned with here . . . is not an agreement between States but an agreement between private law individuals who are nationals of those States. If private law rights are to exist, they must exist as part of some municipal legal system and public international law is not such a system. If public international law is to play a role in providing the governing law which gives an agreement between private law individuals legal force it has to do so by having been absorbed into some system of municipal law.[74]

Unable to rely on the consensual agreement of the private parties as the source of authority, the judge turned to the second source of authority, the State's exercise of judicial powers. Describing the proceedings at The Hague as akin to a domestic "statutory" arbitration, where the jurisdiction of the arbitral tribunal is defined not by any choice or agree-

---

73. A Bill was presented to the Netherlands Parliament which provided that awards of the Iran–US Tribunal should be arbitral awards within the meaning of Dutch law, and not subject to challenge in Dutch courts either for jurisdiction or substance except for compliance with rules of natural justice or on grounds of public policy. The Bill was not proceeded with. Bill entitled "Applicability of Dutch Law to the Awards of the Tribunal sitting in the Hague to hear Claims before Iran and the United States", reprinted in Iranian Assets Litigation Rep. 6, 899 (15 July 1983).

74. [1986] 2 W.L.R. 745, 759.

ment of the parties, he set himself to find the relevant "statute" to govern the present international situation.

This he does as follows:

> The jurisdiction and authority of the tribunal at The Hague was created by an international treaty between the United States and the Republic of Iran, and was within the treaty-making powers of the governments of each of those two countries. Each of the parties was respectively within the jurisdiction and subject to the law-making power of one of the parties to the treaty. Further, the *situs* of all the relevant choses in action are within the jurisdiction of one or other of the two States which are parties to the treaties. Again the municipal legal system of each of the relevant States recognises the competence of the tribunal at The Hague to decide the arbitration proceedings. Accordingly the arbitration proceedings at The Hague are recognised as competent not only by competent international agreements between the relevant States, but also by the municipal laws of those States . . . there is no reason in principle why the curial law of a tribunal cannot derive concurrently from more than one system of municipal law . . . in the present case there are two systems of municipal law with the requisite international competence which give validity to the arbitration proceedings. There is no reason in principle why that validity should not be recognised by the English courts.[75]

This is a lengthy excerpt but I have given it in full to show that the focus has shifted away from the arbitration. There is no question now of the validity of the underlying agreement between the private parties which gave rise to the dishonoured cheques, nor to the absence of any direct agreement between them to refer it to the Claims Tribunal, nor to the validity based on consent of the parties to the resulting award. The enquiry, relying as it does on case law relating to the recognition of decisions of consular courts given in respect of private nationals of States which were not in direct treaty relations with Great Britain,[76] has shifted the focus from consensual autonomy to the competence of the tribunal. If under international law a tribunal is competent, Hobhouse J considers its competence ought to be recognised by English courts. Such competence need not be conferred by treaty, but binds the nationals of the States parties to the treaty and any private party who voluntarily resorts to the arbitral claims tribunal to pursue his claim.

These are resounding principles and exciting news for international lawyers. The *Dallal* decision suggests a route not merely for regularising the relationship of the Iran–US Tribunal with local courts of third States but opens up the prospect of general recognition by local courts of inter-State arbitration. Equating international law with foreign municipal law, the case in effect extends the common law action to enforce a

75. *Idem*, p.761.
76. *The Laconia* (1863) 2 Moore P.C. (N.S.) 161, *Messina* v. *Petrococchina* (1872) L.R. 4 P.C. 144.

foreign judgment[77] to the decision of an international tribunal established by international law. If a bilateral agreement between two States is given such recognition, should the English court not also extend it to judgments of the International Court, which is established by a multilateral treaty to which the majority of States are parties? If it be argued that the recognition is limited to awards affecting the rights of private parties, then surely any arbitral tribunal established by treaty qualifies, whether or not Great Britain is a party to the treaty, provided it purports to decide conclusively issues which otherwise would be decided by the local courts of the contracting states.

So far as the facts of *Dallal* v. *Bank Mellat* are concerned, the treaty between the United States and Iran was confirmed by local legislation of both countries. In the first instance, in the United States it was done by Presidential decree.

On the setting up of the Iran–US Claims Tribunal, in a decree of 24 February 1981 the President suspended all claims for equitable or judicial relief in connection with the claims, and provided that "during the period of suspension all such claims should have no legal effect in any action pending or to be commenced in any court of the United States". The constitutionality of this Presidential decree was upheld by the Supreme Court in *Dames & Moore* v. *Regan Sec. of Treasury*; the Supreme Court there held that Congress had implicitly approved the practice of claim settlement by executive agreement and that the suspension of claims was not an ouster of jurisdiction but effected "a change in the substantive law governing the law suit" and the provision of an "alternative forum, the claims tribunal which is capable of providing meaningful relief".[78] In the words of Justice Rehnquist who delivered the judgment of the Court, "The frozen assets serve as a bargaining chip to be used by the President when dealing with a hostile country." Private law actions by individual claimants could not therefore be allowed to minimise or wholly eliminate this "bargaining chip".

Whilst, in pursuit of the praiseworthy goal of obtaining the release of hostages, criticism of the Presidential decree and suspension of vested rights of action was muted, it is worth pausing to ask how we in the UK would view such action. The government would not have executive power to do so and would have to enact legislation. As Parliament is theoretically capable of doing anything it pleases, presumably by Act of Parliament existing causes of action could be terminated in a manner similar to the American method. It is an interesting speculation whether such interference with vested rights of property and contractual expectations would involve any infringement of the Treaty of Rome in rela-

77. Dicey and Morris, *op. cit. supra* n.70, at p.561.
78. 453 US 654 (1981) 673.

tion to the Common Market or to human rights, particularly the right of property in the First Protocol under the European Convention of Human Rights.

But these speculations apart, is it sufficient to leave such an important extension of jurisdiction into the international field to a common law action? It appears from the decision in the *Dallal* case that there is sufficient scope in such procedure to ensure the application of the safeguards relating to rules of natural justice and local public policy which currently apply for the enforcement of foreign judgments and awards.[79] But what of the broader view of public policy? Should the recognition of a treaty conferring international competence be left to individual litigants' resort to a common law action? Are all such bilateral treaties removing claims of nationals from local courts to inter-State arbitration likely to be ones which, in the words of the judge in the *Dallal* case, the English court will "not frustrate"? Should not the decision to endorse or frustrate a treaty arrangement made between other States be with Parliament? Such endorsement has certainly been required in the case of foreign judgments, as the recent entry into force of the Civil Jurisdiction and Judgments Act 1982 illustrates, and also the UK legislation for foreign arbitral awards giving effect to the New York Convention 1958 and the ICSID Convention.

The fusion of international law with local law is an admirable goal but if it is to be done so as to avoid international conflict surely it ought to be done by observance of constitutional procedure, opportunity for parliamentary debate and taking due account of all interests involved.

V.   CONCLUSION

To summarise:

1. Commercial arbitration, both domestic and international, depends on two sources of authority, the consensual autonomy of the parties and the power of the State to enforce the legal process.

2. Private litigants as a general rule are subject to compulsory adjudication of their disputes by courts. Resort to arbitration arises from the voluntary choice of a more flexible procedure. States are not generally subject to compulsory adjudication; all forms of arbitration are a restriction on their freedom of action.

3. The undertaking to arbitrate comprises three elements: an immediate irrevocable obligation to refer the dispute to arbi-

79. Dicey and Morris, *op. cit. supra* n.70, at p.571; *Dallal* v. *Bank Mellat* [1986] 2 W.L.R. 745, 765.

tration; an obligation to settle the dispute by arbitration in preference and prior to resort to legal proceedings; and an obligation to honour the award of the arbitrator. In inter-State arbitration the State's undertaking to arbitrate probably does not extend to the second obligation and the first and second obligations are given effect solely by operation of the first basis, the consensual autonomy of the parties. The undertaking of the State does not contain a commitment to respect the power of a third State to enforce the award.

4. In international commercial arbitration the undertaking of the State to arbitrate cannot of itself constitute consent to the award being enforced by court proceedings. Such consent may be construed or imputed as consent to enforcement by English courts where the State in the arbitration agreement consents to the applicable law as English law or to the arbitration being held in England, and identifies the arbitration as relating to commercial matters and commercial property. Section 9 of the State Immunity Act 1978 should be so construed.

5. Reference of private party disputes by States to settlement by mixed claims commissions or arbitral claims tribunals involves no consent by the private party to arbitrate unless he subsequently submits his claim to the commission or tribunal. The second basis, the power of the two States to enforce the award of the commission or tribunal should not extend beyond their own courts. If the award of the arbitral claims tribunal is to receive recognition and enforcement in the courts of a third State, that State must be a party to the treaty setting up the claims commission or tribunal and/or enact legislation requiring its courts to give effect as judgments to the awards of such mixed claims commission or arbitral claims tribunal.

[9]

RETALIATION OR ARBITRATION—OR BOTH? THE 1978 UNITED STATES-FRANCE AVIATION DISPUTE

*By Lori Fisler Damrosch**

It began as a very small dispute. Pan American World Airways planned to introduce a service from San Francisco to Paris with a stop in London, using a Boeing 747 aircraft from San Francisco to London and a smaller Boeing 727 aircraft from London to Paris. The change to a smaller plane would have enabled the most efficient and economic use of Pan Am's fleet. In aviation as in railroad terminology, a change along a route to equipment of a different size is called a "change of gauge."[1]

In accordance with French law, Pan Am filed a schedule on February 20, 1978 with the French aeronautical authorities, showing inauguration of the service with change of gauge effective May 1, 1978. The French aeronautical authorities informed Pan Am, however, that, in France's view, the proposed change of gauge at London was not authorized by the United States-France Air Transport Services Agreement (the Agreement).[2] According to the French, the Agreement authorized change of gauge in the territory of the parties subject to conditions specified in the Agreement;[3] but because the Agreement made no mention of change of gauge in third countries, a United States carrier could not undertake such an operation on a route to France unless France gave its consent in the particular case. The French authorities made clear that Pan Am should not expect to obtain such consent unless the United States Government was willing to negotiate with France for an appropriate quid pro quo.

---

* The author is an attorney with the United States Department of State, and was Deputy Agent for the United States in the arbitration discussed in this article. The views expressed are her own and not necessarily those of the Department of State.

[1] Stoffel, *American Bilateral Air Transport Agreements on the Threshold of the Jet Transport Age*, 26 J. AIR L. & COMM. 119, 133 (1959); Lissitzyn, *Change of Aircraft on International Air Transport Routes*, 14 J. AIR L. & COMM. 57 (1947).

[2] 61 Stat. 3445, TIAS No. 1679, as subsequently extended and amended (*see* 1 UST 593, TIAS No. 2106; 2 UST 1033, TIAS No. 2257; 2 UST 1037, TIAS No. 2258; 10 UST 1791, TIAS No. 4336; 13 UST 1860, TIAS No. 5135; 20 UST 2684, TIAS No. 6727).

[3] The Agreement does not use the term "change of gauge." Section VI of the Annex to the Agreement reads:

> (a) For the purpose of the present Section, the term "transshipment" shall mean the transportation by the same carrier of traffic beyond a certain point on a given route by different aircraft from those employed on the earlier stages of the same route.

> (b) Transshipment when justified by economy of operation will be permitted at all points mentioned in the attached Schedules in territory of the two Contracting Parties.

> (c) However, no transshipments will be made in the territory of either Contracting Party which would alter the long range characteristics of the operation or which would be inconsistent with the standards set forth in this Agreement and its Annex and particularly Section IV of this Annex.

786   THE AMERICAN JOURNAL OF INTERNATIONAL LAW   [Vol. 74

Pan Am, and the United States Government, disagreed with the French interpretation. The Agreement's specific provision on change of equipment in the territory of the parties established the conditions under which such operations could take place in those territories, but there were no comparable provisions on third-country change of gauge. Indeed, the United States had always viewed change of gauge as an operational matter left to the managerial discretion of each carrier, unless specific provisions of a bilateral agreement imposed restrictions on the exercise of this discretion. Allowing each carrier to use the most efficient type and size of aircraft in light of differing traffic demands along the segments of a route would promote the declared policy of the United States and France expressed in the Agreement: "to foster and encourage the widest possible distribution of the benefits of air travel for the general good of mankind at the cheapest rates consistent with sound economic principles."[4] In the view of the United States, the text and context of the Agreement, including its negotiating history and a long record of practice under it and similar agreements, led to the conclusion that a third-country change of gauge which did not otherwise violate any conditions imposed by the Agreement was perfectly acceptable. Special consent was not necessary, and accordingly an attempt to prohibit an operation merely because it involved a third-country change of gauge would violate the Agreement.

Intergovernmental consultations and exchanges of diplomatic correspondence in March and April proved fruitless. France demanded an economic concession of equivalent value to the proposed change of gauge, but the United States refused to consider any payment for the exercise of a right that it believed its carriers already enjoyed under the Agreement.[5] Though the issue remained unresolved, Pan Am went ahead and commenced the service with change of gauge as planned, in spite of warnings that France would consider such action a violation of both international law and French domestic law.

On the first day of the new service, May 1, 1978, the French authorities delayed disembarkation of the flight at Orly Airport and questioned the pilot. On the second day they issued a citation. On the third, they refused to allow the passengers to disembark or the waiting passengers to embark; the plane had to return to London. Pan Am then had no choice but to suspend the service: it also commenced an action in French courts to seek a reversal of the French decision denying its right to operate. With each day that went by, it suffered economic losses from its inability to offer the service it had been advertising throughout the spring—and in the meantime Air France was providing direct air service between Paris and Los Angeles.

The United States immediately protested the French actions against Pan

---

[4] *See* section IV of the Annex to the Agreement.

For a recent overview of the development of the policies reflected in aviation agreements negotiated by the United States, see Atwood, *International Aviation: How Much Competition, and How?* (book review), 32 STANFORD L. REV. 1061 (1980).

[5] The proposed change of gauge did not involve the carriage of local traffic between London and Paris, which would have been a new and valuable right subject to bargaining.

Am and proposed on May 4 that an expedited arbitration proceeding could be adopted to resolve the dispute if France persisted in its interpretation of the Agreement.[6] With no satisfactory response received, the U.S. Civil Aeronautics Board ruled on May 9 that France had violated the Agreement.[7] Upon making this finding, the Board set in motion a procedure under part 213 of its Economic Regulations[8] that ultimately could have resulted, on or after July 12, in the retaliatory suspension of all French flights from Paris to Los Angeles. Under the first phase of this procedure the

[6] The Agreement as amended provides in Article X that

> any dispute between the Contracting Parties relative to the interpretation or application of this Agreement or its Annex which cannot be settled through consultation shall be submitted for an advisory report to a tribunal of three arbitrators. . . . The Contracting Parties will use their best efforts under the powers available to them to put into effect the opinion expressed in any such advisory report.

Under arbitral clauses of this type, the principle of recourse to arbitration is agreed in advance, but the modalities of submitting a specific dispute to arbitration must be worked out through the negotiation of an intergovernmental agreement known as a *compromis*. Such an agreement may include, *inter alia*, provisions on selection of the arbitrators, seat of the tribunal, questions to be posed, procedures to be followed, the schedule for the proceedings, and the terms governing the conduct of the parties over the disputed issue during the pendency of the proceedings.

[7] Civil Aeronautics Board Order 78–5–45, Docket 32651.

[8] 14 C.F.R. pt. 213. Part 213, originally proposed by the Civil Aeronautics Board in 1961 to provide a means for controlling the capacity of foreign air carriers if foreign governments controlled the capacity of U.S. carriers, was adopted in somewhat different form in 1970. The version in effect at the time of the U.S.-France dispute authorized the Board to require foreign air carriers to file schedules upon a finding that the public interest so required. In the case of foreign carrier operations subject to an air transport agreement between the United States and a foreign government, the Board could not require filing of schedules unless it found that the carrier's government had impaired, limited, terminated, or denied U.S. operating rights under the agreement or otherwise failed to prevent the denial of fair and equal opportunity to exercise those rights. By entry of a subsequent order, subject to stay or disapproval by the President, the Board could prevent the inauguration of proposed schedules or require the discontinuance of existing schedules.

In 1979 Congress amended section 402(f) of the Federal Aviation Act to include a specific statutory provision on the model of part 213. International Air Transportation Competition Act of 1979, Pub. L. No. 96–192, §9, 94 Stat. 35. Under the new provision, retaliatory measures may be entered summarily and without hearing, subject to the approval of the President. The Senate Commerce Committee's report explains the provision as follows:

> Experience under Part 213 has demonstrated that an effective retaliatory power can and does act as a persuasive deterrent against foreign government restrictions. Moreover, the right of the United States to take proportional countermeasures in response to restrictive action by a foreign government in violation of a bilateral agreement (even when such countermeasures would, in the absence of the foreign government violation, themselves constitute a violation of the agreement) has recently been sustained by an international arbitration tribunal as consistent with recognized international law principles. *Award of Arbitral Tribunal in the International Arbitration between the United States and France*, December 9, 1978.

S. REP. No. 96–329, 96th Cong., 1st Sess. 5–6 (1979). The report also notes the view of the committee that implementation of a retaliatory measure when a foreign government has breached an agreement is consistent with the Board's mandate under section 1102 of the Federal Aviation Act to act consistently with obligations assumed by the United States in intergovernmental agreements.

788   THE AMERICAN JOURNAL OF INTERNATIONAL LAW   [Vol. 74

French carriers (Air France and Union de Transports Aériens) were subjected to a requirement not generally imposed on carriers serving the United States: they were required to file their existing schedules within 7 days and proposed schedules 30 days prior to implementation. The second phase began when the Civil Aeronautics Board entered an order served June 12, which directed the suspension of all Air France flights to Los Angeles within 30 days.[9] Because the French service to Los Angeles was one of the French rights guaranteed by the Agreement, the only basis under international law for suspending it was the alleged prior French breach of the Agreement. On July 11, the day before the suspension was to become effective, a *compromis* of arbitration was signed; in accordance with the *compromis*, the part 213 orders were vacated the same day.[10]

The parties put two questions to the tribunal.[11] First, does a U.S.-designated carrier have the right to change gauge at London on the West Coast-Paris route? Second, did the United States have the right to take the actions it took under part 213? On December 9, 1978, the arbitral tribunal ruled that a U.S.-designated carrier does have the right to change gauge, and that the United States did have the right to take its part 213 action.[12]

The first of these questions is of interest primarily to the aviation community.[13] Underlying the second question, however, are issues going to the heart of the international legal order. How are states to resolve their disputes? When are retaliatory sanctions appropriate for an alleged breach of

[9] Civil Aeronautics Board Order 78–6–82, Docket 32651, 43 Fed. Reg. 25,846 (June 15, 1978). The order was subject to stay or disapproval of the President within 10 days, but was neither stayed nor disapproved: indeed, the interested executive branch agencies (the Departments of State and Transportation) supported the decision to proceed to the implementation of part 213 countermeasures.

[10] Civil Aeronautics Board Order 78–7–33, Docket 32651.

[11] The relevant portion of the *compromis* reads:

> The tribunal is requested to decide the following two questions in accordance with applicable international law and in particular with the provisions of the Agreement:
>
> (A) Does a United States-designated carrier have the right to operate West Coast-Paris service under the Air Services Agreement between the United States and France with a change of gauge in London (transshipment to a smaller aircraft on the outward journey and to a larger aircraft on the return journey)?
>
> The tribunal's decision of this question shall be binding.
>
> (B) Under the circumstances in question, did the United States have the right to undertake such action as it undertook under Part 213 of the Civil Aeronautics Board's Economic Regulations?
>
> The tribunal shall issue an advisory report with respect to this question in accordance with Article X of the Agreement, which shall not be binding.

The *compromis* fixed an expedited schedule for the briefing of the case and requested the tribunal to render its decision no later than December 10, 1978. It also established interim arrangements to permit Pan Am to operate its service with change of gauge on exactly one-half the days between the inception of the dispute and December 10. *See infra*, note 54 and accompanying text.

[12] Case Concerning the Air Services Agreement of 27 March 1946, Arbitral Award of 9 December 1978, 54 ILR 304 (1979) [hereinafter cited as Award].

[13] *See* A. LOWENFELD, AVIATION LAW, ch. II, §5.3 (2d ed. 1980).

an intergovernmental agreement, and under what conditions? If two states have committed themselves in an agreement to submitting disputes concerning its interpretation or application to arbitration, what, if any, unilateral measures may they take before the tribunal is constituted? To what extent may they use the threat or the actual application of such measures to influence the outcome of the negotiations over the terms for submitting the dispute to arbitration or the terms of interim operations pending the outcome of arbitration?

This paper explores some of these issues, using the change-of-gauge arbitration as a case study. In particular, it analyzes the relationship between self-help measures of retaliation and neutral dispute settlement procedures, and discusses how the availability of each can affect the application of the other.

I. RULES ON RESPONSES TO BREACH OF TREATY

Materiality

The Vienna Convention on the Law of Treaties[14] is the logical starting place for an inquiry into the state of the law on permissible responses to a perceived breach of treaty.[15] Under Article 60, a material breach by one party to a treaty entitles the other party to terminate the treaty or suspend its operation in whole or in part. A material breach is defined as a repudiation not sanctioned by other provisions of the Vienna Convention, or a violation of a provision essential to the accomplishment of the object or purpose of the treaty.[16]

With many articles of the Vienna Convention it is relatively easy to ascertain whether the drafters intended to codify existing international

---

[14] UN Doc. A/CONF.39/27 (1969), *reprinted in* 63 AJIL 875 (1969), 8 ILM 679 (1969). The Vienna Convention entered into force on January 27, 1980, but has not been ratified by the United States. However, many of its provisions are considered to be declaratory of customary international law. *See* Briggs, *Unilateral Denunciation of Treaties: The Vienna Convention and the International Court of Justice*, 68 AJIL 51 (1974), and *United States Ratification of the Vienna Treaty Convention*, 73 *id.* 470 (1979). The final preambular paragraph of the convention provides that "rules of customary international law will continue to govern questions not regulated by the provisions of the present Convention."

[15] The word "treaty" is here used in the sense defined by Article 2 (a) of the Vienna Convention on the Law of Treaties: "an international agreement concluded between States in written form and governed by international law, . . . whatever its particular designation." Domestic law considerations, such as whether ratification of the agreement has received the advice and consent of the Senate, are not relevant to this usage of the term.

[16] The relevant provisions of Article 60 of the Vienna Convention read:

1. A material breach of a bilateral treaty by one of the parties entitles the other to invoke the breach as a ground for terminating the treaty or suspending its operation in whole or in part.

. . . .

3. A material breach of a treaty, for the purposes of this article, consists in
   (a) a repudiation of the treaty not sanctioned by the present Convention; or
   (b) The violation of a provision essential to the accomplishment of the object or purpose of the treaty.

law or, alternatively, to create a new rule to take effect between the parties only upon the convention's entry into force. Article 60 does not fall clearly into either of these categories. On the one hand, the International Law Commission noted the lack of consensus among jurists over some of the key concepts addressed in the article and the paucity of state practice to illuminate the issues.[17] On the other hand, the Commission appeared to assume that the basic principle underlying Article 60 was, in the words of Judge Anzilotti's famous dissent in *Diversion of Water from the Meuse*, "so just, so equitable, so universally recognized, that it must be applied in international relations also."[18]

Yet Article 60, whether or not it enunciates existing principles of international law on the points it addresses, cannot—or at least should not—be considered an exclusive statement of the rights under customary international law of a party injured by a breach of treaty. Most important, the article omits any discussion of less than material breaches. By this omission the drafters might have intended to preclude any sanction for nonmaterial breaches. Alternatively, they might have intended only to confirm the right to terminate or suspend a treaty in response to a material breach, and to preclude these drastic measures unless a breach was material, without prejudice to the availability of other lesser responses to lesser breaches. The former interpretation would in effect eliminate any deterrent for a vast category of treaty violations, and runs contrary to good sense.

By reading between the lines of the International Law Commission's commentary, it is fortunately possible to conclude that the Commission did not intend to foreclose appropriate responses to breaches not covered by Article 60's materiality standard. The Commission indirectly recognized that rights of reprisal would be available under international law wholly apart from any codification of the law of treaties.[19] It is not at all clear why the Commission failed to confirm these rights explicitly in the text of the draft articles. In view of the sound policy reasons for preserving a deterrent to minor as well as major treaty breaches, the references to materiality in the text should be read not as excluding entirely the right to respond to minor breaches, but simply as a means to ensure that minor breaches are not used as a pretext for denouncing a treaty which has become inconvenient or for suspending performance of more than proportional obligations.[20]

---

[17] Reports of the International Law Commission on its Seventeenth and Eighteenth Sessions, 21 UN GAOR, Supp. (No. 9) 82–84, UN Doc. A/6309/Rev.1 (1966), *reprinted in* [1966] 2 Y.B. INT'L L. COMM'N 253–55, UN Doc. A/CN.4/Ser.A/1966/Add.1.

[18] PCIJ, ser. A/B, No. 70, at 50 (1937). *See also* A. D. McNAIR, THE LAW OF TREATIES 570–78 (1961); M. WHITEMAN, 14 DIGEST OF INTERNATIONAL LAW 468–78 (1970); RESTATEMENT (SECOND), FOREIGN RELATIONS LAW OF THE UNITED STATES §158; Esgain, *The Spectrum of Responses to Treaty Violations*, 26 OHIO STATE L.J. 1 (1965). For confirmation of the right to suspend performance in the specific case of breach of an air services agreement, see B. CHENG, THE LAW OF INTERNATIONAL AIR TRANSPORT 482 (1962).

[19] The Commission noted that the right to invoke termination or suspension arises "independently of any right of reprisal." [1966] 2 Y.B. INT'L L. COMM'N 255.

[20] The American Law Institute's *Restatement (Second) of the Foreign Relations Law of the United*

The tribunal in the U.S.-France arbitration did not discuss the issue of materiality, though both sides had argued it. France claimed that its denial of the right to change gauge (which in its view did not constitute a breach) was certainly not a violation of a provision "essential to the accomplishment of the object or purpose of the treaty" within the meaning of Article 60, and hence could not supply the legal basis for a U.S. suspension of obligations owed to France. The United States asserted, on the other hand, that the French conduct (which forced Pan Am to abandon an economic method of operation) had effectively grounded Pan Am in violation of the Agreement's essential purpose of providing air services. As a subsidiary point, the United States argued that even a minor breach could justify proportional countermeasures. In finding for the United States on the retaliation issue, the tribunal did not refer to the Vienna Convention or to any purported materiality rule, and thus may well have considered that the right to take proportional countermeasures exists regardless of the materiality of the breach. Let us assume so.

Proportionality

One point to which the tribunal did devote some attention was the question of the proportionality between the alleged breach and the U.S. response. This was an issue the parties had briefed in some detail, not because they differed on the appropriate legal rule,[21] but because they strongly disagreed over the application of the rule to the facts of the case.

France argued that there can be no proportionality between the denial of a right to institute a new and disputed service and the interruption of an undisputed service conducted over many years. Further, in France's view the economic consequences of the Pan Am service and the Air France service were grossly disproportionate.

The United States would have been hard pressed to deny the second point. It thus argued that since the French action had effectively denied Pan Am the right to operate a West Coast-Paris service, it was appropriate to deny the French carrier its rights on a symmetrical route. The tribunal took a slightly different tack:

> In the Tribunal's view, it is essential, in a dispute between States, to take into account not only the injuries suffered by the companies concerned but also the importance of the questions of principle arising from the alleged breach. The Tribunal thinks that it will not suffice, in the present case, to compare the losses suffered by Pan Am on account

---

States confirms in section 158 the right to suspend performance of treaty obligations toward the breaching party as long as the suspension and the violation (apparently whether material or not) involve corresponding provisions or are otherwise reasonably related. Lord McNair notes that retaliatory suspension of a corresponding provision is a common sanction for minor treaty breaches, though he comments that "[t]he precise juridical status of this practice is not clear, and little authority exists." A. D. McNair, *supra* note 18, at 573. *See also* RESTATEMENT, FOREIGN RELATIONS LAW OF THE UNITED STATES (REVISED), Tentative Draft No. 1, April 1, 1980, §345, following Article 60 of the Vienna Convention.

[21] The tribunal described the rule as "well-known." Award, para. 83.

of the suspension of the projected services with the losses which the French companies would have suffered as a result of the counter-measures; it will also be necessary to take into account the importance of the positions of principle which were taken when the French authorities prohibited changes of gauge in third countries. If the importance of the issue is viewed within the framework of the general air transport policy adopted by the United States Government and implemented by the conclusion of a large number of international agreements with countries other than France, the measures taken by the United States do not appear to be clearly disproportionate when compared to those taken by France.[22]

This passage is interesting on several counts. First, it permits states to apply countermeasures that would be disproportionate in an economic sense, in order to enforce a principle. Second, it implies that considerations of principle are all the more weighty when third countries are watching. Figuring third-country reactions into the proportionality formula is novel but sensible, especially in the aviation context. Because of the worldwide network of essentially similar agreements, the way two states interpret and apply their bilateral agreement can have repercussions far beyond the particular case.[23] And apart from questions of aviation practice or policy, a deliberate and effective response to a treaty violation can have, as the tribunal indicated, "an exemplary character directed at other countries": in other words, "the character of a sanction."[24] An overly niggardly approach to proportionality could conceivably detract from the importance of the retaliatory sanction as a deterrent to potential treaty violators. Under this reasoning, the injured party should have an adequate degree of flexibility in assessing the appropriate level of response and should not be subjected to ex post facto censure for having failed to achieve precise equivalence.

Existence of Breach

Though the literature on the law of treaties includes ample discussion of the concepts of materiality and proportionality, another aspect of the problem—the need for a breach as a predicate to retaliation—is hardly discussed at all. One explanation for the dearth of comment may be that the treatise writers have assumed that the condition of a prior breach was so obviously central to the theory of retaliation that it hardly need be discussed. How could a retaliatory breach be justified unless the conduct provoking retaliation was itself a breach?[25]

[22] *Ibid.*

[23] The United States had made an extensive showing of practice under agreements with third countries to support its position on the change-of-gauge issue. The tribunal did not find it necessary to rely on the evidence of third-country practice, and concluded only that this evidence "does not appear inconsistent" with the approach suggested by more direct sources of interpretation. Award, para. 71.

[24] Award, para. 78.

[25] A retaliatory act that is not itself illegal falls into the category of retorsion: an unfriendly act for an unfriendly act. L. OPPENHEIM, 2 INTERNATIONAL LAW 136 (7th ed. H. Lauterpacht, 1952). A retaliatory breach of treaty, however, corresponds to a measure of reprisal under customary international law: the victim state's conduct in derogation from its own international obligations is justified as a response to a prior illegal act.

If the treatise writers have been assuming that only an underlying breach can justify a retaliatory breach, it is time to question that assumption.

The U.S.-France change-of-gauge dispute might have been decided the other way; presumably the French expected the opposite outcome, and the arbitrator of French nationality in an articulate dissent points out the logic of the French position. If either of his colleagues[26] had found the French argument just a shade more persuasive and had cast a different vote on the change-of-gauge issue, would that change in result on the question of treaty interpretation have changed the result on the question of retaliation? If the assumption of the need for an underlying breach is correct, the answer would have to be yes.

For tactical reasons the United States was reluctant to admit even *arguendo* that France might not have committed the first breach, and thus refrained from articulating an explicit theory that the tribunal could have used to approve a retaliatory breach if it found that France had not breached the Agreement. Such a theory can indeed be articulated, and it may well prove more satisfactory than the heretofore unchallenged assumption that only a prior breach can justify a responsive breach.

There are essentially three approaches to the problem: first, that no retaliatory measures should be taken until after an arbitral tribunal has established the existence of a prior breach; second, that retaliatory measures may be implemented pending arbitration at the risk of liability to the other party if the tribunal eventually holds that there has been no breach; and third, that retaliatory measures may be implemented pending arbitration, with liability to the other party or the measure of appropriate reparations to be determined by the retaliating party's good faith rather than by whether it guessed wrong in predicting the tribunal's decision.

The first of these has been advocated by Philip Jessup, who wrote in 1948 that it would be "highly suitable for an international tribunal to pass judgment on the merits of the claim" before an aggrieved state takes retaliatory action.[27] However desirable this approach might be in an ideal world, its shortcomings in today's world are obvious. Tribunals are not always in place to hear disputes or to indicate interim measures of protection; indeed, even when a preexisting agreement calls for arbitration, establishment of the tribunal takes time,[28] and there may be protracted negotiations over the terms of the *compromis* and the regime to govern the conduct of the parties pending the tribunal's decision. If the party allegedly committing the initial breach could enjoy the benefits of its breach without the fear of retaliatory responses during this possibly lengthy period, it would have every incentive

---

[26] The *compromis* provided for the United States and France each to select one arbitrator; they were Thomas Ehrlich and Paul Reuter, respectively. The third arbitrator, chosen by agreement of the parties, was Willem Riphagen, a Dutch international law scholar.

[27] P. JESSUP, A MODERN LAW OF NATIONS 152 (1948). *See also* Borchard, *Declaratory Judgments in International Law*, 29 AJIL 488, 490–91 (1935).

[28] For a discussion of some of the opportunities for delay in the progress of a dispute through arbitration, see Larsen, *Arbitration of the United States-France Air Traffic Rights Dispute*, 30 J. AIR L. & COMM. 231, 237–38 (1964); Larsen, *The United States-Italy Air Transport Arbitration: Problems of Treaty Interpretation and Enforcement*, 61 AJIL 496, 502–03 (1967).

794   THE AMERICAN JOURNAL OF INTERNATIONAL LAW   [Vol. 74

to delay submission of the dispute to arbitration and conclusion of the arbitral proceedings. Because of these realities of international dispute settlement, there is apparently no instance in which a party seeking to terminate its own performance under a treaty on account of the other party's breach has sought prior authorization from an international tribunal.[29]

The second approach was adopted in the 1935 Harvard Draft Convention on the Law of Treaties, which would have permitted provisional suspension of performance of treaty obligations pending a declaration of rights by an international tribunal, with the proviso that "provisional suspension of performance by the party seeking such a declaration will not be justified definitively until a decision to this effect has been rendered by the competent international tribunal or authority."[30] Though the drafters of the Harvard convention recognized that insistence on obtaining a prior arbitral

---

[29] B. SINHA, UNILATERAL DENUNCIATION OF TREATY BECAUSE OF PRIOR VIOLATIONS OF OBLIGATIONS BY OTHER PARTY 210 (1966). *But see* the discussion by the International Court of Justice approving the action of the United Nations General Assembly in invoking South Africa's breach of its international obligations as a ground for terminating South Africa's League of Nations mandate over South West Africa. Legal Consequences for States of the Continued Presence of South Africa in Namibia, [1971] ICJ REP. 16, 46–47.

[30] The Harvard draft convention with commentary is reprinted in 29 AJIL Supp. 662 (1935). The relevant provision, Article 27, is discussed in *id.* at pp. 1077–96 and reads:

> (a) If a State fails to carry out in good faith its obligations under a treaty, any other party to the treaty, acting within a reasonable time after the failure, may seek from a competent international tribunal or authority a declaration to the effect that the treaty has ceased to be binding upon it in the sense of calling for further performance with respect to such State.

> (b) Pending agreement by the parties upon and decision by a competent international tribunal or authority, the party which seeks such a declaration may provisionally suspend performance of its obligations under the treaty *vis-à-vis* the State charged with failure.

> (c) A provisional suspension of performance by the party seeking such a declaration will not be justified definitively until a decision to this effect has been rendered by the competent international tribunal or authority.

The Harvard draft reflected the approach taken by Lauterpacht a few years earlier in discussing self-help remedies in international law. He noted that self-help is not a normal juridical institution, but only a temporary authorization to act in the name of the law. Its use, in the final analysis, must be justified before the law:

> Le "self-help" doit, en fin de compte, se justifier devant la loi, et tout excès ou abus de force entraînera un châtiment. Dans les sociétés où la loi est souveraine, l'individu qui se rend justice à lui-même est strictement responsable devant la loi. . . .

> La thèse d'après laquelle la reconnaissance du "self-help" par le droit national, dans des cas peu nombreux et peu significatifs, justifierait son adoption comme règle générale dans le domaine des relations internationales se heurte donc à de sérieuses objections. Il est également fort grave de placer sur le même plan le "self-help" provisoire, réglementé et justifiable devant les tribunaux, et le "self-help" destiné à faire valoir d'une manière définitive et normale des droits réels ou supposés, sans en référer ensuite à un organisme indépendant chargé de rendre un jugement.

Lauterpacht, *La Théorie des différends non justiciables en droit international,* 34 RECUEIL DES COURS 499, 527–28 (1930 IV).

Thirty-five years later, the International Law Commission, in discussing the draft of the Vienna Convention, noted that some of the Commission's members considered that the right to terminate or suspend a treaty for breach should be made subject to control by compulsory reference to the International Court of Justice. [1966] 2 Y.B. INT'L L. COMM'N 262.

judgment would be unrealistic, they made clear that a party engaging in provisional suspension would do so "at its own risk"; if the tribunal failed to sustain its contentions, the suspending state would itself be in the position of wrongful breach.

> Therefore, under the rule here proposed, it will behoove States not to undertake unilaterally to suspend performance of their treaty obligations *vis-à-vis* a State which they allege to be guilty of breach of the treaty unless they are fairly certain that their allegations are sound and susceptible of being proved to the satisfaction of a competent international tribunal or authority.[31]

Putting states at their peril for a wrong guess may well be inadvisable given the present stage of development of international jurisprudence. There is little continuity among persons acting as arbitrators or judges, no appellate body to harmonize the decisions of ad hoc tribunals, not much of a rule of *stare decisis*, and indeed, considerable uncertainty—as compared to national jurisprudence—concerning the very content of the rules to be applied. In short, there is little to facilitate predictability. How, then, can states be "fairly certain" that an as yet unconstituted tribunal will vindicate their predictions?

It seems preferable to adopt a rule allowing a state to implement countermeasures without risk of later liability when it acts upon a good faith belief that it is the victim of a breach, even though that belief later turns out to be erroneous in light of the results of an arbitration. Good faith could be assessed in light of two sorts of considerations. The first, and probably most important, would be the seriousness of the arguments (though ultimately found unpersuasive) that the retaliating state had adduced in support of its position that the other state committed the prior breach: the closer the case on the issue of underlying breach, the stronger the case for a finding of good faith. The second would be indications of a sincere interest in achieving a prompt and fair resolution of the issue: willingness to consult or to seek third-party assistance through mediation, conciliation, or arbitration would count favorably in this regard.

In contrast, it would be appropriate to hold internationally responsible a retaliating state that advances an insubstantial legal theory concerning the other party's alleged breach, or (though it makes out a plausible but ultimately unavailing argument on underlying breach) that has engaged in dilatory behavior or unwarranted pressure tactics instead of serious efforts to resolve the dispute. Under this approach, states would be enjoined to proceed with caution and in moderation when reacting to a perceived breach, and would be held answerable for frivolous or abusive behavior, but would not be penalized for a good faith but mistaken prediction of the course of development of the law.[32]

---

[31] Harvard draft convention, *supra* note 30, 29 AJIL Supp. at 1095–96.

[32] As a variant on this approach, the Harvard draft approach could be used to enter a finding that retaliation "was not justified" in the absence of prior breach, but good faith would be taken into account in determining whether it would be appropriate for the retaliating party to pay reparation to the other party for any damage caused by the retaliatory acts.

There are, of course, some dangers in this approach. To the extent that it relaxes traditional standards for retaliatory breach, it runs some risk of encouraging (or at least failing to deter) conduct that deviates from solemnly agreed treaty norms. And, to this same extent, it at least arguably impairs the values promoted by the *pacta sunt servanda* rule. But, on the other hand, by stressing the need for a retaliating party to demonstrate its good faith in seeking to resolve the dispute, this approach may well promote resort to neutral dispute settlement mechanisms.

The tribunal in the U.S.-France dispute used language that supports the approach now under discussion (as contrasted with the Jessup or Harvard draft approaches), though it is not entirely clear that that is what the tribunal had in mind. Significantly, the tribunal seems to have separated the question of legality of countermeasures from the question of whether there was an underlying breach: it stated that it is "quite obvious that the lawfulness of the action [of the United States] must be considered regardless of the answer to the question of substance concerning the alleged violation of the 1946 Agreement by the French Government."[33] (The votes cast and separate opinion entered by the arbitrator of French nationality indicate that he had divorced the two questions in his analysis: he dissented from the finding in favor of the United States on the change-of-gauge question but voted for the United States on the question of the legality of the countermeasures.) Further, throughout the discussion of the justification for countermeasures, the tribunal consistently refers to the "alleged breach" or "alleged violation" as giving rise to the other party's right to take responsive action.[34] Finally, good faith seems to have been a highly significant factor in the tribunal's consideration: it appears to have given great weight both to the U.S. conviction that denial of the right to change gauge raised an issue of principle,[35] and to the U.S. good faith efforts to submit the dispute to arbitration and expedite the conclusion of the arbitral proceedings.[36]

The tribunal also devoted considerable attention to the question of whether it is legitimate to invoke countermeasures where there is a preexisting commitment to third-party dispute settlement, and concluded that the presence of an arbitration clause in the Agreement did not preclude the United States from implementing countermeasures during the period until the tribunal was constituted and in a position to indicate interim measures of

---

[33] Award, para. 74.

[34] Award, paras. 74 ("*alleged* violation"); 81 ("a situation . . . which, *in one State's* view, results in the violation of an international obligation by another State"); 82 ("the obligation *allegedly* breached," "the *alleged* violation"); 83 ("the *alleged* breach"); 84 ("a violation of international law *allegedly* committed by the State against which [the countermeasures] are directed") (emphasis added).

Cf. Case Concerning United States Diplomatic and Consular Staff in Tehran, Judgment of May 24, 1980, [1980] ICJ REP. 3, 27–28, *reprinted in* 74 AJIL 746 (1980) (United States countermeasures against Iran were taken "in response to what the United States *believed* to be grave and manifest violations of international law by Iran . . . [emphasis added]"). *But see id.* at 53–55, 63–65, dissenting opinions of JJ. Morozov and Tarazi, arguing that the United States should not have implemented countermeasures when it was looking to the Court for judicial relief.

[35] Award, paras. 77–78, 83, 90.   [36] Award, paras. 91–98.

protection.[37] It concluded that states cannot be deemed to have renounced their right to take countermeasures during the period before the case is submitted: rather, allowing countermeasures during this period "facilitates States' acceptance of arbitration or judicial settlement procedures."[38] In reaching this conclusion, the tribunal touched on the theme of the second half of this article: how the application of countermeasures during the interim period can affect the terms on which a case is submitted to arbitration.

II. RETALIATORY MEASURES AND SUBMISSION TO ARBITRATION

The tribunal's approach raises two interrelated issues. Can retaliation or the threat of retaliation facilitate previously agreed dispute settlement mechanisms, rather than subvert them? Should international law preclude states from resorting to self-help when third-party remedies are either available or pending?

Does Retaliation Undercut or Facilitate Arbitral Resolution?

France could hardly have refused to agree to "the principle of recourse to arbitration,"[39] with or without a U.S. threat of retaliation, since Article X of the Agreement as amended requires arbitration of "any dispute . . . relative to the interpretation or application of this Agreement . . . which cannot be settled through consultation."[40] An arbitration clause of this type, concluded in advance of any dispute at a time when the parties are presumably satisfied with the overall balance struck by the agreement, can greatly facilitate submission of future disputes to arbitration.

Conceivably, such a preexisting dispute settlement clause could be invoked for an abstract legal question of treaty interpretation, before disputed application causes injury to either party. International law scholars have advocated the use of declaratory judgment procedures as a means of preventing injury, and international tribunals have indicated that they believe resolution of this sort of question can under appropriate circumstances be consistent with their judicial function.[41]

Had an anticipatory declaratory judgment procedure been a realistic possibility, the U.S.-France treaty interpretation dispute concerning change of gauge might conceivably have been put to arbitration as early as March 1978, after the French authorities had stated their position that the Pan Am change-of-gauge service would violate the Agreement but before any injury

---

[37] Award, paras. 80, 84–99.   [38] Award, para. 95.

[39] France so agreed by diplomatic note on May 13, 1978, less than 10 days after the United States proposed binding and expedited arbitration and 4 days after the first part 213 order was entered. Award, para. 6.

[40] This provision took its present form when the Agreement was amended by exchange of notes in 1951. 2 UST 1033, TIAS No. 2257. *See* note 6 *supra.*

[41] *See* Borchard, *Declaratory Judgments in International Law*, 29 AJIL 488 (1935); *cf.* Case Concerning the Northern Cameroons (Cameroon v. United Kingdom) (Preliminary Objections), [1963] ICJ REP. 15, 37–38.

798   THE AMERICAN JOURNAL OF INTERNATIONAL LAW   [Vol. 74

had been inflicted.[42] However, the option of arbitrating an issue holds little appeal in the absence of significant injury, either actually incurred or very imminently threatened. Even if pride were not at stake in the risk of an adverse judgment, international arbitration costs the litigants money, and the preparation of the case requires a significant commitment of lawyers' time. It is not realistic to think that states will volunteer to arbitrate an issue unless they can see something tangible to be gained, such as monetary reparation or removal of an obstacle to enforcement of a right. Where injury is only a future possibility, perception of the likelihood of such a gain is not likely.

If only one party has been injured, the expectation of possible gain from arbitration is likely to be asymmetrical in the early stages of a treaty dispute. One party believes itself the victim of unlawful action; the other party enjoys the status quo and has little incentive to participate in facilitating an arbitration that might change that status quo. The aggrieved party can suggest that adjudication will help keep relations amicable; or it can point to a preexisting arbitration treaty or arbitration clause in the treaty in dispute; or, where appropriate, it can invoke the compulsory jurisdiction of the International Court of Justice. But since it is of course rare to find a tribunal already in place at the inception of the dispute with jurisdiction to change the status quo by entering and enforcing interim protective orders, the claimant state will almost always be at a severe disadvantage. It will need the respondent state's cooperation in proceeding to establish the tribunal that will have the authority to change the status quo.

In the U.S.-France dispute, no tribunal was in place. In fact, it was far from clear in May that the dispute would ever reach arbitration. France wanted to settle the dispute through *"négociation,"* which is the word used for "consultation" in the French text of Article X.[43] This insistence on

---

[42] *See* M. HUDSON, INTERNATIONAL TRIBUNALS 120 (1944); G. SCHWARZENBERGER, 1 INTERNATIONAL LAW 586 (1957) ("The fact that international awards and judgments may be of a declaratory character proves that legal interest in international law does not depend on the actual sufferance of damage. . . . [T]he mere danger of an infringement of international rights suffices for this purpose."); *compare* the views of the United States and the United Kingdom on the arbitrability of an incipient controversy over Panama Canal tolls, as set forth in G. HACKWORTH, 6 DIGEST OF INTERNATIONAL LAW 59 (1943). In the *Corfu Channel* case ([1949] ICJ REP. 35), a declaratory judgment was deemed to be appropriate satisfaction for the violation of Albania's sovereignty though Albania had suffered no injury. However, in the *Cameroons* case, the Court did emphasize that the Court

> may pronounce judgment only in connection with concrete cases where there exists at the time of the adjudication an actual controversy involving a conflict of legal interests between the parties. The Court's judgment must have some practical consequence in the sense that it can affect existing legal rights or obligations of the parties, thus removing uncertainty from their legal relations.

[1963] ICJ REP. 33–34. Thus, though consummated injury may not be a requirement for submission of a dispute to adjudication, a concrete controversy is.

[43] The French text of the relevant provision reads: "tout différend entre les Parties contractantes relatif à l'interprétation ou à l'application dudit Accord ou de son annexe qui ne pourrait être réglé par voie de négociations directes sera soumis pour avis consultatif à un Tribunal arbitral de trois membres. . . ."

négociation may well have been prompted in part by a sense that for proper jurisprudential reasons the parties should do everything possible to narrow the issues before submitting them to arbitration, and if possible resolve them.[44] But the United States feared that France might have had other motives: delay worked in favor of France since France benefited from the status quo as it had defined it when it barred the Pan Am service. By prolonging the status quo, perhaps France could induce the United States to "negotiate" a concession, particularly since Pan Am was losing valuable summer revenues each day that the change-of-gauge service was barred.

The United States was not inclined to negotiate a concession for a right that it believed it already enjoyed under the Agreement. Thus, upon finding that France had denied this right, the Civil Aeronautics Board began the part 213 process.[45]

One result of the U.S. action was that France had substantially more interest in a speedy resolution of the dispute than before the entry of the first part 213 order. Thus, the threat of retaliation served as a substitute for effective international judicial mechanisms to enforce a preexisting commitment to arbitrate. In arguing in favor of its part 213 action, the United States spoke of the measures as restoring the balance that had been upset when France unilaterally prevented the operation of the change-of-gauge service.

The part 213 action contributed to balance in another way, since it gave France a grievance as well. France, presumably, was convinced of the illegality of Pan Am's third-country change-of-gauge operation, just as the

---

[44] The jurisprudence of the International Court of Justice and its predecessor, the Permanent Court of International Justice, supports the proposition that in appropriate circumstances a case might even be dismissed if diplomatic consultations had not yet occurred. *See, e.g.,* Mavrommatis Palestine Concessions, [1924] PCIJ, ser. A., No. 2, at 15:

> The Court realises to the full the importance of the rule laying down that only disputes which cannot be settled by negotiation should be brought before it. It recognises, in fact, that before a dispute can be made the subject of an action at law, its subject matter should have been clearly defined by means of diplomatic negotiation.

And *see* dissenting opinion of Judges Spender and Fitzmaurice in the South West Africa Cases (Ethiopia v. South Africa; Liberia v. South Africa), [1962] ICJ REP. 310, 563:

> [R]equirements about "disputes" and "negotiations" are not mere technicalities. They appear in one form or another in virtually every adjudication clause that has ever been drafted, and for good reason. They are inserted purposely to protect the parties, so far as possible, from international litigation that is unnecessary, premature, inadequately motivated, or merely specious.

See also Bourquin, *Dans quelle mesure le recours à des négociations diplomatiques est-il nécessaire avant qu'un différend puisse être soumis à la juridiction internationale?,* in HOMMAGE D'UNE GÉNÉRATION DE JURISTES AU PRÉSIDENT BASDEVANT 43–55 (1960).

[45] The Board found

> that the Government of France has taken action which, over the objections of the United States Government, will impair, limit, terminate, and deny operating rights and deny the fair and equal opportunity of U.S. carriers to exercise the operating rights provided for in the United States-France Air Transport Services Agreement.

Order 78–5–45, *supra* note 7.

800   THE AMERICAN JOURNAL OF INTERNATIONAL LAW   [Vol. 74

United States was convinced of its legality. Neither side could deny that suspension of Air France's Paris-Los Angeles service would have been itself a violation of the Agreement, justifiable under international law only because it responded to an alleged prior breach. Because of France's conviction that it had committed no breach, it saw advantages in arbitrating the legality of the conduct of the United States, and indeed insisted that this question be submitted to the same tribunal that would decide the change-of-gauge issue.[46]

With the field of controversy thus expanded,[47] both sides had something to lose. Each side accordingly looked for ways to lower the risk to itself. Further escalation of retaliatory measures would not have achieved this purpose and might have been counterproductive. Rather, each side tried to find ways to remove from the tribunal's consideration the issue the other side insisted on submitting. France's technique was to claim that the change-of-gauge issue was not yet ripe for adjudication since Pan Am had not exhausted its local remedies in France.[48] The United States took the position that it was inappropriate to arbitrate the legality of threatened countermeasures because neither France nor its carriers had been injured by them,[49] because there was no live dispute after the Civil Aeronautics Board vacated its orders,[50] and because the parties had not had adequate consultations on the issue.[51] In the *compromis* of arbitration each side suc-

---

[46] Each side qualified its consent to arbitration with a reservation of the right to attempt to persuade the tribunal that it should not proceed to the merits of the question in which that party was defendant. *See infra,* notes 48–52 and accompanying text.

[47] Professor Arie David has shown that disputes over treaty termination have a tendency to expand laterally into other aspects of the parties' relationship, which raises the stakes involved in the resolution of the conflict. A. DAVID, THE STRATEGY OF TREATY TERMINATION: LAWFUL BREACHES AND RETALIATIONS (1975). His analysis of the pattern of lateral widening of treaty termination disputes can also be applied to cases of retaliation within a treaty framework. David has pointed out that the adjudicative process, in contrast to the retaliatory process, tends to limit and confine disputes, and thus is inconsistent with the lateral widening phenomenon he sees as usually essential to the resolution of treaty termination conflicts. For this reason, among others, he doubts the utility of adjudication in resolving vital disputes and relegates it to "matters of relatively minor importance." *Id.* at 186–89, 201.

[48] Pan Am had commenced an action in a French administrative tribunal to have set aside the decision denying it the right to operate the service with change of gauge. This action was still pending at the time the arbitral award was rendered.

France argued that the U.S. request for arbitration related essentially to a matter of diplomatic protection of one of its nationals, so that the international law rule of exhaustion should be observed. The United States noted, on the other hand, that the case was not one of espousal but rather of direct injury to the right of the United States to conduct air services through a designated carrier. The United States also argued that the exhaustion rule was waived by the arbitration provisions of the Agreement, and that there was in any event no effective remedy available in France. Though it did not adopt all the arguments made by the United States, the tribunal did rule in favor of the United States on this issue.

[49] *See* note 42 *supra.*

[50] The *Northern Cameroons* case, *supra* note 41, is an example of a dismissal due to the absence of a live controversy between the parties. The classic definition of an international dispute comes from *Mavrommatis Palestine Concessions*: "A dispute is a disagreement on a point of law or fact, a conflict of legal views or of interests between two persons." [1924] PCIJ, ser. A, No. 2, at 11.

[51] *See* note 44 *supra.*

ceeded in reserving the right to argue to the tribunal that the question in which it was defendant should not be answered at all.

The United States also presented a series of arguments on the merits aimed at avoiding a link between the two questions in the event of an adverse ruling on the first: that the U.S. part 213 action was not really a retaliatory breach but merely an unimplemented threat; and that the action was in any event justified, pending submission of the dispute to arbitration, in order to restore the balance upset by France's unilateral action.

Conceivably, the tribunal could have accepted each side's preliminary objections and dissolved itself without adjudicating the merits of either issue.[52] However, it proceeded to the merits on both. There are some hints that considerations of maintaining a balance played a role in the decision to answer both questions and to some extent in the anwers given.[53]

Interestingly, balance was also a major preoccupation of the parties in their negotiations over the terms of submitting the dispute to arbitration. In particular, the parties included in the *compromis* a provision on "interim arrangements that will maintain strict equality of balance between the position of the Government of the United States that Pan American World Airways should be permitted to change gauge during arbitration, and the position of the Government of France that it should not change gauge during this period."[54] The method adopted for maintaining this balance was to establish a fixed date (December 10, 1978) for the conclusion of the arbitral proceedings and to permit Pan Am to operate its change-of-gauge service on exactly one-half the days between the May 1 date of the commencement of the dispute and the expected December 10 date for its final resolution. Though this compromise achieved abstract balance, it was in fact of no benefit to Pan Am: the mid-July date of conclusion of the *compromis* came

[52] The tribunal noted the "request" of the two parties that it answer both questions posed by the *compromis* (Award, para. 22); but it barely acknowledged the express reservation by each party of the right to argue that the other's question should not be answered. Incidentally, there is precedent in international jurisprudence for an applicant party to raise preliminary objections going to jurisdiction or admissibility of a claim. *See* Monetary Gold Removed from Rome in 1943 (Preliminary Question), [1954] ICJ REP. 19, 28–29. In the *Cameroons* case, the Court stated that there may be "an incompatibility between the desires of an applicant, or, indeed, of both parties to a case, on the one hand, and on the other the duty of the Court to maintain its judicial character." [1963] ICJ REP. 29. *But see* Sohn, *The Function of International Arbitration Today*, 108 RECUEIL DES COURS 9, 24 (1963 I): "there are no disputes which by their nature are not suitable for arbitration. If the parties agree that a particular dispute should be submitted to an arbitral tribunal, that tribunal need not enquire whether that dispute is arbitrable."

[53] The French arbitrator in his separate opinion queried whether after the conclusion of the *compromis* France could still claim a sufficient legal interest to ask the second question. He noted, however, that he had answered this question with the tribunal "because a refusal of the Tribunal to answer that question would only have emphasized further an inequality between the Parties visible elsewhere." On the merits of the question, the tribunal noted in sustaining the legality of the U.S. action that the aim of countermeasures is "to *restore equality* between the Parties and to encourage them to continue negotiations with mutual desire to reach an acceptable solution. . . . [T]he United States counter-measures restore in a negative way the *symmetry* of the initial positions." Award, para. 90 (emphasis added).

[54] *Compromis*, para. 3.

too late for Pan Am to carry the summer travelers it had counted on
when it first planned the change-of-gauge service. Thus, even a "balanced"
interim regime turned out to favor the breaching party in the U.S.-France
dispute, despite the steps taken by the United States to counterbalance
France's unilateral action.

The balance metaphor, and the metaphor of first expanding a dispute
through the threat of retaliation and then limiting it for arbitral resolution,
both fit the U.S.-France dispute well. They lead to the tentative conclusion
that retaliation can serve a useful (though not always perfectly successful)
function in the dynamic process of attaining arbitral resolution of a dispute.

Should International Law Preclude Retaliation Pending Arbitration?

The critical legal issue raised by France on the relationship between
retaliation and arbitration is whether a preexisting commitment to arbitrate
—in this case the U.S. commitment rather than the French commitment
—requires a party to refrain from self-help measures pending the outcome
of the proceeding. France contended that resort to retaliatory measures
while negotiations were under way on the terms of the *compromis* of arbitration was not consistent with the assumption that both parties would fulfill
the arbitration commitment in good faith: the U.S. conduct both anticipated
the outcome of the arbitral award and presupposed that arbitration would
be ineffective in redressing the U.S. grievance. France further contended
that invocation of part 213 was an illegitimate application of pressure that
caused France to make concessions it would not otherwise have made on the
terms of the *compromis*.[55] The French position has particular appeal when
the alleged treaty violator believes in good faith that it has committed no
breach. In these circumstances a self-help retaliatory remedy can seem both
presumptuous and precipitous.[56]

---

[55] France claimed that the U.S. application of pressure forced it to make a series of concessions to which it would otherwise not have agreed. These were: (1) submission of the dispute
to arbitration before Pan Am had exhausted local remedies; (2) binding arbitration on the
change-of-gauge question but only an advisory report on the part 213 question; (3) an
expedited schedule for the arbitration; and (4) an interim regime permitting Pan Am to
perform the change-of-gauge operation for part of the period of time before the arbitral
award was to be rendered.

The United States argued in reply that each of the claimed French "concessions" was in fact
illusory. Exhaustion of local remedies was not, under international law, a prerequisite to
submission of this dispute to arbitration (and indeed the tribunal so held; Award, paras.
25–32). In the negotiations for the *compromis*, France never sought anything other than a
binding judgment on the first question and an advisory report on the second. The expedited
schedule for the arbitration and an interim regime permitting change of gauge on half of the
days from the inception of the dispute to the expected date of entry of the award maintained
legal equality of the parties (though in fact, as noted above, text at note 54, Pan Am derived
no benefit from this "equal" arrangement).

[56] *See, e.g.*, the dispute between the United States and the Netherlands during 1974 and
1975, discussed in Lowenfeld, *CAB v. KLM: Bermuda at Bay*, 1 AIR L. 2 (1975–76). In that case,
the United States adopted a new interpretation of a standard clause as a predicate to retaliation,
in circumstances where an arbitral tribunal might well not have ruled in its favor. *See also* H. A.
WASSENBERGH, PUBLIC INTERNATIONAL AIR TRANSPORTATION LAW IN A NEW ERA 110 (1976).

The French position on abstention from retaliation pending arbitration has respectable scholarly authority to support it.[57] In 1934 the Institute of International Law took the position that acts of reprisal are illegal where there is a previously agreed provision between the parties for peaceful settlement of disputes.[58] More recently, Roberto Ago asserted this proposition (citing the Institute's resolution as authority) in a report to the International Law Commission on state responsibility,[59] and the Commission itself appears to have accepted the concept, without analyzing its implications.[60] The concept also draws support from its consistency with the concept that pending arbitration or adjudication states should take no steps to aggravate or extend the dispute; this concept has been developed in International Court rulings on applications for interim protective orders,[61] and some commentators have argued that it constitutes a legal obligation of all states that have made commitments to resolve disputes through third-party methods.[62]

The United States, on the other hand, had argued to the tribunal that the

---

[57] The French based their argument on the proposition that acts of reprisal are not justified where satisfaction can be obtained by other means. As authority they cited the *Naulilaa* arbitration, 2 R. Int'l Arb. Awards 1026-28, and other authorities on the customary international law of reprisals. Arbitration, in the French view, was a means of obtaining satisfaction which should have been exhausted first.

[58] Article 5 of the Institute's resolution read in pertinent part:

> Les représailles même non armeés sont interdites quand le respect du droit peut être effectivement assuré par des procédures de règlement pacifique.
>
> En conséquence, elles doivent être considerées comme interdites notamment:
>
> 1. Lorsqu'en vertu du droit en vigueur entre les parties, l'acte dénoncé comme illicite est de la compétence obligatoire de juges ou d'arbitres ayant compétence aussi pour ordonner, avec la diligence voulue, des mesures provisoires ou conservatoires et que l'Etat défendeur ne cherche pas à éluder cette juridiction ou à en retarder le fonctionnement;
>
> 2. Lorsqu'une procédure de règlement pacifique est en cours, dans les conditions envisagées au 1. . . .

INSTITUT DE DROIT INTERNATIONAL, 38 ANNUAIRE 709 (1934). *See also* 3 RÉPERTOIRE SUISSE DE DROIT INTERNATIONAL PUBLIC 1788 (1975): "La conclusion des traités stipulant l'arbitrage obligatoire pour les différends juridiques exclura les représailles. En effet, on imagine mal des cas où l'autre Etat n'accepterait pas la procédure prévue." The same view is also advocated in Bowett, *Economic Coercion and Reprisals by States*, 13 VA. J. INT'L. 1 (1972); and in E. DUMBAULD, INTERIM MEASURES OF PROTECTION IN INTERNATIONAL CONTROVERSIES 182-84 (1932).

[59] UN Doc. A/CN.4/318/Add.3, at n.15 (Feb. 5, 1979) ("An additional condition [for the legality of reprisals], referred to in article 5 of the Resolution of 1934 of the Institute of International Law, would be that there must not be any provision previously agreed between the parties for peaceful settlement . . .").

[60] Report of the International Law Commission on the Work of its Thirty-first Session, 34 UN GAOR, Supp. (No. 10), UN Doc. A/34/10, at 319 n.579 (1979) ("An additional condition is that there must not be any procedures for peaceful settlement previously agreed upon by the parties").

[61] Electricity Co. of Sofia & Bulgaria, [1939] PCIJ, ser. A/B, No. 79, at 199; Anglo-Iranian Oil Co., [1951] ICJ REP. 89, 93; Case Concerning United States Diplomatic and Consular Staff in Tehran (Order), [1979] ICJ REP. 7, 21, *reprinted in* 74 AJIL 266 (1980), 19 ILM 139 (1980).

[62] *See* E. DUMBAULD, *supra* note 58.

concept of abstention pending arbitration finds no support in state practice and thus has not found its way into the corpus of customary international law, that states must be able to take the steps necessary to preserve their rights and restore the balance of equities before a tribunal is in a position to act, and that (as discussed above) measures such as those taken by the United States can help ensure that the other party's commitment to arbitration is enforced and implemented in a practical, meaningful way.

It is worth considering how this problem will be handled under the Vienna Convention on the Law of Treaties (for the states that are parties and for treaties concluded after the effective date of the convention,[63] since the article in question is apparently not a codification of customary international law). Article 65 of the convention establishes procedures for the termination or suspension of a treaty in the event of breach.[64] A party alleging grounds for termination or suspension, including breach, must notify these grounds to the other party and indicate the responsive measures it proposes to take. Except in cases of special urgency, it may take these measures only after 3 months have elapsed without objection to the proposed response. In the event of objection, the parties are to seek a solution through the means indicated in Article 33 of the United Nations Charter, which, of course, can include arbitration or adjudication.

Apparently, the drafters of the convention intended to limit the sanction of retaliatory suspension of treaty rights within the 3-month period to very urgent cases,[65] but they did not indicate any intent to preclude such measures after this period but before the completion of arbitral or ad-

---

[63] Article 4 of the convention provides:

> Without prejudice to the application of any rules set forth in the present Convention to which treaties would be subject under international law independently of the Convention, the Convention applies only to treaties which are concluded by States after the entry into force of the present Convention with regard to such States.

[64] The relevant provisions of Article 65 read:

> 1. A party which, under the provisions of the present Convention, invokes . . . a ground for impeaching the validity of a treaty, terminating it, withdrawing from it or suspending its operation, must notify the other parties of its claim. The notification shall indicate the measure proposed to be taken with respect to the treaty and the reasons therefor.

> 2. If, after the expiry of a period which, except in cases of special urgency, shall not be less than three months after the receipt of the notification, no party has raised any objection, the party making the notification may carry out . . . the measure which it has proposed.

> 3. If, however, objection has been raised by any other party, the parties shall seek a solution through the means indicated in Article 33 of the Charter of the United Nations.

> 4. Nothing in the foregoing paragraphs shall affect the rights or obligations of the parties under any provisions in force binding the parties with regard to the settlement of disputes.

[65] In light of the argument made in the text at notes 19–20 *supra,* that the convention was not intended to cover countermeasures for nonmaterial breaches, the Article 65 procedure would presumably not apply to such cases. Rather, by virtue of Article 4 (*supra* note 63) and Article 65, paragraph 1 (*supra* note 64), the rules of customary international law would govern.

judicatory procedures.[66] As the United States commented on the International Law Commission's draft that became Article 65, "there is nothing in [this article] which prohibits the claimant party from terminating or withdrawing from the treaty while one or more of the procedures under Article 33 of the Charter are carried out."[67]

Presumably, states becoming parties to the Vienna Convention and concluding treaties after its entry into force can reserve the right in future treaties to terminate or suspend without waiting 3 months if they believe that course will better suit their purposes. But for those states, like the United States, that are not yet parties, the question is whether customary international law does or should constrain their flexibility to act when they have entered into a prior agreement to submit disputes to third-party resolution. The authorities noted above would say that there is such a constraint. But the inherent flaw in this position is obvious from a recent and vivid example.

On November 4, 1979, in flagrant violation of its obligations under customary international law and four international agreements, each of which has a binding dispute settlement clause, the Government of Iran acquiesced in the takeover of the United States Embassy in Tehran and the seizure of 63 hostages by a group of militant students. On November 14, 1979, the United States ordered the blocking of all assets of the Iranian Government in the United States or held by persons subject to the jurisdiction of the United States.[68] The blocking order, though it had additional motivations and legal justifications, can be characterized under international law as a legitimate response by the United States to Iran's manifest violations of its treaty obligations.

Can it plausibly be argued—as the literal wording of the Institute of International Law's 1934 resolution and other authorities noted above seem to contemplate—that the United States should have refrained from any retaliatory response until after dispute settlement proceedings were exhausted? It is true that on November 29, 1979, the United States filed an application with the International Court of Justice for an adjudication of Iran's international responsibility; and on December 15, 1979, the Court ordered provisional measures of protection at the request of the United States—an order Iran flouted.[69] But even if the Court had had the power to enforce its interim order, the entry of the order came 17 days after the U.S. request for interim relief and 41 days after the commencement of the crisis. Surely the United States did not have to initiate an adjudicatory proceeding and wait for an order to be entered and flouted before it could implement responsive and proportional countermeasures. The Iran

---

[66] The International Law Commission considered more restrictive formulations, but concluded that the article as drafted "represented the highest measure of common ground·that could be found among Governments as well as in the Commission on this question." 21 UN GAOR, Supp. (No. 9), UN Doc. A/6309/Rev.1 (1966), *reprinted in* [1966] 2 Y.B. INT'L L. COMM'N 169, 262.

[67] UN Doc. A/6827/Add.2 (1967), *reprinted in* 62 AJIL 567, 574 (1968).

[68] Exec. Order No. 12170, 44 Fed. Reg. 65,729 (1979), *reprinted in* 74 AJIL 428 (1980).

[69] [1979] ICJ REP. 7; *see also* [1980] ICJ REP. 3.

806 THE AMERICAN JOURNAL OF INTERNATIONAL LAW [Vol. 74

example also makes clear that a dispute settlement clause in a treaty that codifies obligations under customary international law should not be regarded as depriving an aggrieved party of its customary international law remedy, retaliatory sanctions.[70]

It is true that the U.S.-Iranian example would probably be considered a "case of special urgency," both under the Vienna Convention and under any customary international rule that might otherwise restrict the victim state's freedom of movement. But other illustrations can also prove the point. Suppose the initial breach does not threaten life or otherwise fall within "extreme urgency," but suppose further that there is no plausible legal justification for the breaching party's conduct. Should the victim state be disadvantaged because it has previously signed a dispute settlement agreement? Must it embark on lengthy and expensive litigation pursuant to that agreement to obtain authorization to suspend its performance in response to the breach? Surely not.

Even where good faith arguments can be made both for and against the existence of a prior breach, the better rule seems to be to permit appropriate, *i.e.*, measured and proportional, self-help measures *pendente lite*, as was done in the U.S.-France case. The dynamics of that case disprove rather than prove the validity of the arguments for a rule constraining the victim state's action. Though the United States did not argue, and the tribunal did not imply, that France might otherwise have failed to live up to its obligation to arbitrate in good faith, the tribunal was persuaded that the U.S. action had a facilitating effect in seeing that the dispute was resolved by arbitration.[71]

The right to retaliate pending arbitration, though important, should not be unqualified. The tribunal in the U.S.-France dispute, while approving the U.S. action during the period before the tribunal came into existence, stated that the "situation changes once the tribunal is in a position to act. To the extent that the tribunal has the necessary means to achieve the objectives justifying the counter-measures, it must be admitted that the right of the Parties to initiate such measures disappears."[72] Furthermore, a qualification implicit in any justification of retaliation is that a responsive countermeasure must be proportional and must cease either when its purpose is achieved or when its continuation would be inconsistent with actions of a functioning tribunal.[73] Another situation at least arguably calling for abstention from retaliatory acts exists when a multilateral treaty establishes an effective

[70] Of course, the U.S.-France Air Transport Services Agreement did not in any respect codify customary international law. However, the distinction between treaties codifying customary international law and treaties *de lege ferenda* has not been made either by the French in their pleadings before the tribunal or in any of the commentary on the question of countermeasures for breach of treaty.

[71] *See* text at note 38 *supra*.   [72] Award, para. 96.

[73] Other qualifications can also be suggested. The United States recently took the position before the International Court that reprisals against the person of diplomats are always unlawful: even if a receiving state believes a diplomat has acted contrary to the sending state's obligations under the Vienna Convention on Diplomatic Relations, it can only expel the diplomat and cannot retaliate by suspending the convention's rules on diplomatic inviolability.

framework for authorizing and legitimizing retaliation as a sanction for breach. Under Article XXIII of the General Agreement on Tariffs and Trade,[74] for example, if one party considers that another party has not carried out its obligations, it may seek authorization from the contracting parties (acting collectively) to suspend the application of equivalent obligations. As a general matter, however, the existence of a dispute settlement clause in a treaty should not require abstention from retaliation during the period before the victim party can obtain satisfaction from a tribunal.

III. CONCLUSION

Under traditional doctrine, the legality of a retaliatory breach of treaty is judged by whether it is a proportional response to a prior material breach. Commentators have also suggested that states should refrain from implementing countermeasures until a tribunal rules on the existence of a breach, at least when there is a preexisting commitment to third-party dispute settlement.

But the experience of states must prove or disprove the soundness of propositions urged in legal debate. The actions of the United States and France, and the judgment of the tribunal they created, suggest refinement or reexamination of some of the views put forth in legal literature. Proportionality might appropriately be judged on a flexible scale, with considerations of principle and of impact on the thinking of third countries as factors in the equation. Materiality of breach may not be relevant at all. Indeed, under some circumstances a responsive breach might be justified even absent a prior breach, if the responding party believes in good faith that a breach has occurred. Finally, since the interplay and even escalation of responses before a dispute reaches a tribunal can serve important purposes, that dynamic process should not be stifled by a blanket rule of abstention from self-help measures pending arbitration.

The U.S.-France dispute, as disputes go, was well suited for arbitral resolution. The dispute became concrete on May 1, 1978 and was fully resolved by December 9 of the same year. Of course, it is impossible to, speculate on what the timing of resolution might have been if the United States had been precluded from implementing countermeasures pending arbitration. Perhaps the best way to handle that question is not to appear to encourage retaliatory responses, but rather to urge the adoption in advance of procedures for the prompt submission of disputes to tribunals which can be convened and which can act on an expedited timetable. When such procedures are in place on a wider basis, states will have less reason to resort to self-help measures.

---

[74] 61 Stat. pts. (5) and (6), TIAS No. 1700. Article XXIII was amended by the Protocol Amending the Preamble and Parts II and III of the GATT, 8 UST 1767, 1787, TIAS No. 3930.

[10]

THE NATURE OF THE IRAN–UNITED STATES CLAIMS TRIBUNAL AND THE EVOLVING STRUCTURE OF INTERNATIONAL DISPUTE RESOLUTION

*By David D. Caron**

The Iran–United States Claims Tribunal[1] has been called "the most significant arbitral body in history";[2] its awards, "a gold mine of information for perceptive lawyers."[3] In a recent international commercial arbitration, however, an arbitrator reportedly stated that decisions of the Tribunal, although on point, were not persuasive because the Tribunal, after all, involves a special type of arbitration. This arbitrator is not alone. A lecturer at the Hague Academy of International Law, speaking on international commercial arbitration, reportedly did not refer to the Tribunal's jurisprudence because he did not find it relevant to his work for the same reason. Viewed as a gigantic experiment in international dispute resolution rather than merely a claims settlement device for this particular group of disputes, the Tribunal thus appears (at least to some) to yield decisions of unclear precedential value. Millions of dollars have been spent on its operation and hundreds of awards rendered, yet an apparently not uncommon perception is that the work of this, in some respects unique, institution is not applicable elsewhere.

* Acting Professor of Law, University of California at Berkeley. Formerly Legal Assistant to Charles N. Brower and Richard M. Mosk, Members, Iran–United States Claims Tribunal. The author wishes to thank George H. Aldrich, Charles N. Brower, Richard M. Buxbaum, John R. Crook, David Feller, Richard M. Mosk, Stefan A. Riesenfeld, Stephen M. Schwebel, Peter D. Trooboff, Albert Jan van den Berg, Jan Vetter and Joachim Zekoll for their comments. He also thanks Joseph Giansiracusa, J.D. Boalt Hall, '89, for his able research assistance.

[1] The Iran–United States Claims Tribunal was established in 1981 pursuant to the Declaration of the Government of the Democratic and Popular Republic of Algeria (hereinafter General Declaration) and the Declaration of the Government of the Democratic and Popular Republic of Algeria concerning the Settlement of Claims by the Government of the United States of America and the Government of the Islamic Republic of Iran (hereinafter Claims Settlement Declaration), collectively referred to as the Algiers Accords. For the text of the Accords, see 1 IRAN–UNITED STATES CLAIMS TRIBUNAL REPORTS [hereinafter IRAN–U.S. C.T.R.] 3 (1981–2), 75 AJIL 418 (1981). As to citation of awards by the Tribunal, see note 123 *infra*.

As to the Tribunal, see generally Brower & Davis, *The Iran–United States Claims Tribunal After Seven Years: A Retrospective View from the Inside*, 43 ARB. J. 16 (1988); THE IRAN–UNITED STATES CLAIMS TRIBUNAL 1981–1983 (R. Lillich ed. 1984) [hereinafter IRAN–UNITED STATES TRIBUNAL]; Stewart, *The Iran–United States Claims Tribunal: A Review of Developments 1983–84*, 16 L. & POL'Y INT'L BUS. 677 (1984); and Selby & Stewart, *Practical Aspects of Arbitrating Claims Before the Iran–United States Claims Tribunal*, 18 INT'L LAW. 211 (1984).

[2] Lillich, *Preface to* THE IRAN–UNITED STATES CLAIMS TRIBUNAL, *supra* note 1, at vii.

[3] Holtzmann, *Some Lessons of the Iran–United States Claims Tribunal*, in 1988 PRIVATE INVESTORS ABROAD—PROBLEMS AND SOLUTIONS IN INTERNATIONAL BUSINESS 16-5 (J. Moss ed.). Indeed, decisions of the Tribunal are cited in a number of Reporters' Notes to the *Restatement (Third) of the Foreign Relations Law of the United States* (1987).

In one sense, the doubt about the relevance of the Tribunal's work reflects a more fundamental uncertainty about the proper place of the Tribunal and its work within traditional categories of international dispute resolution.[4] Like any truly nagging question, that fundamental uncertainty comes to be phrased in various ways. A phrasing frequently used by scholars inquires into the "nature" of the Tribunal.[5] The assumption apparently underlying this question is that there are basically two distinct types of international arbitration:[6] interstate arbitration such as the *Beagle Channel*

[4] A complete discussion of the precedential value that should be given the work of the Tribunal would have several dimensions. The Tribunal's work is potentially significant for various reasons: it is the first major claims tribunal since the interwar period; its orders, awards and much of its workings are open to public (hence scholarly) examination; its docket of approximately 3,850 cases involves issues such as exchange-control regulation, expropriation and expulsion; and it is conducting its work in general in accordance with the UNCITRAL Arbitration Rules (*see infra* notes 26 and 110). This potential significance has been challenged on the ground that combative arbitrators have politicized both the procedural and the substantive decisions of the Tribunal. *See also* M. SORNARAJAH, THE PURSUIT OF NATIONALIZED PROPERTY 202 (1986) ("the jurisprudential value of the awards . . . [is] open to doubt on the ground that they were based on an agreement settling a political dispute and that there was an effort made by the Tribunal to approach issues in a manner favouring compromise"). The significance has also been challenged on the ground that the third-country chairmen have all been drawn from Western countries and thus bring with them the jurisprudential predispositions of their cultures. Both of these challenges are beyond the scope of this article and deserve a separate, extended response. To state my views briefly, however, I do not believe either objection stands up to scrutiny or is substantial. As to the former, I believe the combativeness of the Iranian arbitrators did not politicize substantive decisions, although it is true that, procedurally, extensions of time were more frequently granted to the Iranian parties than many U.S. claimants would have desired. The ingenuity of the Iranians, if anything, only tested and pushed at every aspect of the UNCITRAL Rules. The Tribunal met such tests and, in my opinion, has shown the workability and value of the Rules. On the Tribunal's work in one area of arbitral procedure, see Caron, *Interim Measures of Protection: Theory and Practice in Light of the Iran–United States Claims Tribunal*, 46 ZEITSCHRIFT FÜR AUSLÄNDISCHES ÖFFENTLICHES RECHT UND VÖLKERRECHT 465 (1986).

As to the latter objection, the third-country arbitrators have come from Western countries (two Swedes, two Frenchmen, one Swiss, one Dutchman, one German, one Italian and one Finn), but Iran (or arbitrators appointed by Iran) agreed to the selection of seven of the nine. More importantly, the charge of Western bias is directed really at only one, albeit emotional, issue—expropriation. Even then, the issue in controversy is not what constitutes a taking or whether compensation is due for a taking, but the appropriate standard for determining the amount of compensation.

As the precedential value of an international decision should turn upon its persuasiveness to the next panel, the challenge posed by the uncertainty about the nature of the Tribunal is subtle and indirect. I would speculate that the reluctance of some private international arbitrators to rely on the Tribunal's decisions reflects their intuitive conclusion that the Tribunal involves the classic interstate arbitral process *and* the further intuitive conclusion that the process is therefore particularly politicized. In this sense, a complete discussion of the precedential value of Tribunal awards will require further examination of the challenges to the integrity of the process described above.

[5] *See, e.g., Decisions of the Iran–United States Claims Tribunal*, Remarks of David Lloyd Jones, 78 ASIL PROC. 225, 226 (1984).

[6] During the preparation of this study, I generally found the distinction between public and private international arbitration to be held quite strongly, particularly among civil law scholars accustomed to a more systematic approach to law. Many scholars who stood by it were not altogether sure precisely what factors made an arbitration interstate rather than private, or

arbitration between Chile and Argentina[7] (sometimes referred to here as public international arbitration); and international commercial arbitration such as proceedings between private companies before the International Chamber of Commerce (ICC) (sometimes more broadly referred to here as private international arbitration).[8] Practitioners often regard the inquiry into the nature of the process as irrelevant to lawyering until it is pointed out that many practical questions, such as the enforceability of an award and the ability to challenge an award, turn upon the answer.

As discussed more fully below, a simple inquiry into the legal "nature" of an international arbitral process is too undefined because any one of several aspects could be emphasized. This article in particular examines the relationship of the international legal system and the various municipal legal systems to the arbitrations before the Tribunal, and, in doing so, discusses more broadly the evolving structure of international dispute resolution. I am not concerned here with what *law* the arbitrators might apply *within* the Tribunal, but rather with the positions that will be taken under various *legal systems* on the validity and enforceability of the Tribunal's arbitral awards.

Since practical consequences such as enforceability and recognition can turn upon the nature of an arbitration, it may not be surprising that the Islamic Republic of Iran and the United States have disagreed over which legal system governs the validity of arbitrations before the Tribunal. Indeed, they have disagreed even as to who the parties are for many of the arbitrations.[9] But it is not only the two state parties that have expressed differing views. Advocates as well as scholars have taken a variety of positions on the characterization issue. The Dutch Government proposed legislation in 1984 that would provide clearly for the Dutch legal system to review the validity of the arbitral process.[10] Yet a British judge has stated that "the Dutch Courts would probably . . . wholly decline to recognize the validity in Dutch law of [such] arbitration proceedings" and would therefore declare such proceedings a "nullity."[11] Meanwhile, the United States Court of Appeals for the Ninth Circuit recently affirmed a district court ruling that the New York Convention on the Recognition and Enforcement

---

what insights were gained by the distinction. For many, their intuitive judgment was that arbitrations before the Tribunal have an interstate nature. Another response, reflecting the difficulty of the question more than an answer, was to say that the arbitrations are of a "mixed" or "hybrid" nature.

[7] Argentine-Chile Frontier Case, 16 R. Int'l Arb. Awards 109 (1966) (McNair, Kirwan & Papworth arbs.).

[8] The term "private international arbitration" is used in this article to encompass international commercial arbitration, maritime arbitration and other similar manifestations of private arbitration. On the ICC, see W. CRAIG, W. PARK & J. PAULSSON, INTERNATIONAL CHAMBER OF COMMERCE ARBITRATION (1983). *See generally* Stein & Wotman, *International Commercial Arbitration in the 1980s: A Comparison of the Major Arbitral Systems and Rules*, 38 BUS. LAW. 1685 (1983).

[9] *See infra* text at notes 122–52.   [10] *See infra* text at notes 178–86.

[11] Mark Dallal v. Bank Mellat, [1986] 1 Q.B. 441, 2 W.L.R. 745, 1 All E.R. 239, *noted in* Fin. Times (London), Aug. 21, 1985, at 25, col. 1. *See also* Kunzlik, *Public International Law—Cannot Govern a Contract, Can Authorise An Arbitration*, 45 CAMBRIDGE L.J. 377 (1986).

of Foreign Arbitral Awards "certainly is applicable" to awards rendered by the Tribunal.[12] One Dutch commentator has concluded that its proceedings are not "arbitration" as understood under Dutch law,[13] while another Dutchman has reached the opposite conclusion.[14] Two American lawyers have together argued that the arbitrations are "a-national,"[15] while another, the late Professor Ted Stein, stated that "[t]he *lex fori* of the Tribunal is public international law."[16] Finally, Lady Hazel Fox recently wrote that the Tribunal is the latest example of how "a private party may . . . have its private claims taken up by the State and presented through an interstate arbitration."[17] In short, virtually every possible position on the "nature" of the Tribunal's arbitrations has been put forward.

The analysis of the Tribunal's nature remains incomplete, not from a lack of attention or concern, but because the positions taken tend to rest on intuition supported only by analogies. For example, one position is that the Tribunal, like the International Court of Justice, was established by treaty and that the work of the Tribunal, like that of the Court, therefore has an interstate character. Moreover, the use of undefined terms such as "a-national," "denationalized" and "de-localized," and unclear distinctions such as that between interstate and international commercial arbitration, further confuse the discussion. Consequently, determining the significance of the Tribunal's work requires not only that we examine the Tribunal itself, but also that we understand the larger context and clarify what it means to distinguish between interstate and international commercial arbitration.

Part I introduces the international arbitral process and probes the weakness of the categorical distinction made between interstate and international commercial arbitration. I conclude that the issue is not whether an arbitration has this or that character, as if there existed distinct pigeonholes dictating such an approach. Rather, the proper inquiry should focus on what the parties intended the arbitration to be and what principles of construction should be applied in order to ascertain this intent.

---

[12] Ministry of Defense of Islamic Republic of Iran v. Gould, Inc., 887 F.2d 1357 (9th Cir. 1989). On the district court order of Judge R. A. Gadbois, Jr., No. 87-03673 (C.D. Cal. Jan. 14, 1988), see Lewis, *What Goes Around Comes Around: Can Iran Enforce Awards of the Iran-U.S. Claims Tribunal in the United States?*, 26 COLUM. J. TRANSNAT'L L. 515, 517 n.14 (1988).

[13] Hardenberg, *The Awards of the Iran-US Claims Tribunal Seen in Connection with the Law of the Netherlands*, 1984 INT'L BUS. LAW. 337, *translated from De Uitspraken van het Iran–United States Claims Tribunal naar Nederlands recht bezian*, NEDERLANDS JURISTENBLAD, Feb. 11, 1984, at 167.

[14] Van den Berg, *Proposed Dutch Law on the Iran–United States Claims Settlement Declaration, A Reaction to Mr. Hardenberg's Article*, 1984 INT'L BUS. LAW. 341, *translated from Wetsontwerp Iran–United States Claims Tribunal, Een reactie*, NEDERLANDS JURISTENBLAD, Feb. 11, 1984, at 170.

[15] Lake & Dana, *Judicial Review of Awards of the Iran–United States Claims Tribunal: Are the Tribunal's Awards Dutch?*, 16 L. & POL'Y INT'L BUS. 755 (1984).

[16] Stein, *Jurisprudence and Jurists' Prudence: The Iranian-Forum Clause Decisions of the Iran–United States Claims Tribunal*, 78 AJIL 1, 18 (1984). The thrust of the section that contains this quote, however, is that interpretation of the Algiers Accords is a question of public international law.

[17] Fox, *States and the Undertaking to Arbitrate*, 37 INT'L & COMP. L.Q. 1, 3 (1988).

Part II applies the conclusions of part I to the Iran–United States Claims Tribunal and concludes that Iran and the United States intended that the Dutch legal system govern the validity of the arbitral process and that the awards of the Tribunal be enforceable as Dutch awards. Moreover, so far as the Netherlands is concerned, the process likely is so governed. The significance of this conclusion also is examined. In particular, I do not believe that the decision to create the Iran-U.S. Claims Tribunal foreshadows a wave of such tribunals. The trend in this century has been to replace claims tribunals with lump sum settlements. Although the Iran-U.S. Claims Tribunal demonstrates that circumstances still may yield a tribunal, the trend likely will continue.[18] The significance lies rather in the choice of Iran and the United States to have the Dutch legal system review the validity of the arbitrations. That choice reflects the inadequacy of merely distinguishing between interstate and international commercial arbitration to describe the complexities emerging in practice.

In part III, I speculate on what the nature of the Tribunal's work suggests about the way the structure of international dispute resolution evolves and the significance one means of dispute resolution may have for another. A growing body of literature points to the importance for international law and theories of world legal order of understanding the interrelationships between public and private international law.[19] Examination of the legal character of the Tribunal's work necessarily touches on some aspects of these relationships and illuminates the richness and variety in the international resolution of disputes. Part III posits that the various private, state and interstate mechanisms for the resolution of international disputes have developed in response to the needs of the parties and of the community controlling the mechanisms; that these mechanisms do not operate in isolation but, rather, compete with, and evolve in response to, one another; and that the choices of parties as to the most appropriate mechanism for settling their disputes have led the entire system of dispute resolution to evolve toward greater efficiency and effectiveness.

I. MOVING BEYOND THE DISTINCTION BETWEEN INTERSTATE AND INTERNATIONAL COMMERCIAL ARBITRATION

There are various dimensions within which one might analyze, and hence explore the nature of, a dispute resolution process. Consequently, the focus

---

[18] In the case of the Tribunal, the circumstances were disagreement as to a lump sum settlement amount, coupled with the urgent need to conclude the Accords.

On the general trend toward lump sum settlement, see R. LILLICH & B. WESTON, INTERNATIONAL CLAIMS: THEIR SETTLEMENT BY LUMP SUM AGREEMENTS (1975); and Lillich & Weston, *Lump Sum Agreements: Their Continuing Contribution to the Law of International Claims*, 82 AJIL 69 (1988).

[19] *See, e.g.*, Buxbaum, *The Role of Public International Law in International Business Transactions*, in PUBLIC INTERNATIONAL LAW AND THE FUTURE WORLD ORDER, LIBER AMICORUM IN HONOR OF A. J. THOMAS, JR. 16-1 (J. J. Norton ed. 1987); *Academic Workshop: Should We Continue to Distinguish Between Public and Private International Law?*, 79 ASIL PROC. 352 (1985); and Paul, *The Isolation of Private International Law*, 7 WIS. INT'L L.J. 149 (1988).

of this article should be clear. For example, although all international arbitration rests upon the *consent* of the parties, the point in time relative to the dispute when consent is given, and the scope of that consent, may vary considerably. If consent is the focus, an international court and an ad hoc interstate arbitration can be said to involve the same process. These forums differ, however, as to *party control* over the process, whether that control involves the selection of decision makers or agreement on rules of procedure. This article focuses on two other aspects of the international arbitral process. First, how is the legitimacy or, more relatively, the validity of the arbitral process to be determined? Second, how is the result of the arbitral process to be enforced?[20] Party control is an *internal* aspect of the arbitral process. Validity and enforcement can be viewed as involving the evaluation of different legal systems of the *external* effects to be given the process.

The world internal to an arbitral process is created by the parties. Indeed, municipal arbitration in most countries can be seen simply as an aspect of contract law: the parties to a contract, in this instance an agreement to arbitrate, agree jointly to establish their own means for resolving disputes between them.[21] Similarly, interstate arbitration and private international arbitration are created and defined by the joint will of the parties. In many cases the parties will cooperate in the arbitral proceedings and voluntarily comply with the award. When the parties cooperate in this way, the private arrangement is autonomous in that no legal system need be involved.[22] Such an arbitration is a world unto itself. In any arbitration that is not so ideally cooperative, however, many legal systems may become involved. Generally, they will be those that one or both of the parties or the tribunal invokes. Regardless of whether a legal system becomes involved, however, there will remain a contractual world internal to the arbitration defined by the will of the parties, as that intent is interpreted by the arbitrators.[23]

---

[20] Although one's conclusions regarding the validity of a given arbitral process will often correlate with those regarding enforcement, they need not do so. See discussion on ICSID in text at notes 34–38 *infra*.

[21] Parties are motivated to enter into such arrangements municipally because they perceive the process as more likely to be subject to their control and, perhaps, as faster, less expensive and more confidential than that available in the courts. The key legal issue concerns what external limits the relevant municipal legal system places on the freedom of the parties to contract in this way.

[22] Although such autonomy obtains in most municipal legal systems, it is characteristic of municipal arbitration statutes in many Latin American states that even if the parties include a compromissory clause in a contract, the initiation of arbitration must be reviewed and approved by a municipal court. *See* Garro, *Enforcement of Arbitration Agreements and Jurisdiction of Arbitral Tribunals in Latin America*, 1 J. INT'L ARB. 293, 310–15 (1984).

[23] The parties, in defining the internal world, may make three significant choices regarding "law." First, the parties may designate the law under which the dispute will be decided. Second, the parties may designate the legal system that supervises the arbitral process. Note that it is *essential* to distinguish between the *legal system* governing the arbitration as a process and the *law* applied by the arbitrators to the substance of the dispute to be resolved. Confusion over this distinction is often engendered by the common reference to the legal system governing the arbitration as "the law applicable to the arbitration." Third, the parties may also stipulate the rules of procedure to be used by the tribunal by choosing the procedural law of a state, or, as is

The relationship of the arbitration to the world external to it is governed by a particular legal system, the identity of which depends on the particular relationship in question.[24] The most important relationships between an arbitration and the world external to it arise when a party attempts to have the arbitration agreement enforced, and any resulting award recognized, set aside or enforced. Knowledgeable parties will draft their arbitration agreement and later structure the proceedings so as to ensure that both the agreement and the award will be valid and enforceable.[25] Consequently, the internal and external worlds of an arbitration become intertwined because the designers of the former must anticipate the dictates of the latter.[26]

Although interstate arbitration and international commercial arbitration are thus conceptually similar, there are obvious distinctions between them. They typically involve different sorts of parties, disputes and arbitral institutions. A typical interstate arbitration involves a dispute between two sovereign states, for example, over a boundary, and is conducted before either an ad hoc or an institutional panel.[27] In contrast, the paradigm of interna-

---

more commonly done, the rules of an arbitral institution such as the ICC. All three choices of law are separate and not necessarily the same.

[24] This internal/external model is expressed as a part of the doctrinal view of others. Clive Schmitthoff, for example, writes, "From the viewpoint of doctrine, arbitration contains two elements, a contractual and a judicial element." Schmitthoff, *The Supervisory Jurisdiction of the English Courts*, in INTERNATIONAL ARBITRATION: LIBER AMICORUM FOR MARTIN DOMKE 289, 289 (P. Sanders ed. 1967). The contractual element springs from the will of the parties and is manifested in the internal world of the arbitration. The judicial element arises in every legal system that is touched by the interaction of the arbitration and the world external to it. Hazel Fox recently wrote, "The institution of arbitration, on the one view, derives its force from the agreement of the parties; on another view, from the State as supervisor and enforcer of the legal process." Fox, *supra* note 17, at 1. The internal/external paradigm, at least for the purposes of this study, accurately models the arbitral process.

[25] Professor Park has stated that "an arbitrator must bow to mandatory norms of the country in which he sits." Park, *The* Lex Loci Arbitri *and International Commercial Arbitration*, 32 INT'L & COMP. L.Q. 21, 23 (1983). It may be more accurate to state that it is to the intent of the parties that the arbitrator must bow. Local law very rarely coerces the arbitrator. Instead, by indicating that a motion to set aside would likely be granted, local law encourages the parties to draft an arbitration agreement that will result in compliance of their arbitration with the mandatory provisions of local law. Indeed, Article V(1)(d) of the Convention on the Recognition and Enforcement of Foreign Arbitral Awards, *opened for signature* June 10, 1958, 21 UST 2517, TIAS No. 6997, 330 UNTS 3 [hereinafter New York Convention], states that enforcement of an award can be refused if the "composition of the arbitral authority or the arbitral procedure was not in accordance with the agreement of the parties."

[26] For example, recognizing that the parties would want the award to be enforceable in the external world, the UNCITRAL Arbitration Rules, *reprinted in* 15 ILM 701 (1976) [hereinafter UNCITRAL Rules], an internal set of arbitral rules that parties may adopt, in Article 1(2) provides that those contractual rules are to be superseded by any provision of municipal law that the governing legal system regards as "mandatory."

[27] Because the focus of this article is upon the external view of the process rather than party control, interstate arbitration for the purposes of this article could be ad hoc or within the embrace of an institution such as the International Court of Justice. Although the extent of party control over those processes differs greatly, both types of proceedings are interstate arbitration in the sense that jurisdiction remains consensual.

tional commercial arbitration involves, for example, a contract dispute between two private entities and takes place under the auspices of a private arbitral institution such as the International Chamber of Commerce. The distinction between interstate arbitration and international commercial arbitration is strengthened by the generally separate identity of the groups of practitioners and scholars dealing with them and these specialists' lack of experience with each other's forums.[28]

Distinctions are useful to the extent that they provide a precise, yet simple, model as a foundation for more complex analysis. The distinction between interstate and international commercial arbitration is no exception. Nevertheless, its limits must be appreciated lest any analysis rest on inaccurate assumptions. To move beyond this distinction requires not only a fuller examination of the two types of international arbitration, but also an understanding of why certain institutions, such as the Iran–United States Claims Tribunal, appear to fit neither ideal type.

Interstate Arbitration

The internal world of interstate arbitration typically is created and defined by treaty.[29] The agreement to arbitrate and (where applicable) the treaty establishing the responsible institution are the most relevant treaties. The external world may be of little significance for two reasons.

First, so far as the relationship of the customary international legal system to the arbitration is concerned, the international lawmaking capability of the parties may lead to a merging of the internal/external models. The models can collapse into one because states by their agreements both define the internal world of the arbitration *and* modify the applicable international law. In this sense, international law leaves the structuring and conduct of the arbitration entirely in the control of the parties. Consequently, the prime question is whether by their agreement to arbitrate the state parties intend to adopt, supplement or, instead, replace entirely the customary interna-

---

[28] *See, e.g.,* 1 J. G. WETTER, THE INTERNATIONAL ARBITRAL PROCESS—PUBLIC AND PRIVATE, at xxiv (1979) ("Commercial lawyers regard arbitrations between States as wholly irrelevant; and public international law teachers, advocates and officials view commercial arbitration as an essentially alien process . . ."). However, there is a small group of lawyers and arbitrators who serve in both types of proceedings.

[29] The interstate arbitral process is governed by international law by definition. State parties could agree to remove the dispute entirely from the public international level. For example, state parties in their arbitration agreement could waive their sovereignty and specify that the legal system of a third country will govern the arbitration, just as the latter municipal system might govern private arbitration occurring in that third country. As will be seen, this is precisely what this article contends that Iran and the United States did in the case of the Tribunal. Such an action should be distinguished from those instances in the past when heads of state served as arbitrators of disputes. The arbitration in these cases remained governed by the international legal system. For example, the King of Spain was arbiter in 1906 of a boundary dispute between Honduras and Nicaragua. Nicaragua claimed the award to be a nullity under public international law, an allegation ultimately reviewed and rejected by the International Court of Justice. *See* Arbitral Award Made by the King of Spain (Hond. v. Nicar.), 1960 ICJ REP. 192 (Judgment of Nov. 18).

tional law that governs such processes. Many agreements to ad hoc arbitration are quite brief and are intended to rest upon the pertinent customary international practice.[30] Even a brief agreement, however, may raise the question whether aspects of customary practice have been displaced. For example, state parties often agree that the arbitral award shall be final and binding upon them. Nonetheless, customary international law recognizes that either party may declare the award a nullity when the arbitral process does not satisfy certain fundamental norms of fairness.[31] That a tribunal may not exceed its jurisdiction or be corrupt are examples of such norms.[32] Although states could agree to remove this customary right, the common phrase "the award shall be final and binding upon the parties" does not necessarily constitute such agreement inasmuch as it is "the award" that is challenged by a declaration of nullity.[33] An express example of the removal of the customary right can be found in the, in many ways, innovative Convention establishing the International Centre for Settlement of Investment Disputes (ICSID).[34] That Convention provides a limited mechanism for nullification by a second tribunal[35] and states that the award "shall not be subject to any appeal or to any other remedy except those provided in this Convention."[36]

[30] Indeed, this customary practice was so involved in arbitrations in the first half of this century that international legal scholarship devoted a great deal of energy to its codification. *See, e.g.,* Carlston, *Codification of International Arbitral Procedure,* 47 AJIL 203 (1953).

[31] *See generally* W. M. REISMAN, NULLITY AND REVISION: THE REVIEW AND ENFORCEMENT OF INTERNATIONAL JUDGMENTS AND AWARDS (1971). Of course, the problem with this right is that often no international court has jurisdiction to review the merits of a state's declaration of nullity; thus, the declaration in effect becomes a justification for that state's refusal to comply with the award.

[32] For an example of corruption in modern times, see the discussion of the U.S.-Venezuelan Claims Commission (1866–1888), 2 J. B. MOORE, INTERNATIONAL ARBITRATIONS TO WHICH THE UNITED STATES HAS BEEN A PARTY 1659–92 (1898).

[33] *See* W. M. REISMAN, *supra* note 31, at 421.

[34] Convention on the Settlement of Investment Disputes between States and Nationals of Other States, *opened for signature* Aug. 27, 1965, 17 UST 1270, TIAS No. 6090, 575 UNTS 159 [hereinafter ICSID Convention]. ICSID is unlike classical interstate arbitration in that one of the parties is likely private. In this sense (and see further text at note 216 *infra*), ICSID, like the Tribunal, is an institution that reflects developments not modeled by the traditional distinction. The ICSID Convention, however, nonetheless stands as a valid example of the proposition in the text because the means of reviewing the validity of awards is decided by the mechanisms provided for in the treaty, and not by reliance on or reference to customary international law doctrines such as declarations of nullity.

[35] ICSID Convention, *supra* note 34, Art. 52. For the most recent example of such a nullification proceeding, *see* Amco Asia Corp. v. Republic of Indonesia, No. ARB/81/1: On the Application for Annulment Submitted by the Republic of Indonesia Against the Arbitral Award Rendered on November 20, 1984 (Ad Hoc Committee decision of May 16, 1986, nullifying in part the award on the merits), *reprinted in* 25 ILM 1441 (1986). For further proceedings in the case, see 83 AJIL 106 (1989).

[36] ICSID Convention, *supra* note 34, Art. 53(1).
    This issue was raised vividly in the recent Judgment of the ICJ on jurisdiction in Military and Paramilitary Activities in and against Nicaragua (Nicar. v. U.S.), Jurisdiction and Admissibility, 1984 ICJ REP. 392 (Judgment of Nov. 26). The United States has refused to recognize the proceedings of the Court on the ground that the Court exceeded its jurisdiction. *See* Reisman,

The second reason for the general irrelevance of the external world to interstate arbitration is that the immunities normally afforded to states will preclude the involvement of municipal legal systems. Of course, the treaty defining an interstate arbitration could involve municipal courts. For example, although the validity of an ICSID award is resolved within the ICSID process, ICSID awards are enforceable in the national courts of any state party.[37] In practice, however, resort to municipal courts has been possible only infrequently. Moreover, the agreement of state parties to the use of municipal courts to enforce an arbitral decision is conceptually different from their agreeing that the arbitral process shall be fully subject to a municipal legal system. In the latter case, the municipal system would govern not only enforceability, but also validity.[38] Involvement of municipal courts in either validity or enforcement rests upon a waiver by states of the immunities such courts normally extend to them.

International Commercial Arbitration between Private Entities

The extension of traditional municipal arbitration. As to modern forms of international arbitration, Dr. Mann writes:

> Although, where international aspects of some kind arise, it is not uncommon and, on the whole, harmless to speak somewhat colloquially, of international arbitration, the phrase is a misnomer. In the legal sense no international commercial arbitration exists. Just as . . . every system of private international law is a system of national law, every arbitration is a national arbitration, that is to say, subject to a specific system of national law.[39]

Under this view, international commercial arbitrations are merely private municipal arbitrations that have an international aspect. For such arbitrations, the municipal legal system of the *place of arbitration* governs whether the arbitral award is valid.[40] This governing legal system is often termed the

---

Has the International Court Exceeded its Jurisdiction?, 80 AJIL 128 (1986). The legal issue is whether or not the United States displaced its customary right to nullify an award for this reason by its agreement in Article 94(2) of the UN Charter "to comply with the decision of the International Court of Justice in any case to which it is a party." *See also* W. M. REISMAN, *supra* note 31, at 420–23.

[37] ICSID Convention, *supra* note 34, Art. 54(1). *See, e.g.,* Liberian E. Timber Corp. v. Government of Republic of Liberia, 650 F.Supp. 73 (S.D.N.Y. 1986).

[38] *See, e.g.,* Maritime Int'l Nominees Establishment v. Republic of Guinea, 693 F.2d 1094, 1100 (D.C. Cir. 1982), *cert. denied,* 464 U.S. 815 (1983) (distinguishing between U.S. federal court jurisdiction to enforce and jurisdiction generally over ICSID proceedings). *See generally* Delaume, *ICSID Arbitration and the Courts,* 77 AJIL 784 (1983).

[39] Mann, *Lex Facit Arbitrum,* in INTERNATIONAL ARBITRATION, *supra* note 24, at 157, 159. The de-localized view of arbitration, which challenges Dr. Mann's statement, is considered in the text at notes 50–65 *infra.*

[40] The parties may confuse this general rule by, for example, expressly providing for a *lex arbitri* different from that of the designated place of the arbitration, or by holding all proceedings in, or rendering the award in, a country other than the country of the designated place of arbitration. *See* Mann, *Where Is an Award 'Made'?,* 1 ARB. INT'L 107 (1985).

lex arbitri.[41] "The *lex arbitri* is not necessarily the law governing the substance of the dispute, nor the procedural rules applied by the arbitrators."[42] Rather, it is the legal system that determines whether the award was arrived at properly.[43] An award is said to have the *nationality* of the country where it is rendered; presumably, the place of arbitration is chosen by the parties, or by some other person or institution they have empowered to make that choice. The source of this concept of nationality is territorial; that is, the contract (the agreement to arbitrate) is to be performed within the jurisdiction of a country.[44]

States can take, and have taken, a variety of approaches to their supervision of municipal arbitration. For example, a state may forbid arbitration and refer all disputes to the courts.[45] States may allow arbitration but dictate the precise procedure to be employed, specify which questions are arbitrable and subject all aspects of the arbitration to judicial review.[46] Finally, states may allow the parties to choose how the arbitration is to proceed and

---

[41] *See* Mann, *supra* note 39.   [42] Park, *supra* note 25, at 23.

[43] Hirsch, *The Place of Arbitration and the "Lex Arbitri,"* 34 ARB. J. 43, 44 (1979).

[44] Other dimensions to governance of the arbitral process exist and the courts of the place of arbitration may be requested to intervene in arbitral proceedings in such other ways. These other relationships generally involve securing judicial assistance in furtherance of the arbitral proceedings, including, inter alia, the appointment of arbitrators and the production of evidence. Generally such matters (in particular, matters relating to the composition of the tribunal) are only within the competence of the courts of the place of arbitration. However, assistance in areas such as interim measures might be available to the parties before courts other than those of the place of arbitration. Finally, it is normally reserved to the courts of the place of arbitration to decide questions about liability of the arbitrators to the parties and, not as exclusively, liability of the parties to the arbitrators. The approaches of the various municipal systems on these more detailed questions vary considerably. *See generally* Delaume, *Court Intervention in Arbitral Proceedings,* in RESOLVING TRANSNATIONAL DISPUTES THROUGH INTERNATIONAL ARBITRATION 195 (T. Carbonneau ed. 1984) [hereinafter RESOLVING DISPUTES].

[45] Courts in the United States, for example, were hostile at one time to arbitration. *See, e.g.,* United States Asphalt Ref. Co. v. Trinidad Lake Petroleum Co., 222 F. 1006 (S.D.N.Y. 1915). As caseloads have increased in the United States, however, hostility has given way to encouragement. *See* Burger, *Isn't There a Better Way?,* 68 A.B.A.J. 274, 277 (1982).

[46] For example, until quite recently, this second municipal law approach was exemplified by the law of England and Commonwealth countries that followed English practice. This second approach, known as the "special case" or "case stated" procedure, involves much more extensive judicial supervision and control of the arbitration to ensure not only fundamental fairness but also legally correct results. Under the case-stated procedure, either party may demand that the arbitral panel submit a question of law or fact to the courts. The courts may then hold a hearing with full argument from which appeal may be made. The grounds upon which the court addresses the validity of an award are thus considerably broader. However, the approach is no longer favored in the United Kingdom, having been replaced by the 1979 Arbitration Act, a law that moves toward the third approach—an arbitral process substantially more independent of judicial control.

See Mann, *Some Recent Developments of the English Law of Arbitration,* in IUS INTER NATIONES: FESTSCHRIFT FÜR STEFAN RIESENFELD 187, 190 (1983). *See also* Park, *The Influence of National Legal Systems on International Commercial Arbitration: Recent Developments in English Arbitration Law,* in RESOLVING DISPUTES, *supra* note 44, at 80; Lord Hacking, *Where We Are Now: Trends and Developments Since the Arbitration Act [1979],* 2 J. INT'L ARB. 7 (1985); Jaffe, *The Judicial Trend Toward Finality of Commercial Arbitral Awards in England,* 24 TEX. INT'L L.J. 67 (1989); and Thomas, *The Antaios: The Nema Guidelines Reconsidered,* 1985 J. BUS. L. 200.

limit review to the parties' fundamental interests in a fair process.[47] Although the details vary considerably and differences may be significant, the approach with limited judicial review has come to be the most common.

Under this approach, a statute typically sets forth rules of arbitral procedure. Simultaneously, the statute gives parties the right to displace the statutory procedural scheme by rules of their own choice. Thus, the internal statutory construct is to be applied only if the parties fail to provide otherwise. A frequent caveat in this regard, however, is that *certain* aspects of the national arbitration law will be mandatory. These mandatory provisions are usually those that ensure fundamental fairness; ordinarily, failure to observe these rules will lead to the setting aside of the award.[48] The dominance of the notions of nationality of awards based on the place of the arbitration and judicial review limited to concerns of fundamental fairness has been confirmed and bolstered by their adoption in the 1985 UNCITRAL Model Law on International Commercial Arbitration.[49]

Thus, private parties in international commercial arbitration in effect can control the procedure within statutorily defined limits of fundamental fairness. Effective control devolves upon the parties because it is permitted by the sovereign of the place of arbitration. States in interstate arbitration have such control because of their inherent ability to displace by treaty the regime otherwise provided by customary international law.

---

[47] *See generally* Carbonneau, *American and Other National Variations on the Theme of International Commercial Arbitration,* 18 GA. J. INT'L & COMP. L. 143 (1988) (discussing the evolution of the French, British, Canadian and American approaches).

[48] For example, an arbitral award rendered in the United States may be vacated under § 10 of the U.S. Arbitration Act:

    (a) Where the award was procured by corruption, fraud, or undue means.
    (b) Where there was evident partiality or corruption in the arbitrators . . . .
    (c) Where the arbitrators were guilty of misconduct in refusing to postpone the hearing . . . or in refusing to hear evidence . . . .
    (d) Where the arbitrators exceeded their powers . .

9 U.S.C. § 10 (1988).

[49] UNCITRAL Model Law on International Commercial Arbitration, Art. 34, *adopted* June 21, 1985, *reprinted in* 24 ILM 1302, 1311 (1985) [hereinafter UNCITRAL Model Law]. *See* Report of the U.N. Commission on International Trade Law on the Work of its Eighteenth Session, 40 UN GAOR Supp. (No. 17), UN Doc A/40/17, Ann. 1 (1985). *See generally* H. HOLTZMANN & J. NEUHAUS, A GUIDE TO THE UNCITRAL MODEL LAW ON INTERNATIONAL COMMERCIAL ARBITRATION (1988); McNerney & Esplugues, *International Commercial Arbitration: The UNCITRAL Model Law,* 14 B.C. INT'L & COMP. L. REV. 47 (1986); Herrmann, *UNCITRAL Adopts Model Law on International Commercial Arbitration,* 2 ARB. INT'L 2 (1986); and Broches, *The 1985 UNCITRAL Model Law on International Commercial Arbitration: An Exercise in International Legislation,* 18 NETH. Y.B. INT'L L. 3 (1987).

On previous regional efforts in Latin America and Europe at a uniform municipal model arbitration law, see Domke, *International Arbitration of Commercial Disputes,* in 2 INSTITUTE ON PRIVATE INVESTMENTS ABROAD 131, 136–39 (1960).

That the "fundamental fairness" approach is dominant should not be taken to mean that other approaches to municipal governance of the arbitral process do not exist at present. In particular, arbitration in the socialist countries tends to remain very closely supervised by the courts.

The movement for an anational process. Private parties often are motivated to arbitrate an international dispute for a reason fundamentally different from the reasons that motivate parties to most municipal disputes. On the municipal level, arbitration is attractive because it is perceived to be a desirable alternative to the courts.[50] But on the international level, there often is no alternative to arbitration.[51] In many international situations, neither party will agree to submit all possible disputes to the courts of the other.[52] Arbitration is preferred over litigation in some third state in part because to ascertain whether procedurally and substantively the courts and legal system would be acceptable would take a tremendous effort,[53] and also because foreign court proceedings ultimately require extensive, and possibly costly, use of foreign counsel.[54] Thus, the parties are led to choose arbitration.[55]

Nevertheless, the arbitration alternative does not free the parties entirely from the unknown pitfalls of a foreign legal system; as described above, the system of the place of arbitration will serve as the *lex arbitri*. The desire to free the parties completely from such pitfalls gives rise to one aspect of the anational movement.[56]

---

[50] The arbitration alternative is particularly attractive for smaller cases where the often time-consuming procedural guarantees and appeal structure of a court system are not of particular importance to the parties.

[51] Similarly, domestic labor arbitration, particularly labor grievance arbitration, arguably "is not a substitute for litigation . . . [but] rather, a device by which the parties agree to accept the judgment of a third party instead of fighting the issues out on the picket lines." Brief for Petitioner 32, Textile Workers Union of Am. v. Lincoln Mills of Ala., 353 U.S. 448 (1957).

[52] Smit, *The Future of International Commercial Arbitration: A Single Transnational Institution?*, 25 COLUM. J. TRANSNAT'L L. 9, 10 (1986) ("Rather than permit international disputes to be settled in national courts, many parties often prefer to submit them to a tribunal that is not part of the governmental structure of a particular state"; *id.* at 9); de Vries, *International Commercial Arbitration: A Contractual Substitute for National Courts*, 57 TUL. L. REV. 42 (1982); and Kerr, *Commercial Dispute Resolution: The Changing Scene*, in LIBER AMICORUM FOR LORD WILBERFORCE 111, 128 (M. Bos & I. Brownlie eds. 1987).

[53] The generally recognized expertise of English courts in maritime matters is an exception.

[54] In international commercial arbitration, the necessary reliance on foreign counsel can be greatly reduced. Even if a foreign law is applicable to the substance of the dispute, the normal counsel to the parties usually can operate within the arbitral procedure adopted, generally are better suited to deal with the factual basis of the case and, thus, often need to involve foreign counsel only to advise on selected points of the applicable law or supervising legal system.

[55] Moreover, because the motivations for entering into international and wholly municipal commercial arbitration differ, there can be important differences in the two processes and in the directions in which the processes are evolving. For example, because international commercial arbitration can be the only alternative and large amounts may be in dispute, the parties—rather than desiring a streamlined process to ensure speed and reduce costs, as is often the case stated in the municipal context—may seek to design an arbitral process that quite resembles court proceedings, e.g., by providing for discovery or even appeal.

[56] The movement toward an anational system for private international arbitrations has been the subject of a great deal of commentary in recent years. *See, e.g.,* Paulsson, *Arbitration Unbound: Award Detached from the Law of its Country of Origin,* 30 INT'L & COMP. L.Q. 358 (1981); Park, *supra* note 25. The movement has a number of aims. One is that the legal system of the place of arbitration should no longer govern the arbitral process. Rather, it is argued that the system where enforcement is sought should govern. Another aim is development of a substantive law that is non-national, the *"lex mercatoria." See* Lando, *The "Lex Mercatoria" in International Commercial Arbitration,* 34 INT'L & COMP. L.Q. 747 (1985); and Cremades &

Specifically, although a large number of states allow arbitrating parties to stipulate the procedure to be employed (such as the ICC Rules of Arbitration), this choice does not necessarily assure them a predictable, neutral and effective process. Paulsson offers the following example:

> A majority award is rendered. The losing party moves to set it aside on the grounds that the dissenting arbitrator—who one might suppose was nominated by the said party—had not signed the award. The winning party retorts that the contractually stipulated ICC Rules of Arbitration accept majority awards, and do not require a signature by the dissenting arbitrator. The argument would appear to fail, however, since the law of [the place of arbitration] not only requires that all arbitrators sign the award, but provides that any contractual stipulation to the contrary is invalid.[57]

Paulsson points out that whereas the law of the place of arbitration may be totally appropriate for purely domestic arbitrations,

> the international businessman who had chosen arbitration under a simple set of rules he thought he understood, having ended up at a seat of arbitration selected only for convenience and not out of admiration for any local legal principles, would be deeply shocked to find that the end result of an expensive process in which he had justly prevailed is the utter nullity of his effort.[58]

Furthermore, to the degree that an arbitral award is only enforceable if it has a nationality, the action of the place of arbitration may render the award a nullity throughout the world.[59]

Plehn, *The New "Lex Mercatoria" and the Harmonization of the Laws of International Commercial Transactions,* 2 B.U. INT'L L.J. 317 (1984). For recent critical discussions, see Mustill, *The New "Lex Mercatoria": The First Twenty-Five Years,* in LIBER AMICORUM FOR LORD WILBERFORCE, *supra* note 52, at 149; Highet, *The Enigma of the Lex Mercatoria,* 63 TUL. L. REV. 613 (1989).

The anational arbitration system is similar to the so-called autonomous theory of the nature of private international arbitration. *See* J. RUBELLIN-DEVICHI, L'ARBITRAGE; NATURE JURIDIQUE, DROIT INTERNE ET DROIT INTERNATIONAL PRIVÉ (1965). In essence, the autonomous theory asserts that private parties may take the place of a state in establishing regimes for the resolution of certain disputes. Yet arbitration often depends on states for support during the arbitral process and for enforcement of resulting awards. *See* Wetter, *The Conduct of the Arbitration,* 2 J. INT'L ARB. 7, 27–34 (1985).

[57] Paulsson, *Delocalisation of International Commercial Arbitration: When and Why It Matters,* 32 INT'L & COMP. L.Q. 53, 58 (1983). Paulsson noted that such a provision, albeit "poised for reform," exists in Austria. *Id.* at 59 n.10. *See* Melis, *Arbitration and the Courts in Austria—international aspects,* in THE ART OF ARBITRATION, LIBER AMICORUM FOR PIETER SANDERS 253, 257 (J. C. Schultsz & A. J. van den Berg eds. 1982).

[58] Paulsson, *supra* note 57, at 59.

[59] New York Convention, *supra* note 25. On the Convention, see generally A. J. VAN DEN BERG, THE NEW YORK CONVENTION OF 1958: TOWARD A UNIFORM JUDICIAL INTERPRETATION (1981); Contini, *International Commercial Arbitration: The United Nations Convention on the Recognition and Enforcement of Foreign Arbitral Awards,* 8 AM. J. COMP. L. 283 (1959); Mirabito, *The United Nations Convention on the Recognition and Enforcement of Foreign Arbitral Awards: The First Four Years,* 5 GA. J. INT'L & COMP. L. 471 (1975); Sanders, *A Twenty Years' Review of the Convention on the Recognition and Enforcement of Foreign Arbitral Awards,* 13 INT'L LAW. 269 (1979); and Springer, *The United Nations Convention on the Recognition and Enforcement of Foreign Arbitral Awards,* 3 INT'L LAW. 320 (1969).

The anational movement challenges the burden placed on international commercial arbitration by such vagaries of municipal arbitration. Municipal arbitration statutes were originally drafted, quite understandably, with municipal disputes in mind. Their standards of judicial review followed municipal norms of fairness. The anational movement opposes the tendency of the enforcing state to require that the award have a nationality. Under its approach, an annulment at the place of arbitration would no longer be a global annulment and, in effect, the significance of an award would be determined by the state where enforcement is sought.[60] A common metaphor is that the award "floats" until enforcement seeks to anchor it within a given legal system. Anational arbitration is referred to also as "delocalized arbitration."

Critics of the anational approach argue that arbitral awards must have a nationality; otherwise, "[t]he paradox of a legal obligation independent of a legal order suggests Athena springing full-blown from the head of Zeus . . . ."[61] Proponents counter that no one questions that the validity of an international contract should not turn upon the approval of the state where the contract was formed, particularly when the contract has no other connection with that state. Similarly, the *lex arbitri* should not be permitted to dictate the determinative view of an award because there are often few connections between the place of arbitration and the parties, the dispute or the assets that may satisfy the award.

In support of the enforceability of anational awards under the Convention, see Lake & Dana, *supra* note 15, at 790. Opposed, see A. J. VAN DEN BERG, *supra*, at 28–40. A subcommittee of the American Arbitration Association concluded that "the convention should apply to delocalized arbitration [another term for anational arbitration], but it is to be expected that delocalized awards will be given special scrutiny in the courts of the United States." Sub-Committee on Delocalized Arbitration of the Law Committee of the American Arbitration Association, Report 12 (Feb. 14, 1984) [hereinafter AAA Report]. If, instead of an appropriate law applied fairly, the award were set aside in a country "without a tradition of judicial independence . . . merely to please the bureaucracy . . . . [e]nforcement of such an award [elsewhere] would seem neither improper nor inappropriate." Park, *supra* note 25, at 27–28.

[60] A related objective of the approach is to encourage courts to abstain from applying their law to an international commercial arbitration simply because the award was rendered in that state. An often-argued example is the decision on the appeal of an ICC award, *Götaverken Arendal v. Libyan General National Maritime Transport*, Feb. 21, 1980; for an English translation of extracts, see Paulsson, *supra* note 56, at 385. The Paris Court of Appeal noted that even though the place of arbitration was Paris and the award had been rendered in Paris, Article 11 of the ICC Rules (unaltered by the parties) provided for not even a subsidiary reference to French law: "the place of the arbitral proceedings, chosen only in order to assure their neutrality, is not significant; it may not be considered an implicit expression of the parties' intent to subject themselves, even subsidiarily, to the *loi procédurale française.*" The court concluded that since the award had been "rendered in accordance with proceedings which are not those of French law and which have no attachment whatsoever to the French legal order since the two parties are foreigners, and since the contract was signed and was to be performed abroad, [it] may not be considered French." *Id.* at 386. In this sense, the rhetoric of the anational movement echoes the motivations expressed in the shift in U.S. choice of law from localizing factors to interest analysis.

[61] Park, *supra* note 25, at 27. *See also* Redfern, *The Arbitration Between the Government of Kuwait and Aminoil*, 55 BRIT. Y.B. INT'L L. 78 (1984).

Although nationality of awards may not be a logical necessity, as some critics seem to suggest, there are practical reasons that support the present connection between the rendering of an award and the legal system of the place of arbitration. Most importantly, this connection provides a means for timely judicial review of arbitral awards. Unlike the formation of a contract, the rendering of the award is the final act in arbitral proceedings. Consequently, most municipal arbitration statutes require that a motion to set aside the award must be filed with local courts within a short period—quite often within 3 months of the rendering of the award.[62] This procedure accomplishes two practical goals. First, the losing party need challenge the award only once and therefore is not "forced to litigate issues such as arbitrator corruption in all States where it has assets."[63] Second, and more important, the judicial review of at least certain issues takes place at the most appropriate place and time: where the arbitrators and records are likely to be present and while the recollections and evidence are fresh.

Moreover, this aspect of the anational movement's concerns, although interesting, has been, and will increasingly be, of little practical significance. First of all, prudent parties will desire, and thus intend, that their arbitration be governed by a legal system so that court assistance *during* the proceedings, even though often limited, will be available, and so that the enforceability of the award will be strengthened by the support of the appellation of a nationality. Second, and more important, the problem behind the main impetus to the anational movement, "peculiar and unexpected local norms," is being resolved in ways other than that suggested by the movement's adherents: in part, by the general harmonization of municipal arbitration statutes, and especially, by the trend toward the adoption by states of special statutes that cover international commercial arbitration alone and exclude peculiar local norms.[64] The recently adopted UNCITRAL Model

---

[62] *See, e.g.,* UNCITRAL Model Law, *supra* note 49, Art. 34(3).

[63] Park, *supra* note 25, at 51. *See also* A. J. VAN DEN BERG, *supra* note 59, at 30.

[64] For example, Lord Elwyn Jones, in introducing the bill that eventually eliminated the British "case stated" procedure, *supra* note 46, explained: "The purpose [of the bill] is to remove certain legal obstacles which at present stand in the way of London being used to its full potential as an international centre for arbitration." *See* Kerr, *supra* note 52, at 124. *See also* Bentil, *Making England a More Attractive Venue for International Commercial Arbitration by Less Judicial Oversight,* 5 J. INT'L ARB. 49 (1988). Indeed, the commercial value of being a center of arbitration is generally believed to have spurred this global transformation of municipal arbitration laws.

France, whose courts are argued to have employed anational reasoning in regard to an arbitration (*see supra* note 60), shortly thereafter adopted such a statute. *See* Audit, *A National Codification of International Commercial Arbitration: The French Decree of May 12, 1981,* in RESOLVING DISPUTES, *supra* note 44, at 117. *See also* Carbonneau, *supra* note 47, at 167–73; Carbonneau, *The Elaboration of a French Court Doctrine on International Commercial Arbitration: A Study in Liberal Civilian Judicial Creativity,* 55 TUL. L. REV. 1 (1980); Bellet, *The Evolution of French Judicial Views on International Commercial Arbitration,* 34 ARB. J. 28 (1979).

On the other hand, Belgium has passed a law freeing international arbitrations entirely, i.e., making them anational. *See* van Houtte, *La Loi belge du 27 mars 1985 sur l'arbitrage international,* 1986 REVUE DE L'ARBITRAGE [REV. ARB.] 29 (1986); Vanderelst, *Increasing the Appeal of Belgium as an International Arbitration Forum?—The Belgian Law of March 27, 1985 concerning the Annulment of Arbitral Awards,* 3 J. INT'L ARB. 77 (1986).

Law on International Commercial Arbitration should encourage this approach, as it applies only to international commercial arbitration and affords limited, and only generally accepted, grounds for the setting aside of, or refusal to enforce, an award.[65]

International Arbitration between a State and a Private Entity

Arbitrations that typically are neither interstate nor private illuminate the inadequacy of distinguishing between these processes on the basis of the parties or issues involved, or the public or private nature of the surrounding institutional arrangement. Most such arbitrations involve proceedings between a state and a private entity, an increasingly common configuration of parties and the one faced for the most part by the Iran–United States Claims Tribunal.[66] In these cases, is the arbitration governed by the international legal system as for interstate arbitration, or by a municipal legal system as for international commercial arbitration? Awards reaching one or the other conclusion have been rendered.[67]

---

[65] *See* UNCITRAL Model Law, *supra* note 49, Art. 34. "To the extent that the UNCITRAL draft Model Law . . . with its very limited grounds for review is adopted, [the] reasons for seeking to delocalize arbitration would be reduced in persuasiveness." AAA Report, *supra* note 59, at 6. "Article 34 takes into account the 'mobility' of international commercial arbitration and reduces the legal relevance of the chosen place of arbitration. . . . [I]t contributes to what one may call 'soft delocalization'." Herrmann, *The British Columbia Enactment of the UNCITRAL Model Law*, in UNCITRAL ARBITRATION MODEL IN CANADA 65, 70 (R. Paterson & B. Thompson eds. 1987). As to the grounds for refusing to enforce an award under the UNCITRAL Model Law, see Ungar, *The Enforcement of Arbitral Awards Under UNCITRAL's Model Law on International Commercial Arbitration*, 25 COLUM. J. TRANSNAT'L L. 717 (1987).

[66] *See* Böckstiegel, *States in the International Arbitral Process*, 2 ARB. INT'L 22 (1986).

[67] A caveat to the significance of these arbitral awards can be found in Judge Lagergren's comment in *British Petroleum, infra* note 76, that the "Tribunal is not competent to establish conclusively the nationality of its Award, for this can only be decided by the courts of [the place of arbitration] and of other jurisdictions in which the enforcement of the Award may be sought." 53 ILR at 309. Notably, in this regard the somewhat ambiguous *LIAMCO* award, *infra* note 85, was later the subject of extensive municipal litigation. Implicit in that subsequent litigation, despite the ambiguity of the award itself, is the seemingly unquestioned assumption that the arbitration was governed by Switzerland's legal system. The Swiss Federal Supreme Court, in an action relating to enforcement, noted that "the appeal for annulment permissible under the laws of Geneva was not filed." Libya v. Libyan American Oil Co. (Swiss Federal Supreme Ct., June 19, 1980), *reprinted in* 20 ILM 151, 154 (1981). (As to Swiss laws on the execution issue presented, see generally Lalive, *Swiss Law and Practice in Relation to Measures of Execution against the Property of a Foreign State*, 10 NETH. Y.B. INT'L L. 153 (1979).) Moreover, in a later enforcement action in U.S. courts, Libya itself characterized the award as Swiss, contending that "the Swiss judgment has, in effect, set aside or suspended LIAMCO's arbitral award"; while the United States, as amicus curiae, argued that the award was a foreign arbitral award enforceable under the New York Convention. Brief (June 16, 1980) and Supplemental Memorandum (Nov. 7, 1980) of the United States as *amicus curiae* in Libyan American Oil Co. v. Socialist People's Libyan Jamahirya, *reprinted in* 20 ILM 161 and 164, 165 (1981). The court of appeals, apparently in reliance on the amicus brief, 684 F.2d 1032 (D.C. Cir. 1982), vacated the judgment of the U.S. district court, 482 F.Supp. 1175 (D.D.C. 1980), which also had assumed that the award was the result of foreign rather than international arbitration, but had nonetheless declined to recognize or enforce the award by reason of the act of state doctrine. The award was also recognized in France and Sweden. *See* Procureur de la République v.

The classic discussion of this question in a case is the 1958 arbitration, *Saudi Arabia v. Arabian American Oil Co. (ARAMCO)*.[68] The tribunal concluded that "[a]lthough the present arbitration was instituted, not between States, but between a State and a private American corporation, the Arbitration Tribunal is not of the opinion that the law of the country of its seat [Switzerland] should be applied to the arbitration."[69]

The *ARAMCO* tribunal's conclusion rested in large part on great deference to the sovereign nature of states.

> The jurisdictional immunity of States . . . excludes the possibility, for the judicial authorities of the country of the seat, of exercising their right of supervision and interference in the arbitral proceedings which they have in certain cases. . . .
>
> . . . .
>
> Considering the jurisdictional immunity of foreign States, recognized by international law in a spirit of respect for the essential dignity of sovereign power, the Tribunal is unable to hold that arbitral proceedings to which a sovereign State is a Party could be subject to the law of another State.[70]

This deference to sovereignty reflected the tribunal's estimation of the deference states afforded one another at that time:

> It is true that the practice of the Swiss Courts has limited the jurisdictional immunity of States and does not protect that immunity, in disputes of a private nature, when the legal relations between the Parties have been created, or when their obligations have to be performed in Switzerland. The Arbitration Tribunal must, however, take that immunity into account when determining the law to be applied to an arbitration which will lead to a purely declaratory award. By agreeing to fix the seat of the Tribunal in Switzerland, the foreign State which is a Party to the arbitration is not presumed to have surrendered its jurisdictional immunity in case of disputes relating to the implementation of the "compromis" itself.[71]

Having decided that the Swiss legal system did not govern the arbitration, the panel structured the internal world of the arbitration along the lines of an interstate arbitration. "In such a case, the [internal procedural] rules set forth in the Draft Convention on Arbitral Procedure, adopted by the International Law Commission of the United Nations . . ., should be applied by analogy."[72]

On the other hand, in 1963 the arbitrator in *Sapphire International Petroleums v. National Iranian Oil Co.* decided that the legal system of the place of

---

Société LIAMCO (Trib. gr. inst. Paris 1979), *reprinted in* 106 JOURNAL DU DROIT INTERNATIONAL [JDI] 857 (1979); Libyan American Oil Co. v. Libya (Ct. App. Svea, June 19, 1980), *reprinted in English in* 20 ILM 893 (1981).

[68] Saudi Arabia v. Arabian American Oil Co. (ARAMCO), *reprinted in* 27 ILR 117 (1958) (Sauser-Hall, Badawi/Hassan, Habachy, arbs.).

[69] *Id.* at 155.   [70] *Id.* at 155–56.

[71] *Id.* at 156.   [72] *Id.*

arbitration would govern the arbitration.[73] The parties had agreed to a precise and detailed arbitration clause to be used after an optional conciliation procedure. Cavin, the sole arbitrator, concluded that the parties had "unequivocally shown their mutual desire to use arbitration in order to obtain a decision which will settle once and for all their possible differences."[74] In Cavin's opinion, this desire indicated that the decision "should be subject to the supervision of a State authority, such as the judicial sovereignty of a State."[75]

British Petroleum Exploration Co. v. Libyan Arab Republic[76] was one of three arbitrations between Libya and the nationals of a foreign state that arose out of the Libyan oil nationalizations of the early 1970s.[77] In *British Petroleum*, Judge Lagergren quoted the *ARAMCO* opinion at length but then stated that the tribunal "cannot share the view that the application of municipal procedural law to an international arbitration like the present one would infringe upon such prerogatives as a State party to the proceedings may have by virtue of its sovereign status."[78] Indeed, Judge Lagergren contended, "By providing for arbitration as an exclusive mechanism for resolving contractual disputes, the parties to an agreement, even if one of them is a State, must . . . be presumed to have intended to create an effective remedy"; and the effectiveness of a remedy is certainly greater when the "award [is] founded on the procedural law of a specific [municipal] legal system."[79]

Texaco Overseas Petroleum & California Asiatic Oil Co. v. Libya (TOPCO)[80] involved an arbitration clause identical to the one in *British Petroleum*, yet reached the opposite result of *British Petroleum* and *Sapphire*. Professor Dupuy, the sole arbitrator, cited the result in *Sapphire* with approval but

[73] Sapphire International Petroleums v. National Iranian Oil Co., *reprinted in* 35 ILR 136 (1963) (Cavin, sole arb.). *See also* Suratgar, *The Sapphire Arbitration Award, the Procedural Aspects: A Report and a Critique*, 3 COLUM. J. TRANSNAT'L L. 152 (1964).

[74] *Sapphire*, 35 ILR at 168.   [75] *Id.* at 169.

[76] British Petroleum Exploration Co. v. Libyan Arab Republic (Award on the Merits), *reprinted in* 53 ILR 297 (1973) (Lagergren, sole arb.). A further award was rendered by Lagergren on Aug. 1, 1974, addressing plaintiff's motion to reopen the proceedings; *reprinted in id.* at 375.

[77] *See* von Mehren & Kourides, *International Arbitrations between States and Foreign Private Parties: The Libyan Nationalization Cases*, 75 AJIL 476 (1981). The three arbitrations are significant generally and to this discussion specifically because "[i]t is rare in international arbitration for three arbitrations, with virtually identical factual and legal contexts, to arise and be heard by distinguished international jurists, and to result in awards that thereafter become part of the public domain." *Id.* at 490.

[78] *British Petroleum*, 53 ILR at 309.

[79] *Id.* In support of his holding, Judge Lagergren cited *Sapphire* and Alsing Trading Co. & Svenska Tändsticks Aktiebolaget v. The Greek State, *reprinted in* 23 ILR 633 (1954) (Python, sole arb.). On *Alsing*, see generally Schwebel, *The Alsing Case*, 8 INT'L & COMP. L.Q. 320 (1959).

[80] Texaco Overseas Petroleum Co. & California Asiatic Oil Co. v. Libyan Arab Republic (Award on the Merits) (1977), *reprinted in* 17 ILM 1 (1978) (Dupuy, sole arb.). French original of part II of the Award on the Merits, *reprinted in* 104 JDI 350 (1977). Professor Dupuy at an earlier stage rendered an award on his jurisdiction. TOPCO (Preliminary Award), *reprinted in* 53 ILR 393 (1975) (Dupuy, sole arb.). *See further* Lalive, *Un Grand Arbitrage Pétrolier entre un Gouvernement et deux sociétés privées étrangères*, 104 JDI 319 (1977).

distinguished the case on two bases: (1) *Sapphire* had involved a state enterprise rather than, as was the case in *TOPCO*, the state itself; and (2) the plaintiff in *Sapphire* had sought an enforceable judgment, while the plaintiffs in *TOPCO* "have indicated that they intend that the present arbitration should be an arbitration on matters of principle."[81] Even if a final judgment had been sought, Dupuy suggested that he would have discounted this fact because it was "a consideration relating to enforcement, which is not within the jurisdiction of the Arbitrator."[82] Dupuy then cited the reasoning in *ARAMCO* with approval, adding that its conclusion was further supported in *TOPCO* because the President of the International Court of Justice had appointed the sole arbitrator[83] and the parties had not objected to Dupuy's formulation of the tribunal's rules of procedure, which, inter alia, provided that "the arbitration shall be governed by these Rules of Procedure to the exclusion of the local law."[84]

The third and last Libyan oil nationalization case was *Libyan American Oil Co. v. Libyan Arab Republic* (*LIAMCO*).[85] Of the three, *LIAMCO* was the most unclear about whether the arbitration was governed by the international legal system or by that of the place of arbitration. Mahmassani, the sole arbitrator, wrote only that, given the failure of the parties to agree otherwise, "the City of Geneva shall be the official seat of arbitration" and that "the arbitrator will employ the 1958 United Nations Draft Convention on Arbitral Procedure."[86] The first statement could be read to suggest that the Swiss legal system governed the arbitral process, while the second statement could be read to suggest equally that the international legal system governed.[87]

---

[81] *TOPCO*, 17 ILM at 8.   [82] *Id.*

[83] Dupuy distinguishes *Sapphire*, whose sole arbitrator was to be appointed by the President of the Swiss Federal Tribunal. He implies mistakenly, however, that this designation was an expressly stated basis for the conclusion reached in *Sapphire*. *Id.*

[84] *Id.* at 9.

[85] Libyan American Oil Co. v. Libyan Arab Republic (1977), *reprinted in* 20 ILM 1 (1981) (Mahmassani, sole arb.).

[86] *Id.* at 43.

[87] Von Mehren & Kourides, assuming that Swiss law governed the arbitration, found it interesting that Libya did not challenge the award "because the arbitral procedure was not the law of the situs." Von Mehren & Kourides, *supra* note 77, at 509. However, under the vast majority of municipal arbitration statutes, parties may choose their own internal rules of procedure as long as those rules are not inconsistent with the mandatory provisions of the arbitration statute involved. Thus, there is nothing inherently challengeable about the choice by Mahmassani of the United Nations Draft Convention on Arbitral Procedure. The only reason for challenge on the basis stated would be failure to comply with mandatory provisions, such as registration of the award.

Lake and Dana conclude that the arbitration "must be regarded as a-national" because the choice to use the Draft Convention on Arbitral Procedure was made, according to Mahmassani, "independently of the local law of the seat of arbitration." Lake & Dana, *supra* note 15, at 804. Again, however, Mahmassani's statement is ambiguous in that it does not say that the procedural rules *chosen* would be *applied* even if they were—in some particularities—contrary to local law. Rather, Mahmassani cites *Sapphire* only to support the principle that the rules of procedure are chosen independently of local law.

Arbitrators and commentators have cited one or the other of these cases to justify a variety of inconsistent propositions about the legal system that should govern such arbitrations. Significantly, however, in all of the cases the arbitrators approached the facts before them in the same basic manner: they sought to ascertain the intent of the parties, which not once was set forth clearly in an express provision. Thus, the arbitrators examined subsidiary factors for evidence of intent. It is the facts, or perhaps the starting presumptions of the arbitrators, but not the test of which legal system governs, that led the cases to different results.

As to the difference in starting presumptions of the arbitrators, the 15 years between the *ARAMCO* and *British Petroleum* awards are crucial. That period saw dramatic changes in legal doctrine, which necessarily influenced what the arbitrators thought to be the basic intent of the parties. The 1958 *ARAMCO* award found that even though Saudi Arabia had agreed to making Switzerland the seat of the tribunal, it could not thus be presumed to have surrendered its immunity from Swiss oversight of the arbitration.[88] The 1973 *British Petroleum* award, on the other hand, emphasized that even though one of the parties was a state, it must have intended to create an effective remedy.[89]

This change in attitude from *ARAMCO* to *British Petroleum* can be explained in two ways. First, the panel in *ARAMCO* noted repeatedly that the parties sought only a declaratory judgment. In this sense, they possibly attached less importance to the enforceability of the award.[90] The second and more significant explanation is the emergence of the doctrine of restrictive sovereign immunity in many municipal legal systems during this same period.

The resolution of international legal disputes finds expression in many mechanisms: the International Court of Justice, claims commissions, private

---

At the other end of the spectrum, Redfern suggests that Mahmassani followed the approach of Dupuy in *TOPCO* and regarded *LIAMCO* only as subject to public international law. Redfern, *supra* note 61, at 82.

[88] *ARAMCO*, 27 ILR at 156.

[89] *British Petroleum*, 53 ILR at 309.

Dupuy, the sole arbitrator in *TOPCO*, did not state his view on this point but, rather, confused his jurisdiction to consider enforceability generally with consideration of enforceability as a circumstance evidencing the parties' choice of the legal system to govern the arbitration. In addition, it seems inconsistent that Dupuy cited the number of parties to the ICSID Convention to support his conclusion that UN General Assembly Resolution 1803 continued to reflect the proper standard of compensation in expropriation, 17 ILM at 30, but did not cite the same circumstances to support the apparent willingness of states to enter into enforceable arbitral arrangements.

[90] Dupuy in *TOPCO* also noted that the enforceability of the award in that arbitration was not of practical significance, as the "present arbitration should be an arbitration on matters of principle." 17 ILM at 8. What Dupuy passed over, however, is that, as in *British Petroleum*, the award as to legal principles was only the first stage of an arbitration that ultimately was to decide upon the requested relief of restitution or damages. Thus, the *TOPCO* arbitration ultimately was of more than declaratory character. *See* von Mehren & Kourides, *supra* note 77, at 490–96.

arbitration and municipal courts. The development of these mechanisms is rarely coordinated, yet modifications in any one may, as a stone dropped into water, ripple throughout. The panel in *ARAMCO* noted in 1958 that "[i]t is true that the practice of the Swiss Courts has limited the jurisdictional immunity of States . . . ."[91] It is also true, however, that 1958 marked only the beginning of widespread implementation of the restrictive theory of sovereign immunity. Prior to 1952, a U.S. national's primary mechanism for raising a claim against a foreign government was diplomatic protection.[92] Indeed, the institution of an action in U.S. courts against a foreign state did not become free of executive comment until passage of the Foreign Sovereign Immunities Act in 1976.[93] Although acceptance of the restrictive theory, particularly as to enforcement, is by no means universal, transformations similar to that in the United States occurred in other countries during these decades.[94] Consequently, as the traditional distinctions between a state party and a private party have become less relevant to certain kinds of activity, the likelihood of an effective municipal remedy against state parties has increased dramatically for private parties engaged in international business.[95]

At the same time, companies have often been reluctant to enter into schemes requiring investment in a foreign country unless that investment could be protected.[96] In negotiating arbitration clauses, companies and states are seeking an alternative to the local courts. This alternative can be truly acceptable to private parties only if it provides an effective remedy. Thus, one would expect the circumstances described to lead the parties to choose the legal system of the place of arbitration to govern the arbitral process.

Finally, it should be noted that Lake and Dana offer a third possible legal characterization of arbitrations between states and private entities. They

---

[91] *ARAMCO*, 27 ILR at 156.

[92] *See* Z & F Assets Realization Corp. v. Hull, 311 U.S. 470, 487 (1941).

[93] 28 U.S.C. §§1330, 1332, 1396, 1441, 1602–1611 (1982). During the period 1952–1976, suits could be instituted with the filing by the Department of State of its suggestions on immunity with the court. For a concise history of U.S. practice, see Alfred Dunhill of London, Inc. v. Republic of Cuba, 425 U.S. 682, 698 (1976).

[94] *See, e.g.,* United Kingdom State Immunity Act 1978, ch. 33, *reprinted in* 17 ILM 1123 (1978); Canadian Act to Provide for State Immunity, ch. 95 (1982), *reprinted in* 21 ILM 798 (1982); European Convention on State Immunity (1972), 1972 ETS 74, *reprinted in* 11 ILM 470 (1972); Australian Foreign States Immunities Act 1985, *reprinted in* 25 ILM 715 (1986).

On the current state of sovereign immunity doctrine, see Trooboff, *Foreign State Immunity: Emerging Consensus on Principles*, 200 RECUEIL DES COURS 235 (1986 V). On an agreement to arbitrate as a waiver of sovereign immunity from execution, see *id.* at 388; Fox, *supra* note 17, at 10; and Blessing & Burckhardt, *Sovereign Immunity—A Pitfall in State Arbitration?*, in SWISS ESSAYS ON INTERNATIONAL ARBITRATION 107 (C. Reymond & E. Bucher eds. 1984).

[95] Böckstiegel, *supra* note 66, at 27.

[96] Although I believe this proposition, as qualified, is true, I also note that I am not aware of empirical support for the assertion that business acts cautiously in regard to foreign investment. The qualification "often" recognizes that corporate behavior likely turns also upon the competition within the industry in question and the institutional memory of the specific corporation.

regard arbitrations such as *TOPCO* and *ARAMCO* as anational,[97] a conclusion that apparently rests on the assumption that all "denationalized" arbitration is anational arbitration. This assumption, however, fails to distinguish between two forms of denationalized arbitration: anational arbitration and interstate arbitration. Anational arbitration is denationalized in the sense that it is freed at least somewhat from the supervisory jurisdiction of the legal system where the award was made. Yet the proponents of anational arbitration do not intend that such proceedings also be freed from the jurisdiction of legal systems of states where enforcement may be sought. Interstate arbitration, on the other hand, is totally denationalized.[98] It is governed by the applicable international legal regime and involves municipal courts only to the degree agreed to by the parties. The *ARAMCO* tribunal concluded that Saudi Arabia could not be presumed to have intended to "be subject to the law of another State"; but to regard the *ARAMCO* award as anational would surely subject Saudi Arabia to the legal system of another state—the enforcement state.

The Distinction Distilled: Sovereign Immunity and Intent

The latitude parties enjoy over their agreement to arbitrate allows for great variety in the interstate and international commercial arbitral processes. Private parties choose the place of arbitration and the applicable rules of arbitral procedure, including special rules such as provisions for the production of evidence. States may choose an ad hoc arbitration governed by an international regime (such as in *ARAMCO*) or they may waive at least a part of their immunity and join the private parties in choosing a *lex arbitri*. The consideration arguably most influencing these choices, particularly the agreement of a state to review of the arbitral process by a municipal legal system, is the enforceability of the resulting award.[99] The types of parties and disputes involved often suggest the process preferred by the parties, and thus our intuitive distinction between an interstate and a private commercial process may often be confirmed.

In any particular case, however, the choice suggested as most likely by the circumstances may not be the choice in fact adopted by the parties. Consequently, although it may be convenient or useful to describe a particular type of process as interstate or private, the distinction should be used with care. To determine the legal character of an arbitration, the relevant ques-

---

[97] Lake and Dana first state that *ARAMCO* and *TOPCO* were "denationalized" proceedings, *supra* note 15, at 774. They later conclude that the Iran-U.S. Claims Tribunal, like the International Court of Justice, is "a 'denationalized' adjudicating body, whose actions are governed by the treaty creating it and by its own rules, but not by any national arbitration law," *id.* at 779. They ultimately conclude that because the Tribunal (and implicitly *ARAMCO* and *TOPCO* also) is denationalized, its awards are anational, *id.* at 789.

[98] A similar mixing of these two forms of denationalized arbitrations occurs in Redfern, *supra* note 61, at 77 (text at note 25) and 79–83.

[99] Although it must be remembered that a given country may not be a party to the New York Convention, while a state may have frozen assets at its disposal to set off against a public international award.

tions are: what legal system did the parties intend to govern the validity of the arbitral process? and, if a state is involved, to what degree does the agreement of the parties embody a waiver of the state party's immunities? A legal system will govern the validity of the arbitral process. But inasmuch as the parties themselves choose that legal system, the key factor is their intent.

The awards discussed above suggest several factors that might indicate the intention of the parties about the governing legal system. The content and structure of the arbitration agreement as a whole may serve as such evidence. Thus, Cavin cited the provision for an optional conciliation procedure and the detailed procedural provisions of the arbitration agreement in *Sapphire* to support his conclusion that the parties desired a final solution and that the law of the place of arbitration applied.[100] Likewise, the national or international nature of the appointing authority could be evidence of intent. In the *TOPCO* case, Professor Dupuy found such evidence in the parties' failure to object to the Rules of Procedure he had formulated.[101] In addition to these factors, Delaume suggests that the more the legal system of the place of arbitration reviews both the fairness and the legal correctness of the arbitration, the more likely it is that the state party did not intend to submit itself to that system.[102]

Subsidiary factors evidencing intent need not be examined when the parties have stated it unequivocally in the arbitration clause, even if the subsidiary factors mentioned above indicate the opposite intent. In *Kuwait and the American Independent Oil Co. (AMINOIL)*,[103] the arbitrators noted that the arbitration agreement provided (1) that the proceedings were to be subject to "any mandatory provisions of the procedural law of the place where the arbitration is held";[104] (2) that the parties "expressly waive[d] all rights of recourse to any Court, except such rights as cannot be waived by the law of the place of arbitration";[105] and (3) that the "seat of the arbitration shall be Paris."[106] On the basis of these provisions, the panel concluded that "[w]ith regard to the law governing the arbitral procedure in the broadest sense, it is not open to doubt that the Parties have chosen the French legal system."[107] Without such clear provisions in the arbitral agreement, the subsidiary factors would have suggested the opposite result. In particular, a state rather than a state enterprise was involved, the dispute

---

[100] *Sapphire*, 35 ILR at 168–69.

[101] *See* text at note 84 *supra* and *TOPCO*, 17 ILM at 9.

[102] Delaume, *Arbitration with Governments: "Domestic" v. "International" Awards*, 17 INT'L LAW. 687, 689 (1983):

> In this connection, it may be appropriate to recall that the English Arbitration Act of 1979, abolishing the special case procedure, was enacted for the purpose, among others, of assuring foreign states that . . . they would no longer have to fear that the submission implied acceptance of the judicial supervisory authority of the English Court.

See AAA Report, *supra* note 59, at 5–6.

[103] Kuwait and American Independent Oil Co. (1982), *reprinted in* 21 ILM 976 (1982) (Reuter, Fitzmaurice, Sultan, arbs.).

[104] Art. IV(1), *id.* at 980.   [105] Art. V, *id.*

[106] Art. IV(3), *id.*   [107] *Id.* at 999.

involved rights in natural resources, and the President of the International Court of Justice had been called upon to appoint the presiding arbitrator.[108]

Similarly, their intent would be unmistakable if the parties chose rules such as those of the ICC, since they presuppose that the parties desire a private international arbitral process. Indeed, under the law of several countries, a state's agreement to arbitration within that country's municipal scheme constitutes a waiver of immunities.[109] Normally, the intent to place the arbitration *within* the municipal scheme is apparent because the parties have adopted nationally promulgated private arbitration rules, such as those of the American Arbitration Association, or transnationally promulgated private arbitration rules, such as those of the ICC.

The transition from basing analysis on categories rather than intent will not be as simple for arbitral panels as might initially be thought. Analysis based on intent will require the interpreter of a treaty to be suspicious of traditional pigeonholes for international structures because the parties by their treaty may have constructed a new type of structure. This is not an easy task because an interpreter's preconceived notions of what the parties should have intended can blind the interpreter to what the parties say they intended. In both law and science one can undertake to construct a taxonomy; but in law the categories that can be said to be *naturally* apparent flow from changing circumstances such as the organization of society and the ability of those within the society to interact. This organization is constantly challenged and this ability thus far has increased without major interruption. The challenges may require change in legal categories; often the increasing ability to interact itself provides the means. To squeeze innovative efforts into traditional categories is to constrain society's ability to adapt. The danger that the innovative intent of the parties will be frustrated is particularly acute at a time when the relatively rapid evolution of international law processes may make preheld notions also out-of-date. Treaties are a prime source of innovation in international law and international relations. Subtle doctrinal predispositions will only frustrate objective interpretation and the experimentation necessary to the growth of the international system.

It is this conservative interpretational tendency that has confused analysis concerning the Iran–United States Claims Tribunal. Thus far, this analysis has rested primarily on intuition and analogy. These means of analysis carry

---

[108] Interestingly, in *AMINOIL* it reportedly was the state party, Kuwait, that argued for the arbitration to be governed by French law; AMINOIL argued for an anational process. Redfern, *supra* note 61, at 77. In this sense, it is Kuwait arguably that pressed for a more effective award. *Id.* at 86.

[109] For example, the U.S. Foreign Sovereign Immunities Act recognizes that immunity may be waived, 28 U.S.C. §1605(a)(1) (1982), and the House Report explaining that provision noted that "[w]ith respect to implied waivers, the courts have found such waivers in cases where a foreign state has agreed to arbitration in another country." H.R. REP. No. 1487, 94th Cong., 2d Sess. 6 (1976), 1976 U.S. CODE CONG. & ADMIN. NEWS 6604, 6617. *See generally* Fox, *supra* note 17; Oparil, *Waiver of Sovereign Immunity in the United States and Great Britain by an Arbitration Agreement*, 3 J. INT'L ARB. 61 (1986); Sullivan, *Implicit Waiver of Sovereign Immunity by Consent to Arbitration: Territorial Scope and Procedural Limits*, 18 TEX. INT'L L.J. 329 (1983).

with them many doctrinal predispositions. What is needed, instead, is careful study of what Iran and the United States intended to accomplish in the Algiers Accords. Thus, this article now shifts from the exposition of a general theory to the examination of a specific case.

II. The Legal System Supervising the Iran-U.S. Claims Tribunal

One of the most innovative and intellectually satisfying aspects of the Algiers Accords is that they establish for the Iran–United States Claims Tribunal a rather complete internal world. There is little need for the parties to request assistance from powers external to the Tribunal. The UNCITRAL Arbitration Rules[110] provide for an appointing authority to resolve disputes between the parties over the composition of the Tribunal.[111] More importantly, the Algiers Accords established a fund, the Security Account, with a portion of the Iranian assets that the United States had frozen. With the Algerian Government acting as escrow agent for the Security Account pursuant to the Tribunal's instructions, the Security Account assures the availability of funds to satisfy most awards of the Tribunal.[112]

Nevertheless, to say that there is little need to refer to the world outside the Tribunal is not to say that there is none. Already, a British court has had to consider whether it should recognize an award of the Tribunal as *res judicata*.[113] Moreover, the Security Account may satisfy only the claims of United States nationals, not awards in favor of Iranian nationals or Iranian governmental counterclaimants.[114] Indeed, a current action in U.S. court seeks to enforce such a counterclaim award.[115] In addition, if the Security Account were to become depleted, the unsatisfied beneficiaries might be required to seek enforcement of their awards elsewhere.[116] Finally, a party

---

[110] After 3 years of development involving all interested nations, the UNCITRAL Rules, *supra* note 26, were adopted by the United Nations Commission on International Trade Law (UNCITRAL) on Apr. 28, 1976, and recommended for use without further debate by the General Assembly on Dec. 15, 1976. *See* K. RAUH, DIE SCHIEDS- UND SCHLICHTUNGSORD-NUNGEN DER UNCITRAL (1983); Sanders, *Commentary on UNCITRAL Arbitration Rules*, 2 Y.B. COM. ARB. 172 (1977). Article III(2) of the Claims Settlement Declaration, *supra* note 1, provides that the Tribunal shall use the UNCITRAL Rules "except to the extent modified by the Parties or by the Tribunal." *See* Aksen, *The Iran–United States Claims Tribunal and the UNCITRAL Arbitration Rules—an early comment*, in THE ART OF ARBITRATION, *supra* note 57, at 1.

[111] *See* UNCITRAL Rules, *supra* note 26, Arts. 6–14.

[112] State claimants have achieved similar security in the past by holding on to frozen assets for possible satisfaction of judgments rendered in their favor. The United States, for example, held German assets in this way after World War I and ultimately used a portion of those assets to satisfy awards made by the U.S.-German Mixed Claims Commission in favor of U.S. nationals. *See* Borchard, *The Settlement of War Claims Act of 1928*, 22 AJIL 373 (1928); McHugh, *Settlement of War Claims Act of 1928*, 14 A.B.A.J. 193 (1928).

[113] Mark Dallal v. Bank Mellat, *supra* note 11.

[114] *See* General Declaration, *supra* note 1, para. 7 ("All funds in the Security Account are to be used for the sole purpose of the payments of . . . claims against Iran . . .").

[115] Ministry of Defense v. Gould, Inc., *supra* note 12.

[116] As stated in the brief for the United States as *amicus curiae* in Ministry of Defense v. Gould, Inc., 887 F.2d 1357 (9th Cir. 1989) [hereinafter *Amicus Curiae* Brief]:

dissatisfied with an award may wish to challenge it and have it set aside. Thus, although the Tribunal is substantially less dependent upon the external legal world than many other forms of arbitration, that dependency remains significant.

Another factor in analyzing the Tribunal's relationship to the external legal world is the Tribunal's three primary jurisdictional grants. It must be asked whether the legal system supervising the arbitral process before the Tribunal is a function of the particular basis of jurisdiction. First, the Tribunal may hear "claims of nationals of the United States against Iran and claims of nationals of Iran against the United States"[117] (claims of nationals). Second, the Tribunal has jurisdiction over "official claims of the United States and Iran against each other arising out of [certain] contractual arrangements between them"[118] (official claims). Third, the Tribunal may hear disputes between Iran and the United States concerning the interpretation or performance of any provision of the General Declaration[119] or the interpretation or application of the Claims Settlement Declaration[120] (interpretive disputes). The vast bulk of the disputes falls into the first category, claims of nationals.[121] Moreover, the main point of contention between Iran and the United States, in scholarly commentary and in judicial decisions, has been the legal system governing arbitrations involving claims of nationals. Iran at times has contended that these are interstate arbitrations. The United States, on the other hand, after some consideration, has taken the position that these are more akin to international commercial arbitrations, as they are governed by the legal system of the Netherlands and the resulting awards have Dutch nationality. Iran at other times has joined the United States in characterizing the awards as Dutch. Neither Iran nor the United States has expressed views on the legal system to be applied to the arbitrations involving official claims or interpretive disputes. Consequently, a substantial portion of the evidence regarding intent relates only to the first grant of jurisdiction. As will be seen, however, the analysis set forth below appears to be equally applicable to the official claims and interpretive disputes.

This analysis focuses on three issues: (1) the intention of the state parties to rest the arbitrations involving claims of nationals on the interstate process of diplomatic protection; (2) the intention of the state parties to have the

---

While to date these awards have been paid from the Security Account [and] [a]lthough the United States expects Iran to carry out its obligation to replenish the Security Account in the future, should Iran not do so, the vast majority of private claims before the Tribunal will be dependent on judicial enforcement of Tribunal Awards.

Id. at 7.
[117] Claims Settlement Declaration, *supra* note 1, Art. II(1).
[118] *Id.*, Art. II(2).
[119] *Id.*, Art. II(3); General Declaration, *supra* note 1, para. 17.
[120] Claims Settlement Declaration, *supra* note 1, Art. VI(4).
[121] The Tribunal's docket is composed of approximately 3,761 claims of nationals, 78 official claims and 22 interpretive disputes.

legal system of the Netherlands govern the validity of the arbitrations; and (3) the willingness and ability of the Netherlands to accommodate the desires of the United States and Iran.

Claims of Nationals and Diplomatic Protection

An important preliminary question is whether the arbitrations involving "claims of nationals" are based on claims raised by the nationals themselves or by their governments through the interstate mechanism of diplomatic protection.[122] If these arbitrations are based on diplomatic protection, the long history of this practice would suggest that Iran and the United States intended that they be subject to review under the international legal system.

In the *Dual Nationality* case, decided in 1984, Iran asserted that U.S. nationals who also possessed Iranian nationality (hence the phrase "dual nationals") could not bring claims against Iran before the Tribunal. In support of this position, Iran argued that the arbitrations before the Tribunal were an instance of diplomatic protection. According to Iran, the extensive customary international practice on diplomatic protection, which in Iran's view weighed against the espousal of claims of dual nationals, informed the Algiers Accords.[123] In its Memorial, Iran[124] noted that Article

---

[122] Diplomatic protection is, in the words of the Permanent Court of International Justice, a situation in public international law whereby, "in taking up the case of one of its nationals, by resorting to diplomatic action or international judicial proceedings on his behalf, a State is in reality asserting its own right, the right to ensure in the person of its nationals respect for the rules of international law." Panevezys-Saldutiskis Railway Case (Estonia v. Lithuania), 1939 PCIJ (ser. A/B) No. 76, at 16 (Judgment of Feb. 28). *See also* G. Leigh, *Nationality and Diplomatic Protection*, 20 INT'L & COMP. L.Q. 453, 455 (1971).

[123] Islamic Republic of Iran and United States (Case A18) (Dual Nationality), Dec. 32–A18–FT (Lagergren, Holtzmann (CO), Kashani (DO), Riphagen (CO), Aldrich, Shafeiei (DO), Mangård, Ansari (DO), & Mosk (CO), arbs., Apr. 6, 1984), 5 IRAN-U.S. C.T.R. 251 (1984 I).

Citations to this award and those below include the names of the arbitrators who were members of the panel rendering the award. The Chairman is always listed first, with the other arbitrators following in alphabetical order. Parenthetically following each name is, as appropriate, a letter or letters reflecting the arbitrator's position *vis-à-vis* the Tribunal's award. These symbols are: C, concurring; D, dissenting; CS, concurring via statement by signature; DS, dissenting via statement by signature; CO, concurring opinion; DO, dissenting opinion; SO, separate opinion; and RS, refusal to sign. An indication of dissent or concurrence with a whole award does not necessarily indicate dissent or concurrence with the particular point being discussed in this study.

On dual nationals' claims before the Tribunal, see generally Mahoney, *The Standing of Dual Nationals Before the Iran–United States Claims Tribunal*, 24 VA. J. INT'L L. 695 (1984); Note, *Claims of Dual Nationals in the Modern Era: The Iran–United States Claims Tribunal*, 83 MICH. L. REV. 597 (1984); Leurent, *Problèmes soulevés par les demandes des double nationaux devant le Tribunal des différends irano-américains*, 74 REVUE CRITIQUE DE DROIT INTERNATIONAL PRIVÉ [RCDIP] 273–99, 477–503 (1985); and Rigaux, L'Admissibilité des demandes introduites devant un tribunal international par les binationaux et la décision de l'Iran–United States Claims Tribunal sur cette question (paper presented in The Hague, May 29, 1984).

[124] Memorial of the Islamic Republic of Iran in Case A18 (Oct. 21, 1983) [hereinafter Iranian A18 Memorial], *reprinted in* IRANIAN ASSETS LITIGATION REPORTER [hereinafter I.A.L.R.], Nov. 18, 1983, at 7,503.

II(1) of the Claims Settlement Declaration provides that "an *international* arbitral tribunal (the Iran–United States Claims Tribunal) is hereby established."[125] Although Iran recognized that the "fact that the Tribunal was created by international agreement does not necessarily . . . exclude its having been created in order to settle disputes of national law," it argued that the overall purpose of the Tribunal was to end disputes between the two states, that other jurisdictional categories clearly involved intergovernmental disputes, and that the two states (and not the private parties) had designated the arbitrators and were bearing the expense of the arbitration.[126] The phrase "claims of nationals," in Iran's view, "serves solely to identify" a class of international claims and "does not prejudge the nature of the claims nor the law which should be applied to them."[127] Iran concluded that it is clear from

> the structure, the spirit and the terms of the Declarations, that this tribunal is truly international since it is called upon to settle a dispute between States, arising from the treatment by one of them of the nationals of the other, the solution to which must be found in public international law and not disputes between one State and nationals of the other, which could be resolved by the application of private international law.[128]

Given the international origin of the Tribunal and the prevailing view that individuals are not subjects of international law, "[a]ll this confirms that the provisions concerning the resolution of disputes reflect classical requirements of diplomatic protection."[129]

The United States rebutted this position, arguing that it ignored the most important evidence—what the parties had agreed to in the Accords:

> The Iranian position seems to depend on a combined historical and theoretical analysis of what international tribunals should be. The theory is not derived from the facts of how this Tribunal is constructed. The facts are formed to fit the theory. If the facts don't fit the theory, Iran says that they don't really contradict it, however important the facts are.[130]

The Full Tribunal in its decision in the *Dual Nationality* case observed that "most disputes [before it] involve a private party on one side and a Government or Government-controlled entity on the other." The Tribunal went on to hold that "the object and purpose of the Algiers Declarations was to resolve a crisis in relations between Iran and the United States, not to extend diplomatic protection in the normal sense."[131]

---

[125] *Id.* at 16–17 (emphasis added).

[126] *Id.* At least in the United States, a portion of the costs of the Tribunal is borne by the successful private claimants via a user fee placed by the U.S. Government on the amounts awarded to such claimants. *See* United States v. Sperry Corp. 58 U.S.L.W. 4018 (U.S. Nov. 28, 1989). *See also* the summary of the earlier opinion of the court of appeals in 83 AJIL 86 (1989).

[127] Iranian A18 Memorial, *supra* note 124, at 25–26.

[128] *Id.* at 18.   [129] *Id.* at 31.

[130] 1 U.S. Transcript of the Case A18 Hearing 140 (Nov. 9, 1983).

[131] Case A18 (Dual Nationality), *supra* note 123, at 18–19, 5 IRAN-U.S. C.T.R. at 261.

Despite this decision of the Full Tribunal, Iran has maintained its view that the claims of nationals are indeed the claims of the government of those nationals.[132] In its 1987 decision in Case A21, the Full Tribunal reiterated that "Tribunal awards uniformly recognize that no espousal of claims by the United States is involved in the cases before it."[133] Nonetheless, the Iranian arbitrators continue to file lengthy opinions arguing that the claims of nationals are raised through espousal.[134]

Examination of the Accords supports the Full Tribunal's view that the Tribunal is international in origin but has as its primary purpose the resolution of claims between a private party and a state. The notion of diplomatic protection has structural implications simply not present in the case of the Tribunal.

Classically, for a state to espouse a claim on the basis of diplomatic protection, its national must have exhausted the remedies provided locally by the allegedly offending state.[135] The exhaustion of remedies without redress constitutes a part of the complicity of the second state in the injury to the national of the first state. However, the customary international law requirement that a claimant exhaust local remedies is not without limits.[136] The situation within Iran and between the two countries, for example, affords good reason to conclude that the requirement would have been waived by the Tribunal even if the claims had been presented on the basis of diplomatic protection.[137] Yet the Tribunal has not waived the requirement

---

[132] *See, e.g.,* Memorial of the Islamic Republic of Iran, Case A21, at 15 (May 15, 1986) (interpretive dispute dealing with the duty of the state parties to execute judgments rendered against their nationals), *reprinted in* I.A.L.R., July 25, 1986, at 12,682, 12,693 ("All this confirms that the provisions concerning the resolution of disputes reflect classical requirements of diplomatic protection . . ."). *See also A Recent Review of the Cases at the Hague Tribunal,* Kayhan [Iranian newspaper], June 13, 1984 (U.S. Dep't of State trans.) (statement of an Iranian official after the decision in *Dual Nationality* that "[w]e believe . . . that The Hague arbitration is an international arbitration and the Netherlands' Government has no right to interfere with it").

[133] Islamic Republic of Iran and United States (State Party Responsibility for Awards Rendered Against its Nationals), Dec. 62–A21–FT, para. 12 (Böckstiegel, Holtzmann, Mostafavi (SO), Briner, Aldrich, Bahrami-Ahmadi (SO), Virally, Salans, Ansari (SO), arbs., May 4, 1987), 14 IRAN-U.S. C.T.R. 324, 330 (1987 I).

[134] *See, e.g.,* Concurring/Dissenting Opinion of Assadollah Noori (June 3, 1988) to Leonard & Mavis Daley and Islamic Republic of Iran, AWD 360–10514–1 (Böckstiegel, Holtzmann & Noori (CO/DO), arbs., Apr. 20, 1988); Separate Opinion of Seyed Khalil Khalilian (Feb. 23, 1988) to Lord Corp. and Iran Helicopter Support & Renewal Co., AWD 346–10973–2 (Briner, Aldrich & Khalilian (SO), arbs., Jan. 29, 1988).

[135] *See* Claim of Finnish Shipowners (Fin. v. Gt. Brit.), 3 R. Int'l Arb. Awards 1479 (1934) (Bagge, sole arb.).

[136] *See* Interhandel Case (Preliminary Objections) (Switz. v. U.S.), 1959 ICJ REP. 6 (Judgment of Mar. 21); American Int'l Group v. Islamic Republic of Iran, 493 F.Supp. 522, 525 (D.D.C. 1980) ("It is well settled in international law that where local remedies would be ineffective or meaningless or would not meet the international standard of minimum justice, the alien need not subject himself, in the first instance, to the local courts or administrative tribunals").

[137] *See* Rexnord and Islamic Republic of Iran, AWD 21–132–3, at 8–9 (Mangård, Mosk & Sani (RS), arbs., Jan. 10, 1983), 2 IRAN-U.S. C.T.R. 6 (1983 I); American Int'l Group and Islamic Republic of Iran, AWD 93–2–3, at 9 (Mangård, Ansari (RS) & Mosk (CO), arbs., Dec.

but, instead, has simply held it not to be applicable to the claims of nationals before the Tribunal.[138]

More important than exhaustion of local remedies are aspects of the Accords that indicate in various ways that these claims belong to the national and not to the state, as they would if they were based on diplomatic protection.[139] Article II(1) of the Claims Settlement Declaration does not provide, as might be expected for diplomatic protection, that the Tribunal may decide claims of the United States or Iran brought "on behalf of the interests of its nationals" or "on the basis of injury to its nationals." Rather, the provision provides jurisdiction over the "claims of nationals of the United States and of Iran."

That the claim belongs to the national is substantiated by the fact that the Claims Settlement Declaration provides that the nationals themselves shall present their claims to the Tribunal.[140] Not only have claims of U.S. na-

---

19, 1983), 4 IRAN-U.S. C.T.R. 96 (1983 III); and Time and Islamic Republic of Iran, AWD 139–166–2, at 4 (Riphagen, Aldrich & Shafeiei (DS), arbs., June 29, 1984), 7 IRAN-U.S. C.T.R. 8 (1984 III). *But see* Dissenting Opinion of M. Kashani (Sept. 13, 1984) to Starrett Housing and Islamic Republic of Iran, ITL 32–24–1, at 55 (Dec. 19, 1983), 7 IRAN-U.S. C.T.R., *supra*, at 119. *Cf.* Schwebel, *Some Aspects of International Law in Arbitration Between States and Aliens*, in 1986 PRIVATE INVESTORS ABROAD—PROBLEMS AND SOLUTIONS IN INTERNATIONAL BUSINESS 12-1, 12-8 (J. Moss ed.).

[138] *See, e.g.*, Amoco Int'l Finance Corp. and Islamic Republic of Iran, AWD 310–53–5, para. 21 (Virally, Brower (CO) & Ansari (C/D), arbs., July 14, 1987), 15 IRAN-U.S. C.T.R. 189, 197 (1987 II).

[139] *See* Leigh, *supra* note 122, at 455.

[140] A supplemental clause provides that when the claim is less than $250,000, the claim *may also* be presented by the government of that national. Claims Settlement Declaration, *supra* note 1, Art. III(3). In the event, the claims of U.S. nationals for less than $250,000 were filed by the United States; the typical caption for the claimant read, "The United States of America, on behalf and for the benefit of the [name of private claimant]." The Tribunal, in the spring of 1986 on its own initiative, changed the caption of the claims for less than $250,000 to read, "[name of private claimant], a claim of less than U.S. $250,000 presented by the United States of America." *See, e.g.*, Picker Int'l Corp. and Islamic Republic of Iran, AWD 229–10173–3 (Virally, Brower & Ansari, arbs., May 1, 1986). The Agent for Iran filed Requests for Correction of Award asking that the original caption be reinstated. The Tribunal denied these requests, stating that Article III(3) of the Claims Settlement Declaration indicates that the claim "remains the claim of the national and not of the Government of such national . . . the Government of the national owning such claim merely presents the claim . . . ." *See* Koehler and Islamic Republic of Iran, Dec. 43–11713–1 (Böckstiegel, Holtzmann & Mostafavi (DS), arbs., July 3, 1986), 11 IRAN-U.S. C.T.R. 285 (1986 I). *See also* Trustees of Columbia Univ. and Islamic Republic of Iran, Dec. 42–10517–1 (Böckstiegel, Holtzmann & Mostafavi (DS), arbs., July 3, 1986), 11 IRAN-U.S. C.T.R., *supra*, at 283; Baygell and Islamic Republic of Iran, Dec. 46–10212–2 (Briner, Aldrich & Bahrami-Ahmadi (DS), arbs., Aug. 7, 1986), 11 IRAN-U.S. C.T.R., *supra*, at 300. Since that time, Iranian arbitrators have filed separate opinions arguing that the claims for less than $250,000 are espoused by the United States, and occasionally on their separate opinions have altered the case caption to read "[name of private claimant] presented by THE UNITED STATES OF AMERICA in protection of its national." *See* opinions cited *supra* note 134.

As a precautionary measure, the United States also filed a claim for more than $250,000 for all of the claimants potentially holding claims for less than $250,000 (Case 86). The Statement of Claim in Case 86 was presented "in continuance of the exercise of diplomatic protection of its nationals, acting as parens patriae, trustee, guardian and representative on their behalf."

tionals been filed and argued by those very nationals, but it is also the national that decides whether to withdraw or to accept settlement. Indeed, the Agent for Iran reportedly supported the primacy of the national, arguing that the U.S. Agent may not speak at hearings on the claims of nationals because the United States is not a party to such proceedings.[141]

An example of the importance given to the owner of the claim can be found in the American-Turkish Claims Settlement of 1937, in which numerous claims were rejected almost immediately because they were filed directly with the commission by private counsel representing the nationals. The Agreement of December 24, 1923, between the United States and Turkey establishing the commission provided for governmental espousal of claims. The commission took the position that the direct presentation of claims by nationals was incompatible with the idea of diplomatic protection: "It would, of course, be monstrous to suggest that a government would through some subterfuge pretend to support a claim without having any knowledge of what, if anything, had in some way come before the Commission."[142]

Just as importantly, the Security Account satisfies Tribunal awards *directly* to the benefit of the national who presents the claim and is the named party, and not to the benefit of the government of that national.[143] Indeed, the U.S. Government has been the subject of extensive litigation in the United States because of its efforts to recoup a part of awards to its nationals to cover the administrative expenses of the Tribunal.[144]

A more subtle indicator of the nature of the arbitrations, suggested by David Lloyd Jones, is whether the duties placed on the respondent government flow to the claimant private party or to the private party's state.[145]

This claim, often called the "blanket claim," has not been the subject of any proceedings. "The primary purpose of the filing was to provide a convenient mechanism for dealing with the claims if a lump sum settlement were reached with Iran." Response of the United States, Case A21, at 11 (September 1986), *reprinted in* MEALEY'S LITIGATION REP.—IRANIAN CLAIMS [hereinafter MEALEY'S], Oct. 3, 1986, at 4913, 4919.

[141] *See, e.g.,* Letter from A. Rovine to G. Lagergren (May 28, 1982) ("the Agent of the Islamic Republic of Iran, questioned my right to speak at the conference and stated that my attendance was at the 'courtesy' of his Government"). Indeed, the Tribunal in its awards in such arbitrations lists the U.S. representatives as merely "Also Present."
Likewise, Iran has reportedly characterized as "unwarranted and unjustified" the filing of comments by the U.S. Agent on proposed settlements of such arbitrations. Letter from M. Eshragh to M. Virally (Jan. 9, 1986), *cited in* Response of the United States, *supra* note 140, at 21, *reprinted in* MEALEY'S at 4924.

[142] F. K. NIELSEN & J. MAKTOS, AMERICAN-TURKISH CLAIMS SETTLEMENT 6 (U.S. Government Printing Office, 1937). *See also* 6 J. B. MOORE, A DIGEST OF INTERNATIONAL LAW 616 (1906).

[143] Similarly, it is against the national, and not the government of that national, that the Tribunal's Rules require entry of counterclaims and awards of costs. *See* Introduction and Definitions, para. 3c, Final Tribunal Rules of Procedure, May 3, 1983, *reprinted in* 2 IRAN-U.S. C.T.R. 405, 406 (1983 I); Rules, Arts. 32 and 40, *id.* at 434 and 440.

[144] *See Sperry Corp., supra* note 126.

[145] Jones, *The Iran–United States Claims Tribunal: Private Rights and State Responsibility,* 24 VA. J. INT'L L. 259, 261 (1984) (footnotes omitted). Jones asks:

Speaking in 1983, Jones speculated as to what the Tribunal's response would be to the many claims of nationals based on, for example, the Treaty of Amity between the United States and Iran, in which the duties accepted by each state run to the other. What Jones overlooked, however, is that the Tribunal was intended primarily as a substitute forum for private claimants in U.S. courts. The decision in the *Dual Nationality* case confirms this view.[146] Significantly, United States law provides private parties certain rights under international law otherwise belonging to the state. International law created by treaty is a part of the national law of both Iran[147] and the United States.[148] But "[i]t is only when a treaty is self-executing, when it prescribes rules by which private rights may be determined, that it may be relied upon for the enforcement of such rights."[149] Under U.S. law, the property protection provisions of treaties, such as the Treaty of Amity, have consistently been regarded as self-executing and granting a private right of enforcement.[150] Indeed, this right was recognized by U.S. courts in relation to the Treaty of Amity between the United States and Iran.[151] Richard M. Mosk, an arbitrator with the Tribunal, concluded that if one took into account the existence of these private rights and the impediment they presented to the state parties' conclusion of the Accords, "[i]t does not seem logical that by shifting such disputes to arbitration before this Tribunal the parties to the Algiers Declarations intended to eliminate the substantive

---

Is the Tribunal a private arbitral tribunal created to resolve private law disputes arising under different systems of law and to hear private law claims against Iran and the United States, or is it an international or interstate tribunal charged with the task of ruling on the responsibility of the respondent State under public international law for the conduct which constitutes the subject matter of the claims? If the former is the case, the Tribunal would be required to rule on infringements of private law rights arising in municipal legal systems . . . . On this view, the United States and Iran may be regarded as having referred to a private transnational arbitral tribunal questions of private law which might in other circumstances be justiciable before domestic courts. If the latter is the case, the competence of the Tribunal lies in respect of such claims as are true international claims founded on an alleged breach of international law. On this view, the Tribunal is an international or interstate tribunal dealing with the rights and duties of States under public international law in relation to their activities on the international plane, and is primarily concerned with an exercise in diplomatic protection on behalf of the United States.

[146] The Full Tribunal held in the *Dual Nationality* case, *supra* note 123, at 19, 5 IRAN-U.S. C.T.R. at 261–62:

It seems clear that a major obstacle to the resolution of that crisis was the existence of much litigation in the courts of the United States brought against Iran by citizens of the United States, often involving judicial attachments of Iranian assets. In order to overcome that obstacle and permit the return of these assets and the termination of that litigation, a new substitute forum—this Tribunal—was established.

See also Esphahanian and Bank Tejarat, AWD 31–159–2 (Bellet, Aldrich & Shafeiei (RS/DO), arbs., Mar. 29, 1983), 2 IRAN-U.S. C.T.R. 157 (1983 I) ("the Tribunal has been substituted for the national courts of both countries"; *id.* at 166).

[147] IRANIAN CIVIL CODE Art. 9.   [148] U.S. CONST. Art. VI, cl. 2.

[149] Dreyfus v. Von Finck, 534 F.2d 24, 30 (2d Cir. 1976).

[150] *See* Asakura v. Seattle, 265 U.S. 332 (1924). *See also* R. WILSON, UNITED STATES COMMERCIAL TREATIES AND INTERNATIONAL LAW (1960).

[151] American Int'l Group v. Islamic Republic of Iran, 493 F.Supp. 522, 525 (D.D.C. 1980).

rights of the parties to base a claim on a Treaty of Amity violation or otherwise to invoke that Treaty as applicable law."[152]

Thus, the Tribunal, although international in origin, has before it both intergovernmental claims and claims by nationals of one state party against the government of the other state party. But their choice not to adopt the process of diplomatic protection does not necessarily mean that the state parties intended that the legal system of the place of arbitration rather than the international legal system should govern these arbitrations.

The Intent of Iran and the United States

The intent of a state in any given circumstance can be elusive. In the following analysis, I take the observational standpoint of a tribunal or court and attempt to find the objectively determinable intent of the United States and Iran. In a few instances, I note what sources have told me that U.S. government officials intended or could not have intended. In general, however, the analysis rests upon the agreements between, and the practice of, the two states.

The objectively determinable intent of the state parties initially should be sought in the Algiers Accords themselves. This inquiry should proceed in accordance with the interpretive provisions of the Vienna Convention on the Law of Treaties, in particular, its Article 31(1), which states that "[a] treaty shall be interpreted in good faith in accordance with the ordinary meaning to be given to the terms of the treaty in their context and in the light of its object and purpose."[153]

The Accords contain no express statement on the *lex arbitri* intended by the parties, but three provisions have been referred to by one or the other of the state parties or by commentators. First, Article II(1) of the Claims Settlement Declaration refers to the Tribunal as an "international arbitral

---

[152] Concurring Opinion of Richard M. Mosk at 8 (Dec. 30, 1983) to American Int'l Group and Islamic Republic of Iran, *supra* note 137, 4 IRAN-U.S. C.T.R. at 111. *See also* Separate Opinion of Charles N. Brower at 5 (Mar. 27, 1986) to SEDCO and Islamic Republic of Iran, ITL 59–129–3 (Mangård, Brower (SO) & Ansari (D), arbs., Mar. 27, 1986), 10 IRAN-U.S. C.T.R. 180, 189 (1986 I).

[153] Vienna Convention on the Law of Treaties, Art. 31(1), *opened for signature* May 23, 1969, 1155 UNTS 331, *reprinted in* 8 ILM 679 (1969) (entered into force Jan. 27, 1980).

Iran and the United States on several occasions declared that the Vienna Convention, although not directly applicable, governs interpretation of the Accords. *See, e.g.,* Islamic Republic of Iran and United States (Dual Nationality), *supra* note 123, at 14–15, 5 IRAN-U.S. C.T.R. at 259. The Tribunal has also consistently applied the Vienna Convention. *See, e.g.,* United States and Islamic Republic of Iran (Security Account Issues), Dec. 12–A1–FT, at 3 and 5 (Aug. 3, 1982), 1 IRAN-U.S. C.T.R. 189, 190 (1981–82); Islamic Republic of Iran and United States (Dual Nationality), *supra* note 123; United States and Islamic Republic of Iran (Standby Letters of Credit), AWD 108–A16/582/591–FT, at 15 (Jan. 25, 1984), 5 IRAN-U.S. C.T.R. 57 (1984 I); and United States and Islamic Republic of Iran (Iranian Bank Claims), Dec. 37–A17–FT, at 16 (June 18, 1985), 8 IRAN-U.S. C.T.R. 189 (1985 I). Notwithstanding the views of the state parties, the interpretation provisions of the Vienna Convention would likely be applicable since they are generally regarded "as declaratory of existing law." Jiménez de Aréchaga, *International Law in the Past Third of a Century,* 159 RECUEIL DES COURS 1, 42 (1978 I).

tribunal." Second, Article VI(1) of the same Declaration states that the "seat of the Tribunal shall be The Hague" or any other place agreed to by the state parties. Finally, Article III(2) provides that "the Tribunal shall conduct its business in accordance with the arbitration rules of the United Nations Commission on International Trade Law (UNCITRAL) except to the extent modified by the Parties or by the Tribunal."

The fact that the Tribunal was established by treaty and is thus an "international arbitral tribunal" has greatly influenced the commentators who have challenged review of the Tribunal's awards by Dutch courts. Indeed, Lake and Dana, in pointing to this language, are stressing the same phrase that Iran relied upon in support of its argument on diplomatic protection.[154] As in that argument, this approach confuses origin with purpose. In essence, these commentators find it significant, if not dispositive, that the state parties used a treaty to establish the Tribunal, but they suggest no alternative means by which the state parties might have done so. There appears to be no reason that an arbitral institution of private origin might not hear an interstate arbitration or that an institution of public origin might not hear international commercial arbitrations. Thus, the simple description of the Tribunal as an "international arbitral tribunal" provides little evidence of intent. As we have seen, this phrase did not mean that the parties intended that the claims of nationals be presented on the basis of diplomatic protection; rather, it characterizes the origin of the Tribunal. It also does not necessarily describe the nature of the disputes the institution was intended to adjudicate.

Likewise, locating the Tribunal in The Hague is not by itself a significant piece of evidence as to intent. Although the legal system of the place of arbitration is the *lex arbitri* for international commercial arbitration, the place of arbitration is commonly indicated in purely interstate arbitration as well, without any intent to subordinate the process to the local legal system.

The choice of the UNCITRAL Rules, however, is very significant. Other tribunals have regarded the parties' choice of procedural rules as an indication of intent.[155] The primary alternatives available to the drafters of the Accords were the United Nations Draft Convention on Arbitral Procedure and the UNCITRAL Rules of Arbitral Procedure. The Draft Convention was designed for use in interstate arbitration, while the UNCITRAL Rules were intended for use in international commercial arbitration. In the *ARAMCO* and *TOPCO* arbitrations, the only two arbitrations between a private party and a state in which the *lex arbitri* was found to be international

---

[154] They wrote:

> The Tribunal is a very different institution from the tribunals to which national arbitration laws such as the Dutch Code typically apply. It is not an *ad hoc* entity called into life by a commercial contract to resolve disputes under the contract, but an "International Arbitral Tribunal," established by two sovereign states through an international agreement that has the status of a treaty under international law.

Lake & Dana, *supra* note 15, at 773 (footnotes omitted).

[155] *See, e.g.,* text at note 84 *supra.*

law and not the legal system of the place of arbitration, the arbitrators employed the UN Draft Convention on Arbitral Procedure.[156]

The UNCITRAL Rules chosen by the drafters of the Accords demonstrate both by their general structure and by Article 1(2) specifically that it can be "taken for granted that there is an applicable national law."[157] Article 1(2) provides that "[t]hese Rules shall govern the arbitration except that where any of the Rules is in conflict with a provision of the law applicable to the arbitration from which the parties cannot derogate, that provision shall prevail." Thus, these internal rules of arbitration through Article 1(2) automatically adjust to the nonderogable provisions of the governing municipal arbitration law. Indeed, Article 1(2) assumes that a governing municipal arbitration law exists.[158] In this sense, the presumed intent of parties adopting the UNCITRAL Rules calls for municipal review as clearly as if the choice instead had been the American Arbitration Association Rules or the ICC Rules.[159] However, the presumed intent in the case of the Accords is merely presumptive because the Accords envisioned that their implementation might require modification of the Rules by the state parties or the Tribunal.[160]

Interpretation of the Accords should also take into account that they were drafted in haste and that some clauses may not be the product of full deliberation.[161] To "confirm the meaning resulting from the application of

---

[156] Both *ARAMCO* and *TOPCO* were decided prior to the adoption of the UNCITRAL Rules. Other private arbitration rules, however, were available at the time.

[157] Böckstiegel, *The Relevance of National Arbitration Law for Arbitrators under the UNCITRAL Rules*, 1 J. INT'L ARB. 223, 230 (1984). *See also* Sanders, *supra* note 110, at 179; AAA Report, *supra* note 59, at 5; I. DORE, ARBITRATION AND CONCILIATION UNDER THE UNCITRAL RULES: A TEXTUAL ANALYSIS 45–46 (1986).

[158] The entire UNCITRAL project was directed at developing rules of procedure for international commercial arbitration that would be acceptable worldwide and, in particular, to the developing world. *See* I. DORE, *supra* note 157, at 44; Introduction to Commentary on Preliminary Draft of the UNCITRAL Rules, UN Doc. A/CN.9/97 (1975). Originally, the drafters spread references throughout the Rules to the possible overriding effect of the governing legal system. At the ninth session, however:

> Committee [II] considered the relationship between the Rules and the provisions of the national law applicable to the arbitration. It was agreed that the inclusion only in selected articles of the Rules of a proviso that the particular article was subject to the national law applicable to the arbitration would give rise to arguments *a contrario* in respect of other articles which did not set forth such a proviso. The Committee therefore decided to add to article 1 a general reference to the effect that all provisions in these Rules were subject to the national law applicable to the arbitration.

Report of Committee II, Ninth Session, UN Doc. A/CN.9/IX/CRP.1, para. 12 (1976).

[159] *See supra* text at note 109.   [160] Hardenberg, *supra* note 13, at 338.

[161] As noted by Richard Lillich, "the Claims Settlement Agreement establishing the Tribunal was cobbled together in haste and confusion." Lillich, *supra* note 2, at vii. Indeed, Roberts B. Owen, a principal U.S. negotiator, later wrote that "although the initial draft of the claims settlement declaration [by the United States] was some twenty-five pages long . . . , it was ultimately revised down to about three-and-a-half pages—surely one of the most concise legal documents of its kind ever written." Owen, *The Final Negotiation and Release in Algiers*, in AMERICAN HOSTAGES IN IRAN 297, 312 (P. Kreisberg ed. 1986).

Article 31" and allow for the limitations inherent in textual interpretation, the Vienna Convention directs us to the preparatory work of the Accords. Unfortunately, little is known about the negotiating process. Several sources have indicated to me that more than a few of the American negotiators were unfamiliar with the idea of a *lex arbitri* and did not appreciate that the choice of the UNCITRAL Rules would accord supervisory jurisdiction to the legal system of the Netherlands. Indeed, one must remember that the UNCITRAL Rules were still quite new at the time the Accords were drafted and their UN origin might mistakenly lead one to conclude that they were designed for interstate arbitration rather than private international arbitration.[162] On the other hand, several of the U.S. negotiators had come to the Department of State from private practice and were familiar with international commercial arbitration. The publicly available information on the negotiations indicates that some of the negotiators were familiar with the different processes and confirms at least the willingness of the United States to agree to a private, as well as a public, international arbitral process. In particular, such familiarity and willingness is apparent in the second U.S. negotiating response, given on December 3, 1980, when the United States, in referring to the settlement of claims of its nationals, indicated its agreement "that such arbitration may be conducted, at Iran's election, by and under rules of *the International Chamber of Commerce* or the World Bank's International Center for the Settlement of Investment Disputes" (emphasis added).

Furthermore, the "object and purpose" of the Accords and "surrounding circumstances" also support a private characterization. In part I, I concluded that the trend toward regarding arbitrations between a private party and a state as private reflects the perception that in contract negotiations the private party's need for enforceability of the award often outweighs the state's interest in not waiving whatever immunity it has. The Accords, it is true, did not result from commercial negotiations, but rather memorialize diplomatic efforts to end a crisis in relations between the two countries. For this reason, one may not assume that the state parties were motivated by concerns identical to those of parties contemplating a commercial relationship. Nevertheless, the creation of the Security Account and Article IV(3) of the Claims Settlement Declaration are striking evidence of the importance attached to enforceability.[163] Given the poor, if not hostile, relations be-

---

[162] Consider, for example, the following somewhat ambiguous statement by Warren Christopher, chief U.S. negotiator of the Accords: "The settlement itself was simplified because a reliable body of arbitration law already existed in the United Nations system and could be lifted by reference into the agreement." Christopher, *Introduction*, in AMERICAN HOSTAGES IN IRAN, *supra* note 161, at 1, 10–11.

[163] Article IV(3) provides: "Any award which the Tribunal may render against either government shall be enforceable against such government in the courts of any nation in accordance with its laws." Claims Settlement Declaration, *supra* note 1. Moreover, as Roberts Owen noted:

Although the release of the hostages was far and away the top priority of the U.S. government, we also wanted to avoid, if we possibly could, leaving our claimants without a

tween the two countries, the U.S. concern about enforceability was not illusory. Thus, one probable objective of the United States in negotiating the Accords was to ensure the maximum enforceability of awards. Although the creation of the Security Account went far to satisfy this objective, it arguably is further satisfied by a private, rather than a public, characterization of the arbitrations involving nationals. Moreover, Iran may not have regarded a municipal *lex arbitri* as "an infringement of the prerogatives of the State which is a Party to the arbitration,"[164] since Iran at that time was the defendant in hundreds of lawsuits in the United States.[165] On the other hand, Iran's negotiating position, based on its control over 52 American nationals, was not weak. Indeed, the press of negotiations and the desire to avoid possibly contentious subsidiary issues may explain why the general approach of the UNCITRAL Rules was agreed to with the caveat that the parties or the Tribunal could modify those Rules at a later date.

The Vienna Convention also provides that parties may resort to "any subsequent practice in the application of the treaty which establishes the agreement of the parties regarding its interpretation."[166] This rule of interpretation is particularly appropriate when, as here, it was anticipated that subsequent changes might be made.

After signing the Accords, the state parties closely examined the provisions to which they had agreed and began developing their positions with regard to possible changes.[167] The U.S. State Department recognized, for example, that the provision in the UNCITRAL Rules that the proceedings and resulting awards be kept confidential[168] would hamper dissemination of the Tribunal's developing jurisprudence to other parties.[169]

A key concern was Article VI of the Claims Settlement Declaration, which provides for the seat of the Tribunal to be in The Hague "or any other place agreed by Iran and the United States." A debate commenced in the United States as to whether London might be more suitable.[170] Various U.S. officials wondered whether it was in the best interests of the United States and

---

remedy, and a remedy could be arranged only if Iran could be persuaded, through negotiation, to join in a responsible arrangement for adjudicating the claims. Indeed, for the U.S. government to have abandoned the claimants in the context of the hostage crisis might well have been regarded as a payment of ransom for the hostages' release . . . .

Owen, *supra* note 161, at 301.

[164] *ARAMCO*, 27 ILR at 156.

[165] *See* Hertz, *The Hostage Crisis and Domestic Litigation: An Overview*, in IRAN–UNITED STATES TRIBUNAL, *supra* note 1, at 136.

Iran apparently considered itself in danger of losing such cases, although the U.S. negotiators were aware that the U.S. plaintiffs' actions were vulnerable ultimately to claims of immunity by Iran. *See* Owen, *supra* note 161, at 303–04.

[166] Vienna Convention on the Law of Treaties, *supra* note 153, Art. 31(3)(b).

[167] *See Iran–United States Litigation*, Remarks of Arthur M. Rovine, 77 ASIL PROC. 3 (1983).

[168] UNCITRAL Rules, *supra* note 26, Art. 32(5).

[169] *See, e.g.*, Carter, *Iran–United States Claims Tribunal: Observations on the First Year*, 29 UCLA L. REV. 1076 (1982).

[170] *See, e.g.*, *Symposium on the Settlement with Iran*, 13 LAW. AM. 1, 46 (1981). Indeed, during the negotiation of the Accords, "the United States was inclined to favor London as the site of the proposed international tribunal, [but] the Algerians urged [the United States] to suggest

U.S. nationals for the arbitral process to be governed by the Dutch legal system or by the English legal system, or whether the arbitrations should be subject to a municipal legal system at all.[171] By the time the Agents of the two Governments and the party-appointed arbitrators first met in The Hague in May 1981, the debate within the United States apparently had ended in the belief that the arbitrations should be governed by the Dutch legal system. That this alternative was preferred at that time by the United States is reflected in the fact that it did not seek to change the situation by pursuing modifications in the UNCITRAL Rules.[172] The clearest expression of this position can be found in the U.S. amicus curiae brief of July 1988 in *Ministry of Defense of the Islamic Republic of Iran v. Gould, Inc.:* "Tribunal awards appear to be valid and enforceable under Dutch law and therefore may be considered Dutch awards."[173]

Four events show that Iran also considered the arbitral process to be governed by the Dutch legal system from 1981 until 1984; that Iran reversed this position from 1984 to 1987 when it no longer appeared to be in Iran's interest; and that since 1987 Iran has taken inconsistent positions on the issue.

The decision not to modify Article 1(2) of the UNCITRAL Rules. The parties' choice of the UNCITRAL Rules in the Algiers Accords indicates a common intent that the arbitral process be subject to review by the Dutch courts. The significance of this choice is confirmed by the fact that neither the parties nor the Tribunal exercised their power to modify the approach of the Rules. The Tribunal was formally established in July 1981, and its Rules of Procedure adopted in March 1982.[174] During this 9-month period, the Full Tri-

---

The Hague on the theory that it would be somewhat more palatable to the Iranians." Owen, *supra* note 161, at 313.

[171] At a symposium at the University of Miami Law School on Apr. 14, 1981, Mark Feldman, a lawyer with the U.S. State Department during the negotiation of the Accords, discussed the internal debate in the Department over these concerns and stated his *personal* preference for a process in which national courts would not interfere:

> We are at a stage which raises a very complicated question concerning the law applicable to the proceeding. . . . It is a subtle and difficult thing. We are struggling with it right now. . . . One of the things we will have to try and decide is how to keep the courts of the Netherlands or of England out of these cases.

Symposium, supra note 170, at 38.

[172] Indeed, the statement of Mark Feldman at a second conference held on June 16–18, 1981, reflects this internal consensus:

> At first blush, one might suppose that this arbitration is governed only by international law and that local law is irrelevant . . . . After careful review of the conflicting literature on this subject and the characteristics of this proceeding, the State Department decided that prudence requires that the United States act on the assumption that proceedings conducted in the Netherlands will be governed by Dutch law . . . .

Feldman, *Implementation of the Iranian Claims Settlement Agreement—Status, Issues and Lessons: View from Government's Perspective,* in 1981 PRIVATE INVESTORS ABROAD—PROBLEMS AND SOLUTIONS IN INTERNATIONAL BUSINESS 75, 97–98 (J. Moss ed.).

[173] *See Amicus Curiae* Brief, *supra* note 116, at 39.

[174] Provisionally adopted Mar. 10, 1982; permanently adopted May 3, 1983. *See* note 143 *supra.*

bunal devoted a substantial portion of its time to considering modifications in the UNCITRAL Rules in light of its own concerns and the comments of the state parties.[175] The retention of Article 1(2) in its original form was intentional. It signifies that the Dutch legal system should govern the arbitrations. Indeed, the addition by the Tribunal of Article 1(3), discussed more fully below, only increased the likelihood that Dutch courts could review the awards.[176] Moreover, the Tribunal did not alter, and subsequently has complied with, Article 32(7) of the UNCITRAL Rules, which requires the Tribunal to register its awards in accordance with "the arbitration law of the country where the award is made."[177] There is no indication that either the United States or Iran objected to these actions. Indeed, the subsequent events, described below, suggest that they concurred in them. Even if one of the countries had objected, their agreement in the Accords to authorize the Tribunal to modify the Rules over the objection of one of them would have bound the objecting party.

The tripartite agreement. At the inception of the Tribunal's work, the state parties tended to seek written agreements on broad issues not settled by the Accords. One such effort, begun in May 1981, was the drafting of a tripartite agreement between the United States, Iran and the Netherlands dealing with the status of the Tribunal itself, the privileges and immunities of the arbitrators and staff, the status of the Agents of the two Governments and the relation of the Dutch legal system to the arbitrations conducted before the Tribunal.

As for the Dutch, "[i]t was assumed in the proposals which the Netherlands made in connection with the preparations for the reception of the Tribunal in the Netherlands that the Tribunal would operate as an arbitral body in hearing civil disputes and that Dutch law on Arbitration would therefore apply."[178] As the work of the Tribunal began to pick up pace, the cooperation between Iran and the United States required to conclude the agreement dissipated and the negotiations stalled. The Iranian Agent, in the

---

[175] *See, e.g., Revised UNCITRAL Rules Released for Comment by Tribunal,* I.A.L.R., Feb. 19, 1982, at 4,232.

[176] Article 1(3) of the Declaration, *supra* note 1, provides: "The Claims Settlement Declaration constitutes an Agreement in writing by Iran and the United States, on their own behalfs and on behalf of their nationals submitting to arbitration within the framework of the Algiers Declarations and in accordance with the Tribunal Rules." On the significance of this provision, see text at note 182 *infra.*

[177] Thus, the Tribunal decided on May 3, 1982, to register its awards in accordance with Article 639(1) of the Dutch Code of Civil Procedure, later superseded by the 1986 Netherlands Arbitration Act with Article 1058 of the Dutch Code of Civil Procedure. *See* Manual of the Registry of the Iran–United States Claims Tribunal. The former article of the Dutch Code called for deposit within 8 days at the Registrar of the district where the award was made. The latter calls for deposit "without delay" at the same location. On the new Dutch arbitration law, see generally van den Berg, *The Netherlands,* 12 Y.B. COM. ARB. 3 (1987); and Tebbens, *A Facelift for Dutch Arbitration Law,* 34 NETH. INT'L L. REV. 141 (1987). *See also* Sanders, *A New Law for the Netherlands,* 4 PACE L. REV. 581 (1984).

[178] Explanatory Note of the Ministerie van Buitenlandse Zaken (Foreign Ministry) to a Proposed Bill on "Applicability of Dutch law to the awards of the Tribunal sitting in The Hague to hear claims between Iran and the United States" (July 12, 1983) (unofficial translation by Foreign Ministry).

spring of 1982, for example, reportedly stated in regard to the legal personality of the Tribunal that "granting an independent legal status to the Tribunal is neither required nor warranted."[179]

Owing to the parties' failure to conclude the tripartite agreement, the Dutch Government took a unilateral and less formal approach to those issues the agreement would have resolved. The arbitrators and Secretary-General of the Tribunal were granted the privileges and immunities of a person of ambassadorial rank.[180] Likewise, the Netherlands Government granted the Tribunal the usual immunities of international organizations, a grant cited by the District Court of The Hague in its dismissal of a former Tribunal employee's claim for wrongful discharge.[181] In regard to the arbitrations before the Tribunal involving claims of nationals, the Dutch Foreign Ministry began a slow process of drafting legislation that would formalize and clarify the applicability of the Dutch arbitration law. The Foreign Ministry modeled this legislation on the draft tripartite agreement.

The Iranian challenge of Tribunal awards and the proposed Dutch legislation. The circumstances surrounding the introduction of the proposed Dutch legislation strongly suggest that Iran withdrew its support from the tripartite agreement for reasons other than opposition to the provisions relating to the applicability of Dutch arbitration law. Indeed, on April 8, 1983, Iran invoked Dutch law by requesting that the District Court of The Hague set aside or declare null and void two Tribunal awards.[182] Iran filed other such challenges and by December 2, 1983, had a total of ten challenges pending in Dutch courts.[183] Thus, it appears that until at least the end of 1983, Iran believed that the Dutch legal system governed the validity of Tribunal arbitrations.

This unanimous view of the Tribunal, the United States and Iran ended early in 1984. In July 1983, the Foreign Ministry submitted proposed legislation to the Dutch Parliament on the relation of the Dutch legal system to Tribunal awards. In part, a continuation of legislative efforts initiated within the framework of the stillborn tripartite agreement, the proposal was also a response to the two challenges Iran had filed in April 1983. The Second Chamber of the Dutch Parliament passed the law in February 1984 and sent it to the First Chamber for its concurrence. Iran thereupon reversed its position and adamantly opposed Dutch judicial review of the arbitral process. President Khamenei of Iran said at Friday prayers that the

---

[179] Letter of Arthur Rovine, Agent of the United States, to Christopher Pinto, Secretary-General of the Tribunal (May 28, 1982).

[180] *See* IRAN–UNITED STATES CLAIMS TRIBUNAL, ANNUAL REPORT FOR THE PERIOD ENDING 30 JUNE 1983, paras. 20–22, Anns. VI–IX.

[181] Spaans v. Iran-U.S. Claims Tribunal (Dist. Ct. The Hague, July 9, 1984), *overruling* decision of the Kantonrechter (County Ct. Judge) (The Hague, June 8, 1983), *noted and reprinted in part in* 18 NETH. Y.B. INT'L L. 357 (1987).

[182] *See Iran Appeals Raygo Wagner, Rexnord Awards to Dutch Court,* I.A.L.R., Apr. 15, 1983, at 6,330. The two awards involved were Raygo Wagner Equipment and Star Line Iran, AWD 20–17–3 (Mangård, Mosk & Sani (RS), arbs., Dec. 15, 1982), 1 IRAN-U.S. C.T.R. 411 (1981–82); and Rexnord and Islamic Republic of Iran, *supra* note 137.

[183] For a summary of these challenges, see Lake & Dana, *supra* note 15, at 759–65.

United States had pressured the Dutch Government into preparing legislation that would prejudice Iran before the Tribunal.[184] The Agent of Iran and one of the Iranian arbitrators appeared before the First Chamber to argue against passage of the law. Shortly thereafter, Iran withdrew all ten of its challenges before the Dutch courts so as to remove the motivation for the legislation. The Dutch Government, thereupon, without prejudice to its ability to renew the question if needed, ceased consideration of the legislation.

A letter from M. Eshragh, the Agent of Iran, protesting the proposed legislation after its passage by the Second Chamber suggests two reasons for the change in Iran's position.[185] First, Iran had come to realize that its previous position would be inconsistent with the then-pending and, for Iran, politically sensitive dual nationality proceedings, in which Iran was arguing that the arbitrations were based on diplomatic protection. Second, by clarifying and limiting somewhat the grounds for setting aside an award, the proposed legislation lessened the value to Iran of subordinating the arbitrations to the Dutch legal system because Iran probably realized that its challenges would not be sustained. Simultaneously, this whole series of events likely made Iran increasingly aware that a corollary of its right to challenge awards in Dutch courts was the right of U.S. claimants to enforce them elsewhere, possibly under the New York Convention. Finally, to the degree that the challenges were primarily an Iranian strategy to persuade the Algerian Government, as escrow agent for the Security Account, to withhold payment on awards, that effort had already failed.[186]

Iran's action to enforce the Gould *award in the United States.* Iran's position in favor of characterizing the Tribunal's work as diplomatic protection and against passage of the proposed legislation remained constant from the spring of 1984 until June 1987, when Iran attempted to enforce an award of the Tribunal in the United States under the New York Convention on the ground that the award had Dutch nationality. On June 29, 1984, Chamber Two of the Tribunal had rendered an award in favor of the Ministry of Defence of the Islamic Republic of Iran and against Gould Marketing, the U.S. party, for $3,640,247.13.[187] Gould failed to pay the debt. On June 9, 1987, 20 days shy of the 3-year limit under the New York Convention (9 U.S.C. §207 (1988)), Iran petitioned the U.S. District Court for the Central District of California to enforce the award.[188] Judge Gadbois's order hold-

---

[184] *See* MEALEY'S, Apr. 6, 1984, at 299–300.

[185] *Reprinted in* 5 IRAN-U.S. C.T.R. 405 (1984 I).

[186] Normally, the Algerian Government as escrow agent would order the payment of monies from the Security Account upon receipt of a notification of award from the President of the Tribunal. When challenging awards in 1983, Iran also persuaded Algeria for a time that it should withhold payments on those awards until the challenges to their validity were decided. By November 1983, however, the United States had convinced Algeria that Algeria's function was nondiscretionary and all payment orders were made. *See* I.A.L.R., Nov. 18, 1983, at 7,472.

[187] Gould Marketing and Ministry of Defence of Islamic Republic of Iran, AWD 136–49/50–2 (Riphagen, Aldrich & Shafeiei (CO/DO), arbs., June 29, 1984), 6 IRAN-U.S. C.T.R. 272 (1984 II).

[188] I.A.L.R., July 10, 1987, at 14,407.

ing that U.S. district courts have subject matter jurisdiction over actions to enforce Tribunal awards under the New York Convention, as codified in U.S. law, was recently affirmed by the U.S. Court of Appeals for the Ninth Circuit.[189] Iran's position, however, has not quite come full circle. It still maintains before the Tribunal that the United States espouses the claims of its nationals on the basis of diplomatic protection.[190]

In conclusion, the Accords established a clear presumption that the legal system of the Netherlands would govern the Tribunal's arbitral process. The state parties and the Tribunal confirmed this desire by not modifying the UNCITRAL Rules in this regard. Finally, the subsequent practice and statements of the United States and Iran (although the latter's practice has been somewhat inconsistent) confirm their desire that the Tribunal's arbitrations be subject to review under the Dutch legal system.

Ability and Willingness of the Netherlands to Accommodate the Parties' Desire

Even if the United States and Iran intended that the Dutch legal system govern these arbitrations, the Dutch may not necessarily have been willing or able to accept this role.

As to willingness: The United States and Iran in essence requested that the Netherlands supervise the dispute settlement process they established. If the state parties had sought to place this supervisory role on the Dutch executive branch, the international consent of the Dutch Government would have been required. Whether two countries can avoid obtaining such consent by placing their disputes within the national arbitration scheme presents an issue of constitutional law regarding the respective roles of the executive and judicial branches of that country in foreign affairs.[191] For example, if two countries sought to have the U.S. legal system govern the validity of a border arbitration between them, a strong constitutional argument could be made that the judiciary should abstain from assuming a role that could lead to substantial friction with at least one of the states involved and the concomitant embarrassment of the executive branch.[192] The Netherlands, however, consistent with its long-time role as a mediator of international disputes, apparently did not hesitate to allow its judiciary to supervise the Iran-U.S. Claims Tribunal's proceedings concerning at least the claims of nationals.[193] Instead, the issue has been quite formal: did Iran and the United States create an arbitral process that meets the threshold requirements of arbitration as defined in the Dutch Code of Civil Procedure?[194] In particular, the question whether Article II(1) proceedings are arbitration

---

[189] *Id.*, Apr. 29, 1988, at 15,654.   [190] *See supra* note 132.

[191] Indeed, such direct entry into a national arbitration scheme would not be possible in the United Kingdom where §9 of the Sovereign Immunity Act provides that although a state is not immune from proceedings before UK courts related to an arbitration to which the state agreed, this denial of immunity "does not apply to any arbitration agreement between states."

[192] See, for example, the concerns expressed by the court in Occidental of Umm al Qaywayn v. A Certain Cargo of Petroleum, 577 F.2d 1196, 1203–05 (5th Cir. 1978).

[193] *See supra* text at notes 174–81.

[194] In at least one instance, a municipal court at the place of arbitration has held that the applicable municipal law did not govern an arbitration because the proceedings did not consti-

within the meaning of the Dutch code raises the technical, yet significant, requirement that the agreement to arbitrate shall be in writing and signed by the parties.[195] Van den Berg, referring to the New York Convention, states that the purpose of the written requirement "is to ensure that a party is aware that he is agreeing to arbitration."[196] In this sense, the writing is the objective manifestation of the consent of the parties, the voluntary act that underlies the notion and legitimacy of arbitration.

There can be little doubt that Iran and the United States, the two state parties, knew they were agreeing to arbitration. Moreover, the conduct of Iran from the time of its challenges in the Dutch court indicates that Iran, like the United States, was aware that it had agreed to arbitration governed by the Dutch legal system. Thus, Iran could be regarded as being estopped from raising the issue of its written agreement.[197] Hardenberg argues, however, that for claims of nationals before the Tribunal, there clearly is not an arbitration agreement between the litigants.[198] For support, he cites the Explanatory Note of the Dutch Foreign Ministry accompanying the proposed bill: "Given the absence of voluntary prior contractual agreement between the parties concerned in each individual case and the international nature of the agreement between States underlying the arbitration, doubts may arise as to whether this is indeed arbitration within the meaning of Dutch law."[199] The issue is therefore whether not only the state parties, but also their nationals, can be said to have agreed to arbitration.

---

tute "arbitration" as that term was defined by municipal law and that there was therefore nothing to be governed. *See* SEEE v. Yugoslavia (Swiss Fed. Trib., Sept. 18, 1957), *reprinted in* 47 RCDIP 366 (1958). Doctrinally, the position that there is nothing to be governed could be equated with the setting aside of an award. *Compare* SEEE v. Yugoslavia (Hague Ct. App., Sept. 8, 1972), *reprinted in French in* 1974 REV. ARB. 313, and SEEE v. Yugoslavia (Hoge Raad, Nov. 7, 1975), 1976 Nederlandse Jurisprudentie No. 774, *reprinted in French in* 1978 REV. ARB. 397. *See also* Delaume, *SEEE v. Yugoslavia: Epitaph or Interlude?*, 4 J. INT'L ARB. 25 (1987). Whether such a refusal to review an award should be viewed as the equivalent of setting aside the award or simply as abstention because of concerns with competence is a difficult question that turns upon the specific reason the court feels it cannot or should not examine the award.

[195] The provision of the Dutch Code of Civil Procedure referred to provides that the "arbitration agreement . . . must be made in writing and signed by the parties." Dutch Code of Civil Procedure, Art. 623(1) (unofficial translation prepared by the Asser Institute, 1980). The arbitration agreement is also significant because such a writing is essential to the enforceability of the award, given that the writing requirement is also set forth in the New York Convention, *supra* note 25. In particular, Article IV of the New York Convention requires that to obtain recognition and enforcement, the party applying shall present the award and the arbitration agreement, such agreement, by Article II of the Convention, being in writing by the parties.

[196] A. J. VAN DEN BERG, *supra* note 59, at 171.

[197] To van den Berg, estoppel in the context of the New York Convention would reflect "a fundamental principle of good faith, which principle overrides the formalities required by Article II(2) of the New York Convention." *Id.* at 185.

[198] Hardenberg, *supra* note 13, at 338.

[199] *See* note 178 *supra.* This problem may explain a less specific statement of a U.S. Department of State official some months after the signing of the Accords: "Upon examination of Dutch law, it became apparent that awards rendered pursuant to the Claims Settlement Agreement would not meet certain procedural requirements for valid arbitral awards under the Dutch civil code." Feldman, *supra* note 172, at 98.

One answer is that each state party possesses the authority to agree to arbitration on behalf of its nationals. As van den Berg wrote in response to Hardenberg: "It is arguable that an arbitration agreement can be considered to be present if one regards Iran and the United States as also representing the interests of their subjects when bringing about the *Claims Settlement Declaration*."[200] Indeed, this position is supported by Article 1(3) of the Tribunal's Rules, which provides: "The Claims Settlement Declaration constitutes an Agreement in writing by Iran and the United States, on their own behalfs and *on behalf of their nationals* submitting to arbitration within the framework of the Algiers Declarations and in accordance with the Tribunal Rules."[201]

Although the view of the state as agent is likely sufficient, for this Tribunal one can also find the direct agreement of the nationals to arbitrate. To do so, one must recognize that the Accords manifest a written agreement between Iran and the United States to participate in binding arbitrations of claims brought not only by the other, but also by nationals of the other, even though such nationals were not parties to the Accords. In this sense, the Accords embody a written offer by each state party to the nationals of the other state party to arbitrate certain claims.[202] This offer could be accepted in writing by individual claimants by filing Statements of Claim prior to January 19, 1982. Indeed, each Statement of Claim included an element not normally required by the UNCITRAL Rules, "[a] demand that the dispute be referred to arbitration by the Tribunal."[203] Although it is true that the Algiers Accords compelled U.S. claimants to abandon their proceedings in U.S. courts, the Accords did not compel them to file or defend claims before the Tribunal. As Mr. Justice Hobhouse observed in *Dallal v. Bank Mellat:*

> It was Mr Dallal's voluntary act to commence the proceedings before the Hague tribunal. It is true that he may have had no other alternative under the law of the United States if he wished to pursue his rights as he saw them. But that does not make it any the less a voluntary act.[204]

---

[200] Van den Berg, *supra* note 14, at 343 (emphasis in original).

[201] This provision was added to Article 1 of the UNCITRAL Rules as a part of the Tribunal's modification of those Rules. *See* Tribunal Rules, *supra* note 143, 2 IRAN-U.S. C.T.R. at 408.

[202] Georges Delaume has argued that such a form of agreement would be sufficient for ICSID: "Consent may also result from the investor's acceptance of a unilateral offer from the Contracting State involved, when that State has already consented to ICSID arbitration in relevant provisions . . . of a bilateral treaty with the Contracting State of which the investor is a national." Delaume, *ICSID Arbitration: Practical Considerations,* 1 J. INT'L ARB. 101, 104 (1984). Similarly, although the recent UNCITRAL Model Law on International Commercial Arbitration requires a written agreement to arbitrate, a writing exists if there is "an exchange of statements of claim and defense in which the existence of an agreement is alleged by one party and not denied by another." UNCITRAL Model Law, *supra* note 49, Art. 7(2). *See also* Furnish, *Commercial Arbitration Agreements and the Uniform Commercial Code,* 67 CAL. L. REV. 317, 347 (1979) ("The arbitration agreement should be made amenable to autonomous creation through the same means recognized for the creation of a sales agreement . . .").

[203] Tribunal Rules, *supra* note 143, Art. 18(1)(a), 2 IRAN-U.S. C.T.R. at 422.

[204] Mark Dallal v. Bank Mellat, [1986] 1 All E.R. 239, 254.

A quick response might be that although Dallal's act could be said to be voluntary in that he was not coerced, is an act voluntary when there is no other choice? Yet, as Mr. Justice Hobhouse notes, what choice does any plaintiff have? "Most plaintiffs who commence proceedings are in a similar position. They have to commence proceedings before the appropriate municipal court or else be without legal remedy."[205]

In this connection, it must be recalled that the Tribunal possesses jurisdiction over the claims of nationals of one state party against the other state party, but not vice versa.[206] The Tribunal is unlike a court in that the nationals of each state party may choose to be a plaintiff, but may not be forced to be a defendant. Thus, a written agreement to arbitrate lies in the acceptance by the national of one state party of the other state party's written offer in the Accords, through that national's choice to file a written demand for arbitration.

The Legal Character of Arbitrations before the Tribunal

The question of what legal system governs proceedings before the Tribunal is troublesome because, despite the apparent clarity of the state parties' intent, it does not fit neatly into the pigeonhole normally assigned to international arbitral tribunals created by states. At the beginning of this century, Iran and the United States probably would have intended that the claims of their nationals be espoused via diplomatic protection. They probably would have had no other choice. They certainly had other choices in 1981.

Granting that at the time of the signing of the Algiers Accords the state parties perhaps had not fully developed their negotiating position on the legal system that would apply to the arbitral proceedings, the Accords nonetheless establish a presumption that those involving claims of nationals are governed by the Dutch legal system. Granting also that there was both indecision and confusion about this question for several months following the signing of the Accords, this initial uncertainty is far outweighed by the subsequent practice of both the United States and Iran. Finally, although Iran has opposed Dutch judicial review at times, the Accords clearly provide that the choice of Dutch review cannot be altered without the consent of both state parties or action of the Tribunal itself, requirements that have not been met.

To conclude that Iran and the United States agreed that the Dutch legal system should govern the arbitrations involving claims of nationals does not necessarily mean that the choice promotes the interests of the parties or the Tribunal. Lake and Dana argue that awards do *not* require nationality to be enforceable under the New York Convention (the chief benefit, in their

---

[205] *Id.*

[206] Islamic Republic of Iran and United States (Jurisdiction Over Claims by a State Party Against Nationals of the Other State Party), Dec. 1–A2–FT (Lagergren, Holtzmann, Kashani (D), Bellet, Aldrich, Shafeiei (D), Mangård, Enayat (D) & Mosk, arbs., Jan. 26, 1982), 1 IRAN-U.S. C.T.R. 101 (1981–82).

view, of Dutch review), while the applicability of Dutch law might force claimants to defend against Iranian challenges in lengthy Dutch court proceedings.[207] In addition, they argue that judicial recourse risks renewal of Iranian attempts to have the Algerian Escrow Agent withhold instructions for payment from the Security Account until such challenges are resolved.[208]

Putting aside the fact that it is the intent of the parties and not considerations of policy that determines the *lex arbitri*, the interests of the Tribunal and of international dispute settlement arguably are advanced by Dutch review. The ability to challenge the award at the place of arbitration continues to be appropriate and valuable. Fairness suggests that the losing party should have a primary place in which to question the award immediately, rather than being forced to raise the issue whenever and wherever the winning party seeks enforcement or recognition. Most national laws require that challenges be raised within a limited period after the rendering of the award. This requirement provides a basis for estopping a dilatory objecting party. If there is merit to the challenge, the court may wish to question the arbitrators and to examine the records of the Tribunal. Far less disruption is engendered if such inquiries are made at the place of arbitration rather than at the place of enforcement. Moreover, by providing a mechanism for setting aside fundamentally unfair awards, the state parties bolster the legitimacy of the process and the Netherlands furthers its own interest in continuing to serve as a fair and impartial site for the peaceful legal resolution of disputes.

Last, there is no apparent reason for the conclusion that the Dutch legal system governs the arbitrations involving claims of nationals not to be equally applicable to the arbitrations involving official claims and interpretive disputes. The presumption that the Accords involve the Dutch legal system flows from the choice of the UNCITRAL Rules, a choice that does not distinguish among the various bases of jurisdiction. Nor should we necessarily jump to the conclusion that the state parties would have desired to distinguish the bases of the Tribunal's jurisdiction. In particular, the official claims are based on "*contractual* [not treaty] arrangements between them for the purchase and sale of goods and services." Most, if not all, official claims, although intergovernmental, involve commercial matters.[209] Moreover, the enforceability concerns cited above are also applicable to the official claims. On the other hand, several U.S. and Tribunal officials expressed to me the belief that if the circumstance arose, the state parties would act to block the subjection of proceedings involving official claims and interpretive disputes to the Dutch legal system. A further important difference might be the willingness of the Netherlands to accept these other two categories of disputes for judicial review. The proposed Dutch legislation puts that willing-

---

[207] Lake & Dana, *supra* note 15, at 807.   [208] *Id.* at 808–09.

[209] The qualification "most, if not all," is used in the text to reserve the potentially important question whether the sale of arms by a government, although contractual, is or is not a commercial matter.

ness in some doubt, as it expressly applied only to the arbitrations involving claims of nationals. This single piece of evidence, however, is too slender a reed to bear the conclusion that the Netherlands will not accept the role proposed by the United States and Iran if an issue concerning an official claim or interpretive dispute arises.

III. The Evolving Structure of International Dispute Resolution

In 1914 and 1916, Mr. Mavrommatis obtained concessions from the Ottoman Empire to provide certain public services in Jerusalem and Jaffa. After the First World War, the British Government granted duplicate concessions to a different person. Predictably, a dispute ensued. The Government of Greece eventually espoused the claim of Mavrommatis, its national, against the British Government on the basis of diplomatic protection. Ultimately, the claim was addressed on the public international law level by the Permanent Court of International Justice.[210]

The conventional wisdom is that interstate arbitration, like that involving Mavrommatis, has declined in this century. Parry wrote that "the high noon of international arbitration occurred around the year 1900."[211] Yet further consideration of Mavrommatis's situation tells us that the evolution of international arbitration more generally in this century involves a process far more complex than a mere decline in use.

In the early 1920s, Mavrommatis had few, if any, other options for pursuing his claim. Today, in contrast, he would likely include, as a part of his concession, a clause providing for international commercial arbitration in, for example, Geneva under the UNCITRAL Rules of Arbitration or Paris at the International Chamber of Commerce. In contrast to settlement by the Permanent Court of International Justice, this proceeding would not require the cooperation of the other party and could result in an award enforceable and recognizable around much of the world under the New York Convention.

Many arbitrations at the turn of the century, like the *Mavrommatis* case, involved claims of individuals based on diplomatic protection. That is, many of the disputes were not truly between the two states named as parties.

[210] *See* Mavrommatis Palestine Concessions, 1924 PCIJ (ser. A) No. 2 (Judgment of Aug. 30). My use of the *Mavrommatis* case builds upon Professor Franck's use of the proceeding to illustrate the costs of approaching private disputes as international matters. T. FRANCK, THE STRUCTURE OF IMPARTIALITY 213–14 (1968). "What had been a quarrel between businessmen and an administrator became a dispute pitting Britain against Greece, kingdom against kingdom, national pride against national pride . . . ." *Id.* at 214.

[211] Parry, *Some Considerations upon the Protection of Individuals in International Law*, 90 RECUEIL DES COURS 653, 660 (1956 II). Nor is this piece of wisdom without apparent statistical support. A brief digest of all public international arbitral tribunals yields the following distribution of those tribunals over time: 1776–1800, 7; 1801–1825, 20; 1826–1850, 17; 1851–1875, 66; 1876–1900, 137; 1901–1925, 133; 1926–1950, 41; and 1951–1970, 20. A. M. STUYT, SURVEY OF INTERNATIONAL ARBITRATION 1794–1970 (1976). (Note that these numbers represent tribunals, not claims. Some tribunals heard only one claim; some after World War I heard 20,000.)

Today, depending upon the circumstances, similar claims likely would be handled through lump sum settlement or international commercial arbitration. Thus, the aggregate effect of the change in options described for Mavrommatis is that there quite plausibly has been a shift in dockets. Although further empirical study is necessary to establish the historical proposition, international commercial arbitration clearly has the capacity to take over the adjudication of many of the essentially private disputes previously addressed by the more politically contentious interstate mechanism of diplomatic protection.

The change is striking. In approximately half a century, an elaborate system for the resolution of international commercial disputes has evolved quietly and efficiently. When viewed against the history of international dispute resolution, this recent evolution is more accurately a revolution. Interstate arrangements, municipal court systems and private contractual dispute settlement systems reflect distinct doctrinal categories. In practice, however, they reflect different options for the resolution of disputes. Different groups can control the shape of each process, and they naturally shape and develop the process they control so that it addresses the needs of the group. The processes, although conceptually distinct, do not operate in isolation. Each evolves in response to the needs of the community controlling it and each of the other mechanisms may be affected by such changes. This is not to say that interstate arbitration, international commercial arbitration and municipal legal orders collectively are developing in accordance with some master plan or that they are not duplicating one another or not competing with one another.[212] It is to say that the community of commercial actors operating internationally demanded a more efficient and enforceable system than traditional interstate arbitration. That it was primarily businessmen and private lawyers who built the international commercial

---

[212] One cannot say that there was conscious interaction between the processes of private and public international arbitration during most of this century. Nor can the two processes be said to have been studied comparatively in detail. (A notable early exception in the form of a brief monograph is F. KELLOR & M. DOMKE, ARBITRATION IN INTERNATIONAL CONTROVERSY (1944).) Yet this should not be surprising. The joint existence of the two processes is a rather recent phenomenon, international commercial arbitration generally only having flourished since World War II. Sociologically, even today the two processes remain distinct, in part because, except for certain arbitrators, two very different groups deal with public and private international arbitration. (*See supra* note 28.) For a recent valuable interactive discussion of the two processes, see Vagts, *Dispute-Resolution Mechanisms in International Business*, 203 RECUEIL DES COURS 9, 71–88 (1987 III).

In a practical sense, the lack of attention presented few problems until the Iran–United States Claims Tribunal. The Tribunal brought under one roof both public and private international arbitration and the two groups associated with such proceedings. Government officials found themselves pondering the significance of the nationality of the awards, while private counsel contemplated the effect of declarations of nullity. On procedural matters one can find many instances of citation by the Tribunal of public international arbitral awards as precedent for procedural decisions it took in what it apparently regarded as a private international arbitral matter. In this sense, the Tribunal is serving as a vehicle whereby the groups dealing with public and private international arbitration are getting to know each other and each other's work.

arbitration system from the bottom up, rather than states from the top down, makes it no less of a revolution and all the more striking.

Many forces fueled the emergence of international commercial arbitration. There was an increased need for dispute resolution as the world saw a tremendous expansion of international commerce. Business executives sought security in an environment where previous assurances were no longer thought to suffice. The inability of public international law to adapt quickly to these changing circumstances and satisfy these concerns spurred a search for alternatives. Among other things, the strong tendency to limit standing in interstate arbitration to states did little to satisfy the concerns of the growing number of private international actors.[213]

Thus, as the system that was intended to provide international order proved inadequate and, as important, unresponsive to private international actors, pressures grew within municipal legal systems for more liberal assertions of jurisdiction on the basis of contacts, and for the revision of laws pertaining to the immunity of states from jurisdiction and enforcement. Likewise, efforts were directed at developing international commercial arbitration as an alternative. The success of both international commercial arbitration and transnational litigation was facilitated by the internationalizing of finance and markets, and the consequent dispersal of assets around the world.[214]

The effort to develop a private international arbitral system involved forming (1) a reliable means to enforce both arbitration agreements and arbitral awards, and (2) a fair and predictable arbitration process. From the first, enforcement was seen as the key to a meaningful process. Private international actors in conjunction with their governments used the basic tool of public international law, the treaty, to establish this enforcement regime.[215] In essence, the New York Convention places the coercive power of many of the world's courts at the disposal of private parties so that they may remove actions to, and ultimately implement the decisions of, their private legal systems.

---

[213] The institution of diplomatic protection must always have been somewhat suspect in the mind of the national involved. First, the national had to seek the consent of his or her government to raise the claim; second, the claim on the public plane could become politicized and thus subject to unknown influences; and third, the enforceability of any resulting award was uncertain. Moreover, the enforceability of awards based on diplomatic protection, uncertain as that was, became yet more uncertain after World War II, as the threat of using armed force (which, it has been argued, stood behind the claims commissions at the turn of the century) was, at least in theory, prohibited. *See* Shihata, *Towards a Greater Depoliticization of Investment Disputes: The Roles of ICSID and MIGA*, 1 FOREIGN INVESTMENT L. REV. 1 (1986).

[214] *See, e.g.,* Buxbaum, *supra* note 19. *See also* C. LIPSON, STANDING GUARD: PROTECTING FOREIGN CAPITAL IN THE NINETEENTH AND TWENTIETH CENTURIES (1985).

[215] The private, rather than governmental, hand in the design of the public law aspects of the private international arbitration system arguably is exemplified also by the recent rapid transformation of municipal arbitration statutes, which reduce court interference to a minimum while retaining the imprimatur of the state's endorsement of the validity of the process. *See supra* note 64.

The second dimension, development of a fair and predictable arbitral process, has been a more arduous task. States modernized their municipal laws, and regional efforts at harmonizing such laws were made. The legal profession engaged in massive educational programs and comparative studies of the private arbitration laws of all states. Ultimately, UNCITRAL has sought on a global basis to harmonize the internal and external dimensions of municipally governed arbitration through two ambitious efforts: the 1976 UNCITRAL Rules of Arbitral Procedure and the 1985 UNCITRAL Model Law on International Commercial Arbitration.

If the "top-down" mechanisms of public international arbitration inadequately responded to the needs of the private international community in the first two-thirds of this century, the Iran–United States Claims Tribunal signifies how quickly states have accepted municipally enforceable arbitration in the last third. ICSID can also be viewed in this manner. Like the Tribunal, ICSID originated in a treaty. Unlike the Tribunal, the validity of ICSID proceedings is expressly governed solely by the international regime established by its constituent instrument. Municipal courts of contracting states are expressly barred from reviewing or interfering in ICSID proceedings.[216] ICSID, however, like the international commercial arbitration system, responds to the demand for more effective dispute resolution. It does so by borrowing heavily from the structures of international commercial arbitration. ICSID replaces the traditional public approach of diplomatic protection with a regime permitting private parties to participate directly in arbitrations with states. Likewise, the traditional limitations on enforcement of awards are replaced by a direct private right of enforcement for both state and private parties in the municipal courts of any contracting state.

ICSID and the Tribunal are not isolated examples. The current arbitration between the United States and the Soviet Union over the U.S. Embassy under construction in Moscow rests upon an interlocking net of arbitration clauses, which, by adopting the UNCITRAL Rules of Arbitral Procedure and designating Stockholm as the place of arbitration, apparently establish a process within the supervisory jurisdiction of Sweden and the ambit of the New York Convention. The recent Treaty on Fisheries between the Governments of Certain Pacific Island States and the United States provides that a certain number of fishing licenses will be issued to U.S. nationals each year. Annex II to the Treaty carefully details the grounds upon which a license can be denied in any particular case. Any dispute between the state parties relating to or arising out of the Treaty is subject to arbitration under the UNCITRAL Rules.[217]

The evolution from diplomatic protection to international commercial arbitration and to institutions such as the Tribunal and ICSID is in the international community's interest. The trend away from classic interstate arbitration is desirable politically because it reduces the significance of the

---

[216] *See generally* Delaume, *supra* note 38.
[217] Art. 6.2, Treaty on Fisheries, Apr. 2, 1987, 26 ILM 1048, 1062 (1987).

state as a world actor in areas where the sensitivities of the state need not be implicated. Moreover, the flexibility of private arrangements is coupled with the assurance of harmonized municipal enforcement standards. The resulting low-level national permeation supports the rule of law by its implicit reliance on the existence of independent national judiciaries.[218]

The trend is desirable economically as well. Because the most directly affected parties are involved, both the costs and potential rewards of the process fall to the persons or entities that control it. This cost-benefit allocation promotes efficient decisions about the design and subsequent conduct of arbitral proceedings. Moreover, it is fair to say that the transfer of commercial disputes to the more enforceable process of private international arbitration not only prevents essentially private disputes from rising to the level of international conflict, but also furthers international investment and economic cooperation.

Finally, the transfer of certain disputes to private arbitration does not leave interstate arbitration bereft of content. Rather, it brings more clearly into focus what have always been the central tasks (and the major limitations) of interstate arbitration. Interstate arbitration has worked very well for resolving boundary disputes but not as well for disputes involving central interests of the state, such as the use of force. Although the volume of interstate arbitration may be less than it was at the turn of the century, international resolution of disputes *generally* is likely at an all-time high. Since these new mechanisms now address disputes that previously were elevated to the level of interstate arbitration by diplomatic protection, it would not be surprising to learn that true interstate arbitration in fact has remained relatively constant. Understanding this evolution helps strip away the false belief that somehow international arbitration accomplished much more in the past.

Understanding the evolution also lays bare what yet needs to be done and suggests directions for doing so. The development of alternative systems for international commercial disputes is in many respects far along, but the broad area of torts, in particular those involving the environment and human rights, appears to be at quite a different stage, dependent at present on transnational litigation (perhaps facilitated by treaty) or interstate fact-finding commissions. In this connection, it should be borne in mind that the foundation of the success of international commercial arbitration, the New York Convention, is not strictly limited to commercial matters.

---

[218] Arbitration awards may be brought directly before the courts of 82 countries under the New York Convention. UNCITRAL, Status of Conventions, UN Doc. A/CN.9/325 (May 17, 1989). Moreover, although one cynically might speculate that a local judge in some instances would feel constrained to contact his or her foreign ministry for "guidance," in time judges likely will fill the roles given. On the other hand, recognizing once again the evolutionary interplay of the various mechanisms, a counterbalancing consequence of globally elevating the international role of national judiciaries may be that as they are called upon to address more disputes with an international flavor, the more likely it will be that judicial doctrines will arise to assure deference to, and thereby enable courts to avoid embarrassment of, the executive.

IV. CONCLUSION

The arbitral proceedings before the Iran–United States Claims Tribunal involving claims of nationals are governed by the legal system of the Netherlands. This conclusion does not sit easily with the prevailing tendency to think that the proceedings of a tribunal formed by treaty to resolve a crisis between two countries are an interstate process not subject to interference by municipal legal orders. The tension between this conclusion and intuition is all the more striking, as the support for the former is extensive, if not overwhelming. The prevailing tendency nonetheless persists because it rests upon a categorical distinction between public and private international dispute resolution that in the past reflected practice quite faithfully. This distinction, however, no longer adequately describes the variations in international dispute resolution. The inadequacy of the distinction is problematic particularly for the interpreters of treaties because it may lead them unconsciously to force the innovative features of a treaty into the pigeonholes of the past. Thus, unconscious reliance upon this distinction should be replaced with a case-by-case examination of the mechanism the parties intended to create. Where this is done, innovation through treaty is protected, and a means for the development of international organization preserved.

The desire to innovate is driven by the perception that existing mechanisms do not fulfill the needs of the parties. To the parties, the various mechanisms are not separate doctrines but, rather, alternatives that should be measured against their needs. In this way, the parties' needs fuel the evolution of these mechanisms. Two particularly important dimensions to international dispute resolution in which innovation has occurred are the means of reviewing the validity of the result and the means of gaining enforcement of the result. The emergence of specific machinery such as the Tribunal and ICSID, and the increasing incidence of transnational litigation involving states and international commercial arbitration with state parties —all concurrent with an arguably decreasing need to rely on diplomatic protection—indicate that the various private, state and interstate mechanisms for the resolution of international disputes should not be viewed as operating in isolation, but as competing with, and evolving in response to, one another. To be sure, this evolving system is not the result of a master plan; rather, it is the Darwinian consequence of numerous separate demands. A continuing task of scholarship is to inform the soundness of such demands, to make them more coherent and, consequently, to help guide the evolving structure of international dispute resolution.

[11]

Strengthening GATT Procedures
for Settling Trade Disputes

Ernst-Ulrich Petersmann

HE INFLUENCE of an international organization 'depends not on fiat but on the confidence that its practice inspires. Confidence will not flourish unless the rule of law is observed in the development of practice. And for confidence to grow, interpretation must be consistent with legal principles and with the promotion of progressive economic objectives.' So has written Sir Joseph Gold, for many years General Counsel at the International Monetary Fund (IMF), on the legal and institutional aspects of the international monetary system.

In trying to fathom the General Agreement on Tariffs and Trade (GATT), the language used in the treaty's text, in interpretations of its provisions and in reports on disputes between member countries can be mystifying. One recent example is a panel report on a major trade dispute which summarized its analysis of the trade-distorting effects of variable import levies in the following formula: 'Expressed more briefly, the Panel noted that, since $G+F+E=C+A$, only if $F+E$ equalled C would A equal G.'[1]

This article accordingly begins with a few introductory comments on the difficulties of understanding the GATT legal system and of ensuring its consistent interpretation and application. It goes on to describe the contribution of GATT dispute-settlement procedures to the maintenance of legal certainty and overall consistency in the GATT legal system, then lists a number of remaining procedural weaknesses and discusses some proposals for improvements in the GATT dispute-settlement system.[2]

DIFFICULTIES IN INTERPRETING GATT LAW

There are many stories about the often cryptic wording and inherent complexity of GATT law and GATT practice. Congressmen in the United States have groaned that 'anyone who reads the GATT is likely to have his sanity impaired'.[3] The

ERNST-ULRICH PETERSMANN: Counsellor in the Office of Legal Affairs, Secretariat of the General Agreement on Tariffs and Trade (GATT), Geneva, and Lecturer in International and European Trade Law, University of the Saarland, Saarbrücken, Federal Republic of Germany.

56   ERNST-ULRICH PETERSMANN

presumably small number of people who have ever succeeded in reading the full text of the General Agreement — many provisions of which have been drafted 'with Anglo-Saxon discursiveness'[4] (such as the 23 paragraphs of Article XVIII extending over eight narrow-typed pages plus a two-page Annex) — may have shared the conclusion of one expert that 'only the learned can communicate with it and then only in code'.[5] After the reading, they may have been told by a GATT practitioner that 'this legal situation . . . bears no relation to the facts'[6] and '[breaches of rules] have in some cases become so frequent and so tolerated that the rules are now simply traps for the unwary, inexpert or naive'.[7]

Even economic specialists on the GATT have complained that 'only ten people in the world understand it and they are not telling anybody'.[8] The few legal experts that have elaborated systematic treatises on the GATT have described it as a 'puzzle'[9] and have been critical of the apparent contradiction between the legalistic style of the General Agreement, drafted for the most part in precise and justiciable language resembling a tax code, and the GATT's sometimes overly pragmatic 'diplomat's jurisprudence'[10] and 'institutional inability to maintain compliance with the rules'.[11] Those engaged in commercial diplomacy often perceive it as 'an enduring irony that while governments have dealt with international trade issues through the GATT for more than thirty years, businesses actually encountering trade problems in the market-place think of the GATT, to the extent that they think of it at all, as something remote and ineffectual. Like apartment dwellers living on different floors, the GATT and the business community have co-existed all this time, but largely in isolation from one another.'[12]

The introductory quotation from a recent GATT dispute-settlement report illustrates what a reading of the central GATT dispute-settlement provision of Article XXIII confirms beyond doubt: the GATT dispute-settlement provisions are no exception to the general difficulty of understanding GATT law. During the preparatory work on the GATT in Geneva back in 1947, one delegate characterized a draft of Article XXIII by saying that, 'of all the vague and woolly punitive provisions that one could make, this seems to hold the prize place. It appears to me that what it says is this. In this wide world of sin there are certain sins which we have not yet discovered and which, after long examination, we cannot define; but there being such sins, we will provide some sort of punishment for them if we find out what they are and if we find anybody committing them. The only definite thing in the whole Article . . . is the type of punishment which can be visited upon these offenders. It seems to me that this is something like Pirandello's play *Six Characters in Search of an Author*, only it is rather the other way round. Here it is one punishment in search of six sins.'[13] In comparison with the dispute-settlement provisions of other international economic organizations, Article XXIII appears indeed to be unique in admitting complaints not only in the case of a violation of specific GATT obligations but also when certain government measures, entirely legal in themselves, 'nullify or impair any benefit accruing under this Agreement'.[14]

GATT DISPUTE-SETTLEMENT PROCEDURES 57

The main economic function of international agreements on the use of transparent, non-discriminatory and least-distortive policy instruments, such as the GATT and the IMF Articles of Agreement, is to assist each contracting party (member country) in increasing its national gains from trade by means of general rules designed to reduce international transaction costs, to secure market access and to enhance undistorted competition. A major function of dispute-settlement procedures is to increase legal certainty and, thereby, to act as an incentive for shifting resources from protective into productive uses. These economic objectives can be achieved only to the extent that the international rules are known, understood and respected not only by governments but also by private traders, producers, investors and consumers and to the extent that they are consistently construed and applied over time. If governments and those engaged in international trade do not remain convinced that observance of the rules promotes their national and individual self-interests, the rules may cease to be respected. And if the rules are not set in a framework of an effective 'legal system' of mutual 'checks and balances', ensuring that the public good of legal certainty and undistorted international competition is not unduly sacrificed to short-term exigencies and special interests, the rules may prove incapable of playing their crucial role. International legal disciplines designed to constrain the abuse of discretionary powers in trade and monetary policy cannot remain effective if their interpretation and observance are considered to lie within the discretion of the governments whose powers the rules were designed to constrain.

General rules promoting legal certainty and undistorted competition, consistently construed and applied over time, have been likened by economists to a stock of capital continuously yielding profits. Like Gresham's Law on the replacement of good money by the bad, inconsistent interpretations and violations of the rules may entail a vicious circle of 'bad laws driving out good laws'. If governments no longer observe the legal disciplines that make mutual economic gains possible, other governments may be tempted or pressurized to follow such precedents; and even private economic agents may wonder why they should continue to observe international trade rules.

Most international economic agreements therefore include (i) provisions and procedures for their consistent interpretation, application and further development, (ii) supervisory mechanisms for the review, judgment and correction of conduct inconsistent with the rules and (iii) mechanisms for the prevention and settlement of disputes.[15] Virtually all international economic organizations — albeit, in the case of the GATT, only since 1981 (34 years after its inception) — have set up legal services systematically enhancing the transparency, consistency and development of their respective primary and 'secondary' multilateral treaty law as well as its implementation in the national legal systems of member countries. Both the GATT (Article X[3][b]) and the IMF Agreement (Article VIII [2][b]) attempt to enhance the effectiveness of their respective international rules by providing also for the review and enforcement of national trade and monetary regulations by domestic courts. The numerous regular publications by the legal services, for instance those of the IMF and the European Community, continuously documenting, explaining and supervising the evolution of IMF law and Community law, have been instrumental in enabling individuals and domestic courts to invoke, apply and enforce in domestic courts precise and unconditional international legal obligations.[16]

By contrast, the domestic foreign-trade laws of many GATT member countries explicitly authorize executive trade restrictions in violation of GATT rules; and the domestic courts in most GATT member countries do not permit private individuals to invoke GATT rules in the courts and to rely on their observance by governments. The reasoning of the courts in the United States and the European Community,[17] for instance, indicates that the judges have not remained unimpressed by the mercantilist notions of some GATT provisions (as on 'trade concessions') and perceive 'GATT pragmatism' as an expression of 'power-oriented' rather than 'rule-oriented' trade policies, hindering the judicial application and enforcement of precise and unconditional GATT obligations.

The General Agreement and the central GATT dispute-settlement procedures under Article XXIII apply in principle to all tariff and non-tariff measures affecting trade. The comprehensive scope of the GATT is reflected also in a decision adopted at the end of the Tokyo Round of multilateral trade negotiations of 1973-79 in which 'the Contracting Parties reaffirm their intention to ensure the unity and consistency of the GATT system . . . as a whole'.[18] This view of GATT law, as a comprehensive system, has strengthened the disposition of various GATT panels on trade disputes (i) to find legal solutions under the articles for newly arising problems of international trade regulation, (ii) to construe the General Agreement and the additional Tokyo Round agreements or codes in a mutually consistent manner and (iii) to apply a 'teleological approach', choosing the interpretation which best serves the purpose and continued effectiveness of a GATT provision.

The actual application of GATT law depends to a large extent on its interpretation and the legal methods of interpretation used. Even the best intentioned *ad hoc* interpretation of a GATT dispute-settlement panel — if adopted without knowledge of the 700 or so GATT interpretations and GATT reports adopted over the last four decades[19] and without regard to the established principles of international treaty interpretation[20] or to the essential principles of international dispute-settlement procedures[21] — may prove to have disintegrating precedent-creating effects and may be criticized as having been reached in an unprincipled and therefore arbitrary manner 'like a khadi under a tree dispensing justice according to considerations of individual expediency'.

Since, in the words of the economist F.A. Hayek, 'it is of the essence of legal thinking . . . that the lawyer strives to make the whole system consistent',[22] the

GATT DISPUTE-SETTLEMENT PROCEDURES 59

traditional GATT policy of avoiding anything smacking of 'legalism', including the setting up of a GATT legal office until 1981, is another 'puzzle' and may have weakened the necessary 'system-building' of the GATT.

In particular, 'the European Community's policy quite openly consists in playing down the legal substance of the GATT'[23] and, too, in portraying the GATT as merely a framework of 'soft law' and a forum for negotiations, thereby putting into doubt the legally binding character of GATT law.[24] This legal misconception has been espoused even by the Community's Court of Justice in Luxembourg, which directly applies and enforces many prohibitions of the Treaty of Rome, the 'constitution' of the Community (such as Articles 30, 34 and 95), and of the free trade agreements with countries in the European Free Trade Association (EFTA) which have the same wording as the equivalent GATT prohibitions (such as Articles III and XI[1]). But the Court refuses to observe these international GATT obligations in respect of third GATT contracting parties on the ground that judicial observance of GATT legal disciplines might render the Community 'defenceless' and that 'respect for the provisions of the GATT by the contracting parties depends above all upon the fact that each can count upon the others observing the agreement only if it does so itself'.[25] Apparently the Court's judges believe that the limited trade-policy powers of the European Community include the right to regulate the foreign-trade activities of Community citizens in open violation of the Community's precise and unconditional GATT legal obligations for the use of transparent, non-discriminatory and least-distortive policy instruments, the observance of which would allow Community traders, producers and consumers to buy and sell goods in the best markets, to compete among each other without discriminatory trade distortions, to benefit from a transparent and welfare-increasing conduct of the common commercial policy and to rely on the rule of law within the Community.[26]

After the formation of the European Economic Community in 1958 up to 1970, the use of the central GATT dispute-settlement procedures under Article XXIII strongly declined.[27] In the 1970s, the GATT dispute-settlement procedures continued to meet with criticism. The United States Congress, for instance, complained that 'today many GATT principles are observed more in the breach'.[28] In the Trade Act of 1974, Congress therefore mandated the President of the United States to seek improvements in the procedures. In 1979, 1982 and 1984, the GATT Contracting Parties adopted a number of improvements to the GATT dispute-settlement system.[29] The ministerial declaration of 1986 on the Uruguay Round negotiations also envisages that, 'in order to ensure prompt and effective resolution of disputes to the benefit of all contracting parties, negotiations shall aim to improve and strengthen the rules and the procedures of the dispute-settlement process, while recognizing the contribution that would be made by more effective and enforceable GATT rules and disciplines'.[30] Since negotiations on, and proposals for, such improvements are dependent on how one

60   ERNST-ULRICH PETERSMANN

assesses the past performance of the GATT dispute-settlement procedures, the following comments discuss first the past experience with GATT Article XXIII and only subsequently some proposals for reforms.

MAJOR BENEFITS OF GATT PROCEDURES FOR SETTLING
TRADE DISPUTES

An evaluation of GATT dispute-settlement procedures not only has to take into account the contribution of the procedures to (i) the settlement of a large number of trade disputes. It is also necessary to note that the procedures tend to promote important goals of the GATT trading system such as (ii) rule-oriented trade policies in compliance with GATT obligations, (iii) the maintenance of continued reciprocity and 'equity' in the face of changing circumstances, (iv) agreed further development of the GATT legal system and (v) the exclusion of the customary law of unilateral 'reprisals'. These points are successively elaborated in the ensuing discussion.

Resolution of a Large Number of Disputes

There exists no official classification of GATT 'dispute-settlement proceedings' or of 'trade disputes'. The General Agreement contains some 30 provisions
     obliging contracting parties to hold bilateral and multilateral consultations
on restrictive trade measures in specific instances (for example, Articles
VI[7], XII[4], XVI[1], XIX[2], XXII, XXIII[1] and XXVIII) or
     providing for other multilateral procedures that can be used for the
settlement of disputes (for example, Articles XII[4], XIX[3], XXIII[2],
XXIV[7] and [10], XXV[5] and XXVIII[4]).
Between 1948 and October 1987, more than 100 formal complaints were instituted under the central dispute-settlement provision of Article XXIII.[31] But these formally notified Article XXIII complaints are only the tip of the iceberg. A large number of additional complaints were dealt with in consultations under Articles XXII and XXIII.[32] Since 1980, some twenty formal complaints have been submitted under the dispute-settlement provisions of the various GATT codes, concluded at the end of the Tokyo Round negotiations in 1979.[33] More than 90 per cent of the altogether more than 50 working-party and panel reports under Article XXIII have been adopted and implemented. Even in the case of the four panel reports (relating to Spanish restrictions on soyabean oil, Canadian restrictions on the sale of gold coins, the European Community's production subsidies on canned fruit and the Community's tariff preferences for citrus products) not adopted under Article XXIII, the complaining party withdrew its complaint or agreed on a settlement of the dispute. Complaints instituted by developing countries were on

GATT DISPUTE-SETTLEMENT PROCEDURES 61

average no less successful than those brought by developed countries. And the very small number of complaints not supported by GATT panels or working parties suggests that the problem of unjustified 'procedural harassment', well known in domestic anti-dumping and countervailing-duty proceedings, does not present a problem in the GATT.

There is no other international organization, including the European Community, with such a large number and successful record of multilateral dispute-settlement proceedings among states. Moreover, international trade conflicts in the GATT are often only a reflection of prior domestic conflicts in the formation of national policy between, on the one hand, trade-policy commitments under the GATT and, on the other, domestic pressures for protectionist departures from GATT rules for the benefit of special interests. Thus 'tacit collusion' among the disputing governments can rather often be seen in GATT dispute-settlement decisions leading to the confirmation of legal interpretations that were espoused by the 'losing' government itself in the national-policy deliberations prior to the dispute; the 'losing' government then gladly avails itself of the GATT dispute-settlement decision in order to resist domestic protectionist pressures. And there are also instances showing that GATT dispute-settlement proceedings can be completed more rapidly than domestic judicial proceedings on the very same issue. In the 1977 case on the suspension of customs liquidation by the United States,[34] for instance, the GATT working party, established at the request of Japan, confirmed within only three weeks the legal interpretation shared also by the United States Administration that a prior decision by the US Customs Court was inconsistent with GATT Article VI(4). This GATT ruling successfully assisted the appeal lodged by the Administration itself to the US Court of Customs and Patent Appeals which then repealed the lower-court decision in compliance with the GATT ruling.

Promotion of the 'Rule of Law' and Economic Welfare

More than 90 per cent of all complaints under Article XXIII are 'violation complaints'; that is, complaints in which the applicant country asserts 'the failure of another contracting party to carry out its obligations under this Agreement' (Article XXIII[1][a]) and requests the withdrawal of the measures concerned. The Agreed Description of the Customary Practice of the GATT in the Field of Dispute Settlement, which is the Annex to the Understanding Regarding Notification, Consultation, Dispute Settlement and Surveillance adopted in 1979, confirms this right to specific performance of GATT obligations by stating that, 'in the absence of a mutually agreed solution, the first objective of the Contracting Parties is usually to secure the withdrawal of the measures concerned if these are found to be inconsistent with the General Agreement. The provision of compensation should be resorted to only if the immediate withdrawal of the measure is impracticable and as a temporary measure pending the withdrawal of the measures which are inconsistent with the General Agreement.'[35] The terms of reference regularly request panels — usually composed of diplomats from national delegations to the GATT in Geneva — to examine the complaint 'in the light of the relevant GATT provisions'. Virtually all GATT panels focus on this legal examination of the compatibility of the disputed measures with GATT law. Most of the GATT dispute-settlement decisions under Article XXIII have led to the withdrawal of those measures which were found to be inconsistent with GATT law and have contributed to the 'rule of law' in international trade. The GATT dispute-settlement proceedings have thereby become one of the most important operational activities of the GATT.

By promoting rule-oriented rather than power-oriented trade policies and dispute settlements, GATT law and its enforcement through the GATT dispute-settlement procedures protect contracting parties from protectionist pressures not only by foreign governments but also by domestic pressure groups. In spite of their lack of 'political clout' (also due, *inter alia*, to their reduced GATT commitments and their political dependence on the voluntary Generalized System of Preferences [GSP]), small developing countries have also used Article XXIII successfully in order to enforce their GATT rights and, for instance, to resist protectionist pressures on them to accept 'voluntary' restraints on their exports of particular products.[36]

Since restrictions of 'foreign trade' operate by restricting the freedoms and property rights of domestic traders, producers and consumers and redistribute income among domestic groups at considerable net cost to the restricting economy, observance of GATT law is of constitutional significance for the rule of law also in domestic legal systems. GATT law does not hinder any contracting party from attaining any policy objective.[37] It only prescribes the use of transparent, non-discriminatory and least-distortive policy instruments for whatever policy objectives a contracting party wants to pursue. Thus observance of GATT law does not prevent any contracting party

from deciding autonomously on its national level of trade protection (see Article XXVIII),

from introducing safeguard measures (as under Articles XII and XVIII to XXI),

from regional economic integration (as under Article XXIV) or

from intervening in its domestic economy by means of production subsidies (Article XVI[1]), state trading (Article XVII), taxes and other regulations (Article III).

GATT law ranks the various instruments of trade and economic policy in almost the same way as economic theory suggests.[38] Hence, as John Maynard Keynes emphasized in his 'Proposals for an International Currency or Clearing Union' of

1942, 'it is an advantage, and not a disadvantage, of the scheme that it invites the member states to abandon that licence to promote indiscipline, disorder and bad-neighbourhood which, to the general disadvantage, they have been free to exercise hitherto'.[39] Ultimately, the GATT legal disciplines for the use of transparent, non-discriminatory and least-distortive policy instruments can be conceived as an extension to the foreign-trade sector of national economies of the Western constitutional principles of transparent policy making, non-discrimination, limited government, individual liberties and judicial review.[40]

Rule-oriented Promotion of Reciprocity and Equity

Following the precedent set by numerous bilateral trade agreements concluded before World War II, Article XXIII also admits 'non-violation complaints'; that is, complaints whenever

'any contracting party should consider that any benefit accruing to it directly or indirectly under this Agreement is being nullified or impaired or that the attainment of any objective of the Agreement is being impeded as the result of . . . (b) the application by another contracting party of any measure, whether or not it conflicts with the provisions of this Agreement, or (c) the existence of any other situation' (Article XXIII[1][b] and [c]).

The drafting history indicates that these non-violation complaints were mainly designed to protect the mutual balance of advantages resulting from reciprocal trade negotiations and from 'schedules of concessions' (Article II), not only against trade restrictions specifically prohibited in the substantive GATT provisions but also against other kinds of 'nullification or impairment'. GATT contracting parties were considered to be entitled not only to the observance by other contracting parties of express legal GATT obligations but also to a broader kind of balance of rights and obligations and commercial opportunities deriving therefrom.

The GATT Contracting Parties have only cautiously used this 'common law jurisdiction' on a case-by-case basis in order to prevent the circumvention of tariff concessions through governmental measures not prohibited by the General Agreement and, thereby, to preserve the balance of the original exchange of concessions. Thus GATT law has been construed to confer not only a right to the observance and specific performance of GATT provisions, including the right to compensation in case of direct withdrawal of tariff concessions (Article XXVIII). An additional 'benefit accruing under this Agreement' in terms of Article XXIII (1), recognized and protected under GATT law, has been the 'reasonable expectation' (*bona fide*) that the competitive advantages deriving from tariff concessions under Article II will also not be nullified or impaired by the concession-granting country in an indirect way through the subsequent introduction of a governmental

International Dispute Settlement

64   ERNST-ULRICH PETERSMANN

measure which, although not inconsistent with the General Agreement, (i) upsets the competitive relationship between the bound 'concession product' and directly competitive products from other origins and (ii) could not be reasonably anticipated by the complaining party at the time of the tariff negotiations.[41] A case in point is a 1985 panel report on a complaint by the United States, which found that the unforeseeable introduction of production aids in the European Community for certain canned fruit had nullified or impaired benefits accruing to the United States from prior tariff concessions granted by the Community on these products under Article II.

There are important procedural and substantive differences between violation complaints and non-violation complaints. A violation of a GATT rule is presumed to have adverse competitive effects on other contracting parties (*'prima facie* nullification or impairment') and entails a legal obligation to withdraw the illegal measure. By contrast, a non-violation complaint implies a more far-reaching burden of proof on the part of the complaining party (for example, demonstration of 'reasonable expectations' and subsequent 'upsetting of competition'). And the Contracting Parties may only recommend, but not prescribe in a legally binding manner, the withdrawal of the distorting but lawful measure. If the recommendation to remove the competitive distortion is not followed, they may only authorize the adversely affected contracting party to suspend the application of equivalent GATT obligations or concessions towards the country that has impaired the tariff concessions.

The GATT obligations for the use of market-conforming policy instruments (i.e. tariffs) proceed from the assumption that comparative advantage and undistorted competition are the most efficient allocators of production and consumption not only within countries but also between countries. But, given worldwide government interventions in agricultural and mineral commodity trade, the General Agreement also contains provisions for 'measures designed to attain stable, equitable and remunerative prices' of certain primary products (Article XXXVI[4]) and for the maintenance of 'an equitable share of world export trade' in subsidized primary products (Article XVI[3]). Other GATT provisions relating to 'unfair trade' (such as Articles VI and XVI[4]) are also sometimes construed as resting in part on considerations of equity.

Some dispute-settlement reports under Article XXIII have contributed to a rule-oriented interpretation of these ambiguous provisions by elaborating general criteria, legal presumptions or procedural rules for the burden of proof, as with the trade-distorting effects of export subsidies. The 1958 panel report concerning French assistance to exports of wheat and wheat flour, for instance, concluded that export subsidies causing a large increase in exports justify the assumption of 'more than an equitable share of world export trade'.[42] And the four 1976 panel reports on income-tax practices proceeded from a similar assumption that the export subsidies could be presumed to result 'in the sale of such product for export at a price lower than the comparable price charged for the like product to buyers in the domestic market' (Article XVI[4]).[43] The principles, procedures and legal presumptions (as for *'prima facie* nullification or impairment') for violation complaints and non-violation complaints under Article XXIII were developed through the GATT dispute-settlement proceedings on a case-by-case basis and finally codified in the Agreed Description of the Customary Practice of the GATT in the Field of Dispute Settlement adopted in 1979.

Agreed Further Development of the GATT Legal System

According to the *dictum* of Mr Justice Holmes in the United States in the landmark case of *Missouri v. Holland* (1920), 'a constitutive instrument will call into life a being, the development of which could not have been foreseen completely by the most gifted of its begetters'.[44] To be put into practice, general GATT rules have to be interpreted by the 125 countries participating in the GATT legal system and to be applied by domestic executive, legislative and judicial organs to concrete circumstances. By contrast to IMF Article XXIX and World Bank Article IX, the General Agreement does not explicitly provide for a special procedure for 'authoritative interpretations' of its articles. The GATT dispute-settlement procedures have provided one among several other procedural means for adopting agreed interpretations whenever divergent views on the interpretation and application of GATT rules arise. They have thus helped to prevent each individual contracting party from asserting a right to the unilateral final interpretation of GATT rules.

The principles and rules of interpretation, evolved under international treaty law (especially in Articles 31 and 32 of the 1969 Vienna Convention on the Law of Treaties) and under international customary law, reserve a considerable margin of discretion to the parties of multilateral treaties to interpret the treaty provisions with due regard to the special objectives and inherent structures of the treaty concerned. The GATT's 'diplomat's jurisprudence', under Article XXIII, continues to be characterized by the trend of attributing considerable importance to the intentions of the contracting parties at the time of the drafting of the General Agreement and by interpreting some GATT obligations restrictively. But, presumably influenced by the gradual evolution of the GATT into a worldwide framework agreement and international trade organization of unlimited duration, GATT dispute-settlement reports and rulings also make increasing use of the methods of interpretation prescribed in the Vienna Convention, which considers preparatory work only as a supplementary means of interpretation and does not even mention the interpretative rule of *in dubio pro libertate*.

Thus the primary importance of the objective meaning of the treaty text, seen in its context and in the light of the treaty objectives, has been acknowledged in various panel reports. And interpretations contributing to the achievement of GATT objectives have been preferred. The agreed GATT practice since 1947 (through references, for instance, to previous panel reports) has become a generally recognized means of interpretation of GATT law. As an indication of 'the agreement of the parties regarding its interpretation' (Article 31[3][b] of the Vienna Convention), it tends to reduce the weight given to the historical intentions of the drafters 40 years ago. This is in accordance with the principle of international law that the authors of a treaty can attribute to the text any meaning they choose by subsequent decisions.

The interpretations and obligations determined in GATT dispute-settlement reports become legally binding only through the adoption of the report by the competent GATT body and, arguably, only in respect of the parties to the dispute. But the rule-oriented nature of most panel reports and of the concept of nullification or impairment (Article XXIII) — which does not require the determination of 'trade damage' but only of the impairment of trade opportunities protected under the General Agreement[45] — has contributed to the recognition that GATT dispute-settlement reports and decisions often acquire a more general paradigmatic significance for the future 'administration of justice' in similar cases.

Moreover, treaty texts are often open to different possible interpretations and the agreed choice of one over another possible interpretation also contains an element of law-creation. The more the historical views of the drafters fade behind the current views of contracting parties, the more agreed interpretations and rule-applications in the context of dispute-settlement procedures can amount to a further development of GATT law. Similar to the development of English common law and equity law based on judicial precedent and derived from general principles and social needs, rather than from fixed and inflexible rules, GATT dispute-settlement procedures have enabled the GATT Contracting Parties over the last four decades to give more precision to many GATT obligations, to make GATT rules more effective thereby and to preserve GATT law as an objective legal order, notwithstanding departures from some obligations by individual member countries from time to time.

The fairly satisfactory operation of the GATT dispute-settlement proceedings has contributed to the maintenance of confidence in the GATT legal system and has reduced the incentives for alternative power-oriented trade policies. Just as most countries have introduced systematic foreign-trade legislation for a transparent, non-discriminatory and market-conforming conduct of trade policy only after their accession to the GATT, in the course of domestic implementation of GATT obligations, the interpretations agreed in GATT dispute-settlement procedures have contributed to the further development not only of GATT law (see, for example, the use by the 1979 GATT Subsidies Code[46] of legal criteria elaborated in prior GATT dispute-settlement reports) but also of the domestic implementing legislation and national trade practices.

Successful Combination of Various Means of Dispute Settlement

In international state practice, it has become customary to distinguish between different modes of dispute settlement, such as 'seeking a solution by negotiation, enquiry, mediation, conciliation, arbitration, judicial settlement, resort to regional agencies or arrangements or other peaceful means' (see Article 33 of the United Nations Charter). Each of these means of dispute settlement also has a long tradition in the field of international trade relations and specific features designed to fit different situations and to maximize the chances of dispute settlement by successive or alternative use of different means.

The GATT dispute-settlement system differs from that of other multilateral agreements and international economic organizations in that it makes full use of almost all of these different methods of dispute settlement and provides also for the — very rarely used — possibility of international sanctions by authorizing a contracting party to suspend the application to another contracting party of trade concessions or other obligations under the GATT (for example, Articles XII[4] and XXIII[2]). Only the possibility, provided for in the 1948 Havana Charter for an International Trade Organization, of requesting the International Court of Justice to give an advisory opinion was not taken over into the General Agreement. But observance of GATT rules may be controlled through the municipal courts and legal systems of contracting parties which 'shall maintain or institute . . . judicial, arbitral or administrative tribunals or procedures for the purpose, *inter alia*, of the prompt review and correction of administrative action relating to customs matters' (Article X[3]). Thus foreign exporters frequently resort to the domestic courts, as in the United States and the European Community, for judicial review of anti-dumping, countervailing-duty and other safeguard proceedings.

Notwithstanding the absence of a provision for recourse to an international judicial body, the GATT dispute-settlement provisions, and their successful application in GATT practice over the last four decades, constitute one of the most effective and original dispute-settlement systems existing in any international economic organization. GATT practice appears to confirm that the existence of these special treaty provisions on dispute settlement and enforcement excludes the right of contracting parties to rely on the international customary law methods of dispute settlement such as 'retorsion' and 'reprisals'.

Negotiation as a form of dispute settlement serves the purpose of achieving agreed solutions without the participation of neutral third parties. Most dispute-settlement clauses in international treaties, including the GATT's Article XXIII and the dispute-settlement provisions of the various GATT codes, provide that the dispute may be submitted to other forms of settlement only after the attempt to solve the dispute by consultation or negotiation has failed.

68   ERNST-ULRICH PETERSMANN

Good offices, enquiry, mediation and conciliation are characterized by the agreed participation of neutral third parties in the settlement of disputes and by the recommendatory nature of the contribution from the third party which may act merely as a 'go-between' (good offices), contribute to the impartial clarification of disputed facts (enquiry) or help the parties more actively in reconciling their divergent views by submitting proposals *ex aequo et bono* or based on existing law (mediation and conciliation).

Proposals from a neutral third party may be easier to accept than when they come directly from the opponent. Mediation and conciliation procedures have also the advantage of being very flexible. The neutral third party is not bound by existing law, but can take additional circumstances into account. The disputing parties retain a large degree of autonomy and are free to reject the recommendations submitted to them for the solution. And the proposed compromises or 'package deals' may be based on considerations of equity and may be accompanied by additional services (such as financial aid offered by the World Bank in its mediation in the 1951-61 dispute between India and Pakistan on the division of the waters of the Indus basin), which makes mediation and conciliation particularly suited to non-justiciable political disputes. Mediators and conciliators, however, may also put their own relations with the parties at risk. Conciliators, who act in their individual capacity and not as representatives of their state or organization, may enjoy more freedom of action than mediators and may find it easier to de-politicize the conflict.

Mediation and conciliation are often considered inappropriate in the context of multilateral agreements that aim to establish a uniform legal order. The reason is that, while mediators and conciliators may initially act as a sort of legal adviser in justiciable disputes, any compromise solutions achieved in the process of mediation or conciliation may have a weakening effect on the legal order. While the confidentiality and voluntary acceptance of mediation and conciliation proposals may strengthen their effectiveness and may avoid a loss of prestige for the 'losing' party, they are less likely to serve as a precedent for future disputes and their rejection may put the rule of law into doubt. In spite of the large number of international treaties providing for the possibility of conciliation, only a few conflicts have actually been submitted to it.

In dispute-settlement proceedings under Article XXIII, the complaining countries insist, almost invariably, on third-party adjudication of their rights through the reports of independent GATT panels and subsequent decisions of the GATT Council. Only in a very few cases have GATT disputing parties availed themselves of the existing possibility of requesting good offices (those, say, of the Director-General), factual enquiries (by, say, independent experts) or efforts at conciliation (through, say, GATT working parties). Arbitration through a GATT panel report, which both parties to the dispute accepted as binding without adoption of the report by the GATT Council, has been requested only once under

GATT DISPUTE-SETTLEMENT PROCEDURES 69

Article XXIII, namely by the United States and the European Community in order to resolve their 'chicken war' in 1962-63. [47]

SOME WEAKNESSES IN EXISTING GATT PROCEDURES FOR SETTLING TRADE DISPUTES

Most problems in past GATT dispute-settlement proceedings have arisen from disagreements over, and imbalances in, certain substantive GATT legal disciplines (such as Article XVI) rather than from deficiencies in the GATT dispute-settlement procedures. The Tokyo Round negotiations have shown that the willingness to accept more stringent dispute-settlement procedures (for example, as part of various GATT codes) may depend on whether agreement can be reached in giving the GATT's substantive rules more precision and making GATT legal disciplines more balanced (for example, by terminating 'waivers' granted to only certain contracting parties). If consensus on rule-oriented trade policies is lacking (as with the rules on agricultural import restrictions and export subsidies), reforms of GATT dispute-settlement procedures may also fail to induce more rule-oriented trade policies.

The GATT ministerial declaration of 1982 records the agreement of the Contracting Parties 'that the Understanding on Notification, Consultation, Surveillance and Dispute Settlement negotiated during the Tokyo Round provides the essential framework of procedures for the settlement of disputes among contracting parties and that no major change is required in this framework, but that there is scope for more effective use of the existing mechanism and for specific improvements in procedures'. [48] This ministerial declaration and the action taken by the Contracting Parties on 30 November 1984 provide for various improvements in the GATT dispute-settlement procedures, proceeding from the common understanding that 'procedural improvements can lead to improvements in the quality of panel reports'. [49]

Today there appear, at least on paper, to be hardly any real deficiencies in the GATT dispute-settlement procedures. The present procedures, if effectively used, have proven capable of producing adequate settlements of disputes. Yet there persist a few procedural problems in the actual panel process which could be addressed within the existing framework and through additional amendments of the procedures.

Delays in the Establishment and Work of Panels

If consultations do not yield a settlement of the dispute, the complaining party can invoke Article XXIII(2) and request the establishment of a panel to examine the complaint and to assist the Contracting Parties to deal with the matter. The 1979 Understanding provides that 'the Contracting Parties would decide on its establishment in accordance with standing practice . . . after the contracting party concerned had had an opportunity to study the complaint and respond to it before the Contracting Parties' and 'the panel should be constituted as promptly as possible and normally not later than thirty days from the decision by the Contracting Parties'. Panels 'should aim to deliver their findings without undue delay, taking into account the obligation of the Contracting Parties to ensure prompt settlement. In cases of urgency, the panel would be called upon to deliver its findings within a [specified] period, normally three months from the time the panel was established.' The Annex to the Understanding notes that 'in most cases the proceedings of the panels have been completed within a reasonable period of time, extending from three to nine months'.

The 1984 decision on dispute-settlement procedures, noting that 'experience has shown these time targets are seldom met', makes provision for the following procedural improvements 'on a trial basis' so as to better ensure the formation of panels and the completion of panel work in a timely manner:

'In the event that panel composition cannot be agreed within thirty days after a matter is referred by the Contracting Parties, the Director-General shall, at the request of either party and in consultation with the Chairman of the Council, complete the panel by appointing persons from the roster of non-governmental panelists to resolve the deadlock, after consulting both parties. . . Panels should continue to set their own working procedures and, where possible, panels should provide the parties to the dispute at the outset with a proposed calendar for the panel's work. Where written submissions are requested from the parties, panels should set precise deadlines, and the parties to a dispute should respect those deadlines.'

'Justice delayed is justice denied.' In GATT practice, requests for the establishment of a panel, however, have usually been granted by the GATT Council within two months (that is, at the first or second Council meeting after the request) and the average period of time since 1948 for the adoption of panel reports by the GATT Council has been ten months after the request for the establishment of the panel. [50] These time periods appear reasonable and shorter than the average time of proceedings before, for example, the International Court of Justice or the European Community's Court of Justice. Most of the causes of past delays have been dealt with in subsequent amendments to the GATT dispute-settlement procedures, such as:

(a) the explicit understanding of 1979 'that complaints and counter-complaints in regard to distinct matters should not be linked' (such linkage by the United States had delayed by several years the establishment of the four panels on the 1973 complaints relating to certain tax practices in the United States and the European Community and the adoption of their reports);

(b) the authorization given in 1984 to the Director-General to complete the composition of a panel at the request of either party if the parties could not agree on the composition of the panel within 30 days (the latter disagreement had delayed the work of several panels);

(c) the provision in the 1982 ministerial declaration that 'the Director-General shall inform the Council of any case in which it has not been found possible to meet the time-limits for the establishment of a panel' (which may act as a disincentive for abusive delays);

(d) another provision in the 1982 ministerial declaration, which has facilitated the composition of several GATT panels since then, that 'where experts are not drawn from Geneva, any expenses . . . shall be met from the GATT budget'; and

(e) the request in the 1984 decision to set and respect precise deadlines for written submissions to panels (disregard of such deadlines by the disputing parties had considerably delayed several panel proceedings).
Some other causes of delay could usefully be addressed through additional procedural provisions. For instance:

The occasional efforts by the defendant party to influence the outcome of the panel proceeding by insistence on special terms of reference (for instance, excluding the examination by the panel of certain controversial legal aspects), and the delays caused by lengthy negotiations on such terms of reference, could be avoided by recognizing a right of the complaining party to the use of standard terms of reference, unless both parties agree on special terms of reference within a fixed period of time.

Following the precedent of the 1979 Agreed Description of the Customary Practice of the GATT in the Field of Dispute Settlement, an 'agreed description of the customary working procedures of panels', including an explicit procedural requirement to conclude the written and oral panel proceedings within a period of normally three months, might expedite the panel deliberations and discourage the occasional practice of too infrequent panel meetings or of Geneva-based panel members being reassigned to other countries before the end of the panel proceeding.

Since the request for the establishment of a GATT panel evidences the failure of the preceding consultations to resolve the issue and a desire for an independent examination of the complaint 'in the light of the relevant GATT provisions' (standard terms of reference), the requirement in the 1979 Understanding that panels should continue to give the parties 'adequate opportunity to develop a mutually satisfactory solution' should be construed in a manner preventing undue delays in the elaboration of the panel report. Pending its adoption, the report is still of an advisory nature, anyhow, and in no way hinders the disputing parties from agreeing on a settlement of the dispute.

Some opportunities for the defendant country to delay the dispute-settlement process are difficult to remove through procedural reforms. Due to the considerable imbalance in certain GATT obligations (as a result, for instance, of the 'waiver' for agricultural trade restrictions of the United States) and to well-known divergencies in the interpretation of some GATT rules (such as Articles XI[2], XVI, XXI and XXIV), some contracting parties tend to prefer negotiations and agreement on more adequate new rules in lieu of quasi-adjudicative panel procedures for the settlement of certain GATT-related trade disputes. A 'right to a panel' has been formally recognized in various GATT codes, but not yet explicitly by all contracting parties in respect of Article XXIII, even though it seems to have been recognized *de facto* in GATT practice relating to Article XXIII. Delays in the formation of panels have occurred mostly in complaints against the United States (such as those relating to the Domestic International Sales Corporation, the Wine Equity and Export Expansion Act of 1984 and the trade embargo affecting Nicaragua) and the European Community (such as those relating to certain tax practices in three Community countries, value-added taxes and tariff preferences for Mediterranean citrus products). Even new factual information and arguments, presented by the defendant party as late as sixteen months after the first panel meeting,[51] may be rejected and ignored by the panel only at the risk of having the debate later re-opened and adoption of the panel report possibly opposed in the GATT Council. Avoidance of delaying tactics and of 'abuse of procedures' depends ultimately on the political will to promote national self-interests through rule-oriented cooperation on GATT matters and cannot be completely secured through reforms of the dispute-settlement procedures.

Inadequate Panel Reports

Prior to the 1976 panel reports on certain tax practices in the United States, Belgium, France and the Netherlands, panel and working-party reports under Article XXIII were almost invariably adopted by the GATT Contracting Parties without lengthy debates on the report's legal conclusions. The four panel reports concerning tax practices were finally adopted in December 1981 subject to an 'understanding' which corrected some of the panel conclusions.[52] Since 1981, four panel reports presented under Article XXIII and three panel reports presented to the Subsidies Committee under the dispute-settlement procedures of the GATT Subsidies Code have not (yet) been adopted.

Apart from the 1986 panel report on the Wine Equity Act in the United States, adoption of which was blocked by the United States because the European Community opposed the adoption in the Subsidies Committee of the 1983 panel report concerning the European Community's subsidies to exports of pasta products, the opposition to the adoption of all the other above-mentioned panel reports is explained on grounds of allegedly inadequate reasoning by the panelists or because of differences of view on the interpretation of the substantive GATT rules concerned. From the point of view of GATT dispute-settlement procedures, such opposition does not present a problem if it is shared by a 'relevant' number of contracting parties. This was the situation in the case of the three panel reports relating to Belgian, Dutch and French tax practices, the 1981 panel report on Spanish restrictions on the sale of soyabean oil and the 1985 panel report on the Community's tariff preferences for certain Mediterranean citrus products. The need for adoption of panel reports by the politically responsible GATT body provides a legal and political 'filter' for panel reports and enables the rejection of reports which are widely considered as 'opaque, questionable and incomplete'[53] and as inconsistent with previously accepted interpretations of GATT law.

The establishment of a GATT legal office in 1981 has reduced the risk of panel reports overlooking recognized principles of GATT law, treaty interpretation and dispute-settlement procedures. But the influence of the GATT legal office is limited to the 'persuasive force' of its legal advice to the panel members who remain responsible for the panel proceeding, for the elaboration of the panel report and for its presentation to the competent GATT body. The 1985 panel report on the European Community's tariff preferences for certain Mediterranean citrus products is illustrative of another problem. 'Creative' interpretations, which admittedly go beyond past GATT precedents[54] and rely more on factual assessments of trade-policy results ('practical operation of the preferences', 'trade damage') than on normative general criteria for the assessment of trade-policy actions, run the risk of being criticized by GATT contracting parties as being inconsistent with the rule-oriented GATT concept of 'nullification or impairment' and as rendering the GATT dispute-settlement proceedings unpredictable.[55]

National and international courts and arbitration bodies proceed from the principle that tribunals may not reach a finding of *non liquet* on the ground 'that the law is non-existent, or controversial, or uncertain and lacking in clarity'.[56] The lack of *non liquet* decisions by international courts and arbitration bodies 'reveals clear support for a rule that international law does not prohibit a court from deciding a case even if it finds absence or obscurity of pre-existing law'.[57] The 1983 panel report on the European Community's subsidies to exports of wheat flour presents one of the very rare exceptions to this international practice due to the finding of the panel 'that it was unable to conclude as to whether the increased share has resulted in the EEC having "more than an equitable share" in terms of Article 10 [of the Subsidies Code], in light of the highly artificial levels and conditions of trade in wheat flour, the complexity of developments in the markets, including the interplay of a number of special factors the relative importance of which it was impossible to assess, and, most importantly, the difficulties inherent in the concept of "more than equitable share"'.[58] Given the merely advisory nature of panel reports and the panel mandate to assist the responsible GATT body in the rule-oriented resolution of the dispute through clear panel findings of fact and of law, this refusal to apply GATT rules was criticized by several contracting parties as being unwarranted; since it frustrated the right to a legal examination of the complaint by an independent expert body, it was also criticized as being tantamount to a 'denial of justice'.

The 1983 panel report on the European Community's subsidies to exports of pasta products illustrates still another problem. The panel finding that the discontinuance in 1979 of the 1960 United States reservation to Article XVI(4) had rendered illegal certain export subsidies came as a surprise to several contracting parties who had accepted the GATT Subsidies Code on the assumption of the continued admissibility of these export subsidies. Thus even a legally correct panel interpretation may fail to provide an acceptable basis for the politically responsible GATT body to resolve the political problem resulting from an apparent misunderstanding at the time of the negotiation of a GATT code.

More than half of all complaints under Article XXIII(2), or under the corresponding provisions of the GATT codes, have related to agricultural trade restrictions. Tariffs, quotas and taxes have been the most frequent targets of complaints. Apart from the panel report on Spanish restrictions on the sale of soyabean oil, these complaints have generally led to a satisfactory settlement of the dispute albeit, in the case of the 1976 tax panel reports, only after considerable delay. The more than ten complaints since 1978 under Article XXIII or under the Subsidies Code relating to agricultural subsidies have revealed a lack of consensus on the interpretation of GATT subsidy provisions, which has prompted increasing controversies over panel reports in this field. The more the differences of view over the interpretation of the subsidy rules become entrenched and politicized, the more difficult it can become for contracting parties to accept differing legal interpretations in panel reports in this field.

Delays in the Adoption and Implementation of Panel Reports

In the early years of the GATT, the Contracting Parties decided on the adoption of some working-party and panel reports under Article XXIII by majority votes, pursuant to Article XXV(4). Since the 1950s, adoption by consensus, including the two disputing parties, has become the customary practice. In the ministerial declaration of 1982, 'the Contracting Parties reaffirmed that consensus will continue to be the traditional method of resolving disputes; however, they agreed that obstruction in the process of dispute settlement shall be avoided' and that 'this does not prejudice the provision on decision-making in the General Agreement'. Hence majority decisions remain legally admissible. The legal principle that no one should be a judge in his own cause (*nemo debet esse judex in propria causa*) seems to be recognized in all national legal systems. In 1925 an advisory opinion was given by the Permanent Court of International Justice that the rule of unanimity in the League of Nations had to be construed in a dispute-settlement proceeding 'subject to the limitation that the votes cast by representatives of the interested Parties do not affect the required unanimity. . . The well-known rule that no one can be judge in his own suit holds good.' [59] In view of this, a chairman of the GATT Council might, arguably, feel entitled likewise to propose that persistent obstruction by the 'losing' party alone to the adoption of a panel report does not affect the 'consensus'. Adoption of panel reports is considered to imply that the legal interpretations and conclusions of the panel, including the legal obligation 'to secure the withdrawal of the measures concerned if these are found to be inconsistent with the General Agreement', [60] are given legal force in terms of Article XXIII(2).

In GATT disputes under Article XXIII(2), which could not be resolved through the preceding consultations, the average period of time from the date of the Article XXIII(2) complaint to the date of the adoption of the report has been ten months since 1948, as already mentioned, and it has been about fourteen months since 1979. The average time between the date of the Article XXIII(2) complaint and the date of implementation of the panel findings has been about two years. [61] There appear to be only two completed cases relating to rather special circumstances (namely, the dairy quotas imposed by the United States Congress in 1951 and the United States' sugar restrictions against Nicaragua imposed in 1983) in which the defendant country (both times the United States) took no action to implement the findings of a report adopted under Article XXIII(2). In both cases, however, the disputed measures were later brought into conformity with GATT law (by means of a GATT waiver granted in 1955 for the American dairy quotas and, arguably, by the American invocation of Article XXI *vis-à-vis* Nicaragua). In only one case (the American dairy quotas) was retaliatory action pursuant to Article XXIII(2) requested and authorized, even though apparently not applied. The GATT ministerial declaration of 1982 includes various provisions designed to ensure the timely adoption of rulings or recommendations under Article XXIII, which 'shall be aimed at achieving a satisfactory settlement of the matter in accordance with GATT obligations'. It also provides for the periodic review by the GATT Council of the action taken pursuant to such rulings or recommendations and obliges the contracting party concerned to report on its implementing action.

If the disputing countries have informed the GATT Council of the settlement of their dispute or of the elimination of the disputed trade measure, the Council has only 'taken note' of panel reports if the defendant country objected to the adoption of the report (as happened with the 1985 panel reports on the European Community's production aids for canned fruit and on discriminatory Canadian taxes on gold coins). This Council practice is understandable in view of the bilateral adversary nature of GATT dispute-settlement proceedings, even though the submission of the panel report to the Council confers an additional multilateral dimension to the dispute, which could warrant adoption of panel reports with legal interpretations and clarifications of GATT law of general importance. This could also contribute to avoiding the present unsatisfactory situation of several GATT panel reports being published (in one case with mistakes) in private journals, but, due to their non-adoption by the competent GATT body, not in generally available GATT publications.

IMPROVING DISPUTE-SETTLEMENT PROCEDURES THROUGH ANOTHER 'UNDERSTANDING'?

Suggestions for changes and improvements in GATT dispute-settlement procedures depend on the broader view one has of the functions of GATT rules, of GATT dispute-settlement mechanisms and of government at large. If one views 'the history of civilization . . . as a gradual evolution from a power-oriented approach towards a rule-oriented approach',[62] and understands the GATT obligations for the use of transparent, non-discriminatory and welfare-increasing policy instruments as an extension to the field of foreign trade of the basic principles of democratic constitutionalism,[63] then one may also be prepared to conclude that the GATT legal system serves important 'domestic policy functions' for the maintenance of transparent policy making, non-discrimination, a welfare-increasing division of labour, undistorted competition, limited government and other basic constitutional principles in the domestic legal system of many GATT contracting parties.[64] From this perspective, observance of GATT rules for non-discriminatory trade competition contributes to the maximization not only of the national economic welfare of each contracting party but also of the equal protection of the economic freedoms and property rights of their citizens, which are the legal prerequisites of voluntary, mutually-beneficial economic transactions and of a welfare-maximizing division of labour, both within and among countries.

By contrast, there is what Andrew Shonfield described as the traditional French view that states are in practice bound to seek their exclusive national advantage in any international encounter and that an adversary relationship is the natural one; treaties simply disguise this fact and should, therefore, be interpreted in the narrowest possible way, in order to minimize the constraints which they impose on national freedom of manoeuvre.[65] If one subscribes to this view, then one will rather be inclined to consider international trade, as well as GATT legal disciplines, as a 'zero sum game' in which 'what is given to someone has to be taken away from somebody else', to quote J.B. Colbert, France's Minister of Finance under Louis XIV. From this perspective, GATT dispute-settlement procedures may be conceived as a threat to the 'national freedom of manoeuvre' and to the bureaucratic discretion of using trade-policy instruments in a non-transparent, discriminatory and mutually impoverishing way for the benefit of protectionist interests.

Most of the perceived problems of GATT dispute-settlement procedures have arisen in proceedings relating to agricultural trade and involving the United States and/or the European Community. The scope for procedural improvements designed to lessen these problems depends, therefore, on the positions of these two trading powers.

Since the inception of the GATT, and also of the IMF Agreement, the United States has tended to perceive the GATT and the IMF Agreement as a means of using justiciable international rules to constrain discretionary executive powers and 'to protect governments in the exercise of their sovereign powers against the pressure of interest groups which want these powers exercised to their own benefit'.[66] Hence the United States, as well as many other GATT contracting parties, expects GATT dispute-settlement proceedings to produce equally binding adjudicative findings on rights and duties under the GATT, notwithstanding the simultaneous American insistence on its 'sovereign power' to disregard GATT obligations and GATT panel findings.

By contrast, the European Community has tended to perceive GATT legal disciplines for non-discriminatory trade competition rather as a potential threat to the Community's preferential arrangements with more than 100 countries, to its systematic import protection and export subsidies for agricultural products and to the Treaty of Rome's delegation of exclusive discretionary trade-policy powers to the Community executives (Article 113). Since the Community's Court of Justice has recognized that GATT law is legally binding on the Community as an 'integral part of the Community legal system', with legal precedence over 'secondary' Community law, the Community's executives do not have the 'sovereign power' under Community law to ignore GATT obligations deliberately. Hence, due to their different attitude towards several substantive GATT obligations and to their more stringent internal legal constraints resulting from GATT law, the Community's executives are more reluctant to accept adjudicative interpretations of their GATT obligations and, thereby, also of their common commercial-policy powers.

Litigation in the GATT for ensuring 'reciprocity', 'fair trade' and avoidance of real trade warfare is a domestic political necessity for the United States executive, prescribed by Section 301 of the Trade Act of 1974 and politically imperative for demonstrating to Congress the executive's active enforcement of American rights. On the other hand, avoidance of GATT dispute-settlement findings against the European Community's preferential and agricultural trade policies may be perceived as a political need by the Community executives, necessary for the deflection of conflicts not only in the GATT but, above all, within the Community. The Community's traditional preference for a 'diplomatic' rather than 'adjudicative' settlement of GATT disputes over 'politically sensitive' trade restrictions (as on agricultural, steel and textile products) appears to reflect less an anti-legal attitude than a (rightly or wrongly) perceived political need resulting

78   ERNST-ULRICH PETERSMANN

from the much more stringent legal position of GATT law within the Community compared with most other GATT contracting parties (including the United States). [67]

Given this traditional opposition by the European Community, and to a lesser extent by Japan, to proposals for establishing a 'GATT tribunal' or for otherwise strengthening the adjudicative features of the GATT dispute-settlement procedures, the most realistic objective of 'negotiations . . . to improve and strengthen the rules and the procedures of the dispute-settlement process', envisaged in the ministerial declaration on the Uruguay Round negotiations, might be another understanding by the Contracting Parties recording agreed clarifications and improvements of the existing procedures. The 'evolutionary approach' of an understanding, codifying and clarifying practices that have gradually evolved and proven useful in GATT dispute-settlement proceedings, offers various advantages compared with an alternative 'legislative approach' aimed at negotiating a new international agreement on GATT dispute settlement:

(a) The focus would be on 'real problems' that have actually emerged in past GATT practice in the field of dispute settlement.

(b) Due regard to the customary GATT practice in dealing with such problems could contribute to avoiding politicized discussions on abstract legal questions (such as a 'right to a panel', 'automatic adoption' of panel reports, avoidance of 'wrong cases' and special-and-more-favourable treatment of developing countries in GATT dispute-settlement proceedings).

(c) The risk of a possible weakening of the existing procedures as a result of newly negotiated, but possibly over-ambitious and ineffective, reforms could be reduced.

(d) The common understanding, normative force and precedent-creating effects of the established procedures could be strengthened.

(e) And political attention should not be diverted from the fact, emphasized already in the GATT ministerial declaration of 1982, that a 'more effective use of the existing mechanism' and improvements in the substantive legal framework of the GATT are more important for the strengthening of the GATT dispute-settlement system than any further 'tinkering' with real or imaginary deficiencies in the present dispute-settlement procedures.

GATT practice relating to dispute settlement has considerably evolved since the 1979 Understanding and Agreed Description of the Customary Practice of the GATT in the Field of Dispute Settlement. While there are no simple procedural solutions to many of the practical difficulties in GATT dispute-settlement proceedings, resulting from differing interpretations of substantive GATT rules (such as Articles XI, XVI, XXI and XXIV) and 'lack of political will' to implement certain panel findings in this field, a number of procedural issues might usefully be addressed and given more precision in a new Understanding or a revised Agreed Description of the Customary Practice of the GATT in the Field of Dispute Settlement.

GATT DISPUTE-SETTLEMENT PROCEDURES 79

(a) The formal recognition in various GATT codes (such as Article 18 of the Subsidies Code) of a legal right to the establishment of a panel could be extended to all Article XXIII disputes in accordance with the standing GATT practice, recognized already in the 1979 Understanding, that the Contracting Parties have always established a panel on request pursuant to Article XXIII(2).

(b) The occasional shortage of suitable panelists, *inter alia* due to the American or European nationality of qualified panelists in disputes relating to the United States and/or the European Community or to Geneva-based diplomats being reassigned to other countries before they can acquire much GATT experience, could be overcome and the 'professionalization' of panels could be promoted by making permanent the 'roster of non-governmental panelists' which was established in 1985 on a trial basis for a period of one year.

(c) Delays and potential obstruction due to the defendant country's insistence on 'special terms of reference' could be avoided by formal recognition of a right of the complaining country to the use of the standard terms of reference, unless both parties agree on special terms of reference within a fixed period of time, or of a right of the Chairman of the GATT Council to decide on the terms of reference after consultations with the two disputing parties.

(d) Since Article XXIII(2) complaints can be submitted only after the failure of prior consultations to resolve the dispute, an additional mediation or conciliation requirement could result in unduly prolonging the dispute-settlement process (as illustrated by the cumbersome mandatory conciliation phase pursuant to Article 17 of the GATT Subsidies Code). Hence mediation and conciliation should remain separated from the panel process and should not be made mandatory. The relationship between Article XXIII and the special dispute-settlement procedures of the GATT codes could be clarified and made more uniform (as regards, for instance, the requirement set out in some codes to 'complete the dispute-settlement procedures under this Agreement before availing themselves of any rights which they have under the GATT, including invoking Article XXIII thereof').[68]

(e) The time limits for establishing panels and determining their terms of reference and composition and for completing the panel work could be specified and tightened, with the possibility of extensions subject to approval by the Chairman of the GATT Council and of disincentives in case of non-observance of the time limits. GATT contracting parties could be requested not to reassign to other countries Geneva-based diplomats serving as panelists before the end of the panel proceeding.

(f) The legal function of panels 'to examine the matter in the light of the relevant provisions of the General Agreement' could be more clearly separated from their additional function set out in the 1979 Understanding to 'consult regularly with the parties to the dispute and give them adequate opportunity to develop a mutually satisfactory solution', for example by entrusting the latter function to the chairman of the panel only and by stipulating that completion of the panel report shall not be delayed by such consultations. It could also be specified that panel recommendations for the settlement of disputes must be in conformity with the GATT obligations of contracting parties unless the panels have been specifically authorized to submit other compromise solutions.

(g) Elaboration of an 'agreed description of the customary working procedures of panels' could relieve panels of the present requirement to 'set up their own working procedures' and thereby contribute to the shortening and uniformity of panel proceedings.

(h) The legal consistency of panel reports could be promoted by formal recognition of the practice evolved since the establishment of the Legal Office of the GATT Secretariat that the Legal Adviser to the GATT Director-General must advise the panel on all legal aspects of the dispute and must participate in all panel meetings.

(i) The already-existing possibility for the disputing parties to agree to binding arbitration (for example, prior acceptance of panel findings as legally binding without the need for Council approval) or to request a legal opinion by the GATT Director-General could be explicitly confirmed and encouraged.

(j) Following the salutary evolution in the early 1950s from working parties (including the disputing parties) to panels, a comparable recognition of the elementary legal principle that no one should be a judge in his own cause could help to overcome the recent problem of 'blockage' in the GATT Council of the adoption of a panel report by the 'losing' party. The resultant risks for the excluded parties to the dispute would be small. Any serious objections to the panel report would in all likelihood be shared by other contracting parties. GATT practice indicates also that the risk of retaliatory measures in case of disregard of panel findings is small and cannot be avoided by 'blockage' of a report's adoption.

(k) Review of the implementation of panel reports, based on reports on action taken by the disputing parties, could be made a regular item of GATT Council meetings (independent of explicit requests by the complaining party) or could be made the task of a special GATT working party under the responsibility of the GATT Council.

(l) Provision could be made for the regular publication and de-restriction of panel reports unless the GATT Council decides to keep non-adopted reports restricted to government use.

GATT DISPUTE-SETTLEMENT PROCEDURES 81

STRENGTHENING JUDICIAL REVIEW AT DOMESTIC LEVEL?

During the negotiations on the Havana Charter for an International Trade Organization, whose trade-policy provisions were later incorporated into the General Agreement, it was agreed that the legal obligations should be as precise as possible and justiciable in the International Court of Justice. At the same time, the political imperatives of 'pragmatism' were taken into account by a large number of 'escape clauses', permitting the withdrawal of concessions and unilateral safeguard measures subject to various substantive and procedural requirements, such as 'to maintain a general level of reciprocal and mutually advantageous concessions not less favourable to trade than that provided for in this Agreement' (Article XXVIII[2]). The provision in Article 96 of the Havana Charter for advisory opinions on legal questions by the International Court of Justice was not taken over into the General Agreement, due *inter alia* to a widespread distrust then among the diplomats of lawyers and the pronounced British preference for men of 'sound economic judgment' capable of appraising 'economic facts'.[69] Yet since the 1940s, GATT law and many international trade issues have evolved into such complex matters, making it questionable whether traditional diplomatic procedures are still an adequate means for settling comprehensive trade disputes and making it questionable, too, whether diplomats temporarily based in Geneva can still acquire within a few years the knowledge of GATT law and GATT practice necessary for them to serve as effective panel members.

Thus there have been an increasing number of proposals over the past years for a separate international agreement establishing an international judicial body with jurisdiction over specified inter-governmental trade disputes,[70] for authorizing the GATT to commence dispute-settlement proceedings on its own initiative,[71] for advisory opinions by the International Court of Justice or by an independent Advocate-General on GATT legal disputes[72] or for enabling private access to international GATT dispute-settlement procedures (similar perhaps to the 1965 Convention establishing the International Center for the Settlement of Investment Disputes administered by the World Bank).[73]

It is true that an international tribunal serving as a neutral arbiter for the rule-oriented, rather than power-oriented, settlement of international trade disputes could contribute to creating the international equivalent of a 'government of laws, not men', for the trading system. European Community law reflects most clearly this constitutional ideal and the underlying economic and legal insight that liberal trade and the rule of law among states are no less advantageous than within states. It suggests, too, that the basic principles of democratic constitutions — such as the rule of law, limited delegation of government powers, judicial review, non-discrimination and equal protection of freedoms and property rights — can be rendered more effective in the increasingly important foreign-trade sectors of national economies by international legal disciplines based on the GATT. But

82   ERNST-ULRICH PETERSMANN

apart from the above-mentioned opposition by the European Community and Japan against 'transforming the GATT into a tribunal', other countries also appear to be reluctant to yield powers of binding adjudication and enforcement to an international tribunal removed from democratic control and without direct citizen access.

If the economic proposition is true that trade restrictions are essentially redistribution of income among domestic groups by means of taxing and regulating individual freedoms and property rights in a very costly and often surreptitious manner reducing national economic welfare,[74] then the availability of judicial review at domestic level could prove to be more important, and politically more acceptable, than judicial review at international level. A major legal function of GATT law is to place precise and justiciable legal constraints on the powers of governments to tax and regulate the foreign-trade transactions of their citizens and, thereby, to protect the decentralized decision-making processes of traders, producers and consumers from non-transparent, discriminatory and welfare-reducing trade distortions. Accordingly, a stronger enforcement of GATT rules might be achieved most effectively by their agreed incorporation in domestic legal systems, enabling private economic agents themselves to invoke precise and unconditional GATT obligations in domestic courts against illegal trade restrictions.

Article X(3)(b) of the GATT commits 'each contracting party [to] maintain . . . judicial, arbitral or administrative tribunals or procedures for the purpose, *inter alia*, of the prompt review and correction of administrative action relating to customs matters'. The practical experience with domestic judicial review of such customs matters and anti-dumping and countervailing-duty actions seems to confirm that the real effectiveness of many GATT rules, or of corresponding obligations under the Treaty of Rome, depends to a large extent on domestic law and on judicial review by domestic courts.[75] International trade conflicts usually originate from and reflect domestic conflicts between,

> on the one side, the national economic, political and legal self-interest in a transparent, non-discriminatory and welfare-increasing conduct of trade policy in compliance with GATT law and,

> on the other side, protectionist pressures from special interests for income redistribution through non-transparent and discriminatory trade restrictions.

From this perspective, GATT legal disciplines for the use of transparent, non-discriminatory and least-distortive policy instruments can be seen, in Jan Tumlir's words, as a 'second line of constitutional entrenchment' of basic national constitutional principles, such as transparent policy making ('government by discussion'), limited government, non-discriminatory taxation and regulation, judicial review and equal protection of individual freedoms and property rights. If the ultimate function of the GATT legal disciplines for non-discriminatory market access and for trade competition is to protect equal freedoms and property rights in a way maximizing the national gains from trade, then the domestic courts (such as the Court of International Trade in the United States and the Court of Justice of the European Community) appear to be more suitable agencies for judicial review of foreign trade restrictions than international tribunals. And if the main weakness of the 'crumbling international trading system'[76] consists in the non-observance of basic GATT rules by insufficiently constrained executives, then a more effective domestic judicial review of executive trade restrictions could be of importance not only for rendering Articles X(3), XIX and XXIII more effective but also for the achievement of the broader objectives of the Uruguay Round negotiations.

Is it Utopian to assume that those governments and private 'rent seekers' which collude in circumventing GATT legal disciplines may be prepared to accept — for example, as part of a GATT safeguard code, elaborating Article XIX (the GATT's main escape clause) — more stringent legal disciplines for, and domestic judicial review of, their own 'grey area' trade measures? The historical example of the GATT codes shows that governments may actually consider it to be in their own self-interest to use inter-governmental agreements for correcting deficiencies in their domestic decision-making processes. Collectively, as a sort of inter-governmental cartel against protectionist pressure groups, they can better resist the domestic pressures from import-competing producers. Inter-governmental agreements on trade-liberalizing measures are less exposed to domestic pressures than unilateral government decisions at national level. And the reciprocal opening of market access mobilizes additional political support for trade liberalization from export industries.[77] The incorporation of GATT codes in the domestic foreign-trade laws of major GATT contracting parties has made some of these additional GATT legal disciplines justiciable by domestic courts[78] and, thereby, has enabled domestic traders and consumers to protect more effectively their individual rights and self-interests in transparent policy making and in non-discriminatory trade competition.

Making protectionist violations of GATT rules (such as discriminatory import or export restraints in violation of Articles XI and XIII) contestable in domestic courts would also reduce the incentives for protectionist 'rent seeking' and increase the risks of 'grey area' trade measures outside the rule of law. This could further de-politicize the protectionist producer bias in the making of trade policy and increase the real ability of policy makers to pursue transparent, non-discriminatory and welfare-increasing trade policies benefiting the majority of their electorate. Similar to the customs-union law of the European Community, which is directly enforceable by Community citizens in domestic courts against protectionist trade restrictions of their own governments, domestic justiciability of precise and unconditional GATT legal disciplines for transparent and non-discriminatory trade-policy making would contribute to the prevention and resolution of trade conflicts within countries and, thereby, also among countries.

84   ERNST-ULRICH PETERSMANN

Recognition of the domestic-policy functions of international commitments for the use of transparent, non-discriminatory and welfare-increasing policy instruments, and of the primarily domestic nature of most 'international' trade conflicts, leads to the conclusion that the strengthening of the domestic dispute-settlement procedures of GATT contracting parties could be a more important objective of the Uruguay Round negotiations than additional improvements in the international GATT dispute-settlement procedures. The basic constitutional function of independent domestic courts is to ensure the consistent application of the law and to constrain abuses of power and of the many 'asymmetries' in domestic political and economic processes. Non-transparent, discriminatory and mutually impoverishing 'grey area' trade measures, and the international trade conflicts generated therefrom, are signs of 'constitutional failure' in the foreign-trade sectors of national economies. Government decisions to subsidize and protect selected producers by taxing and restraining domestic consumers and traders through welfare-reducing import restrictions should be taken in a transparent, non-discriminatory and politically accountable manner. They should be subject to the same constitutional guarantees of 'due process' and judicial review as other, more efficient and more effective instruments of taxation and regulation. Since the self-imposed GATT legal obligations for the public choice of transparent and least-distortive instruments of protection and for the maintenance of non-discriminatory competition are functionally equivalent to constitutional rules, their justiciability by domestic courts would strengthen not only the observance of GATT law but also the domestic constitutional systems of Western democracies at large.

---

1. The first quotation is from Joseph Gold, 'Keynes on Legal Problems of International Organizations', in his *Legal and Institutional Aspects of the International Monetary System*, Volume II (Washington: International Monetary Fund, 1984) p. 860. The second quotation is from 'EEC Production Aids Granted on Canned Fruit and Dried Grapes: Report by the Panel', Document L/5778, GATT Secretariat, Geneva, 1985, p. 21. This report has not been adopted.

2. The views expressed in this article are strictly personal. Helpful comments on an earlier draft from Ake Lindén and Frieder Roessler, colleagues in the Legal Office of the Secretariat of the General Agreement on Tariffs and Trade (GATT), are gratefully acknowledged. The article, completed early in 1987, is to appear in a collection of essays to be published by Macmillan Press in London as Hugh Corbet and Guillermo de la Dehesa (eds), *The European Community and the Uruguay Round Negotiations*.

3. Senator Eugene D. Millikin, in the United States Congress, Senate Finance Committee Hearings on the GATT in 1951 (p. 92), cited in John H. Jackson, *World Trade and the Law of GATT* (Indianapolis, Kansas City and New York: Bobbs-Merrill, 1969) p. vii.

4. Pierre Pescatore, formerly a Judge in the Court of Justice of the European Community, in his introduction to Meinhard Hilf, Francis Jacobs and Ernst-Ulrich Petersmann (eds), *The European Community and the GATT* (Deventer: Kluwer, 1986) p. xv.

5. Herbert Feis, a former economic adviser to the State Department, Washington, cited in Jackson, *World Trade and the Law of GATT*, *op. cit.*, p. vii.

6. Comment by Sir Eric Wyndham White, the first Director-General of the GATT, on certain GATT obligations, cited in *ibid.*, p. 191.

GATT DISPUTE-SETTLEMENT PROCEDURES 85

7. Jackson, 'The Jurisprudence of International Trade: the DISC Case in GATT', *American Journal of International Law*, Washington, October 1978, pp. 747-48.

8. Richard N. Gardner, *In Pursuit of World Order* (New York: Praeger, 1964) p. 148.

9. See, for example, Jackson, 'The Puzzle of GATT', *Journal of World Trade Law*, Geneva, March 1967, p. 131, and Robert E. Hudec, 'The GATT Legal System: a Diplomat's Jurisprudence', *Journal of World Trade Law*, September 1970, p. 615.

Also see Olivier Long, *Law and its Limitations in the GATT Multilateral Trade System* (Dordrecht: Martinus Nijhoff, 1985), in which the former GATT Director-General writes that GATT law is 'a subject matter difficult to grasp in all its implications by those not involved with it on a day-to-day basis'.

10. Hudec, 'The GATT Legal System: a Diplomat's Jurisprudence', *loc. cit.*

11. Jackson, 'The Jurisprudence of International Trade', *loc. cit.*, p. 748.

12. William N. Walker, 'Private Initiative to Thwart the Trade in Counterfeit Goods', *The World Economy*, London, March 1981, p. 31. Mr Walker was Deputy Special Representative for Trade Negotiations in the United States Administration in 1975-77.

13. See Preparatory Committee of the United Nations Conference on Trade and Employment, Document EPCT/B/PV/33, United Nations, Geneva, 26 June 1947, p. 42.

14. For a useful compilation of all international dispute-settlement provisions and procedures, see Karin Oellers-Frahm and Norbert Wühler, *Dispute Settlement in Public International Law*, Texts and Materials (Berlin, Heidelberg, New York and Tokyo: Springer, 1984).

15. For a comparative analysis of the dispute-settlement procedures of international economic organizations, see for example Pieter van Dijk (ed.), *Supervisory Mechanisms in International Economic Organizations* (Antwerp, Boston, Frankfurt and London: Kluwer, 1984).

16. Among the more than 100 IMF publications by the former General Counsel at the IMF, see for example Gold, *The Fund Agreement in the Courts*, published by the International Monetary Fund in three volumes, 1962, 1982 and 1986. On the interpretation and application of European Community law in the courts, see the commentary on the Treaty of Rome edited by members of the European Community's legal service, Hans von der Groeben, Hans von Boeck, Jochen Thiesing and Claus-Dieter Ehlermann (eds), *Kommentar zum EWG-Vertrag*, second edition (Baden-Baden: Nomos, 1983), in two volumes.

17. See, for example, the discussion of the pertinent 'GATT case law' of the courts in the United States and the European Community in the contributions of Meinhard Hilf, Robert E. Hudec, Marc Marescau and Ernst-Ulrich Petersmann in Hilf, Jacobs and Petersmann (eds), *op. cit.*, pp. 58-59, 108 *et seq.*, 157-58, 173 *et seq.*, 196 *et seq.* and 237 *et seq.*

18. See *General Agreement on Tariffs and Trade: Basic Instruments and Selected Documents*, 26th Supplement (Geneva: GATT Secretariat, 1980) p. 201, hereafter cited as *BISD*.

Whenever referring to the contracting parties acting jointly, it is GATT practice to use the words 'contracting parties' in capitals, as required by Article XXV(1). In this article, however, initial capitals are used when referring to the contracting parties as a whole.

19. On the legal evolution of the GATT system since the drafting of the General Agreement, see the loose-leaf publication prepared by the author, *GATT Analytical Index: Notes on the Drafting, Interpretation and Application of the Articles of the General Agreement* (Geneva: GATT Secretariat, 1986).

20. See, for example, Denys Simon, *L'interprétation judicaire des traités d'organisations internationales* (Paris: A. Pedone, 1981) and Ian Sinclair, *The Vienna Convention on the Law of Treaties*, second edition (Manchester: Manchester University Press, 1984).

21. See, for example, V.S. Mani, *International Adjudication: Procedural Aspects* (The Hague. Boston and London: Martinus Nijhoff, 1980).

22. F.A. Hayek, *Law, Legislation and Liberty*, Volume 1 (London: Routledge & Kegan Paul, 1973) pp. 66 and 94 *et seq.* It seems to be no accident that almost all systematic textbooks on the GATT have been written by lawyers (for example, John H. Jackson, Kenneth W. Dam, Robert E. Hudec, Thierry Flory, Edmond McGovern and Olivier Long, although Dr Dam and Dr Long are also economists).

23. See Pescatore, *loc. cit.*, p. xvi.

86   ERNST-ULRICH PETERSMANN

24. Hence, even today, 40 years after the inception of the GATT, lectures on GATT law to officials in the European Community are sometimes introduced by a sentence like the following: 'It should not need to be emphasized, but unfortunately has to be, that, however complicated, the arrangement [that is to say, the GATT] is nevertheless a legally binding one.' This quotation is taken from Edmond McGovern, 'Dispute Settlement in the GATT: Adjudication or Negotiation?', in Hilf, Jacobs and Petersmann (eds), *op. cit.*, p. 75.

25. For a critical review of the 'GATT case law' of the Court of Justice, see Petersmann, 'Application of GATT by the Court of Justice of the European Communities', *Common Market Law Review*, The Hague, October 1983, pp. 397 and 424-37. The quotations in the text are from Judge Ulrich Everling, 'The Law of the External Economic Relations of the European Community', in Hilf, Jacobs and Petersmann (eds), *op. cit.*, pp. 85 and 97. In both GATT law and IMF law, the breach of an obligation by one member does not entitle other members to retaliate unilaterally against the violator by disregarding their GATT or IMF obligations; only a very few provisions, which have been used rarely in GATT practice since 1948 (for example, Articles XIX[3] and XXVIII[3]), authorize resort to self-help subject to specified procedures and substantive criteria.

26. The mercantilist perception of the GATT legal disciplines for non-discriminatory trade competition as a 'threat' to the freedom of action of the European Community, rather than as a self-imposed legal restraint of the discretionary commercial-policy powers of the Community in order to promote transparent, non-discriminatory and welfare-increasing trade-policy making, seems to be shared also in the Commission which is 'very pleased with the Court's views' on the GATT and has never invoked the Article 169 procedures (non-fulfilment of Treaty obligations, including GATT obligations recognized to be binding on the Community) against the increasing number of discriminatory 'grey area' trade restrictions inconsistent with GATT law (for example, bilateral 'voluntary' export restraints). See Ehlermann, 'Application of GATT Rules in the European Community', in Hilf, Jacobs and Petersmann (eds), *op. cit.*, pp. 127, 135 and 139.

27. For details, see Hudec, *The GATT Legal System and World Trade Diplomacy* (New York: Praeger, 1975) pp. 193 *et seq.*

28. Senate Committee on Finance, Senate Report No. 93-1298, 93rd Congress, 2nd Session, 1974, p. 83.

29. See *BISD*, 26th Supplement (1980), pp. 210 *et seq.*, 29th Supplement (1983), pp. 13 *et seq.*, and 31st Supplement (1985), pp. 9 and 10.

30. See *BISD*, 33rd Supplement (1987), p. 25.

31. For chronological and country lists of these disputes, see the *GATT Analytical Index*, *op. cit.*, under Article XXIII. These lists do not include various GATT complaints in which Article XXIII was not explicitly invoked or where consultations were held under Article XXIII(1) without formal notification to the GATT.

32. For a survey, see the *GATT Analytical Index*, *op. cit.*, under Articles XXII and XXIII. Many of these consultations were not notified to the GATT.

33. For a survey, see the *GATT Analytical Index*, *op. cit.*, under Article XXIII, Section 34.

34. *BISD*, 24th Supplement (1978), p. 134.

35. *BISD*, 26th Supplement (1980), p. 216.

36. See, for instance, the successful complaints in 1978 by Hong Kong against Norway (*BISD*, 27th Supplement [1981], p. 119) and in 1979 by Chile against the European Community (*BISD*, 27th Supplement, p. 98) against discriminatory import restrictions imposed after the refusal by these developing countries to accept 'voluntary' export restraints.

37. See, for example, Frieder Roessler, 'The Scope, Limits and Functions of the GATT Legal System', *The World Economy*, September 1985, pp. 287-98.

38. For an explanation of this point, see Jan Tumlir, 'GATT Rules and Community Law', in Hilf, Jacobs and Petersmann (eds), *op. cit.*, pp. 4 *et seq.*

39. This quotation is taken from J.K. Horsefield (ed.), *The International Monetary Fund 1945-1965*, Volume III (Washington: International Monetary Fund, 1969) p. 36.

40. This has been emphasized in Tumlir, 'GATT Rules and Community Law', *loc. cit.*, pp. 1 and 14. For an elaboration of this argument, see Petersmann, *Constitutional Functions of International Economic Law* (Fribourg: Fribourg University Press, 1988).

GATT DISPUTE-SETTLEMENT PROCEDURES 87

41. For a survey of the GATT practice relating to 'non-violation complaints' since the Chilean complaint in 1950 against certain Australian subsidies, see the *GATT Analytical Index, op. cit.,* under Article XXIII.

42. See *BISD*, 7th Supplement (1959), pp. 52 and 53 (paras 19 and 23).

43. See *BISD*, 23rd Supplement (1977), pp. 125, 135 and 145.

44. Volume 252 of the judgments of the United States Supreme Court, 1920, p. 416.

45. See, for instance, the 1985 panel report on 'EEC Production Aids Granted on Canned Fruit and Dried Grapes', *op. cit.,* which accords with various previous panel reports: 'The Panel was of the view that it was not necessary to establish statistical evidence of trade damage in order to make a finding of nullification and impairment under Article XXIII. . . Benefits accruing from bound tariff concessions under Article II also encompass future trading opportunities. Consequently, complaints by contracting parties regarding nullification and impairment should be admissible even if there was not yet statistical evidence of trade damage. . .'

46. The formal title of the Subsidies Code is the Agreement on Interpretation and Application of Articles VI, XVI and XXIII of the General Agreement on Tariffs and Trade.

47. See *BISD*, 12th Supplement (1964), p. 65.

48. *BISD*, 29th Supplement (1983), pp. 13-14. This rather positive evaluation of the GATT dispute-settlement procedures seems to be shared by most observers of GATT law. See, for example, Jackson, 'GATT as an Instrument for the Settlement of Trade Disputes', *Proceedings of the American Society of International Law* (Washington: American Society of International Law, 1967) p. 155: 'The costs of the GATT procedure for dispute settlement are probably as minimal as any known procedure of dispute settlement between nations in the world today, and the returns and values achieved from the GATT procedure are considerably higher than most, if not all, of the other dispute-settlement procedures.'

49. *BISD*, 31st Supplement (1985), p. 9.

50. See *Review of the Effectiveness of Trade Dispute Settlement under the GATT and the Tokyo Round Agreements* (Washington: United States International Trade Commission, 1985) pp. 57 and 58.

51. See 'EEC Production Aids Granted on Canned Fruit and Dried Grapes', *op. cit.*, p. 12.

52. See GATT Council Minutes, Document C/M/154, GATT Secretariat, Geneva, 1982, and *BISD*, 28th Supplement (1982), p. 114.

53. See Jackson, 'The Puzzle of GATT', *loc. cit.*, p. 764.

54. See Document L/5776, GATT Secretariat, Geneva, 1985, para. 4(35). This panel report has not been adopted.

55. On the risks of using GATT dispute-settlement procedures for legislative purposes or for 'result-oriented' decisions *ex aequo et bono*, not explicitly requested by the disputing parties, see also the remarks in Gold, 'Keynes on Legal Problems of International Organizations', *loc. cit.*

56. Hersch Lauterpacht, 'Some Observations on the Prohibition of "Non Liquet" and the Completeness of the Law', *Festschrift Verzijl* (The Hague: Martinus Nijhoff, 1958) p. 199. See also Article 4 of the French Code Civil: 'Le juge qui refusera de juger, sous prétexte du silence, de l'obscurité ou de l'insuffisance de la loi, pourra être poursuivi comme coupable de déni de justice.'

57. Julius Stone, 'Non Liquet and the Function of Law in the International Community', *British Yearbook of International Law* (London: Stevens, 1959) pp. 124 and 159.

58. GATT Document SCM/42 of 21 March 1983, p. 40. This panel report was not adopted.

59. Permanent Court of International Justice, Series B No. 12, 21 November 1925, pp. 31 and 32.

60. *BISD*, 26th Supplement (1980), p. 216.

61. See *Review of the Effectiveness of Trade Dispute Settlement under the GATT and the Tokyo Round Agreements, op. cit.*, p. 64.

62. Jackson, 'Perspectives on the Jurisprudence of International Trade: Costs and Benefits of Legal Procedures in the United States', *Michigan Law Review*, Ann Arbor, April 1984, pp. 1570 and 1571.

63. In this sense, see Tumlir, 'International Economic Order and Democratic Constitutionalism', *Ordo*, Stuttgart, Vol. 34, 1983, pp. 71-83.

88   ERNST-ULRICH PETERSMANN

64. See, for example, Heinz Hauser, 'Domestic Policy Foundation and Domestic Policy Function of International Trade Rules', *Aussenwirtschaft*, Zurich, September 1986, pp. 171-84; Roessler, 'The Constitutional Function of International Economic Law', *Aussenwirtschaft*, September 1986, pp. 467-74; and Petersmann, 'Trade Policy as a Constitutional Problem: On the "Domestic Policy Functions" of International Trade Rules', *Aussenwirtschaft*, September 1986, pp. 405-39.

65. Andrew Shonfield (ed.), *International Economic Relations of the Western World 1959-1971* (London: Oxford University Press, for the Royal Institute of International Affairs, 1976) p. 101.

66. Tumlir, 'Strong and Weak Elements in the Concept of European Integration', in Fritz Machlup, Gerhard Fels and Hubertus Müller-Groeling (eds), *Reflections on a Troubled World Economy*, Essays in Honour of Herbert Giersch (London: Macmillan, for the Trade Policy Research Centre, 1983) pp. 29 and 47; and Petersmann, 'International and European Foreign Trade Law', *Common Market Law Review*, September 1985, pp. 441 and 458-59.

67. See Ehlermann, 'Application of GATT Rules in the European Community', *loc. cit.*, p. 135: 'It is easy enough to assume direct effect [of GATT law] where the legislator can in fact exclude it; not nearly so easy where such effect is constitutionally laid down — which is of course the case in the Community, as opposed to the United States.' See also Hudec, 'Legal Issues in US-EC Trade Policy: GATT Litigation 1960-1985', in Robert E. Baldwin, Carl Hamilton and André Sapir (eds), *Issues in US-EC Trade Relations* (Chicago: University of Chicago Press, for the National Bureau of Economic Research, forthcoming), where it is rightly noted that the Community's 'internal powers are more exposed to charges of legal irregularity than is true of most other GATT members. International obligations tend to have greater legal effects internally, and once such obligations are found applicable it is much more difficult for Community organs to change them.' See also Roessler, 'L'Attitude des Etats-Unis et de la CEE devant le Droit du GATT', in Jacques Bourrinet (ed.), *Les Relations Communauté Européenne-Etats-Unis* (Paris: Edition Economica, 1987) pp. 43 *et seq.*

68. Article 20(11) of the 1979 Agreement on Implementation of Article VII of the General Agreement (the Customs Valuation Code). Similar exhaustion of remedy requirements are to be found in Article 14(23) of the 1979 Agreement on Technical Barriers to Trade and in Article 15 of the 1979 Agreement on Implementation of Article VI of the General Agreement (the revised Anti-dumping Code). See *The Texts of the Tokyo Round Agreements* (Geneva: GATT Secretariat, 1986) pp. 18, 95 and 141.

69. See Preparatory Committee of the United Nations Conference on Trade and Employment, Document EPCT/C.6/W.77, United Nations, Geneva, 1947.

70. See, for example, Jackson, 'Governmental Disputes in International Trade Relations: a Proposal in the Context of GATT', *Journal of World Trade Law*, January 1979, pp. 13 *et seq.*; *GATT Plus: a Proposal for Trade Reform*, Report of the Special Advisory Panel to the Trade Committee of the Atlantic Council (Washington: Atlantic Council, 1976); and *Remaking the System of World Trade: a Proposal for Institutional Reform*, a Report of the Panel on International Trade Policy and Institutions (Washington: American Society of International Law, 1976).

71. See *GATT Plus, op. cit.*, pp. 52 and 53, and Miriam Camps and William Diebold, *The New Multilateralism: Can the World Trading System be Saved?* (New York: Council on Foreign Relations, 1983) pp. 28 and 64.

72. See Guy Ladreit de Lacharrière, 'Case for a Tribunal to Assist in Settling Trade Disputes', *The World Economy*, December 1985, pp. 339, 348, 350 and 351. Lacharrière was Vice President of the International Court of Justice in the Hague from 1985 to 1987, having been a judge in the Court since 1982.

73. Jackson, Jean-Victor Louis and Mitsuo Matsushita, *Implementing the Tokyo Round: National Constitutions and International Economic Rules* (Ann Arbor: University of Michigan Press, 1984) pp. 207 *et seq.*

74. See, for example, Richard Blackhurst, 'The Economic Effects of Different Types of Trade Measures and their Impact on Consumers', in *International Trade and the Consumer* (Paris: OECD Secretariat, 1986) pp. 96 *et seq.*

75. See, for example, J. Michael Finger, Keith H. Hall and Douglas R. Nelson, 'The Political Economy of Administered Protection', *American Economic Review*, December 1982, pp. 452-66, where it is demonstrated that the 'rule-oriented', technical, 'low' policy tracks of anti-dumping and

GATT DISPUTE-SETTLEMENT PROCEDURES 89

countervailing-duty proceedings have been less exposed to protectionist pressures and 'back room deals' compared with the discretionary, political, 'high' policy tracks of other safeguard measures (Article XIX of the GATT), where decisions are less circumscribed by rules. See also Tumlir, 'International Trade Regimes and Private Property Rights: a US Perspective', in Helmut Hesse, Erich Streissler and Gunther Tichy (eds), *Aussenwirtschaft bei Ungewissenheit* (Tübingen: J.C.B. Mohr, 1985) p. 328: 'Regimes requiring constant management by diplomacy must deteriorate over time. They are as bound by precedent as any legal system, but their precedents, created by negotiation between sovereign governments, rather than by judges constrained by the logic of the law, are unprincipled and cumulatively erode the foundations of the regime.'

76. See Jackson, 'The Crumbling Institutions of International Trade', *Journal of World Trade Law*, January 1978, pp. 93 *et seq.*

77. See Roessler, 'The Constitutional Function of International Economic Law', *loc. cit.*, p. 310.

78. See the detailed analysis in Jackson, Louis and Matsushita, *op. cit.*

Part VI
Judicial Settlement

[12]

DECLINE OF THE OPTIONAL CLAUSE[1]

By PROFESSOR C. H. M. WALDOCK, C.M.G., O.B.E., Q.C.

§ 1. *Introduction*

THE Optional Clause represents the compromise adopted at the First Assembly of the League of Nations to resolve the deadlock between those States which advocated that the jurisdiction of the proposed Permanent Court of International Justice should from the outset be made compulsory for all legal disputes and those which contended that the acceptance of the Court's jurisdiction should be left to the subsequent decision of each individual State.[2] The opponents of automatic compulsory jurisdiction, amongst whom were the Great Powers, let it be understood that they had it in mind, after signing the Statute of the Court, to enter into bilateral or multilateral treaties by which they would accept the Court's compulsory jurisdiction for specified classes of legal disputes *vis-à-vis* the particular parties to those treaties.[3] They were unwilling, however, in the Statute to commit themselves in advance either as to the classes of legal disputes or as to the States with respect to which they would bind themselves to accept the Court's jurisdiction. Their objection to arming the proposed Court, in the Statute itself, with a general power of compulsory jurisdiction over all parties to the Statute and for all legal disputes was thus both *ratione materiae* and *ratione personae*.[4] The compromise—the Optional Clause— was to give each party to the Statute the option, either at the time of signing or ratifying the Statute or at any time afterwards, to make a unilateral declaration by which, on the basis of reciprocity, it recognized the Court's compulsory jurisdiction and also the power to define the classes of legal disputes with respect to which the declaration was to apply.

In 1945 a similar divergence of opinion manifested itself in regard to the compulsory jurisdiction of the new International Court, and received the same solution. The Committee of Jurists, which prepared a draft of the new Statute for consideration by the San Francisco Conference, presented two alternative texts on the question of compulsory jurisdiction, one reproducing the Optional Clause and the other investing the Court automatically

---

[1] For the Optional Clause see Hudson, *Permanent Court of International Justice*, 2nd ed. (1943), pp. 449–82; Oppenheim, *International Law*, vol. ii (7th ed., by Lauterpacht, 1952), pp. 58–65; Lauterpacht in *Economica*, 10 (1930), pp. 137–72; Hambro in this *Year Book*, 25 (1948), pp. 133–53; Vulcan in *Acta Scandinavica*, 18 (1947–8), pp. 30–55.

[2] See Hudson, op. cit., pp. 190–193.

[3] Cf. Sir Cecil Hurst (Great Britain), *Records of First Assembly* (1920), Committee 1, p. 380.

[4] See the discussion in the Committee of Jurists on reciprocity, ibid., p. 312, especially the observation of M. Huber.

DECLINE OF THE OPTIONAL CLAUSE   245

with compulsory jurisdiction for all legal disputes.[1] The Committee, without elaborating the point, drew attention to the possibility of mitigating the rigour of the second alternative by allowing States, as in the General Act of Geneva of 1928, to make a limited number of authorized reservations. Even so, and although the great majority of States at the San Francisco Conference were in favour of a general system of compulsory jurisdiction, its introduction proved to be impossible owing to the objections of the Soviet Union and the United States. Neither of these two States was at that time in a position to accept a Statute which invested the Court automatically with compulsory jurisdiction for legal disputes, and, since the Statute was to be an integral part of the Charter of the United Nations, insistence by the majority on a general system of compulsory jurisdiction would have excluded these two key States from the United Nations.[2] Accordingly, the optional system whereby each State individually makes its decision whether or not to accept compulsory jurisdiction was maintained in the new Statute.[3]

If there had been no Optional Clause in the Statute, it would still have been open to States gradually to develop the Court's compulsory jurisdiction by treaty, either bilateral or multilateral. Even with the Optional Clause, the primary method of accepting compulsory jurisdiction is by treaty, and the greater part of the Court's compulsory jurisdiction is derived from this source. As a rule, however, the compulsory jurisdiction derived from treaties is either limited to two particular States or, in the case of multilateral treaties, to a particular subject-matter. The importance of the Optional Clause is that it provides a simple means of accepting compulsory jurisdiction generally for all legal disputes and as against any State undertaking the same obligation. Its purpose was not merely to provide a possible basis for the judicial settlement of disputes, but also, through the multiplication of declarations by individual States, to promote between the parties to the Statute a general system of compulsory jurisdiction. The latter purpose has been achieved only to a very limited extent. The high-water mark of the Optional Clause jurisdiction of the old Court was in 1934, in which year no less than 42 States had declarations in force recognizing its compulsory jurisdiction under the Clause.[4] After that date, although some new States adhered, others allowed their declarations to

---

[1] United Nations Conference on International Organization (hereinafter referred to as U.N.C.I.O.), vol. xiv, pp. 667–8.

[2] Report of Rapporteur of Committee IV/1, U.N.C.I.O., vol. xiii, pp. 390–2.

[3] Moreover, it was provided in Article 36 (5) that declarations made under the old Statute and still in force should be deemed, as between parties to the new Statute, to be acceptances of the compulsory jurisdiction of the new Court for the period which they have still to run and in accordance with their terms.

[4] See Hudson, op. cit., p. 473; according to Hudson these 42 declarations were equivalent to 861 bilateral agreements between the States concerned for the acceptance of compulsory jurisdiction.

expire, and the total number bound under the Clause gradually decreased. The experience of the new Court has been similar. In 1947, one year after its establishment, there were 25 States bound by the Optional Clause.[1] By 1952–3 this number had been increased to 37,[2] but the number has since decreased and the *Year Book* of the Court for 1954–5 shows only 32 States with effective declarations under the new Optional Clause.[3] Belgium, Bolivia, Brazil, Guatemala, and Iran have either cancelled their declarations or allowed them to expire. The historical record does not, therefore, justify any great optimism as to the possibility that by degrees the Optional Clause may bring about a general system of compulsory jurisdiction. Today, despite the almost universal support for compulsory jurisdiction at the San Francisco Conference, fewer than half the Members of the United Nations are adherents to the Optional Clause, and of these many have qualified their acceptances of the Optional Clause by the insertion of numerous limitations, reservations, and conditions in their declarations.

Even more disturbing is the increasing tendency on the part of States subscribing to the Optional Clause so to frame their declarations as to leave themselves largely free, when an actual dispute arises, to accept or decline jurisdiction as they think fit. The chief devices employed for this purpose are (1) time-limit clauses making the declarations terminable merely by notice to the Secretary-General of the United Nations, and (2) reservations by which it is sought to retain the right, by a future act effected after the declaration has come into force, to exclude from the acceptance of compulsory jurisdiction particular cases or categories of case at the will of the State concerned. The reciprocity prescribed by the Optional Clause, while it equalizes the position between States employing these devices and other States subscribing to the Clause, multiplies the prejudicial effect of the devices in undermining the system of compulsory jurisdiction. The object of the present article is, first, to focus attention on these devices; secondly, to examine the operation of the principle of reciprocity with respect to them; and thirdly, to point out that criticism of these devices, however well-founded in theory, must also take account of the really indefensible advantage given by the Statute and Rules of Court to States which prefer to stay outside the Optional Clause as against those which undertake its obligations. As a preliminary, however, to dealing with these matters, it is necessary to consider the freedom of a State to fix unilaterally the terms of its declaration under the Optional Clause, the nature of the juridical bond established between States by their declarations, and the meaning of the 'condition of reciprocity' contained in the Optional Clause.

[1] See *Year Book of the International Court of Justice, 1946–7*, pp. 221–8.
[2] Ibid., *1952–3*, pp. 171–82.
[3] Ibid., pp. 189–200; Portugal also has since adhered to the Optional Clause.

§ 2. *The freedom to fix unilaterally the terms of declarations under the Optional Clause*

Paragraph 2 of Article 36 of the Statute—the Optional Clause—reads:

'The States parties to the present Statute may at any time declare that they recognize as compulsory *ipso facto* and without special agreement, in relation to any other State accepting the same obligation, the jurisdiction of the Court in all legal disputes concerning:[1]

 (a) the interpretation of a treaty;

 (b) any question of international law;

 (c) the existence of any fact which, if established, would constitute a breach of an international obligation;

 (d) the nature or extent of the reparation to be made for the breach of an international obligation.'

As between any two States which have made declarations under the Optional Clause, their reciprocal obligation to accept the Court's compulsory jurisdiction is constituted by the joining together of their two declarations through the Clause. Each is free to frame the terms of its declaration without consulting the other, and the fixed element in the legal relation between them is to be found in the Clause.

The fixed element in the Optional Clause itself, even under the new Statute, is comparatively small. In the old Statute a wide freedom of choice was deliberately left to the individual State in order to make it as easy as possible for States to subscribe to compulsory jurisdiction under the Clause. The idea was that, if a large number of States could be induced to make declarations, it would only be a matter of time before there was general acceptance of the principle of compulsory jurisdiction for all States. Accordingly, the old Statute in terms permitted acceptance of the compulsory jurisdiction of the Court *in all or any* of the four classes of legal disputes listed in the Clause. The Statute expressly envisaged the possibility of declarations being limited, for example, to disputes concerning 'the interpretation of a treaty' or 'any question of international law'. With one exception, States did not in practice make use of this liberty to limit their declarations to one, or more, of the listed classes of legal disputes. The one exception was Iran, who limited her Declaration in 1930 to disputes with regard to situations or facts relating directly or indirectly to the application of treaties or conventions accepted by Iran, that is, to the first of the classes of disputes listed in Article 36 (2).[2] The new Statute, however,

---

[1] The old Statute here read: 'in all or any of the classes of legal disputes', but the words 'or any of the classes of' were cut out of the new Statute at the San Francisco Conference; see below, p. 248.

[2] Indeed, Iran further limited her declaration by confining the applicable treaties or conventions to those subsequent to her declaration, and was on that ground held by the Court to be entitled to decline a judicial settlement of the *Anglo-Iranian Oil Company* case (*I.C.J. Reports*, 1952, p. 93).

appears to exclude the possibility of making a declaration which does not comprise all the four listed classes of legal disputes. In the new text of Article 36 (2) the words 'or any of the classes of' have been omitted from the phrase 'in all or any of the classes of legal disputes concerning', &c. The change of wording, which was made not in the Committee of Jurists but in a sub-committee of the San Francisco Conference,[1] was deliberate and was explained as being 'favourable to the jurisdiction of the Court, *since it eliminates the distinctions which the present text seems to make'*. Accordingly, it now appears that a declaration must *at least purport to embrace all the four listed classes of legal disputes* even though it may still be open to a State, by the insertion of conditions and reservation, to retract from these listed classes very large categories of matters. On this basis a declaration similar to the Iranian declaration of 1930 seems now to be incompatible with the Statute.[2]

Paragraph 3 of Article 36 of the new Statute, repeating a similar paragraph of the old Statute, adds a rider to the Optional Clause which provides:

'The declarations referred to above may be made unconditionally or on condition of reciprocity on the part of several or certain States, or for a certain time.'

But the fact that Article 36 specifically permits the inclusion of a condition of reciprocity on the part of designated States and of a limit upon the duration of the declaration does not mean that other forms of reservation, limitation, or condition are excluded. It seems from the first to have been recognized that the Optional Clause authorizes the making of any reservations, limitations, or conditions which are not incompatible with the basic provisions of the Statute. Thus, in 1921 the Netherlands confined its declaration to future disputes, and excepted disputes in regard to which the parties had agreed to have recourse to another form of peaceful settlement, although Article 36 made no mention of either exception. The League of Nations, with the object of encouraging adherence to the Optional Clause, actually drew attention to the possibility of making reservations.[3] In 1929 the United Kingdom made a declaration containing a limitation *ratione temporis*, three express reservations, and a condition.[4] The United Kingdom's example was followed in numerous other declarations and it was never suggested in any case either by the parties or by the Court that such limitations, reservations, or conditions were open to objection under the terms of the Statute. In short, it was a recognized interpretation of the

---

[1] U.N.C.I.O., vol. xiii, pp. 557–8.

[2] The Iranian declaration itself continued in force in virtue of paragraph 5 of Article 36, which maintained declarations made under the old Statute *in accordance with their terms*. Iran, however, has since terminated her declaration.

[3] *Records of the Fifth Assembly*, Third Committee, p. 199.

[4] For the text of the declaration see Hudson, op. cit., p. 689.

DECLINE OF THE OPTIONAL CLAUSE   249

Statute that States had an inherent right to qualify their acceptance of the Court's jurisdiction under the Optional Clause by limitations, reservations, and conditions.

The White Paper[1] presenting the United Kingdom's 1929 declaration to Parliament explained that Article 36 had been regarded as admitting any kind of reserve or exception 'because the jurisdiction of the Court may be accepted "in all *or any*" of the classes of legal disputes enumerated'. The reason why Article 36 was interpreted in this way seems, however, to have been the broader one which has been indicated above. The fundamental purpose of the Optional Clause being to encourage the acceptance of jurisdiction by unilateral act, it was assumed that each State possessed a wide liberty to fix for itself the limits of the jurisdiction to which it was willing to submit. At any rate, despite the deletion of the words '*or any*' from the new text of the Optional Clause, the same freedom to make reservations undoubtedly exists under the new Statute. The subcommittee of the San Francisco Conference which, by making this change in the Optional Clause, withdrew the right to pick and choose amongst the four enumerated classes of legal disputes, emphasized that the right to make reservations is inherent in Article 36:[2]

'As is well known, the Article has consistently been interpreted in the past as allowing States accepting the jurisdiction of the Court to subject their declarations to reservations. The Subcommittee has considered such interpretation as being henceforth established. It has, therefore, been considered unnecessary to modify paragraph 3 in order to make express reference to the right of States to make such reservations.'

Accordingly, while it is no longer open to a State, in accepting compulsory jurisdiction under the Optional Clause, to differentiate between the classes of legal disputes listed in the Clause, it may still, in other ways, differentiate between the categories of disputes with respect to which it accepts the Clause. It may still, by limitations, reservations, and conditions, except large categories of disputes from its acceptance of compulsory jurisdiction.

As to time-limits on the duration of declarations, which are expressly authorized by Article 36 (3) of the Statute, States have interpreted the authority to make declarations 'for a certain time' as giving them complete freedom in limiting the duration of their declarations.[3] Only ten States set no time-limit to their declarations, and the remainder have adopted a variety of forms of time-limit. Some have simply made their declarations for specific periods of 5, 10, or 15 years and have then either renewed them or allowed them to lapse. Others have made their declarations terminable on 6 or 12 months' notice to the Secretary-General of the

---

[1] Misc. No. 12 (1929), Cmd. 3452.   [2] U.N.C.I.O., vol. xiii, p. 558.

[3] See Hudson, op. cit., pp. 472–3; see also the texts of declarations under the new Statute in the *Year Book of the International Court of Justice, 1954–5*, pp. 189–200.

League/United Nations, or even immediately on notice to the Secretary-General. Others, yet again, combining the two main forms, have made their declarations for a period of 5 or 10 years and thereafter until notice of termination is given to the Secretary-General. The differing periods for which declarations are current raise awkward questions of reciprocity which will be discussed later.[1]

The fixed element, it has been said above, in the reciprocal obligation established between two States by their unilateral declarations is the Optional Clause. The Clause does not, however, stand by itself. It forms an integral part of the Statute which governs the exercise of all the Court's jurisdiction. Accordingly, quite apart from paragraphs 3, 4, and 5 of Article 36, which specifically relate to declarations under the Optional Clause, all the provisions of the Statute, so far as they have any bearing on the Court's contentious jurisdiction, are necessarily brought into the agreements established between States by adherence to the Optional Clause. For example, the rules as to the appointment of a judge *ad hoc*, the right of other parties to the Statute to intervene in a case, and the power of the Court to decide any dispute as to its jurisdiction, are automatically incorporated into the obligation accepted by a State making a declaration under the Clause. Moreover, the bulk of the statutory provisions which are thus incorporated into the obligation established between States under the Optional Clause appear to have a fixed content, since they form part of the settled constitution of the Court. It does not appear to be open to States in their unilateral declarations, any more than in their Special Agreements, to make their acceptance of jurisdiction conditional upon the non-application of constitutional provisions of the Court's Statute. The Court is required both by Article 92 of the Charter and Article 1 of the Statute to function in accordance with the Statute. Indeed, the old Court, even though it was not bound by such an express injunction to observe the Statute, held in the *Free Zones* case[2] that it had no power to depart from the terms of the Statute on the proposal of the parties to a case. The Optional Clause, therefore, although it leaves to the individual State a large discretion as to the terms on which it accepts compulsory jurisdiction, does not permit a State to make a declaration which is incompatible with the fixed constitutional provisions of the Court's Statute.[3]

§ 3. *The nature of the juridical bond under the Optional Clause*

M. Fernandez of Brazil, when he first suggested an option as a means of resolving the deadlock on the issue of the voluntary or compulsory nature

---

[1] See below, pp. 278–9.

[2] *Free Zones of Upper Savoy and the District of Gex* (1929), P.C.I.J., Series A, No. 22, p. 12.

[3] The rigidity of the Statutory provisions, of course, extends only to those provisions which are categorical in form and do not allow a measure of choice to the State or States concerned.

of the Court's jurisdiction, proposed that the jurisdiction Article of the Statute should have two alternative versions, one providing for a compulsory and the other for a voluntary system of jurisdiction.[1] On adhering to the Statute, a State would simply specify which version of the Article it subscribed to. If this proposal had been adopted, the juridical bond linking the States which subscribed to the compulsory version would have been an ordinary treaty obligation resulting from their common acceptance of a fixed treaty provision. The Assembly of the League, however, preferred to maintain a single text of the jurisdiction Article, voluntary in form, and in a special clause to provide what was really an additional Protocol of Compulsory Jurisdiction to which States could separately adhere by an independent and unilateral act.[2] The Assembly's formula was, perhaps, more scientific than that of M. Fernandez, but it also involved a more complicated form of juridical bond between the States which subscribed to the Court's compulsory jurisdiction.

States subscribing to the Optional Clause 'declare that they recognize as compulsory *ipso facto* and without special agreement, *in relation to any other State accepting the same obligation*, the jurisdiction of the Court in all legal disputes', &c. These declarations undoubtedly constitute 'international engagements' binding on the State concerned in relation to any other State also making a declaration under the Optional Clause. The question is whether such an 'international engagement' is constitutionally to be regarded as founded upon a unilateral legislative act done *vis-à-vis* the Court, or as founded upon a bilateral, consensual transaction effected by the joining together of the declarations of any given pair of States through the Optional Clause. Nor is this question purely academic, since the unilateral or bilateral character of the 'engagement' may have legal consequences and, notably, with regard to the right to terminate the engagement.[3]

The text of the Optional Clause—'declare that they recognise as compulsory . . . *in relation to any other State* [French text *à l'égard de tout autre État*] accepting the same obligation'—is not crystal clear on the point whether the declaration is to be regarded as made *vis-à-vis* the Court or *vis-à-vis* the other declarants. The majority of States which have made their declarations in French have substituted the words *vis-à-vis de tout autre état* for the words of the Clause, which perhaps suggests that they conceived of their declarations as directed at the other declarants rather than at the Court. More conclusive is the fact that, under the original Statute, the declarations were not notified to the Registrar of the Court but

---

[1] *Records of the First Assembly* (1920), Committee 1, p. 553.

[2] Ibid., pp. 566 and 440.

[3] In this connexion it may obviously be of critical importance to determine how far the law of treaties applies to this class of international engagement; see below, pp. 263–5.

to the Secretary-General of the League of Nations, who was in no sense an officer of the Court, since the Court was not an organ of the League. The Secretary-General in turn registered the declarations under Article 18 of the Covenant expressly as belonging to the category of 'international engagement or acts by which nations or their governments intend to establish *legal obligations between themselves and another State, nation or government*'.[1] The position is similar under the new Statute, declarations being notified to the Secretary-General and registered by him as 'international agreements' under Article 102 of the Charter.[2] Admittedly, the Court is now an organ of the United Nations, but there can be no doubt that the Secretary-General receives the declarations not as an officer of the Court but as a depositary of instruments relating to an international agreement.

The Permanent Court of International Justice referred to the legal nature of declarations under the Optional Clause principally in two cases: *Phosphates in Morocco (Preliminary Objection)* and *The Electricity Company of Sofia and Bulgaria (Preliminary Objection)*. In the *Phosphates* case,[3] the Court pointed out that the making of a declaration is a unilateral act and seemed to imply that this may be a relevant consideration in interpreting its terms. On the other hand, it also stressed the reciprocal nature of the obligations resulting from the declarations of the two parties. In the *Electricity Company of Sofia* case[4] the Court was quite explicit as to the contractual nature of the obligation resulting from the declarations. In this case Belgium invoked, first, a general treaty of arbitration with Bulgaria and, secondly, the Belgian and Bulgarian declarations under the Optional Clause, as bases for the jurisdiction of the Court. In considering whether Belgium was entitled to rely on both possible sources of jurisdiction simultaneously, the Court repeatedly referred to the declarations as constituting a jurisdictional agreement between Belgium and Bulgaria on the same plane as the general treaty of arbitration. Moreover, the dissenting Judges took the same view of the nature of the legal nexus created between the two States by their declarations. Judges Anzilotti and Urrutia said in terms that the Belgian and Bulgarian Declarations resulted in an *agreement between the two States* accepting the compulsory jurisdiction of the Court, while Judge Hudson referred to Belgium and Bulgaria as being bound *inter se*.[5]

In the *Anglo-Iranian Oil Company* case[6] the new Court had occasion to consider the legal nature of declarations under the Optional Clause in connexion with the interpretation of the Iranian declaration. Iran contended

---

[1] *League of Nations Treaty Series*, vol. 1 (1920), p. 8.

[2] See *United Nations Treaty Series*, vol. 1 (1946–7), Note by the Secretariat, p. xvi; notification to the Secretary-General is expressly directed by Article 36 (4) of the new Statute.

[3] (1938): Series A/B, No. 74, at p. 22. [4] (1939): Series A/B, No. 77.

[5] At pp. 87, 103, and 121 respectively. [6] *I.C.J. Reports*, 1952, p. 93.

DECLINE OF THE OPTIONAL CLAUSE   253

that the declarations do not set up a contractual relation between the States concerned but that, to the extent to which they coincide, they create obligations for each State *vis-à-vis* the Court. The United Kingdom, on the other hand, contended that any given pair of declarations sets up an essentially contractual relation between the States concerned. The Court, in dealing with a United Kingdom argument that the Iranian declaration must, if possible, be so interpreted as to give meaning to all the words, commented:[1]

'It may be said that this principle should in general be applied when interpreting the text of a treaty. But the text of the Iranian Declaration is not a treaty text resulting from negotiations between two or more States. It is the result of unilateral drafting by the Government of Iran, which appears to have shown a particular degree of caution when drafting the text of the Declaration. It appears to have inserted, *ex abundanti cautela*, words which, strictly speaking, may seem to have been superfluous.'

It will be noted that the Court, while emphasizing the unilateral *drafting* of the instrument, did not deny its legal character as a *treaty text*. Nevertheless, it does seem from this passage and from the passage from the *Phosphates in Morocco* judgment which has already been cited,[2] that for the purpose of interpreting their terms the unilateral origin of the individual declarations will be taken into account.

It is true that so careful a judge as Sir Arnold McNair, in his separate Opinion in the same case,[3] referred to the Optional Clause as 'in the nature of a *standing invitation made on behalf of the Court* to Members of the League of Nations to accept as compulsory, on the basis of reciprocity, the whole or any part of the jurisdiction of the Court as therein defined'. But it would be reading too much into this somewhat figurative description of the operation of the Optional Clause to treat it as saying that declarations are to be regarded as made in relation to the Court rather than in relation to the other declarant States. At any rate, Judges Alvarez and Read had no doubt that declarations create consensual agreements between each pair of States making them. The former said of the Iranian declaration:[4]

'The declaration is a multilateral act of a special character; *it is the basis of a treaty made by Iran* with the States which had already adhered and with those which would subsequently adhere to the provisions of Article 36, paragraph 2, of the Statute of the Court.'

Judge Read's language was similar:[5]

'Admittedly, it was drafted unilaterally. On the other hand, it was related, in express terms to Article 36 of the Statute, and to the declarations of other States which had already deposited or might in the future deposit, reciprocal declarations. It was intended to establish *legal relationships with such States, consensual in their character*, within the régime established by the provisions of Article 36.'

[1] At p. 103.   [2] Page 252, n. 3, above.   [3] At p. 116.   [4] At p. 125.
[5] At p. 142.

The origins and the treaty character of the Optional Clause, the role of the Secretary-General of the United Nations in receiving and registering notices of declarations under the Optional Clause, the practice of States in making their declarations, and the jurisprudence of the Court, it is considered, leave no real doubt of the consensual nature of the juridical bond established between States by their declarations. This is not to deny the unilateral character of the act by which a State gives its adherence to the obligations of the Optional Clause. The settlement of the terms of its declaration is not a matter for negotiation with other States but is entirely within its own discretion so long as it keeps within the framework of the Statute. The unilateral making of the instrument, the Court has said, may affect the application to it of the ordinary principles of treaty interpretation. But the making of the instrument is a unilateral act only in the same sense that adhering to a pre-existing treaty or ratifying a previously negotiated treaty text is a unilateral act. Judge Alvarez, indeed, termed a declaration under the Optional Clause a 'multilateral act of a special character'. It is multilateral in the sense that it results in relations with a number of States; but the relation between any given pair of States which have made declarations is not, it is believed, precisely of the same character as that which exists between the parties to a multilateral treaty. The relation between two States under the Optional Clause appears to be more a bilateral than a multilateral relation. The declarations or any other subsequent acts of other adherents to the Optional Clause have no bearing on the obligations of the two States *inter se* and, so far as the actual obligation to accept the Court's jurisdiction is concerned, there is little mutuality among the collective body of the States adhering to the Clause. On the other hand, the relation is not exclusively bilateral because, as previously mentioned, the whole Statute is brought in with the Optional Clause and, under Article 62, parties to the Statute with a legal interest which may be affected by the decision may apply to intervene in the case. Thus, while the relation established between States by their declarations is for most purposes bilateral, it also has a multilateral aspect. The easiest course is, perhaps, to call it a consensual relation which is *sui generis*.

§ 4. *The condition of reciprocity*

A considerable number of the declarations of adherence to the Optional Clause contain a formal statement that they are made 'on condition of reciprocity'. A good number use a double reciprocity formula: *'in relation to any other State accepting the same obligation, that is to say, on condition of reciprocity'*. These phrases were inserted in the earliest declarations *ex abundanti cautela* when jurisdiction under the Optional Clause was still

DECLINE OF THE OPTIONAL CLAUSE   255

untried, and the general opinion is that they are otiose.[1] This certainly appears to be the case since the principle of reciprocity is laid down in the Optional Clause itself, under which every declaration is expressed to operate only 'in relation to any other State *accepting the same obligation*'. Reciprocity, in short, is a basic constitutional provision of the Statute applying to every declaration—even to a declaration, like that of Nicaragua, expressed to be made 'unconditionally'.

Paragraph 3 of Article 36, it has already been seen,[2] provides that a declaration may be made 'unconditionally or on condition of reciprocity on the part of several or certain States or for a certain time'. This paragraph does not relate to 'reciprocity'. It simply authorizes States to accept compulsory jurisdiction under the Optional Clause for limited periods, and to make their liability to jurisdiction conditional on compulsory jurisdiction having been also accepted by a particular number of other States or by particular named States. The reference in paragraph 3 to a 'condition of reciprocity on the part of several or certain States' is, indeed, a legacy from a special preoccupation of the Brazilian delegate, M. Fernandez, in the 1920 Committee of Jurists. Brazil considered it impolitic to venture on a unilateral acceptance of compulsory jurisdiction unless some at least of the Great Powers did likewise. Accordingly, M. Fernandez proposed the following formula for the Optional Clause:[3]

'They may adhere unconditionally or conditionally to the Article providing for compulsory jurisdiction, *a possible condition* being reciprocity on the part of a certain number of Members or, again, of a number of Members including such and such specified Members.'

Although M. Fernandez's version of the Optional Clause itself was dropped in favour of the one which now appears in the Statute, the 'condition of reciprocity' on the part of several or certain States was included in paragraph 3 in order to satisfy him. Afterwards Brazil did in fact make her declaration subject to a condition of reciprocity on the part of two, at least, of the Great Powers, but she is the only State to have resorted to this form of condition. Such a condition, as will be appreciated, is not really a 'condition of reciprocity' but rather a condition that the declaration is not to be in force unless and until a certain number of States or certain named States have accepted compulsory jurisdiction under the Optional Clause.

The condition of reciprocity, as has been said, is inherent in every declaration under the Optional Clause, being introduced therein by the words in paragraph 1 'in relation to any other State *accepting the same obligation*'. Taken literally, the words 'accepting the same obligation' might

---

[1] E.g. Hudson, op. cit., p. 465.   [2] Page 248 above.
[3] *Records of the First Assembly* (1920), Committee 1, p. 553.

seem to imply that one State is bound to another under the Optional Clause only when the obligations assumed in their respective declarations are exactly, or at least broadly, the same. But such an interpretation of the words would have been highly prejudicial to the development of compulsory jurisdiction under the Optional Clause in view of the number and variety of the limitations, conditions and reservations which have in fact been inserted by many States in their declarations. The effect would have been to divide the States adhering to the Optional Clause into small groups whose members had made the same or similar declarations, and to make the members of each group bound *inter se* to accept the Court's compulsory jurisdiction but not bound to accept it at all in relation to members of any other group with declarations having somewhat different terms. Indeed, a few States, having made limitations, conditions, or reservations peculiar to themselves, would have adhered to the Optional Clause and yet not have been liable to compulsory jurisdiction at the suit of any State. That the Optional Clause should have such an effect was clearly not intended by those who drafted it in 1920, and the 'condition of reciprocity' contained in the Clause has in practice been interpreted in a quite different way.

The words 'in relation to any other State accepting the same obligation' appear to have been inserted in the Optional Clause simply for the purpose of limiting a State's liability to accept the Court's jurisdiction at the suit of another State to *cases when the dispute falls within a category of disputes covered by both their declarations*. The roots of the Optional Clause go back beyond the 1920 Committee of Jurists to the Hague Peace Conference of 1907, at which an energetic attempt was made to secure the adoption of the principle of compulsory arbitration for legal disputes. The majority of States at the Conference were prepared to accept compulsory arbitration of all legal disputes subject to the reservation of disputes 'involving vital interests, independence or honour'. But, recognizing the sweeping nature of the exception created by this reservation, the majority were further prepared to accept compulsory arbitration *without any reserve* for disputes in regard to pecuniary claims and in regard to conventions dealing with seven stated categories of matters.[1] In addition, they were prepared to specify in a separate Protocol other categories of matters considered to be susceptible of forming the subject of an agreement for compulsory arbitration without any reserve. Finally, the Protocol was to enumerate the States which, on condition of reciprocity, immediately undertook this obligation with regard to one or more of the specified matters, and these States were to be entitled to extend their undertaking subsequently to other matters on the list by registering their acceptance of the obligation at an inter-

---

[1] *Actes et Documents* (1907), vol. ii, pp. 136 ff.

DECLINE OF THE OPTIONAL CLAUSE

national bureau situated at The Hague.[1] The procedure envisaged was that that Protocol should have annexed to it a table on which the specified matters would be set out in columns and then in each column would be indicated the particular States which subscribed to compulsory arbitration in regard to the particular matter listed in that column. Under Article 1, each State entering its name in one or more of the columns undertook to accept compulsory arbitration without reserve '*with respect to each of the other signatory Powers whose reciprocity in this regard is indicated in the same manner in the table*'.[2] In short, the reciprocity which the delegates had in mind at the 1907 Conference was simply that each State would be under an obligation to submit to compulsory arbitration without reserve in relation to any other State for those categories of disputes with respect to which both States had accepted that obligation.

There can be little doubt that the condition of reciprocity inserted in the Optional Clause in 1920 was intended to be of the same kind. The Optional Clause, in the form in which it appears in the 1920 Statute of the Court, allowed States the choice of accepting compulsory jurisdiction 'in all or any' of specified categories of legal disputes, with the resulting possibility that they might be found to have accepted it with respect to different categories. The condition of reciprocity expressed in the words 'in relation to any other State accepting the same obligation' was intended simply to limit the obligation to cases where both States had subscribed to the Optional Clause in regard to the particular class of legal dispute in question. It does not seem that the draftsmen of the 1920 Statute then had in mind the question of reciprocity in regard to conditions and reservations or to time-limits. In practice, however, the divergencies in the declarations of States under the Optional Clause have arisen from the insertion of differing conditions, reservations, and time-limits, not from the acceptance of jurisdiction specifying different categories of legal disputes. Consequently, it is in connexion with conditions, reservations, and time-limits that the problem of reciprocity has proved primarily to be of interest and importance. In these connexions, as previously indicated, the words of the Optional Clause 'in relation to any other State *accepting the same obligation*', if literally applied, would have the effect of confining compulsory jurisdiction under the Clause to States making declarations in identic terms. The words have not, however, been treated as laying down a condition that *exactly or even broadly the same obligation of compulsory jurisdiction must have been accepted by each State*. The words 'in relation to any other State accepting the same obligation' have rather been interpreted as requiring that there shall be complete reciprocity in the operation of compulsory jurisdiction under

---

[1] The draft proposals also contemplated the addition of new matters to the list and the subsequent adherence to the Protocol of other States; ibid.   [2] Ibid., at pp. 161–2.

258   DECLINE OF THE OPTIONAL CLAUSE

the Optional Clause *as between two States which have accepted the obligation in different terms*. This interpretation emerges very clearly from the attitude of States before the Court and from the jurisprudence of the Court.

The first case in which reciprocity in relation to conditions and reservations was discussed was the case of the *Phosphates in Morocco*,[1] in which Italy filed an Application against France in respect of the alleged confiscation by the latter of an Italian national's phosphate licences without compensation. France's declaration contained a limitation of her acceptance of compulsory jurisdiction to disputes 'which may arise after the ratification of the present declaration with regard to situations or facts subsequent to such ratification'. Italy's declaration contained a condition requiring a previous attempt to have been made to settle the dispute through the diplomatic channel, but did not include a limitation *ratione temporis* in the same terms as the French limitation. France lodged a preliminary objection to jurisdiction both on the ground of her own limitation *ratione temporis* and on the ground of the Italian condition concerning prior recourse to the diplomatic channel. In invoking the Italian condition precedent, France referred to the words 'in relation to any other State accepting the same obligation' as creating a condition of reciprocity, and Italy did not contest France's right to rely on the Italian condition precedent.

France also invoked the principle of reciprocity in connexion with her limitation *ratione temporis*. She pointed out that the ratification of her unilateral declaration on 25 April 1931 did not by itself place her under any obligation whatever *vis-à-vis* Italy and that, owing to the requirement of reciprocity, the juridical bond between France and Italy under the Optional Clause only arose some five months later, on 7 September 1931, when Italy's declaration also became effective by ratification. She then proceeded to argue that, for the purpose of applying the limitation *ratione temporis* in her own declaration, the relevant date was not 25 April 1931, the date which she herself had specified in the declaration, but 7 September 1931, the date when the two States first became mutually bound under the Optional Clause. Italy objected that, even if the date of the Italian ratification was the date on which the two States first became mutually bound, the date for applying the French limitation *ratione temporis* must be the date actually specified in the French declaration, namely, the date of the French ratification. Reciprocity, while it might require the French limitation to be applied equally to both States in accordance with its terms, could not have the effect of applying it in an altered form by arbitrarily substituting another date for the date actually specified in the French limitation. France, taking the view that the difference of date was not, in fact, of any practical consequence in the case, did not press her argument. The Court equally

[1] (1938): Series A/B, No. 74.

considered the difference in date to be immaterial and expressed no opinion on the point. It is, however, believed to be clear that the French contention concerning the date for applying her limitation *ratione temporis* was ill-founded and that the Italian view of the operation of reciprocity in such cases was correct.[1]

Neither France nor Italy in this case appears to have had any doubt that the operation of the principle of reciprocity with respect to conditions and limitations is to make any condition or limitation found in the declaration of one party to a dispute both binding on and available to the other party for the purpose of their mutual relations under the Optional Clause. Similarly, the Court said, with reference to a difference between the French and Italian limitations *ratione temporis*:[2]

> 'This [the Italian] declaration does not contain the limitation that appears in the French declaration concerning the situations or facts with regard to which the dispute arose; *nevertheless, as a consequence of the condition of reciprocity stipulated in Article 36 (2) of the Statute of the Court it is recognized that this limitation holds good between the parties.*'

In point of fact, it seems open to question whether reciprocity was the true ground for applying a limitation contained in the *defendant's* own declaration. The true ground would seem to be the fundamental rule that a State can never be brought before the Court except on the conditions on which it has consented to jurisdiction.[3] The principle of reciprocity only needs to be brought in when the defendant State is objecting to jurisdiction on the basis of a limitation, condition, or reservation contained in the *plaintiff* State's declaration.

In the *Phosphates in Morocco* case, therefore, the Court's pronouncement on the operation of reciprocity in regard to limitations may not have been strictly relevant to the facts of that case. The same cannot, however, be said of a similar pronouncement in the *Electricity Company of Sofia and Bulgaria* case,[4] in which the Court had again to consider the operation of the 'condition of reciprocity' in the context of a limitation *ratione temporis*. This time, the declaration of the defendant State, Bulgaria, was unconditional and the limitation *ratione temporis* was contained in that of the plaintiff

---

[1] The French limitation *ratione temporis* was so designed as to exclude (*a*) all disputes existing prior to 25 April 1931, and (*b*) disputes subsequent to 25 April 1931, with regard to situations or facts prior to that date. The Italian limitation was so designed as to exclude all disputes existing prior to 7 September 1931 but to include all disputes arising after that date without regard to the date of the situations or facts out of which they arose. Consequently, neither the French nor Italian declarations excluded a dispute arising after 7 September 1931, the date of Italy's ratification, with respect to situations or facts after 25 April 1931, the date of France's ratification. Yet the French contention would have denied the Court's jurisdiction over this class of dispute.

[2] At p. 22.

[3] In the *Mavrommatis Palestine Concessions* case the Court had said that its jurisdiction is 'invariably based on the consent of the respondent' and only exists in so far as this consent has been given: (1924), Series A, No. 2, p. 16.   [4] (1939): Series A/B, No. 77, 80–82.

DECLINE OF THE OPTIONAL CLAUSE

State, Belgium. Bulgaria, invoking the principle of reciprocity, claimed the benefit of Belgium's limitation *ratione temporis* and objected to jurisdiction. The Court thereupon said:[1]

'Although this limitation does not appear in the Bulgarian Government's own declaration, it is common ground that in consequence of the condition of reciprocity laid down in paragraph 2 of Article 36 of the Court's Statute and repeated in the Bulgarian declaration, it is applicable between the Parties.'

Several of the dissenting Judges[2] also referred to the operation of reciprocity, all of them treating the limitations, conditions and reservations in the declaration of one party as automatically read into that of the other party. After this case, therefore, it could be regarded as settled that, in virtue of the reciprocity laid down in the Optional Clause, a defendant State can always rely upon a limitation, condition, or reservation in its opponent's declaration.[3]

In the *Anglo-Iranian Oil Company* case[4] the new Court made a brief pronouncement on the operation of reciprocity. The declarations of both the plaintiff State, the United Kingdom, and the defendant State, Iran, contained a limitation *ratione temporis* together with other reservations. In addition, Iran's Declaration contained words restricting her acceptance of jurisdiction absolutely to disputes concerning matters relating to the application of treaties accepted by Iran. The Court said:[5]

'By these Declarations, jurisdiction is conferred on the Court only to the extent to which the two declarations coincide in conferring it. As the Iranian Declaration is more limited in scope than the United Kingdom Declaration, it is the Iranian Declaration on which the Court must base itself. This is common ground between the Parties.'

In this case, again, Iran without invoking the principle of reciprocity was fully entitled, as defendant, to object to being brought before the Court except within the limits set by the terms and conditions of her own Declaration. The above pronouncement has, therefore, to be understood simply as underlining that, owing to the principle of reciprocity, the

---

[1] At p. 81.

[2] E.g., Judges Anzilotti (at p. 87), Urrutia (at p. 103), Van Eysinga (at p. 109), and Hudson (at p. 121).

[3] In the *Electricity Company of Sofia and Bulgaria* case the Belgian declaration was ratified on 10 March 1926 and, in applying the limitation *ratione temporis*, the Court said (at p. 81): 'The Parties agree that the date on which the dispute arose was June 24, 1937, i.e. after 10 March, 1926,—the date of the establishment of the juridical bond between the two States under Article 36 of the Court's Statute.' Here the Court's judgment, although correct in substance, appears to be founded on wrong reasoning. 10 March 1926, the date of the Belgian ratification, was the relevant date for applying the limitation *ratione temporis*, not because it was the date of the establishment of the juridical bond between the two States, but because it was the date specified in the Belgian declaration as the date by reference to which disputes were excluded *ratione temporis* from its acceptance of the Optional Clause. The date of the establishment of the juridical bond under the Optional Clause could not, as such, have any bearing upon the scope of the Belgian limitation *ratione temporis*.

[4] *I.C.J. Reports*, 1952, p. 93.   [5] At p. 103.

DECLINE OF THE OPTIONAL CLAUSE   261

declarations of both parties must always be taken into account and that the Court's jurisdiction in any given case is the highest common factor of the two declarations. The general rule, therefore, is that jurisdiction under the Optional Clause is conferred on the Court *'only to the extent to which the two declarations coincide in conferring it'*. Judge McNair, looking at the question of reciprocity rather from the point of view of what has to be shown in a concrete case, said in his individual Opinion:

'the declarations of both States [must] *concur in comprising the dispute in question within their scope.'*

This formulation of the applicable principle, it will be appreciated, comes close to the original concept of reciprocity which inspired those who drafted the Optional Clause in 1920.

The attitude of States in cases before the Court and the jurisprudence of the Court itself thus establish that the 'condition of reciprocity' contained in the Optional Clause does not mean that both States must have accepted the same or even broadly the same measure of compulsory jurisdiction. It means two things. Primarily, it means that if compulsory jurisdiction under the Optional Clause is to apply to a particular dispute, both States must have made a declaration which comprises that dispute within its scope. As a corollary, it also means that a party to a dispute whose own declaration comprises that dispute within its scope is always entitled to invoke a condition, reservation, or limitation in its opponent's declaration for the purpose of excluding the particular dispute from the application of the Optional Clause.

§ 5. *Time-limits as escape clauses*

The majority of States, as previously mentioned, have taken advantage of the authority given in Article 36 (3) of the Statute to make their declarations 'for a certain time' and have placed a variety of time-limits upon the currency of their declarations. The time-limits with which this article is particularly concerned are those under which the declaration is expressed to be terminable by notice to the Secretary-General. Before examining them, however, it is necessary to consider (1) what may conveniently be called the rule in the *Nottebohm* case, and (2) the general principle in regard to unilateral termination of a declaration.

The rule in the Nottebohm case

In the *Nottebohm* case (Preliminary Objection)[1] Guatemala's declaration was expressed to be valid for a period of five years from 27 January 1947, and was therefore due to expire on 26 January 1952. Liechtenstein's declaration was revocable on twelve months' notice but, notice of revocation not

[1] *I.C.J. Reports,* 1953, p. 111.

having been given, was in full force. On 17 December 1951, that is, about five and a half weeks before Guatemala's declaration was due to expire, Liechtenstein filed an Application presenting a case against Guatemala. The latter lodged a preliminary objection to jurisdiction on the basis that after the expiry of her declaration the Court had no power to hear any case against Guatemala under the Optional Clause, even although the Application might have been filed during the period of the currency of her declaration. She did not dispute that at the date when the Liechtenstein Application was filed the Court became regularly seized of jurisdiction over the case. She claimed that her declaration must be understood as relating generally to the administration of justice by the Court, not merely to the seizing of the Court with jurisdiction to administer justice, with the result that the expiry of the declaration terminated the Court's power to administer justice in the case.

The Court rejected Guatemala's interpretation of the effect of her declaration, pointing out that it was an entirely novel one. In both the *Losinger & Co.*[1] and *Phosphates in Morocco* cases[2] the declaration of the defendant State had expired shortly after the filing of the Application in the case. Yet, although in each case the defendant State had raised other objections to jurisdiction, it had never thought to claim that the expiry of its declaration involved automatically the removal of the case from the Court's list. These were both cases of the simple expiry of a time-limit specified in the declaration. The Court could also have adduced the *Anglo-Iranian Oil Company* case,[3] decided in the previous year, as another example. Iran's declaration was terminable on notice, and after the filing of the United Kingdom's Application in the case Iran did terminate her declaration by notice to the Secretary-General of the United Nations. Iran raised every possible ground of objection to the Court's jurisdiction but she did not rely on the subsequent termination of her declaration as precluding the Court from further considering the case. The Court held in the *Nottebohm* case that the Optional Clause and the declarations of States thereunder relate to the seising of the Court with jurisdiction, not to the adjudication of the suit. It said:[4]

'The purpose of Article 36, paragraph 2, and of the declarations relating thereto, is to regulate the seizing of the Court: under the system of the Statute the seizing of the Court by means of an Application is not *ipso facto* open to all States parties to the Statute, it is only open to the extent defined in the applicable Declarations. This being so, the lapse of a Declaration, by reason of the expiry, before the filing of the Application, of the period fixed therein makes it impossible to invoke that Declaration in order to seize the Court.

The seizing of the Court is thus dominated by the Declarations emanating from the

---

[1] (1936): Series A/B, No. 67.
[3] *I.C.J. Reports*, 1952, p. 93.
[2] (1938): Series A/B, No. 74.
[4] At p. 122.

parties when recourse is had to the compulsory jurisdiction in accordance with Article 36, paragraph 2. But the seizing of the Court is one thing, the administration of justice is another. The latter is governed by the Statute, and by the Rules which the Court has drawn up by virtue of the powers conferred upon it by Article 30 of the Statute. *Once the Court has been regularly seized, the Court must exercise its powers, as these are defined in the Statute.* After that, the expiry of the period fixed for one of the Declarations on which the Application was founded is an event which is unrelated to the exercise of the powers conferred on the Court by the Statute, *which the Court must exercise whenever it has been regularly seized* and whenever it has not been shown, on some other ground, that it lacks jurisdiction or that the claim is inadmissible.' (Italics added.)

Accordingly, when an Application has been regularly filed in a particular case while the declarations of both States were current, the subsequent lapse of one of the declarations, whether by the expiry of a fixed period or by notification to the Secretary-General under the terms of the declaration, does not deprive the Court of jurisdiction over that case. On the other hand, the prior lapse of a declaration, by however brief a space of time, suffices to prevent the establishment of the Court's jurisdiction by means of an Application based upon the expired declaration.

Unilateral termination of a declaration

The making of a declaration, it has been seen,[1] is a unilateral act; it does not, however, follow that the unmaking of a declaration is equally a unilateral act at the free discretion of the State concerned. The declaration, once made, sets up consensual relations with other States and the question necessarily arises whether a State can have any right to terminate its declaration except in accordance with an express term of the declaration. This question was raised in 1938 when Paraguay, whose declaration of 1933 contained no provision for its own termination, notified the Secretary-General of the League of a recent decree which purported to withdraw the declaration. Paraguay's attempt to rescind her declaration was motivated by the fear that Bolivia might file an Application under the Optional Clause in the Gran Chaco boundary dispute, and Bolivia, not unnaturally, notified the Secretary-General of her 'most formal reservations as to the legal value of the decree'.[2] Bolivia at the same time requested that her reservations should be communicated to other signatories of the Statute, and five other States then also made reservations as to the legal effects of Paraguay's purported cancellation of her declaration.[3] Bolivia and these five States all had made declarations for specific periods of years which had not yet expired. They did not enlarge upon their reasons for contesting Paraguay's right to terminate her declaration, but two of them, the Netherlands and Czechoslovakia, did indicate that they regarded the question as being governed by the law relating to the termination of treaties. This would

[1] Pp. 252–4 above.   [2] (1938–9): *P.C.I.J.*, Series E, No. 15, p. 227.   [3] Ibid.

normally mean that a State having a declaration without any provision for its termination would not be entitled to cancel it as against other States having declarations for fixed periods except with their consent. Otherwise, termination of the declaration would not be justifiable except by reference to one of the special rules concerning the termination of treaties, such as the doctrine of *rebus sic stantibus*; moreover, under the final paragraph of Article 36 of the Statute it would be for the Court to decide any dispute as to the validity of a purported cancellation of a declaration.[1]

The Court, as it happened, never had occasion to consider the legal effect of Paraguay's attempted cancellation of her declaration. The Registry continued to include Paraguay amongst the States which had declarations under the Optional Clause, drawing attention at the same time to the Paraguayan instrument of cancellation of 1938 and to the reservations in regard to it made by Bolivia and the other five States. When the Statute of the new Court was drawn up, Paraguay took no action to clarify the position in regard to her declaration, despite the fact that paragraph 5 of Article 36 of the new Statute provides that declarations under the old Statute 'which are still in force shall be deemed, as between the parties to the present Statute, to be acceptances of the compulsory jurisdiction of the International Court of Justice *for the period which they have still to run and in accordance with their terms*'. The Registry of the new Court appears, in consequence, to have felt itself obliged to maintain Paraguay's 1933 declaration in the list of operative declarations under the Optional Clause, while again drawing attention to the notice of cancellation and to the reservations made in regard to that notice. The only possible interpretation of the Registry's action is that it considers the legal effect of a cancellation of a declaration which has no time-limit to be open to question.

The reservations of Bolivia and the other five States in 1938 and the cautious attitude of the Registry in regard to the Paraguayan notice of cancellation are believed to have been well founded. A State which, having the right to make its declaration only 'for a certain time', chooses to make it without time-limit, is in a position analogous to that of a State which has entered into a bilateral treaty of indefinite duration. If two States both have declarations without time-limit, their position *vis-à-vis* each other seems clearly to be that of parties to a bilateral treaty of indefinite duration, and any right which either State may have to put an end to their mutual obligation to accept the compulsory jurisdiction of the Court under the Optional Clause can only derive from the general law concerning the termination of treaties. The agreement between the two States, which is

---

[1] Sweden, in reserving her position in regard to Paraguay's notification of the cancellation of the Paraguayan declaration, emphasized that it would be for the Court to determine the legal effect of the notification. (1938–9): *P.C.I.J.*, Series E, No. 15, p. 227.

DECLINE OF THE OPTIONAL CLAUSE   265

constituted by their parallel acceptances of the Optional Clause, contains no reference to a right arbitrarily to terminate their mutual obligation under the Clause simply by giving notice to the Secretary-General. Nor can such a right be implied in Article 36 of the Statute, paragraph 3 of which clearly contemplates an indefinite commitment unless provision for a time-limit is made when a State makes its declaration.

The same reasoning applies to the case of a State whose declaration is either made for a specific period of years or is expressed to be terminable after a specific period of notice and which nevertheless purports, regardless of the terms of the declaration, to cancel it immediately by notice to the Secretary-General. The legitimacy of terminating any declaration otherwise than in accordance with its terms must, on principle, hinge upon the rules governing the termination of treaties. This is borne out by the fact that when France, the United Kingdom, and other Commonwealth States notified the Secretary-General of the League in September 1939 that they would 'not regard their acceptances of the Optional Clause as covering disputes arising out of events occurring during the present hostilities', they formulated the grounds on which they justified their action in a manner strongly to imply that they were invoking the doctrine of *rebus sic stantibus*.[1] At the date in question the declarations of these States were valid for fixed periods which had not yet expired, and they clearly did not consider themselves to have the right unilaterally to terminate or vary their declarations except on principles analogous to those governing the termination or variation of treaties. Even so, a number of neutral States made reservations in regard to the legal effect of the action taken by these States.[2]

On principle, therefore, there is no right of unilateral termination of a declaration under the Optional Clause unless the right has been expressly reserved in the declaration. On the same principle also there is not, in the absence of an express term, any right of unilateral variation of a declaration previously made and still in force. It is probable that the condition of reciprocity laid down in the Optional Clause gives a State the right to rely on a time-limit in another State's declaration for the purpose of terminating the particular obligation between them. But this important question will be deferred until Section 7 below.

Reservation of a right to terminate on giving notice

A number of States have interpreted the words 'for a certain time' (*pour un délai déterminé*) in paragraph 3 of Article 36 as authorizing them to make

---

[1] *League of Nations Official Journal*, 1939, pp. 407–10; ibid., 1940, p. 44. These States alleged that the conditions which prevailed at the time of their acceptance of the Optional Clause no longer existed.

[2] Belgium, Brazil, Denmark, Estonia, Haiti, Netherlands, Norway, Peru, Sweden, Switzerland, and Thailand: *League of Nations Official Journal*, 1939, p. 410; ibid., 1940, pp. 45–47.

266   DECLINE OF THE OPTIONAL CLAUSE

declarations which have no set period but are to remain in force until notice of their termination is given. Thus in the 1954–5 *Year Book of the Court* two declarations are expressed to be terminable after twelve months' notice, four declarations after six months' notice, and ten declarations immediately on notice to the Secretary-General. Little objection can be taken to the six declarations the expiry of which is subject to a specific period of notice. Although the right to terminate gives the States concerned some chance of manœuvring to avoid jurisdiction in an impending dispute, any other State engaged in a dispute with one of them will always be in a position to know a reasonable time beforehand exactly on what date its opponent's liability to compulsory jurisdiction will terminate, and can shape its course of action accordingly. Very different, however, is the position of a State engaged in a dispute with one of the States whose declarations are terminable immediately on notice being given to the Secretary-General. At any moment and without any warning this State may find that its opponent has withdrawn the dispute from the compulsory jurisdiction of the Court simply by notifying the Secretary-General of the immediate termination of its declaration. Such a use by an opponent of its right to terminate its declaration with immediate effect, in order to remove a current dispute from the jurisdiction of the Court, could only be defeated with certainty by the premature filing of an Application at the outset of the dispute. A State, for reasons of comity, is normally reluctant to drag another State before the Court without first making a serious attempt to arrange the matters in dispute by diplomatic negotiations.[1] But a State confronted with the possibility that its opponent may at any moment terminate its adherence to the Optional Clause takes the risk of losing its remedy under the Clause altogether if it does not promptly file an Application as soon as a dispute exists. One objection to declarations immediately terminable by a mere notice to the Secretary-General is, therefore, the pressure which they put on States to institute proceedings under the Optional Clause without first exhausting the possibilities of settlement out of Court.

Declarations containing this form of time-limit are, however, open to the more fundamental objection that they tend to undermine the whole purpose of the Optional Clause. So long as the State concerned sees itself only as a potential plaintiff, it will maintain its declaration in order that it may be in a position to bring any opponent compulsorily before the Court.

[1] In the absence of a specific provision to that effect in one of the declarations, the prior exhaustion of diplomatic means of settlement is not a condition of the exercise of the Court's jurisdiction under the Optional Clause. It appears that there must have been sufficient interchanges between the parties to establish the existence of a 'dispute'; but that is all that the Statute requires. See *Electricity Company of Sofia and Bulgaria* case (1939): *P.C.I.J.*, Series A/B, No. 77, at p. 83; see also Hudson, op. cit., pp. 413–16.

DECLINE OF THE OPTIONAL CLAUSE   267

But the moment it sees a serious possibility that it may itself be brought compulsorily before the Court as defendant—and especially in a case where one of its so-called 'vital interests' is involved—it will be tempted promptly to terminate its declaration and put itself out of its opponent's reach. Thus, the right to terminate the declaration immediately by the mere giving of notice may be used *not so much as a means of terminating the general obligation of the State concerned to compulsory jurisdiction under the Optional Clause, but as a means of withdrawing from the Court's compulsory jurisdiction a particular dispute after it has arisen.* In short, the right to terminate the declaration may be used to serve much the same purpose as the reservation of 'matters affecting vital interests, independence and honour' commonly found in the arbitration treaties concluded in the period between the First Hague Peace Conference and the establishment of the Permanent Court of International Justice. Under the latter form of reservation, as was pointed out at the Second Hague Peace Conference,[1] the arbitration provided for by the treaty was compulsory only in form, since the moment a dispute arose a party had the right to exclude the dispute from the operation of the treaty by applying the reservation. Under that form of reservation the right to specify the dispute as excluded from the agreement to arbitrate was exercisable even after the other State had already invoked the agreement, and the compulsory arbitration professedly established by the treaty was completely illusory. The reservation of a right to terminate a declaration under the Optional Clause does not go to the same lengths in destroying the obligation to accept compulsory jurisdiction. The difference is that under the rule in the *Nottebohm* case[2] the exercise of the right to terminate the declaration is ineffective to withdraw a particular dispute from the Court if the other State has already invoked the compulsory jurisdiction of the Court by filing an Application. This difference is a material one, since the compulsory jurisdiction accepted in the declaration is very much a reality up to the moment when notice of termination is given.[3] It is, indeed, only this fact, that the compulsory jurisdiction has its full effects until notice of termination is given, which prevents a declaration in this form from being regarded as totally incompatible with the Optional Clause. Nevertheless, there is a danger that the right to terminate the declaration may be used as a general escape-clause to prevent a particular current dispute from being submitted to the Court.

The warning signs in State practice are clear. Australia, faced with the

---

[1] E.g., by Von Bieberstein, the German delegate: *Actes et Documents* (1907), vol. ii, pp. 51 and 53.   [2] See above, p. 261.

[3] In the *Anglo-Iranian Oil Company* case, Iran failed to cancel her declaration until *after* the filing of the United Kingdom's Application and would, in consequence, have been subject to compulsory jurisdiction in that case had she not been able to establish that the particular dispute was not covered by the terms of her declaration.

possibility of a Japanese Application in her pearl fisheries dispute with Japan, terminated her declaration in 1954 and issued a fresh one accepting compulsory jurisdiction for disputes concerning sedentary fisheries of the Australian continental shelf only, on condition that a *modus vivendi* was first agreed between the parties to cover the interim period before the final decision of the Court.[1] Admittedly, the State concerned did not seek to withdraw the dispute altogether from the Court. It did, however, terminate its existing declaration apparently for the purpose of making special provision for a current dispute, and it could with equal facility have terminated its declaration as a means of withdrawing the dispute altogether from the Court. In October 1955 the United Kingdom appears in fact to have terminated its declaration for the purpose of excluding a current dispute from its acceptance of compulsory jurisdiction. It notified the termination of a declaration *made only five months previously* and issued another one containing a new reservation excluding 'disputes in respect of which arbitral or judicial proceedings are taking, or have taken, place with any State which, at the date of the commencement of the proceedings, had not itself accepted the compulsory jurisdiction of the International Court of Justice'. The terms of this reservation indicate that the United Kingdom's sudden alteration of its declaration had reference to the break-down of the Buraimi Arbitration a few weeks before owing to the wholesale bribery of potential witnesses by the Saudi Arabian Government and that the new reservation was introduced specifically to exclude the Buraimi dispute. Admittedly, the circumstances were somewhat special and the United Kingdom had the best of reasons for acting as it did. Nevertheless, its action provides a striking illustration of how a declaration terminable on notice may be terminated *ad hoc* for the purpose of declining jurisdiction in a current dispute. Two further examples may be given. The first is Iran's termination of her declaration shortly after the filing of the United Kingdom's Application in the *Anglo-Iranian Oil Company* case, which has already been referred to on page 262 above. It is reasonable to suppose that Iran's action was taken with a view to putting herself in the best possible posture of defence against the United Kingdom in the event of Iran being able, by her preliminary objections, to defeat the latter's initial Application to the Court. The other example is the very recent termination of India's declaration immediately after the filing of the Portuguese declaration in the dispute concerning Portugal's claim to rights of passage over Indian territory. India promptly reissued her declaration with a new reservation of 'matters of domestic jurisdiction' in the subjective United States form of 'matters which are essentially within the domestic jurisdiction of' India as determined by India.

[1] See *Year Book of the International Court of Justice*, *1953-4*, p. 210.

The three States mentioned in the previous paragraph as having terminated their declarations and reissued them with new reservations were States of the British Commonwealth, whose declarations are modelled on Great Britain's original declaration in 1929. The United Kingdom has, indeed, the chief responsibility for introducing a form of declaration which now threatens seriously to weaken the Optional Clause. The United Kingdom can plead in extenuation that its introduction of declarations terminable by notice was more by inadvertence than by design. Its original declaration was expressed to be valid 'for 10 years and thereafter until such time as notice may be given to terminate the acceptance'. Consequently, there was nothing ambiguous or half-hearted about its original acceptance of compulsory jurisdiction. The United Kingdom bound itself for ten years certain, and the provision in regard to notice of termination was inserted merely as a convenient means of extending the period beyond ten years without express renewal rather than as a means of acquiring freedom to contract in and out of the Optional Clause as its interests might require. Nevertheless, when the ten years had passed, its declaration became terminable on notice and it was in the position of being able to contract in and out of the Optional Clause as its interests dictated. The declarations of India and the Dominions had the same form of time-limit, and by the end of September 1939 all had become terminable at any moment simply by notice to the Secretary-General of the League. Meanwhile, in 1930 Iran and in 1938 Iraq had adopted this form of time-limit and in due course their declarations also became immediately terminable by notice. The next development was in April 1940, when the Union of South Africa notified the Secretary-General of the termination of her original declaration and issued a fresh declaration, which simply said that it was to remain in force 'until notice of termination is given'.[1] In the case of South Africa, this formula was a mere restatement of her existing position under the Optional Clause after the expiry of the ten-year period. But the issue of a declaration which boldly provided that it was to be immediately terminable from the very first moment of its signature drew attention to a possible method of subscribing to compulsory jurisdiction under the Optional Clause with an absolute minimum of actual commitment to submit to jurisdiction.

Up to the present the South African form of time-limit has only been copied by the United Kingdom and by India in new declarations which, like that of South Africa, replaced existing declarations which were already terminable on notice. In principle, however, the new declarations of these three States of the British Commonwealth have to be regarded as independent of the earlier declarations which they replace and, assuming that they are compatible with Article 36 of the Statute, they provide precedents for

[1] (1939–45): Series E, No. 16, p. 326.

270 DECLINE OF THE OPTIONAL CLAUSE

accepting compulsory jurisdiction under the Optional Clause while reserving the right to repudiate it again at any moment and without any warning. Whether these declarations are compatible with Article 36 depends on whether a declaration for no certain period and terminable by simple notification to the Secretary-General falls within the authority given in paragraph 3 of Article 36 to make declarations 'for a certain time' (*pour un délai déterminé*). The States concerned would presumably invoke the maxim *id certum est quod certum reddi potest* as bringing their declarations within paragraph 3, and there does not, in fact, seem to have been any disposition to challenge their validity. The danger is that, on the basis of these precedents, it may become normal for new declarations not to be made for any certain period but merely until notice of their revocation is given. As it is, in the post-war period five further States, the Netherlands and the Philippines (1946), France (1949), Liberia (1952), and Portugal (1955), have made declarations in the original British Commonwealth form for a specific period of years and thereafter until notice of termination is given.[1] By 1958 eleven declarations, nearly one-third of all those in force, will be immediately terminable by notice. The flexibility of this form of declaration and the freedom of manœuvre which it gives may lead to its extended use, especially if there should be any lessening of confidence in the Court. If this occurs, compulsory jurisdiction under the Optional Clause will have become an extremely fragile instrument for the judicial settlement of disputes and an institution very different from that hoped for by those who devised the Clause.

§ 6. *Reservations as escape clauses*

Article 36, as previously mentioned,[2] contains no provision concerning the insertion of limitations, reservations and conditions in declarations accepting the Optional Clause, and this omission has been interpreted as giving complete freedom to insert any special term not incompatible with the fixed constitutional provisions of the Statute. The liberal use made by States of the power to restrict the scope of their declarations by limitations, conditions and reservations is to be regretted because of the large inroad which it makes into what was hoped to be a general system of compulsory jurisdiction. It is not, however, entirely pernicious in its effect so long as the matters excluded from acceptance of the Optional Clause are fixed in the declarations themselves by reference to determinate, objective, criteria. This is, for example, the case with the frequently found limitation to future disputes, which usually takes the double form of limiting the acceptance to 'all disputes arising after the ratification of the present declaration with

---

[1] See *Year Book of the International Court of Justice, 1954–5*, pp. 192–6. Portugal's declaration will presumably appear in the *1955–6 Year Book* of the Court.   [2] Page 248 above.

DECLINE OF THE OPTIONAL CLAUSE   271

regard to situations or facts subsequent to the said ratification'. Most 'subsequent disputes' will relate to situations or facts which have a history going back some years, and a loose interpretation of the limitation might result in a drastic curtailment of the matters covered by the declaration. But the limitation is objectively stated and the Court has had no difficulty in keeping it within bounds by holding that a prior situation or fact, if it is to bring the limitation into play, must be one which is 'the source of the dispute'.[1] A State cannot, therefore, by a specious invocation of tenuous connexions between a recent 'dispute' and a past 'situation or fact', use this form of limitation as a general escape clause.

Some reservations are open to criticism on the ground that the criteria, although objective, are so broadly stated as to leave doubts as to their true scope. Such is the case with the common reservation of 'disputes in regard to which the Parties to the dispute have agreed or shall agree to have recourse to other methods of pacific settlement'.[2] Others give some opportunity for delaying tactics, for example, the reservation of the right to 'suspend judicial proceedings under certain conditions in the case of disputes under consideration by the Security Council'.[3] But the application of these reservations is to be determined by objective criteria and there is no basic inconsistency with the principle of compulsory jurisdiction.

Subjective reservations concerning matters of domestic jurisdiction

The inconsistency with the principle of compulsory jurisdiction comes when the application of a reservation to a particular dispute or category of disputes is not pre-determined by the words of the reservation but is left for subsequent determination at the discretion of the State concerned. The obvious example is the reservation which was introduced by the United States in 1946[4] and which excludes

'disputes with regard to matters which are essentially within the domestic jurisdiction of the United States of America as determined by the United States of America.'

This unblushingly subjective form of reservation appears to reserve the right, whenever a dispute arises, to determine it to be a dispute 'with regard to matters which are essentially within the domestic jurisdiction of the United States of America' and thereby exclude it from the scope of the United States acceptance of compulsory jurisdiction. In consequence, the declaration does not finally define beforehand the matters in regard to which the United States accepts jurisdiction; the declaration leaves the definition

---

[1] *Electricity Company of Sofia and Bulgaria* case (1939): Series A/B, No. 77, at p. 82.

[2] See Lauterpacht in *Economica*, 10 (1930), p. 145.

[3] Found in the declarations of most Commonwealth States. The opportunity for chicane provided by this reservation is limited by the power of the Security Council to remove the dispute from its agenda for the express purpose of bringing the Court's compulsory jurisdiction into play.   [4] *Year Book of the International Court of Justice, 1946–7*, p. 217.

until after a case has arisen, and leaves it then not to the determination of the Court but to the United States itself.

This form of 'domestic jurisdiction' reservation was examined at some length by the present writer in the previous volume of this *Year Book*,[1] where the conclusion was reached that it is open to the Court to hold that a declaration which contains this form of reservation has no legal force as a declaration under the Optional Clause. This view of the United States declaration can, it was suggested, be taken on two grounds. First, the reservation is scarcely compatible with paragraph 6 of Article 36 of the Statute, under which it rests with the Court to decide any dispute as to its jurisdiction, and this paragraph appears to be part of the fixed constitution of the Court. Secondly, the reservation of what appears to be a general right to exclude from the scope of the declaration any dispute at any time at the will of the State concerned can scarcely be regarded as a genuine 'recognition' of the Court's compulsory jurisdiction within the meaning of the Optional Clause. It would serve no purpose to re-examine here all the considerations advanced in the earlier paper for holding that a declaration which contains the United States form of 'domestic jurisdiction' reservation lacks the quality of a valid declaration under the Optional Clause. By looking only at the form and not the substance of the United States reservation, it may perhaps be possible to reconcile it with the letter, although not the spirit, of Article 36 (6) of the Statute. In form the reservation does not deny the competence of the Court to decide any dispute as to its jurisdiction; it merely excludes from the United States acceptance of jurisdiction all disputes which come within the category of 'disputes with regard to matters which are essentially within the domestic jurisdiction of the United States of America as determined by the United States of America'. If in a particular case no such 'determination' is made by the United States, *cadit quaestio*. If, on the other hand, such a determination is made and is disputed, the Court remains competent to 'decide' the dispute even although it must do so in favour of the United States by reason of the terms of the reservation.[2] The substance of the matter is that the United States has invested itself with the power, through the use of this reservation, to prevent the Court from examining whether the United States acceptance of compulsory jurisdiction applies in any given case.[3]

[1] Vol. 31 (1954), pp. 131–7.

[2] It would also be competent to decide the question whether there had been a 'determination' by the United States bringing the reservation into play.

[3] It is tempting to suggest an intermediate interpretation which would leave the Court power to decide whether a 'determination' of matters essentially of domestic jurisdiction was a possible one in the particular case, having regard to established principles of international law. Such an interpretation appears, however, to be excluded by the abundant evidence that the United States intended its reservation to give it the complete right to insist upon its own determination of matters essentially of domestic jurisdiction. In the *Anglo-Iranian Oil Company* case (*I.C.J.*

DECLINE OF THE OPTIONAL CLAUSE   273

If the United States form of reservation is held to be compatible with the letter of Article 36 (6), it does not remove the second ground of objection to the reservation. The State concerned arrogates to itself a general power to veto the application of compulsory jurisdiction whenever a particular dispute arises. This form of escape clause is infinitely more pernicious than a right to terminate the declaration immediately on notice, *since it seeks to defeat the Court's compulsory jurisdiction even after the Application has been filed in the case*. If, as the United States appears to intend, the 'determination' that the dispute concerns a matter essentially of domestic jurisdiction is to be made after an Application has been filed, it has retroactive effect and avoids the operation of the rule in the *Nottebohm* case.[1] Thus, under this form of escape clause, the establishment of the Court's jurisdiction in any particular case will depend on the willingness of the State concerned to submit to jurisdiction after the case has arisen, and the professed acceptance of compulsory jurisdiction in the declaration is illusory.[2] Regrettably, five other States[3] have already adopted this form of escape clause despite its wide condemnation by jurists.[4]

Subjective reservations concerning multilateral treaties

The United States declaration contains another potentially subjective reservation because it excludes

'disputes arising under a multilateral treaty, unless (1) all Parties to the treaty affected by the decision are also Parties to the case before the Court, or (2) the United States of America specially agrees to jurisdiction'.

The effect of this reservation is far from clear. It was introduced into the United States declaration in the Senate, and the *travaux préparatoires* of the reservation do not indicate what exactly was its object.[5] Hudson takes the view that the Court would probably interpret the reservation by reference to Articles 62 and 63 of the Statute, which deal with the right of a third State to intervene in a case.[6] Article 62 allows a State to apply for leave to intervene when it 'consider[s] that it has an interest of a legal nature which may be affected by the decision in the case'. Article 63, on the other

---

Reports, 1952, p. 107) the Court held that recourse may be had to the *travaux préparatoires* of a declaration under the Optional Clause in order to ascertain the true intention.

[1] Page 261 above.

[2] In the previous volume of this *Year Book*, 31 (1954), pp. 133–4, the writer suggested that the declaration may be regarded as forming a useful basis for establishing jurisdiction on the principle of *forum prorogatum* rather than as a true acceptance of the Optional Clause.

[3] Mexico (1947), Pakistan (1948), France (1949), Liberia (1953), and India (1956).

[4] E.g. Preuss in *American Journal of International Law*, 40 (1946), pp. 720–36; Hudson, ibid., 41 (1947), pp. 9–14; Wilson, *The International Law Standard in Treaties of the United States* (1953), p. 44; Oppenheim, *International Law*, vol. 2 (7th ed., by Lauterpacht, 1952), pp. 62–63.

[5] See Wilcox in *American Journal of International Law*, 40 (1946), pp. 714–16, and Quincy Wright, ibid., 41 (1947), pp. 445–52.

[6] In *American Bar Association Journal*, 32 (1946), p. 832.

hand, gives a State an absolute right to intervene in a case whenever the construction of a multilateral treaty to which it is a party is in question. Hudson interprets Article 63 as laying down that, when the meaning of any multilateral convention is in issue in a case, every party to it has 'an interest of a legal nature which may be affected by the decision'. On that basis he concludes that in any case involving the interpretation of a multilateral treaty to which the United States is a party, the reservation requires every party to the treaty to have become a party to the case before the Court will be invested with compulsory jurisdiction over the United States. Lauterpacht expresses the same view of the effect of the reservation.[1] If this view is correct it means in practice that the reservation precludes the United States from being brought before the Court in a case involving the construction of a multilateral treaty unless it specifically consents to jurisdiction after the case has arisen.[2]

Dr. F. O. Wilcox maintains that the Senate did not have in mind so sweeping a reservation.[3] He suggests that by the words 'Parties to the treaty affected by the decision', the Senate meant parties 'directly affected' or 'legally affected' by the decision. On this basis, the reservation would not require all parties to the treaty, by reason only of their general interest in the construction of the treaty, to become parties to the case. Only those parties 'directly' or 'legally' affected by the decision as to the construction of the treaty would be required to be parties to the case. The distinction between parties 'directly' or 'legally' affected by the decision as to the meaning of the treaty and parties merely interested in the decision by reason of their general rights and obligations under the treaty, does not seem to be an easy one to draw. If a narrow interpretation is adopted of 'Parties affected by the decision', the effect of the reservation will be very small—much smaller than appears to have been intended by the Senate. If a broad interpretation is adopted, the practical effect will be much the same as under Hudson's view which has been set out above; the Court's jurisdiction will in each instance depend on an express submission to jurisdiction by the United States. If, as may well be the case, Dr. Wilcox's view of the meaning of the reservation is correct,[4] the uncertainty and difficulty attendant on its

---

[1] See Oppenheim, op. cit., p. 63.

[2] States do not intervene in a dispute between other States unless they believe that a substantial interest of their own is at risk in the case. It will also be observed that the reservation requires all parties to the treaty to be parties to the case; but the United States itself would not be a 'Party to the case before the Court' *unless the Court already had jurisdiction over the United States with respect to the case.*

[3] See *American Journal of International Law*, 40 (1946), pp. 714–16. Dr. Wilcox acted as assistant to the Foreign Relations Committee of the Senate.

[4] Professor Quincy Wright supports Dr. Wilcox and seems even to go somewhat farther; see *American Journal of International Law*, 41 (1947), pp. 445–52. By elaborate and not altogether convincing reasoning, he seems to conclude that the real point of the reservation is to guard against an arbitrary exercise by the Court of its discretion, under Article 62, to refuse intervention by a

DECLINE OF THE OPTIONAL CLAUSE   275

application will still leave the legal effect of the reservation obscure and the establishment of the Court's jurisdiction dependent on the will either of third States or of the United States itself. The reservation has been generally condemned as tending to withdraw from the Court, at the will of the United States, a large fraction of the legal disputes covered by the Optional Clause, because a sensible proportion of international disputes 'arise under a multilateral treaty'. Nor does the United States appear to have had any solid reasons for making the reservation, which seems only to have been inspired by vague fears and misconceptions as to the working of the Optional Clause in a case arising under a multilateral treaty. If adopted by other States, the reservation might seriously prejudice the effectiveness of the Optional Clause system of compulsory jurisdiction in a most important sphere of legal disputes. Fortunately, it has so far been adopted only by Pakistan.[1]

Reservation of a right to vary by giving notice

Attention has been drawn above[2] to the use that may be made of a right to terminate a declaration, by notice to the Secretary-General, for the purpose of varying the terms of the declaration. Portugal in a recent declaration, dated 19 December 1955,[3] has introduced a new escape device. She has made her declaration for one year and from then on until notice of termination is given and has, in addition, reserved the right at any time to exclude from the scope of her declaration 'any given category or categories of disputes by notifying the Secretary-General of the United Nations and with effect from the moment of such notifications'. By this reservation Portugal appears to have arrogated to herself the right to vary the scope of her acceptance of compulsory jurisdiction at any time during the currency of her declaration and with respect to any categories of disputes.

A reservation in the Portuguese form sets up a position analogous to that under a declaration immediately terminable on notice, and is open to all the same objections. The State concerned, as soon as it sees the possibility that an attempt may be made to start proceedings against it in regard to a particular matter, is able to take avoiding action by notifying the Secretary-General of the exclusion of that category of matters from its declaration. At first sight, indeed, this form of reservation appears to render the acceptance of compulsory jurisdiction completely illusory. Such

---

third State which considers itself to have an interest of a legal nature affected by the decision. Apart from the fact that when the case involves the construction of a multilateral treaty the Court under Article 63 has no such discretion, it may be doubted whether the Senate had any appreciation of the subtle argument advanced by Professor Wright.

[1] Pakistan declaration of 1948; see *Year Book of the International Court of Justice, 1954–5,* p. 196.   [2] At pp. 265–8.

[3] Presumably to be published in the *1955–6 Year Book of the International Court of Justice.*

would certainly be the case if retroactive effect were claimed for any future notification of a reservation, and a declaration which made this claim could hardly be regarded as an acceptance of the Optional Clause at all. The Portuguese reservation, however, expressly states that any future reservation is to have effect only from the date on which it is notified to the Secretary-General. This means that Portugal's acceptance of compulsory jurisdiction holds good with respect to any category of matters until the exclusion of that category has been notified to the Secretary-General. Accordingly, under the rule in the *Nottebohm* case,[1] the filing of an Application with respect to any particular matter within the category would be effective to bind Portugal to submit to the Court's jurisdiction, and the subsequent notification of a reservation would be of no avail to put a stop to the proceedings. The introduction of this form of reservation is nevertheless to be condemned as tending to frustrate the purpose of the Optional Clause in the same way and to much the same extent as a provision whereby a declaration is made immediately terminable by notice to the Secretary-General. A declaration, like that of Portugal, in which both these forms of escape clause are combined, must be regarded as hardly more than a nominal acceptance of compulsory jurisdiction.

Other reservations of broad and uncertain scope

A number of other reservations leave the scope of the compulsory jurisdiction accepted by the State concerned in considerable uncertainty. Amongst these, attention may be drawn to two reservations made respectively by Salvador in 1921 and Israel in 1950.[2] The Salvador reservation excludes 'disputes or differences concerning points or questions *which cannot be submitted to arbitration in accordance with the political constitution of Salvador*'. The Israel declaration is a strange one, for it excepts all disputes which 'involve a legal title created or conferred by a government or authority other than the Government of the State of Israel or an authority under the jurisdiction of that Government'. Space does not permit an examination of the legal effect of these reservations. It may, however, be observed that the Salvador reservation would appear to mean that Salvador, if she wishes, may vary the scope of her acceptance of the Optional Clause by amending her Constitution.

§ 7. Reciprocity and escape clauses

The primary meaning of the condition of reciprocity contained in the Optional Clause, it has been seen in § 4 above, is that for the Optional Clause jurisdiction to apply to a particular dispute, both States must have

---

[1] See above, p. 261.
[2] *Year Book of the International Court of Justice, 1954–5*, at pp. 191 and 193, respectively.

DECLINE OF THE OPTIONAL CLAUSE   277

made a declaration which comprises the particular dispute within its scope. It was also seen[1] that the operation of the condition of reciprocity had been worked out with special reference to conditions, reservations and limitations in regard to which reciprocity means that a State may always invoke a provision in its opponent's declaration for the purpose of excluding a particular dispute from the application of the Optional Clause jurisdiction. It is, therefore, beyond question that an escape clause in the form of a reservation operates in a particular dispute not only in favour of the State which made it but also in favour of its opponent. A reservation, for example, by State *A* of disputes in regard to matters which are essentially within its domestic jurisdiction as determined by itself, if it is not invalid, arms every other State with the power, whenever a dispute arises with State *A*, to 'determine' the matters in issue to be within its own domestic jurisdiction and, by so doing, to oust the Court's compulsory jurisdiction. The principle of reciprocity requires that escape clauses in the form of reservations should work both ways. It was, however, pointed out in the previous volume of this *Year Book*[2] that in the case of subjective reservations of this kind the reciprocity may be more apparent than real. One State, by reason of its legal convictions or its other interests, may find it impossible to designate a certain class of matters as 'matters essentially of domestic jurisdiction', whereas another State may have less scruples about pursuing a purely opportunist policy in determining a matter to be a matter within its domestic jurisdiction for the sole purpose of avoiding compulsory jurisdiction in an individual case. This is in itself an additional objection to the admissibility of subjective reservations in declarations under the Optional Clause.

The Portuguese reservation, which asserts a right to qualify the acceptance of compulsory jurisdiction at any time by notifying new reservations, brings out the importance of the bilateral rather than multilateral character of the reciprocal obligations established between States under the Optional Clause.[3] The condition of reciprocity confers upon every other State adhering to the Clause the right, *vis-à-vis* Portugal, to qualify its acceptance of compulsory jurisdiction by notifying new reservations. But any such notification of a new reservation would be ineffective to alter the obligations of the State concerned under the Optional Clause with respect to any State other than Portugal. The right to make the new reservation has its sole foundation in the right to complete reciprocity with Portugal, and exists only with respect to Portugal. Reciprocity requires, but only requires, that each State should have the right to make new reservations *excluding particular categories of disputes with Portugal* from its acceptance of compulsory jurisdiction under the Optional Clause.

[1] Page 257 above.   [2] 31 (1954), at p. 135.   [3] See above, p. 254.

278   DECLINE OF THE OPTIONAL CLAUSE

The operation of reciprocity in regard to time-limits has not, as yet, provoked much discussion. It is inherent in the Optional Clause system of compulsory jurisdiction that it requires both States to be simultaneously subject to the Clause before the jurisdiction can be invoked. In other words, the system requires reciprocity of obligation to exist at the date when the Application is filed in a case, which means that both declarations must be current at that date. Both declarations must concur in comprising the date of the filing of the Application within the periods of their validity. In regard to the time factor, therefore, reciprocity primarily means that the duration of the mutual obligations—the juridical bond—between any two States under the Optional Clause is limited to the joint period during which both declarations are in force. For example, in the *Electricity Company of Sofia and Bulgaria* case,[1] Bulgaria's declaration, made in 1921, was without time-limit, while that of Belgium, made on 10 March 1926, was to run for a period of fifteen years; and Judge Anzilotti referred to the two declarations as combining to create an agreement between the two States whose duration was fifteen years from 10 March 1926.

There is, however, another aspect of reciprocity in regard to time-limits which seems to deserve attention, since it may well assume importance in view of the increasing number of declarations which are immediately terminable on notice to the Secretary-General. Reciprocity would seem to demand that in any given pair of States each should have the same right as the other to terminate the juridical bond existing between them under the Optional Clause. This is so even in the ordinary case where State *A*'s declaration is without time-limit while State *B*'s is for a period of five or ten years. State *B* at the end of the period may choose whether to renew or to terminate its obligations towards State *A* under the Optional Clause. State *A* may reasonably contend that, while not retracting its general acceptance of the Optional Clause, it also is entitled at the end of the period to choose whether or not to continue its particular obligations towards State *B*. It is one thing to hold that a unilateral declaration made without time-limit binds the State concerned indefinitely toward other States which have made similar declarations. It is quite another thing to hold that such a unilateral declaration is binding indefinitely towards other States which have not undertaken the same commitment. The inequality in the positions of the two States under the Optional Clause, if the principle of reciprocity is not applied to time-limits, becomes absolutely inadmissible when State *A*'s declaration is without time-limit while that of State *B* is immediately terminable on notice to the Secretary-General. It would be intolerable that State *B* should always be able, merely by giving notice, to terminate at any moment its liability to compulsory jurisdiction *vis-à-vis* State *A*, whilst the

[1] (1939): Series A/B, No. 77.

latter remained perpetually bound to submit to the Court's jurisdiction at the suit of State *B*. The Court has not yet had occasion to examine this aspect of the operation of reciprocity in relation to time-limits. In the light, however, of its interpretation of the condition of reciprocity in regard to reservations, the Court, it is believed, must hold that under the Optional Clause each State, with respect to any other State, has the same right to terminate its acceptance of compulsory jurisdiction as is possessed by that other State.

The point can, perhaps, be illustrated by considering the declarations of Norway, Sweden and the United Kingdom in the year 1950, when the United Kingdom filed its Application in the *Anglo-Norwegian Fisheries* case.[1] At that date, the United Kingdom's declaration was terminable on notice to the Secretary-General, while those of both Norway and Sweden had fixed time-limits expiring in 1956. Assuming the application of reciprocity to time-limits, Norway would then have been entitled to give notice to the Secretary-General of the termination of her declaration with respect to the United Kingdom in virtue of the right of termination contained in the latter's declaration. If she had done so before the filing of the United Kingdom's Application in the case, she would have defeated the Application. *On the other hand, the termination of her declaration vis-à-vis the United Kingdom would have left her declaration in full force vis-à-vis Sweden.* A question might be raised as to whether Norway's termination of her declaration would operate only with respect to the United Kingdom or also with respect to all other States which had reserved a right of termination upon notice to the Secretary-General. It seems clear, however, that if Norway had purported to terminate her obligation under the Optional Clause only with reference to the United Kingdom and on the basis of a right derived reciprocally from the United Kingdom's declaration, Norway's declaration would remain in full force with respect to other States. The relations established between States under the Optional Clause, as has been emphasized,[2] are of a bilateral rather than multilateral character. A notification to the Secretary-General intended to alter State *A*'s obligations with respect only to State *B* has no effect therefore on State *A*'s obligations under the Optional Clause with respect to other States. To allow a State, on the ground of reciprocity in regard to time-limits, the right to terminate its obligations under the Optional Clause with reference only to a particular State or States may add to the complexity of the Optional Clause system. To refuse it such a right would, however, be to establish a gross inequality between States in regard to the termination of their obligations under the Optional Clause.

[1] *I.C.J. Reports*, 1951, p. 116.
[2] See above, p. 254.

§ 8. *The position of a State which refrains from making a declaration*

A State which is a party to the Statute of the Court but does not make a declaration under the Optional Clause is in a highly favoured position. Acceptance of the Statute by itself carries no liability to appear in front of the Court in a contentious case at the suit of another State. Before it can come under any liability to appear as defendant in a case, a State must specifically have accepted the Court's contentious jurisdiction either by treaty or by unilateral declaration under the Optional Clause. On the other hand, the mere fact that a State is a party to the Statute gives it the power, under the Optional Clause, at any moment to put itself into the position of being able instantly to bring before the Court any States which have already subscribed to the Optional Clause in any case covered by the terms of their declarations. Being a party to the Statute, it has the right under the Optional Clause *at any time and without reference to any other State* to make a declaration recognizing the compulsory jurisdiction of the Court in relation to States which also subscribe to the Optional Clause. If it does so, it automatically has the right to use the procedure provided in Article 40 (1) of the Statute and Article 32 (2) of the Rules and, by filing an Application with the Registrar, may at once bring before the Court compulsorily any other State which subscribes to the Optional Clause in any case covered by the terms of its own and its opponent's declarations. The making of the declaration, its deposit with the Secretary-General of the United Nations and the filing of the Application can all be effected within a single day. Assuming that the case in fact falls within the terms of the declarations of the plaintiff and defendant States, the filing of the Application establishes immediately and conclusively the jurisdiction of the Court over the case. Accordingly, so far as concerns the power to institute proceedings under the Optional Clause against another State, a party to the Statute which refrains from making a declaration is in almost the same position as the State which in good faith has undertaken a general obligation to submit to compulsory jurisdiction for a substantial, or even indefinite, period of years.

There is, in consequence, a glaring inequality in the position of a State which does and a State which does not make a declaration under the Optional Clause. The former State, for practical purposes, is continuously liable to be brought before the Court compulsorily at the suit of the latter, whereas the latter is not liable to be brought before the Court at the suit of the former unless and until it chooses to initiate proceedings before the Court as plaintiff and makes a declaration under the Optional Clause *ad hoc* expressly for that purpose. This fundamental lack of reciprocity between the positions of States which do and States which do not make declarations is aggravated by the fact that it seems to be open to a State which is driven to make a declaration in order to institute proceedings as plaintiff, to exploit its opponent's general commitment under the Optional Clause without itself undertaking much more than a nominal commitment. Thus, the Statute and the Rules do not in terms preclude a State which hitherto has held itself entirely aloof from the Optional Clause from making a declaration for a token period of 12, 6, or even 3 months for the sole purpose of instituting proceedings against another State in a particular case, and from then filing an Application in the case. On the expiry of the token period, while the rule in the *Nottebohm* case[1] would maintain the Application before the Court until a final judgment had been pronounced in the case, the plaintiff State, by the lapse of its declaration, would have regained its former total immunity from process under the Optional Clause. Similarly, the Statute and Rules do not in terms preclude a State which is anxious to submit a particular case to the Court from making a declaration expressed only to run 'until notice of termination is given', leaving itself free to put an end to its acceptance of the Optional Clause as soon as it has achieved its object. Indeed, the letter of the Statute might be claimed to permit a State to make a declaration today, file an Application in a particular case immediately afterwards, and tomorrow give notice to terminate the declaration. Opportunism so flagrant would, it is believed, be open to challenge on the grounds of a manifest lack of *bona fides* in making the declaration and of a total absence of reciprocity between the States concerned. But, leaving aside such a *reductio ad absurdum* case, it seems clear that a State may hold aloof for years from the compulsory jurisdiction of the Court under the Optional Clause and then make a declaration *ad hoc* for a particular case in a form which involves it in only a very transient acceptance of the Clause.

Admittedly, a State which makes a declaration even for a very brief period exposes itself during that period to the risk of being dragged before the Court by any State which has subscribed to the Optional Clause, and this risk might cause some States to hesitate before venturing on a declaration under the Optional Clause. Since, however, a State is free, by reservations and conditions, to place drastic limits upon the categories of matters covered by its declaration, it could usually so frame the latter as to include the particular dispute in which it sought to be plaintiff and yet exclude other disputes in respect of which it felt itself to be vulnerable. Indeed, if the United Kingdom's declaration of 1946 regarding the boundaries of British Honduras is a valid form of declaration, it may be open to a State in terms to limit the scope of its declaration to the category of matters with which the particular case in which it seeks to be plaintiff is concerned. Again, such a very particular and opportunist declaration may

---

[1] See above, pp. 261–3.

be open to challenge on the ground of a manifest lack of reciprocity between the two States under the Optional Clause. But a State which does not go to quite such absurd lengths can quite easily frame the scope of its declaration so as to enable it to take advantage of the Optional Clause jurisdiction for a particular case, without exposing itself to any substantial risk of being forced into Court under the Clause in another case.

Under the Optional Clause, therefore, the State which refrains from making a declaration may sit immune on the side-lines and yet, when the moment is favourable, descend for a brief space of time on to the field of play to pounce upon one of the unsuspecting States already there and afterwards speedily return to its secure seat on the side-lines. The result is that so long as a fair number of States are subscribers to the Optional Clause, which is the position today, there is really no point at all in adhering to the Clause in advance of an actual case. The State which does not make a declaration now has the best of both worlds. It is not, therefore, to be wondered at that, despite the very large majority at the San Francisco Conference in favour of giving the new International Court of Justice compulsory jurisdiction for all legal disputes, there have been so few new subscribers to the Optional Clause. Still less is it to be wondered at that there has been an increasing tendency amongst those States which have subscribed to the Optional Clause to introduce into their declarations escape or hedging clauses leaving them the maximum freedom of manœuvre when faced with the threat of proceedings in an actual case. Indeed, the highly privileged position of the State which does not make a declaration goes a long way to justify the use of declarations immediately terminable by notice and even attempts to frame reservations which will enable the State concerned, if it thinks fit, to decline jurisdiction in individual cases. Regrettable and retrograde though these devices may be, it seems idle to make a great outcry about them without first doing something to ensure a greater degree of reciprocity between States which regularly subscribe to the Optional Clause and States which prefer normally to stay immune from compulsory jurisdiction.

A State has, in fact, a means of protecting itself against the State which remains outside the Optional Clause and then suddenly has recourse to it for the purpose of starting proceedings in a particular case. It need only insert in its own declaration a reservation excluding ' all disputes with a State which at the date of the ratification of the declaration has not accepted the Optional Clause, except disputes which arise after the acceptance of the Optional Clause by that State and with regard to situations or facts subsequent to the said acceptance'. Such a reservation would simply be the normal formula for a limitation *ratione temporis* so drawn as to exclude disputes already in existence at the date of any subsequent declaration by another State, instead of the usual exclusion of disputes already in existence at the date of the State's own declaration. The double form of reservation—'disputes which arise after the acceptance of the Optional Clause with regard to situations or facts subsequent to the said acceptance'—would effectively prevent a State from making a declaration under the Optional Clause for the sole purpose of starting proceedings in a particular case.[1] Alternatively, the reservation might be framed on the lines of the amendment to the Statute which is suggested on p. 286 below.

If it is true that the making of a temporary declaration for the purpose of taking an individual case to the Court has not yet been a feature of State practice under the Optional Clause, there is a real risk of such a development. On 19 December 1955, Portugal made a declaration valid for twelve months and thereafter until notice of termination is given, deposited the declaration with the Secretary-General on the same day, and within three days had filed an Application against India in regard to alleged Portuguese rights of passage over Indian territory. It can, no doubt, be urged in Portugal's favour that she had only recently become a party to the new Statute. Moreover, India's declaration was terminable by notice to the Secretary-General. Even so, her lightning declaration and Application in this case sets an ominous precedent and illustrates the possibilities of abuse of the Optional Clause in an individual case by a State not itself previously liable to compulsory jurisdiction.[2]

§ 9. *The Optional Clause system today*

That there has been a sensible decline in the quality of State practice under the Optional Clause is manifest. If the tendencies discussed in the present article continue, the large majority of declarations will become terminable either immediately or on short notice, while a number will contain particular escape clauses. There appears even to be some danger that the attitude of States towards the Optional Clause may degenerate into one of pure opportunism, declarations being made, cancelled and varied as the immediate interests of each State may dictate. It is, therefore, proposed to conclude this article with a brief reappraisal of the Optional Clause system of compulsory jurisdiction.

The Optional Clause came into existence for the very reason that some

---

[1] At the same time, the reservation would not cut out new disputes arising in regard to past situations or facts, unless the past situation or fact was the *source* of the dispute in the sense that it had really started the dispute. Thus, the limitation would only cut out disputes which were already developing before the second State made its declaration.

[2] The immediate filing of Portugal's Application raises in addition an interesting question of reciprocity, since in her declaration she reserved the right at any time in the future to make reservations. The immediate filing of the Application, in part at least, stultified India's reciprocal right to make use of this reservation in Portugal's declaration.

284 DECLINE OF THE OPTIONAL CLAUSE

States, especially the Great Powers, would not undertake in advance to submit legal disputes of any importance to settlement by an independently elected tribunal administering international law. It constituted an invitation to States to pluck up courage and undertake this commitment even if only for a trial period and even if only for a limited range of disputes. The mistake, if it was a mistake,[1] was to make the undertaking of this commitment a wholly unilateral act, and then to give an almost complete discretion to each State as to when and for how long and on what conditions it would undertake the commitment. The virtual absence of any restrictions as to the terms on which a State might adhere to the Optional Clause, while it might open the gate to a larger circle of adherents, was calculated to give full rein to those nervous fears and political inhibitions which weigh upon Governments called upon to submit the interests of their State to determination by an independent, external, authority. It was also calculated to make State practice under the Optional Clause sensitive to the barometer of international confidence in (1) the Court as a judicial tribunal and (2) the order and stability of international affairs.

After 1920, as confidence in the Court grew, a slowly widening circle of States adhered, and the prospect of establishing eventually a general system of compulsory jurisdiction through the Optional Clause did not appear altogether visionary. The adherence of Great Britain in 1929 provided a strong stimulus to acceptance of the Optional Clause by other States. At the same time, however, it provided a sharp reminder of the distance which had yet to be travelled before complete submission to the judicial process became an integral part of the international order. Great Britain was a State with large and varied interests at stake and she made free use of the power given in the Optional Clause to frame the terms of her submission to jurisdiction to suit her own circumstances. Other States followed her example; and as the limitations, reservations and conditions multiplied, the ambit of the Optional Clause system of jurisdiction contracted. Meanwhile, the rapid deterioration in international relations in the 1930's resulted in a general waning of confidence in international action, and a number of States which had accepted the Optional Clause for limited periods allowed their acceptances to lapse.

At the San Francisco Conference there seems to have been little disposition to remove the serious weaknesses inherent in the Optional Clause by reason of the virtually unrestricted power permitted to each individual State of framing the conditions of its adherence to the Clause. The question was raised in a sub-committee by Canada and Australia, the latter

---

[1] It is arguable that the almost invincible repugnance of many States to submitting their interests to decision by an external body made it essential to give the widest possible discretion in the framing of declarations under the Optional Clause, if there was to be any prospect of a general acceptance of compulsory jurisdiction.

DECLINE OF THE OPTIONAL CLAUSE   285

proposing that there should be an exhaustive list of permitted reservations, on the lines adopted in the General Act of Geneva of 1928.[1] But the sub-committee voted in favour of maintaining the existing text of the Optional Clause, while it also emphasized that this text had been interpreted as authorizing the making of reservations. When another Great Power with large and varied interests at stake, the United States, brought itself to adhere to the Optional Clause in 1946, it also made free use of its right unilaterally to frame the conditions of its acceptance of the Clause. It is debatable, as has been pointed out above,[2] whether the United States did not in fact go beyond even the wide liberty of making reservations which the Optional Clause allows. However that may be, the conclusion is almost inevitable that the fabric of the Optional Clause system of jurisdiction has been more weakened by the introduction into it of the United States reservations than it has been strengthened by the adhesion of another Great Power. There has been no such general widening of the circle of States bound by the Optional Clause as might compensate for the de-preciation in the quality of acceptances of the Clause under the new Statute.

It is comparatively easy to point out the technical defects of the Optional Clause and to suggest remedies. First, there is the absurdity of a system of compulsory jurisdiction which permits a right of immediate termination of the obligation by unilateral act. The remedy would be to tighten up the time-limit provision in Article 36 (3) and to require declara-tions to be made for not less than a specified minimum period. The ideal minimum would be five years, but something a little less stringent may be more in keeping with the coy attitude of States towards the Optional Clause. A provision requiring declarations to be made either for a mini-mum period of two years or until not less than one year's notice of ter-mination is given could hardly be considered unduly strict and yet would prevent the opportunist contracting in and out which is possible under the present Statute.

Secondly, there is the virtually unfettered power to restrict the scope of declarations by limitations, reservations and conditions. The remedy would be that proposed by Canada and Australia, namely, to allow only specified kinds of authorized exceptions, on the lines of the General Act of Geneva. The General Act list leaves open a decidedly wide range of reservations but it does, at least, attempt to exclude vague and subjective reservations such as now threaten to undermine the Optional Clause system.[3]

---

[1] Report of Sub-committee D of Committee 1 of Commission IV; U.N.C.I.O., vol. xiii, p. 558.   [2] Pp. 271–5.

[3] Article 39 of the General Act reads as follows:

'1. In addition to the [condition of reciprocity], a Party, in acceding to the present General

Thirdly, there is the anomaly that a State which has deliberately remained outside the Optional Clause system may yet by a stroke of the pen put itself into a position instantly to institute proceedings under the Clause. Opinions may differ as to whether any provision should be introduced into the Statute to put an end to this anomaly, since the 'condition of reciprocity' would make any restriction imposed on a newcomer operate both ways. Moreover, as pointed out above,[1] it is already possible for a State, if it wishes, to guard against an opportunist declaration on the part of an outsider by means of an appropriate limitation *ratione temporis*. It is, however, believed that a specific statutory provision is desirable because the present position is both palpably unfair to States which are genuine adherents to the Optional Clause system and is a positive encouragement to other States to remain outside the system. An appropriate rule is not easy to formulate, but the insertion at the end of Article 36 (2) of a proviso on the following lines might, perhaps, serve:

'Provided that for a period of two years after the date when any such declaration comes into force it shall not have effect with respect to a dispute concerning matters which were the subject of differences between the Parties during the two years immediately preceding that date.'

Such a provision would cut out the worst kinds of opportunism without making too large an inroad into the Court's jurisdiction over 'past' disputes.

The technical weaknesses of the Optional Clause are matters which merit attention even although, in the present state of international relations, there may not be much prospect of removing them by amendment of the Statute of the Court. It would, however, be naïve to suppose that these weaknesses are a principal cause of the decline of the Optional Clause system of jurisdiction. During the life of the present Court the extreme tension between the Soviet and the Western blocs, the revolutionary political changes in some parts of the world, and the greater fluidity of international law itself, have combined to create an international climate unfavourable to the development of the Optional Clause system. These influences have not left the Court itself altogether untouched, and it may

Act, may make his acceptance conditional upon the reservations exhaustively enumerated in the following paragraph. These reservations must be indicated at the time of accession.
    '2. These reservations may be such as to exclude from the procedure described in the present Act:
        a. Disputes arising out of facts prior to the accession either of the Party making the reservation or of any other Party with whom the said Party may have a dispute;
        b. Disputes concerning questions which by international law are solely within the domestic jurisdiction of States;
        c. Disputes concerning particular cases or clearly specified subject-matters, such as territorial status, or disputes falling within clearly defined categories.'

[1] Page 282.

DECLINE OF THE OPTIONAL CLAUSE   287

be doubted whether the new Court has yet gained for itself the full measure of confidence which the old Court enjoyed. At any rate, until a greater sense of security and solidarity has returned to the international community, expansion of the Court's compulsory jurisdiction by unilateral action under the Optional Clause is hardly to be expected. The immediate objective must rather be to prevent the further deterioration of State practice in framing the terms of declarations, which, if not checked, may bring the whole system into disrepute and produce not an expansion but a contraction of the Court's compulsory jurisdiction under the Optional Clause. If this objective is achieved, the Optional Clause may still serve the useful, if limited, purpose of providing a basis for the exercise of the Court's jurisdiction in a number of particular cases.

[13]

Settlement of Disputes Arising Out of the Law of the Sea Convention

LOUIS B. SOHN*

INTRODUCTION

On the last day of the Caracas session of the Third Conference on the Law of the Sea a group of States presented a working paper on the settlement of law of the sea disputes.[1] It was the result of informal consultations held by a group of more than thirty States, from all the regions of the world, during the last month of the Conference.[2] The working paper set out various possible alternatives, together with notes indicating relevant precedents. The hope was expressed that the working paper might serve as a framework for further discussions at the next session of the Conference.

The proposals included in the working paper are based on a long tradition of submission to arbitration or judicial settlement of disputes relating to the interpretation or application of international

---

* Bemis Professor of International Law, Harvard University.
1. U.N. Doc. A/CONF.62/L.7 (1974). *See also* 71 DEP'T STATE BULL. 418 (1974).
2. The Co-Chairmen of the Working Group were Ambassadors Reynaldo Galindo Pohl (El Salvador) and R.L. Harry (Australia); Professor Louis B. Sohn (U.S.A.) acted as Rapporteur. 71 DEP'T STATE BULL. 394 (1974); Borgese, *The Law of the Sea*, 7 THE CENTER MAGAZINE, November/December, 1974, at 25, 33. *See also* the statement by Ambassador Galindo Pohl, Aug. 29, 1974, U.N. Doc. A/CONF.62/SR.51, at 3 (prov. ed. 1974).

agreements.[3] Many current multilateral and bilateral treaties contain provisions on dispute settlement as a matter of routine.[4] In
the law of the sea negotiations the settlement of disputes issue
has been discussed primarily in connection with the provisions relating to the seabed;[5] some proposals have also been made with
respect to the settlement of disputes relating to fisheries.[6] Apart
from the original proposals of Malta which provided for an International Maritime Court,[7] there was practically no discussion in the
preparatory work for the Conference of the question of an overall provision for dispute settlement until the very end, when the
United States raised the issue.[8] The Caracas Working Group took

---

3. Already in 1890, the Washington Conference of American States
called for obligatory arbitration of all controversies concerning "the validity, construction and enforcement of treaties." SCOTT, INTERNATIONAL CON
FERENCES OF AMERICAN STATES 40 (1931). A similar provision was included
by the Second Conference of American States in the 1902 treaty of arbitration. *Id.* at 100. *See also* the widely imitated treaty between Argentina
and Italy of September 18, 1907 which provided for the arbitration of differences concerning interpretation and application of conventions. An Italian initiative in the 1870's led to the insertion in many bilateral treaties
of the so-called compromissory clauses providing for submission to arbitration of questions concerning the interpretation and application of these treaties. For a list of these early treaties, *see* H. CORY, COMPULSORY ARBITRA
TION OF INTERNATIONAL DISPUTES 22-24 (1932).

4. More than two hundred such provisions have been collected by the
Secretariat of the United Nations in the volume A SURVEY OF TREATY PROVI
SIONS FOR THE PACIFIC SETTLEMENT OF INTERNATIONAL DISPUTES 1949-1962
(U.N. Publ. 66.V.5) (1966) (hereinafter cited as U.N. Survey). A systematic collection of such provisions may be found in H. BLIX & J. EMERSON,
THE TREATY MAKER'S HANDBOOK (1973) (hereinafter cited as BLIX). *See
also* Comment, *Toward Peaceful Settlement of Ocean Space Disputes: A
Working Paper,* 11 SAN DIEGO L. REV. 733 (1974).

5. For a summary of the early proposals, *see* Sohn, *A Tribunal for the
Sea-Bed or the Oceans,* 32 ZEITSCHRIFT FÜR AUSLÄNDISCHES ÖFFENTLICHES
RECHT UND VÖLKERRECHT 253 (1972). The latest alternative proposals are
reproduced in 2 Report of the Committee on the Peaceful Uses of the Sea-
Bed and the Ocean Floor beyond the Limits of National Jurisdiction, 28
U.N. GAOR, Supp. 21, at 130-36, U.N. Doc. A/9021 (1973).

6. The 1958 Geneva Convention on Fishing and Conservation of the Living Resources of the High Seas contained in articles 9-11 elaborate provisions for dispute settlement. [1966] 17 U.S.T. 138, T.I.A.S. No. 5969, 559
U.N.T.S. 285. *See also* recent proposals by the United States, U.N. Doc. A/
AC.138/SC.II/L.9 (1972); Japan, U.N. Doc. A/AC.138/SC.II/L.12 (1972);
and Australia and New Zealand, A/CONF.62/C.2/L.57/Rev. 1 (1974).

7. Malta: Draft Ocean Space Treaty, ch. xxvi, U.N. Doc. A/AC.138/53;
21 U.N. GAOR, Supp. 21, at 105, 176, U.N. Doc. A/8421 (1971).

8. United States, Draft Articles for a Chapter on the Settlement of Disputes, U.N. Doc. A/AC.138/97 (1973). In introducing this proposal, Mr.
Stevenson made the following statement (69 DEP'T STATE BULL. 412, 414
(1973)):

 Our general view is that a system is needed that insures, to the
 maximum possible extent, uniform interpretation and immediate
 access to dispute-settlement machinery in urgent situations while
 at the same time preserving the flexibility of states to agree to re-

this United States proposal into account, but proceeded independently from it on the basis of a special questionnaire elaborated at one of its early sessions.[9] Early in its proceedings the Working Group decided positively that the future Law of the Sea Convention should include effective dispute settlement provisions, which should be contained in a separate chapter of the Convention, without prejudice to special provisions which might be contained in other chapters of the Convention. In particular, the Working Group prepared alternative provisions on the following subjects:

1. Obligation to settle disputes under the Convention by peaceful means.
2. Settlement of disputes by means chosen by the parties.
3. Clause relating to other obligations with respect to dispute settlement.
4. Clause relating to settlement procedures not entailing a binding decision.
5. Obligation to resort to a means of settlement resulting in a binding decision.
6. The relationship between general and functional approaches.
7. Parties to a dispute.
8. Local remedies.
9. Advisory jurisdiction.
10. Law applicable.
11. Exceptions and reservations to the dispute settlement provisions.

The subsequent sections of this paper will deal seriatim with these questions.

OBLIGATION TO SETTLE DISPUTES UNDER THE CONVENTION BY PEACEFUL MEANS

The Charter of the United Nations provides in article 2(3) that all Members of the United Nations "shall settle their disputes by

---

solve their disputes by a variety of means. We have noted in particular the wishes of many states to resolve disputes on the basis of procedures agreed on a regional basis. What has emerged in our consideration of this question is the idea of dispute settlement by general, regional, or special agreement but with a law of the sea tribunal which would be available in cases where states do not agree to settle the disputes through other procedures.

9. The papers of the Working Group have not been published, and no official minutes have been kept. The references to the proceedings of the Group in this article are based on the author's notes and recollections.

peaceful means in such a manner that international peace and security, and justice, are not endangered." In addition, article 33(1) imposes an obligation on the "parties to any dispute, the continuance of which is likely to endanger the maintenance of international peace and security," to seek a solution, first of all, "by negotiation, inquiry, mediation, conciliation, arbitration, judicial settlement, resort to regional agencies or arrangements, or other peaceful means of their own choice."

It would seem unnecessary to repeat these obligations in any other international instrument, and they should be implied in any dispute which might arise, regardless of its subject-matter. Nevertheless, some States would like to see in the Law of the Sea Convention an explicit reference to the duty to settle a dispute through the peaceful means indicated in article 33 of the Charter. They did point out the fact that the important document forming the basis of the law of the sea negotiations, the Declaration of Principles Governing the Sea-Bed and the Ocean Floor, and the Subsoil Thereof, beyond the Limits of National Jurisdiction, proclaimed in paragraph 15 that the "parties to any dispute relating to activities in the area and its resources shall resolve such dispute by the measures mentioned in Article 33 of the Charter of the United Nations and such procedures for settling disputes as may be agreed upon in the international regime to be established."[10] Similar provisions are contained in various international agreements and in some proposals made during the law of the sea negotiations.[11]

In view of the fact that the Declaration on Principles of International Law concerning Friendly Relations and Cooperation among States in accordance with the Charter of the United Nations, which was adopted by the General Assembly in 1970, contained an elabora-

---

10. Adopted by G.A. Res. 2749 (XXV), 25 U.N. GAOR, Supp. 28, at 24-25, U.N. Doc. A/8028 (1971).

11. *See, e.g.*, the Vienna Convention on the Law of Treaties, of May 23, 1969, article 65(3), U.N. Doc. A/CONF. 39/27 (1969), 63 AMERICAN J. INT'L LAW 875 (1969); Treaty of Friendship and Neighbourly Relations between Iraq and Turkey, of March 29, 1946, art. 5(1), 37 U.N.T.S. 226; Treaty of Friendship between Turkey and Transjordan (now Jordan), of January 11, 1947, article 4, 14 U.N.T.S. 49. *See also* the Geneva Convention on Fishing and Conservation of the Living Resources of the High Seas, of April 29, 1958, article 9(1), [1966] 17 U.S.T. 138, T.I.A.S. No. 5969, 559 U.N.T.S. 285. It may be noted that a Canadian Working Paper on International Regime and Machinery contained the following comment: "While the future sea-bed treaty should provide for the resolution of disputes in accordance with Article 33 of the UN Charter it is essential that further procedures for the settlement of disputes should be included in the treaty." U.N. Doc. A/AC.138/59 (1971); 26 GAOR, Supp. 21, at 218, U.N. Doc. A/8421 (1971). A similar statement is contained in a Polish Working Paper, U.N. Doc. A/AC.138/44, para. 24 (1971); 26 GAOR, Supp. 21, at 81, U.N. Doc. A/8421 (1971).

[VOL. 12: 495, 1975] *Law of The Sea Convention*
SAN DIEGO LAW REVIEW

tion of the obligation embodied in article 2(3) of the U.N. Charter, it has been suggested that reference should be also made to that Declaration.[12] Others would prefer to have no reference to the Declaration or at most to include such a reference only in a preambular phrase.

Consequently, the Working Group proposed the following alternative texts:[13]

Alternative A

The Contracting Parties shall settle any dispute between them relating to the interpretation or application of this Convention through the peaceful means indicated in Article 33 of the Charter of the United Nations.

Alternative B

[Having regard to the Declaration on Principles of International Law concerning Friendly Relations and Cooperation among States in accordance with the Charter of the United Nations,] the Contracting Parties shall settle any dispute between them relating to the interpretation or application of this Convention by peaceful means in conformity with the Charter of the United Nations.

SETTLEMENT OF DISPUTES BY MEANS CHOSEN BY THE PARTIES

A reference to article 33 of the Charter implicitly includes the enumeration in that article of means of settlement to be used by the parties. That article also makes clear that the parties are free to use, in the first place, any peaceful means of their own choice. Nevertheless it was considered desirable to confirm explicitly the right of the parties to choose freely any peaceful means they consider suitable for the settlement of a particular dispute, and to list the means which might, or should be, used.[14]

Consequently, the Working Group suggested the following alternative texts, the first of which puts an emphasis on the obligation to consult on the choice of appropriate means:[15]

---

12. The text of the Declaration was approved by G.A. Res. 2625 (XXV), 25 U.N. GAOR, Supp. 28, at 121-24, U.N. Doc. A/8028 (1970). It is referred to in the Declaration of Principles Governing the Sea-Bed, *supra* note 10, at para. 6.

13. U.N. Doc. A/CONF.62/L.7, at 2 (1974).

14. Similar provisions are contained in the Antarctic Treaty, of December 1, 1959, article 11(1), [1961] 12 U.S.T. 794, T.I.A.S. No. 4780, 402 U.N.T.S. 71; and in the Single Convention on Narcotic Drugs, of March 30, 1961, art. 48(1), [1967] 18 U.S.T. 1407, T.I.A.S. No. 6298, 520 U.N.T.S. 204. *See also* the United States proposal in U.N. Doc. A/AC.138/97, art. 1 (1973).

15. U.N. Doc. A/CONF.62/L.7, at 4 (1974).

Alternative A

If any dispute arises between two or more Contracting Parties relating to the interpretation or application of this Convention, those Parties shall consult together with a view to the settlement of the dispute by negotiation, inquiry, mediation, conciliation, arbitration, judicial settlement, recourse to special procedures provided for by an international or regional organization, or other peaceful means of their own choice.

Alternative B

The parties to the dispute may agree to settle the dispute by any peaceful means of their own choice, including negotiation, mediation, inquiry, conciliation, arbitration, judicial settlement, or recourse to special procedures provided for by an international or regional organization.

CLAUSE RELATING TO OTHER OBLIGATIONS WITH RESPECT TO DISPUTE SETTLEMENT

A difficult question arises with respect to the relationship between the new provision for dispute settlement and previous obligations on the subject which have been contracted by the parties to the dispute. Many States are already bound by various treaties on the pacific settlement of disputes binding them to submit all disputes to arbitration or judicial settlement.[16] Many States have also agreed in a variety of treaties to settle certain categories of disputes by means specified in those treaties.[17] Obligations under many of these two categories of treaties are likely to overlap with obligations under the dispute settlement provisions of the Law of the Sea Convention. The concept of freedom of choice, discussed in the preceding section of this paper, also requires that the parties should be free to agree after a dispute has arisen that it be referred to a new procedure specially tailored to the circumstances of this dispute.[18]

---

16. For a collection of such treaties, see UNITED NATIONS, SYSTEMATIC SURVEY OF TREATIES FOR THE PACIFIC SETTLEMENT OF INTERNATIONAL DISPUTES, 1928-1948 (U.N. Publ. 1949.V.3).

17. *See* U.N. Survey, *supra* note 4.

18. In a similar spirit, the Charter of the United Nations provides in article 95, which is contained in the Chapter relating to the International Court of Justice, that:

> Nothing in the present Charter shall prevent Members of the United Nations from entrusting the solution of their differences to other tribunals by virtue of agreements already in existence or which may be concluded in the future.

See also Geneva General Act for the Pacific Settlement of International Disputes, of September 26, 1928, revised April 28, 1949, art. 29(1), 93 L.N.T.S. 345, 71 U.N.T.S. 101; European Convention for the Pacific Settlement of Disputes, of April 29, 1957, art. 28(1), 320 U.N.T.S. 243; Treaty Establishing the European Economic Community, March 25, 1957, art. 219, 298 U.N.T.S. 3. The United States proposal on the subject was limited to agreements providing for arbitration. U.N. Doc. A/AC.138/97, art. 3 (1973).

The objection was raised that the parties may have agreed or may agree to submit the dispute merely to a procedure of mediation or conciliation, and that a party is free to reject the results of such a procedure. In such a case, the dispute will not be really settled, and it would, therefore, be dangerous to oust the procedure embodied in the Law of the Sea Convention in favor of such an unreliable means of dispute settlement. To meet this objection, it was agreed that an outside procedure shall be exclusive only in cases in which it entails a binding decision, and a different solution was provided for procedures not entailing a binding decision. (See the following section with respect to such solution.)

Finally, there was a difference of opinion on the question whether the Law of the Sea Convention's procedure should have an automatic precedence over other procedures, or whether, on the contrary, the prior procedures should automatically be applied. In either case, the parties may agree, before or after the dispute has arisen, which of the procedures shall apply.

Consequently, the Working Group agreed on the following alternative texts:[19]

Alternative A

If the parties to a dispute [agree to resort to a procedure entailing a binding decision or] have accepted, through a general, regional, or special agreement, or some other instruments, an obligation to resort to arbitration or judicial settlement, any party to the dispute shall be entitled to refer it to [such procedure or to] arbitration or judicial settlement in accordance with that agreement or instruments in place of the procedures specified in this Convention.

Alternative B

The provisions of this Convention relating to dispute settlement shall not apply to a dispute with respect to which the parties are bound by an agreement, or other instruments, obliging them to submit that dispute to another procedure entailing a binding decision.

Alternative C

Notwithstanding the provisions of any agreement or other instruments in force between them, the Contracting Parties shall, unless they otherwise agree, apply the procedures laid down in this Convention to any dispute relating to its interpretation or application.

---

19. U.N. Doc. A/CONF.62/L.7, at 5 (1974). It may be noted that the phrase "procedure entailing a binding decision" is used here in preference to the phrases "compulsory dispute settlement procedure" or "binding procedure," both of which are less accurate.

Clause Relating to Settlement Procedures Not Entailing a Binding Decision

In order not to frustrate the provisions on dispute settlement contained in the Law of the Sea Convention, it is necessary to regulate any resort to mediation, conciliation or any other procedure not entailing a binding decision. The parties may agree to exhaust first those other procedures, and in such a case it is necessary to defer to their preference. If the parties have agreed to a time-limit for the purpose, that time-limit has to be observed.[20] If there are no such agreements, and one party has resorted to some other procedure, the other party should have the right to refer the dispute to the procedures under the Law of the Sea Convention either at its complete discretion or after the first procedure has not led to any result within a reasonable time.[21]

Taking these considerations into account, the Working Group agreed on the following alternative texts:[22]

Alternative A

Where a Contracting Party which is a party to a dispute relating to the interpretation or application of this Convention has submitted that dispute to a dispute settlement procedure not entailing a binding decision, the other party or parties to the dispute may at any time refer it to a dispute settlement procedure provided for by this Convention, unless the parties have agreed otherwise.

Alternative B

Notwithstanding any agreement to refer a dispute to a procedure not entailing a binding decision, any Contracting Party which is a party to a dispute relating to the interpretation or application of this Convention, which is required by this Convention to be submitted on the application of one of the parties to a dispute settlement procedure entailing a binding decision, may refer the dispute at any time to that procedure.

Alternative C

The right to refer a dispute to the settlement procedure provided for by this Convention for obtaining a binding decision may be exercised only after the expiration of the time-limit established by the parties in an agreement to resort to a dispute settlement procedure which does not entail a binding decision, or, in the absence of such a time-limit, if [within a period of _____ months] [within a reasonable time, taking into account the relevant circumstances] that procedure has not been applied or has not resulted in a settlement of the dispute.

---

20. *See, e.g.*, the Convention on Transit Trade of Land-Locked States, of July 8, 1965, art. 16(1), [1968] 19 U.S.T. 7383, T.I.A.S. No. 6592, 597 U.N.T.S. 42.

21. *See, e.g.*, the Geneva General Act for the Pacific Settlement of International Disputes, *supra* note 18, art. 29(2).

22. U.N. Doc. A/CONF.62/L.7, at 7 (1974).

[VOL. 12: 495, 1975]   *Law of The Sea Convention*
                                        SAN DIEGO LAW REVIEW

OBLIGATION TO RESORT TO A MEANS OF SETTLEMENT
RESULTING IN A BINDING DECISION

Once it is agreed that the disputes relating to interpretation or application of the Law of the Sea Convention should be submitted to a procedure resulting in a binding decision, several roads are open. The three main alternatives considered by the Working Group were arbitration, a special Law of the Sea Tribunal and the International Court of Justice.[23]

Many agreements concluded in the maritime field provide for submission of disputes to arbitration.[24] A special tribunal has been proposed, in particular, in connection with seabed disputes;[25] the U.S. proposed in 1973 that a Law of the Sea Tribunal be established.[26] Many treaties provide also that disputes relating to their interpretation and application shall be submitted to the International Court of Justice;[27] a dispute may be submitted either to the full Court or to a special chamber of the Court.[28]

Arbitration is the most flexible of the three methods and allows the parties to tailor the membership of the tribunal to the special circumstances of the case. On the other hand, States have been reluctant to accept foolproof provisions for the establishment of an arbitral tribunal;[29] and there have been many cases in which arbi-

---

23. Similar three alternatives are provided for in the Convention on the Protection of the Marine Environment of the Baltic Sea Area, of March 22, 1974, art. 18, 13 INT. LEGAL MATERIALS 546, 552 (1974).

24. *See, e.g.*, the IMCO Convention for the Prevention of Pollution from Ships, of November 2, 1973, art. 10 and Protocol II, IMCO Doc. MP/CONF/WP.35 (1973), 12 INT'L LEGAL MATERIALS 1319, 1441 (1973); Convention for the Prevention of Marine Pollution from Land-Based Sources, of June 4, 1974, art. 21 and Annex B, 13 INT'L LEGAL MATERIALS 352 (1974). *See also* London Fisheries Convention, of March 9, 1964, art. 13 and annex II, 581 U.N.T.S. 57.

25. *See* 28 U.N. GAOR, Supp. 21, Vol. II, at 130-36, U.N. Doc. A/9021 (1973).

26. U.N. Doc. A/AC.138/97 (1973).

27. Most of these treaties are listed in [1973-1974] I.C.J.Y.B. 81-94.

28. Such a chamber could be created for law of the sea disputes. *See* arts. 26-29 of the Statute of the Court, and arts. 24-27 of the Rules of the Court, as amended in 1972. 2 INTERNATIONAL COURT OF JUSTICE, ACTS AND DOCUMENTS CONCERNING THE ORGANIZATION OF THE COURT 9-10 (1972).

29. *See, e.g.*, the *Model Rules on Arbitral Procedure*, prepared by the International Law Commission, 13 U.N. GAOR, Supp. 9, at 5-8, U.N. Doc. A/3859 (1958). A proposal that the General Assembly commend these Rules to the attention of Member States had to be modified, and the General As-

tral tribunals run into membership and procedural difficulties which have prevented an effective decision.[30] It often takes many months before an arbitral tribunal is able to function, and it cannot deal effectively with cases requiring speedy emergency action.

The International Court of Justice can quickly enact provisional measures to preserve the respective rights of the parties to the dispute. Under its new rules of procedure, it can deal as expeditiously with a case as the parties will allow. The Court has had vast experience in interpreting international agreements, and in recent years has shown great flexibility with respect to both procedural and substantive law. While the Court has sometimes been considered as too conservative, it is less likely to be so in applying a new Law of the Sea Convention representing a new stage in the development of international law. On the other hand, it can be argued that the Law of the Sea Convention will contain many technical provisions requiring not good generalists, but judges with special competence in law of the sea problems. Many questions which might arise under the Law of the Sea Convention will relate not to international law but to various administrative problems of the new regime which require a tribunal with an administrative rather than strictly legal approach, a tribunal resembling more French *Conseil d'Etat* or the Court of Justice of the European Communities than an arbitral tribunal or the International Court of Justice. The final difficulty relates to the possible parties before the Court (see *infra*). If it is decided that the law of the sea dispute settlement procedure should be open not only to States but also to international organizations, public and private legal persons, and even to individuals, they could not be given access to the International Court of Justice without a drastic amendment to its Statute.[31]

A special Law of the Sea Tribunal would avoid most of these difficulties. Being a permanent tribunal, it would be able to function expeditiously, especially in emergency cases. It could be opened to any parties to a dispute, under conditions specified in its statute. It would be composed of persons with special competence in various fields covered by the Law of the Sea Convention, and in addition it might have attached to it specially qualified tech-

---

sembly merely brought them to the attention of Member States. 13 U.N. GAOR, Annexes, Agenda Item No. 57, at 4-7 U.N. Doc. A/3983 (1958); and G.A. Resolution 1262 (XIII), of November 14, 1958, 13 U.N. GAOR, Supp. 18, Vol. I, at 53, U.N. Doc. A/4090 (1958).

30. For an analysis of the mishaps which can befall international arbitral tribunals, *see* CARLSTON, THE PROCESS OF INTERNATIONAL ARBITRATION (1946).

31. At present, article 34(1) of the Statute provides that only States may be parties in cases before the Court.

nical assessors who could be called upon to participate in cases within their field of competence.[32] Functioning within the framework of the Law of the Sea Convention and under its authority, the Tribunal should be able to ensure that the guiding principles of the Convention and its spirit are properly observed.[33]

The Working Group found it necessary to present the following alternatives for the three main options, as well as a text combining them in one complex formula:[34]

Alternative A.1

Any dispute which may arise between two or more Contracting Parties regarding the interpretation or application of this Convention shall be submitted to arbitration at the request of one of the parties to the dispute.

Alternative A.2

Any dispute between two or more Parties to this Convention concerning the interpretation or application of this Convention shall, if settlement by negotiation between the Parties involved has not been possible, and if these Parties do not otherwise agree, be submitted upon request of any of them to arbitration as set out in annex . . . to this Convention.

Alternative B.1

Any dispute between two or more Contracting Parties relating to the interpretation or application of this Convention shall be submitted, at the request of any of the parties to the dispute, to the Law of the Sea Tribunal to be established in accordance with the annexed Statute.

Alternative B.2

Notwithstanding the submission of a dispute to a procedure not entailing a binding decision, any Contracting Party which is party to a dispute relating to the interpretation or application of this Convention, which is required by this Convention to be submitted on the application of one of the parties to a dispute settlement procedure entailing a binding decision, may refer the dispute at any time to the Law of the Sea Tribunal.

Alternative C.1

Any dispute arising between Contracting Parties concerning the interpretation or application of this Convention which is not settled by negotiation shall be referred to the International Court of Justice by the application of any party to the dispute.

---

32. *See* U.S. proposal, A/AC.138/97, arts. 4-5 (1973).

33. The Treaty Instituting the European Coast and Steel Community, of April 18, 1951, provided in article 31 that the function of the Court established by that Treaty was "to ensure the rule of law in the interpretation and application" of that Treaty and of its implementing regulations. 261 U.N.T.S. 140.

34. U.N. Doc. A/CONF.62/L.7, at 8-13 (1974).

Alternative C.2

Any dispute arising between Contracting Parties concerning the interpretation or application of this Convention shall be referred by application of any party to the dispute to a chamber to be established in accordance with the Statute of the International Court of Justice to deal with the Law of the Sea disputes.

Alternative D

Subject to the provisions of this Chapter, any party to a dispute relating to the interpretation or application of this Convention shall be entitled to refer such dispute at any time to [the dispute settlement procedures entailing a binding decision which are provided for in this Convention] [arbitration] [the tribunal established under this Convention] [the International Court of Justice].

THE RELATIONSHIP BETWEEN GENERAL AND FUNCTIONAL APPROACHES

The acceptance of over-all dispute settlement procedures depends to a large extent on the solution of the problem of its relationship to special, functional procedures devised for such areas as seabed and fishing. Before the concept of an over-all dispute settlement machinery was developed, certain "vested rights" were established in several functional areas. There seems to be a general acceptance of a Seabed Tribunal and various proposals have been advanced to deal with difficult fishing problems. How can these functional approaches be reconciled with the more general procedure to be embodied in the dispute settlement chapter of the Convention?

The simplest approach would be to divide the field on functional lines. Wherever the Convention provides for a special procedure—as for instance, with respect to the seabed or fisheries—this special procedure would apply, and the general approach would be restricted to areas not covered by special procedures. The general procedures might also apply in cases where there are conflicts between various uses, for instance, between seabed exploitation and fishing, or between navigation and seabed exploitation.

At the other extreme, should a Law of the Sea Tribunal be established it might replace all the functional procedures. To facilitate, however, different approaches in various fields, separate functional chambers might be established for each field. Any special jurisdiction contemplated in a functional chapter would thus be transferred to the appropriate chamber of the Tribunal. Variety and flexibility would thus be preserved, without a proliferation of special commissions and tribunals. To facilitate this approach, it has been suggested (as noted *supra*) that technical experts or assessors be attached to the Tribunal. Such experts could function semi-independently, as special committees dealing in a preliminary fashion with scientific and technical questions, leaving to the Tribunal only such issues as cannot be resolved on the technical level. Alternatively, the experts might function as assessors, participating in all stages of the proceedings, but without the right to vote. It is quite likely that in either case, the Tribunal would rely heavily on the findings and the advice of the experts and would try to mesh them with its own conclusions derived from the language and spirit of the Convention.

A third approach has also been considered which relies on a two-step procedure. In some cases, for instance, if there is a separate seabed tribunal, an appeal to the Law of the Sea Tribunal might be allowed in specified categories of cases. Thus an appeal would be possible if the decision on the lower level is challenged on such grounds as lack of jurisdiction, infringement of basic rules of procedure, misuse of power (in French administrative law—*abus de pouvoir* or *detournement de pouvoir*), or a violation of the Convention.[35] In other cases, where the functional chapters place reliance on fact-finding commissions (for instance, with respect to fishing, pollution or scientific research), the findings of fact thus made either might be considered conclusive or might result in a shift in the burden of proof.[36]

In this case also the Working Group found it necessary to present a variety of options, with the following alternatives:[37]

Alternative A.1

When a party to a dispute objects to a decision arrived at through a specialized dispute settlement procedure[38] provided for in this

---

35. For analogous provisions, see the Treaty Establishing the European Community, *supra* note 18, art. 173; and the Statute of the Administrative Tribunal of the United Nations, as revised in 1953 and 1955, art. II(1), U.N. Doc. AT/11/Rev. 2 (U.N. Publ. 62.X.3) (1962).

36. For a parallel approach, see the Agreement for the Establishment of the Indo-Pacific Fisheries Council, *as amended* in 1961, art. XIII, 418 U.N.T.S. 334, 348; the International Olive Oil Agreement, of April 20, 1963, art. 35, 495 U.N.T.S. 381, 383. A proposal by Australia and New Zealand concerning highly migratory species provides for reference by the tribunal of scientific and technical questions to a group of experts. U.N. Doc. A/CONF.62/C.2/L.57/Rev. 1, art. 9(A) (1974).

37. U.N. Doc. A/CONF.62/L.7, at 14-15 (1974).

38. It is envisaged that provisions relating to special procedures which may be required in such functional fields as fishing, sea-bed, marine pollution, scientific research, will be set out either in a separate part of the dispute settlement chapter or within the chapter to which they relate [footnote in original text of Working Group proposal].

507

Convention, that party may have recourse to the dispute settlement procedure entailing a binding decision provided for in this chapter on any of the following grounds:

(a) lack of jurisdiction;

(b) infringement of basic procedural rules;

(c) misuse of powers; or

(d) violation of the Convention.

Alternative A.2

Whenever this Convention provides for a specialized procedure, without allowing further recourse to the dispute settlement procedure entailing a binding decision, this chapter shall not apply.

Alternative B.1

1. Before resorting to the dispute settlement procedure entailing a binding decision provided for in this chapter, the parties to any dispute relating to chapters _____ of this Convention [*e.g.*, those relating to fishing, pollution, or scientific research] may agree to refer it to a special fact-finding procedure in accordance with the provisions of annex ___.

2. In any procedure entailing a binding decision under this chapter, the findings of fact made by the fact-finding machinery shall be considered conclusive [unless one of the parties presents positive proof that a gross error has been committed].

or

2. Should the findings of fact made by the fact-finding machinery be challenged by a recourse to the dispute settlement procedure provided for in this chapter, the party challenging such facts shall bear the burden of proof.

Alternative B.2

1. At the request of any party to a dispute relating to chapters _____ of this Convention [*e.g.*, those relating to fishing, pollution or scientific research], the dispute shall be referred to a special fact-finding procedure in accordance with the provisions in annex ___.

2. If any party to the dispute considers that the fact-finding decision is not in accordance with the provisions of this Convention, it may appeal to the dispute settlement procedure provided for in this chapter.

Alternative C.1

1. The Law of the Sea Tribunal, to be established in accordance with the annexed statute shall establish special chambers to deal with disputes relating to chapters _____ of this Convention. Each chamber of the Tribunal shall be assisted in the consideration of a dispute by four technical assessors sitting with it throughout all the stages of the proceedings, but without the right to vote. These assessors shall be chosen by each chamber from the list of qualified persons prepared pursuant to the statute of the Tribunal. [Their opinion on scientific and technical questions shall be considered by the chamber as conclusive.]

2. Each chamber shall deal with the dispute in accordance with the special procedure prescribed for that chamber by the statute of the Tribunal, taking into account the special requirements of each category of cases.

Alternative C.2

1. When a dispute submitted to the Law of the Sea Tribunal involves scientific or technical questions, the Tribunal shall refer

such matters to a special committee of experts chosen from the list of qualified persons prepared in accordance with the statute of the Tribunal.

2. If the dispute is not settled on the basis of the committee's opinion, either party to the dispute may request that the Tribunal proceed to consider the other aspects of the dispute, taking into consideration the findings of the committee and all other pertinent information.

PARTIES TO A DISPUTE

It is quite difficult for some States to reconcile themselves to the idea of a dispute settlement machinery resulting in a binding decision. One cannot be surprised, therefore, that they balk even more when it is suggested that this machinery should be open not only to States but also to other entities, or even individuals. Others believe, however, that several categories of law of the sea disputes are likely to go beyond the usual State-to-State framework. The Charter of the United Nations departed from traditional international law by recognizing the rights of individuals and the United Nations has slowly developed machinery to protect these rights, at least in cases of gross violations.[39] It would be incongruous to deny the minimal procedural rights to individuals in the new Law of the Sea Convention which is meant to provide new vistas of international law. There need not be, however, a complete break with the past, and appropriate conditions might be imposed on the use by legal entities and individuals of the facilities established under the Law of the Sea Convention.[40] These conditions might be different for international intergovernmental organizations, international nongovernmental organizations, other legal entities and individuals.

The Working Group decided to present on this subject the following stark alternatives:[41]

Alternative A

1. The dispute settlement machinery shall be open to the States parties to this Convention.

2. The conditions under which the machinery shall be open to other States, international intergovernmental organizations, [non-

---

39. L. SOHN & T. BUERGENTHAL, INTERNATIONAL PROTECTION OF HUMAN RIGHTS 1-19, 505-22, 772-856 (1973).

40. *See, e.g.,* the restrictions included in article 173 of the Treaty Establishing the European Economic Community, *supra* note 18.

41. U.N. Doc. A/CONF.62/L.7, at 17 (1974).

governmental international organizations having a consultative relationship with the United Nations or a specialized agency of the United Nations or any other international organization], and natural and juridical persons shall be laid down [by . . . .] [in an annex to this Convention], but in no case shall such conditions place the parties in position of inequality.

Alternative B

The dispute settlement machinery shall be open to the States parties to this Convention [and to the Authority, subject to the provisions of article . . . .]

LOCAL REMEDIES

One of the oldest rules of international law is the rule requiring exhaustion of local remedies before a resort to international remedies.[42] It has been considered appropriate that ordinarily a State should not be internationally responsible if an adequate remedy might have been obtained in its courts. On the other hand, if no such remedy exists or it is insufficient, too slow or likely to be biased, international law allows this requirement to be skipped.[43] There are also some international agreements which completely dispense with the requirement that local remedies be exhausted.[44]

Consequently, the Working Group suggested the following alternatives:[45]

Alternative A

A Contracting Party which has taken measures alleged to be contrary to this Convention shall not be entitled to object to a request for submission of a dispute to the dispute settlement procedure under this chapter solely on the ground that any remedies under its domestic law have not been exhausted.

Alternative B.1

The Contracting Parties shall not be entitled to submit a dispute to the dispute settlement procedure under this chapter, if local remedies have not been previously exhausted, as required by international law.

Alternative B.2

1. In the case of a dispute relating to the exercise by the coastal State of its enforcement jurisdiction in accordance with this Con-

---

42. The rule on exhaustion of local remedies, and the closely related rules on denial of justice, can be traced at least to the ninth century. *See* SOHN & BUERGENTHAL, *supra* note 39, at 32-40.

43. *See generally* F. GARCÍA-AMADOR, L. SOHN & R. BAXTER, RECENT CODIFICATION OF THE LAW OF STATE RESPONSIBILITY FOR INJURIES TO ALIENS 72-78, 261-70, 362, 366, 400-01 (1974). *See also* Geneva General Act, *supra* note 18, arts. 31-32.

44. *See, e.g.*, Convention relating to Intervention on the High Seas in Cases of Oil Pollution Casualties, of November 29, 1969, art. VIII(2), Br. Parl. Papers, Cmnd. 4403 (1970); 2 Lay, Churchill & Nordquist, NEW DIRECTIONS IN THE LAW OF THE SEA: DOCUMENTS 592 (1973).

45. U.N. Doc. A/CONF.62/L.7, at 18-19 (1974).

[VOL. 12: 495, 1975]

Law of The Sea Convention
SAN DIEGO LAW REVIEW

vention, the occasion [subject matter] of which, according to the domestic law of the coastal State, falls within the competence of its judicial or administrative authorities, the coastal State shall be entitled to request that the submission of the dispute to the means of dispute settlement provided for in this chapter be delayed until a decision with final effect has been pronounced, within a reasonable time, by the competent authority.

2. In such a case, the party to the dispute which desires to resort to the procedure for dispute settlement provided for in this chapter may not submit the dispute to such procedure after the expiration of a period of one year from the date of the aforementioned decision.

[3. When the case has been submitted to the settlement procedure under this chapter, the party challenging the findings of fact by the judicial authorities of the coastal State shall bear the burden of proof.]

ADVISORY JURISDICTION

To further facilitate the coordination between domestic and international remedies, it has been suggested that it would be desirable to allow domestic tribunals to request the Law of the Sea Tribunal for an advisory opinion authoritatively interpreting the provision of the Convention which is at issue in the domestic forum. Some delegations would prefer a binding ruling similar to those given by the Court of Justice of the European Communities in analogous situations.[46] A domestic tribunal would be authorized to request such an opinion only if its own law authorizes such a reference to an international authority. The Law of the Sea Tribunal may either be bound to give such an advisory opinion or the matter may be entirely at its discretion, depending on the circumstances of the case, the seriousness of the issues involved, and the need to maintain uniform jurisprudence.

Consequently, the Working Group agreed on the following proposal, embodying the basic options:[47]

If a court of a Contracting Party has been authorized by the domestic law of that Party to request the Law of the Sea Tribunal to give an advisory opinion [a ruling] on any question relating to the interpretation or application of this Convention, the Law of the Sea Tribunal may [shall] give such an opinion [ruling].

46. Treaty Establishing the European Economic Community, *supra* note 18, art. 177.
47. U.N. Doc. A/CONF.62/L.7, at 20 (1974).

LAW APPLICABLE

One of the basic reasons for the acceptance of an international tribunal for the settlement of treaty disputes is that the treaty itself embodies the law to be applied by the tribunal, and that, consequently, the discretion of the tribunal to apply rules of customary international law would be quite narrowly circumscribed. In areas of the law as controversial in recent years as the law of the sea, some States found it even necessary to modify their previous acceptances of the jurisdiction of the International Court of Justice in order to avoid premature decisions while the law was in the process of revision.[48] However, once the law is codified and developed to the satisfaction of all the States concerned in the new Law of the Sea Convention, that convention will constitute the law to be applied and previous anxieties will disappear.

Some delegations did not think it necessary to single out the new Law of the Sea Convention as the only law applicable. They expressed the view that once that convention comes into effect it will form a chapter of general international law, and it should be sufficient to state quite simply that the law of the sea dispute settlement machinery should decide in accordance with applicable international law. They pointed out that even if priority should be given to the Law of the Sea Convention, other rules of international law would also have to be applied from time to time, and the Convention will have to be interpreted in accordance with the rules of international law relating to interpretation.

A question was also raised about the content of the "law of this Convention." Is it limited to the text of the Law of the Sea Convention only, or does it also embody the regulations enacted thereunder as well as regional arrangements and public or private contracts concluded pursuant to the Law of the Sea Convention? Some delegations would also like to preserve the right of the parties to agree that a dispute be decided *ex aequo et bono*.[49] Finally, some delegations suggested that the dispute settlement machinery should be expressly given the function to ensure that the law of the Law of the Sea Convention would be observed in the interpretation and application of that Convention.[50]

Taking these proposals into consideration, the Working Group

---

48. *See, e.g.,* the recent declarations by Australia, Canada and the Philiippines. [1973-1974] I.C.J.Y.B. 49-51, 53-54, 73-74.

49. The Statute of the International Court of Justice contains such provision in art. 38(2).

50. For a similar provision, *see* the Treaty Establishing the European Economic Community, *supra* note 18, art. 164.

proposed the following alternatives concerning the law applicable and a separate provision on equity jurisdiction.[51]

Alternative A

In any dispute submitted to it the dispute settlement machinery shall apply the law of this Convention, and shall ensure that this law is observed in the interpretation and application of this Convention.

Alternative B

In any dispute submitted to it, the dispute settlement machinery shall apply, in the first place, the law of this Convention. If, however, the dispute relates to the interpretation or application of a regional arrangement or public or private agreement concluded pursuant to this Convention, or to regulations adopted by a competent international organization, the dispute settlement machinery shall apply, in addition to the Convention, the rules contained in such arrangements, agreements, or regulations, provided the regulations are not inconsistent with this Convention.

Alternative C

Any dispute submitted to the dispute settlement procedure established by this Convention shall be decided in accordance with applicable international law.

Alternative D

In any dispute submitted to it, the dispute settlement machinery shall apply:

(a) the provisions of this Convention;

(b) the rules and regulations laid down by the competent international authority;

(c) the terms and conditions of the relevant contracts or other legal arrangements entered into by the competent international authority.

Equity Jurisdiction

The provisions of this chapter shall not prejudice the right of the parties to a dispute to agree that the dispute be settled *ex aequo et bono.*

EXCEPTIONS AND RESERVATIONS TO THE DISPUTE SETTLEMENT PROVISIONS

Some delegations believe that the integrity of the compromise package to be embodied in the Law of the Sea Convention needs to be preserved at all cost and that effective dispute settlement provisions are needed, applicable without exception to all parts of the

---

51. U.N. Doc. A/CONF.62/L.7, at 20-21 (1974).

Convention.[52]   Others would like to allow exceptions with respect to some parts of the Convention, or, alternatively, to limit binding decisions to specified chapters or articles of the Convention.[53]   The extreme approach of making the provisions on dispute settlement merely optional[54] was rejected by the Working Group in favor of a compromise proposal allowing specified exceptions to be enumerated exhaustively in the Convention.[55]   While some would allow such exceptions with respect to all procedures, others would allow them only insofar as procedures leading to a binding decision are concerned, thus prohibiting reservations with respect to conciliation, mediation and similar procedures.

For the moment, the Working Group has limited itself to listing exceptions which were suggested by various delegations.   It did not try to draft them in a final, more precise form; nor did it consider the desirability or the danger of particular formulations.[56]

The following options and alternatives were listed by the Working Group:[57]

Alternative A

The provisions of this chapter shall apply to all disputes relating to the interpretation and application of this Convention.

Alternative B.1

The dispute settlement machinery shall have no jurisdiction to render binding decisions with respect to the following categories of disputes:

(a) Disputes arising out of the normal exercise of regulatory or enforcement jurisdiction, except when gross or persistent violation of this Convention or abuse of power is alleged.[58]

(b) Disputes concerning sea boundary delimitations between States.

---

52. Many international agreements provide for an over-all dispute settlement machinery, without exceptions. *See, e.g.,* BLIX, *supra* note 4, at 117.

53. For an example of this approach, see Vienna Convention on the Law of Treaties, *supra* note 11, art. 66.

54. At the 1958 Law of the Sea Conference a separate optional protocol on dispute settlement was adopted; not many countries ratified it.   450 U.N.T.S. 169. For a criticism of this approach, *see* the statement by Ambassador Galindo Pohl, U.N. Doc. A/CONF.62/SR.51, at 4 (prov. ed. 1974).

55. A similar method was adopted in drafting the Geneva General Act, *supra* note 18, art. 39.

56. As Ambassador Galindo Pohl has noted, certain fundamental or constitutional problems facing some States need to be taken into account, allowing them to protect their vital interests through "exceptions which had to be determined with the greatest care." U.N. Doc. A/CONF.62/SR.51, at 4-5 (prov. ed. 1974).

57. U.N. Doc. A/CONF.62/L.7, at 22-24 (1974).

58. The precise drafting and implications of this exception will require further examination in the light of the substantive provisions of this Convention [footnote in original text of Working Group proposal].

[VOL. 12: 495, 1975]   *Law of The Sea Convention*
                                        SAN DIEGO LAW REVIEW

(c) Disputes involving historic bays or limits of territorial sea.

(d) Disputes concerning vessels and aircraft entitled to sovereign immunity under international law, and similar cases in which sovereign immunity applies under international law.

(e) Disputes concerning military activities [unless the State conducting such activities gives its express consent].

(f) . . . .

(g) . . . .

Alternative B.2

The dispute settlement machinery shall have no jurisdiction with respect to the following categories of disputes:

(a) Disputes arising out of the normal exercise of discretion by a coastal State pursuant to its regulatory and enforcement jurisdiction under this Convention, except in cases involving an abuse of power.[59]

(b) Disputes concerning sea boundary delimitations between adjacent and opposite States, including those involving historic bays and the delimitation of the adjacent territorial sea.

(c) Disputes concerning vessels and aircraft entitled to sovereign immunity under international law, and similar cases in which sovereign immunity applies under international law.

(d) Disputes concerning military activities [unless the State conducting such activities gives its express consent.]

(e) . . . .

(f) . . . .

Alternative C.1

1. In ratifying this Convention, acceding to it, or accepting it, a State may declare that it does not accept the jurisdiction of the dispute settlement machinery to render binding decisions with respect to one or more of the following categories of disputes:

[(a)-(g) as in Alternative B.1.]

2. If one of the Contracting Parties has made such a declaration, any other Contracting Party may enforce the same exception in regard to the Party which made the declaration.

Alternative C.2

1. In ratifying this Convention, acceding to it, or accepting it, a State may declare that it does not accept the jurisdiction of the dispute settlement machinery with respect to one or more of the following categories of disputes:

[(a)-(f) as in Alternative B.2]

2. If one of the Contracting Parties has made such a declaration, any other Contracting Party may enforce the same exception in regard to the Party which made the declaration.

---

59. The precise drafting and implications of this exception will require further examination in the light of the substantive provisions of this Convention [footnote in original text of Working Group proposal].

Conclusion

The working paper prepared by the Working Group on the settlement of the law of the sea disputes is only provisional in character and limited to outlining the basic alternatives. It needs to be completed and various issues need to be further clarified. However, once an agreement is reached on the basic elements it should be relatively easier to arrive at a solution of the less essential points.[60] It is hoped that the suggestions of the Working Group will facilitate the final settlement.

In conclusion, it might be useful to note some of the important reasons for including in the Law of the Sea Convention effective dispute settlement provisions: [61]

1. Effective legal procedures for dispute settlement are necessary to avoid political and economic pressures. While the larger and richer countries can apply extra-legal, political and economic pressures to achieve their ends, it is especially important for small countries and for developing countries to have disputes directed into legal channels where the principle of equality before the law prevails.

2. It is important to achieve a large measure of uniformity in the interpretation and application of the new Convention. Otherwise, the compromise arrived at with such great difficulty will quickly disintegrate, and the efforts of many years of negotiation would come to naught.

3. The system of dispute settlement must be an integral part of the Law of the Sea Convention. An optional protocol would be a totally inadequate way of dealing with the problem. An attempt to relegate dispute settlement to an optional protocol might jeopardize the ratification and even the signing of the Convention. For many countries, the adjustments made for the sake of obtaining an agreement on the Law of the Sea Convention are only justifiable if effective means are provided to avoid the political and even military confrontations which otherwise might occur.[62]

---

60. Statement by Ambassador Galindo Pohl, August 29, 1974, *supra* note 56, at 4.

61. For a similar list, *see* Ambassador Galindo Pohl's statement, *id.*

62. *See, e.g.,* the following statement by Ambassador Stevenson, July 11, 1974, 71 Dep't State Bull. 232, 235 (1974):

[My] government believes that any law of the sea treaty is almost as easily susceptible of unreasonable unilateral interpretation as are the principles of customary international law. This is particularly true when we consider that the essential balance of critical portions of the treaty, such as the economic zone, must rest upon impartial interpretation of treaty provisions. One of the primary motivations of my government in supporting the negotiation

[VOL. 12: 495, 1975]   *Law of The Sea Convention*
                                          SAN DIEGO LAW REVIEW

4. The injunction of the Charter of the United Nations that international disputes must be settled "by peaceful means in such a manner that international peace and security, and justice, are not endangered" cannot be complied with unless effective means are actually provided for such a settlement in the far-ranging Law of the Sea Convention which will decide the fate of some 70% of the earth surface covered by seas and oceans. The more encompassing the solutions are, the more the Convention lays down novel principles for the solution of current and future problems, the more it is necessary to provide for the stability of the new regime through generally accepted, effective and flexible means for the settlement of law of the sea disputes.

---

of a new law of the sea treaty is that of making an enduring contribution to a new structure for peaceful relations among states. Accordingly, we must reiterate our view that a system of peaceful and compulsory third-party settlement of disputes is in the end perhaps the most significant justification for the accommodations we are all being asked to make.

[14]

INVOKING INTERNATIONAL HUMAN RIGHTS LAW IN DOMESTIC COURTS*

*Richard B. Lillich***

Table of Contents

The purpose of this monograph is to describe and evaluate the status of international human rights law—both conventional and customary—in domestic courts. The focus is on the principles and rules governing cases arising in the federal and state courts of the United States, since they generally are representative of the problems that courts face elsewhere. Moreover, as will be evident, United States courts in the past decade have been the prime movers in the development of this body of international law. To the extent that the monograph has a thesis, it is that there is plenty of international human rights law extant, that domestic courts increasingly are being briefed on such law, and that they either are taking or should take this law into account in reaching their decisions. Hence lawyers—including international human rights specialists, all too

---

* An earlier version of this article was prepared for and published by the American Bar Association's Standing Committee on World Order Under Law, with whose kind permission this somewhat revised and updated version is now published.

** Howard W. Smith Professor of Law and President, Procedural Aspects of International Law Institute. A.B., Oberlin College, 1954; LL.B. with Specialization in International Affairs, Cornell Law School, 1957; LL.M. (in International Law) and J.S.D., New York University School of Law, 1959, 1960. The author is a Member of the Advisory Board of the Urban Morgan Institute of Human Rights and the author or editor of over 20 books, the most recent being THE HUMAN RIGHTS OF ALIENS IN CONTEMPORARY INTERNATIONAL LAW (1984).

many of whom often have concentrated exclusively upon the development and use of international procedures to promote and protect human rights—no longer can ignore the enforcement possibilities afforded by domestic courts.

I. A Brief Overview of the Status of International Law in Domestic Courts

One of the few references to international law in the United States Constitution is found in article VI, section 2, which provides that "all Treaties made, or which shall be made, under the Authority of the United States, shall be the supreme Law of the Land; and the Judges in every State shall be bound thereby, any Thing in the Constitution or Laws of any State to the Contrary notwithstanding."[1] Under this provision, which is the only one in the Constitution that speaks to the relation of international law to municipal law in domestic courts, a self-executing treaty when proclaimed by the President (or a non-self-executing treaty when implemented by Congress) supersedes all inconsistent state and local laws.[2] Additionally, under the "last-in-time" rule a self-executing treaty will supersede earlier inconsistent federal laws.[3]

The other major source of international law—customary international law—is not mentioned in the Constitution, but the Supreme Court has ruled that it is "part of our law, and must be ascertained and administered by the courts of justice of appropriate jurisdiction, as often as questions of right depending upon it are duly presented for their determination."[4] Having the same status as treaty law,[5] it also supersedes all inconsistent state and local laws[6] and, at least in principle, earlier inconsistent federal laws and international agreements.[7] "[A]s in the case of treaties, American courts

---

1. U.S. Const. art. VI, § 2.
2. *See* Asakura v. Seattle, 265 U.S. 332, 341 (1924) (construing U.S. Const. art. VI, § 2); Ware v. Hylton, 3 U.S. (3 Dall.) 198, 236-37 (1796) (same).
3. *See* Whitney v. Robertson, 124 U.S. 190, 194 (1888); *see also* 1 Restatement of Foreign Relations Law of the United States (Revised) § 135 comment c, at 79-80 (Tent. Draft No. 6, 1985) [hereinafter cited as Restatement].
4. The Paquete Habana, 175 U.S. 677, 700 (1900).
5. *See* 1 Restatement, *supra* note 3, § 102 comment j, at 33.
6. *Id.* §§ 131(1), 135 comment e, at 81.
7. There seem to have been no cases in which a rule of customary international law was challenged on the ground that it is inconsistent with an earlier statute or international agreement of the United States. Since international customary law and an international agreement have equal authority in international law (§ 102, Comment j) and both are law of the United States (§ 131), arguably later customary

will give effect to the obligations of the United States under customary international law; at the behest of affected private parties, courts will prevent violations of international law by the States or by lower federal officials.''[8]

Under the dualist approach to international law, however, subsequent federal laws will prevail over both conventional and customary international law when the two conflict.[9] Thus the United States may breach an international obligation and become responsible internationally—as it did when Congress enacted the Byrd Amendment which, under the last-in-time rule, required the President to violate United Nations sanctions against Southern Rhodesia (now Zimbabwe)—and yet not be answerable for such a breach in domestic

---

law should be given effect as law of the United States, even in the face of an earlier law or agreement. . . . But customary law is made by practice, consent or acquiescence of the United States, usually acting through the President alone, and it has been argued that the sole act of the President ought not to prevail over a law of the United States. . . . Courts in the United States will hesitate to conclude that a principle has become a rule of customary international law if they are required to give it effect in the face of an earlier inconsistent statute.

Id. § 135 reporters' note 4, at 83.

For contrasting views on the an earlier version of section 135 and the reporters' note therein, compare Henkin, *International Law as Law in the United States*, 82 MICH. L. REV. 1555, 1561-67 (1984) (supportive), with Goldklang, *Back on Board the Paquete Habana: Resolving the Conflict Between Statutes and Customary International Law*, 25 VA. J. INT'L L. 143 (1985) (critical). For a lively debate on the subject, see Murphy, *Customary International Law in U.S. Jurisprudence—A Comment on Draft Restatement II*, INT'L PRACTITIONER'S NOTEBOOK, No. 20, at 17 (Oct. 1982); Paust, *Reply to John Murphy's Comment on Incorporating Customary International Law in U.S. Jurisprudence*, INT'L PRACTITIONER'S NOTEBOOK, No. 21, at 18 (Jan. 1983); Goldklang, *Customary International Law and U.S. Laws*, INT'L PRACTITIONER'S NOTEBOOK, No. 22, at 16 (Apr. 1983); Paust, *When Customary International Law Clashes with a Domestic Statute*, INT'L PRACTITIONER'S NOTEBOOK, No. 23, at 10 (July 1983).

8. L. HENKIN, FOREIGN AFFAIRS AND THE CONSTITUTION 223 (1972). For a discussion about when international agreements and customary international law create rights that individuals may invoke in domestic courts, see 1 RESTATEMENT, *supra* note 3, § 131 reporters' note 4, at 63-66. *See also infra* text accompanying note 25.

In the recent case of Hanoch Tel-Oren v. Libyan Arab Republic, 517 F. Supp. 542 (D.D.C. 1981), *aff'd per curiam*, 726 F.2d 774 (D.C. Cir. 1984), *cert. denied*, 53 U.S.L.W. 3612 (1985), one judge on appeal contended that international human rights law could be invoked only in those rare instances where individuals *explicitly* were granted a ''cause of action.'' 726 F.2d at 801 (Bork, J., concurring). Two subsequent cases generally adhere to this line of reasoning. *See* Frolova v. U.S.S.R., 761 F.2d 370 (7th Cir. 1985); Handel v. Artukovic, 601 F. Supp. 1421 (C.D. Cal. 1985). For criticism of this approach, which as a practical matter would restrict such lawsuits to situations involving perhaps a handful of self-executing treaties, see D'Amato, *What Does Tel Oren Tell Lawyers? Judge Bork's Concept of the Law of Nations Is Seriously Mistaken*, 79 AM. J. INT'L L. 92 (1985). *See also* Schneebaum, *The Enforceability of Customary Norms of Public International Law*, 8 BROOKLYN J. INT'L L. 289 (1982); *cf. infra* text at and accompanying note 165.

9. *See* The Over the Top, 5 F.2d 838, 842 (D. Conn. 1925); *see also* 1 RESTATEMENT, *supra* note 3, § 135(1)(a). *See generally* Lillich, *The Proper Role of Domestic Courts in the International Legal Order*, 11 VA. J. INT'L L. 9, 12-18 (1970).

courts.[10] Moreover, by refusing to apply an obviously self-executing treaty, or by not granting an individual the standing to challenge United States laws that allegedly conflict with international law, domestic courts not only deny litigants redress, but also impliedly condone conduct for which the United States may become responsible internationally.[11] The judiciary thus must rethink and revise a number of its restrictive rules before it truly can be said that international law is part of domestic law.

II.   A BRIEF DESCRIPTION OF THE ORIGINS AND DEVELOPMENT OF INTERNATIONAL HUMAN RIGHTS LAW

The notion that all human beings enjoy certain basic human rights is an outgrowth of the traditional international law governing State Responsibility for Injuries to Aliens.[12] As developed by state practice and numerous arbitral decisions during the nineteenth and early twentieth centuries, this body of law required all states to adhere to an "international minimum standard" of procedural and substantive justice in their treatment of aliens. This international minimum standard—"whether aliens [were] treated in accordance with ordinary standards of civilization"[13]—was repeatedly invoked by the United States on behalf of its citizens abroad, be it in cases of extended incarceration,[14] cruel and inhuman punishment,[15] or arbitrary expulsion.[16]

---

10. Diggs v. Shultz, 470 F.2d 461, 465-67 *passim* (D.C. Cir. 1972), *cert. denied*, 411 U.S. 931 (1973); *see* 1 RESTATEMENT, *supra* note 3, § 135(1)(b). "[A]lthough subsequent legislation may supersede an earlier rule of [customary] international law or provision of an international agreement as domestic law, the United States remains bound by the rule or agreement internationally." *Id.* § 135 comment b, at 79.

11. This statement is not to suggest that, when a domestic court finds a treaty to be non-self-executing or denies an individual standing to bring suit to enforce an international agreement, it thereby expressly violates the United States's international obligations. Rather, by so acting, a court bypasses a decision on the merits and thus deprives the United States of the opportunity either to put matters right or to demonstrate to the world community that it has adhered to its international commitments. A complaint in an international forum or a diplomatic claim—both of which could have been avoided—thus may follow, with the United States facing possible liability under State Responsibility principles.

12. *See generally* Lillich, *Duties of States Regarding the Civil Rights of Aliens,* 161 RECUEIL DES COURS (Hague Academy of International Law) 329, 339-56 (1978-III).

13. Roberts Case (U.S. v. Mex.), United States and Mexican General Claims Comm., Opinions of Commissioners 1926-1927, at 100 (1927), 4 R. Int'l Arb. Awards 77 (1927).

14. *See, e.g.,* Halstead Case (U.S. v. Mex.) (1868), in 4 J. MOORE, HISTORY AND DIGEST OF THE INTERNATIONAL ARBITRATIONS TO WHICH THE UNITED STATES HAS BEEN A PARTY 3243 (1898).

15. *See, e.g.,* Baldwin Case (U.S. v. Mex.), in 4 J. MOORE, *supra* note 14, at 3235.

16. *See generally* 4 J. MOORE, *supra* note 14, at 3333-59.

When the United States signed the UN Charter in 1945, thereby adhering to the human rights provisions of articles 55 and 56 of the Charter, it thus was extending its longstanding recognition of an "international minimum standard" to include all human beings rather than just aliens.[17] Similarly, by signing subsequent international human rights instruments such as the Universal Declaration of Human Rights,[18] the UN Covenant on Civil and Political Rights[19] and the American Convention on Human Rights,[20] the United States was reaffirming its commitment to the basic civil and political rights contained therein.[21] In considering the domestic enforcement of the norms found in the various international human rights instruments,[22] therefore, it should be remembered that, while the history of United States adherence to such norms is not necessarily of recent vintage, only in the past few decades have domestic courts been asked to apply them as part of conventional or customary international law. Thus the application process, chronologically speaking, is still in its infancy. The following sections will take up the major problems that have arisen in the cases decided to date and, it is hoped, anticipate some of the questions that will arise in future litigation.

III. The Status of the UN Charter in Domestic Law

The UN Charter, having been ratified by the United States, is the supreme law of the land. Article 1(3) lists among the UN's main

---

17. *See generally* Lillich, *supra* note 12, at 391-99.

18. Universal Declaration of Human Rights, *signed* Dec. 10, 1948, G.A. Res. 217A, U.N. Doc A/180, at 71 (1948), *reprinted in* R. Lillich, International Human Rights Instruments § 440.1 (1985).

19. International Covenant on Civil and Political Rights, *adopted* Dec. 16, 1966, *entered into force* Mar. 23, 1976, G.A. Res. 2200, 21 U.N. GAOR Supp. (No. 16) at 52, U.N. Doc. A/6316 (1966), *reprinted in* R. Lillich, *supra* note 18, § 170.1.

20. American Convention on Human Rights, *opened for signature* Nov. 22, 1969, *entered into force* July 18, 1978, O.A.S.T.S. No. 36, *reprinted in* R. Lillich, *supra* note 18, § 190.1.

21. State Responsibility for Injuries to Aliens Law protected only the civil rights of aliens, there being uniform agreement at customary international law that political rights could be claimed only by the citizens of a state. Its reach, moreover, did not extend to what are now called economic, social and cultural rights. While international human rights law embraces all of the above rights, civil and, to a lesser extent, political rights are the two types that have been (or are likely to be) invoked in domestic courts and hence are the focus of this monograph. *See generally* Lillich, *Civil Rights*, in 1 Human Rights in International Law: Legal and Policy Issues 115 (T. Meron ed. 1984); Humphrey, *Political and Related Rights*, in *id.* at 171.

22. For the text, reservations, states parties, United States action, selected bibliography and federal and state court decisions citing the 45 principal international human rights treaties, agreements and declarations of especial interest to the United States, see R. Lillich, *supra* note 18.

CINCINNATI LAW REVIEW [Vol. 54

purposes the achievement of international cooperation "in promoting and encouraging respect for human rights and for fundamental freedoms for all without distinction as to race, sex, language, or religion."[23] Similarly, in accordance with article 55(c) the UN has the duty to promote "universal respect for, and observance of, human rights and fundamental freedoms for all without distinction as to race, sex, language, or religion."[24] Finally, under article 56 all members of the UN "pledge themselves to take joint and separate action in cooperation with the Organization for the achievement of the purposes set forth in Article 55."[25]

Under the principles first enunciated in *Foster v. Nielson*,[26] the status of the human rights clauses of the UN Charter in domestic law turns upon whether or not they were intended to be self-executing,[27] since "[i]t is only when a treaty is self-executing, when it prescribes rules by which private rights may be determined, that it may be relied upon for the enforcement of such rights."[28] Yet attempts to go

---

23. U.N. CHARTER art. 1, para. 3.

24. U.N. CHARTER art. 55.

25. U.N. CHARTER art. 56.

26. 27 U.S. (2 Pet.) 253, 314 (1829).

27. A treaty (or a provision thereof) is said to be self-executing and, hence, under article VI, § 2, the supreme law of the land "equivalent to an act of the legislature, whenever it operates by itself without the aid of any legislative provision." *Foster,* 27 U.S. (2 Pet.) at 314. More fully defined, a self-executing treaty is one "which prescribes by its own terms a rule for the Executive or for the courts or which creates obligations [or rights] for individuals enforceable without legislative implementation." Evans, *Self-Executing Treaties in the United States of America,* 30 BRIT. Y.B. INT'L L. 178, 185 (1951).

While there is general agreement about the effects of a self-executing treaty, there is considerable confusion about the *criteria* to be used in determining whether a treaty is self-executing in the first place. *See* United States v. Postal, 589 F.2d 862, 876 (5th Cir. 1979) ("The self-execution question is perhaps one of the most confounding in treaty law."). A 1948 memorandum by the Department of State concluded that "it seems quite clear that a precise definition of a self-executing treaty is not possible. It is believed that in each instance it will be necessary to consider the facts of the particular case before reaching a decision." 14 M. WHITEMAN, DIGEST OF INTERNATIONAL LAW 309 (1970). For recent attempts to clarify the question, see *infra* text at and accompanying notes 33 & 68.

28. Dreyfus v. Von Finck, 534 F.2d 24, 30 (2d Cir.), *cert. denied,* 429 U.S. 835 (1976). In Manningham Mills v. Congoleum Corp., 595 F.2d 1287 (3d Cir. 1979), the Third Circuit noted that:

> A treaty of the United States is a contract with another nation which becomes the law of this country. Like private rights under law, a treaty may confer rights capable of enforcement, but this is not the general rule. . . . [U]nless a treaty is self-executing, it must be implemented by legislation before it gives rise to a private cause of action.

Id. at 1298 (citation omitted); *cf. supra* text at and accompanying note 8.

While there is some disagreement about the *effects* of a self-executing treaty, there is considerable confusion about the *criteria* to be used in determining whether a treaty is

beyond the words of the human rights clauses of the Charter and ascertain the actual "intent of the parties"[29]—specifically, whether or not the drafters intended the clauses to be self-executing—have proved futile. "Nothing in the documents of the [San Francisco] conference," one commentator has concluded, "indicates that the framers even considered the direct legal impact of the human rights clauses on the domestic law of the members."[30] Since relatively few countries have adopted the doctrine of self-executing treaties,[31] this state of affairs is not surprising; indeed, with the vast majority of countries having no such concept in their jurisprudence and little interest in the mechanics by which other countries fulfill their international legal obligations under a treaty, efforts to ascertain the "intent of the parties" to most multilateral treaties have only marginally greater chances of success than medieval attempts to capture the unicorn.[32] For this and other reasons, Professor Riesenfeld maintains that the "intent of the parties" really has no relevancy to the question of self-execution. "The intent of the parties to an international treaty," he suggests,

---

self-executing in the first place. *See infra* text at and accompanying notes 29, 33-34 & 68. The best discussion of the problems involved may be found in Riensenfeld, *The Doctrine of Self-Executing Treaties and* U.S. v. Postal: *Win at Any Price?*, 74 AM. J. INT'L L. 892 (1980).

29. Whether a particular treaty provision is self-executing depends upon the intent of the parties, i.e., whether they intended that the treaty be applied directly as if it were a statute, or that it be applied only indirectly as if it were a statute, or that it be applied only indirectly through implementing legislation. The intent of the parties may be established by reference to the terms of the treaty and to its legislative and drafting history.

International Human Rights Treaties: Hearings Before the Senate Comm. on Foreign Relations, 96th Cong., 1st Sess. 314, 315 (1979) (letter from Robert B. Owen, Legal Advisor, Department of State, to Senator Jacob K. Javits) (citing 15 M. WHITEMEN, *supra* note 24, at 302-16) [hereinafter cited as *Hearings*]. For statements that it is the intent of the United States, not the parties, which determines whether or not a treaty is to be considered self-executing in the United States, see *infra* text at notes 33-34.

30. Schluter, *The Domestic Status of the Human Rights Clauses of the United Nations Charter*, 61 CALIF. L. REV. 110, 130 (1973). *See generally* Huston, *Human Rights Enforcement Issues of the United Nations Conference on International Organization*, 53 IOWA L. REV. 272 (1967).

31. Among them are Argentina, Austria, Belgium, Cyprus, Egypt, France, Germany (Federal Republic of), Greece, Italy, Japan, Luxemborg, Malta, Mexico, the Netherlands, Spain, Switzerland, Turkey and the European Communities. *See Hearings*, *supra* note 29, at 291, 293 n.23 (memorandum submitted by Dean Norman Redlich on behalf of Freedom House); Riesenfeld, *supra* note 28, at 896.

32. *Cf. Hearings*, *supra* note 29, at 298, 299 n.8 (supplementary statement to letter from Oscar M. Garibaldi to Senator Frank Church) ("The 'intention of the parties' criterion is not always realistic, because a contracting State which has no system of automatic incorporation will not often be interested in the internal arrangements of the other Parties.").

is relevant only to the question of whether private individuals shall have the right of protection in domestic courts against violations of a treaty provision. Whether this result is to be achieved by legislation or by the treaty itself is a question of constitutional law and not within the purview of the intent either of all parties to the treaty or of a particular ratifying power.[33]

The American Law Institute's *Restatement of the Foreign Relations Law of the United States (Revised)*, never mentioning the "intent of the parties," takes the same approach. "In the absence of special agreement," it states by way of comment, "how the United States carries out its international obligations is ordinarily for it to decide. Accordingly, *the intention of the United States determines whether an agreement is to be self-executing in the United States* or should await implementing legislation."[34]

In any event, domestic courts, faced with determining the domestic impact of the human rights clauses of the UN Charter,[35] have held repeatedly that they are non-self-executing. In an early decision that has become the leading case in point, *Sei Fujii v. California*, the California District Court of Appeals struck down a provision of the California Alien Land Law, under which land transferred to an alien not eligible for citizenship escheated to the state, on the ground that the racially-motivated statute ran afoul of the nondiscriminatory provisions found in article 55(c) of the UN Charter.[36] The California

---

33. Riesenfeld, *supra* note 28, at 895-96.

   From a survey of the copious literature it emerges that the concept of self-executing treaties is in need of clarification. It has separate international and domestic constitutional aspects. The international aspect focuses on the issue of whether the treaty aims at the immediate creation of rights and duties of private individuals which are enforceable and to be enforced by domestic tribunals. The domestic constitutional aspect deals with the question whether and under what circumstances such enforceability and enforcement needs separate legislative action to accomplish this aim.

Id. at 896-97; *cf. supra* text at note 29.

34. 1 RESTATEMENT, *supra* note 3, § 131 comment h, at 58 (emphasis added); *see also supra* text accompanying note 29.

35. While all three branches of the federal government may have reason to assess whether a particular treaty is self-executing, ultimately the determination by the judiciary is the one that counts. *See* 1 RESTATEMENT, *supra* note 3, § 131 comment h, at 58:

   After the agreement is concluded, the President often must decide in the first instance whether the agreement is self-executing, whether existing law is adequate to enable the United States to carry out its obligations, or whether he shall seek further legislation. Congress may also consider whether new legislation is necessary and what it shall provide. Whether an agreement is to be given [effect] without further legislation is an issue that a court must decide when a party seeks to invoke the agreement as law.

Id.

36. 217 P.2d 481 (1950), *aff'd*, 38 Cal. 2d 718, 242 P.2d 617 (1952).

Supreme Court, while affirming the judgment, did so exclusively on the ground that the statute violated the equal protection clause of the fourteenth amendment.[37] It specifically rejected the lower court's reasoning, observing that there was nothing in articles 55 and 56

> to indicate that these provisions were intended to become rules of law for the courts of this country upon the ratification of the Charter.
>
> The language used in Articles 55 and 56 is not the type customarily employed in treaties which have been held to be self-executing and to create rights and duties in individuals.
>
> . . . .
>
> [Articles 55 and 56] lack the mandatory quality and definiteness which would indicate an intent to create justiciable rights in private persons immediately upon ratification . . . .
>
> The humane and enlightened objectives of the United Nations Charter are, of course, entitled to respectful consideration by the courts and Legislatures of every member nation, since that document expresses the universal desire of thinking men for peace and for equality of rights and opportunities. The Charter represents a moral commitment of foremost importance, and we must not permit the spirit of our pledge to be compromised or disparaged in either our domestic or foreign affairs. We are satisfied, however, that the Charter provisions relied on by plaintiff were not intended to supersede existing domestic legislation, and we cannot hold that they operate to invalidate the alien land law.[38]

The notion that even the norm of nondiscrimination found in article 55(c) does not provide a rule of law for domestic courts has surfaced repeatedly in subsequent cases. In *Camacho v. Rogers*, a federal district court ruled that "the very wording of Article 55 shows that it is not intended to be self-executing," and that in any event "[t]he question of whether Article 55 is self-executing has been fully discussed in *Sei Fujii v. State* and as appears there the answer is that it is not."[39] This view was echoed in *Diggs v. Dent*,[40] where another

---

37. 38 Cal. 2d 718, 725, 242 P.2d 617, 622 (1952).

38. *Id.* at 722-25, 242 P.2d at 621-22. The Supreme Court of Michigan used similar reasoning in an earlier case involving the enforceability of the UN Charter provisions. *See* Sipes v. McGhee, 316 Mich. 614, 25 N.W.2d 638 (1947), *rev'd,* 334 U.S. 1 (1948). There it noted that the "pronouncements [of the Charter] are merely indicative of a desirable social trend and an objective devoutly to be desired by all well-thinking peoples." *Id.* at 628, 25 N.W.2d at 644.

39. 199 F. Supp. 155, 158 (S.D.N.Y. 1961) (citation omitted).

40. Civ. No. 74-1292 (D.D.C. May 14, 1975), *reprinted in* 14 INTERNATIONAL LEGAL MATERIALS 797, 804 (1975), *aff'd sub nom.* Diggs v. Richardson, 555 F.2d 848 (D.C. Cir. 1976). For an excellent critique of the district court's decision, see 24 KAN. L. REV. 395 (1976).

federal district court ruled that, while the Charter imposed "definite" international obligations on the United States,

> [T]reaties do not generally confer upon citizens rights which they may enforce in the courts. It is only when a treaty is "self-executing" that individuals derive enforceable rights from the treaty, without further legislative or executive action. . . . The provisions of the Charter of the United Nations are not self-executing and do not vest any of the plaintiffs with any legal rights which they may assert in this court.[41]

On appeal, the United States Court of Appeals for the District of Columbia affirmed, stating that even if the Charter imposed a binding international obligation on the United States "that obligation does not confer rights on the citizens of the United States that are enforceable in court in the absence of implementing legislation."[42]

The above approach to the human rights clauses of the UN Charter, while early on receiving some support in academic writings,[43] has been roundly criticized by most commentators.[44] It should be noted too that "[t]he decision [in *Fijii*] was not appealed to the Supreme Court of the United States, so the point remains unsettled for the country as a whole."[45] Thus, while this writer is extremely doubtful whether the Supreme Court—at least as presently

---

41. 14 INTERNATIONAL LEGAL MATERIALS 804 (1975).

42. 555 F.2d at 850. For commentary on the *Diggs* case, see Newman & Burke, *Diggs v. Richardson: International Human Rights in U.S. Courts*, 34 NAT'L LAW. GUILD PRAC. 52 (1977); Note, *Individual Enforcement of Obligations Arising Under the United Nations Charter*, 19 SANTA CLARA L. REV. 195 (1979); Comment, *Public Interest Litigation and United States Foreign Policy*, 18 HARV. INT'L L.J. 375 (1977).

43. *See, e.g.*, Hudson, *Charter Provisions on Human Rights in American Law*, 44 AM. J. INT'L L. 543 (1950).

> [T]he Charter's provisions on human rights have not been incorporated into the municipal law of the United States so as to supersede inconsistent State legislation, because they are not self-executing. They state general purposes and create for the United States only obligations to cooperate in promoting certain ends. . . . [Thus], [a]part from action taken by Congress to implement them, the application of the Charter's human rights provisions is not for a court to undertake.

Id. at 545.

44. Schluter remarks that the Fujii court applied an unnecessarily strict standard in determining that articles 55 and 56 were not self-executing. "The court failed . . . to observe that other American courts have applied less definite and less detailed treaty provisions than those [that it chose] to cite." Schluter, *supra* note 30, at 147; *see also* Asakura v. Seattle, 265 U.S. 332 (1924); *infra* text at note 50 (quoting *Asakura*).

On the domestic legal effect of the human rights clauses of the UN Charter, see especially Schachter, *The Charter and the Constitution: The Human Rights Provisions in American Law*, 4 VAND. L. REV. 643 (1951); Sohn, *The Human Rights Law of the Charter*, 12 TEX. INT'L L.J. 129 (1977); Note, *supra* note 42.

45. Finch, *The Need to Restrain the Treaty-Making Power of the United States Within Constitutional Limits*, 48 AM. J. INT'L L. 57, 72 (1954).

constituted—would hold the human rights clauses to be self-executing if it were to be presented with the question, a few observers of the Court now believe that "[i]t is unlikely that [*Fujii*] . . . would be decided the same way today."[46] Such assertions have been supported by various combinations of the following arguments.

First, it is argued that "[a]lthough [an expansive] construction of the human rights clauses . . . clearly goes beyond the actual intent of the framers of the Charter, so does the construction of the American and other constitutions in judicial practice."[47] The point here is that the Charter's human rights provisions could be rendered enforceable by an enlightened judiciary determined to encourage social progress. In considering this interpretive approach,

> [o]ne could point towards a number of legislative or constitutional analogies in the United States. Section 1 of the Fourteenth amendment, for example, is "self-executing" in the sense that courts apply the Due Process Clause or the Equal Protection clause without legislative implementation. But note, on the other hand, that Section 5 of that amendment gives Congress the power to enforce it "by appropriate legislation." That is, the same text at once constitutes applicable "law" upon which private parties may rely in litigation, and provides a basis for federal legislation.[48]

Such a reading of the Charter's human rights clauses finds support in the principle enunciated by the Supreme Court in *Asakura v. Seattle*,[49] namely, that "[t]reaties are to be construed in a broad and liberal spirit, and, when two constructions are possible, one restrictive of rights which may be claimed under it, and the other favorable to them, the latter is preferred."[50]

Second, it is doubtful whether it can be maintained today—as it was argued successfully in *Fujii*[51]—that the Charter's human rights clauses are too vague and indefinite to establish binding legal obligations enforceable in domestic courts. Apart from the fact that "the concept of human rights . . . has a core of meaning provided by

---

46. Schluter, *supra* note 30, at 162 n.291.

47. *Id.* at 162-63.

48. H. STEINER & D. VAGTS, TRANSNATIONAL LEGAL PROBLEMS 584 n.31 (2d ed. 1976).

49. 265 U.S. 332 (1924).

50. *Id.* at 342. The Supreme Court reaffirmed this principle in Factor v. Laubenheimer, 290 U.S. 276 (1933), noting that "if a treaty fairly admits of two constructions, one restricting the rights which may be claimed under it, and the other enlarging it, the more liberal construction is to be preferred." *Id.* at 293-94; *see also* Kolovrat v. Oregon, 336 U.S. 187, 193 (1961) ("This Court has many times set its face against treaty interpretations that unduly restrict rights a treaty is adopted to protect.").

51. *See supra* text at note 39.

a continuously developing body of general principles [long] recognized by . . . international customary law,''[52] any vagueness that may have characterized articles 55 and 56 in 1945 "has been eliminated in large measure through subsequent adoption by the United Nations of various international human rights instruments that give juridical content to [these articles].''[53] Specifically, the Universal Declaration, discussed below, is now widely regarded as containing a universally recognized catalog of the human rights the UN deems fundamental.[54] Furthermore, "the International Covenant on Civil and Political Rights, and the International Covenant on Economic, Social and Cultural Rights evidence an unprecedented international consensus on the meaning of the concept of human rights.''[55] Considering the foregoing, plus the fact that the Charter's

---

52. Schluter, *supra* note 30, at 123; *see supra* text at notes 12-16.

53. Sarosdy, *Jurisdiction Following Illegal Extraterritorial Seizure: International Human Rights Obligations as an Alternative to Constitutional Stalemate,* 54 TEX. L. REV. 1439 (1976).

54. Whether the Universal Declaration now reflects customary law and hence must be applied by domestic courts (*see supra* text at note 4) is discussed at notes 128-92 *infra.* The present question is a related yet distinct one, namely, whether the Declaration has become so widely accepted as an authoritative interpretation of the UN Charter's human rights clauses that, reading it into the Charter, a domestic court might find them to be self-executing. *See* Comment, *Self-Executing Treaties and the Human Rights Provisions of the United Nations Charter: A Separation of Powers Problem,* 25 BUFFALO L. REV. 773, 783-84 (1976); *cf.* Sarosdy, *supra* note 53, at 1465; Schluter, *supra* note 30, at 144-49.

This contention, commonly called the Newman-Berkeley thesis after its leading proponent, former Judge (again Professor) Newman of the University of California at Berkeley, has been raised by amici several times in recent years. *See* Brief of the International Human Rights Law Group as Amicus Curiae Urging Affirmance at 9-13, Doe v. Plyler, 628 F.2d 448 (5th Cir. 1980); Brief for Amnesty International-U.S.A., International League for Human Rights, and the Lawyers' Committee for International Human Rights as Amicus Curiae at 7-9, Filartiga v. Pena-Irala, 630 F.2d 876 (2d Cir. 1980); *cf.* Brief of the International Human Rights Law Group, the Council on Hemispheric Affairs and the Washington Office on Latin America as Amicus Curiae at 10-13, Filartiga v. Pena-Irala, 630 F.2d 876 (2d Cir. 1980).

To date no court has passed upon the thesis. The *Filartigo* court stated:

> Appellants "associate themselves with" the argument of some of the *amici curiae* that their claim arises directly under a treaty of the United States, Brief for Appellants at 23 n.*, but nonetheless primarily rely upon treaties and other international instruments as evidence of an emerging norm of customary international law, rather that [sic] independent sources of law.

630 F.2d at 880 n.7; *cf.* Henkin, *The Constitution at Sea,* 36 ME. L. REV. 201, 209 n.31 (1984) ("The United States . . . is a party to the U.N. Charter which includes general human rights obligations, and it may be bound by some of the provisions of the Universal Declaration of Human Rights, either as elaborations of the Charter obligation or under customary international law.'').

55. Note, *supra* note 42, at 209. The Newman-Berkeley thesis described in note 54 *supra* can be expanded to embrace not only the Universal Declaration but also the UN Covenant on Civil and Political Rights and other relevant international human rights instruments. The latter, of course, also may contribute to the development of customary international law norms enforceable as such by domestic courts. *See infra* text at and accompanying note 156.

human rights clauses are in any event "no vaguer than any number of well-known constitutional and statutory expressions which have been left to the Courts to apply,"[56] it is not unreasonable to suggest that the *Fujii* determination that articles 55 and 56 are non-self-executing may be "ripe for overruling."[57]

Third, even if one acknowledges that the language in these articles is too general to be self-executing as to all human rights guaranteed by the Universal Declaration and the two Covenants, the "all or nothing" approach to the interpretation of the Charter taken in *Fujii* must be rejected. In view of the widespread and indeed universal support for the nondiscrimination norm contained in article 55(c),[58] it can be argued persuasively that "the nondiscrimination element in Article 55 is a self-sustaining and definite rule of law even if other human rights are not specified clearly enough to be protected on the basis of the Charter provisions."[59] This argument finds support in the fact that the International Court of Justice, in its Advisory Opinion in the *Namibia* case,[60] noted that signatories of the Charter had pledged themselves "to observe and respect, in . . . [territories] having an international status, human rights and fundamental freedoms for all without distinction as to race," and that to deny human rights on the basis of race was "a flagrant violation of the purposes and principles of the Charter."[61] Many jurists believe, reasoning from this advisory opinion, that at the very least the prohibition of racial discrimination contained in the Charter is general in nature and binding on all states.[62]

---

56. Schachter, *supra* note 44, at 655; *see infra* text accompanying note 69.

57. Note, *supra* note 42, at 209.

58. *See* I. BROWNLIE, PRINCIPLES OF PUBLIC INTERNATIONAL LAW 596-98 (3d ed. 1979); M. McDOUGAL, H. LASSWELL & L. CHEN, HUMAN RIGHTS AND WORLD PUBLIC ORDER 581-611 *passim* (1980); McDougal, Lasswell & Chen, *The Protection of Respect and Human Rights: Freedom of Choice and World Public Order*, 24 AM. U.L. REV. 919, 1034-86 (1975). *See generally* W. McKEAN, EQUALITY AND DISCRIMINATION UNDER INTERNATIONAL LAW (1983).

59. Schluter, *supra* note 30, at 148. "At the very least, the fact that the articles prohibit distinctions made in the enjoyment of human rights and fundamental freedoms on the grounds of race, sex, language or religion has never been questioned." Note, *supra* note 42, at 209; *cf. 1* RESTATEMENT, *supra* note 3, § 702(f) comment a, at 469. (only racial—not, e.g. sexual—discrimination prohibited by customary international law). *See infra* text at and accompanying notes 62 & 80.

60. Advisory Opinion on the Continued Presence of South Africa in Namibia (South West Africa), 1971 I.C.J. 16.

61. *Id.* at 57.

62. *See, e.g.,* Schwelb, *The International Court of Justice and the Human Rights Clauses of the Charter*, 66 AM. J. INT'L L. 337 (1972). Human rights lawyers advanced this argument in Motion for Leave to File Brief Amicus Curiae and Brief of the International Human Rights Law Group at 14-18, Bob Jones Univ. v. United States, 461 U.S. 574 (1983) (decided on statutory construction grounds). *See supra* text accompanying note 59.

Fourth, even taking into account the general nature of the language in articles 55 and 56, it seems clear that whatever human rights norms are generated by the Charter must be given effect domestically by member states, including the United States, if they are to fulfill their legal obligations under the treaty.[63] Over 150 years ago, Secretary of State Livingston stated,

> The Government of the United States presumes that whenever a treaty has been duly concluded and ratified by the acknowledged authorities competent for that purpose, an obligation is thereby imposed upon *each and every department of the Government,* to carry it into complete effect, according to its terms, and that on the performance of this obligation consists the due observance of good faith among nations.[64]

Thus domestic courts, being one of the "departments" of government, are "obliged to construe and apply [articles 55 and 56] in the normal exercise of their jurisdiction"[65] so as to render them effective, *i.e.,* to deem them self-executing.

Finally, it is arguable that two decisions during the past decade concerning the enforceability of international law in domestic courts may have paved the way for an eventual rejection of the *Fujii* rationale by the Supreme Court. In 1974, in *People of Saipan ex rel.*

---

63. During the Ford and Carter Administrations, the United States consistently took the position that the human rights clauses of the UN Charter have legal effect and thus must be complied with by all countries, including the United States. Thus the Acting Legal Adviser of the Department of State, Geroge Aldrich, observed in 1974 that "members of the United Nations have a legal duty to promote respect for and protection of human rights around the world. . . . The Charter of the United Nations and the Universal Declaration of Human Rights are the basic texts in this field. I would point, in particular, to articles 55 and 56 of the United Nations Charter. . . . The United States recognizes these obligations and is determined to live up to them." 1974 Digest of United States Practice in International Law 125 (1975).

President Carter himself reaffirmed this position in his March 1977 address to the UN, declaring, "The solemn commitments of the United Nations Charter, of the United Nations Universal Declaration for Human Rights, of the Helsinki Accords, and of many other international instruments must be taken just as seriously as coimmercial or security agreements." 1977 Pub. Papers 444, 450-51; *see also* Address by Assistant Secretary of State for Human Rights and Humanitarian Affairs Patricia Derian, Lawyers' Committee for Civil Rights Under Law (Mar. 16, 1978) ("the position of the United States that the provision of Articles 1, 55 and 56 of the United Nations Charter embody mutual recognition by all parties that every person without distinction is entitled under the Charter to respect for his or her human rights and fundamental freedoms").

64. Letter from Secretary of State Livingston to Mr. Serurier, June 3, 1833, *reprinted in* 2 F. Wharton, Digest of the International Law of the United States 67 (1887) (emphasis added).

65. Wright, *National Courts and Human Rights — The Fujii Case,* 45 Am. J. Int'l L. 62, 75 (1951).

Guerrero v. United States Department of Interior, [66] the United States Court of Appeals for the Ninth Circuit adopted a more satisfactory test for determining whether a treaty is self-executing. [67] In holding that the UN Trusteeship Agreement over Micronesia provided the plaintiffs with "direct, affirmative, and judicially enforceable rights" to challenge the execution of a lease purportedly in violation of that agreement, the court of appeals noted

> The extent to which an international agreement establishes affirmative and judicially enforceable obligations without implementing legisla-

---

66. 502 F.2d 90 (9th Cir. 1974), *cert. denied,* 420 U.S. 1003 (1975). The *Saipan* court cited M. McDougal, H. Lasswell & J. Miller, The Interpretation of Agreements and World Public Order (1967) as supporting authority for its "test" of whether a treaty is self-executing. *Cf.* McDougal, *Comment,* 45 Am. Soc'y Int'l L. Proc. 101, 102 (1951) ("'[T]his word 'self-executing' is essentially meaningless, and . . . the quicker we drop it from our vocabulary the better for clarity and understanding.").

67. Earlier approaches to determining whether a treaty is self-executing are mentioned briefly in the text accompanying note 27 *supra. See also* Comment, *Criteria for Self-Executing Treaties,* 1968 Ill. L.F. 238. The following passage from a memorandum submitted to the Senate Foreign Relations Committee by Dean Redlich summarizes them as follows:

> The traditional formulation of the concept of the self-executing treaty appears in *Foster v. Neilson.* In that case, Justice Marshall based the distinction between self-executing and non-self-executing treaties on whether the language of the instrument operates by itself as a rule of law or is contractual and requires implementation.
>
> . . . .
>
> Since *Foster,* analysis under the concept of self-execution has developed along three lines. The first, objective test is that formulated in *Foster.* The court looks to the language of the treaty and, most frequently, compares it to that of a statute to determine whether the provision prescribes a rule that is sufficiently definite and mandatory for a court to rely upon it as it would a statute.
>
> The second, subjective test inquires into the intent of the drafters or parties to a treaty to answer the question of whether the treaty is self-executing or executory. Even if the court finds implementing language, some authority exists under this test for the proposition that some provisions may be self-executing while others may not be. Particularly in the case of multilateral agreements, the presence or absence of implementing language is not controlling because those provisions may have been included for the benefit of States that do not have constitutions which operate automatically to make treaties the "supreme law of the land."
>
> Finally, courts have used a subject matter test in which the inquiry is directed to the question of whether the treaty of necessity requires Congressional implementation to be effective. The test amounts to a delegation of powers analysis in which the court determines to which branch of government the subjects encompassed by the treaty have been allocated by the Constitution. However, this last test cannot be determinative in attempting to assess the self-executing or non-self-executing nature of [human rights treaties] . . . because the only instances in which subject matter could be conclusive would be those cases in which implementation required an appropriation from the federal treasury or involved a criminal penalty.

Hearings, supra note 29, at 291, 292 (citing 27 U.S. (2 Pet.) 253 (1829) (memorandum submitted by Dean Norman Redlich on Behalf of Freedom House).

tion must be determined in each case by reference to many contextual factors: the purposes of the treaty and the objectives of its creators, the existence of domestic procedures and institutions appropriate for direct implementation, the availability and feasibility of alternative enforcement methods, and the immediate and long-range social consequences of self- or non-self-execution.[68]

Under this test, a strong case can be made that articles 55 and 56 are self-executing. While, as has been pointed out,[69] it appears impossible to ascertain the objectives of the drafters of the UN Charter in this regard, it is clear that under article 1(3) one of the major purposes of the Charter is to "[promote] and [encourage] respect for human rights and fundamental freedoms for all without distinction as to race, sex, language, or religion." Moreover, it has become evident that, since "alternative enforcement methods" to protect these rights are not generally available on the international level, continuing to construe the UN Charter's human rights clauses as non-self-executing on the domestic level may result, at least in the absence of implementing legislation, in serious deprivations of internationally-recognized human rights. Therefore, using the *Saipan* test an enlightened court someday may reject *Fujii* and conclude that the Charter grants individuals at least a hard core of judicially enforceable human rights.

A second case which contains hints that *Fujii* may be ripe for overruling is *Diggs v. Shultz,*[70] where former Congressman Diggs sued for injunctive relief and for a declaratory judgment that the Byrd Amendment, permitting the United States to resume the importation of chrome from Southern Rhodesia (now Zimbabwe) in violation of UN Security Council Resolution 232 imposing sanctions, was null and void.[71] While ultimately holding that under the last-in-time rule the Byrd Amendment prevailed,[72] the United States

---

68. 502 F.2d at 97 (citing M. McDougal, H. Lasswell & J. Miller, The Interpretation of Agreements and World Public Order (1967)). Significantly, the court of appeals noted that "the substantive rights guaranteed through the Trusteeship Agreement are not precisely defined. However, we do not believe that the agreement is too vague for judicial enforcement. Its language is no more general than such terms as 'due process of law,' 'seaworthiness,' 'equal protection of the law,' 'good faith,' or 'restraint of trade,' which courts interpret every day." *Id.* at 99; *see supra* text at note 56.

69. *See supra* text at notes 29-30.

70. 470 F.2d 461 (D.C. Cir. 1972), *cert. denied,* 411 U.S. 931 (1973).

71. *Id.* at 463-64.

72. The United States Court of Appeals for the District of Columbia, brushing aside plaintiffs' somewhat strained argument that the Byrd Amendment did not expressly compel the President to end the domestic observance of UN sanctions, observed that neither legislative history nor any amount of statutory interpretation could change the obvious purpose and effect of the Byrd Amendment. It was clearly

Court of Appeals for the District of Columbia reversed the district court's determination that the plaintiffs lacked standing to bring the action. In so doing, the court of appeals stated that the plaintiffs were "unquestionably within the reach of [the] purpose [of Security Council Resolution 232] and among its intended beneficiaries;" that the plaintiffs were injured "in fact;" and that there was a "logical nexus" between the plaintiffs' claimed injuries and the "challenged [congressional] action."[73] These remarks, although not directly relevant to the question of the UN Charter's self- or non-self-executing nature, at least severely restrict one of the doctrines the judiciary traditionally has invoked to dismiss actions based upon alleged statutory violations of United States treaty obligations.[74] Thus it should be much easier in the future to raise test cases based upon the self-executing nature of the Charter's human rights clauses, especially when Security Council resolutions are involved.[75]

---

a measure which would make—and was intended to make—the United States a certain treaty violator. The so-called options given to the President are, in reality, not options at all. In any event, they are in neither case alternatives which are appropriately to be forced upon him by a court.

Under our constitutional scheme, Congress can denounce treaties if it sees fit to do so, and there is nothing the other branches of government can do about it. We consider that this is precisely what Congress has done in any case.

Id. at 466-67.

The court of appeals' holding was especially disappointing in view of the fact that the treaty obligation in question flowed from the UN Charter, specifically article 25 in which members "agree to accept and carry out the decisions of the Security Council." Some years earlier Professor Sohn, contending, "[t]he obsolete doctrine that international law is not controlling in United States courts when confronted with a later statute is a product of the jurisprudence of a period when international law was quite different from what it is today," had urged the courts to modify the "last-in-time" rule so that at least "the rules derived from the [UN] Charter prevail not only over earlier law but also over later statute." Sohn, *Comment*, 63 AM. SOC'Y INT'L L. PROC. 180 (1960). The plaintiffs in *Diggs v. Shultz* raised a variation of this argument—unsuccessfully. *See* 470 F.2d at 465, n.4. A frontal attack on the last-in-time rule's applicability when the UN Charter is the treaty involved still awaits making.

73. 470 F.2d at 464.

74. The importance of the court of appeals' holding in this regard may be gleaned from the fact that the United States subsequently argued, fortunately in vain, that on this score *Diggs v. Shultz* "was wrongly decided." *See* Diggs v. Richardson, 555 F.2d 848, 850 (D.C. Cir. 1976).

75. One commentator has suggested that

The *Diggs* decision has potentially two areas of innovative effect. The first is in its expansion [of] the concept of standing in the federal courts. The second is in increasing the likelihood that international organizations may promulgate resolutions which may be relied on in domestic courts to challenge the actions of administrative agencies.

Note, *supra* note 42, at 214.

Despite the optimism created in human rights circles by the above two cases,[76] here as elsewhere in the law one must beware of the wish becoming the parent of the thought. True, the human rights clauses of the UN Charter—at least insofar as the non-discrimination norm contained in article 55(c) is concerned—certainly would seem to be self-executing under either the traditional[77] or more recent[78] test. Moreover, support for such an interpretation may be found in the *Restatement of the Foreign Relations Law of the United States (Revised)*, which seems to support a presumption that most treaties are self-executing.[79] Yet, unlike some of his more activist colleagues, this writer does not believe it an opportune time to orchestrate a test case, given the present composition of the Supreme Court. Furthermore, in view of the hesitant attitude most lower court judges

---

As to standing, see *infra* text at note 219. On the question of whether Security Council resolutions may be self-executing, see Note, *Security Council Resolutions in United States Courts*, 50 IND. L.J. 83 (1974). *Cf. Diggs v. Richardson*, 555 F.2d at 850. "[I]t is unlikely that a U.S. court in the near future will hold a UN Security Council resolution to be a self-executing obligation directly enforceable in such fashion. The language in *Diggs v. Richardson*, in fact, points in the other direction." R. LILLICH & F. NEWMAN, INTERNATIONAL HUMAN RIGHTS: PROBLEMS OF LAW AND POLICY 475 (1979).

76. The foothold gained in . . . *Diggs* . . . and the *Saipan* case appears to be firmly established and presages well for the future of our courts as forums increasingly . . . aware of their obligation to realize that violations of international law are not merely political matters to be settled through diplomatic channels by the states involved, but also worthy of redress by [sic] injured individuals in the domestic courts.

Note, *supra* note 42, at 216. *But see infra* text accompanying note 181.

77. *See supra* text accompanying notes 27 & 67.

78. *See supra* text at notes 66-70; *see also* Riesenfeld, *supra* note 28, at 900-01.

A treaty provision which by its terms and purpose is *meant* to stipulate the immediate and not merely progressive creation of rights, privileges, duties, and immunities cognizable in domestic courts and is *capable* of being applied by the courts without further concretization *is* self-executing by virtue of the constitutional mandate of Article VI of the U.S. Constitution.

Id. (emphasis in original).

79. Section 131 of the *Restatement* provides

(3) Courts in the United States are bound to give effect to international law and international agreements of the United States, *except* that a "non-self-executing" agreement will not be given effect as law in the absence of necessary legislation.

(4) An international agreement is "non-self-executing" *if the agreement manifests an intention that it shall not become effective as domestic law without the enactment of implementing legislation,* or in those rare cases where implementing legislation is constitutionally required.

1 RESTATEMENT, *supra* note 3, § 131 (emphasis added).

The reporters' commentary to these subsections makes the point more clearly: "In general, agreements that can be readily given effect by executive or judicial bodies, federal or state, without further legislation, are deemed self-executing, *unless a contrary intention is manifest.*" *Id.* § 131 reporters' note 5, at 67 (emphasis added).

display towards international law in general, he seriously doubts whether one of them will take the lead and hold that the human rights clauses of the UN Charter are self-executing, even with respect to the basic nondiscrimination norm contained in article 55(c).[80] Such arguments are being made—and should be made—in appropriate cases today, but in all likelihood the judiciary will have to experience more international human rights law consciousness-raising before they are accepted and the rationale behind *Fujii* rejected.

IV. The Status of Other Human Rights Treaties in Domestic Law

As is common knowledge, the United States has an exceptionally poor ratification record insofar as international human rights treaties are concerned. The Genocide Convention[81] has languished in the Senate now for over three decades, and no action is contemplated in the near future on the four human rights treaties—the UN Covenant on Civil and Political Rights,[82] the UN Covenant on Economic, Social and Cultural Rights,[83] the Racial Discrimination Convention,[84] and the American Convention on Human Rights[85]—which President Carter sent to the Senate in 1978.[86] Yet, the United States currently is a party to at least eleven international human rights instruments other than the UN Charter,[87] at least two

---

80. For the most recent decision holding that the Charter's human rights clauses are non-self-executing and hence "do not confer rights on individual citizens," see Frolova v. U.S.S.R., 761 F.2d 370 (7th Cir. 1985). Even otherwise enlightened judges continue to take this position. *See, e.g.,* Lareau v. Manson, 507 F. Supp. 1177, 1187-89 n.9 (D. Conn. 1980) (Cabranes, J.), *aff'd in part and modified in part,* 651 F.2d 96 (2d Cir. 1981); *cf.* Filartiga v. Pena-Irala, 630 F.2d at 881, 882 n.9.

81. Convention on the Prevention and Punishment of the Crime of Genocide, *opened for signature* Dec. 9, 1948, *entered into force* Jan. 12, 1951, 78 U.N.T.S. 277, *reprinted in* R. Lillich, *supra* note 18, § 130.1.

82. *See supra* note 19.

83. International Covenant on Economic, Social and Cultural Rights, *adopted* Dec. 16, 1966, *entered into force* Jan. 3, 1976, G.A. Res. 2200, 21 U.N. GAOR Supp. (No. 16) at 49, U.N. Doc. A/6316 (1966), *reprinted in* R. Lillich, *supra* note 18, § 180.1.

84. International Convention on the Elimination of All Forms of Racial Discrimination, *adopted* Dec. 21, 1965, *entered into force* Jan. 4, 1969, 660 U.N.T.S. 195, *reprinted in* R. Lillich, *supra* note 18, § 160.1.

85. *See supra* note 20.

86. Message of the President Transmitting Four Treaties Pertaining to Human Rights, S. Exec. Doc. No. 95-C, D, E and F, 95th Cong., 2d Sess. (1978); *see* U.S. Ratification of the Human Rights Treaties: With or Without Reservations? (R. Lillich ed. 1981). The Foreign Relations Committee held informational hearings on the four treaties in 1979 but has taken no action on them. *Hearings, supra* note 29.

87. *See* R. Lillich, *supra* note 18, §§ 20.1—120.1.

of which have been invoked in domestic courts on the ground that they contain self-executing provisions.[88]

By far the most litigation has centered around the Protocol Relating to the Status of Refugees,[89] which the United States ratified in 1968 and which incorporates by reference the provisions of the Refugees Convention of 1951.[90] Article 1(A)(2) of the latter defines "refugee" to include, inter alia, any person who, "owing to well-founded fear of being persecuted for reasons of race, religion, nationality, membership of a particular social group or political opinion, is outside the country of his nationality and is unable, or owing to such fear, is unwilling to avail himself of the protection of that country." Among the various rights accorded refugees by the convention is the important one of *non-refoulment*. Article 33(1) provides that "[n]o Contracting State shall expel or return ("refouler") a refugee in any manner whatsoever to the frontiers of territories where his life or freedom would be threatened on account of his race, religion, nationality, membership of a particular social group or political opinion." This treaty provision offered the refugee seeking asylum considerably more substantive protection than that afforded him by the parallel statutory provision found in section 243(h) of the Immigration and Nationality Act of 1952.[91] Therefore, if it were considered self-executing the Protocol, being last-in-time, would prevail over the statute to the benefit of the refugee. Yet, despite the apparent self-executing character of articles 1(A)(2) and 33(1)[92] and the obvious differences in language between the statute and the Protocol, the Immigration and Naturalization Service (INS) stoutly maintained that "the Protocol does not require a change in the

---

88. In this regard, recall the late Professor Evans' reminder that "the controversy over the case of *Fujii v. California* does not mean that a self-executing treaty cannot do what the [lower court] sought to accomplish by resort to the United Nations Charter." Evans, *supra* note 27, at 189. Too often *Fujii* is viewed as rendering *all* international human rights treaties non-self-executing, clearly an erroneous reading of the case. *See supra* text at notes 66-69.

89. Protocol Relating to the Statute of Refugees, *signed* Jan. 21, 1967, *entered into force* Oct. 4, 1967, 19 U.S.T. 6223, T.I.A.S. No. 6577, 606 U.N.T.S. 267, *reprinted in* R. Lillich, *supra* note 18, § 110.1.

90. Convention Relating to the Status of Refugees, *opened for signature* July 28, 1951, *entered into force* Apr. 22, 1954, 189 U.N.T.S. 137, *reprinted in* R. Lillich, *supra* note 18, § 280.1.

91. Immigration and Nationality Act of 1952, § 243(h), 8 U.S.C. § 1253(h) (1976); *see* Carliner, *The Implementation of Human Rights Under the U.S. Immigration Law*, in International Human Rights Law and Practice 133, 139 (J. Tuttle ed. 1978).

92. Frank, *Effect of the 1967 United Nations Protocol on the Status of Refugees in the United States*, 11 Int'l Law. 291, 296 (1977).

standards under which claims of persecution are to be decided."[93]

Counsel for numerous (mainly Haitian) refugees challenged the INS view of the Protocol's status in a series of cases.[94] In *Sannon v. United States,*[95] for instance, they argued—and the United States District Court for the Southern District of Florida held—that a regulation issued by the Attorney General regarding the procedure an alien must follow to obtain political asylum either had been misconstrued or was invalid under the Protocol. The district court, without explicitly deciding whether or not the Protocol was self-executing, ruled that the interpretation of the regulation urged by the Attorney General found "no justification in the Protocol, in logic or in fairness,"[96] and in so ruling noted that "were it not for the Protocol petitioners would have no grounds for objecting to their exclusion."[97] Similarly, in *Pierre v. United States,*[98] the United States Court of Appeals for the Fifth Circuit held that a statutory provision which prohibited certain aliens from entering the United States was not applicable to appellants, stating that "application of [the statute to those aliens] would render the [Protocol] meaningless as a practical matter."[99] Numerous other cases, the most significant perhaps being *Coriolan,*[100] saw domestic courts either applying the Protocol in "last-in-time" fashion or otherwise assuming sub silentio that it was self-executing.[101]

---

93. Carliner, *supra* note 91, at 140. "No court has reversed this view to date [1978]. Applicants for asylum and for stays of deportation on grounds of human rights have largely been left to the exercise of discretion by the administrative agencies. As we have seen, its exercise has been heavily influenced by political and foreign policy considerations." *Id.* For an early plea to bring the statute into line with the Protocol, see Comment, *Immigration Law and the Refugee—A Recommendation to Harmonize the Statutes With the Treaties,* 6 CALIF. W. INT'L L.J. 129 (1975).

94. The issues raised in these cases are set out in Kramer, *Due Process Rights for Excludable Aliens Under United States Immigration Law and the United Nations Protocol Relating to the Status of Refugees—Haitian Aliens, A Case in Point,* 10 N.Y.U. J. INT'L L. & POL'Y 203 (1977), and Lieberman & Krinsky, *Political Asylum and Due Process of Law: The Case of the Haitian Refugees,* 33 NAT'L LAW. GUILD PRAC. 102 (1976).

95. 427 F. Supp. 1270 (S.D. Fla.), *vacated mem.,* 566 F.2d 104 (5th Cir. 1977); *see also* Sannon v. United States, 460 F. Supp. 458 (S.D. Fla. 1978) (same case on remand).

96. 427 F. Supp. at 1276.

97. *Id.* at 1274.

98. 525 F.2d 933 (5th Cir. 1976).

99. *Id.* at 935; *cf.* Pierre v. United States, 547 F.2d 1281, 1287-89 (5th Cir.), *vacated and remanded,* 434 U.S. 962 (1977) (statutory provision consistent with Protocol).

100. Coriolan v. Immigration & Naturalization Serv., 559 F.2d 993, 996-97 (5th Cir. 1977); *see* Note, *Coriolan v. Immigration and Naturalization Service: A Closer Look at Immigration Law and the Political Refugee,* 6 SYR. J. INT'L L. & COM. 133 (1978).

101. *See, e.g.,* Kashani v. Immigration & Naturalization Serv., 547 F.2d 376, 379 (7th Cir. 1977); Kan Kam Lin v. Rinaldi, 361 F.2d 1229 (3d Cir.) (per curiam), *cert. denied,*

388   *CINCINNATI LAW REVIEW*   [Vol. 54

The upshot of these cases was that Congress, in the Refugee Act of 1980, rewrote section 243(h)[102] with the intention of bringing it into conformity with article 33(1).[103] While lower court cases since then differ on whether or not the Protocol is self-executing,[104] they routinely treat it as a "policy backdrop" against which the Act should be construed.[105] Moreover, the Supreme Court recently took a somewhat similar approach in the *Stevic* case.[106] Thus, although one might have thought that under the "last-in-time" rule the Protocol, even if self-executing, lost its bite after the Act took effect in 1980, it continues to be invoked and taken into account today. The net result is that significant progress has been made in upgrading the law applied by domestic courts in refugee matters, progress achieved in large measure by astute counsel using international human rights law contained in an arguably self-executing treaty.

The second treaty that was argued to contain self-executing provisions was the Protocol of Buenos Aires,[107] which amended the

---

419 U.S. 874 (1974); *In re* Sindona, 450 F. Supp. 672, 694 (S.D.N.Y. 1978); Ming v. Marks, 367 F. Supp. 673, 676-81 (S.D.N.Y. 1973), *aff'd on opinion below,* 505 F.2d 1170, 1171-72 (2d Cir. 1974) (per curiam), *cert. denied,* 421 U.S. 911 (1975).

102. Refugee Act of 1980, Pub. L. No. 96-212, §§ 201(a), 203(e), 94 Stat. 102, 107 (codified as amended at 8 U.S.C. §§ 1101(a)(42)(A), 1253(h)(1) (1982)). *See generally* Martin, *The Refugee Act of 1980: Its Past and Future,* 3 MICH. Y.B. INT'L LEGAL STUD., TRANSNATIONAL LEGAL PROBLEMS OF REFUGEES 91 (1982).

103. *But see* Helton, *Political Asylum Under the 1980 Refugee Act: An Unfulfilled Promise,* 17 U. MICH. J.L. REF. 243, 250-53 (1984) (critical of INS's continued adherence to "clear probability of persecution" standard). The Supreme Court recently upheld the INS interpretation of revised § 243(h), finding no merit in the "argument that this construction is inconsistent with the Protocol." Immigration & Naturalization Serv. v. Stevic, 104 S. Ct. 2489, 2500 n.22 (1984).

104. *Compare* Bertrand v. Sava, 684 F.2d 204, 218-19 (2d Cir. 1982) (non-self-executing) *with* Fernandez-Roque v. Smith, 539 F. Supp. 925, 935 n.25 (N.D. Ga. 1982) (probably self-executing).

105. *See, e.g.,* Haitian Refugee Center v. Smith, 676 F.2d 1023, 1038 n.35 (5th Cir. 1982); *see also* Orantes-Hernandez v. Smith, 541 F. Supp. 351, 365 n.15 (C.D. Cal. 1982) ("Whether or not the Protocol is self-executing, plaintiffs are clearly entitled to rely on it as persuasive authority and to urge the Court to construe the Refugee Act of 1980 . . . consistently with the Protocol's provisions."); *infra* text at and accompanying note 216.

106. *See supra* text accompanying note 103. Whether the Protocol is self-executing or not is now squarely before the Supreme Court in Jean v. Nelson, 544 F. Supp. 973 (S.D. Fla. 1982), *aff'd in part and rev'd in part,* 711 F.2d 1455 (11th Cir. 1983), *dismissed in part and rev'd in part,* 727 F.2d 957 (11th Cir.) (en banc), *cert. granted,* 105 S. Ct. 563 (1984). *See* Brief of Amici Curiae the Procedural Aspects of International Law Institute, the International Human Rights Law Group, the International League for Human Rights and the Center for Constitutional Rights at 27-43, *Jean v. Nelson.*

107. Protocol of Amendment to the Charter of the Organization of American States (Protocol of Buenos Aires), *signed* Feb. 27, 1967, *entered into force* Feb. 27, 1970, 21 U.S.T. 607, T.I.A.S. No. 6847, *reprinted in* R. LILLICH, *supra* note 18, § 120.1. *See generally* Buergenthal, *The Revised OAS Charter and the Protection Human of Rights,* 69 AM J. INT'L L. 828 (1975).

Charter of the Organization of Amercian States.[108] In *Plyler v. Doe,*[109] where the lower federal courts and ultimately the Supreme Court struck down as violative of the equal protection clause a Texas statute effectively used to deny free elementary school education to the children of undocumented aliens, plaintiffs contended that the statute also ran afoul of article 47 of the Protocol.[110] This article provides, inter alia, that:

> The Member States will exert the greatest efforts, in accordance with their constitutional processes, to ensure the effective exercise of the right to education, on the following bases:
> a.   Elementary education, compulsory for children of school age, shall also be offered to all others who can benefit from it. When provided by the State it shall be without charge.[111]

Faced with this innovative argument, the United States District Court for the Eastern District of Texas side-stepped deciding whether the above provision was self-executing; rather, it used article 47(a) as support for its alternative holding that the Texas statute infringed upon an area that had been preempted by federal laws regulating immigration and the education of the disadvantaged children. After setting out several of the latter, the district court added tha⁺ "[t]he federal government's commitment to expanding educational opportunity is also evidenced in [article 47(a) of] the Protocol of Buenos Aires."[112] On appeal, the United States Court of Appeals for the Fifth Circuit not only ignored the argument by one of the amicus curiae that article 47(a) was self-executing,[113] but, after noting in

---

108. CHARTER OF THE ORGANIZATION OF AMERICAN STATES, *signed* April 30, 1948, *entered into force* Dec. 13, 1951, [1952] 2 U.S.T. 2394, T.I.A.S. No. 2361, 19 U.N.T.S. 3.

109. 458 F. Supp. 569 (E.D. Tex. 1978), *aff'd,* 628 F.2d 448 (5th Cir. 1980), *aff'd,* 457 U.S. 202 (1982).

110. *Id.* at 592; *cf.* Kane & Velarde-Munoz, *Undocumented Aliens and the Constitution: Limitations on State Action Denying Children Access to Public Education,* 5 HASTINGS CONST. L.Q. 461, 504 & 505 n.367 (1978).

111. Protocol of Amendment to the Charter of the Organization of American States (Protocol of Buenos Aires), *signed* Feb. 27, 1967, *entered into force* Feb. 27, 1970, 21 U.S.T. 607, T.I.A.S. No. 6847, *reprinted in* R. LILLICH, *supra* note 18, § 120.

112. 458 F. Supp. at 592. *But see infra* text at note 115.

113. *See* Brief of the International Human Rights [Law] Group as Amicus Curiae Urging Affirmance at 3-23 *passim,* Doe v. Plyler, 628 F.2d 448 (5th Cir. 1980); *accord* Kane & Velarde-Munoz, *supra* note 110. The Department of Justice filed an amicus brief addressed only to the equal protection issue. *See* 628 F.2d at 450 n.3. *But cf.* Letter from H. Rowan Gaither, Office of the Legal Adviser, U.S. Dep't of State, to Sam Williamson, Esq. (Dec. 23, 1974) (conveying that Department's opinion that article 47(a) was "not intended to be read as an obligation imposed upon the various states of the United States except in the most general manner of goals which the Federal government would hope could be attained"). The court of appeals undoubtedly would have given "great weight" to this letter had it been called to its attention. *See* 2 RESTATEMENT, *supra* note 3, § 326(2).

dictum that "the Protocol of Buenos Aires . . . has never been considered self-executing,"[114] reversed the district court's alternative federal preemption holding on the ground that article 47(a) "does not indicate a clear commitment to educating children illegally in the country."[115]

The Supreme Court, even if it had addressed arguments beyond the equal protection clause, thus would have received very little assistance on the self-execution question from either of the above opinions. However, it would have found some muddled discussion of the issue followed by a square holding that article 47(a) was non-self-executing in the related case of *In re Alien Children Education Litigation*, which it had joined with *Plyler* for purposes of briefing and oral argument.[116] There, presented with the argument that article 47(a) was a self-executing treaty provision which invalidated the Texas statute under the supremacy clause, the United States District Court for the Southern District of Texas ran through the litany of self-execution and concluded that it "was not intended to be self-executing; it was 'not addressed to the judicial branch of our government.' "[117] As it then explained:

> Article 47(a) is no doubt sufficiently direct to imply the intention to create affirmative and judicially enforceable rights. The article read as a whole, however, belies that construction. Article 47 begins with the statement that "The Member States will exert the greatest efforts, in accordance with their constitutional processes, to insure the effective exercise of the right to education. . . ." This is not the kind of promissory language which confers rights in the absence of implementing legislation. The parties have engaged to perform a particular act, that is, to exert the greatest efforts to advance the cause

---

114. 628 F.2d at 453. Nor, of course, had it ever been held to be non-self-executing, save in the related case of *In re* Alien Children Educ. Litig., 501 F. Supp. 544 (S.D. Tex. 1980), *aff'd unreported mem.* (5th Cir. 1981), *aff'd sub nom.* Plyler v. Doe, 457 U.S. 202 (1982), which the court of appeals footnotes only in connection with the equal protection issue. *See* 628 F.2d at 450 n.5.

115. *Id.* at 454; *cf. supra* text at note 112.

116. 501 F. Supp. 544 (S.D. Tex. 1980), *aff'd unreported mem.* (5th Cir. 1981), *aff'd sub nom.* Plyler v. Doe, 457 U.S. 202 (1982). In the interest of full disclosure, it should be recorded that the present writer testified as an expert witness on international law for the plaintiffs in this case, arguing, inter alia, that article 47(a) was self-executing. The expert witness for Texas was Professor Covey T. Oliver, whose contrary views may be found in Oliver, *The Treaty Power and National Foreign Policy as Vehicles for the Enforcement of Human Rights in the United States*, 9 HOFSTRA L. REV. 411 (1981).

On the growing use of expert testimony in such cases, see 1 RESTATEMENT, *supra* note 3, § 133 comment c, at 75; Baade, *Proving Foreign and International Law in Domestic Tribunals*, 18 VA. J. INT'L L. 619 (1978); Panel, *Proving International Law in a National Forum*, 70 AM. SOC'Y INT'L L. PROC. 10 (1976). *See also infra* text accompanying note 162.

117. 501 F. Supp. at 590 (quoting Diggs v. Richardson, 555 F.2d at 851).

of education. They have not contracted to provide free public education to all children of school age within the country. The court concludes that Article 47 of the amended Charter of the Organization of American States is a non-self-executing treaty and that it does not invalidate inconsistent state laws.[118]

The above paragraph initially acknowledges that an interpretation of article 47(a) "in accordance with the ordinary meaning"[119] of the text leaves "no doubt" that it is "sufficiently direct to imply the intention to create affirmative and judicially enforceable rights." Yet, somewhat surprisingly in view of such apparent certainty, the district court then purports to examine the article "as a whole,"[120]

---

118. *Id.* (citations omitted). In a footnote the district court adds the following dictum:
> The court is aware of other problems with the plaintiffs' position that Article 47 is supreme domestic law. Having reached the conclusion that Article 47 is a non self-executing treaty provision, it is unnecessary to discuss such issues as the effect of the "Bricker-like" reservation made by the Senate at the time of ratification and whether the United States may legislate in the area of human rights through the exercise of the treaty power.

Id. at 590 n.119.

On the first point, the reservation to the OAS Charter states simply that "none of its provisions shall be considered as enlarging the powers of the Federal Government of the United States or limiting the powers of the several states of the Federal Union with respect to any matters recognized under the Constitution as being within the reserved powers of the several states." *See* CHARTER OF THE ORGANIZATION OF AMERICAN STATES, *signed* Apr. 30, 1948, *entered into force* Dec. 13, 1951, [1952] 2 U.S.T. 2394, T.I.A.S. No. 2361, 19 U.N.T.S. 3. Putting aside the question of whether or not the reservation is effective vis-a-vis the later Charter amendments contained in the Protocol of Buenos Aires, it does little more than express the fundamental proposition that the Charter cannot be interpreted to reallocate the powers granted to the federal government and the states by the United States Constitution. *See* 2 RESTATEMENT, *supra* note 3, § 302 comment d, at 19 & reporters' note 3 at 23-24. Given the supremacy clause and decisions of the Supreme Court both before and after Missouri v. Holland, 252 U.S. 416 (1920), the reservation cannot serve to justify state action which violates the Charter. *Cf.* L. HENKIN, *supra* note 8, at 143-48. Similar considerations apply with respect to the phrase "in accordance with their constitutional processes" in the preambulatory part of article 47. *See infra* text accompanying note 120.

On the second point, surely at this late date there is no longer any doubt whatsoever that "the United States may legislate in the area of human rights through the exercise of the treaty power." *See* 2 RESTATEMENT, *supra* note 3, § 302 reporters' note 2, at 22-23. For the authoritative article on this point, see Henkin,᠎ *The Constitution, Treaties, and International Human Rights,* 116 U. PA. L. REV. 1012 (1968).

119. 2 RESTATEMENT, *supra* note 3, § 325(1).

120. Actually, in addition to article 47(a) the district court examines only the preambulatory part of article 47, which requires states to "exert the greatest efforts, in accordance with their constitutional processes, to ensure the effective exercise of the right to education." It does not quote or discuss articles 47(b) and 47(c) dealing with middle-level and higher education respectively, both of which are less concrete and specific than article 47(a) and hence, by contrast, serve to underscore the mandatory character of the latter's requirement that elementary education *shall be* free and compulsory for all children of school age. *See* 501 F. Supp. at 590.

finds language which it apparently thinks points in the opposite direction, and ultimately jumps to a conclusion contrary to its initial impression and certainly at odds with the ordinary meaning of article 47(a). Perhaps the influence of *Fujii*, which the district court cites,[121] was too strong for it to resist. In any event, since the *Plyler* Court found it unnecessary to pass upon the question, domestic courts are without authoritative guidance as to whether or not article 47(a) of the Protocol of Buenos Aires is self-executing.

Aside from the Refugees Protocol and the Protocol of Buenos Aires, the international human rights treaties ratified by the United States do not appear to lend themselves to self-executing arguments.[122] On the distant horizon, of course, are the four human rights treaties which President Carter submitted to the Senate in 1978. Unhappily, with each treaty came a recommendation that the Senate, in giving its advice and consent, adopt a declaration stating that the treaty's substantive provisions are non-self-executing.[123] As many of the provisions in the treaties, expecially the UN Covenant on Civil and Political Rights, appear to be self-executing in nature, to attempt to emasculate their potential domestic impact in this fashion is most unfortunate.[124] While the legal effect of such declarations is debatable,[125] at the very least

---

121. *See id.*

122. A statement borne out by the recent case of Handel v. Artukovic, 601 F. Supp. 1421 (C.D. Cal. 1985), which holds two law of war conventions to be non-self-executing. *Id.* at 1424-26.

123. *See supra* note 86.

124. *See generally* Weissbrodt, *United States Ratification of the Human Rights Covenants*, 63 MINN. L. REV. 35, 66-72 (1978).

> The effect of this declaration is to deprive American courts of their most potent technique for contributing meaningfully to the interpretation of the Human Rights Covenants. If the Covenants are self-executing, litigants may use these treaties to support their positions. In furthering their specific interests, litigants may discover many possible applications for the Covenants that might otherwise be overlooked by the slow moving and very rudimentary international enforcement procedures established by the Covenants. With a whole world to watch, the international procedures can probably be expected to focus only on the most serious human rights problems. If the Covenants are self-executing, however, every lawyer in the United States is potentially a watchdog for human rights. The final result of making the Covenants not self-executing can only be to diminish substantially the impact of the treaties in the United States.

Id. at 67-68.

125. Professor Weissbrodt, for instance, believes that "the propriety and legality of the proposed declarations are at least questionable." *Id.* at 68; *cf.* Risesenfeld, *supra* note 28, at 901.

> In the absence of a valid *reservation*, even a formal *declaration* of a party as to the nature and import of a multilateral treaty would not be conclusive on either the international or—at least in the United States—the domestic judicial level. Nothing in prior practice compels or supports a different conclusion.

they would be accorded "great weight"[126]—in all likelihood nearly conclusive weight—by domestic courts.[127] Thus international human rights lawyers anxious to use domestic courts to enforce to the fullest the rights guaranteed in the treaties should help mobilize public and congressional support against these self-defeating declarations.[128]

V. THE STATUS OF CUSTOMARY INTERNATIONAL HUMAN RIGHTS LAW IN THE DOMESTIC LAW

Unlike many areas of international law, treaties rather than custom have been the principal source of international human rights law. Today, however, the customary international law of human rights is becoming increasingly important, especially since it binds all states and not, as in the case of treaty law, just those states parties to a particular treaty. In the United States, moreover, customary international law, while not mentioned in the Constitution, is part of the law of the land to be determined and applied by the courts whenever appropriate in making a decision.[129]

The starting point in ascertaining what international human rights norms have been received into customary international law—and therefore are rules of decisions for domestic courts—commonly is thought to be the Universal Declaration of Human Rights,[130] a UN General Assembly resolution adopted in 1948 without a dissenting

---

Id. (emphasis in original); *see also* Note, *The Domestic Legal Effect of Declarations that Treaty Provisions Are Not Self-Executing,* 57 TEX. L. REV. 233 (1979).

126. *See supra* text accompanying note 113.

127. *See Hearings, supra* note 29, at 278 (Schachter); *id.* at 280 (Anderegg); *id.* at 285 (Inman); *id.* at 288 (Henkin); *id.* at 294 (Redlich); *id.* at 300-01 (Garibaldi); *id.* at 315 (Owen); *see also id.* at 348-49.

> [Some persons] . . . have suggested that there might be some constitutional objec-
> tions to these declarations. I do not think there would be constitutional objec-
> tions. I think should the Senate wish to attach such declarations, however, the
> courts would not necessarily be bound by them. They would not be reservations;
> they would not be part of the treaties; therefore, they would not be the supreme
> law of the land. Nevertheless, they would be a very cogent and incisive bit of
> legislative history to which a court later on interpreting the treaty would certainly
> refer.

Id. (Lillich).

128. Speaking of certain proposed reservations (but in a context relevant to the declarations), the Legal Adviser of the Department of State acknowledged in 1979 that, "if the Senate should decide that they are not necessary, I think the administration would be willing to dispense with them. Then we would be, in effect, bringing about a more rigorous civil rights regime and there would be no possible criticism that we were not fulfilling the treaties as a whole." *Id.* at 42 (Owen). Whether the Reagan Administration subscribes to this approach is doubtful.

129. *See supra* text at note 4.

130. *See supra* note 18.

vote. At the time of its adoption the United States, a strong supporter of the resolution, nevertheless made it clear that since the Declaration was not a treaty it gave rise to no binding legal obligations whatsoever.[131] A contemporary commentator reflected this view when he described the Declaration as "the first and easiest step leading to [an] International Bill of Rights. It implements the Charter by defining human rights in a maximum program of a legally nonbinding character."[132]

According to Professor Humphrey, who was one of the Declaration's drafters, in the three decades since its adoption "the Declaration has been invoked so many times both within and without the United Nations that lawyers now are saying that, whatever the intention of its authors may have been, the Declaration is now part of the customary law of nations and therefore is binding on all states."[133] This view, first advanced solely by legal scholars[134] but subsequently supported by the resolutions of international conferences,[135] state practice,[136] and even court deci-

---

131. *See* 3 U.N. GAOR 934, U.N. Doc. A/177 (1948).

132. Kunz, *The United Nations Declaration of Human Rights*, 43 AM. J. INT'L L. 316, 322 (1949). Another such commentator remarked that it was "fortunate that the courts have before them the [Declaration] as a guide to the interpretation of Article 56. . . . While not a treaty, the Declaration is of great interpretative value, manifesting the opinion of the United Nations as to the scope of human rights and fundamental freedoms." Wright, *supra* note 65, at 77. His remarks foreshadowed the Newman-Berkeley thesis described *supra*, text accompanying note 54.

133. Humphrey, *The International Bill of Rights: Scope and Implementation*, 17 WM. & MARY L. REV. 527, 529 (1976). Humphrey himself now believes that the Declaration is "part of the customary law of nations and therefore is binding on all states. The Declaration has become what some nations wished it to be in 1948: the universally accepted interpretation and definition of the human rights left undefined by the Charter." *Id.* The second sentence lends additional support to the Newman-Berkeley thesis described *supra*, text accompanying note 54.

134. In addition to Humphrey, see M. McDougal, H. Lasswell & L. Chen, *supra* note 58, at 274, 325 & 338; Sohn, *supra* note 44, at 133; Waldock, *Human Rights in Contemporary International Law and the Significance of the European Convention*, in THE EUROPEAN CONVENTION ON HUMAN RIGHTS 1, 15 (Brit. Inst. Int'l & Comp. L. Ser. No. 5, 1965).

135. In 1968, Human Rights Year, the Assembly for Human Rights, a meeting of non-governmental organizations, adopted the Montreal Statement, which included the assertion that the "Universal Declaration of Human Rights . . . has over the years become part of customary international law." Montreal Statement of the Assembly for Human Rights 2 (1968), *reprinted in* 9 J. INT'L COMM. OF JURISTS 94, 95 (1968). Also adopted in 1968 by a UN sponsored International Conference on Human Rights was the Proclamation of Teheran, which stated that "the Universal Declaration of Human Rights . . . constitutes an obligation for members of the international community." Declaration of Teheran, Final Act of the International Conference on Human Rights 3, at 4, para. 2, 23 U.N. GAOR, U.N. Doc. A/CONF. 32/41 (1968).

136. Statements by members of the United States Executive Branch suggest that the Declaration sets forth internationally recognized human rights. *See, e.g.,* R. LILLICH,

sions,[137] now appears to have achieved widespread acceptance. Indeed, the suggestion has been made that the Declaration has "the attributes of *jus cogens*,"[138] certainly an overly enthusiastic assertion in the opinion of the present writer if it is intended to imply that *all* the rights enumerated in the Declaration now constitute peremptory norms of international law.[139]

The Use of International Human Rights Norms in U.S. Courts 18-19 (Dep't of Justice 1980). Of prime importance is former President Carter's assertion that

> [t]he Declaration is the cornerstone of a developing international consensus on human rights. It is also the authoritative statement of the meaning of the United Nations Charter, through which member nations undertake to promote, respect and observe human rights and fundamental freedoms for all, without discrimination.

1978 Pub. Papers 2090. The second sentence lends further support to the Newman-Berkeley thesis described in the text accompanying note 54 *supra*.

137. *See infra* text at note 151 & accompanying note 170.

138. M. McDougal, H. Lasswell & L. Chen, *supra* note 58, at 274. The peremptory norms of international law, *jus cogens,* are explained thus:

> Some rules of international law are accepted and recognized by the international community of states as peremptory, permitting no derogation, and prevailing over and invalidating international agreement and other rules of international law in conflict with them. Such a peremptory norm is subject to modification only by a subsequent norm of international law having the same character.

1 Restatement § 102 comment k, at 33.

139. As the *Restatement* cautions, "much uncertainty prevails as to the bounds of *jus cogens* . . ." 2 Restatement, *supra* note 3, § 331(2) comment e at 117. Certainly not all of the norms contained in the Declaration have achieved such status. In addition to the obligations of member states under the UN Charter,

> [i]t has been suggested that norms that create "international crimes" and obligate all states to proceed against violations are also peremptory. . . . This might include rules prohibiting genocide, slave-trading and slavery, apartheid and other gross violations of human rights, and perhaps attacks on diplomats.

1 *id.* § 102 reporters' note 6 at 42; *see also* Domb, *Jus Cogens and Human Rights,* 6 Israel Y.B. Human Rights 104, 116-21 (1976); Whiteman, *Jus Cogens in International Law, With a Projected List,* 7 Ga. J. Int'l & Comp. L. 609, 625 (1977). For discussion about whether the prohibition of torture constitutes *jus cogens,* see *infra* text accompanying note 151.

Prof. Higgins, writing about human rights treaties but reasoning along lines applicable to the Declaration, takes a similar selective approach.

> [T]he suggestion has been made that human rights treaties have the character of *jus cogens*. There certainly exists a consensus that certain rights—the right to life, to freedom from slavery or torture—are so fundamental that no derogation may be made. . . . This being said, neither the wording of the various human rights instruments nor the practice thereunder leads to the view that all human rights are *jus cogens*.

Higgins, *Derogations Under Human Rights Treaties,* 48 Brit. Y.B. Int'l L. 281, 282 (1976-1977).

In seeking to determine what human rights protected by the Declaration and the Covenant on Civil and Political Rights have achieved *jus cogens* status, a good starting point is the list of rights that article 4(2) of the latter makes non-derogable, i.e., rights that a state may not suspend even in time of war or national emergency. They are contained in articles 6, 7, 8(1)(2), 11, 15, 16 and 18 of the Covenant. *Cf. infra* text accompanying notes 156 & 178.

Insofar as the United States is concerned, perhaps the most explicit recognition that at least parts of the Declaration now reflect customary international law is found in the United States memorial to the International Court of Justice in the *Hostages Case*.[140] After marshalling traditional international law precedents to demonstrate "that States have an international legal obligation to observe certain minimum standards in their treatment of aliens," the memorial added a brief passage about the nature and scope of fundamental human rights:

> It has been [contended] that no such standard can or should exist, but such force as that position may have had has gradually diminished as *recognition of the existence of certain fundamental human rights has spread throughout the international community.* The existence of such fundamental rights for all human beings, nationals and aliens alike, and the existence of *a corresponding duty on the part of every State to respect and observe them, are now reflected, inter alia, in the Charter of the United Nations, the Universal Declaration of Human Rights and corresponding portions of the International Covenant on Civil and Political Rights.* . . .
>
> In view of the *universal contemporary recognition that such fundamental human rights exist* . . . Iran's obligation to provide "the most constant protection and security" to United States nationals in Iran includes *an obligation to observe those rights.*[141]

As evidence of the fundamental human rights to which all individuals are entitled and which all states must guarantee, the memorial cited articles 3, 5, 7, 9, 12 and 13 of the Declaration,[142] plus articles 7, 9, 10 and 12 of the UN Covenant on Civil and Political Rights.[143]

Since under the "mirror image" principle the United States, as well as Iran, has an international obligation to live up to the above provisions, the question next becomes whether this obligation can be enforced domestically as well as internationally. The answer does

---

140. Case Concerning United States Diplomatic and Consular Staff in Tehran (U.S. v. Iran), 1980 I.C.J. 3.

141. Memorial of the Government of the United States of America at 71, Case Concerning United States Diplomatic and Consular Staff in Tehran (U.S. v. Iran), 1980 I.C.J. 3 (emphasis added) [hereinafter cited as U.S. Memorial].

142. U.S. Memorial, *supra* note 141, at 71 n.3 & 72 n.2. These articles cover, respectively, the right to life, liberty and security of person; the prohibition of torture and cruel, inhuman or degrading treatment or punishment; the right to equality before the law and to nondiscrimination in its application; the prohibition of arbitrary arrest and detention; the right to privacy; and the right to freedom of movement.

143. *Id.* at 71 n.4 & 72 n.2. These articles cover, respectively, the prohibition of torture and cruel, inhuman or degrading treatment or punishment; the right to liberty and security of person and the prohibition of arbitrary arrest and detention; the right to be treated with humanity during detention; and the right to freedom of movement.

not turn upon the self- or non-self-executing nature of the Declaration, since it is not a treaty, but upon whether the Declaration, or at least parts thereof, being evidence of customary international law, can be used in domestic courts either to supplement or invalidate state or federal statutes. Under *The Paquete Habana*,[144] there is no doubt that the Declaration, to the extent that it reflects customary international law, is part of our law and therefore should be directly enforceable in domestic courts. Until recently, however, attempts to invoke it in such fashion uniformly had been unsuccessful.[145]

A major breakthrough in the use of customary international human rights law occurred in 1980 when the United States Court of Appeals for the Second Circuit handed down its eloquent and far-reaching decision in *Filartiga v. Pena-Irala*,[146] a decision that has done as much to assist the development of this body of international law as *Fujii* did to retard it. In *Filartiga*, two Paraguayan plaintiffs brought an action in a federal district court against another citizen of Paraguay for the torture and death of their son and brother, basing their claim on the Alien Tort Statute, a federal statute dating back to the original Judiciary Act of 1789, which provides "The district courts shall have original jurisdiction of any civil action by an alien for a tort only, committed in violation of the law of nations or a treaty of the United States."[147] Since the plaintiffs did not argue that their action arose directly under a treaty to which the United

---

144. 175 U.S. 677 (1900).

145. For a typical case dismissing an action grounded upon the Declaration, see Jamnr Prods. Corp. v. Quill, 51 Misc. 2d 501, 509-10, 273 N.Y.S.2d 348, 356 (Sup. Ct. 1966). It must be remembered, of course, that such cases were decided before the Declaration or parts thereof could be deemed to have become part of customary international law.

146. 630 F.2d 876 (2d Cir. 1980); *see also* Blum & Steinhardt, *Federal Jurisdiction over International Human Rights Claims: The Alien Tort Claims Act After Filartiga v. Pena-Irala*, 22 HARV. INT'L L.J. 53 (1981); Note, *The Exhaustion of Local Remedies Rule and Forum Non Conveniens in International Litigation in U.S. Courts*, 13 CORNELL INT'L L.J. 351 (1980); Comment, *Torture as a Tort in Violation of International Law: Filartiga v. Pena-Irala*, 33 STAN. L. REV. 353 (1981).

147. Judiciary Act, ch. 20, § 9, 1 Stat. 73 (1789) (current version at 28 U.S.C. § 1350 (1982)). Plaintiffs also invoked general federal question jurisdiction under 28 U.S.C. § 1331 (1982). Since the complaint alleged a violation of customary international law, which is part of domestic law, jurisdiction presumably could have been based upon that statute too. *See* Brief for Amnesty International-U.S.A., International League for Human Rights, and the Lawyers' Committee for International Human Rights as Amicus Curiae at 21, *Filartiga v. Pena-Irala*; Memorandum for the United States as Amicus Curiae at 25 n.49, *Filartiga v. Pena-Irala*. The court of appeals recognized that "our reasoning might also sustain jurisdiction under the general federal question provision, 28 U.S.C. § 1331 (1982). We prefer, however, to rest our decision upon the Alien Tort Statute, in light of that

States was a party,[148] jurisdiction under the statute turned upon whether or not torture now violates "the law of nations," i.e., customary international law. The district court, in an unreported decision, felt constrained by precedent to dismiss the complaint on the ground that " 'the law of nations,' as employed in Section 1350, [excludes] that law which governs a state's treatment of its own citizens."[149] In short, it ruled that torture of a Paraguayan in Paraguay did not violate customary international law.

On appeal, the court of appeals reversed, holding that "an act of torture committed by a state official against one held in detention violates established norms of the international law of human rights, and hence the law of nations."[150] Among the appropriate sources of international law to which it looked, pride of place went to article 5 of the Universal Declaration. The right to be free from torture, wrote Chief Judge Kaufman, "has become part of customary international law, *as evidenced and defined by the Universal Declaration . . . which states, in the plainest of terms, 'no one shall be subjected to torture.' "[151] The court of appeals also found the Declara-

---

provision's close coincidence with the jurisdictional facts presented in this case." 630 F.2d at 887 n.22.

Since plaintiffs were aliens, the basis of jurisdiction was unimportant in *Filartiga*: the court of appeals' dictum about federal question jurisdiction, however, remains important in actions brought by United States plaintiffs. Unfortunately, in a recent case where such plaintiffs relied upon § 1331 the district court, ignoring the above dictum, held that it lacked jurisdiction. Handel v. Artukovic, 601 F. Supp. 1421, 1421 (C.D. Cal. 1985). "Although two recent circuit court opinions, *Filartiga* and Judge Edwards' concurrence in *Tel-Oren*, have found that 28 U.S.C. § 1350 creates a private right to sue for violations of the law of nations, it is clear that the result would be different if section 1331 rather than section 1350 were the applicable jurisdictional statute." 601 F. Supp. at 1421.

For the excellent suggestion that "Congress should consider amending [the Alien Tort Statute] to allow lawsuits brought by U.S. citizens as well as aliens," see *The Phenomenon of Torture: Hearings on H.J. Res. 605 Before the Subcomm. on Human Rights and International Organizations of the House Comm. on Foreign Affairs*, 98th Cong., 2d Sess. 247 (1984) (statement of Michael H. Posner, Esq., Exec. Dir., Lawyers Committee for International Human Rights). Mr. Posner notes "This can be done simply by deleting the words 'by an alien' from section 1350." *Id.*

148. *Cf. supra* text accompanying note 54.

149. 630 F.2d at 880.

150. *Id.* At the time of the alleged act the defendant was Inspector General of Police in Asuncion, Paraguay. *Id.* at 878.

151. *Id.* at 882 (emphasis added). For a fuller discussion of the prohibition of torture contained in article 5 of the Declaration, see Lillich, *supra* note 21, at 126-30. Recall that the United States Memorial in the *Hostages Case* twice cited article 5. *See supra* text at and accompanying note 142. *See also* Memorandum for the United States as Amicus Curiae at 16, *Filartiga v. Pena-Irala*, where the United States relied upon article 5 of the Declara-

tion on Torture,[152] another UN General Assembly resolution adopted in 1975 without a dissenting vote, particularly relevant.[153] "These UN declarations are significant," it declared, "because they specify with great precision the obligations of member nations under the Charter."[154] They were, to paraphrase the court of appeals, authoritative statements of the international community creating expectations of adherence which, in conjunction with contemporary state practice, have generated a binding rule of customary international law.[155] Overwhelming evidence that such state practice proscribes torture was found in "numerous international treaties and

---

tion to support its contention that "[i]nternational custom . . . evidences a universal condemnation of torture."

While the court of appeals nowhere specifically addresses the question of whether the prohibition of torture constitutes *jus cogens, see supra* notes 138-39 and accompanying text, its language points in that direction. *See, e.g.,* 630 F.2d at 890 ("Among the rights universally proclaimed by all nations . . . is the right to be free of physical torture. Indeed, for purposes of civil liability, the torturer has become—like the pirate and the slave trader before him—*hostis humani generis,* an enemy of all mankind.") The present writer, in an affidavit submitted on the plaintiffs' behalf, *see id.* at 879 n.4, had averred that, "like piracy, slavery and genocide before it, the prohibition against torture is not a peremptory norm of international law," i.e., *jus cogens.*

152. Declaration on the Protection of All Persons from being Subjected to Torture and Other Cruel, Inhuman or Degrading Treatment or Punishment, *adopted* Dec. 9, 1975, G.A. Res. 3452, 30 U.N. GAOR Supp. (No. 34) at 91, U.N. Doc. A/1034 (1975), *reprinted in* R. LILLICH, *supra* note 18, § 480.1. On December 10, 1984, the thirty-sixth anniversary of the signing of the Universal Declaration, the UN General Assembly adopted a Convention Against Torture and Other Cruel, Inhuman or Degrading Treatment or Punishment, which not only codifies the norms of customary international law expressed in the Declaration on Torture (and confirmed in *Filartiga*), but also provides for procedures to implement its prohibition of torture.

153. 630 F.2d at 882 & n.11 (entire Declaration on Torture set out in margin). The United States Memorial in the *Hostages Case* cited this Declaration. U.S. Memorial, *supra* note 141, at 72 n.2. *See also* Memorandum for the United States as Amicus Curiae at 17, *Filartiga v. Pena-Irala,* where the United States contended that it "confirms that international custom outlaws torture."

154. 630 F.2d at 883; *cf. supra* note 54 and accompanying text (setting out Newman-Berkeley thesis).

155. [I]t has been observed that the Universal Declaration of Human Rights "no longer fits into the dichotomy of 'binding treaty' against 'non-binding pronouncement,' but is rather an authoritative statement of the international community." *E. Schwelb, Human Rights and the International Community* 70 (1964). Thus, a Declaration creates an expectation of adherence, and "insofar as the expectation is gradually justified by State practice, a declaration may by custom become recognized as laying down rules binding upon the States." 34 U.N. ESCOR [Supp. (No. 8) 15, U.N. Doc. E/cn.4/1/610 (1962) (memorandum of Office of Legal Affairs, U.N. Secretariat)]. Indeed, several commentators have concluded that the Universal Declaration has become, *in toto,* a part of binding, customary international law. 630 F.2d at 883.

accords,''[156] in "modern municipal—i.e., national—law as well,''[157] and in the works of jurists.[158] On the basis of this extensive examination of the sources from which customary international law is derived, the court of appeals had no difficulty in reaching its conclusion that "official torture is now prohibited by the law of nations. The prohibition is clear and unambiguous, and admits of no distinction between treatment of aliens and citizens.''[159]

Important as *Filartiga* is in establishing that torture violates customary international law, the case is even more significant in

---

156. *Id.* at 883-84 (citing American Convention on Human Rights, art. 5(2), *supra* note 20; UN Covenant on Civil and Political Rights, art. 7, *supra* note 19; European Convention for the Protection of Human Rights and Fundamental Freedoms, art. 3, *signed* Nov. 4, 1950, 213 U.N.T.S. 222 (entered into force Sept. 3, 1953), *reprinted in* R. LILLICH, *supra* note 18, § 500.1). Like the plaintiffs, the court of appeals relied upon these international human rights treaties "as evidence of an emerging norm of customary international law, rather [than] independent sources of law." 630 F.2d at 880 n.7; *cf. supra* note 55 and accompanying text.

One should not overlook the importance of treaties as a source of emerging customary international law norms. There is ample language in the decisions of the International Court of Justice to support the late Judge Baxter's observation that "Treaties that do not purport to be declaratory of customary international law at the time they enter into force may nevertheless with the passage of time pass into customary international law." Baxter, *Treaties and Custom*, 129 RECEUIL DES COURS (Hague Academy of International Law) 25, 57 (1970-II); *accord* 1 RESTATEMENT, *supra* note 3, § 102 reporters' note 5, at 40-41. For the application of this principle to international human rights treaties, see Lillich, *supra* note 12, at 397-99.

Recall also that the United States Memorial in the *Hostages Case* twice cited article 7 of the UN Covenant on Civil and Political Rights. *See supra* text at and accompanying note 143. See also Memorandum for the United States as Amicus Curiae at 13, *Filartiga v. Pena-Irala*, where after citing the three international human rights treaties mentioned in the first paragraph of this footnote the United States concluded, "This uniform treaty condemnation of torture provides a strong indication that the proscription of torture has entered into customary international law." It furthermore contended, "These treaty provisions, in conjunction with other evidence, are persuasive of the existence of an international norm that is binding as a matter of customary law on all nations, not merely those that are parties to the treaties." *Id.* at 13 n.28, (citing A. D'AMATO, THE CONCEPT OF CUSTOM IN INTERNATIONAL LAW 103, 124-28 (1971)).

The test suggested in the last paragraph of the text accompanying note 139 *supra* for determining whether a particular right protected by an international human rights treaty may have achieved the status of *jus cogens*, namely whether the treaty makes the right non-derogable, also is useful for determining whether the right has passed into customary international law in the first place. All three treaties mentioned in the first paragraph of this footnote forbid derogation from the prohibition of torture. *Cf. supra* text accompanying note 139; *infra* text accompanying note 178.

157. 630 F.2d at 884.

158. Three law professors in addition to the present writer submitted affidavits on the plaintiffs' behalf unanimously agreeing that "the law of nations prohibits absolutely the use of torture as alleged in the complaint." *Id.* at 879 & n.4; *cf. infra* text accompanying note 162.

159. *Id.* at 884.

demonstrating to lawyers the growing importance of customary international human rights law and graphically illustrating how they should go about proving it in cases before domestic courts. Moreover, the decision reflects the willingness of one of the most highly respected courts in the United States to use such law, when proven, in reaching its decision.[160] Thus it is not surprising that the case already has generated further international human rights law litigation,[161] certainly a positive development if parties invoking *Filartiga's* teachings do so carefully and conservatively, thus avoiding a potential backlash either from the courts[162] or the body politic.[163] For, as Judge Kaufman cautioned in a subsequent magazine article, the case's holding

---

160. *Nota bene*: The court of appeals used customary international law in *Filartiga* only to decide whether it had federal jurisdiction under the Alien Tort Statute, *not* as a rule of decision to judge whether the alleged wrong was actionable. The choice of law question— the law of the forum, customary international law or Paraguayan law—was left for the district court on remand. *See id.* at 889.

In the event, Pena took no further part in the action and the district court entered a default judgment. In fixing damages, however, the court held "that it should determine the substantive principles to be applied by looking to international law." Filartiga v. Pena-Irala, 557 F. Supp. 860, 863 (E.D.N.Y. 1984). It ultimately awarded, inter alia, punitive damages in the amount of $10 million. *Id.* at 867.

161. *See, e.g.*, Siderman de Blake v. Republic of Argen., No. CV 82-1772-RMT (MCx) (C.D. Cal. Sept. 28, 1984) (alleging torture by Argentina) (available on LEXIS).

For a misguided attempt to establish that acts of "international terrorism" violate customary international law and hence are actionable under the Alien Tort Statute as construed in *Filartiga*, see Hanoch Tel-Oren v. Libyan Arab Republic, 517 F. Supp. 542 (D.D.C. 1981), *aff'd per curiam*, 726 F.2d 774 (D.C. Cir. 1984), *cert. denied*, 53 U.S.L.W. 3612 (1985). Since even cursory research by counsel would have revealed that customary international law as yet contains no general prohibition of terrorism, *compare* R. LILLICH, TRANSNATIONAL TERRORISM: CONVENTIONS AND COMMENTARY xv-xvii (1982) *with* Note, *Terrorism as a Tort in Violation of the Law of Nations*, 6 FORDHAM INT'L L.J. 236 (1982), plaintiffs would have been better advised never to have initiated the action, which afforded the district court and two judges on appeal the opportunity to question *Filartiga*. Even Professor D'Amato, who begins a recent article by stating, "I want to take brief issue with those persons who feel that it was a severe mistake for the plaintiffs to bring their case in a United States court in the first place," D'Amato, *supra* note 8, at 92-93, ends up a dozen pages later admitting, "I am not sure, as a matter of strategy, that the *Tel-Oren* case was worth bringing in the first place." *Id.* at 105.

162. Note the gratuitous aside by one judge on appeal in *Hanoch Tel-Oren* where, after setting out his views on why the political question doctrine should make Alien Tort Statute cases non-justiciable, the learned jurist remarks that "[c]ourts ought not to serve as debating clubs for professors willing to argue over what is or what is not an accepted violation of the law of nations." 726 F.2d at 827 (Robb, J., concurring). *But see* Statute of the International Court of Justice, art. 38(1)(d) (authoritatively establishing "the teachings of the most highly qualified publicists of the various nations, as subsidiary means for the determination of rules of law," a position uniformly taken by domestic courts and recently endorsed by American Law Institute). *See* 1 RESTATEMENT, *supra* note 3, § 102 reporters' note 1, at 35-36; 1 *id.* § 102(d) reporters' note 1, at 46; *cf. supra* text accompanying note 158.

163. Such as occurred during the early 1950's in the aftermath of *Fujii*. Although racial factors were at work in the land then, they find their parallel today in the electorate's

that torture is a violation of customary international law for Alien Tort Statute purposes is a relatively narrow one;[164] it should not be misread or exaggerated to support sweeping assertions that all (or even most) international human rights norms found in the Universal Declaration or in international human rights treaties have ripened into customary international law enforceable in the domestic courts.[165]

Two subsequent cases indicate the possibilities and pitfalls of invoking customary international human rights law post-*Filartiga* and hence warrant mention. The first, *Fernandez v. Wilkinson*,[166] involved a Cuban refugee from the "freedom flotilla" who the Immigration and Naturalization Service had determined was ineligible for admission into the United States because he had been convicted of a crime involving moral turpitude.[167] During exclusion proceedings in July 1980, an immigration judge determined that Fernandez was indeed excludable and ordered his deportation, pending which he

---

apparent tolerance, if not acceptance, of the Reagan Administration's downgrading of human rights in the foreign policy decisionmaking process.

164. Kaufman, *A Legal Remedy for International Torture?*, N.Y. TIMES, Nov. 9, 1980, § 6 (Magazine), at 44, 52.

> [There are] doctrinal limitations as to the numbers and kinds of cases that will be brought after *Filartiga*. The courts will not be transformed into some kind of roaming human-rights commission; the broad response to the phenomenon of torture, of course, is best left to the policy makers in the other branches of government. Nor is the United States, by empowering our courts to hear international claims of torture, engaging in messianic moral imperialism. While Americans feel strongly about freedom of speech and of the press, for instance, we are not required to open our courts to hear complaints alleging denials of these rights by foreign governments. Such rights are not yet universal, and we would be arrogant and self-righteous to apply them to all societies. The right to be free from torture, however, is one of the few absolute standards of international law, a right that exists regardless of the economic or social organization of a society.

Id.

165. Speaking of the fundamental human rights now guaranteed to individuals as a matter of customary international law, the United States in *Filartiga* correctly noted that not "all such rights may be judicially enforced. Indeed, it is likely that only a few rights have the degree of specificity and universality to permit private enforcement." Memorandum for the United States as Amicus Curiae at 6, *Filartiga v. Pena-Irala*. Too, "[w]e do not suggest that every provision of these treaties states a binding rule of customary international law." *Id.* at 14.

> The courts are properly confined to determining whether an individual has suffered a denial of rights guaranteed him as an individual by customary international law. Accordingly, *before entertaining a suit alleging a violation of human rights, a court must first conclude that there is a consensus in the international community that the right is protected and that there is a widely shared understanding of the scope of this protection.*

Id. at 22 (emphasis added).

166. 505 F. Supp. 787 (D. Kan. 1980), *aff'd on other grounds sub. nom.* Rodriguez-Fernandez v. Wilkinson, 654 F.2d 1382 (10th Cir. 1981).

167. *See* 8 U.S.C. § 1182(A)(9) (1982).

was detained in the federal penitentiary at Leavenworth, Kansas, a maximum security institution. Since the United States was unable to make the necessary arrangements to return him and other excludable aliens to Cuba, Fernandez remained in protective detention in December 1980, at which time he sought a writ of habeas corpus. His counsel argued that his continued confinement, without bail and without having been charged with or convicted of a crime in the United States, violated his constitutional rights under the fifth and eighth amendments.

After surveying the cases interpreting the constitutional and statutory provisions,[168] the United States District Court for the District of Kansas observed that, although Fernandez's detention constituted "arbitrary detention,"

> [d]ue to the unique legal status of excluded aliens in this country, it is an evil from which our Constitution and statutory laws afford no protection. . . . [I]n the case of unadmitted aliens detained on our soil, but legally deemed to be outside our borders, the machinery of domestic law utterly fails to operate to assure protection.[169]

Yet all was not lost! Responding to an imaginative argument by the amicus curiae that Fernandez's continued detention contravened "fundamental human justice as embodied in established principles of international law,"[170] the district court broke new international human rights law ground by holding that "[customary] international law secures to petitioner the right to be free of arbitrary detention and that his right is being violated."[171] It stated that:

> Our review of the sources from which customary international law is derived clearly demonstrates that arbitrary detention is prohibited by customary international law. *Therefore, even though the indeterminate detention of an excluded alien cannot be said to violate the United States Constitution or our statutory laws, it is judicially remedial as a violation of international law.*[172]

---

168. The key case, which the district court attempted to distinguish, is Mezei v. Shaughnessy, 345 U.S. 206 (1952) (5-4 decision), where the Supreme Court held that the 20-month detention of an excluded alien pending his deportation was not unlawful. The continued validity of *Mezei* is at issue in Jean v. Nelson, 544 F. Supp. 973 (S.D. Fla. 1982); *aff'd in part and rev'd in part,* 711 F.2d 1455 (11th Cir. 1983), *dismissed in part and rev'd in part,* 727 F.2d 957 (11th Cir.) (en banc), *cert. granted,* 105 S. Ct. 563 (1984).

169. 502 F. Supp. at 795.

170. *Id.* (citing Universal Declaration and the American Convention on Human Rights).

171. *Id.* Note that the district court based its decision upon customary international law. "The most important source of international law is international treaties. At present, the United States has ratified and is party to only a few human rights treaties. Petitioner does not assert that his detention is in direct violation of a treaty to which the United States is a party." *Id.*

172. *Id.* at 798 (emphasis added).

Accordingly, the United States was ordered to terminate petitioner's arbitrary detention within ninety days.

The district court's decision, building upon *Filartiga*, represented another significant step forward in that for the first time a domestic court used customary international human rights law as a rule of decision to uplift domestic law, to provide a greater measure of protection than that accorded by the Constitution or federal statutes.[173] Also, the decision, treating the Universal Declaration as not just *evidence* but rather "an important *source* of international human rights,"[174] found yet another of the Declaration's rights—the prohibition of arbitrary detention contained in article 9[175]—to be part of customary international law.[176] Although the contours and content of this right are less clear than is the case with torture,[177] certainly the district court was correct in holding the basic core prohibition against arbitrary detention to constitute a part of customary international law.[178]

---

173. As might occur analogously if the United States ratified the four human rights treaties without attaching the proposed non-self-executing declarations. *See Hearings, supra* note 29, at 349 (Lillich); *supra* text at notes 123-28.

174. 505 F. Supp. at 797 (emphasis added); *cf. supra* text accompanying note 151.

175. Article 9 provides, "No one shall be subjected to arbitrary arrest, detention or exile." For discussion of this article, see Lillich, *supra* note 21, at 136-39.

176. *Cf.* Judgment of June 10, 1954, Court of First Instance, Courtrai (Belgium), 1954 U.N.Y.B. Human Rights 21 (court also relied upon Universal Declaration in ordering release from detention).

177. *See generally* Marcoux, *Protection from Arbitrary Arrest and Detention Under International Law,* 5 B.C. Int'l & Comp. L. Rev. 345 (1982). Unlike the prohibition of torture, it is not *jus cogens.* Lillich, *supra* note 21, at 139; see supra text at and accompanying notes 138-39.

178. In addition to article 9 of the Universal Declaration, the court cited, inter alia, similar language in article 7(3) of the American Covention on Human Rights, *supra* note 20, article 9(1) of the UN Covenant on Civil and Political Rights, *supra* note 19, and article 5 of the European Convention for the Protection of Human Rights and Fundamental Freedoms, *supra* note 155. Although noting that the United States was not a party to any of these treaties, it considered them "indicative of the customs and usages of civilized nations." 505 F. Supp. at 797.

Additional support for the prohibition of arbitrary detention could have been obtained from the nascent practice of the Human Rights Committed under article 9(1). *See* Lillich, *supra* note 21, at 138 n.132. *See generally* Hassan, *The International Covenant on Civil and Political Rights: Background and Perspectives on Article 9(1),* 3 Denver J. Int'l L. & Pol'y 153 (1973). Also, resort to the far more developed practice of the European Commission and the European Court of Human Rights under article 5 would have been helpful. Lillich, *supra* note 21, at 137 n.125. However, the district court did not avail itself of these and other evidences of "the customs and usages of civilized nations." Indeed, although it paraphrased *Filartiga* about how to discern the principles of customary international law, *see* 505 F. Supp. at 798, in practice it showed far less sophistication than the Court of Appeals for the Second Circuit on this score.

On appeal, the United States Court of Appeals for the Tenth Circuit did not directly address the district court's holding, instead construing the relevant statutory provisions to require Fernandez's release from continued detention.[179] In dictum, however, it considered at length "the serious constitutional questions involved if the statute were construed differently."[180] Noting that "[d]ue process is not a static concept," the court of appeals thought it proper "to consider international law principles for notions of fairness as to propriety of holding aliens in detention. No principle of international law is more fundamental than the concept that human beings should be free from arbitrary imprisonment."[181] Citing the Universal Declaration and the American Convention on Human Rights in support of this position, it concluded that its construction of the statute was "consistent with accepted international law principles that individuals are entitled to be free of arbitary imprisonment."[182] Thus, while not applying customary international law directly, the court of appeals used it indirectly in determining the protection afforded by domestic law.[183]

Further support for the proposition that the prohibition now reflects custorary international law may be found in the fact that the United States memorial in the *Hostages Case* cited both article 9 of the Universal Declaration and article 9 of the Covenant on Civil and Political Rights. *See supra* text at and accompanying notes 142-43.

Cutting the other way, however, is the fact that states may derogate from this prohibition, unlike the one against torture, under all three treaties mentioned in the first paragraph of this footnote. *Cf. supra* text accompanying notes 139 & 156. The United States District Court for the Northern District of Georgia ignored this argument, advanced by the government in Defendants' Reply Memorandum in Opposition to Habeas Corpus Petition at 26-27, when in dictum it concluded that prolonged arbitrary detention violates customary international law. *See* Fernandez-Roque v. Smith, 567 F. Supp. 1115, 1122 n.2 (N.D. Ga. 1983). For earlier dictum to the same effect, see Soroa-Gonzales v. Civiletti, 515 F. Supp. 1049, 1061 n.18 (N.D. Ga. 1981); *cf.* Palma v. Verdeyen, 676 F.2d 100, 106 n.5 (4th Cir. 1982) (dictum). *Contra* Jean v. Nelson, 544 F. Supp. 973 (S.D. Fla. 1982), *aff'd in part and rev'd in part*, 711 F.2d 1455 (11th Cir. 1983), *dismissed in part and rev'd in part*, 727 F.2d 957 (11th Cir.) (en banc), *cert. granted*, 105 S. Ct. 563 (1984).

179. *See* 654 F.2d at 1386.

180. *Id.*

181. *Id.* at 1388.

182. *Id.* at 1390.

183. For an excellent essay contrasting the district court's approach with that of the court of appeals, see Martineau, *Interpreting the Constitution: The Use of International Human Rights Norms*, 5 HUM. RTS. Q. (1983). The author concludes:

At first blush it may appear that the Tenth Circuit retreated from a bold assertion by the district court of the *binding* effect of international norms on the United States courts. It might be concluded that international human rights norms will have less impact on federal courts under the Tenth Circuit's analysis than they would under the district court's approach. That approach appears to open the door to the use of international human rights law as a basis for rules of decision.

The second significant post-*Filartiga* case, mentioned above in the section on human rights treaties that arguably contained self-executing provisions, is *In re Alien Children Education Litigation.*[184] In addition to arguing that article 47(a) of the Protocol of Buenos Aires was self-executing, plaintiffs asserted that the article, along with article 26(1) of the Universal Declaration[185] and similar provisions in various other international human rights instruments,[186] reflected an emerging rule of customary international law guaranteeing children free elementary school education. Although acknowledging that "[t]hese human rights instruments recognize the right of all persons to literacy or to a free primary education,"[187] the district court concluded "that the right to education, while it represents an important international goal, has not acquired the status of [customary] international law."[188] Thus the plaintiffs had not shown the existence of a rule of decision arising from customary international law that could be used to invalidate the inconsistent Texas statute denying free elementary school education to the children of undocumented aliens.

Admittedly, the right to education is not nearly as crystallized, much less as important, as the prohibitions of torture and arbitrary

---

In contrast, the Tenth Circuit's decision would seem disappointing to human rights advocates because it rejects the strong position adopted by the lower court. Yet the definitional approach of the Tenth Circuit is a strong, practicable method for incorporating international human rights principles via interpretation of constitutional language, and may, in the long run, be far preferable to an approach which seeks the direct incorporation of international human rights norms into domestic law.

Id. at 103 (citing contrary view of Hassan, *The Doctrine of Incorporation: New Vistas for the Enforcement of Human Rights?*, 5 HUM. RTS. Q. 68 (1983)). The reasons why the indirect use of international human rights norms may be strategically more profitable over the long haul are canvassed in the next section.

184. 501 F. Supp. 544 (S.D. Tex. 1980), *aff'd unreported mem.* (5th Cir. 1981), *aff'd sub nom.* Plyler v. Doe, 457 U.S. 202 (1982).

185. Article 26(1) provides, inter alia, that "[e]veryone has the right to education. Education shall be free, at least in the elementary and fundamental stages."

186. Among them article 13(2)(1) of the UN Covenant on Economic, Social and Cultural Rights, *supra* note 83; article XII of the American Declaration of the Rights and Duties of Man, *signed* May 2, 1948, IACHR, HANDBOOK OF EXISTING RULES PERTAINING TO HUMAN RIGHTS, O.A.S. Off. Rec. OEA/Ser.L/V/II.60, doc. 28, rev. 6, at 21, 23 (English ed. 1983), *reprinted in* R. LILLICH, *supra* note 18, § 430.1; article 4(a) of the Convention Against Discrimination in Education, *adopted* Dec. 14, 1961, *entered into force* May 22, 1962, 429 U.N.T.S. 93, *reprinted in* R. LILLICH, *supra* note 18, § 330.1. While the United States has signed the American Declaration, it is not a party to either of the above treaties. Indeed, it has not even signed the latter.

187. 501 F. Supp. at 594.

188. *Id.* at 596.

detention. Yet, the provisions in the instruments involved by the plaintiffs, especially article 26(1) of the Universal Declaration, certainly are clear, precise and easily distinguishable from other provisions in these same instruments that are aspirational in nature.[189] The district court's failure to articulate and apply a conceptualistic framework for determining whether the right to education has been received into customary international law,[190] its inability to appreciate that distinctions should be drawn between the status under such law of the various rights set out in the Declaration,[191] and its confusion about the nature and enforceability of international law in general (and international human rights law in particular)[192] all come as a distinct disappointment in contrast to the sophisticated approach displayed by the *Filartiga* court. While reasonable men may differ

---

189. Mentioning articles 24, 25 and 27(a) of the Universal Declaration, which admittedly are of an aspirational nature, the district court proceeds in "guilt by association" fashion to find article 26(1) to be "an important international goal" but not yet a right having "the status of international law." *Id.* at 596. More appropriately it could have referred to articles 5 and 9 which are no more direct and specific than article 26(1) but which were held to reflect customary international law in *Filartiga* and *Fernandez v. Wilkinson.* Like the prohibitions of torture and arbitrary detention, moreover, the right to education found in article 26(1) also is spelled out in a number of other international human rights instruments, thus distinguishing it from the aspirational rights set out in the articles cited by the district court.

190. Nowhere in this brief section of its opinion does the district court set out its jurisprudential approach to ascertaining customary international law; it merely quotes extensively from The Paquete Habana, 175 U.S. 677 (1900), and then proceeds to its conclusory holding. 501 F. Supp. at 595-96. One explanation for this brevity may be that the court thought its treatment of the self-executing character of article 47(a) of the Protocol of Buenos Aires dispositive of this issue too. If so, then the point needs making that, assuming arguendo a treaty provision like article 47(a) is non-self-executing, it does not necessarily follow that the right set out in the treaty, read in conjunction with similar provisions in other international human rights instruments, does not reflect customary international law.

191. *See supra* text accompanying note 189.

192. The district court supported its conclusion that the right to education has not acquired the status of international law for purposes of enforcement in domestic courts by reference to "the nature of international law," which it intimates should be enforced on a state-to-state basis through the diplomatic process. Thus it stated, "To the extent that the United States is neglecting its pledge to promote human rights or to exert the greatest efforts to further educational opportunities, an alien's government may call the United States to answer before an international tribunal." *Id.* at 596. Why the possibility of state-to-state remedies (available, of course, only when aliens are involved) should bar domestic courts from enforcing customary international law rights the court does not explain. Its misunderstanding of the role of domestic courts in the enforcement, much less the development, of customary international law is profound, harking back to Banco Nacional de Cuba v. Sabbatino, 376 U.S. 398 (1964), which it quotes approvingly. *See* 501 F. Supp. at 596; *see also* Lillich, *supra* note 9, at 32-33. *See generally* R. FALK, THE ROLE OF DOMESTIC COURTS IN THE INTERNATIONAL LEGAL ORDER (1964).

about whether customary international law now recognizes a right to free elementary school education,[193] few persons reading the court's opinion are likely to regard it as a jurisprudential contribution to the development of customary international human rights law.

VI. Using International Human Rights Law to Infuse United States Constitutional and Statutory Standards

Far more likely than a court's holding that the human rights clauses of the UN Charter are self-executing—far more likely even than a court's holding that a particular article of the Universal Declaration now reflects customary international law—is the possibility that a court will regard international human rights law as infusing United States constitutional and statutory standards with its normative content. This "indirect incorporation" of both conventional and customary international human rights law is an exceptionally interesting and promising approach warranting greater attention than it has received of late.[194] Professor Schachter astutely observed over thirty years ago that "it would be unrealistic to ignore the influence . . . of the Charter as a factor in resolving constitutional issues which have hitherto been in doubt."[195] His recommendation has been followed in a growing number of federal and state cases which, with increasing frequency in recent years, have referred explicitly to the Charter, the Declaration, or other international human rights instruments to determine the content and reach of rights guaranteed by domestic law.[196]

In *Oyama v. California*,[197] a case decided as far back as 1948, two justices of the United States Supreme court, concurring in a case striking down a portion of the California Alien Land Law as con-

---

193. For a recent student note concluding that it does, see Case Comment, *Plyler v. Doe and the Right of Undocumented Alien Children to a Free Public Education*, 2 B.U. Int'l L.J. 513, 523-32 (1984); *cf. supra* text at and accompanying notes 164-65.

194. An excellent survey and analysis of the seminal post-World War II civil rights cases wherein private parties, organizations such as the ACLU and even the United States government used this approach, with far more effect than is generally recognized, is Lockwood, *The United Nations Charter and United States Civil Rights Litigation: 1946-1955*, 69 Iowa L. Rev. 901 (1984). For recent scholarly support of the present writer's view in this regard, see the numerous articles gathered in *id.* at 901 n.1. By far the most insightful is Christenson, *Using Human Rights Law to Inform Due Process and Equal Protection Analyses*, 52 U. Cin. L. Rev. 3 (1983). *See also* Hartman, *'Unusual' Punishment: The Domestic Effects of International Norms Restricting the Application of the Death Penalty*, 52 U. Cin. L. Rev. 655 (1983).

195. Schachter, *supra* note 42, at 658.

196. Courts in other countries also have used the Charter as a guide to public policy. *See, e.g., In re* Drummond Wren, [1945] 4 D.L.R. 674 (High Ct. Ont.).

197. 332 U.S. 633 (1948).

trary to the fourteenth amendment, remarked that the statute's "inconsistency with [article 55(3) of] the Charter, which has been duly ratified and adopted by the United States, is but one more reason why the statute must be condemned."[198] How could the United States "be faithful to [its] international pledge," two other concurring justices inquired, "if state laws which bar land ownership and occupancy by aliens on account of race are permitted to be enforced?"[199] While none of the four justices asserted that an inconsistency between a provision of the Charter and a state law automatically invalidated the latter, they believed, as a district court judge later concluded, that "the fact that an article of the United Nations Charter is incongruent with a state law is an argument against the validity of such law."[200] In a similar case decided in 1949, the Supreme Court of Oregon, in *Namba v. McCourt,* held the Oregon Alien Land Law violative of the equal protection clause of the fourteenth amendment.[201] The court pointed out that "significant changes . . . in our relationship with other nations and other people,"[202] specifically alluding to article 55 of the UN Charter, was one of the factors it had taken into account in reaching its decision.[203]

Over the years, various groups and scholars have stressed the important interpretative function the human rights clauses of the Charter could and should have. Thus the Commission to Study the Organization of Peace stated nearly two decades ago that the clauses, even if not deemed to be self-executing, "can assist in more liberal interpretation of constitutional and legislative provisions, thus enlarging the sphere of the domestic protection of human rights."[204] From

---

198. *Id.* at 673 (1948) (Murphy, J. & Rutledge, J., concurring).

199. *Id.* at 650 (Black, J., & Douglas, J., concurring).

200. United States v. Vargas, 370 F. Supp. 908, 914-15 (D.P.R. 1974), *vacated and remanded,* 558 F.2d 631 (1st Cir. 1977); *cf.* Lockwood, *supra* note 194, at 920 ("It should be underscored here that the four justices who joined in the concurrences expressed no doubts that the Charter provisions were self-executing. Nowhere did they express a concern that the judicial branch was hamstrung to apply the Charter provisions until the legislative branch passed implementing legislation.").

201. 185 Or. 579, 204 P.2d 569 (1949).

202. *Id.* at 604, 204 P.2d at 579.

203. For a fascinating account of this important decision, which "was lost in the wake of the *Sei Fujii* cases," see Lockwood, *supra* note 194, at 923. Without a doubt he is correct in concluding that "[h]ad *Namba* [rather than *Fujii*] proven to be the seminal case for striking down an alien land law, postwar human rights jurisprudence in America . . . might have included creative use of the Charter to inform constitutional analysis." *Id.* at 924; *cf. infra* text at notes 206-07.

204. COMMISSION TO STUDY THE ORGANIZATION OF PEACE, 18TH REPORT, THE UNITED NATIONS AND HUMAN RIGHTS 4 (1968).

410   *CINCINNATI LAW REVIEW*   [Vol. 54

a slightly different perspective, a law review writer has observed that, "since lawyers are widely reluctant to confess that the values established by the national constitutions fall below any requirement of the Charter, they will rarely explicitly rely on the Charter. This reluctance may eventually lead the courts to more liberal interpretation of the basic rights and freedoms embodied in the constitution."[205]

It is interesting to note that if the human rights clauses of the UN Charter are viewed as tools for clarifying expanding constitutional and statutory rights rather than as norms capable of direct enforcement in and of themselves, the spectre of *Fujii* becomes considerably less haunting. There seems little doubt that the California Supreme Court's opinion in that case was an overreaction to the intermediary appellate court's unabashed reliance on the UN Charter. Had the latter, like the Supreme Court of Oregon in *Namba*,[206] simply cited the Charter's human rights clauses as persuasive authority for a holding based upon the equal protection clause of the fourteenth amendment, rather than using them to establish an independent rule of decision for the case, the California Supreme Court never would have had to embark on its somewhat crabbed analysis of the purposes and meaning of the Charter provisions.[207] If international human rights lawyers today not only argue that the human rights clauses in the UN Charter are self-executing, but also invoke them indirectly in a manner that gradually increases the judiciary's consciousness of their existence and, perhaps more importantly, their potentially enlightening influence, chances are that the results sought by the intermediary appellate court in *Fujii* eventually will be achieved, albeit through an indirect route.[208]

The same approach applies with respect to the Universal Declaration. Although it has been invoked twice recently in direct fashion to help establish rules of customary international human rights law— in *Filartiga* and *Fernandez v. Wilkinson*—the Declaration's principal usefulness has been and most likely will remain that of assisting

---

205. Schluter, *supra* note 27, at 157 n.268. For a recent attempt to convince United States constitutional law professors that international human rights norms should become a significant factor in constitutional decision-making, see Lillich & Hannum, *Linkages Between International Human Rights and U.S. Constitutional Law*, 79 Am. J. Int'l L. 158 (1985). *See also* MATERIALS ON INTERNATIONAL HUMAN RIGHTS AND U.S. CONSTITUTIONAL LAW (H. Hannum ed. 1985) (teaching materials designed to supplement leading United States constitutional law casebooks).

206. *See supra* note 203 and accompanying text.

207. *See supra* text accompanying note 36.

208. *Cf. supra* text accompanying note 183.

domestic courts indirectly. Numerous litigants and judges already have invoked the Declaration for precisely this purpose.[209] Some decisions even have cited the Declaration as a reason for extending economic and social rights.[210] Thus it is likely that, as with the human rights clauses of the UN Charter, the provisions of the Declaration will have their greatest impact on domestic law in the future by influencing the courts' approach to constitutional and statutory standards.[211]

Finally, numerous other international human rights instruments afford the same opportunities for infusing human rights norms into such standards that the UN Charter and the Universal Declaration provide. As mentioned above, no domestic court explicitly has held the Refugees Protocol to be self-executing,[212] yet, as the United States Court of Appeals for the Fifth Circuit recently wrote, "[t]he obligations of the United States as set forth in the Protocol have informed the asylum policy of the United States as expressed in 8 U.S.C. § 1253(h)."[213] So, too, have the UN Standard Minimum Rules for the Treatment of Prisoners[214] helped the United States District Court for the District of Connecticut to define what constituted overcrowded prison conditions for eighth amendment purposes.[215]

As suggested at the outset of this section, international human rights law, at least until the United States ratifies more self-executing

---

209. The cases are collected in R. LILLICH, *supra* note 18, § 440.6-440.7. This looseleaf service, which is updated annually, lists all federal and state court decisions citing the 45 principal international human rights instruments of especial interest to the United States.

210. *See, e.g.*, Copeland v. Secretary of State, 226 F. Supp. 20, 31 n.16 (S.D.N.Y.), *vacated and remanded*, 378 U.S. 588 (1964); Pauley v. Kelley, 255 S.E.2d 859, 864 (W. Va. 1979).

211. *See* Schwelb, *The Influence of Universal Declaration of Human Rights on International and National Law*, 53 AM. SOC'Y INT'L L. PROC. 217, 219 (1959). This conclusion is supported by the fact that courts in other countries have relied upon the Declaration in civil and political rights cases. *See, e.g., In re* Bukowicz, 1953 Y.B. HUM. RTS. 21 (UNITED NATIONS) (BELGIUM); PUBLIC PROSECUTOR v. F.A.v.A., 1951 Y.B. HUM. RTS. 251, 252 (United Nations) (Netherlands); *In re* Pietras, 1951 Y.B. HUM. RTS. 14, 15 (United Nations) (Belgium).

212. *See supra* text at note 104.

213. Haitian Refugee Center v. Smith, 676 F.2d 1023, 1029 n.8 (5th Cir. 1982); *see supra* note 105 and accompanying text.

214. United Nations Standard Minimum Rules for the Treatment of Prisoners, *adopted* E.S.C. Res. 663(c), 24 U.N. ESCOR, Supp. (No. 1) 11, U.N. Doc. E/3048 (1957), *reprinted in* R. LILLICH, *supra* note 18, § 450.1.

215. Lareau v. Manson, 507 F. Supp. 1177 (D. Conn. 1980); *see also* Sterling v. Cupp, 290 Or. 611, 623 n.21, 625 P.2d 123, 131 n.21 (1981). The Supreme Court subsequently held that "double-bunking," prohibited by article 9(1) of the UN Standard Minimum Rules, to which the Court did not refer, was compatible with the eighth amendment. Rhodes v. Chapman, 452 U.S. 337 (1981).

human rights treaties or more norms in the Universal Declaration ripen into customary international law, may serve an important function shaping the content and reach of constitutional and statutory standards. At the very least, through the invocation of the established principle of statutory interpretation that "an Act of Congress ought never to be construed to violate the law of nations, if any other possible construction remains,"[216] it should have substantial impact in many cases involving statutory construction.[217] Thus, while the infusion process may offend some purists, to the lawyer anxious to obtain results it offers significant as well as virtually limitless possibilities for achieving greater protection of the rights of individuals.[218]

VII. CONCLUSION

Using domestic courts to enforce international human rights law, whether directly or indirectly, is a new and growing area of human rights advocacy that presents both challenges and opportunities. In

---

216. Murray v. Schooner Charming Betsy, 6 U.S. (2 Cranch) 64, 118 (1804); *accord* Lauritzen v. Larsen, 345 U.S. 571, 578 (1953); *see* 1 RESTATEMENT, *supra* note 3, § 134. British courts follow the same rule of interpretation with the results recommended in the text. "[S]ince there is a presumption that Parliament does not intend to break the international obligations of the United Kingdom, ambiguous provisions in Acts of Parliament will be construed by the courts to conform so far as possible with the Convention." McBride & Brown, *The United Kingdom, the European Community and the European Convention on Human Rights,* 1981 Y.B. EUR. L. 167, 177; *see also* Duffy, *English Law and the European Convention on Human Rights,* 29 INT'L & COMP. L.Q. 585 (1980).

217. *See, e.g.,* Orantes-Hernandez v. Smith, 541 F. Supp. 351, 365 n.15 (C.D. Cal. 1982); *cf.* Immigration & Naturalization Serv. v. Stevic, 104 S. Ct. 2489, 2500 n.22 (1984). Amicus curiae in the *Bob Jones Case* advanced the argument that the Internal Revenue Code required interpretation consistent with the international law norm against racial discrimination. Motion for Leave to File Brief Amicus Curiae and Brief of the International Human Rights Law Group at 9-10, Bob Jones Univ. v. United States, 461 U.S. 574 (1983). The Court, which decided the case on statutory construction rather than constitutional grounds, found it unnecessary to consider this argument.

An analagous statutory construction argument raising the impact of the above norm and also the Refugees Protocol on the Refugee Act of 1980 has been made in the Brief of Amici Curiae the Procedural Aspects of International Law Institute, the International Human Rights Law Group, the International League for Human Rights and the Center for Constitutional Rights at 43-45, 54-55, Jean v. Nelson, 53 U.S.L.W. 3417 (1984).

218. *See supra* text accompanying note 183. For other writers recommending this approach, see *supra* note 194. *See also* Burke, Coliver, de la Vega & Rosenbaum, *Application of International Human Rights Law in State and Federal Courts,* 18 TEX. INT'L L.J. 291, 295, 322-28 (1983); Greenburg, *The Widening Circles of Freedom,* 8 HUM. RTS (No. 3), Fall 1979, at 10, 45; Hoffman, *The Application of International Human Rights Law in State Courts: A View from California,* 18 INT'L LAW. 61, 63 (1984); Linde, *Comment,* 18 INT'L LAW. 69 (1984). *See generally Proceedings: Conference on International Human Rights Law in State and Federal Courts,* 17 U.S.F.L. REV. 1 (1982).

addition to the substantive problems addressed in this article, many procedural difficulties—carrying such labels as standing,[219] sovereign immunity,[220] act of state[221] and the political question doctrine[222]—confront the private party seeking to invoke international human rights law in the domestic context. While words of

---

219. The leading standing case is Diggs v. Shultz, 470 F.2d 461 (D.C. Cir. 1972), *cert. denied*, 411 U.S. 931 (1973), where the United States Court of Appeals for the District of Columbia held that former Congressman Diggs and other plaintiffs had standing to challenge the Byrd Amendment as violating UN Security Council Resolution 232. This holding so troubled the Ford Administration that the United States subsequently argued, unsuccessfully, that on this point *Diggs* was "wrongly decided." Diggs v. Richardson, 555 F.2d 848, 850 (D.C. Cir. 1976). The two cases are discussed in Lillich, *The Role of Domestic Courts in Promoting International Human Rights Norms*, 24 N.Y.L. SCH. L. REV. 153, 165-68, 172-76 (1978).

For a recent case holding that a nonprofit membership corporation organized to assist Haitian refugees had standing to challenge the United States interdiction of visaless Haitians on the high sees, see Haitian Refugee Center v. Gracey, 600 F. Supp. 1396, 1401-03 (D.D.C. 1985).

220. The leading sovereign immunity case is Letelier v. Republic of Chile, 488 F. Supp. 665 (D.D.C.), *judgment awarded*, 502 F. Supp. 259 (D.D.C. 1980), a suit in the United States District Court for the District of Columbia arising out of the assassination in Washington, D.C. of the former Chilean foreign minister, Orlando Letelier. The Chilean government, who the plaintiffs alleged had ordered the assassination because Letelier outspokenly opposed the ruling junta, claimed that the Foreign Sovereign Immunities Act, 28 U.S.C. §§ 1602-1611 (1982), deprived the court of jurisdiction. The court, correctly, disagreed. *See* 488 F. Supp. at 683; *see also* 21 VA. J. INT'L L. 251 (1981). Certainly the FSIA was not designed to thwart adjudication of cases arising out of human rights violations and should not be so construed. *Cf.* Youngblood, *1980 Survey of International Law in the Second Circuit*, 8 SYR. J. INT'L L. & COMM. 159, 203-04 (1980). Efforts by plaintiffs to enforce the judgment against the assets of LAN, the Chilean National Airline, have been rebuffed. *See* Letelier v. Republic of Chile, 575 F. Supp. 1217 (S.D.N.Y. 1983), *rev'd*, 748 F.2d 790 (2d Cir. 1984). For a recent case wherein the United States Court of Appeals for the Seventh Circuit held that "under the FSIA the Soviet Union was entitled to sovereign immunity," see Frolova v. U.S.S.R., 761 F.2d 370 (7th Cir. 1985).

221. In Filartiga v. Pena-Irala, 630 F.2d 876 (2d Cir. 1980), the defendant argued on appeal that "[i]n the conduct complained of is alleged to be the act of the Paraguayan government, the suit is barred by the Act of State doctrine." *Id.* at 889. The United States Court of Appeals for the Second Circuit found it unnecessary to decide the question, but in dictum expressed doubt "whether action by a state official in violation of the Constitution and laws of the Republic of Paraguay, and wholly unratified by that nation's government, could, properly be characterized as an act of state." *Id.; see* Comment, *supra* note 146, at 363-67.

The court of appeals' dictum as to the nonapplicability of the act of state doctrine is fine as far as it goes, but it does not go far enough. The rationale underlying the doctrine, as formulated in Banco Nacional de Cuba v. Sabbatino, 376 U.S. 398 (1964) assuredly does not preclude United States courts from adjudicating cases involving serious human rights violations by foreign governments officials—period! *See* Lillich, *supra* note 219, at 159-62; *cf.* 1 RESTATEMENT, *supra* note 3, § 469 comment c at 361.

222. The political question doctrine undoubtedly is and will remain the most serious obstacle to private parties seeking to litigate international human rights law issues in United States courts. *See, e.g.,* Hanoch Tel-Oren v. Libyan Arab Republic, 726 F.2d 774, 823

caution may be in order,[223] however, counsels of despair should be taken in stride.[224] Although it would be "a grave mistake to think that courts are the only forums in which human rights law is made or developed,"[225] considerable progress has been made during the past decade in enforcing such law in domestic courts. With imaginative ideas,[226] thorough research,[227] sound judg-

---

(D.C. Cir. 1984)(Robb, J., concurring). For a pungent critique of this tired old doctrine now pleaded "whenever governmental or administrative or political expediency counsels against judicial review of an otherwise quintessentially justiciable dispute," see Gordon, *American Courts, International Law and Political Questions Which Touch Foreign Relations*, 14 INT'L LAW. 297, 329 (1980).

223. As mentioned above, some cases, like Hanoch Tel-Oren v. Libyan Arab Republic, 726 F.2d 774 (D.C. Cir. 1984), are not worth bringing. *Cf.* Martin v. International Olympic Comm., 740 F.2d 670, 673 n.1 (9th Cir. 1984), where the highly speculative argument that the failure to include 5,000 and 10,000 meter track events for women at the Olympic Games violated international human rights law was, fortunately in the opinion of the present writer, not raised properly on appeal, thereby depriving the Ninth Circuit of the opportunity to reject it and perhaps in dictum doing international human rights law more harm than good.

Note that Professor Newman, who filed an *amicus* brief in Diggs v. Richardson, 555 F.2d 848 (D.C. Cir. 1976), arguing that the human rights clauses of the UN Charter were self-executing, has admitted candidly that "[o]ne of the terrible things that happened was that Judge Leventhal took the occasion to announce to everybody that United States Nations Security Council resolutions were not self-executing. Well, if Kathy [Burke] and I had anticipated that result we wouldn't have filed that brief, because the case set a terrible precedent. . . . The holding may well have been the result of the *amicus* brief." Newman, *Keynote Address*, 17 U.S.F.L. REV. 2, 8-9 (1982).

224. *Cf.* Christenson, *The Uses of Human Rights Norms to Inform Constitutional Interpretation*, 4 HOUS. J. INT'L L. 39, 54 (1981):

> Professor Covey Oliver has argued that human rights advocates sometimes overstate or, more precisely, fail to shape their arguments with sufficient skill to guard against losing ground if an appellate court can easily dismiss the argument. I disagree with his conclusion if it counsels timidity in the face of Bricker Amendment-type retaliation, even though I agreee with his tactical point. The use of human rights norms to support constitutional claims can be crafted with better skill. . . . This [indirect incorporation] argument is less vulnerable to attack than one which claims, in the alternative, that a discriminatory law must fall because it violates a treaty standard which is not clearly self-executing or it violates a customary international law when it is questionable whether that international norm is part of federal common law. Presenting a vulnerable, alternative ground to the highest court is the same as inviting the Court to reject it, especially when it is not necessary to a decision.

Id. (citing Oliver, *supra* note 116).

225. The harder, less immediately rewarding, but more important pursuit of international human rights, as of other policies, occurs not in the courts, but in persuading those responsible for policymaking, in the Congress, the State Department, and the White House that Americans care about human rights abroad as well as at home.

Linde, *supra* note 218, at 81.

226. *See, e.g.*, the litigation possibilities sketched out in Burke, Coliver, de la Vega & Rosenbaum, *supra* note 218, at 325-28.

227. For an example of a judicial disaster that might have been avoided had minimal

ment[228] and skillful advocacy,[229] substantial new gains await the making.[230]

---

research been undertaken prior to the commencement of suit, see Hanoch Tel-Oren v. Libyan Arab Republic, 726 F.2d 774 (D.C. Cir. 1984). *See also supra* text accompanying note 161.

228. *But see supra* text accompanying note 223.

229. Skillful advocacy, as Dean Christenson wisely counsels, involves the careful crafting of international human rights law arguments. *See supra* text accompanying note 224. Committed but over-enthusiastic human rights advocates, like the one who opined that "I do not believe that it is critical for practitioners to be overly concerned about the precise legal status of the international norms they present to a . . . court," Hoffman, *supra* note 218, at 62, actually invite the judicial backlash against the invocation of international human rights law that two concurring opinions in *Hanoch Tel-Oren* and several more recent decisions may presage. *See supra* text accompanying notes 8 & 162.

230. As this issue of the *Review* was going to print, the Supreme Court reached its decision in *Jean v. Nelson*, referred to by Professor Lillich, *supra*, at notes 106 and 168. *See* Jean v. Nelson, 105 S. Ct. 2992 (1985). The majority opinion in *Jean* affirmed the decision of the court of appeals without reaching the question of whether the Protocol Relating to the Status of Refugees is self-executing. *Cf. supra* note 106. Similarly, Justice Rehnquist found no need to consider the continuing viability of Mezei v. Shaughnessy, 345 U.S. 206 (1952). *Cf. supra* note 168. Justice Marshall in dissent, however, argued at length for abandonment of the *Mezei* doctrine. *See* 105 S. Ct. at 3005-09 (Marshall, J., dissenting). [Ed.]

[15]

The Time Has Come for an International Criminal Court

M. Cherif Bassiouni *

Introduction

The end of the "Cold War" presents an historic opportunity to advance the international rule of law by establishing an international criminal court to preserve peace, advance the protection of human rights and reduce international and transnational criminality.

The idea for such a court is not new and the efforts to establish it have increased over the years. All of the precedents, however, have been *ad hoc* international tribunals which ceased to exist when the specific function or purpose for which they were designed ended. But the important legal fact is that they existed, albeit with all the weaknesses and shortcomings of having been hastily established, created for a single adjudicating purpose and temporary in nature. Nevertheless, these precedents are the backdrop of international experience which must now ripen into a permanent international adjudicating structure designed to apply international criminal law with consistency and objectivity, and by means of fair process.

Historical Background

It can be said that the first international criminal court was established in 1474 in Breisach, Germany, where 27 judges of the Holy Roman Empire judged and condemned Peter von Hagenbach for his violations of the "laws of God and man" because he allowed his troops to rape and kill innocent civilians and pillage their property.[1] Since then, a number of similar precedents have taken place and moreover,

---

*   Professor of Law, President, International Human Rights Law Institute, DePaul University; President, International Association of Penal Law; President, International Institute of Higher Studies in Criminal Sciences.
    1.   G. SCHWARZENBERGER, INTERNATIONAL LAW AS APPLIED BY INTERNATIONAL COURTS AND TRIBUNALS 462 (1968). *See also* M.H. KEEN, THE LAWS OF WAR IN THE LATE MIDDLE AGES 23-59 (1965).

a number of initiatives for a permanent international criminal court
have been developed. (*See* Appendix I for the chronology of these
initiatives.)

-After World War I, the Treaty of Versailles provided for the prosecution of Kaiser Wilhelm II[2] and for an international tribunal to try
German war criminals.[3] After the war, the Kaiser fled to the Netherlands
where he obtained refuge, but the Allies, who had no genuine interest
in prosecuting him, abandoned the idea of an international court.[4]
Instead, they allowed the German Supreme Court sitting at Leipzig
to prosecute a few German officers.[5] The Germans criticized the proceedings because they were only directed against them and did not
apply to Allied personnel who also committed war crimes. More troublesome, however, was the Allies' failure to pursue the killing of a
then estimated 600,000 Armenians in Turkey.[6] The 1919 Commission
on the Responsibilities of the Authors of the War and on the Enforcement of Penalties for Violations of the Laws and Customs of War,
which investigated the responsibility of those who violated the laws of
war, recommended the prosecution of responsible Turkish officials and
by doing so, the notion of "crimes against humanity" became a legal
reality.[7] Strange as it may seem today, the United States, at that time,
opposed such prosecution on the technical legal argument that no such
crime yet existed under positive international law.[8] Consequently, the
Treaty of Sèvres (1920), which was to serve as a basis for Turkish
prosecutions, was never ratified,[9] and its replacement, the Treaty of

---

2. Treaty of Peace Between the Allied and Associated Powers and Germany
(Treaty of Versailles), 28 June 1919, 11 Martens NOUVEAU RECUEIL DES TRAITES (3d)
323, art. 227.

3. *Id.*, art. 228.

4. *See generally* J.F. WILLIS, PROLOGUE TO NUREMBERG (1982); *see also*, Wright,
The Legality of the Kaiser, 18 AM. POL. SCI. REV. 121 (1919).

5. *See* C. MULLINS, THE LEIPZIG TRIALS (1921). The two major prosecutions
were "The Dover Castle," (*reprinted in* 16 AM. J. INT'L L. 704 (1922)), and "The
Llandovery Castle," (*reprinted in* 16 AM. J. INT'L L. 708 (1922)).

6. *See generally* Dadrian, *Genocide as a Problem of National and International Law:
The World War I Armenian Case and its Contemporary Legal Ramifications*, 14 YALE J. INT'L
L. 221 (1989).

7. Report of the Commission on the Responsibilities of the Authors of the
War and on Enforcement of Penalties for Violations of the Laws and Customs of
War, Conference of Paris 1919, Carnegie Endowment for International Peace, Division
of International Law, Pamphlet No. 32 (1919), *reprinted in* 14 AM. J. INT'L L. 95
(Supp. 1920).

8. *Id.*, Dissent of the United States, at 58 (of Pamphlet No. 32).

9. The Treaty of Peace Between the Allied Powers and Turkey (Treaty of

Lausanne (1923), gave the Turks amnesty.[10] Thus, the first of many mass killings in this century — atrocities now commonly referred to as genocide[11] — remained unpunished. Nevertheless, one can assume that the granting of amnesty constituted implicit legal blameworthiness; i.e., amnesty is only granted for a crime. The reluctance to recognize

---

Sèvres), 10 August 1920, 15 AM. J. INT'L L. 179 (Supp. 1921) (not ratified). *See* in particular arts. 226-230. Article 226 provides:

> The Turkish Government recognises the right of the Allied Powers to bring before military tribunals persons accused of having committed acts in violation of the laws and customs of war. Such persons shall, if found guilty, be sentenced to punishments laid down by law. This provision will apply notwithstanding any proceedings or prosecution before a tribunal in Turkey or in the territory of her alies.
>
> The Turkish Government shall hand over to the Allied Powers or to such one of them as shall so request all persons accused of having committed an act in violation of the laws and customs of war, who are specified either by name or by the rank, office or employment which they held under the Turkish authorities.

See generally Matas, *Prosecuting Crimes Against Humanity: The Lessons of World War I*, 13 FORD. INT'L L. J. 86 (1989).

10. In fact, the treaty did not even address the question of prosecuting war criminals. Treaty of Peace between the Allied Powers and Turkey (Treaty of Lausanne), 24 July 1923, 28 L.N.T.S. 11, *reprinted in* 18 AM. J. INT'L L. 1 (Supp. 1924). *See generally*, Garner, *Punishment of Offenders Against the Laws and Customs of War*, 14 AM. J. INT'L L. 70 (1920).

11. *See* Convention on the Prevention and Suppression of the Crime of Genocide, 9 Dec. 1948, 78 U.N.T.S. 277, *reprinted in* 45 AM. J. INT'L L. 7 (Supp. 1951). Article II defines genocide as follows:

> In the present Convention, genocide means any of the following acts committed with intent to destroy, in whole or in part, a national, ethnical, racial, or religious group, as such:
> (a) Killing members of the group;
> (b) Causing serious bodily or mental harm to members of the group;
> (c) Deliberately inflicting on the group conditions of life calculated to bring about its physical destruction in whole or in part;
> (d) Imposing measures intended to prevent births within the group;
> (e) Forcibly transferring children of the group to another group.

On its face, this definition excludes mass killings which are committed without the accompanying intent to destroy a group "in whole or in part." *See* Bassiouni, *Introduction to the Genocide Convention*, in 1 M.C. BASSIOUNI, INTERNATIONAL CRIMINAL LAW: CRIMES 281 (1986). *See also*, E. ARONEAU, LE CRIME CONTRE L'HUMANITE (1961); P. DROST, THE CRIME OF STATE (1959); Bassiouni, *International Law and the Holocaust*, 9 CAL. W.J. INT'L L. 201, 250 (1979); Lemkin, *Genocide as a Crime Under International Law*, 41 AM. J. INT'L L. 145 (1944).

"crimes against the laws of humanity" in the post-World War I era as prosecutable and punishable international crimes came back to haunt the very same Allies, and particularly the United States, after World War II.

-In 1937, the League of Nations adopted a Convention Against Terrorism. The Protocol to this Convention contained a Statute for an International Criminal Tribunal; however, India was the only country to ratify it and the Convention never entered into effect.[12] Since then, the world has been plagued with all sorts of terror-violence, producing significant victimization, and as a consequence, a number of international Conventions on the subject have been adopted but none contained a provision for the establishment of an international criminal court as did the 1937 Convention.[13] Once again the short-sightedness of public officials prevented the taking of that additional step which many felt to be necessary.[14]

-After World War II, the Allies established two international tribunals — at Nuremberg[15] and Tokyo[16] — to try major war criminals; however,

---

12. Convention for the Creation of an International Criminal Court. Opened for signature at Geneva, Nov. 16, 1937, League of Nations O.J. Spec. in Supp. No. 156 (1938), League of Nations Doc. C.547(I).M.384(I).1937V. (Never entered into force); *reprinted in* 7 INTERNATIONAL LEGISLATION (1935-37), 878 (M. Hudson ed. 1972).

13. *See* Convention for the Suppression of Unlawful Seizure of Aircraft, 16 Dec. 1970, 860 U.N.T.S. 105; Convention for the Suppression of Unlawful Acts Against the Safety of Civil Aviation, 23 Sept. 1971, 974 U.N.T.S. 177; Convention on the Prevention and Punishment of Crimes Against Internationally Protected Persons, Including Diplomatic Agents, 14 Dec. 1973, T.I.A.S. No. 8532; International Convention Against the Taking of Hostages, 18 Dec. 1979, G.A. Res. 34/145 (XXXIV), 34 U.N. GAOR Supp. (No. 46), at 245, U.N. Doc. A/34/146; Protocol for the Suppression of Unlawful Acts of Violence at Airports Serving Civil Aviation, 24 Feb. 1988, 27 I.L.M. 627 (1988); Convention and Protocol from the International Conference on the Suppression of Unlawful Acts Against the Safety of Maritime Navigation, 10 Mar. 1988, I.M.O. Doc. SVA/CON/15.

14. *See* INTERNATIONAL TERRORISM AND POLITICAL CRIMES, (M.C. Bassiouni ed. 1975). In particular, *see* "Final Document: Conclusions and Recommendations" (of the participants to the International Conference on Terrorism and Political Crimes, held at the International Institute of Higher Studies in Criminal Sciences, June 4-16, 1973), at xi-xxii.

15. Agreement for the Prosecution and Punishment of Major War Criminals of the European Axis (London Agreement), 8 Aug. 1945, 82 U.N.T.S. 279, 59 Stat. 1544, E.A.S. No. 472 (entered into force, 8 Aug. 1945), and the annexed Charter of the International Military Tribunal (Nuremberg). *See generally*, TRIAL OF THE MAJOR WAR CRIMINALS: PROCEEDINGS BEFORE THE INTERNATIONAL MILITARY TRIBUNAL (1949), known as the "Blue Series." The ensuing trials were published under the title, TRIALS OF WAR CRIMINALS BEFORE THE NUREMBERG MILITARY TRIBUNAL (1949), known as the

the absence of a strong precedent in the post-World War I era weakened the legality of the process. Even worse was the absence of prosecution of Allied military personnel for war crimes. These and subsequent prosecutions became tainted with the claim of "victor's vengeance," although the legitimacy of prosecuting such offenders by far outweighed the legal weaknesses of the process and certainly outweighed non-prosecution. Subsequent to Nuremberg and Tokyo, the Allies established war crimes tribunals in their respective zones of occupation in Germany and tried over 20,000 war criminals.[17] Germany then took over the task of prosecuting offenders found in its territory.[18] Formerly occupied countries of Europe also prosecuted Germans and their own nationals who collaborated with the occupiers. In some countries, the process continues. Suffice it to recall: Israel's Nazi and Nazi Collaborators (Punishment) Law,[19] under which there were two landmark

---

"Green Series." For an account of the trial and the accused, *see* E. DAVIDSON, THE TRIAL OF THE GERMANS (1966). For a legal appraisal and description of the proceedings, *see* R. WOETZEL, THE NUREMBERG TRIALS IN INTERNATIONAL LAW (1960); J. KEENAN & B. BROWN, CRIMES AGAINST INTERNATIONAL LAW (1950); S. GLUECK, WAR CRIMINALS, THEIR PROSECUTION AND PUNISHMENT (1944).

16. International Military Tribunal for the Far East: (a) Special Proclamation: Establishment of an International Military Tribunal for the Far East; (b) The Charter of the International Military Tribunal for the Far East, Tokyo, 19 Jan. 1946 (General Order No. 1), as amended 26 Apr. 1946, T.I.A.S. No. 1589, *reprinted in* 4 TREATIES AND OTHER INTERNATIONAL AGREEMENTS OF THE U.S.A., 1776-1949 20 (C.I. Bevans ed. 1968).

17. "Control Council Law No. 10" (Punishment of Persons Guilty of War Crimes, Crimes Against Peace and Against Humanity), adopted at Berlin, 20 Dec. 1945, OFFICIAL GAZETTE OF THE CONTROL COUNCIL FOR GERMANY, No. 3, Berlin, 31 Jan. 1946, *reprinted in* 1 B. FERENCZ, AN INTERNATIONAL CRIMINAL COURT 488 (1980). *See* A. MAUNOIR, LA REPRESSION DES CRIMES DE GUERRE DEVANT LES TRIBUNAUX FRANCAIS ET ALLIES (1956); HISTORY OF THE UNITED NATIONS WAR CRIMES COMMISSION (Wright ed. 1948); Bierzanek, *War Crimes: History and Definition*, in 1 A TREATISE ON INTERNATIONAL CRIMINAL LAW 559 (M.C. Bassiouni and V.P. Nanda eds. 1973); Cowles, *Trial of War Criminals (non-Nuremberg)*, 42 AM. J. INT'L L. 299 (1948). In the post-Nuremberg prosecutions conducted in the occupied zones, the U.S. prosecuted 1814 persons (450 executed); the U.K. 1085 (240 executed); France, 2107 (109 executed). *See* Bierzanek, *War Crimes: History and Definition*, in 3 M.C. BASSIOUNI, INTERNATIONAL CRIMINAL LAW: ENFORCEMENT, (1987). The U.S.S.R. is estimated to have prosecuted over 10,000 persons in Germany. No information is available on the number of persons executed. The United Nations War Crimes Commission also reported a number of other prosecutions in and throughout the European countries at war with Germany in World War II.

18. *See* Weinschenck, *Nazis Before German Courts: The West German War Crimes Trials*, 10 INT'L LAW. 515 (1976).

19. Nazi and Nazi Collaborators (Punishment) Law-5710 (1950) 4 LAWS OF

prosecutions, Eichmann[20] (convicted in 1961) and Demjanjuk[21] (convicted in 1989); in Yugoslavia where Artukovic — extradited in 1988 from the United States — was executed in 1989;[22] in France, where Barbie was convicted for the second time in 1989;[23] in the United States denaturalization and deportation of World War II criminals continues;[24] and in Canada, where a 1987 law permits prosecution of persons charged with war crimes and crimes against humanity;[25] the first case was decided in 1989.[26] Prosecution of similar violations as those occurring after World War II has not taken place on any sort of consistent basis, notwithstanding many reported cases in regional conflicts and other conflicts of a non-international character.[27] For

---

THE STATE OF ISRAEL No. 64, at 154. *See* U.N. YEARBOOK ON HUMAN RIGHTS 163 (1950) for the English translation of that law.

20. Attorney General of Israel v. Eichmann (Israel Dist. Court of Israel 1962), 36 I.L.R. 277 (1962). *See generally* G. HAUSER, JUSTICE IN JERUSALEM (1966).

21. Extradited from the U.S. to Israel, In re Extradition of Demjanjuk, 612 F. Supp. 544 (N.D. Oh. 1985), *aff'd*, Demjanjuk v. Petrovsky, 776 F.2d 571 (6th Cir. 1985), *cert. denied* 475 U.S. 1016 (1986).

22. Artukovic v. Rison, 628 F. Supp. 1370 (C.D. Calif. 1986), *aff'd*, 784 F.2d 1354 (9th Cir. 1986).

23. *See* Matter of Barbie, Gaz. Pal. Jur. 710 (France Cass. crim. Oct. 6, 1983). *See also* Le Gunehec, "Affaire Barbie" *Gazette du Palais*, No. 127-128, 106e anneé, Mercredi 7-Jeudi 8 Mai, 1985; and Angevin, "Enseignements de L'Affaire Barbie en Matiere de Crimes Contre l'Humanité," *La Semaine Juridique*, 62e anneé, No. 5, 14 Dec. 1988 p. 2149; Doman, *Aftermath of Nuremberg: The Trial of Klaus Barbie*, 60 COLO. L. REV. 449 (1989).

24. On the revocation of naturalization, *see* 8 U.S.C. § 1451 (1988). *See also Alleged Nazi War Criminals: Hearings Before the Subcommittee on Immigration, Citizenship and International Law of the House Committee on the Judiciary*, 95th Cong., 1st Sess. 59 (1977). And *see generally*, A. RYAN, QUIET NEIGHBORS: PROSECUTING NAZI WAR CRIMINALS IN AMERICA (1984) (examining the issue of war criminals who emigrated to the United States and who now must confront their past).

25. *See* Act to amend the Criminal Code, ch. 37, 1987 Can. Stat. 1107. (*See* in particular § 1.96.). Also, Australia and the United Kingdom have passed or considered similar legislation. In Australia: War Crimes Act 1988, No. 3 of 1989, 25 Jan. 1989; In the U.K. *see* WAR CRIMES: REPORT OF THE WAR CRIMES INQUIRY (Presented to Parliament by the Secretary of State for Home Department by Command of Her Majesty, July 1989).

26. The Queen v. Imre Finta, Court File No. 30/88 (Sup. Ct. of Ontario, 1990).

27. *See generally* Mudge, *Starvation as a Means of Warfare*, 4 INT'L LAW. 228 (1969-1970) [Biafra; Nigeria]; KAMPUCHEA: DECADE OF THE GENOCIDE (K. Kiljunen ed. 1984); Frank & Rodley, *After Bangladesh: The Law of Humanitarian Intervention by Military Force*, 67 AM. J. INT'L L. 275 (1973); and Commentary, *International Crimes Tribunal in Bangladesh*, 11 INT'L COMM. JUR. REV. 29 (N. MacDermot ed. 1973); Paust &

example, only one conviction arose out of the Vietnam War.[28]

-In 1948, the Genocide Convention recognized the jurisdiction of an international criminal court, should one be established, but the Convention did not require that such a court be established.[29] Since 1948, however, mass killings have gone unpunished, including those resulting from the internal conflicts in Biafra (Nigeria), Bangladesh and Kampuchea, where the killing is still ongoing.[30]

-As a result of the post-World War II prosecutions, the United Nations established a Committee for the codification of "Offences Against the Peace and Security of Mankind"[31] and also to develop the statute for an international criminal court. In 1951, such a draft statute was prepared[32] and in 1953, it was amended,[33] but it has been tabled by

---

Blaustein, *War Crimes Jurisdiction and Due Process: The Bangladesh Experience*, 11 VAND J. TRANS. L. 1 (1978); The Asia Watch Committee, KHMER ROUGE ABUSES ALONG THE THAI-CAMBODIAN BORDER (1989). *See also* L. KUPER, GENOCIDE (1981).

28. U.S. v. Calley, 46 C.M.R. 1131 (1973), *aff'd* 48 C.M.R. 19 (1973); *see also* 2 L. FRIEDMAN, THE LAW OF WAR: A DOCUMENTARY HISTORY 1703 (1972).

29. Convention on the Prevention and Punishment of the Crime of Genocide, *supra* note 11, art. IV.

30. *See supra* note 27.

31. *See generally* Williams, *The Draft Code Against the Peace and Security of Mankind*, in 1 M.C. BASSIOUNI, INTERNATIONAL CRIMINAL LAW: CRIMES 109 (1986).

32. Draft Statute for an International Criminal Court (Annex to the Report of the Committee on International Criminal Court Jurisdiction, 31 Aug. 1951), 7 U.N. GAOR Supp. (No. 11), U.N. Doc. A/2136 (1952), at 23. *See also* subsequent Reports of the Committee on International Criminal Jurisdiction, U.N. Doc. A/2186 and U.N. Doc. A/2186/Add. 1. The discussions of the Sixth Committee and of the General Assembly until the end of 1952 encompassed all three reports (U.N. Doc. A/2136, U.N. Doc. A/2186, U.N. Doc. 2186/Add.1). *See also* Historical Survey of the Question of International Criminal Jurisdiction, Memorandum by the Secretary-General, A/CN.4/7/Rev.1 (1949), *reprinted in* 1 B. FERENCZ, AN INTERNATIONAL CRIMINAL COURT 399 (1980). The chronology of relevant U.N. documents, reports and resolutions are: Report of the International Law Commission on the Question of International Criminal Jurisdiction, U.N. Doc. A/CN.4/15 (1950); Report of the International Law Commission to the U.N. General Assembly on the Question of International Criminal Justice, 5 U.N. GAOR Supp. (No. 12), at 18, U.N. Doc. A/1316 (1950); Report of the Sixth Committee to the U.N. General Assembly concerning the Report of the International Law Commission on the Question of International Criminal Jurisdiction (U.N. Doc. A/1316), 5 U.N. GAOR, U.N. Doc. A/1639 (1950); Report on the International Criminal Jurisdiction, 7 U.N. GAOR Supp. (No. 11), U.N. Doc. A/2136 (1951) (Final).

33. Report of the 1953 Committee on International Criminal Jurisdiction to the Sixth Committee, 9 U.N. GAOR Supp. (No. 12), at 23, U.N. Doc. A/2645 (1953); Report of the Sixth Committee to the U.N. General Assembly considering the (Final) Report of the 1953 Committee on International Criminal Jurisdiction (U.N.

the General Assembly ever since.

-In 1972, the *Apartheid* Convention provided for the establishment of an international criminal jurisdiction.[34] In 1980, at the request of the Commission on Human Rights, I prepared a draft statute for an international criminal tribunal to prosecute *apartheid* violators, but the project thus far has not been acted upon.[35]

-In 1989 and 1990, the General Assembly requested the International Law Commission to report on the establishment of an international criminal court to prosecute persons engaged in the international trafficking of drugs.[36] Pursuant to that call, the International Institute of Higher Studies in Criminal Sciences (Siracusa), in cooperation with the United Nations Crime Prevention Branch and the Italian Ministry

---

Doc. A/2645), 9 U.N. GAOR Supp., U.N. Doc. A/2827/Corr. 1 (1954); G.A. Res. 898 (X), U.N. Doc. A/RES./266 (1954) (tabling the Report of the 1953 Committee on International Criminal Jurisdiction); G.A. Res. 1187 (XII), 12 U.N. GAOR (1957) (tabling the Report of the Sixth Committee on International Criminal Jurisdiction, U.N. Doc. A/3771 (1957)).

34. International Convention on the Suppression and Punishment of the Crime of *Apartheid*, G.A. Res. 3068 (XXVIII), 28 U.N. GAOR Supp. (No. 30), at 75, U.N. Doc. A/9030 (1973), *reprinted in* 13 I.L.M. 50 (1974), arts. V, IX.

35. U.N. Doc. E/CN.4/AC.22/C.R.P. 19 (1980), "Study on ways and means of insuring the implementation of international instruments such as the International Convention on the Suppression and Punishment of the Crime of *Apartheid*, including the establishment of the international jurisdiction envisaged by the Convention," U.N. Doc. E/CN.4/1426, (1980). *See also* Bassiouni & Derby, *Final Report on the Establishment of an International Criminal Court for the Implementation of the Apartheid Convention and Other Relevant International Instruments*, 9 HOFSTRA L. REV. 523 (1981).

36. G.A. Res. 43/164 (1988) and 44/39 (1989). And, in particular, *see* Agenda item 152 entitled *International Criminal Responsibility of Individuals and Entities Engaged in Illicit Trafficking in Narcotic Drugs Across National Frontiers and Other Transnational Criminal Activities Establishment of an International Criminal Court with Jurisdiction Over Such Crimes, Report of the Sixth Committee to the General Assembly*, U.N. Doc. A/44/770 (1989). *See also Adoption of a Political Declaration and a Global Programme of Action*, Draft global programme of action by the Bureau of the *Ad Hoc* Committee of the Seventeenth Special Session of the General Assembly (Item 14 of the provisional agenda), U.N. Doc. VA/S-17/AC.1/L.2 (1990), which at paragraph 80 provides:

> Since the International Law Commission has been requested to consider the question of establishing an international criminal court or other international trial mechanism with jurisdiction over persons alleged to be engaged in illicit trafficking in narcotic drugs across national frontiers, the Administrative Committee on Co-ordination shall consider, in its annual adjustments to the United Nations system-wide action plan on drug abuse control requested by the General Assembly in its resolution 44/141 of 15 December 1989, the report of the International Law Commission on the question.

See generally, 84 AM. J. INT'L L. 930, 930-933 (1990).

of Justice, convened a committee of experts in June 1990 to prepare
such a draft statute. The Committee approved the document I prepared[37]

---

37. The Draft Statute for an International Criminal Court is based on the
earlier proposal prepared by this author for the United Nations to prosecute *apartheid*
violators. *See supra* note 35. Thereafter the Draft Statute was amended and published
in M.C. BASSIOUNI, A DRAFT INTERNATIONAL CRIMINAL CODE AND DRAFT STATUTE FOR
AN INTERNATIONAL TRIBUNAL (1987). In preparation for the Siracusa meeting the Draft
Statute was discussed at a meeting convened by Senator Arlen Specter:

> But, the ILC is not the only forum for discussion of this proposal. Commencing
> later [sic] month in Italy, the International Institute of Higher Studies in
> Criminal Sciences in cooperation with the United Nations Crime Prevention
> Branch on Penal Codes will focus primary attention on the issue of creation
> of an international criminal court. And, in August, the United Nations' 8th
> Congress on Crime Prevention will also focus debate on the creation of such
> a court. Clearly, the progress made on the need for and creation of inter-
> national criminal court has taken a quantum leap forward.
>
> In sum, it is clear that there is broad agreement on the definition and threat
> posed by drugs and drug trafficking leading to the United Nations adoption
> on December 20, 1988 of the Convention against the Illicit Traffic in Narcotic
> Drugs and Psychotropic Substances. In spite of several international conven-
> tions on aviation, maritime safety and hostage-taking, there is less agreement
> on the definition of terrorism. While both represent a very serious problem
> to safety and security, the development of a regional international criminal
> court focusing on drugs and international drug trafficking, in my view, offers
> a start in establishing and developing the international criminal court system.
>
> In closing, I wish to support the effort of the forthcoming fora in their efforts
> to create an international criminal court. In the months ahead I shall be
> introducing a new legislative proposal to move the United States closer to a
> more active role in the formulation of an international criminal court.
>
> Mr. President, I would be gravely remiss if I did not recognize the extensive
> scholarship contributed by Cherif Bassiouni, professor of law at DePaul
> University College of Law to the development of an international criminal
> court and code. Professor Bassiouni's counsel and dedication have been a
> source of inspiration and guidance to this Senator and indeed to the community
> of international criminal lawyers and scholars. His competence and vision as
> an international criminal law scholar are universally shared. I thank him
> publicly for his contributions and leadership in this matter and look forward
> to greater cooperation with him in the formulative period ahead.

136 CONG. REC. S8080 (daily ed. June 18, 1990) (statement of Sen. Specter).
And also, after the Siracusa Conference:

> [A] special committee of experts organized by the International Institute of
> Higher Studies in Criminal Sciences under the auspices of the Italian Ministry
> of Justice and in cooperation with the United Nations Crime Prevention and

with minor changes and the text was submitted to the Eighth United
Nations Congress on Crime Prevention and the Treatment of Offenders
held in Havana, Cuba, August-September, 1990.[38]
-The Eighth Congress debated the subject and that discussion was
summarized in its report as follows:

> There was a need to develop clear ideas and a firm attitude
> on international co-operation, free of isolationism while re-
> specting the sovereignty of States. Some delegations considered
> that the threat of major international crimes necessitated the
> establishment of an international criminal court. It would serve
> as an instrument for the defence of international peace and
> security, without which the sovereignty of some States, par-
> ticularly small States, could be placed in jeopardy.[39]

The Congress, however, resolved as follows:

> The International Law Commission should be encouraged to
> continue to explore the possibility of establishing an inter-
> national criminal court or some other international mechanism
> to have jurisdiction over persons who have committed offences
> (including offences connected with terrorism or with illicit
> trafficking in narcotic drugs or psychotropic substances), in
> accordance with General Assembly resolution 44/39 of 4 De-
> cember 1989. Similarly, and in the light of the report that
> the International Law Commission will submit on this par-
> ticular subject to the General Assembly at its forty-fifth session,
> the possibility might be considered of establishing an inter-
> national criminal court or appropriate mechanism with each
> and all of the procedural and substantive arrangements that
> might guarantee both its effective operation and absolute re-
> spect for the sovereignty and the territorial and political in-
> tegrity of States and the self-determination of peoples. States

Criminal Justice Branch held a symposium in Siracusa, Italy. The Institute
urged establishment of the court, drafted a model statute for such a court and
presented its recommendations to the Eighth United Nations Congress on the
Prevention of Crime and the Treatment of Offenders which met in August.

136 CONG. REC. S18160 (daily ed. Oct. 25, 1990) (statement of Sen. Specter).

38.   U.N. Doc. A/Conf. 144/NGO 7, *Draft Statute: International Criminal Tribunal*
(1990), Item 5, *reprinted in* 15 NOVA L. REV. 375 (1991). *See also* Bassiouni, A Comprehensive Strategic Approach on International Cooperation for the Prevention, Control
and Suppression of International and Transnational Criminality, Including the Establishment of an International Criminal Court, 15 NOVA L. REV. 353 (1991).

39.   *Report of the Eighth United Nations Congress on the Prevention of Crime and the
Treatment of Offenders*, U.N. Doc. A/Conf. 144/28, at 227, (1990).

could also explore the possibility of establishing separate international criminal courts of regional or sub-regional jurisdiction in which grave international crimes, and particularly terrorism, could be brought to trial and the incorporation of such courts within the United Nations system.[40]

-In July 1990, the International Law Commission completed a report and submitted it to the 1990 session of the General Assembly.[41] It expressed a positive view on the feasibility of such a court with jurisdiction over "Crimes Against the Peace and Security of Mankind."[42]

All these efforts have brought us closer to realizing the expectations of so many who believe that some form of international adjudication for international and transnational crimes may be forthcoming. But so far the political will of the world's major powers has been lacking, and progress toward that goal is slow though growing.

Political, Practical and Technical Legal Considerations

The obstacles to the establishment of an international criminal court fall essentially into three categories: (1) political; (2) practical; and, (3) legal-technical. Of these three, the political factor is the most significant, followed by the practical one, while the legal-technical one does not pose any serious difficulties.

The political factor stems essentially from objections generated by those who adhere to a rigid conception of sovereignty, even though such conceptions have been *dépassé* in so many other areas of international law, particularly with respect to the international and regional protections of human rights embodied in conventional and customary international law. The real opposition, however, comes from government officials who fear two types of situations.

The first is the risk that they and other senior officials, especially heads of state, can be called to answer for their acts which may constitute international violations and which would be subject to the Court's jurisdiction. This is not surprising in view of the fact that the Nuremberg[43] and Tokyo[44] international military tribunals, and the United Nations'

---

40. *Id.*, at 193-4.

41. *See supra* note 36, and accompanying text.

42. International Law Commission, Forty Second Session, U.N. Doc. A/CN.4/430/Add.1 (1990) *Eighth Report on the Draft Code of Crimes Against the Peace and Security of Mankind.*

43. *See supra* note 15.

44. *See supra* note 16.

subsequent affirmation of the Nuremberg principles, removed the immunity of heads of states and negated other defenses, such as "obedience to superior orders."[45]

Since World War II a number of instances have come to world public attention indicating that heads of state and senior government officials have engaged in or supported the commission of such international crimes as aggression, war crimes, crimes against humanity, genocide, *apartheid*, slavery and slave-related practices, international trafficking in drugs, aircraft hijacking, kidnapping of diplomats, taking of civilian hostages and torture. And while the world community expresses abhorrence of some of these crimes, and outrage about others, little if anything is done, other than pious denunciations, and occasionally, some condemnatory resolutions by the United Nations and other international bodies.

The political problem is obvious. Heads of states and senior government officials have historically wanted to shield themselves from any form of international accountability. Their successors and even their opponents so frequently cover up for them for fear that they too may find themselves in a similar situation, or because they feel that domestic political peace may warrant it. This was evident when Bangladesh did not carry out its intended prosecution of Pakistanian military personnel after the independence of that region, which was once part of Pakistan.[46] It was also the case when Argentina, after prosecuting some officers for the estimated 15,000 *desaparecidos* between 1976-1983, passed an amnesty law on December 29, 1990.[47]

During the "cold war" (1948-1989) countries on both sides of the then "iron curtain" perceived the exigencies of national security at precluding consideration of an international criminal court that would deal with such international crimes as aggression and terrorism. But the real reason was that the two superpowers engaged in acts violating international criminal law, as did their surrogates, satellites and respective friendly countries. Exaggerated as these claims of national

---

45. *See Affirmation of the Principles of International Law Recognized by the Charter of Nuremberg Tribunal* G.A. Res. 95 (I) U.N. Doc. A/64 Add. 1 (1946); *Principles of International Law Recognized in the Charter of the Nuremberg Tribunal and in the Judgment of the Tribunal* (International Law Commission), 5 U.N. GAOR (No. 12), 11 U.N. Doc. A/1316 (1950). Also, in 1968, the United Nations adopted the *Convention on the Non-Applicability of Statutory Limitations to War Crimes and Crimes Against Humanity*, 26 Nov. 1968, 754 U.N.T.S. 73, *reprinted in* 8 I.L.M. 68 (1969).

46. *See* Frank & Rodley, Paust & Plaustein, *supra* note 27.

47. *See* Timerman, *Fear Returns to Argentina* New York Times, Jan. 5, 1991, at 13, col. 1.

security were, and certainly as they now appear to be, the argument
of national security was frequently used to rationalize the commission
of international crimes ranging from aggression to torture. Even now,
public officials in countries which resort to, or allow torture, rationalize
it on the grounds of national security or public necessity.[48] Strange as
it may seem, the efforts of public officials to shield themselves from
accountability, whether heads of state or simple police officers, has
consistently been the same for as long as there is a record of these
occurrences. They invariably argue that their action was necessary in
order to protect or save the nation, or to advance its vital or national
security interests.

Another argument advanced against such a court, as well as another
risk perceived by public officials, is the apprehension that an international adjudication body can, for purely political reasons, embarrass
governments and public officials. But surely sufficient safeguards could
be developed to prevent such possibilities, much as certain mechanisms
have been developed in domestic legal systems to avoid abuse of power
through prosecutorial misconduct and abuse of prosecutorial discretion.
Such issues as well as other legal-technical issues cannot be raised *a
priori* to oppose the realization of the idea. They are valid concerns to
be raised in the context of drafting the norms and provisions of an
international criminal court system so as to develop appropriate safeguards. It is, therefore, more likely that this argument is raised in
order to obfuscate the fact that the former one (to shield public officials)
is the real reason for the opposition to the idea.

Practical questions are also raised with frequency and have a ring
of authenticity to them, particularly to the non-initiated. Among these
questions are: where to locate the Court; how to secure the presence
of the accused to stand trial; how to select judges, etc. These and other
practical questions are no different than those which faced the drafters
of the 1899 Hague Convention establishing the Permanent Court of
Arbitration,[49] or those of the 1920 Permanent Court of International
Justice and of the 1945 International Court of Justice, respectively part
of the League of Nations and United Nations Charters. Granted, these
tribunals were not set up for purposes of individual criminal prosecutions
and that there are peculiar problems to this type of adjudication, but

---

48. *See generally* Bassiouni & Derby, *The Crime of Torture*, in 1 M.C. BASSIOUNI,
INTERNATIONAL CRIMINAL LAW: CRIMES 363 (1986); TORTURE IN THE EIGHTIES (An
Amnesty International Report, 1984).

49. Convention for the Pacific Settlement of Disputes, July 29, 1899, 32 Stat.
1799.

14   IND. INT'L & COMP. L. REV.   [Vol. 1:1

political sensitivities about all forms of international adjudication are similar. That is why both the PCIJ and the ICJ provide for the Member-States the choice of compulsory or voluntary submission to jurisdiction.[50] In the case of an international criminal court having jurisdiction over individuals, it would seem that these political sensitivities should be of a lesser nature, except, of course, when it comes to prosecuting public officials for crimes having political overtones or which are committed pursuant to state-policy and particularly if the international criminal court were to have exclusive jurisdiction.

The Draft Statute for an International Criminal Tribunal, which I prepared in 1980 and which was revised and reviewed by the 1990 Siracusa Committee of Experts and then submitted to the Eighth United Nations Congress,[51] addresses these concerns without compromising the basic values and goals sought to be achieved by such a Tribunal. Clearly, other solutions to practical and legal technical questions can be developed, but the point is that these problems are not as difficult to resolve as some government officials claim. They are not, therefore, a valid reason for the refusal of establishing an international criminal court.

Legal-technical issues are easily resolvable and many thoughtful models have been developed by the League of Nations, the United Nations, non-governmental organizations and individual scholars.[52] (Some of these questions are discussed below when the ''Proposed Model'' is examined.)

Recent Developments

In the last three years, the question of establishing an international criminal court has emerged at the highest political levels in the world and renewed interest has been expressed by world leaders and by the United Nations.[53]

As early as 1987, President Gorbachev expressed support for such a court, but with jurisdiction limited to terrorism.[54] In the United

---

50. *See* Statute of the International Court of Justice, art. 36. For a case which examines the Court's jurisdictional issues, *see* MILITARY AND PARAMILITARY ACTIVITIES IN AND AGAINST NICARAGUA 1986. I.C.J. 14. *See generally,* Maier, *Appraisals of the ICJ's Decision: Nicaragua v. United States,* 81 AM. J. INT'L L. 77 (1987).

51. *See supra* notes 37-39.

52. *See e.g., supra* notes 32, 33 and 35, *infra* note 71 and the Appendix.

53. *See supra* notes 36-42 and accompanying text and *infra* notes 54-56, 65 and accompanying text.

54. Pravda Sept. 16, 1987.

States, Senator Arlen Specter has been, since 1986, a constant advocate of such a court,[55] as have Congressmen Leach and Kastenmeier in the House.[56] In fact, the United States Congress has urged the establishment of an international criminal court, but only with regard to international terrorism and international trafficking in drugs. In 1986, as part of the Omnibus Diplomatic Security and Antiterrorism Act of 1986,[57] Congress called upon the President to "consider including on the agenda for these negotiations [regarding an international convention to prevent and control all aspects of international terrorism,] the possibility of eventually establishing an international tribunal for prosecuting terrorists."[58] Also, in 1988, Congress passed the Anti-Drug Abuse Act of 1988,[59] which also asserts the need for some sort of international tribunal to handle cases of drug trafficking. It provides that:

> It is the sense of the Senate that the President should begin discussions with foreign governments to investigate the feasibility and advisability of establishing an international criminal court to expedite cases regarding the prosecution of persons accused of having engaged in international drug trafficking or having committed international crimes.[60]

Even more recently, Congress, at the behest of Senator Specter, amended the "Foreign Operations, Export Financing, and Related Programs Appropriations Act, 1991,"[61] and provided:

(a)   The Congress finds that—

---

55. *Supra* note 37; *see also* Appendix II.

56. H.R. Con. Res. 66, 100th Cong., 2d Sess. (1989). In recognition of the efforts of Congressmen Leach and Kastenmeier, Senator Specter stated in the *Congressional Record*, October 25, 1990, *supra* note 37:

First and foremost, I wish to recognize the great contribution made by Congressman Jim Leach, Congressman Bob Kastenmeier and their staffs on behalf of this legislation regarding the creation of an international criminal court. Their efforts in the House of Representatives have served as inspiration for this Senator to continue ahead in the unchartered waters surrounding this issue. Their House Concurrent Resolution 66, which they introduced on March 2, 1989, served as a source of reassurance to my past resolutions and in my crafting of amendment No. 3068.

57. PUB. L. No. 99-399 (1986).

58. *Id.*, Title XII - Criminal Punishment of International Terrorism; § 1201 (Encouragement for Negotiation of a Convention) (d).

59. PUB. L. No. 100-690 (1988).

60. *Id.*, Title IV International Narcotics Control, § 4108 (International Criminal Court) (a).

61. PUB. L. No. 101-513 (1990).

(1) the international community has defined as criminal conduct in various international conventions, certain acts such as war crimes, crimes against humanity, torture, piracy and crimes on board commercial vessels, aircraft hijacking and sabotage of aircraft, crimes against diplomats and other internationally protected persons, hostage-taking, and illicit drug cultivation and trafficking;

(2) in spite of these international conventions, the effective prosecution of those who commit criminal acts has been seriously obstructed in certain cases because of problems of extradition and differences between the legal and judicial systems of individual nations;

(3) the jurisdiction of the International Court of Justice extends only to cases involving governments, and not to individual criminal cases;

(4) the concept of an international criminal court has been under consideration in the United Nations and other international fora for many years, including proposals and reviews undertaken in 1990 by the United Nations General Assembly, the International Law Commission, and the Eighth United Nations Congress on the Prevention of Crime and the Treatment of Offenders;

(5) the international military tribunals established in Nuremburg, Germany, and Tokyo, Japan, following World War II also establish a precedent for international criminal tribunals; and

(6) there is growing movement among nations of the world to formulate their economic, political and legal systems on a multilateral basis.

(b) It is the sense of Congress that—

(1) the United States should explore the need for the establishment of an International Criminal Court on a universal or regional basis to assist the international community in dealing more effectively with criminal acts defined in international conventions; and

(2) the establishment of such a court or courts for the more effective prosecution of international criminals should not derogate from established standards of

due process, the rights of the accused to a fair trial
and the sovereignty of individual nations.

(c) The President shall report to the Congress by October
1, 1991, the results of his efforts in regard to the establishment of an International Criminal Court to deal with
criminal acts defined in international conventions.

(d) The Judicial Conference of the United States shall report
to the Congress by October 1, 1991, on the feasibility
of, and the relationship to, the Federal judiciary of an
International Criminal Court.[62]

As for the Bush Administration, it has stressed international cooperation against terrorism and trafficking in drugs, but it seems, at
this point, reluctant to support an international court to prosecute such
offenders.[63] (For a chronology of U.S. developments regarding an international criminal court *see* Appendix II.)

As for other countries, France and the United Kingdom have an
ambiguous position. At the 1990 Eighth United Nations Congress on
Crime Prevention and Treatment of Offenders, their representatives
joined efforts to lobby other Western European countries against a
resolution calling for the establishment of an international criminal
court, though both countries had previously voted favorably on two
resolutions in the General Assembly in 1989-90 supporting such an
idea.[64] On the positive side, sixteen Caribbean and Latin American
countries have been supporting the idea since 1989. Trinidad and
Tobago has been in the forefront of this question, led by Prime Minister
A.N.R. Robinson, and since 1990, Columbia's President C. Oaviria
Trujillo has also strongly supported the idea.[65] In response to such

---

62. *Id.*, § 599 E (International Criminal Court).

63. On terrorism and drugs, *see e.g.*, Bassiouni, *Effective National and International
Action Against Organized Crime and Terrorist Criminal Activities*, 4 EMORY INT'L L. REV. 9
(1990); Bassiouni, *Critical Reflections of International and National Control of Drugs*, 18 DEN.
J. INT'L L. & POL. 311 (1990).

64. *See supra* note 36. At the Eighth United Nations Congress, *see supra* notes
38-40 and accompanying text; a number of countries made statements supporting the
idea of an international criminal court. They are: Brazil, Colombia, Czechoslovakia,
Israel, Poland, Romania, Trinidad and Tobago, U.S.S.R. and Yugoslavia.

65. Agenda Item 152, referred to *supra* note 36, was introduced at the request
of Trinidad and Tobago, *see* G.A. Res. A/44/195 (1989) and in the Annex, an
explanatory memorandum by Ambassador Margorie Thorpe stated, in part, as follows:

The desirability and feasibility of an international criminal court to deal

International Dispute Settlement

18   IND. INT'L & COMP. L. REV.   [Vol. 1:1

strong interest, the Organization of American States has begun studying the possibility of a Regional Criminal Court for the Americas.[66] The Caribbean and Latin American countries show particular eagerness for such a Court and they are understandably dismayed to see the disinterest and opposition of other countries (particularly the U.S.) that are quick to accuse them of not doing enough to control international trafficking in drugs and terrorism.

Current international interests, however, seem to focus only on drugs and terrorism. What is needed instead is an international criminal

---

with international criminal offences was the subject of much discussion even before the establishment of the Nuremberg International Military Tribunal on 8 August 1946. It was envisaged then that the jurisdiction of an international criminal court would cover individuals charged with violations of certain rules of international law such as genocide. Such a proposal was formalized in 1951 and revised in 1954 by the Committee on International Criminal Jurisdiction, established pursuant to General Assembly resolutions 489 (V) of 12 December 1950 and 687 (VII) of 5 December 1952 . . . .

The establishment of an international criminal court with jurisdiction to prosecute and punish individuals and entities who engage in, *inter alia*, the illicit trafficking in narcotic drugs across national borders would serve to bolster the legal process whereby such offenders are prosecuted and punished and would also contribute substantially to the progressive development and codification of international law.

With regard to Columbia, as Senator Specter notes in the *Congressional Record*:

Colombia is a vivid case in point. Extraditions to the United States have had some positive effect on traffickers. But, these same extraditions represent a serious political problem for the leadership of Colombia. Thus, in his August 7, 1990, Inauguration address, President Cesar Oaviria Trujillo vowed to "explore the possibility of creating an international or regional criminal jurisdiction to fight narco-trafficking and other related crimes that surpass international borders."

136 CONG. REC. S18160 (daily ed. October 25, 1990).

66. The Inter-American Juridical Committee of the OAS at its 1990 session, held in Rio de Janeiro, Brazil (*see* document OEA/Ser. G, CP/doc.2113/90, Nov. 7, 1990, page 53). The motion to examine this topic was presented by the Argentine member of the Committee, Dr. Jorge R. Vanossi, who was subsequently appointed rapporteur together with Professor M. Vieira from Uruguay. In his introductory statement, Dr. Vanossi made reference to the work undertaken by the International Institute of Higher Studies in Criminal Sciences, and to the preparatory work submitted by Dr. Bassiouni (*see* 1990 Session of the Inter-American Juridical Committee, August 18 meeting, Minute No. 12). These documents will be an important source for the Committee, which is expected to begin examination of the topic at the 1991 July-August session. This information was provided by Ambassador Hugo Caminos, Assistant Secretary General for Legal Affairs, who is following this question at the OAS.

court with universal jurisdiction to prosecute all or most of the 22 categories of international crimes covered by conventional and customary international law, including, but not limited to:[67] aggression (crimes against peace); war crimes; crimes against humanity; genocide; *apartheid*; slavery and slave-related practices; torture; unlawful human experimentation; piracy; hijacking and sabotaging of aircraft; kidnapping of diplomats and other internationally protected persons; taking of hostages; and, criminal damage to the environment. The International Law Commission has taken such a position in its 1990 Report to the General Assembly, though the list of international crimes it has developed is different from the one proposed above by this writer.[68]

The ILC's 1990 position on such a Court is stated as follows:

1. *Competence of the Court*

(a) *Jurisdiction limited to the crimes mentioned in the Code or jurisdiction as to all international crimes?*

(i) *Versions submitted*

5. On this topic, the Special Rapporteur submits the following versions:

Version A: There is established an International Criminal Court to try natural persons accused of crimes referred to in the draft Code of crimes against the peace and security of mankind.

Version B: There is established an International Criminal Court to try natural persons accused of crimes referred to in the draft Code of crimes against the peace and security of mankind, or other offences defined as crimes by the other international instruments in force.

---

67. *See* M.C. BASSIOUNI, INTERNATIONAL CRIMES: DIGEST/INDEX OF INTERNATIONAL INSTRUMENTS 1815-1985 (1986). *See also* statement of Senator Specter, *supra* note 37:

> Modern international criminal law can be said to have commenced in 1815 at the Congress of Vienna with efforts to abolish slavery. Since then 317 international instruments on substantive international criminal law have been agreed to covering international crimes such as aggression, war crimes, crimes against humanity, apartheid, torture, piracy on board commercial vessels, aircraft hijacking, kidnapping of diplomats and other internationally protected persons, taking of civilian hostages and environmental damages to name a few.

68. *See* the International Law Commission's latest report (from its Forty-First Session) to the General Assembly, U.N. Doc. A/CN.4/L.443 (1990).

(ii) *Commentary*

6.   The question is whether international criminal jurisdiction will be limited to the crimes referred to in the draft Code of crimes against the peace and security of mankind, or whether it will also encompass other international crimes which do not fall within that category. As is well known, the Code does not cover all international crimes. Among those not mentioned therein are the dissemination of false or distorted news, or false documents, by persons knowing that they will have an adverse effect on international relations; insults to a foreign State; the counterfeiting of currency, practiced by one State to the detriment of another State, and the theft of national or archaeological treasures; the destruction of submarine cables; international trafficking in obscene publications, etc.

7.   Accordingly, the concept of an international crime is broader than that of a crime against the peace and security of mankind; it covers a wider field which includes all other international crimes in addition to those defined in the draft Code.

8.   The question, therefore, is whether the jurisdiction of the Court is limited to crimes against the peace and security of mankind, or whether the Court will deal with all international crimes.

9.   It would seem preferable to confer the broadest possible jurisdiction upon the Court; otherwise, it would be necessary to establish two international criminal jurisdictions, which would lead to complications.

(b) *Necessity or non-necessity of the agreement of other States*

(i) *Versions submitted*

Version A: No person shall be tried before the Court unless jurisdiction has been conferred upon the Court by the State in which the crime was committed, or by the State of which such person is a national, or by the State against which the crime was directed, or of which the victims were nationals.

Version B: Any State may bring before the Court a complaint against a person if the crime of which he is accused was committed in that State, or if it was directed against that State, or if the victims are nationals of that State. If one of the said States disagrees as to the jurisdiction of the Court, the Court shall resolve the issue.

(ii) *Commentary*

11. Version A is based on article 27 of the draft statute prepared by the 1953 Committee on International Criminal Jurisdiction.[69] Is it appropriate? From the legal point of view, nothing prohibits a State from punishing crimes against its own security, even if such crimes are committed abroad by foreigners. Moreover, in the vast majority of cases, this solution would lead to requesting the consent of Governments guilty of having organized or tolerated criminal acts.[70]

Such a court is not only possible, it is quite feasible. All of the foreseeable problems and difficulties have been thoughtfully dealt with by a number of experts who have prepared detailed studies and examined alternative solutions to the various legal and practical questions.[71]

---

69. *See* Report of the 1953 Committee on International Criminal Jurisdiction, *Official Records of the General Assembly, Ninth Session, Supplement No. 12* (A/2645), annex, article 27.

70. International Law Commission, Forty Second Session, U.N. Doc. A/CN.4/430/Add.1 (1990) *Eighth Report on the Draft Code of Crimes Against the Peace and Security of Mankind.*

71. *See e.g.*, B. FERENCZ, AN INTERNATIONAL CRIMINAL COURT (1980), which provides a documentary examination of the historical evolution of international crimes and the establishment of an international criminal court. Some scholars see the problem both in terms of the political will of the most powerful governments and of the lack of scholarly consensus on the broader issue of the scope and content of international criminal law. *See e.g.*, Friedlander, *The Enforcement of International Criminal Law: Fact or Fiction,* 17 CASE W. RES. J. INT'L L. 79 (1985) (wherein the author re-examines Georg Schwarzenberger's query about the existence of international criminal law); Friedlander, *The Foundations of International Criminal Law: A Present Day Inquiry,* 15 CASE W. RES. J. INT'L L. 13 (1983); Green, *Is There an International Criminal Law,* 21 ALBERTA L. REV. 251 (1983); Green, *New Trends in International Criminal Law,* 11 ISR. Y.B. HUM. RTS. 9 (1981); Green, *An International Criminal Code — Now?* 3 DALHOUSIE L.J. 560 (1976); Dinstein, *International Criminal Law,* 5 ISR. Y.B. HUM. RTS. 55 (1975); Wright, *The Scope of International Criminal Law,* 15 VA. J. INT'L L. 562 (1975). *See generally* Derby, *A Framework for International Criminal Law,* in 1 M.C. BASSIOUNI, INTERNATIONAL CRIMINAL LAW: CRIMES 33 (1986); Schwarzenberger, *The Problem of International Criminal Law,* 3 CURRENT LEGAL PROBLEMS 263 (1950); Report of the International Law Commission on Questions of International Criminal Jurisdiction, U.N. Doc. A/CN.4/15 (1950). *See also* Bassiouni & Derby, *Final Report on the Establishment of an International Criminal Court for the Implementation of the Apartheid Convention and Other Relevant Instruments,* 9 HOFSTRA L. REV. 523 (1981); Kos-Rabcewicz-Zubkowski, *La Creation d'une Cour Pénal Internationale et l'Administration Internationale de la Justice,* 1977 CAN. Y.B. INT'L L. 253;

Alternative Models

The formulae presented in the scholarly literature and proposals advanced by different organizations range from the position of the Association Internationale de Droit Pénal, which since 1926, has urged the establishment, by way of a treaty-statute (much like the Nuremberg Charter and Tokyo Statute), of a universal, as opposed to a regional, international criminal court having jurisdiction over all international crimes, to that of the International Law Association, which has advocated an International Commission of Inquiry (*See* Appendix I). Alternative approaches are based on an expanded concept of jurisdiction discussed, since the 1970's, within the Council of Europe under the rubrique "*L'Espace Judiciaire Européen*", which is still under consideration, and which has inspired the Commission of the Andean Parliament

---

Kos-Rabcewicz-Zubkowski, *The Creation of an International Criminal Court*, in INTERNATIONAL TERRORISM AND POLITICAL CRIMES 519 (M.C. Bassiouni ed. 1975); Grebing, *La Creation d'une Cour Pénal Internationale: Bilan et Perspectives*, 45 REV. INT'LE DE DROIT PÈNAL 435 (1974); Miller, *Far Beyond Nuremberg: Steps Toward an International Criminal Jurisdiction*, 61 KY. L.J. 925 (1973); Dautricourt, *The Concept of International Criminal Court Jurisdiction — Definition and Limitations of the Subject*, in 1 A TREATISE ON INTERNATIONAL CRIMINAL LAW 636 (M.C. Bassiouni & V.P. Nanda eds. 1973); J. STONE & R. WOETZEL, TOWARD A FEASIBLE INTERNATIONAL CRIMINAL COURT (1970); Klein & Wilkes, *United Nations Draft Statute for an International Criminal Court: An American Evaluation*, in INTERNATIONAL CRIMINAL LAW 573 (G.O.W. Mueller & E. Wise eds. (1965)); Ambion, *Organization of a Court of International Criminal Jurisdiction*, 29 PHIL L. J. 345 (1954); P. CARJEU, PROJET D'UNE JURIDICTION PENALE INTERNATIONALE (1953); Wright, *Proposal for an International Criminal Court*, 46 AM. J. INT'L L. 60 (1952); Finch, *Draft Statute for an International Court*, 46 AM. J. INT'L L. 89 (1952); Yeun-Li, *The Establishment of an International Criminal Jurisdiction: The First Phase*, 46 AM. J. INT'L L. 73 (1952); A. SOTTILE, THE PROBLEM OF THE CREATION OF A PERMANENT INTERNATIONAL CRIMINAL COURT (1951); Pella, *Towards an International Criminal Court*, 44 AM. J. INT'L L. 37 (1950); Pella, *Plan d'un Code Repressif Mondial*, 6 REV. INT'LE DE DROIT PÉNAL 148 (1935). *See* Symposium issue 45 REV. INT'LE DE DROIT PÉNAL, Nos. 3-4 (1974) (containing contributions for the Fifth U.N. Congress on Crime Prevention and the Treatment of Offenders, Geneva, 1-12 Sept. 1975; Symposium issue 20 REV. INT'LE DE DROIT PÉNAL, No. 1 (1949) (regarding the various U.N. drafts); Symposium issue (with articles by Donnedieu de Vabres and Francis Biddle) 19 REV. INT'L DE DROIT PÉNAL, No. 1 (1948); Symposium issue 17 REV. INT'LE DE DROIT PÉNAL, Nos. 3-4 (1936). *See Draft Statute for an International Commission of Criminal Inquiry and a Draft Statute for an International Criminal Court*, International Law Association, 60th Conference, Montreal, Aug. 29 - Sept. 4, 1982, in *Report of the 60th Conference of the International Law Association* (1983); *Draft Statute for an International Criminal Court*, Work Paper, Abidjan World Conference on World Peace Through Law, Aug. 26-31 (1973); *Draft Statute for an International Criminal Court*, Foundation for the Establishment of an International Criminal Court (Wingspread Conference, Sept. 1971).

to consider the "*Espacio Judiciario Andino.*"[72] These approaches substitute expanded regional criminal jurisdiction for the idea of regional or international adjudicating bodies. Thus, national criminal courts and national structures of administration of criminal justice would remain competent but they would be able to act even when the crime was not committed within their territory. In fact, these schemes are not really designed to expand the adjudication system, but they are a subterfuge for allowing law enforcement agencies, now limited by territorial jurisdiction, to operate outside it. These approaches, while strengthening law enforcement, do not accomplish the many goals of international or regional adjudication, and consequently, should not be regarded as valid alternatives. In addition, these schemes are fraught with dangers to procedural safeguards on the extra-territorial activities of law enforcement.

The establishment of an international criminal court, whether universal or regional, can be based on exclusive jurisdiction for certain crimes or on concurrent or alternative jurisdiction with that of the state having criminal jurisdiction. The jurisdictional mechanisms are, of course, to be established by the treaty-statute.

The establishment of an international criminal court could admittedly be based on various models including, but not limited to:

    i.   Expanding the jurisdiction of the International Court of Justice to include questions of interpretation and application of conventional and customary international criminal law, and providing for compulsory jurisdiction under Article 36 of the Statute of the International Court of Justice for disputes between states arising out of these questions;

    ii.   Establishing an international commission of inquiry, either as an independent organism, as part of the international criminal court or as an organ of the United Nations. Such a commission would investigate and report on violations of international criminal law, taking into account the proposal of the International Law Association and existing United Nations experiences with fact-finding and inquiry bodies which have

---

72. *See generally,* Graefrath, *Universal Criminal Jurisdiction and an International Criminal Court,* 1 EUROPEAN J. INT'L L. 67, 81-85 (1990); *see also* Mosconi, *L'Accordo di Dublino del 4/12/79, Le Comunita Europee e La Repressione del Terrorisimo,* in LA LEGISLAZIONE PENALE 543 (1986); Van Den Wyngaert, *L'Espace Judiciarie Européen Face à L'Euroterrorisme et la Sauvegarde des Droits Fondamentaux,* 3 REV. INT'LE DE CRIMINOLOGUIE ET DE POLICE TECHNIQUE 289 (1980).

developed over the years;

iii. Establishing an international (universal) criminal jurisdiction along the lines of the 1953 United Nations Draft Statute
for Establishment of an International Criminal Court[73] or the
1980 Draft Statute for the Establishment of an International
Criminal Jurisdiction to Implement the International Convention on the Suppression and Punishment of *Apartheid*
Convention;[74]

iv. Establishing Regional International Criminal Courts.

The Proposed Model

This model could be used for a (Universal) International
Criminal Court, as well as for a Regional International Criminal Court, the latter being only limited in geography to State-
Parties from the region. The highlights of this proposal are
as follows:

1. Establishment of the Tribunal

    a. The Tribunal would be established pursuant to a multilateral
        convention (hereinafter referred to as the ''Convention'') open
        to all States.

    b. The States-Parties to the Convention would agree on the es-
        tablishment of the Tribunal whose location will be determined
        by the Convention.

    c. The Tribunal would have an independent international legal
        personality and would sign a host-country agreement with the
        host-state. The Tribunal will thus have extra-territoriality for
        its location and immunity for its personnel.

    d. The Tribunal's costs and facilities, including detentional fa-
        cilities would be paid on a pro-rata basis by the State-Parties
        to the convention.

    e. The Tribunal as an international organization would be granted
        jurisdiction by the State-Parties to prosecute certain specified

---

73. *See supra* note 33.
74. *See supra* note 35.

offences embodied in the Annex to the Convention and would
have the authority to detain those accused, and those convicted
of the charges.

2. Jurisdiction of the Tribunal and Applicable Law

    a. The jurisdiction of the Tribunal would be over persons for
those offences defined in the Annex to the Convention, as
amended, from time to time. [This would permit expanding
the list of crimes depending upon need, and also to allow State-
Parties to acquire confidence in the Tribunal.]

    b. The Court could have exclusive jurisdiction for some crimes
and derivative jurisdiction over others by virtue of a transfer
of the proceeding[75] from a State-Party to the Convention,
provided the State-Party has jurisdiction on the basis of territoriality, active or passive personality. [This would avoid the
sovereignty problems that some claim would exist if the Tribunal would have exclusive or original jurisdiction. It would
also serve to circumvent problems of mandatory national prosecution if the laws of the state where the crime occurred so
require. Transfer of proceedings may also be done in a way
that would be similar in legal nature to a change of venue.
This approach coupled with the possibility of transfer of the
offender back to the state where the crime occurred would also
avoid many domestic legal difficulties.] Nothing, however, precludes the State-Parties from conferring exclusive jurisdiction
for certain crimes to the Tribunal. Thus, each State-Party that
has original jurisdiction based on territoriality, active or passive
personality would not lose jurisdiction, but merely transfer the
criminal proceedings to the Tribunal.

    c. To avoid problems of what substantive law to apply, the Tri-
bunal would use the substantive law of the transferring state
or of the state where the offence was committed and its own
procedural rules which would be part of the Convention and
promulgated prior to the Tribunal's entry into function.[76] [The

---

75. *See e.g.*, European Convention on the Transfer of Proceedings in Criminal
Matters, 15 May 1972, E.T.S. No. 73. *See also* M.C. BASSIOUNI & E. MÜLLER-RAPPARD,
EUROPEAN INTER-STATE CO-OPERATION IN CRIMINAL MATTERS (1987).

76. The procedural rules would be on the basis of general principles of international law and in accordance with internationally protected human rights, particularly
the International Covenant on Civil and Political Rights, G.A. Res. 2200A (XXI),

Tribunal's procedural rules would incorporate international human rights standards of due process and assure uniformity of procedural treatment of all persons. The application of the substantive law of the state where the offence was committed is fair, and would assuage any exacerbated feelings of sovereignty that such a state may have in allowing the Tribunal to prosecute those accused of committing crimes in their territory.]

3. Prosecution

a. The Tribunal's Procurator-General would act as the Chief Prosecutor, but could be assisted by a prosecuting official of the transferring state whose law is to be applied. [This too would reinforce the change of venue approach and prevent the claim that State-Parties totally relinquished jurisdiction.]

b. Prosecution would commence on the basis of a criminal complaint brought by a State-Party (thus supporting State-Parties' sovereignty). In addition, a State-Party that does not have subject matter or *in personam* jurisdiction, or that does not wish to bring a criminal complaint within its own jurisdiction, may petition the Procurator-General of the Tribunal to inquire into the potential direct prosecution by the Tribunal. [This relieves a State-Party from pressures in certain cases.] In such cases, the request by a State-Party would be confidential, and only after the Procurator-General of the Tribunal has deemed the evidence sufficient will the case for prosecution be presented to an Inquiry Chamber of the Tribunal *in camera* for its action. In such a situation, the Tribunal's Procuracy and the Inquiry Chamber would be acting as an international judicial board of inquiry.[77] Once the Inquiry Chamber has decided to allow

16 Dec. 1966 and the Inter-American Convention on Human Rights, O.A.S. Official Records Ser. K/XVI/1.1 Doc. 65, Rev. 1, Cor. 1 (Jan. 7, 1970), 22 Nov. 1969; and the European Convention for the Protection of Human Rights and Fundamental Freedoms, Nov. 4, 1950, 213 U.N.T.S. 262, No. 5.

77. *See* "Draft Statute for an International Commission of Criminal Inquiry and a Draft Statute for an International Criminal Court," International Law Association, 60th Conference, Montreal, Aug. 29-Sept. 4, 1982, in *Report of the 60th Conference of the International Law Association* (1983). For efforts to initiate such a commission *see* U.N. Security Council Resolution 672 (1990) and Bassiouni, *Iraq's Human-Rights Toll*, CHRISTIAN SCIENCE MONITOR, Nov. 26, 1990 at 19, which provides in part:

Recently, the Security Council resolved to establish an ad hoc commission to investigate Israel's killing of some 20 Palestinians at Jerusalem's Temple

prosecution, it would authorize the Procurator-General to issue an indictment and request the surrender of the accused from the State where the accused may be found. If that state is a State-Party, it would be bound to surrender the accused. Any other state may do so by the special treaty with the Tribunal or on the basis of comity.

c. The Convention would include provisions on surrendering the accused to the Tribunal and providing the Tribunal with legal assistance (including administrative and judicial assistance) for the procurement of evidence, both tangible and testimonial.[78]

d. By virtue of the Convention, an indictment by the Inquiry Chamber, will be recognized by all State-Parties in much the same way as other forms of recognition of foreign penal judgments. [National legislation could be amended whenever necessary to provide for such recognition.]

4. Conviction

a. Upon conviction, the individual may be returned to the surrendering state, which will carry out the sentence on the basis of provisions in the Convention, which would be in the nature of "transfer of prisoners" agreements.[79] Alternatively, the convicted person can be transferred to any other State-Party on

---

Mount. Appropriate as that is, no one who views human rights as universal can fail to note that the same measure was not resolved for Iraqi violations — or, for that matter, for other more serious ones. Lest one forgets, 1.5 million people have been killed by the Khmer Rouge in Cambodia, with muted condemnation by powers quick to condemn Israel and now Iraq. We must not have different scales to weigh human-rights violations, scales dependent upon who the violator or the victim may be.

The tragic incidents in the Middle East can be an opportunity to enhance human-rights protections by serving as an impetus to the establishment of an impartial, permanent fact-finding commission. The time has come to do something more than express selective verbal condemnations.

78. See e.g., The European Convention on Mutual Legal Assistance, Apr. 20, 1959, E.T.S. No. 30; see M.C. BASSIOUNI & E. MÜLLER-RAPPARD, supra note 75. See generally Ellis & Pisani, The United States Treaties on Mutual Assistance in Criminal Matters in 2 M.C. BASSIOUNI, INTERNATIONAL CRIMINAL LAW: PROCEDURE 151 (1986).

79. See e.g., The European Convention on Transfer of Sentenced Persons, Mar. 21, 1983, E.T.S. No. 112. See Epp, The European Convention on Transfer of Prisoners, in 2 M.C. BASSIOUNI, INTERNATIONAL CRIMINAL LAW: PROCEDURE 253 (1986), and Bassiouni, Transfer of Prisoners Between the United States, Mexico, and Canada. Id., at 239. See M.C. BASSIOUNI & E. MÜLLER-RAPPARD, supra note 75.

the same legal basis, or the Tribunal may place the convicted person in its own detentional facilities, which would be established by the Convention in accordance with a host-state agreement between the Tribunal and the state wherein the detentional facility would be established. [This provides a first option to the State-Party where the crime was committed, to execute the sentence, as well as a second option of allowing the transfer to another State-Party in order to avoid the pressures and problems that the detention of certain offenders can engender or to have the Tribunal execute the sentence. A number of States are already bound by treaties on transfer of prisoners and the practice is well under way among more than thirty countries.]

b.   A conviction by the Tribunal would be recognized by all State-Parties on the basis of a provision in the Convention establishing recognition for such judgments similar to existing agreements on the same subject.

Other states may recognize such a judgment by special arrangement with the Tribunal or on the basis of their domestic laws which could be made to include recognition of the Tribunal's penal judgments. [This would expand the network of cooperating states to include those states which may not become State-Parties but who would be willing to cooperate with the Tribunal in some respect.]

5.   Composition of the Court

a.   The Tribunal would consist of as many judges as there are State-Parties to the Convention, but not less than thirteen. There would be at least four Chambers of three judges each and a Presiding Judge. The judges would be drawn by lot and sit in rotation on the various chambers.

b.   One of the chambers would act as the Inquiry Chamber while the other chambers would be adjudicating chambers.

6.   Appeal

To provide for the right of appeal, the Tribunal sitting *en banc* with a panel of nine judges would hear appeals excluding those judges who decided the merits of the case.

7.   Selection of Judges

Each State-Party would appoint a judge from the ranks of its judiciary or from distinguished members of the bar or from academia. The judges would be persons of high competence, knowledgeable in international criminal law, and of high moral character. Appointment of judges and their tenure would be established by the Convention.

8. Rules of the Tribunal

The Tribunal would be authorized to enact rules of practice and procedures before it.

9. Standing Committee of State-Parties

The State-Parties would hold an annual conference to review the Tribunal's work and the Convention for purposes of amending it whenever needed and to ensue full compliance by the State-Parties.

10. The Organs of the Tribunal

These organs shall consist of:

The Court

1. The Court shall consist of twelve judges, no more than two of whom shall be of the same nationality, who shall be elected by the Standing Committee of States-Parties from nominations submitted thereto.

2. Nominees for positions as judges shall be of distinguished experts in the fields of international criminal law or human rights and other jurists qualified to serve on the highest courts of their respective states who may be of any nationality or have no nationality.

3. Judges shall be elected by secret ballot and the Standing Committee of States-Parties shall strive to elect persons representing diverse backgrounds and experience with due regard to representation of the major legal and cultural systems of the world.

4. Elections shall be coordinated by the Secretariat under the supervision of the presiding officer of the Standing Committee of States-Parties and shall be held whenever one or more vacancies exist on the Court.

5. Judges shall be elected for the following terms: four judges for four-year terms, four judges for six-year terms, and four judges for eight-year terms. Judges may be re-elected for any term at any time available.

6. No judge shall perform any public function in any state.

7. Judges shall have no other occupation or business than that of judge of this Court. However, judges may engage in scholarly activity for remuneration provided such activity in no way interferes with their impartiality and appearance of impartiality.

8. A judge shall perform no function in the Tribunal with respect to any matter in which he may have had any involvement prior to his election to this Court.

9. A judge may withdraw from any matter at his discretion, or be excused by a two-thirds majority of the judges of the Court for reasons of conflict of interest.

10. Any judge who is unable or unwilling to continue to perform functions under this statute may resign. A judge may be removed for incapacity to fulfill his functions by a unanimous vote of the other judges of the Court.

11. Except with respect to judges who have been removed, judges may continue in office beyond their term until their replacements are prepared to assume the office and shall continue in office to complete work on any pending matter in which they were involved even beyond their term.

12. The judges of the Court shall elect a president, vice-president and such other officers as they deem appropriate. The president shall serve for a term of two years.

13. Judges of the Court shall perform their judicial functions in three capacities:
    a. Sitting with other judges as the Court *en banc*;
    b. Sitting in panels of three on a rotational basis in chambers; and
    c. Sitting individually as supervisors of sanctions.

14. The salary of judges shall be equal to that of the judges of the International Court of Justice.

15. The Court *en banc* shall, subject to the provisions of this Statute, adopt rules governing procedures before its chambers and the Court *en banc*, and provide for establishment and rotation of chambers.

16. The Court *en banc* shall announce its decisions orally in

full or in summary, accompanied by written findings of fact and conclusions of law at the time of the oral decision or within thirty days thereafter, and any judge so desiring may issue a concurring or dissenting opinion.

17. Decisions and orders of the Court *en banc* are effective upon certification of the written opinion by the Secretariat, which is to communicate such certified opinion to parties forthwith.

18. The Court *en banc* may, within thirty days of the certification of the judgment, enter its decisions without notice.

19. No actions taken by the Tribunal may be contested in any other forum than before the Court *en banc*, and in the event that any effort to do so is made, the Procurator shall be competent to appear on behalf of the Tribunal and in the name of all States-Parties of this Statute to oppose such action.

20. States-Parties agree to enforce the final judgments of the Court in accordance with the provisions of this Statute.

The Procuracy

1. The Procuracy shall have the Procurator as its chief officer and shall consist of an administrative division, an investigative division and a prosecutorial division, each headed by a deputy Procurator, and employing appropriate staff.

2. The Procurator shall be elected by the Standing Committee of States-Parties from a list of at least three nominations submitted by members of the Standing Committee, and shall serve for a renewable term of six years, barring resignation or removal by two-thirds vote of the judges of the Court *en banc* for incompetence, conflict of interest, or manifest disregard of the provisions of this Statute or material rules of the Tribunal.

3. The Procurator's salary shall be the same as that of the judges.

4. The deputy procurators and all other members of the Procurator's staff shall be named and removed by the Procurator at will.

The Secretariat

1. The Secretariat shall have as its chief officer the Secretary,

who shall be elected by a majority of the Court sitting *en banc* and serve for a renewable term of six years barring resignation or removal by a majority of the Court sitting *en banc* for incompetence, conflict of interest or manifest disregard of the provisions of this Statute or material rules of the Tribunal.

2. The Secretary's salary shall be equivalent to that of the judges.

3. The Secretariat shall employ such staff as appropriate to perform its chancery and administrative functions and such other functions as may be assigned to it by the Court that are consistent with the provisions of this Statute and the rules of the Tribunal.

4. In particular, the Secretary shall twice each year:

    a. Prepare budget requests for each of the organs of the Tribunal; and

    b. Make and publish an annual report on the activities of each organ of the Tribunal.

5. The Secretariat staff shall be appointed and removed by the Secretary at will.

6. An annual summary of investigations undertaken by the Procuracy shall be presented to the Secretariat for publication, but certain investigations may be omitted where secrecy is necessary, provided that a confidential report of the investigation is made to the Court and to the Standing Committee and filed separately with the Secretariat. Either the Court or the Standing Committee may order by majority vote that the report be made public.

The Standing Committee

1. The Standing Committee shall consist of one representative appointed by each State-Party.

2. The Standing Committee shall elect by majority vote a presiding officer and alternate presiding officer and such other officers as it deems appropriate.

3. The presiding officer shall convene meetings at least twice each year of at least one week duration, each at the seat of the Tribunal, and call other meetings at the request of a majority vote of the committee.

4. The Standing Committee shall have the power to perform the functions expressly assigned to it under this Convention, plus any other functions that it determines appropriate in furtherance of the purposes of the Tribunal that are not inconsistent with the Convention, but in no way shall those functions impair the independence and integrity of the Court as a judicial body.

5. In particular, the Standing Committee may:

a. Offer to mediate disputes between States-Parties relating to the functions of the Tribunal; and

b. Encourage states to accede to the Convention.

6. The Standing Committee shall propose to States-Parties international instruments to enhance the functions of the Tribunal.

7. The Standing Committee may exclude from participation representatives of States-Parties that have failed to provide financial support for the Tribunal as required by this Statute or States-Parties that failed to carry out their obligations under this Statute.

8. Upon request by the Procuracy, or by a party to a case presented for adjudication to a chamber of the Court, the Standing Committee may be seized with a mediation and conciliation petition. In that case, the Standing Committee shall within 60 days decide on granting or denying the petition, from which decision there is no appeal. In the event that the Standing Committee grants the petition, Court proceedings shall be stayed until such time as the Standing Committee concludes its mediation and conciliation efforts, but not for more than one year except by stipulation of the parties and with the consent of the Court.[80]

Conclusion

We no longer live in a world where narrow conceptions of jurisdiction and sovereignty can stand in the way of an effective system of

---

80. M.C. Bassiouni, *supra* note 37, at 236-44, and *Draft Statute: International Criminal Tribunal*, *supra* note 38.

international cooperation for the prevention and control of international and transnational criminality. If the United States and the Soviet Union can accept mutual verification of nuclear arms controls, then surely they and other countries can accept a tribunal to prosecute not only drug traffickers and terrorists, but also those whose actions constitute such international crimes as aggression, war crimes, crimes against humanity and torture.

Many of the international crimes for which the Court would have jurisdiction are the logical extension of international protection of human rights.[81] Without enforcement, these rights are violated with impunity. We owe it to the victims of these crimes and to our own human and intellectual integrity to reassert the values we believe in by at least attempting to prosecute such offenders. When such a process is institutionalized, it can operate impartially and fairly. We cannot rely on the sporadic episodes of the victorious prosecuting the defeated and then dismantle these *ad hoc* structures as we did with the Nuremberg and Tokyo tribunals. The permanency of an international criminal tribunal acting impartially and fairly irrespective of whom the accused may be is the best policy for the advancement of the international rule of law and for the prevention and control of international and transnational criminality.

An international criminal court will surely be established one day. In the meantime, however, we will have to remain with the bitter realization that, if it had existed earlier, it could have deterred certain people and thus prevented some victimization. The conscience of world leaders should be bothered by this prospect, especially when they oppose the idea on the basis that it might infringe on jealously guarded notions of sovereignty.

Justice Robert Jackson as Chief Prosecutor at the Nuremberg International Military Tribunal stated in his opening speech: "This principle of personal liability is a necessary as well as a logical one if International Law is to render real help to the maintenance of peace . . . . Only sanctions which reach individuals can peacefully and effectively be enforced . . . . [T]he idea that a State . . . commits crimes, is a fiction. Crimes always are committed only by persons."[82] It is

---

81. *See* Bassiouni, *The Proscribing Function of International Criminal Law in the Processes of International Protection of Human Rights*, 9 YALE J. WORLD PUB. ORDER 193 (1982), *reprinted in* 1 M.C. BASSIOUNI, INTERNATIONAL CRIMINAL LAW: CRIMES, 15 (1986).

82. 1 THE TRIAL OF GERMAN MAJOR WAR CRIMINALS: PROCEEDINGS OF THE INTERNATIONAL MILITARY TRIBUNAL SITTING AT NUREMBERG GERMANY, 82-83 (1946).

unconscionable at this stage of the world's history, and after so much human harm has already occurred, that abstract notions of sovereignty can still shield violators of international criminal law or that the limited views and lack of vision and faith by government officials can prevent the establishment of such an important and needed international institution. The time has come for us to think and act in conformity with the values, ideals and goals we profess.

Appendix I

I. Establishment of an International Criminal Court

A. OFFICIAL TEXTS

1. Convention for the Pacific Settlement of International Disputes (First Hague, I), signed at The Hague, 19 July 1899, 26 MARTENS NOUVEAU RECUEIL DES TRAITES (2d) 720, 32 Stat. 1779, T.S. No. 342 (entered into force 4 Sept. 1900).

2. Convention Relative to the Establishment of an International Prize Court (Second Hague, XII), signed at The Hague, 18 Oct. 1907, 3 MARTENS NOUVEAU RECUEIL DES TRAITES (3d) 688 (never entered into force).

3. Treaty of Peace with Germany (Treaty of Versailles), signed at Versailles, 28 June 1919, 11 MARTENS NOUVEAU RECUEIL DES TRAITES (3d) 323 (entered into force 10 Jan. 1920).

4. Convention for the Creation of an International Criminal Court, opened for signature at Geneva, 16 Nov. 1937, League of Nations O.J. Spec. in Supp. No. 156 (1938), League of Nations Doc. C.547 (I).M.384(I).1937, (1938) (never entered into force).

5. Agreement for the Prosecution and Punishment of Major War Criminals of the European Axis (London Agreement), signed at London, 8 Aug. 1945, 82 U.N.T.S. 279, 59 Stat. 1544, E.A.S. No. 472 (entered into force, 8 Aug. 1945), ANNEX, Charter of the International Military Tribunal (Nuremberg).

6. International Military Tribunal For the Far East Proclaimed at Tokyo, 19 Jan. 1946 and amended 26 Apr. 1946, T.I.A.S. No. 1589 (entered into force 19 Jan. 1946), ANNEX Charter of the International Military Tribunal for the Far East (Tokyo).

7. Control Council Law No. 10 (Punishment of Persons Guilty of War Crimes, Crimes Against Peace and Against Humanity), adopted at Berlin, 20 Dec. 1945, Official Gazette of the Control Council for Germany, No. 3, Berlin, 31 Jan. 1946.

8. Draft Statute for an International Criminal Court (Annex to the Report of the Committee on International Criminal Jurisdiction, 31 Aug. 1951), 7 GAOR Supp. 11, U.N. Doc. A/2136 (1952) at 23.

9. Revised Draft Statute for an International Court (Annex to the Report of the Committee on International Criminal Jurisdiction, 20

Aug. 1953), 9 GAOR Supp. 12, U.N. Doc. A/2645 (1954), at 21.

10. Draft Statute for the Creation of an International Criminal Jurisdiction to Implement the International Convention on the Suppression and Punishment of the Crime of Apartheid, 19 Jan. 1980, U.N. Doc. E/CN.4/1416.

B. UNOFFICIAL TEXTS

1. Report on the Creation of an International Criminal Jurisdiction, by V.V. Pella to the Interparliamentary Union, XXII Conference, held in Berne and Geneva, 1924, in *L'Union Interparliamentaire. Compte Rendu de la XXII Conference tenue a Berne et a Geneva en 1924, publie par le Bureau Interparliamentaire*, 1925, *see also L'Union Interparliamentaire. Compte rendu de la XXIII Conference tenue a Washington et a Ottowa en 1925* (1925).

2. Projet D'Une Cour Criminelle Internationale, adopted by the International Law Association at its 34th Conference in Vienna, Aug., 1926, *The International Law Association, Report of the 34th Conference, Vienna, Aug. 5-11, 1926* (1927).

3. Project of the International Association of Penal Law, in *Actes du Premier Congres International de Droit Pénal, Bruxelles, 26-29 June 1926* (1927) and Projet de Statut pour la Creation d'une Chambre Criminelle au Sein de la Cour Permanente de Justice Internationale, presented by the International Association of Penal Law to the League of Nations in 1927, 5 REVUE INTERNATIONAL DE DROIT PÉNAL (1928).

4. Constitution et Procedure D'un Tribunal Approprie pur juger de la Responsabilite des Auteurs des Crime de Guerre, presente a la Conference des Preliminaires de Paix par la Commission des Responsabilites des Auteurs de la Guerre et Sanctions, III, *La Paix de Versailles* (1930).

5. Project for the Establishment of a Convention for the Creation of a United National Tribunal for War Crimes, established by the United Nations War Crimes Commission, 1944, *see* UNITED NATIONS WAR CRIMES COMMISSION (Wright ed. 1948).

6. *L'Union Interparliamentaire. Compte rendu de la XXVII Conference tenue a Rome en 1948* (1949).

7. Draft Statute for an International Criminal Court, in J. STONE AND R. WOETZEL, TOWARD A FEASIBLE INTERNATIONAL CRIMINAL COURT (1970).

8. Draft Statute for an International Criminal Court, *Foundation for the Establishment of an International Criminal Court* (Wingspread Conference, September 1971).

9. Draft Statute for an International Criminal Court, *Work Paper, Abidjan World Conference on World Peace Through Law, Aug. 26-31,* (1973).

10. Draft Statute for an International Commission of Criminal Inquiry and a Draft Statute for an International Criminal Court, International Law Association, 60th Conference, Montreal, Aug. 29-Sept. 4, 1982, in *Report of the 60th Conference of the International Law Association* (1983).

II. *Instruments on the Codification of Substantive International Criminal Law*

A. OFFICIAL TEXTS

1. 1954 Draft Code of Offences Against the Peace and Security of Mankind. 9 U.N. GAOR Supp. No. 9, U.N. DOC. A/2693.

2. *Draft* International Criminal Code, Presented by the AIDP to the 6th U.N. Congress on Crime Prevention and the Treatment of Offenders (Caracas, 1980). U.N. Doc. E/CN.4/NGO 213. Updated in M.C. BASSIOUNI, A DRAFT INTERNATIONAL CRIMINAL CODE AND DRAFT STATUTE FOR AN INTERNATIONAL CRIMINAL TRIBUNAL (1987).

Appendix II

CHRONOLOGY OF CONTEMPORARY U.S. POSITIONS ON THE ESTABLISHMENT OF AN INTERNATIONAL CRIMINAL COURT*

13 Feb. 1978: Resolution adopted by the House of Delegates of the American Bar Association. It urges the US State Department to open negotiations for a convention for the establishment of an International Criminal Court, with jurisdiction expressly limited to a) hijacking, b) violence aboard aircraft, c) crimes against diplomats and internationally protected persons, and d) murder and kidnapping.

13 Mar. 1986: Statement of Secretary of State George Schultz before the Foreign Operations Subcommittee of the Senate Committee on Appropriations. The agenda is "Foreign Assistance and Related Programs Appropriations for Fiscal Year 1987." Schultz responds to Senator Specter during his testimony that "we need to be working on the web of law that can operate here, and in conjunction with others around the world to say to terrorists that they have no place to hide and they are going to get prosecuted."

25 June 1986: Senator Specter presents Amendment 2187 on the Senate floor and comments on his proposal. The amendment states in part that "rampant terrorism by its very nature threatens world order and thereby all civilized nations and their citizens; any and every nation has the right, under current principles of international law, to assert jurisdiction over offenses considered to be 'universal crimes', such as piracy and slavery, in order to protect sovereign authority, universal values, and the interests of mankind." Specter, in the amendment, also suggests that the President establish an international criminal court that would have jurisdiction over the crime of international terrorism. He acknowledges that because of issues of sovereignty, various nations might be reluctant to act together on such an initiative. He argues nevertheless that "if these crimes were prosecuted in a world tribunal, there could be no question that such prosecutions . . . would have much greater force and much greater weight than those prosecutions in an individual state." The amendment was agreed to.

---

* This chronology was prepared by Charles Bataglia, Assistant to United States Senator Arlen Specter. It was slightly edited by the author.

27 Aug. 1986: Public Law 99-399, the Omnibus Security and Terrorism Act mandates the President to consider "the possibility of eventually establishing an international tribunal for prosecuting terrorists." This Act also includes an amendment (Chapter 113A) to Part I of title 18, United States Code which defines and stipulates penalties for terrorist acts abroad committed against US nationals.

16 June 1988: Testimony of Secretary of State George Schultz before the Foreign Operations Subcommittee of the Senate Committee on Appropriations. The agenda is "Foreign Assistance and Related Programs Appropriations for fiscal Year 1989." Senator Specter asks Secretary Schultz whether it would be "useful" to "push ahead with an international tribunal for the trial of these kinds of international criminals [terrorists]." Secretary Schultz replies that "it may be an important possibility," and notes that "over a period of years now more and more usefulness of the rule of law in getting at terrorism and drug trafficking."

1988: Senator Specter includes a provision in the Omnibus Anti-Drug Abuse Act calling on the President to pursue negotiations to establish an international criminal court with jurisdiction over international drug trafficking.

2 Mar. 1989: House Concurrent Resolution 66, submitted by Congressman Jim Leach of Iowa. The resolution calls for "the creation of an International Criminal Court with jurisdiction over internationally recognized crimes of terrorism, illicit narcotics trafficking, genocide, and torture, as those crimes are defined in various international conventions."

15 Mar. 1989: Floor Statement by Senator Specter on international terrorism. Specter recalls that in a 1986 amendment to the Omnibus Diplomatic Security and Antiterrorist Act and in Section 4108 of the 1988 Omnibus Anti-Drug Abuse Act, Congress called on the President to pursue negotiations to establish an international court with jurisdiction over terrorism and drug trafficking. He goes on to say that his discussions with various foreign leaders have persuaded him that "the civilized international community is prepared to speak with one voice to condemn terrorism." The creation of an international criminal court, he concludes, "would be an eloquent expression of that condemnation."

15 Mar. 1989: Testimony of Secretary of State Baker before the Subcommittee on Foreign Operations of the Committee on Appropriations. Senator Specter asks Secretary Baker what he thinks of the possibility of an international court. Secretary Baker calls the idea "interesting,"

but says it has "some fundamental problems." For instance, there are
the questions of who would conduct the investigations, who would bring
the prosecutions, and the exact composition of the court. Still, Baker
admits "we could probably reach some sort of a United States position
on that and then after some period of time, perhaps an international
agreement." He concludes that the idea of an international court is
worthy of further consideration.

Autumn 1989: The United Nations places the question of establishing
an international criminal court for illicit drug traffickers on the Fall
agenda of the UN General Assembly.

20 Nov. 1989: UN General Assembly Agenda Item 152 (44th session,
Sixth [Legal] Committee). This resolution, following three days of
intense debate, requests that the International Law Commission address
the possibility of establishing "an international criminal court or other
criminal trial mechanism," the jurisdiction of which would include
illicit trans-national drug trafficking.

18 June 1990: Floor Statement by Senator Specter. Specter describes
a symposium held at his request to discuss the creation of an international criminal court. At the 10 May 1990 symposium chaired by
Professor M.C. Bassiouni, 13 international criminal law scholars and
government officials joined by Congressmen Bob Kastenmeier and Jim
Leach, expressed a consensus that "a regional international criminal
court of limited scope and powers had the potential for making a
significant contribution in the area of narcotics trafficking and should
be further explored." Specter includes in the Congressional Record a
copy of the written consensus drafted at the symposium.

24-28 June 1990: The Draft Statute for an International Criminal
Tribunal prepared by Professor M.C. Bassiouni and discussed at the
May 10 symposium is presented to a special committee of experts
organized by the International Institute of Higher Studies in Criminal
Sciences. A model draft statute to establish an international criminal
tribunal is prepared and in August, 1990 the Committee submits it to
the Eighth United Nations Congress on Crime Prevention and the
Treatment of Offenders.

16 July 1990: Draft Report of the International Law Commission on
the work of its 42nd session in Geneva (1 May - 20 July 1990). In
Chapter II, Part C of this report, the Commission considers, and agrees
in principle with, the idea of establishing a permanent international
criminal court "to be brought into relationship with the United Nations
system." The commission notes that there are at least three possible

models: 1) an international criminal court with exclusive jurisdiction, 2) concurrent jurisdiction between an international criminal court and national courts, and 3) an international criminal court having only a review competence. Professor S. McCaffery of the U.S. and a member of the ILC supports the report.

7 Aug. 1990: President Cesar Oaviria Trujillo of Colombia, who had planned to attend the Siracusa meeting of June 1990 (but sent three representatives who briefed him on it), vowed in his inaugural address to "explore the possibility of creating an international or regional criminal jurisdiction to fight narco-trafficking and other related crimes that surpass international borders."

4 Sept. 1990: Testimony of Secretary of State Baker before the House Foreign Affairs Committee points out that "defendants of the nature of Saddam Hussein or for that matter Pol Pot" do not answer to any judicial authority, Congressman Leach asks Secretary Baker to look seriously at the idea of creating an international criminal court. Secretary Baker replies that he thinks "the suggestion is a good one" and wonders "why that's not something that had been looked at before, if indeed it hasn't been."

10 Sept. 1990: Testimony of Under Secretary of State Robert Kimmitt before House Foreign Affairs Committee. Kimmitt states that the Leach and Specter proposals would be "enormously complex" undertakings, noting, for instance, that if the State Department wanted to go forward on these proposals, it would have to come to the Senate for advice and consent first. Still, Kimmitt expresses "no disagreement at all" on the mechanism and the principle involved in the Leach proposal. He adds, in fact, that he would like to bring in lawyers in other agencies and departments who are working right now on the Gulf situation. Kimmitt concludes that "the time is probably riper than ever to look closely at that situation." (international criminal jurisdiction).

11 Sept. 1990: By a vote of 97 to 2, the US Senate endorsed the idea of trying Saddam Hussein before an international tribunal.

19 Sept. 1990: During Congressional Testimony, Congressman Gus Yatron asked John Bolton, Assistant Secretary of State for the Bureau of International Organization Affairs, for his comment on House Concurrent Resolution 66, the House measure promoting the proposed court. Bolton said that the Department of State was open to discussing the merits of the court.

19 Oct. 1990: By unanimous consent, the Senate passes an amendment to the FY 91 Foreign Operations Appropriations bill. The amendment calls for the President to report to the Congress by October 1, 1991, the results of his efforts in regard to the establishment of an International Criminal Court to deal with criminal acts defined in international conventions. It also requires the Judicial Conference of the United States to report to the Congress by October 1, 1991 on the feasibility of, and the relationship to, the Federal Judiciary of an international criminal court.

25 Oct. 1990: In conference on the FY 91 Foreign Operations Appropriations bill, House conferees recede to the Senate's position on the Specter amendment. The bill passes the Congress and is signed into law by the President on

5 Nov. 1990: President Bush signs into Law the FY 91 Foreign Operations Appropriations which includes the Specter amendment.

1990: The U.S. is among the sponsors of the UN General Assembly declaring the nineties as the Decade of International Law.

[16]

The Proliferation of Adjudicatory Bodies:
Dangers and Possible Answers
Sir Robert Y. Jennings
former President of the International Court of Justice

I take it that my task, this morning, on this question of proliferation of international tribunals, is to throw out problems rather than to offer solutions. I can say at once that I have no simple solutions for this problem. I will try to be a little provocative from time to time, and you must not mind too much if I say something that politically is not quite correct.

The Quiet Revolution in International Law

The first thing I wanted to say is to point out something which is very often not noticed so much today, that is the quiet revolution that has been going on in international law as a whole in the last couple of decades or so, and with accelerating vigor. I mean of course the way in which international law has recently, in the perspective of the history of international law, radically changed in character. What I am thinking of is especially evident in the field of treaty law.

Most governments make a lot of treaties every year, and an increasing number of them are not the old political kind of treaties one used to read about in history books; they are treaties that affect the life of every one of us daily in our ordinary occupations. These are interpreted and applied by municipal courts and there, I think, is a very big change, certainly in my time as an international lawyer. More and more, international law is a little doubtfully international law as it were; the boundary between municipal law and international law has been breaking down. To take an example, the great body of air law: one can still give a lecture on the international law of the air, but if you wanted to advise an air company, for example, on what is happening in the real world, just to be an international lawyer would not be very much use. You would have to know at least some municipal law and about its enforcement by municipal courts. You would have to be something of a comparativist. And you would certainly have to be something of a private international lawyer, as well as a public international lawyer.

So that is the first thing I wanted to do; to put the problem in the perspective of the very considerable change in the nature of international law and the breaking down of those old barriers. The idea I was taught as an undergraduate that public international law was something on a special plane of its own and quite different from municipal law and the work of municipal courts, is no longer even approximately true. So it is not surprising perhaps that, in this crucial and new context, there has been a proliferation of adjudicating tribunals of various kinds.

Reasons Requiring the Establishment of New Tribunals

There are a number of reasons for having more tribunals. There is of course the regional idea; that is people sometimes prefer a local tribunal. One recently established tribunal of that kind is the Badinter Commission, established under the auspices of the Peace Conference on Yugoslavia, where there was the feeling that security within Europe was a European problem. It was perhaps unfortunate that the first big problem that occurred before it turned out not to be

2

European at all, but universal. The efforts were about as successful as all the other efforts — whether on a regional or a universal scale — in dealing with that problem of the former Yugoslavia which is still with us.

But there is this idea, and I think it is reasonable, that local tribunals sometimes can understand the local requirements better than more general tribunals. One may think, for example, of the criticisms that used to be levelled against the ICJ about the *Asylum* case by South American states, which felt that the local tradition of asylum in an embassy was not really properly understood by what was then, a predominantly European court. On the other hand, it is also true that it is possible for a universal court to understand local variations. I think the chamber of the ICJ in the *Honduras/El Salvador* case coped pretty well with the problem of *uti possidetis juris*; indeed, it was difficult not to understand it after all the explanations we heard from counsel in the course of that case.

This regional prejudice, however, is very capricious. I am thinking of disputes in which I was somewhat involved, between Argentina and Chile. In the most recent arbitration concerning a part of the long frontier between them — with which arbitration I had nothing to do, because I was a judge on the ICJ by then — I gathered that the parties agreed that it was better to have a Latin American tribunal, because that seemed reasonable in the circumstances, since it was a Latin American matter. But in the earlier one, the *Beagle Channel* case, when it came to the choosing of the court which was a sort of a compromise between arbitration and the International Court, I remember very well at a meeting in London, the counsel from both sides have agreed upon one basic principle: that was "no Latin Americans," because the feeling then was that, any Latin American would be *parti pris* in this very well-known and debated for eighty or ninety years dispute between Chile and Argentina. So, the regional idea for new tribunals is a capricious one. You can never be quite sure how it will work, except that one way or another, it will produce more and more tribunals. I am sure of that.

Perhaps this is the place to mention one disturbing development, at least very disturbing to my mind. That is the idea, that comes, I suppose, from Muslim fundamentalism and that has been embodied recently in a *fatwa* issued in Saudi Arabia, that Muslim countries are not to go to any tribunal other than one which applies Mahometan law. Now this, of course, is a challenge to the universality principle of our system of international law. Obviously, one cannot go into this, but I just wanted to mention it. I find it a very disturbing challenge and one which demands a lot of serious thought.

Then there are courts and tribunals established for special subjects, such as the courts of human rights. The European Court of Human Rights, for example, was established on a European basis because of the European Convention and because it was possible to provide machinery with teeth to enforce human rights in this regional group, which was not possible on a larger basis. That is obviously a very good reason for having a special, regional tribunal.

There are many other new tribunals of course, but I cannot go through a whole list of the examples because there as so many. I do not know if anybody has a complete list. That should be almost the first thing we ought to do, to get a comprehensive list of these international tribunals. One of a different kind is the World Trade Organization tribunals recently invented, but I confess I do not know a great deal about them. But there seems to be a rather different

3

idea, that is members of the tribunals should be experts in this particular subject and it includes, which seems more unusual if I got it right, the possibility of making policy decisions and not merely the application of a system of law. If I am right, we have here what could be a very important new development.

There are also the international criminal courts, the proposed general one, the one for former Yugoslavia and the one for Rwanda; the last two, peculiar tribunals because they were established by the Security Council under the machinery for the keeping of the peace. Thus, they are purely *ad hoc* and should come to an end when their purpose is accomplished. But how far the tribunals will assist in establishing peace in those regions remains to be seen. There is one problem that I would like to mention, at least to me it seems to be a problem, and this would apply also, I think, to the proposal in the International Law Commission for a permanent tribunal. I understand that a policy decision was made to go ahead with the tribunal before the work on the code of law it is to apply was accomplished. There was supposed to be a code of international humanitarian criminal law and this is not forthcoming and so we will have a tribunal without it. That, I think, is going to raise very considerable problems in certain cases, especially in the offenses like murder which are common to the municipal law systems. I suppose in international criminal law, they are thinking of murder with the added factor of a sort of illegitimate policy behind it.

Another point on these new tribunals I would like to mention is that I think we have to be careful — if I may put it that way, I said I might be a bit provocative — of the arrogance of public international lawyers. What I mean is: Is it right that most of these tribunals, except the trade ones, seem to be jobs for public international lawyers? There is little sign, even in the Law of the Sea tribunals for example, of the use of other disciplines and other kinds of experts. If I could just illustrate it in a sort of personal way, the first time I appeared as a counsel in an international arbitration was in the *Encuentro* or *Palena* case between Argentina and Chile. The tribunal had a retired professor of international law and indeed former President of the ICJ, Lord McNair as its president, but the other two members: one of them was the Secretary of the Royal Geographical Society, not a lawyer at all, and the other one was a soldier and an engineer. That, I am bound to say, was one of the best tribunals I ever had anything to do with. I discovered the hard way that it is very important not to underestimate the military. The soldier arbitrator had rather played the ignorant soldier in all the preparations up to the actual hearings, but when addressing the tribunal one realized that he was producing all the documents just at the right moment to the president from the pile in front of him, and the frightening thing was that he not only produced the one you mentioned but also had ready all the others you were going to mention. As for the Secretary of the Royal Geographical Society, he was able to exclude one legal argument. The Argentineans were very concerned that the Chileans were bringing a lot of evidence of the allegiance and nationality of people who lived in this rather remote area of the Andes. We — I was for Argentina — were concerned about it because Chileans of course had always gone to Argentina for work, and there was indeed a place on the Atlantic coast with a larger population of Chileans than Argentineans, so we were naturally bothered by this evidence and objected. McNair was impressed as a lawyer with the objections, not so the geographer. He said he did not understand the legal objection, but as a geographer he wanted to know about "land-use." It was a good point, and all that evidence was thus admitted before the tribunal. That is one of the illustrations of the use of other disciplines. One can think that in the law of the sea surely, one ought to use more experts, such as maritime surveyors and hydrographers, not merely as advisers but as members of the court; but that is not very popular with international lawyers, I fear.

The Dangers of Proliferation

There are thus various good reasons for producing more tribunals of different kinds, but the problem really is the possible dangers that could arise from this proliferation. I think the main point can be put this way: looking at it as a whole, you see that this proliferation has been flourishing, but without system. It is simply that tribunals have been thought of and produced from time to time for local or other reasons, but the result as a whole is a mess. And to put it in better words, there is a recent article written by my colleague Judge Shahabuddeen, whom I quote:

> The adjudicating machinery on the international plane consists of a number of tribunals, some instituted on a bilateral basis, others on a multilateral basis, but with nothing to hold them together in a coherent system. They all make decisions which can influence the development of international law. If that influence can amount to law-making in the case of all of them, the absence of hierarchical authority to impose order is a prescription for conflicting precepts.

Now, that is probably the main danger of proliferation, the fragmentation of international law; and by fragmentation I do not mean the very proper local variations for particular purposes. It so happens that the Strasbourg Court of Human Rights has produced for me the ideal case to illustrate this danger. In the last few weeks, in the case of *Loizidou v. Turkey*, a complaint against Turkey was brought by Cyprus before the European Court about the alleged difficulty of a Cypriot national of the Greek community who wanted to visit the family property in the Turkish part of Cyprus. The question first before the Court was a question of competence or jurisdiction. The Convention has a clause providing for declaration by governments accepting the jurisdiction of the Strasbourg Court and that clause is, word for word, based on Article 36(2) of the Statute of the ICJ, the optional clause. So the same machinery was provided and governments that wish to accept the jurisdiction of the Court did so by making a declaration. Most of them, and apparently practically all of them, if they wished to accept the jurisdiction, did so unconditionally by simply filing a declaration. Turkey acted differently. It agreed to the application of the Convention and the competence of the Court in respect of "matters coming within Article 1 of the Convention and performed within the boundary of the national territory of the Republic of Turkey," a reservation obviously intended to exclude the northern part of Cyprus from the jurisdiction of the tribunal.

The decision of the Court on this matter — the merits have not yet come before the Court — was that it did have jurisdiction and the reasoning was as follows. First, other governments in accepting the Court's jurisdiction had accepted it without reservation. Therefore, in the light of this consistent practice, the making of reservations was not permissible. The Court went on to say that the decisions of the ICJ to this matter, which of course had been pleaded before them, were irrelevant because of the special character of the Strasbourg Court. The surprising thing to me is that it is not unlike the famous separate opinion of Judge Lauterpacht, where he felt that the "automatic" reservation of France to its optional declaration was invalid and void because contrary to the Statute. He agreed, however, with the majority of the Court that the reservation was unseverable and that therefore the French attempt to create jurisdiction was itself invalid. To the contrary, the Strasbourg Court decided that the Turkish "invalid" reservation was severable and therefore Turkey must be taken to have accepted the competence of the Court without any reservation at all. The passage of the Court's decision that I want to mention is:

> The fundamental difference in the role and purpose of the respective tribunals [that is Strasbourg and the Hague], coupled with the existence of a practice of unconditional acceptance, provided a compelling basis for distinguishing Convention practice from that of the International Court.

Now, of course, one can say this is merely a question of jurisdiction, and not of substance, but there are red lights there. It indicates the tendency of particular tribunals to regard themselves as different, as separate little empires which must as far as possible be augmented. Of course, one can appreciate that the Strasbourg Court, applying and interpreting the European Convention, is in a different position from the ICJ applying a universal system of international law. It might be acceptable to rely on the regional differences for a question of jurisdiction; but obviously, there is a possibility that the technique might also be extended to matters of substance. This could lead to a law of human rights increasingly different from the universal system, which is part of general international law, and under the custody of the ICJ. I merely point out the danger. I have no solution, all I can say is that I am sure this tendency will increase rather than decrease. We ought to be thinking about it.

Possible Answers

Coming back to this question of the control raised by Judge Shahabuddeen, what can we do about this glut of tribunals with no hierarchical pattern? We do not even have a list of these different tribunals anywhere easily available, much less an analysis. Well, one thinks immediately of the ICJ, the principal judicial organ of the United Nations, as possibly providing the head of some sort of hierarchy, a court of last resort, of appeal, review or cassation. But there are difficulties about that and the principal one is Article 34(1) of the Statute of the Court, which says that only states may be parties before the Court. It means that for the contentious jurisdiction at any rate, it is not easy to think of any machinery for tribunals dealing with other entities than states having recourse to the Court. It may happen incidentally sometimes in a contentious case. It did happen in the Guinea-Bissau case. The Court did pass upon an arbitral award which was, according to the agreement establishing the arbitration, to have been final. The Court confirmed the validity of the award, but it did hear the case. So there is a sort of precedent there. The other difficulty with the International Court's attempt to control these other tribunals would be that, according to Article 34(1), it does not have contentious jurisdiction over any of the international organizations which exist in the international sphere. This is a most extraordinary position. It is extraordinary that you have this UN system of law, a universal system of international law, you have a principal judicial organ of the United Nations and no state or government can cite an international organization before the ICJ; for example, in regard of allegedly *ultra vires* activities. Maybe the International Court itself is not the proper instrument, but there ought to be some way of getting international organizations, as well as other entities, before the tribunals.

6

I had the privilege in the UN Congress in New York, a few weeks ago, to hear the very remarkable speech by Ambassador Owada about the tension in international relations between the requirements of stability and the requirements of justice. I think it was one of the most important things that has been said about international law by anybody for quite a long time. I cite only one paragraph just to show the problem:

> The single most important fact behind this change is that the world today suffers from the dichotomy that has come to exist between the fast-growing socio-economic reality that entrepreneurs as individuals engage in activities on a global basis and the equally stark reality that the competence to regulate these activities are still compartmentalized by nations states, within the system based on the Westphalian legal order.

Article 34(1) of the Statute of the International Court is the embodiment of the Westphalian legal order. I suppose something can be done. Another colleague on the Court, Judge Guillaume has suggested that there might be a possibility of reference by other tribunals to the Court, corresponding to Article 177 of the Rome Treaty. They might be encouraged to ask the Court for advice on questions of international law. The advisory jurisdiction of the ICJ is much more flexible, and it could accommodate a procedure of reference. Whether tribunals would in fact refer is perhaps doubtful; but at any rate, even if there were the possibility, it might serve as a beginning for some sort of order and system.

We have a proliferation of adjudicating bodies of various kinds, but we still do not have that political machinery, that Ambassador Owada was calling for, to control activities on the international plane. In the domestic sphere, we have tribunals or courts which have compulsory jurisdiction. That works for the simple reason that you also have political bodies within their own sphere controlled by constitutional and administrative law; political bodies that make decisions for political or administrative reasons and not for legal reasons; for reasons of statesmanship, for reasons of policy, for reasons of expediency and convenience, for reasons of general wisdom and need to change things. We do not have that in the international sphere, except to an inadequate extent. There is the Security Council, but even the Security Council has only been able to begin activities of that kind recently, has relatively little experience and, in any case, it is practically all we have got. I do think that the call of international lawyers for more and more tribunals, for more and more activity by international lawyers needs to be balanced by a call for more and more thinking about the need for political decisions, wise political decisions on the international plane. There are summits and so on, but we need something better and it seems to me that we ought to be thinking not only of the sort of tribunals that we might need, but we ought as well to be thinking about the other kind of decisions that are needed in a healthy international society.

7

Part VII
Agencies

[17]

THE PLACE OF INTERNATIONAL LAW IN THE SETTLEMENT OF DISPUTES BY THE SECURITY COUNCIL

By Rosalyn Higgins *

The place of law in the settlement of disputes by the Security Council is a topic which has already occasioned debate. Many lawyers contend that law plays a minimal rôle in the work of the Council. That organ is, they point out, essentially a political body. It operates in a different way from a judicial body such as the International Court of Justice, and frequently ignores the law of nations. Oscar Schachter, writing in this JOURNAL in 1964, has offered another view, pointing to subtle ways in which the influence of law can still make itself felt in the work of the Security Council, by providing a common language, by applying principles to specific cases, and by determining new points of community interest.[1] The purpose of this article is to examine, in the light of recent years, some of the limitations within which this legal endeavor takes place, and to see whether law has any real function in the settlement of disputes.

The Security Council may be a political body, but its rôle is defined by the United Nations Charter, which is a legal instrument, a treaty between nations. Further, Article 1 of the Charter declares a major purpose of the United Nations to be the resolution of disputes "in conformity with the principles of justice and international law." What does it mean for a political body to act within a legal framework, and to have to provide solutions to disputes that are in conformity with the law?

I

Use of the law by the Security Council is necessarily ambivalent, because the Security Council itself is really a dual concept; it is each of the individual members, stating its case, and also the sum total of the members acting in the name of the organ. Thus, when we speak of law in the Security Council, we are really speaking of two things: law as it is invoked by the claimants to a dispute, and law as it is employed by the organ itself, when passing its decision. The members of the Security Council are, at one and the same time, both participants and decision-makers. And it is hardly surprising that each uses the law rather differently.

One or more members of the Security Council may themselves be involved in the dispute upon which the Council is called to adjudicate. The Charter itself sought to differentiate these two rôles by providing in Article

* The Royal Institute of International Affairs, London. This article is based on a Paper given before the Cambridge University International Law Club on Feb. 14, 1969.

[1] Oscar Schachter, "The Quasi-Judicial Rôle of the Security Council and the General Assembly," 58 A.J.I.L. 960–965 (1964).

1

2   THE AMERICAN JOURNAL OF INTERNATIONAL LAW   [Vol. 64

27(3) that a member must abstain from voting where the Council is taking a decision for the pacific settlement of a dispute to which it is a party. However, this provision has been unable to stop the blurring, over the years, of the position of protagonists and impartial organ for two main reasons. First, it has become increasingly difficult to identify "the parties" to a dispute. In an increasingly interdependent world, states find it hard to stand aside from the disputes of others. Even if they are not involved directly as the major protagonists in the controversy, they may well be involved indirectly, in the sense that they have interests at stake. Second, a member is enjoined to abstain from voting on a resolution for the pacific settlement of a dispute to which it is a party. But frequently a member of the Security Council is able to deny that it is party to a dispute, or to assert that the matter is a "situation" but not a "dispute," or that the decision in question falls under Chapter VII; that is to say, action with respect to threats to the peace, breaches of the peace and acts of aggression. Accordingly, the disqualification from voting, which would serve to limit the dual rôle of members as participants and decision-makers, is rarely used.

It has become more and more rare for a member to make the formal claim of the existence of a dispute, and rarer still for abstentions from voting, for the reason enumerated in Article 27(3), to take place. Indeed, there have only been eight cases where the issue was debated, and demands made for abstentions in voting, and none since 1951.[2] On occasion, however, a member has taken it upon itself to abstain without the matter being formally raised.[3]

The United Kingdom participation in voting on the Rhodesian question can be explained on the grounds that it does not regard itself as a party to a dispute, and the measures taken fall under Chapter VII rather than Chapter VI. But one may also recall that in 1968 Ethiopia did not feel it necessary to abstain on a vote on South West Africa in the Security Council[4]— though her case with Liberia before the Court rested on the existence of a dispute with South Africa—and, even more blatantly, the Soviet Union cast a veto at the end of a debate on her invasion of Czechoslovakia, even though no measures under Chapter VII were envisaged. Nor was her right to do so challenged. No doubt a factor here was Russia's assertion that there was no "dispute," and Czechoslovakia's unwillingness to characterize it as such.

---

[2] Thus no practice is listed in this regard in Supp. No. 2, Vol. II of the Repertory of Practice of United Nations Organs, covering the period 1956–1959. The Repertory also notes certain developments in procedure which have facilitated the ability to avoid a vote as to whether a matter is a dispute or a situation. These include the expressing of unanimous approval without vote; the withdrawing of draft resolutions in favor of agreed statements by the President, summarizing proceedings; and non-participation in a vote while at the same time indicating that this was not an abstention in application of the provision. II Repertory of Practice of United Nations Organs 84.

[3] E.g., Argentina did not participate in the voting on the Eichmann question. Security Council, 15th Year, Official Records, 868th Meeting. Non-participation and abstention are treated as identical for purposes of Art. 27(3).

[4] Security Council Res. 245 (1968).

In everything that we can usefully say, therefore, the difficulties which flow from the duality of the Security Council must be borne in mind. The significance of this duality is nonetheless not to be exaggerated. The central problem remains that members of the Security Council are not prepared to assume the political consequences of sitting in judgment on fellow members that are parties to a dispute. So far as the parties to a dispute themselves are concerned, it is a commonplace that they use international law as a means of furthering their political case. If law is not a fig leaf to cover disagreeable political realities, it is a tactical device, a weapon in the armory of rhetoric. But one must also be sure to see the other side of the coin. The other side of the coin is that reference to legal principle, whether that of the Charter or of general international law, ensures that partisan states will at least have to justify their views on grounds that are acceptable to others. International law is the common language. Further, reference to law may here provide a bridge between states with diverse cultures and ideologies.[5]

There can still arise, however, cases—fortunately exceptional—where, though law provides a common language, the reality behind that language is of total divergency. One can thus on occasion have the sort of *Alice Through the Looking Glass* situation that one had in the Security Council debate of the Russian invasion of Czechoslovakia. The Soviet Union sought to justify her action as a response to an invitation under the Warsaw Pact, and as collective self-defense under Article 51 of the Charter: both understandable arguments, even if not plausible in the light of facts as we know them. But the use of the law as a common language completely breaks down when the Soviet Union roundly condemns the Security Council's interest in Czechoslovakia in language which is completely inapplicable to the position of the Council, and applicable solely to the conduct of the Soviet Union. The Soviet representative, in denying the right of the Security Council to examine the situation, turned legal language on its head, and admonished "all states strictly to observe the principles of respect for sovereignty and independence, and of the inadmissibility of aggression, direct or otherwise."[6] When the reiteration of legal principles is so inappropriate to the facts, they cease to serve as a language which men can hold in common.

These are some of the problems raised by the use of law made by the parties to a dispute. Turning now to look at the use of law by the Security Council *qua* organ, the Charter does, of course, envisage that the Security Council may contribute to the settlement of a dispute by calling upon the parties to go before the International Court. Article 33 provides that the Security Council shall, when it deems necessary, call upon the parties to settle their disputes by means which include arbitration and judicial settlement; and Article 36(3) stipulates that "legal disputes should as a general rule be referred by the parties to the International Court of Justice." But, as the years have gone by, the Security Council has been less and less in-

---

[5] Schachter, *loc. cit.* above, p. 962.
[6] Security Council, 23rd Year, Official Records, 1441st Meeting.

4   THE AMERICAN JOURNAL OF INTERNATIONAL LAW   [Vol. 64

clined to throw its weight behind this method of settling disputes. It was not always so: the original resolution adopted by the Council on August 1, 1947, in the Indonesian case, for example, called upon the parties to settle their disputes "by arbitration or by other peaceful means."[7] At the early stages of the Kashmir dispute the Security Council recommended arbitration. In neither case was the recommendation acted upon. Only in the *Corfu Channel* case has the Security Council made a formal recommendation that the matter should be settled by the International Court. And it is true that in recent years even individual members of the Security Council, let alone the Security Council *qua* organ, have been increasingly reluctant to suggest reference to the Court. The Communist nations have always refused to use the Court;[8] the newer nations have been convinced, since the *South West Africa* Judgment of 1966, that the Court cannot help in the solution of their problems; and the Western nations find it impolitic to urge reference to the Court.

The Security Council, therefore, finds itself unable to recommend the reference of legal aspects of disputes to the Court; and thus it faces these legal issues itself. In making its decisions, it is comparatively rare for the Security Council to be asked to pass on the correctness of legal propositions as such. More usually, it is presented by the parties to the dispute with justifications of action they have taken based on two impeccably correct legal propositions. It is for the Security Council to decide which of the legal propositions happened to accord with the facts of the case. (This, of course, is not unique to the Council. Courts find themselves in the same position.) Thus State A will claim that State B has used force illegally and aggressively; and State B will reply that it has acted in self-defense. The Council is not called upon to choose between these two legal propositions— they are two sides of the same coin;[9] rather it is asked to decide which applies to the facts before it.

Very occasionally, however, the Council is called upon to pronounce upon the validity of a legal proposition as such, rather than its applicability to the particular case. Thus in 1951 the Security Council was faced with two countervailing claims as between Egypt and Israel. Egypt had closed the Suez Canal to Israeli ships, and to ships going to or from Israel. To the charge that the Constantinople Convention of 1888 provides that the Canal shall be open to all nations save those with whom the riparian state might find itself at war, Egypt replied that she *was* at war with Israel and was

---

[7] *Ibid.*, 2nd Year, 173rd Meeting, p. 1703. The Linggadjati Agreement had itself provided that any dispute as to its terms should be settled by arbitration. On this, and other early recommendations for arbitration, see Goodrich and Simons, The United Nations and the Maintenance of International Peace and Security 325–329.

[8] Except in the case of the Cuban complaint about the Punta del Este decisions, where Cuba, backed by the Soviet Union, asked the Security Council to request an Advisory Opinion from the Court. Security Council, 17th Year, Official Records, 992nd–998th Meetings.

[9] For a fully elaborated argument that all legal norms are in fact "matching opposites," see McDougal, "Some Basic Theoretical Concepts about International Law: A Policy Oriented Framework of Enquiry," 4 Journal of Conflict Resolution 337–354 (1960).

entitled to exercise rights of visit and search in the Canal. Yet there had been no armed hostilities between the countries since 1949. The question now arose as to whether one country which has signed an armistice with another can claim nonetheless to exercise rights of belligerency. The Security Council had to examine the traditional rules concerning armistices, which certainly indicated that rights of belligerency can continue until a final peace; had to evaluate this in the light of the postwar tendency for long-term and indefinite armistices to replace the traditional treaty of peace; and had to scrutinize the particular armistice regime referred to, in this case the 1949 Armistice agreed under the auspices of the Security Council itself. The Security Council found, in a direct confrontation of the legal issues, that no claim of belligerency was permitted under an armistice which envisaged only progress to peace and expressly prohibited a return to hostilities and which, moreover, was arrived at as the result of a decision by the Security Council itself under Article 40 of the Charter.

How authoritative is this decision of the Security Council? On the one hand, the Security Council has no authority to make binding interpretations of the legal positions of states without their consent. On the other hand, the resolution which incorporated the interpretation was of itself a binding resolution to which Article 25 applied. This point is emphasized by Professor Halderman.[10] He refers to a New Zealand demand that Egypt carry out the Security Council resolution of September 1, 1951, on passage through the Canal, and notes that the Egyptian Delegation asked "What are these obligations? What article of the Charter has Egypt contravened?" Professor Halderman continues:

> The correct answer must be "none" . . . Any suggestion that the United Nations might develop a role under which majorities could apply such decisions to other states while the states composing the majority, at the same time, denied the right of the United Nations to apply such measure against themselves, would seem to run counter to basic legal propositions such as that any rule of law must be reciprocal in character, capable of being applied equally and dispassionately to all concerned, and that law must have a general basis of acceptance on the part of those members of the community in which it is supposed to apply.

These remarks seem to come near decrying, *per se*, majority decisions. It is constitutional limitations which prevent majority decisions from degenerating into "tyranny of the majority." Moreover, such decisions of the Security Council are not, in fact, taken and applied by "majorities" so far as the United Nations membership as a whole is concerned, but rather by a small, delegated group of 15 authorized to act on behalf of the general membership. Nor do the Security Council members, when so acting, deny the right of the United Nations to apply such measures against themselves: the norm which they enunciated on the compatibility of belligerent rights with a particular armistice regime established under Article 40 would be relevant to any comparable circumstances in which they might find them-

[10] In his valuable book, The United Nations and the Rule of Law 67–68 (1966).

selves. Again, to state that a rule of law must be reciprocal does not mean that an existing norm is to be denied because in a particular case one party to a dispute chooses not to heed it. And the proposition that law must have a general basis of acceptance on the part of those members of the community in which it is supposed to apply is relevant mainly to the notion of regional customary law. It cannot be taken to mean that no legal obligations exist unless all the parties in a geographical region are in agreement. In any event, all of these points go considerably beyond what seemed to be the original issue under discussion; namely, the authority of the Security Council to pronounce upon the validity of legal norms while passing binding decisions under Article 25 of the Charter. A way out of the dilemma may perhaps be found by recognizing that the Security Council may make authoritative and binding interpretations of Members' legal obligations under the Charter, even if not of such legal obligations as are not covered by the Charter. Is the right of passage through the Suez Canal an obligation covered by the Charter? As such it is not. But the Security Council is the organ responsible for the maintenance of international peace and security and was responsible for the carrying out of the Armistice established under Article 40. And Article 2(4) may also be a relevant injunction. Even more difficult is the case where a dispute does not greatly threaten international peace, where the Security Council has not been previously involved and where the legal issues are not easily brought within the scope of the Charter. The Security Council membership was generally agreed, in the debates on the Eichmann question, that the kidnaping of Eichmann by Israeli agents was an offense against Argentina's sovereignty which merited reparation by Israel.[11] So it was possible to avoid asking, in clear terms, whether the Security Council's decision to this effect was in fact legally authoritative.

There now also arise situations which fall somewhat between the two categories of (a) deciding which of two correctly stated legal principles apply to the particular circumstances, (b) whether a legal proposition is or is not correct. This is the case when, in its attempts to resolve a dispute, the Security Council makes recommendations which indirectly pass on legal questions. The application of legal rules to particular circumstances forms part of United Nations practice and, over a period of time, becomes part of the stream of authoritative decisions which are looked to as a source of law. Moreover, as Schachter has observed:

> Considerations of equity and equal treatment will tend to favor its application in "equivalent" situations; moreover, the reasons which impelled its adoption in the one case are likely to have some influence in other cases.[12]

This being so, and given the nervousness of governments about creating

---

[11] But it was not agreed as to what constituted "appropriate reparation." The United States thought an apology was sufficient, while Argentina wanted the return of Eichmann and the punishment of the Israelis concerned. Security Council, 15th Sess., Official Records, 865th–868th Meetings, and Security Council Res. 138 (1960).

[12] Schachter, *loc. cit.* 964.

precedents, it behooves Security Council members to pay the greatest attention to the legal implications of this class of resolutions. It is clear, however, that the pressure of events sometimes prevents this from being done. The result can be the assertion of legal principle based upon insufficient scrutiny or confused understanding. To take first an example of inadequate scrutiny:

After the June war of 1967 the General Assembly adopted a resolution [13] which called upon Israel not to alter the status of Jerusalem. The assumption has grown out of that resolution—the terms of which have been subsequently confirmed [14] by the Security Council—that Jordan has a legal title in Old Jerusalem which is preferable to that of Israel's. Jordan holds Old Jerusalem by virtue of her military action against Israel in 1948. It is perhaps arguable that she has now obtained a title through occupation, notwithstanding the clauses in the Jordan-Israel Armistice which stress that the Armistice itself confers no legal title to territory demarcated by it. But there was no discussion at all within the Security Council of this point; or of the question whether, if Jordan was in occupation of Old Jerusalem but without title to it, it could be legally dispossessed by a country claiming to have responded in self-defense to an attack by Jordan. These are very difficult and very complex questions. It is not my purpose here to provide answers to them,[15] but rather to point out that resolutions which by implication take a stand on those questions have been passed without proper consideration of the legal issues involved.[16]

To turn now to resolutions affecting legal rights and duties which may be based on misunderstanding: again, the June war affords an example. And even those nations which most pride themselves on respect for, and knowledge of, international law, can be party to this. At the heart of the Arab-Israel problem there is an intractable political and strategic problem: Which should come first in time, Israeli withdrawal from the Arab territories which she holds, or Egyptian recognition of Israel and formal acknowledgment of peace? But what is particularly disturbing to the lawyer is the way in which the notion of territorial acquisition has become deliberately blurred with that of military occupation. Nearly all of the arguments advanced have spoken of the prohibition in Article 2(4) as requiring Israeli withdrawal from the occupied territories. Article 2(4) makes it clear, by implication at least, that an aggressor should not be allowed to retain the

---

[13] General Assembly Res. 2253 (ES-V).

[14] Security Council Res. 252 (1968).

[15] Though see Eli Lauterpacht, Jerusalem and the Holy Places, Monograph for Anglo-Israel Association, 1968; Julius Stone, No Peace-No War in the Middle East, published by Australian Branch, I.L.A.; and S. Shepard Jones, "The Status of Jerusalem: Some National and International Aspects," Law and Contemporary Problems, Winter, 1968.

[16] Equally, the General Assembly purported to terminate the mandate for South West Africa without adequate discussion of the legal issues: for doubts as to the validity of the Assembly action, see Higgins, "The International Court and South West Africa: The Implications of the Judgment," International Affairs, Oct. 1966, pp. 573–599, at 598–599. For a detailed discussion of the legal aspects of revocation, see Dugard, "The Revocation of the Mandate for South West Africa," 62 A.J.I.L. 78–97 (1968), and Marston "Termination of Trusteeship," 18 Int. and Comp. Law Q. 1–40 (1969).

fruits of his aggression. But this article provides no clear guidance on the problem of a state which has responded to a threat of annihilation, and in so doing has taken the fight into the enemy's territory. Now it may well be, as Professor R. Y. Jennings has suggested,[17] that there are compelling policy reasons why, even in these circumstances, the victorious state should not be permitted permanently to retain these territories; but we cannot pretend that it is Article 2 of the Charter which answers this problem.

More important has been the general failure in debate, and in the text of Security Council resolutions, to distinguish between claiming title to territory and legitimate military occupation of it. A sharp distinction must be drawn between the situation in Jerusalem and the situation in the rest of the territories which are presently occupied, for in the latter there is no claim to annexation or title.[18] And there is nothing in either the Charter or general international law which leads one to suppose that military occupation, pending a peace treaty, is illegal. The Allies, it will be recalled, did not claim title to Berlin in 1945; but neither did they withdraw immediately they had entered it. The law of military occupation, with its complicated web of rights and duties, remains entirely relevant, and until such time as the Arab nations agree to negotiate a peace treaty, Israel is in legal terms entitled to remain in the territories she now holds.

II

This leads us on to a second question: We have noted that the political discretion of the Security Council is circumscribed by law—the law of the Charter as a whole, and the injunction in Article 1(1) that disputes be settled "in conformity with . . . international law." But not only is the Council enjoined to decide "in conformity with the principles of international law" but also "the principles of justice." This raises the problem of the compatibility of law and justice. This is a problem which is more meaningful to some lawyers than to others. To those lawyers who perceive law primarily as fixed rules to be applied to situations, the dichotomy between "law" and "justice" can be a very real one, though it is a dichotomy which they may feel it is not in their power to redress.[19] Others, perceiving law as a decision-making process, feel that, as reliance on past decisions (rules) is to be tempered by the need for reconciliation with community objectives, the identification of law with justice is largely in the decision-makers' hands.[20] A middle view is also possible, whereby law is, but is not only, a decision-making process. It has, it is argued, a many-faceted rôle.

[17] The Acquisition of Territory 52–67.

[18] For detailed arguments on this point, see R. Higgins, "The June War: The United Nations and Legal Background," Journal of Contemporary History (July, 1968) 252–273, at 269–272.

[19] See, for example, the views of Judge Sir Gerald Fitzmaurice, as discussed in R. Higgins, "Policy Considerations and the International Judicial Process," 17 Int. and Comp. Law Q. 58 (1968).

[20] This view, of course, permeates the writings of Myres McDougal and his associates. See, particularly, McDougal, "Some Basic Theoretical Concepts about International Law: A Policy Oriented Framework of Enquiry," 4 Journal of Conflict Resolution 337 (1960).

While this has the advantage of avoiding "the tendency of unrestricted 'rule skepticism' to dissolve the objective quality of legal obligation," [21] it leaves open the possibility that law, while making minor concessions to pacify discontented groups in society, in the main continues to sustain the prevailing order, including existing injustices.[22]

If, *arguendo,* discrepancies can exist between law and justice, and bearing in mind the injunction of Article 1(1) of the Charter, is the Security Council thus given a discretion to "bend" the rules of international law when justice seems to require it in the settlement of disputes? No less an authority than Kelsen has suggested this: he contends [23] that the terms of a settlement recommended by the Security Council under Article 37(2) or Article 38 of the Charter need not be in conformity with international law. Article 37(2), it will be recalled, authorizes the Security Council to recommend such terms of settlement as it may consider appropriate. Taking both this and the reference to "justice" in Article 1 into account, Kelsen concludes that the Security Council is authorized to recommend a settlement which might involve an infringement upon the rights which one or another party has under existing international law, if the Security Council considers such a settlement as "just" or as "appropriate." I myself would venture to differ from this view. I do not believe that the term "appropriate" in Article 37(2) was inserted in contradistinction to "international law" in Article 1. Rather, it was intended by the term to provide broad discretion *within* the framework of the principles of international law. So far as "justice" is concerned, there is no evidence in the *travaux préparatoires* that the framers of the Charter saw any great distinction between law and justice: the terms were used almost synonymously, even if somewhat redundantly; and our own views that justice and law may not always run entirely in harness should not lead us to give great weight to this supposed deliberate dichotomy in the Charter context.

III

This is not, of course, to dispose of the matter. Does the requirement to decide in accordance with the principles of international law unreasonably hamper the Security Council in the settlement of disputes? Would it be better if it could decide them in accordance with "the principles of justice" alone? The principles of justice, while a laudable goal, would seem to be considerably more subjective as a yardstick than the principles of general international law. Some, it is true, have from time to time argued that all reference to law in the Security Council is unhelpful. It is an argument most usually advanced by governments when they know their legal case to be weak. Thus at the time of the British intervention in Suez the Prime Minister informed the Security Council that he thought it was "not particularly helpful" to think about the legal aspects of the case. And when

---

[21] Such a view would seem to be held by Richard Falk. See, for example, his review article, "The Reality of International Law," XIII World Politics 354 (1961).

[22] See Falk, Review in 10 A. J. Comp. Law 297 (1961).

[23] Kelsen, The Law of the United Nations 385.

Egypt was in 1947 urging that British troops should withdraw from the Suez Canal Zone, notwithstanding a treaty with Britain which authorized their presence, the Egyptian representative stated:

> I have refrained from relying on juridical considerations. I have done so because I believe the Security Council is not limited to settlement of the legal aspect of a dispute brought before it. The Council is not called upon to adjudicate on the legal rights of the parties. Its mission—I shall say its higher mission—is to preserve peace and security, to see that conditions prevail in which peaceful and friendly relations may obtain among nations.[24]

Again, in discussion of the *Corfu Channel* case before the Security Council, the Brazilian representative stated:

> In the examination of disputes and situations, the Council is not restricted, as a Court or Tribunal would be, to the consideration of proofs, facts, circumstances and laws. Our function is political, not juridical. Our consideration of a dispute or situation should limit itself to that part of the one or the other which may endanger the maintenance of international peace and security.[25]

The claim that the Council is not restricted to the consideration of law is unexceptional. But one notices that it can also go beyond "facts" and "circumstances." The implication—a curious one—is that only legal bodies are concerned with "facts" and "circumstances" while, mysteriously, political bodies may move beyond them. Occasionally, emphasis on the political activity of the Security Council is used to avoid specific legal requirements. Thus when in 1947 the Security Council was debating whether the question of the hostilities between Indonesia and The Netherlands should be put upon the agenda, China suggested: "I think it would be dangerous to talk too much about legalities. . . . If we pay too much attention to legalities, we shall become involved. . . . Emphasis on legalities might have very serious and undesirable political consequences."[26] One must recall that here the context was procedural. There is surely no justification for ignoring Charter law in a procedural question, where there does not even exist the rationalization of providing a "just" settlement.

Some, therefore, feel that the law hampers the Security Council in its search for peace. But there are other reasons, too, why some feel that law is not necessarily the most desirable yardstick to be used by the Security Council in the settlement of disputes. Many of the new nations, for example, see—on certain occasions if not on others—the law as solidification of the *status quo*, and a *status quo* which is not always acceptable to them.[27] They feel, in particular, that the international law prohibitions on

[24] Security Council, 2nd Year, Official Records, 179th Meeting, p. 1861.
[25] *Ibid.*, No. 32, p. 687 ff.   [26] *Ibid.*, Part 2, 173rd Meeting, p. 1685.
[27] For a discussion of the issues where such feelings most commonly arise, see Higgins, Conflicts of Interests (Bodley Head), Ch. 2. Professor Falk has written: "Law tends to sustain the prevailing order-preferring old injustices to new solutions; the legal process makes minor concessions to pacify discontented groups in society, but concentrates its energy upon the maintenance of an atmosphere favorable to elite groups." 10 A. J. Comp. Law 297 (1961).

the use of force are inequitable in that the United Nations has failed to provide a satisfactory and concurrent means of political change. True, Article 14 refers to the peaceful adjustment of situations deemed likely to impair the general welfare or friendly relations among nations, including situations resulting from a violation of the provisions of the Charter. But this is an authority limited to the General Assembly, and one which it has not very successfully harnessed. Thus it could come about that the Indian entry into Goa in 1963, which many Western nations viewed as a clearly illegal use of force beyond one's own boundaries, was not condemned by the Security Council, for many nations felt that it was inequitable that the United Nations had been able to devise no means of getting Portugal to negotiate with India, in an era of decolonization, over the Portuguese enclave on the Indian subcontinent.

Such is the psychological need for legal justification, that the upshot is frequently not an overt rejection of the legal norm in question, but rather an implicit revision of it. Resolutions on colonial questions frequently include clauses which seek, in effect, to relax the strictly limited Charter authorization of force. Similar attempts have been made in the course of the work of the Special Committee on Principles of International Law concerning Friendly Relations and Co-operation among States.[28] Thus in the case of Rhodesia, and indeed Southern Africa as a whole, the Afro-Asian Members of the United Nations have seen the traditional rules of non-intervention working to their disadvantage; and the last two resolutions on Rhodesia,[29] which have received the affirmative vote of all the Permanent Members, contain clauses by which the Council "urges all States Members of the United Nations to render moral and material assistance to the people of Southern Rhodesia in their struggle to achieve their freedom and independence." Attempts are thus made to revise the common understanding on the use of force to permit not only the existing right of revolution, but the right and indeed the duty of third parties to aid such revolutions.

IV

There are equally those who believe that the Security Council views "justice" as synonymous with the *status quo ante*, but that the *status quo ante* is not necessarily the *status juris*, even under established international law. This argument was heavily relied on by Israel in 1956, when she sought to impose conditions upon her withdrawal from Egyptian territory. She indicated that to go back to the position prior to the invasion of Suez, a situation deemed "just" by most states, would be to revert to an illegal closure of the Suez Canal and the Gulf of Aqaba to Israeli shipping, and an exposure to illegal incursions across her borders. Was it the duty of the United Nations (in this case the General Assembly, but the same principle holds for the Security Council) to redress the last illegality with which it was faced—Israel's invasion of Egypt—or to restore the over-all *status juris?*

[28] See particularly the consideration of the four principles enumerated in par. 5 of General Assembly Res. 2181 (XXI), which is reported in A/6799, General Assembly, 22nd Sess., Official Records, Agenda item 87.

[29] Security Council Res. 253 (1968) and 232 (1967).

The Security Council has consistently chosen to deal, so far as mandatory decisions are concerned, with only the immediately prior illegality. For the settlement of the underlying issues by the establishment of an acceptable *status juris*, it has preferred to recommend that the parties resort to negotiation or mediation, though the Council has often offered its own good offices. This is a very understandable practice, and perhaps it is an inevitable one. But it does lead to a cluster of "hard core" cases where, though hostilities may be terminated, there remains the very real danger that they will flare up again because the underlying problems have not been resolved. This is to some extent [30] true of the Arab-Israel situation and also of the long-standing conflict between India and Pakistan over Kashmir. The reluctance of the Security Council to settle disputes by indicating legal over-all settlements is closely tied in with the question of whether the Council will regard it as proper, in reaching its decisions, to go back in time beyond the immediate illegality before it. Thus in March of last year the Security Council strongly condemned Israel for violating the cease-fire by striking deep into Jordanian territory in a large-scale military action.[31] Israel had indeed illegally violated the cease-fire, and the Security Council was unanimous in its condemnation. But the Council had failed equally to condemn Jordan for the initial Al Fatah raids into Israel which had led to the Israeli retaliation—a failure which occurred partly because of the protection of the Arab position by the Soviet veto (a protection which the United States is, quite properly, unwilling to exercise on behalf of Israel), and partly because the present composition of the Security Council ensures a sympathetic hearing for the Arab case. The outbreak of fighting between India and Pakistan in 1965 points to some of the same problems, though the two cases are not quite on all fours. The initiation of fighting by Pakistan was not, in this case, a retaliation against prior raids by Indian guerrillas: but it was embarked upon because Pakistan felt that no progress had been made since 1950 in settling the Kashmir dispute, and that the Security Council's recommendations for a plebiscite had never been carried out. In agreeing to the ordered cease-fire,[32] Pakistan made it clear that she deemed a long-term solution imperative, and that she would withdraw from the United Nations if the Security Council did not mobilize its resources in this direction. As we know, the Tashkent Agreement was reached through the good offices of the Soviet Union, and it provides but a starting point to dealing with a dispute which still remains unsolved.

We have noted, then, that the Council is usually reluctant to recommend long-term solutions to disputes, to go beyond calling for an end to hostilities. There are, of course, exceptions to this proposition: at the end of the second Dutch military action against Indonesia in 1949 the Security Council specified in some detail the agreement which should form the basis of a

---

[30] But not wholly true; the U.N. has sometimes sought a middle course, such as requiring Israel to withdraw from Egypt in 1956, but ensuring, through the placing of UNEF along the armistice line and at Sharm-el-Sheikh, an amelioration of the initial situation.

[31] Security Council Res. 248 (1968).   [32] Security Council Res. 211 (1965).

settlement. But this is unusual. Chapter VI on the Pacific Settlement of Disputes does, perhaps, place an emphasis on solutions reached by the parties themselves. Article 33 provides that the Council shall call upon parties to a dispute, the continuation of which is likely to endanger peace, to seek a solution by negotiation, enquiry, mediation, conciliation, arbitration, judicial settlement, or other means of their own choice. However, by the terms of Article 36(1), the Security Council may "at any stage of a dispute of the nature referred to in Article 33" (*i.e.*, the continuation of which is likely to endanger peace) "recommend appropriate procedures or methods of adjustment"; and in Article 37 it is provided that, if the parties fail to settle a dispute through any of the means listed in Article 33, the Security Council may recommend appropriate procedures or methods of adjustment (*i.e.*, employ Article 36) or—and here we move away from procedure and on to substance—recommend such terms of settlement as it may consider appropriate. Understandably, and very probably also correctly, the Council has usually felt that there is little to be gained from doing this, as any recommended settlement has to be one which both parties can agree upon between themselves. Only in the exceptional circumstances of an Indonesian-Dutch-type situation, where one party is under particular pressure because it has lost the support of all its major allies, can an imposed settlement work. Article 39 of the Charter leads in the same direction: here, once the Security Council has determined there is a threat to the peace, a breach of the peace, or an act of aggression, it can decide, before embarking upon enforcement action, to "make recommendations." The same considerations obtain.

V

Much of the Security Council's "third-party" rôle, as we have seen, is to try to urge the parties themselves to reach agreement. The Security Council has frequently sought to bridge the gulf between getting the parties to agree between themselves, and making its own recommendations, by appointing a Special Representative of the Security Council. Thus the series of Special Representatives in Kashmir sought to find common ground between India and Pakistan, and the Security Council would approve their suggestions. Or again, as in the present Arab-Israel situation, the Council can provide a broad list of political and legal propositions and appoint a Special Representative to work out with the parties how these are to be implemented.

Nonetheless, the question must be asked: Is third-party settlement in general, and reference to law in particular, really possible or desirable? Conventional wisdom in the Western world urges the desirability of more third-party settlement, in particular by the International Court of Justice.[33]

---

[33] See C. W. Jenks, The Prospects for International Adjudication, Ch. 1, esp. pp. 76–112; see also Professor Franck's comment that "The failure of the International Community to develop a system of third party law-making comparable to that of the National Community may well prove to be the fatal error of our civilization." The Structure of Impartiality 46.

But there are those who reject entirely this method of going about things: There is no necessary antipathy between international law and systems analysis.[34] However, the particular school led by Dr. John Burton, of University College, London, views the rôle of law as positively unhelpful. Conflict occurs, he contends, where there is non-systemic behavior; and

> The remedy is not to introduce an outside agent or set of "normative laws" to control such behaviour, but to provide States with the theories, insights and rules that enable them to achieve their goals without running into the self-defeating conflicts inherent in non-systemic behaviour.[35]

He believes that law may impose behavior in the short term, but cannot actually settle disputes, because disputes occur because of non-systemic behavior, which can be rectified only by the removal of all misconceptions between the parties, who will have to make adjustments *inter se*. It is further argued that reference to international law is a hindrance in this process, because it is static and lacks the necessary flexibility; and that attempts at imposition of these rules by a third party are doomed to failure, and can not properly be deemed either conflict resolution or the settlement of disputes. My own belief is that the legal process is considerably more flexible and dynamic than these arguments would lead us to believe. Dr. Burton speaks only of "traditional rules" and takes no note of the function of policy-oriented jurisprudence as a factor in the promotion of systemic behavior.

Within the framework of any one dispute a state may, it is true, find an unsatisfactory outcome imposed by legal consideration. But one surely views the matter through too short a perspective if one fails to see that there are considerations concerning the long term which may militate in favor of its accepting a solution resting on international law. What may, as such, be seen as an unacceptable result can become more acceptable if other considerations, other carrots and sticks, beyond the scope of the case in question are also brought into consideration. And, of course, high among these other long-term considerations is the interest which most states feel in having disputes resolved by reference to legal standards rather than force. The proposition that legal decisions cannot resolve disputes, because they fail to accommodate the interests of one of the parties, therefore seems to be altogether too broadly stated. If a nation accepts the compulsory jurisdiction of the International Court of Justice, it *has* decided that, in the long term, it is willing to have solutions "imposed" upon it by law in certain circumstances. One can agree that states regard certain issues as so vital that they will not submit them to any third-party adjudication, without accepting that all forms of third-party settlement are always therefore unacceptable to the parties. So it is with the Security Council, for Members of the United Nations have agreed that the Security

---

[34] Indeed, there can be fruitful co-operation between the two disciplines. See, for example, the collaboration between Falk and his colleagues at the Woodrow Wilson Center, Princeton University.

[35] J. W. Burton, Systems, States, Diplomacy and Rules 222 (1968); and Conflict and Communication 148–200 (1909).

Council shall have the authority to recommend, in conformity with international law, settlements to disputes. In fact, the "third-party" element in Security Council practice is much exaggerated. Frequently resolutions are drafted only after consulting the parties to the dispute to see what common ground may be discovered between them. Thus the November, 1968, resolution on the Middle East, adopted unanimously, represented weeks of work by Lord Caradon, the British representative, to discover what principles the two sides could in fact agree upon as a starting point to settlement of the dispute. The possibility of a veto has the advantageous side effect that such sustained diplomatic efforts are now made well in advance of the vote.

Where solutions to disputes between the parties are agreed between them, there is every likelihood that they will be, as the Charter requires, "in conformity with the principles of . . . international law." Exceptions to this must be rare, though one thinks of the case of Cyprus before independence, where the Security Council was faced with a dispute between Greece and Turkey.[36] Cyprus now argues that the arrangements made, to which she herself was a party, are contrary to general international law. Under the terms of the Zurich and London Agreements, a draft constitution with certain entrenched clauses was devised for Cyprus, the aim being to provide safeguards for the Turkish Cypriot minority on the island. The Agreements also provided that, should these constitutional provisions be altered, the co-signatories—Greece, Turkey and the United Kingdom—would have the right to intervene to restore the *status quo ante*. The government of Archbishop Makarios has apparently found the original constitution unworkable, and declares that, notwithstanding it was itself a signatory, the Agreement was illegal because it is contrary to *jus cogens*, the peremptory norms of international law, to arrange for states to intervene upon the territory of others.

VI

A further question now presents itself: Is the "political" element so paramount in disputes which come before the Security Council as to render impossible third-party settlement under the law? There are, I think, two points to be made. The first is that it is a fallacy to assume—though it is commonly done—that "certain kinds of disputes are obviously inherently political, invested with a sort of mask of Cain which alienates them forever"[37] from the scope of legal reasoning. While many lawyers agree that "political" questions should not receive "legal" answers, it is noticeable that what one sees as a political question another sees as a legal one. The impossibility of consistent, objective practical application should make one wary of the thesis.[38] The second point is that in any event, there is of course a very substantial difference between the use, the employment, of international law by the Security Council, on the one hand, and by a purely

[36] See General Assembly, Official Records, 6th–13th Sessions; and Cmnd. Paper 679 (Misc. No. 4), H.M. Stationery Office, 1959.

[37] A fallacy elegantly noted by Franck, *op. cit.* 171.

[38] This is a theme which I have elaborated in "Policy Considerations and the International Judicial Process," 17 Int. and Comp. Law Q. 58 (1968).

16 THE AMERICAN JOURNAL OF INTERNATIONAL LAW [Vol. 64

judicial body such as the International Court of Justice, on the other. The International Court is enjoined to settle disputes by discovering the better legal position of the parties before it, drawing upon the accepted sources of international law. The Security Council is to settle disputes by encouraging the parties to agree between themselves, or by recommending solutions itself. It has a wide political discretion, and all that is required of it is that its solutions should be "in conformity with the principles of . . . international law." It can even recommend adjustments, if these are compatible with international law. This political operation *within* the law, rather than decision according *to* the law, which is the Court's function, allows the Council to address itself to problems with a very considerable number of facets, which it is better equipped to do than a purely judicial body.[89] But if there are twenty possible solutions or fifty, a political body may be better equipped to provide the answer within a broad framework of legally acceptable solutions.[40]

Accepting that the Court and the Security Council have different rôles to play in the settlement of disputes, and accepting further that law, though used differently, is an element in the solutions offered by the Security Council, to what extent is the rôle of the Security Council adjudicative? It is for the Council to make political decisions which are in accordance with international law, not to find legal answers. Disputes come before the Security Council either because their continuation would be likely to endanger international peace (Chapter VI) or because they are causing a threat to, or breach of, the peace. There is nothing in the U.N. Charter which requires states to assert non-compliance with the Charter or with general international law as a basis for Security Council competence. This has been one of the great popular debating points on the handling of the Rhodesian question by the United Nations. Why, it has been asserted, should the Security Council act in respect of Rhodesia when, being a non-member, it is in breach of no Charter obligations; nor is it in breach of international law, rebellion against the Crown not offending the law of nations? This is to miss the legal point. The Security Council may legally act when a certain situation, namely, a threat to the peace, exists. And it is for the Council, and the Council alone, to determine the existence of such a threat.[41] Whether one agrees with its judgment is both another point and beside the point.

[89] Franck has suggested that an appropriate way to decide whether issues are suitable for adjudication is to see whether a legal answer to them would be fully dispositive of the dispute. Where there are innumerable possible solutions to a controversy, the answering of particular legal claims may not be a helpful method of approach: "What makes a judicial determination of the status of lobsters . . . and nautical signals relatively easy for a Court is the clear duality of choice. Each issue poses only two credible alternatives." *Op. cit.* 185.

[40] Milton Katz, in his book, The Relevance of International Adjudication (1968), writes interestingly of "political decisions made with a sense of law." See Ch. VI, pp. 145–160.

[41] See R. Higgins, "International Law, Rhodesia and the UN," 23 World Today 94 (1967); and McDougal and Reisman, "Rhodesia and the United Nations: The Lawfulness of International Concern," 62 A.J.I.L. 1 (1968).

But even though states do not have to assert non-compliance with the Charter or international law as a basis for Security Council competence, they frequently choose to do so, advancing this as a substantive charge. The reason is not hard to find: the behavior of a state is not easily challenged on grounds of "policy"; it is clearly preferable, if one wishes to gain the support of those not directly involved, to show it as a departure from legal obligations.[42] States look to the Security Council to vindicate those of their actions which they regard as based on good legal grounds. By and large, however, the Security Council has declined the rôle of adjudicator. Oscar Schachter has claimed that the Security Council was never intended to act in a "quasi-judicial" rôle.[43] He is here using the term "quasi-judicial" to mean "adjudicative" because he is certainly among those who believe that the political actions of the Security Council contain some law-creating elements. And it is because he uses the term in this way that his view appears to stand in such marked contrast with that of Kelsen, who has an entire section of his book on *The Law of the United Nations* entitled "The Quasi-Judicial Settlement of Disputes by the Security Council." The Security Council's function, then, is not to act as watchdog to adjudicate on breaches of the Charter or international law by Members. These are relevant to it only insofar as they may be the causes of a threat to international peace. The Council has tended to adopt resolutions or decisions aimed at bringing about a settlement while avoiding any determination of guilt. It apparently feels, in the great majority of cases, that a settlement is more likely to ensue if one particular party is not branded as having acted "illegally," as being the "wrongdoer." That there is some strength in this view is undeniable; but cynics may also note that it is most likely to be advanced by countries who do not themselves, for political reasons, wish to be put in the position of condemning another nation. Thus India refused to vote for the Security Council resolution condemning the Soviet Union for its intervention in Czechoslovakia, declaring that the function of the Security Council was to achieve a withdrawal of Soviet troops, and that therefore the judgment of illegality and condemnation should be removed.[44] This is, if you like, a movement away from the attempted settlement of disputes by adjudication towards the attempted settlement of disputes by a bargaining process. The technique is closer to that of labor bargaining, within a legal framework, than to judicial adjudication. This raises acute problems for the state which believes its actions to be legally impeccable. It sees itself subjected to illegal acts by its adversary, and, when seeking a clear denunciation by the Security Council, finds that it can achieve at most a resolution admonishing both parties to desist from all illegal acts. Thus, when Israel brings claims against its Arab neighbors, the resolutions warn both Israel and the Arabs to heed their legal obligations; India and Pakistan are conjoined as addressees by the Council, though each would wish the Security Council to condemn the other. The Security Council may be right

[42] Schachter, *loc. cit.* 960–961.   [43] *Ibid.*
[44] Security Council, 23rd Year, Official Records, 1443rd Meeting.

in its judgment that a settlement would not be brought nearer by attributing legal guilt to one party, but this practice does present grave difficulties to the states concerned. Their governments have to explain to domestic opinion why it continues to be useful to go to the Security Council, and to heed it, when that body is unwilling publicly to support what they perceive as a legally valid case. And once domestic opinion moves against reference to the United Nations, as it seems to be doing in Israel, then a long-term settlement becomes that much harder to achieve. This seems an inescapable dilemma. Further, when deciding to avoid attributions of guilt, the Security Council has taken into consideration the fact that criticism, in legal terms, of a particular country may in fact mobilize public opinion in that country, if there is a free press, against the actions of its government, and thus contribute to a rapid settlement of the dispute. The resolutions will also have some impact upon the officials in the country concerned. Certainly the U.N. resolutions concerning Britain's legal position at the time of Suez, 1956, acted in this way. So it is a very fine point in judgment, in any particular case, as to whether it is useful for the Council to adopt an adjudicative rôle or one of compromise bargaining. Is the Soviet Union to be exempt from legal criticism because, having no free press, her public opinion cannot be reached? It is difficult to know, when debating this question of adjudication by the Security Council, whether the chicken or the egg comes first. Oscar Schachter has asked in these pages [45] whether it is only in those cases which are regarded as the most intractable that the Security Council permits itself the luxury of attributing legal guilt?—the repeated condemnation of Rhodesia for UDI, South Africa for *apartheid,* and Portugal for its colonial policy come to mind. Or is it the other way round: Has the assigning of legal guilt to those countries in fact stiffened their resistance to accepting any proposed settlement? When making decisions the Security Council is normally very anxious not to damage its own authority, and it usually feels that its calls, for example, for a cease-fire in the Middle East or the Indian subcontinent will be more easily achieved if guilt is not attributed. But it has been suggested that it appears to regard certain cases as *so* difficult—South Africa, Portugal—that it is willing to demand, as a legal requirement, a pattern of behavior by the addressed state which it knows will not be forthcoming.

The Security Council thus labors under a myriad of difficulties when seeking to settle disputes in accordance with international law. To say that the Council, being a political body, ignores international law, is at once an exaggeration and uninstructive. Clearly, its use of the law is very different from that of the International Court. It is constantly faced with the choice of arranging compromises or acting in a quasi-adjudicative manner; and the arguments in favor of either course may be very finely balanced. It would be comforting to think that they have been fully thought through.

[45] *Loc. cit.* 965.

Part VIII
The Future of International Dispute Settlement

[18]

Legalized Dispute Resolution:
Interstate and Transnational

Robert O. Keohane, Andrew Moravcsik,
and Anne-Marie Slaughter

International courts and tribunals are flourishing. Depending on how these bodies are defined, they now number between seventeen and forty.[1] In recent years we have witnessed the proliferation of new bodies and a strengthening of those that already exist. "When future international legal scholars look back at . . . the end of the twentieth century," one analyst has written, "they probably will refer to the enormous expansion of the international judiciary as the single most important development of the post–Cold War age."[2]

These courts and tribunals represent a key dimension of legalization. Instead of resolving disputes through institutionalized bargaining, states choose to delegate the task to third-party tribunals charged with applying general legal principles. Not all of these tribunals are created alike, however. In particular, we distinguish between two ideal types of international dispute resolution: interstate and transnational. Our central argument is that the formal legal differences between interstate and transnational dispute resolution have significant implications for the politics of dispute settlement and therefore for the effects of legalization in world politics.

Interstate dispute resolution is consistent with the view that public international law comprises a set of rules and practices governing *interstate* relationships. Legal resolution of disputes, in this model, takes place between states conceived of as unitary actors. States are the subjects of international law, which means that they control access to dispute resolution tribunals or courts. They typically designate the adjudicators of such tribunals. States also implement, or fail to implement, the decisions of international tribunals or courts. Thus in interstate dispute resolution, states act as gatekeepers both to the international legal process and from that process back to the domestic level.

---

1. Romano 1999, 723–28. By the strictest definition, there are currently seventeen permanent, independent international courts. If we include some bodies that are not courts, but instead quasi-judicial tribunals, panels, and commissions charged with similar functions, the total rises to over forty. If we include historical examples and bodies negotiated but not yet in operation, the total rises again to nearly one hundred.
2. Ibid., 709.

International Organization 54, 3, Summer 2000, pp. 457–488

In transnational dispute resolution, by contrast, access to courts and tribunals and the subsequent enforcement of their decisions are legally insulated from the will of individual national governments. These tribunals are therefore more open to individuals and groups in civil society. In the pure ideal type, states lose their gatekeeping capacities; in practice, these capacities are attenuated. This loss of state control, whether voluntarily or unwittingly surrendered, creates a range of opportunities for courts and their constituencies to set the agenda.

Before proceeding to our argument, it is helpful to locate our analysis in the broader context of this special issue of *IO*. Legalization is a form of institutionalization distinguished by obligation, precision, and delegation. Our analysis applies primarily when obligation is high.[3] Precision, on the other hand, is not a defining characteristic of the situations we examine. We examine the decisions of bodies that interpret and apply rules, regardless of their precision. Indeed, such bodies may have greater latitude when precision is low than when it is high.[4] Our focus is a third dimension of legalization: delegation of authority to courts and tribunals designed to resolve international disputes through the application of general legal principles.[5]

Three dimensions of delegation are crucial to our argument: independence, access, and embeddedness. As we explain in the first section, independence specifies the extent to which formal legal arrangements ensure that adjudication can be rendered impartially with respect to concrete state interests. Access refers to the ease with which parties other than states can influence the tribunal's agenda. Embeddedness denotes the extent to which dispute resolution decisions can be implemented without governments having to take actions to do so. We define low independence, access, and embeddedness as the ideal type of interstate dispute resolution and high independence, access, and embeddedness as the ideal type of transnational dispute resolution. Although admittedly a simplification, this conceptualization helps us to understand why the behavior and impact of different tribunals, such as the International Court of Justice (ICJ) and the European Court of Justice (ECJ), have been so different.

In the second section we seek to connect international politics, international law, and domestic politics. Clearly the power and preferences of states influence the behavior both of governments and of dispute resolution tribunals: international law operates in the shadow of power. Yet within that political context, we contend that institutions for selecting judges, controlling access to dispute resolution, and legally enforcing the judgments of international courts and tribunals have a major impact on state behavior. The formal qualities of legal institutions empower or disempower domestic political actors other than national governments. Compared to interstate dispute resolution, transnational dispute resolution tends to generate more litigation, jurisprudence more autonomous of national interests, and an additional source of pressure for compliance. In the third section we argue that interstate and transna-

---

3. Abbott et al., this issue, tab. 1, types I–III and V.
4. Hence we do not exclude types II and V (Abbott et al., tab. 1, this issue) from our purview.
5. See Abbott et al., this issue.

tional dispute resolution generate divergent longer-term dynamics. Transnational dispute resolution seems to have an inherently more expansionary character; it provides more opportunities to assert and establish new legal norms, often in unintended ways.

This article should be viewed as exploratory rather than an attempt to be definitive. Throughout, we use ideal types to illuminate a complex subject, review suggestive though not conclusive evidence, and highlight opportunities for future research. We offer our own conjectures at various points as to useful starting points for that research but do not purport to test definitive conclusions.

A Typology of Dispute Resolution

Much dispute resolution in world politics is highly institutionalized. Established, enduring rules apply to entire classes of circumstances and cannot easily be ignored or modified when they become inconvenient to one participant or another in a specific case. In this article we focus on institutions in which dispute resolution has been delegated to a third-party tribunal charged with applying designated legal rules and principles. This act of delegation means that disputes must be framed as "cases" between two or more parties, at least one of which, the defendant, will be a state or an individual acting on behalf of a state. (Usually, states are the defendants, so we refer to defendants as "states." However, individuals may also be prosecuted by international tribunals, as in the proposed International Criminal Court and various war crimes tribunals.[6]) The identity of the plaintiff depends on the design of the dispute resolution mechanism. Plaintiffs can be other states or private parties—individuals or nongovernmental organizations (NGOs)—specifically designated to monitor and enforce the obligatory rules of the regime.

We turn now to our three explanatory variables: independence, access, and embeddedness. We do not deny that the patterns of delegation we observe may ultimately have their origins in the power and interests of major states, as certain strands of liberal and realist theory claim. Nevertheless, our analysis here takes these sources of delegation as given and emphasizes how formal legal institutions empower groups and individuals other than national governments.[7]

Independence: Who Controls Adjudication?

The variable *independence* measures the extent to which adjudicators for an international authority charged with dispute resolution are able to deliberate and reach legal

---

6. We do not discuss the interesting case of international criminal law here. See Bass 1998.

7. This central focus on variation in the political representation of social groups, rather than interstate strategic interaction, is the central tenet of theories of international law that rest on liberal international relations theory. Slaughter 1995a. Our approach is thus closely linked in this way to republican liberal studies of the democratic peace, the role of independent executives and central banks in structuring international economic policy coordination, and the credibility of commitments by democratic states more generally. See Keohane and Nye 1977; Moravcsik 1997; Doyle 1983a,b; and Goldstein 1996.

judgments independently of national governments. In other words, it assesses the extent to which adjudication is rendered impartially with respect to concrete state interests in a specific case. The traditional international model of dispute resolution in law and politics places pure control by states at one end of a continuum. Disputes are resolved by the agents of the interested parties themselves. Each side offers its own interpretation of the rules and their applicability to the case at issue; disagreements are resolved through institutionalized interstate bargaining. There are no permanent rules of procedure or legal precedent, although in legalized dispute resolution, decisions must be consistent with international law. Institutional rules may also influence the outcome by determining the conditions—interpretive standards, voting requirements, selection—under which authoritative decisions are made.[8] Even where legal procedures are established, individual governments may have the right to veto judgments, as in the UN Security Council and the old General Agreement on Tariffs and Trade (GATT).

Movement along the continuum away from this traditional interstate mode of dispute resolution measures the nature and tightness of the political constraints imposed on adjudicators. The extent to which members of an international tribunal are independent reflects the extent to which they can free themselves from at least three categories of institutional constraint: selection and tenure, legal discretion, and control over material and human resources.

The most important criterion is independent selection and tenure. The spectrum runs from direct representatives of unconstrained national governments to a more impartial and autonomous process of naming judges. Judges may be selected from the ranks of loyal politicians, leading members of the bar, and justice ministries; or they may be drawn from a cadre of specialized experts in a particular area of international law. Their tenure may be long or short. After serving as adjudicators, they may be dependent on national governments for their subsequent careers or may belong to an independent professional group, such as legal academics. The less partisan their background, the longer their tenure; and the more independent their future, the greater the independence of adjudicators.

Selection and tenure rules vary widely. Many international institutions maintain tight national control on dispute resolution through selection and tenure rules.[9] Some institutions—including the UN, International Monetary Fund, NATO, and the bilateral Soviet–U.S. arrangements established by the Strategic Arms Limitation Treaty (SALT)—establish no authoritative third-party adjudicators whatsoever. The regime creates instead a set of decision-making rules and procedures, a forum for interstate bargaining, within which subsequent disputes are resolved by national representatives serving at the will of their governments. In other institutions, however, such as the EU, governments can name representatives, but those representatives are assured

---

8. Helfer and Slaughter 1997.

9. Even less independent are ad hoc and arbitral tribunals designed by specific countries for specific purposes. The Organization for Security and Cooperation in Europe, for example, provides experts, arbiters, and conciliators for ad hoc dispute resolution. Here we consider only permanent judicial courts. See Romano 1999, 711–13.

TABLE 1. *The independence continuum: Selection and tenure*

Level of independence	Selection method and tenure	International court or tribunal
Low	Direct representatives, perhaps with single-country veto	UN Security Council
Moderate	Disputants control ad hoc selection of third-party judges	PCA
	Groups of states control selection of third-party judges	ICJ, GATT, WTO
High	Individual governments appoint judges with long tenure	ECJ
	Groups of states select judges with long tenure	ECHR, IACHR

long tenure and may enjoy subsequent prestige in the legal world independent of their service to individual states. In first-round dispute resolution in GATT and the World Trade Organization (WTO), groups of states select a stable of experts who are then selected on a case-by-case basis by the parties and the secretariat, whereas in ad hoc international arbitration, the selection is generally controlled by the disputants and the tribunal is constituted for a single case.

In still other situations—particularly in authoritarian countries—judges may be vulnerable to retaliation when they return home after completing their tenure; even in liberal democracies, future professional advancement may be manipulated by the government.[10] The legal basis of some international dispute resolution mechanisms, such as the European Court of Human Rights (ECHR), requires oversight by semi-independent supranational bodies. The spectrum of legal independence as measured by selection and tenure rules is shown in Table 1.

Legal discretion, the second criterion for judicial independence, refers to the breadth of the mandate granted to the dispute resolution body. Some legalized dispute resolution bodies must adhere closely to treaty texts; but the ECJ, as Karen Alter describes in this issue, has asserted the supremacy of European Community (EC) law without explicit grounding in the treaty text or the intent of national governments. More generally, institutions for adjudication arise, as Abbott and Snidal argue in this issue, under conditions of complexity and uncertainty, which render interstate contracts necessarily incomplete. Adjudication is thus more than the act of applying precise standards and norms to a series of concrete cases within a precise mandate; it involves interpreting norms and resolving conflicts between competing norms in the context of particular cases. When seeking to overturn all but the most flagrantly illegal state actions, litigants and courts must inevitably appeal to particular interpretations of such ambiguities. Other things being equal, the wider the range of considerations the body can legitimately consider and the greater the uncertainty concerning the proper interpretation or norm in a given case, the more potential legal independence it possesses. Where regimes have clear norms, single goals, and narrow scope—as in, say, some purely technical tasks—we expect to see limited legal

10. For a domestic case of judicial manipulation, see Ramseyer and Rosenbluth 1997.

discretion. Where legal norms are valid across a wide area—as in the jurisprudence of the ECJ, which is connected to the broad, open-ended EC—there is more scope to promulgate general principles within the context of specific cases.[11] Similarly, greater legal independence exists where cross-cutting interpretations are plausible, such as over the scope of legitimate exceptions to norms like free trade, nonintervention, and individual rights. For instance, GATT and WTO dispute resolution bodies, or human rights courts, are increasingly being called upon to designate the margin of appreciation granted to national governments in pursuing legitimate state purposes other than free trade or human rights protection.

The third criterion for judicial independence, *financial and human resources*, refers to the ability of judges to process their caseloads promptly and effectively.[12] Such resources are necessary for processing large numbers of complaints and rendering consistent, high-quality decisions. They can also permit a court or tribunal to develop a factual record independent of the state litigants before them and to publicize their decisions. This is of particular importance for human rights courts, which seek to disseminate information and mobilize political support on behalf of those who would otherwise lack direct domestic access to effective political representation.[13] Many human rights tribunals are attached to commissions capable of conducting independent inquiries. The commissions of the Inter-American and UN systems, for example, have been active in pursuing this strategy, often conducting independent, on-site investigations.[14] Indeed, inquiries by the Inter-American Commission need not be restricted to the details of a specific case, though a prior petition is required. In general, the greater the financial and human resources available to courts and the stronger the commissions attached to them, the greater their legal independence.

In sum, the greater the freedom of a dispute resolution body from the control of individual member states over selection and tenure, legal discretion, information, and financial and human resources, the greater its legal independence.

Access: Who Has Standing?

Access, like independence, is a variable. From a legal perspective, access measures the range of social and political actors who have legal standing to submit a dispute to be resolved; from a political perspective, access measures the range of those who can set the agenda. Access is particularly important with respect to courts and other dispute-resolution bodies because, in contrast to executives and legislatures, they are "passive" organs of government unable to initiate action by unilaterally seizing a dispute. Access is measured along a continuum between two extremes. At one extreme, if no social or political actors can submit disputes, dispute-resolution institutions are unable to act; at the other, anyone with a legitimate grievance directed at

11. Weiler 1994.
12. Helfer and Slaughter 1997.
13. Keck and Sikkink 1998.
14. Farer 1998.

government policy can easily and inexpensively submit a complaint. In-between are situations in which individuals can bring their complaints only by acting through governments, convincing governments to "espouse" their claim as a state claim against another government, or by engaging in a costly procedure. This continuum of access can be viewed as measuring the "political transaction costs" to individuals and groups in society of submitting their complaint to an international dispute-resolution body. The more restrictive the conditions for bringing a claim to the attention of a dispute-resolution body, the more costly it is for actors to do so.

Near the higher-cost, restrictive end, summarized in Table 2, fall purely interstate tribunals, such as the GATT and WTO panels, the Permanent Court of Arbitration, and the ICJ, in which only member states may file suit against one another. Although this limitation constrains access to any dispute-resolution body by granting one or more governments a formal veto, it does not permit governments to act without constraint. Individuals and groups may still wield influence, but they must do so by domestic means. Procedures that are formally similar in this sense may nonetheless generate quite different implications for access, depending on principal-agent relationships in domestic politics. Whereas individuals and groups may have the domestic political power to ensure an ongoing if indirect role in both the decision to initiate proceedings and the resulting argumentation, state-controlled systems are likely to be more restrictive than direct litigation by individuals and groups.

In state-controlled systems, the individual or group must typically lobby a specialized government bureaucracy, secure a majority in some relevant domestic decision-making body, or catch the attention of the head of government. State officials are often cautious about instigating such proceedings against another state, since they must weigh a wide range of cross-cutting concerns, including the diplomatic costs of negotiating an arrangement with the foreign government in question. Such indirect arrangements for bringing a case are costly, prohibiting government action to serve extremely narrow or secondary interest groups.

In other cases, state action under such arrangements can be considered prohibitively expensive because of the government's role as a veto player. The most obvious circumstance is one in which individuals and groups seek to file suit challenging the actions of their home state. (This is generally the type of litigation before most human rights and many regional economic integration bodies—which do not restrict access to states.) Although, in theory, an individual or group could secure access to international adjudication by mustering a large enough domestic bloc to override the outright hostility of the state, this rarely occurs in practice.

Within these constraints, GATT/WTO panels and the ICJ differ in their roles toward domestic individuals and groups. In the GATT and now the WTO, governments nominally control access to the legal process, yet in practice injured industries are closely involved in both the initiation and the conduct of the litigation by their governments, at least in the United States. A firm or industry group, typically represented by an experienced Washington law firm, will lobby the U.S. Trade Representative to bring a claim against another country allegedly engaging in GATT violations. The industry lawyers may then participate quite closely in the preparation of the suit and

TABLE 2. *The access continuum: Who has standing?*

Level of access	Who has standing	International court or tribunal
Low	Both states must agree	PCA
Moderate	Only a single state can file suit	ICJ
	Single state files suit, influenced by social actors	WTO, GATT
High	Access through national courts	ECJ
	Direct individual (and sometimes group) access if domestic remedies have been exhausted	ECHR, IACHR

wait in the halls for debriefing after the actual proceeding. In the ICJ, by contrast, individual access is more costly. The ICJ hears cases in which individuals may have a direct interest (such as the families of soldiers sent to fight in another country in what is allegedly an illegal act of interstate aggression). However, these individuals usually have little influence over a national government decision to initiate interstate litigation or over the resulting conduct of the proceedings. As in the WTO, finally, individuals are unable to file suit against their own government before the ICJ. Because the ICJ tends to handle cases concerning "public goods" provision across national jurisdictions, such as boundary disputes and issues concerning aggression, the groups influenced by ICJ decisions tend to be diffuse and unorganized, except through the intermediation of national governments.

Near the permissive end of the spectrum is the ECJ. Individuals may ultimately be directly represented before the international tribunal, though the decision to bring the case before it remains in the hands of a domestic judicial body. Under Article 177 of the Treaty of Rome, national courts may independently refer a case before them to the ECJ if the case raises questions of European law that the national court does not feel competent to resolve on its own. The ECJ answers the specific question(s) presented and sends the case back to the national court for disposition of the merits of the dispute. Litigants themselves can suggest such a referral to the national court, but the decision to refer lies ultimately within the national court's discretion. Whether the interests involved are narrow and specific—as in the landmark *Cassis de Dijon* case over the importation of French specialty liquors into Germany—or broad, the cost of securing such a referral is the same. As Karen Alter shows in her article in this issue, different national courts have sharply different records of referral, but over time national courts as a body have become increasingly willing to refer cases to the ECJ. These referrals may involve litigation among private parties rather than simply against a public authority.[15]

15. It therefore remains unclear, on balance, whether the EC or the ECHR provides more ready access. Whereas the EC system under Article 177 allows only domestic courts, not individuals, to refer cases, the EC does not require, as does the ECHR and all other human rights courts, that domestic remedies be exhausted.

Also near the low-cost end of the access spectrum lie formal human rights enforcement systems, including the ECHR, the IACHR, the African Convention on Human and People's Rights, and the UN's International Covenant on Civil and Political Rights. Since the end of World War II we have witnessed a proliferation of international tribunals to which individuals have direct access, though subject to varying restrictions. Even in the ECHR, a relatively successful system, individual access broadened slowly over time. Under the "old ECHR"—the one that existed prior to very recent reforms—individuals could bring cases themselves only if the government being sued had previously accepted an optional clause in the convention recognizing individual petition; otherwise only states could file petitions. This clause was initially accepted by only a few countries and not by all until the 1980s. NGOs and other third parties were excluded; anonymous petitions were not permitted. Any complaint to the system had, moreover, to be reviewed by the European Human Rights Commission before being passed on to the court—assuming that the government had accepted compulsory jurisdiction. Only if the commission decided in favor of referring the case would it finally be heard before the ECHR.

Although this process only rarely constituted an outright barrier to a suit, it could be time consuming. Recent reforms have abolished this intermediate step. The new ECHR, by contrast, gives individuals direct access to the court without any domestic or international intermediary.[16] Even so, however, it continues to require that any individual or group exhaust all national remedies before appealing to the system, typically meaning that litigants must first sue in a lower national tribunal and appeal the resulting judgment up the chain of administrative tribunals and domestic courts. The path to international dispute resolution is thus long, costly, and uncertain, even in this permissive environment; the process can take six to eight years and requires substantial legal expertise.

The Inter-American, UN, and nascent African systems of formal human rights enforcement are in some ways more permissive. As in the new ECHR, individual petition is mandatory. Under the IACHR, other actors have standing to bring suit on behalf of individuals and groups whose rights may be being violated. Indeed, the individuals and groups need not even consent to the suit, and anonymous petitions are permitted. The IACHR Commission has also adopted a very broad and permissive interpretation of what it means to exhaust domestic remedies.[17] Under the African Charter on Human and People's Rights, individuals and states may submit complaints, which will be heard if a majority on a commission so decide. The commission will soon be able to send cases on to the future African Court of Human and People's Rights only if the state against which a claim is being brought has accepted an op-

16. In response to the widespread success of the individual petition mechanism in Europe, the growth of the number of states party to the convention, and an increasing backlog of cases, the Council of Europe had sought to improve upon the existing judicial review machinery. After months of arduous negotiation, a majority of states signed Protocol 11, which, once ratified, will abolish the European Commission on Human Rights and create a permanent European Court of Human Rights. For a discussion of both systems, see Moravcsik 2000.

17. Sands, Mackenzie, and Shany 1999, 233–45.

tional clause. As under the ECHR, domestic remedies must be exhausted. The UN requires individual petitions to trigger a process, though NGOs may be involved in the process. Whereas in the ECHR context, the commission took a relatively permissive attitude toward references to the court, this was not so in the Americas. For many years, the IACHR Commission declined to refer cases to the court—to the point where the court admonished the commission for failing to fulfill its "social duty to consider the advisability of coming to the Court."[18]

Among world courts and tribunals, the Central American Court of Justice, established in 1991 as the principal judicial organ of the Central American Integration System, offers the easiest access. Any state, supranational body, or natural or legal person can bring suit against a state party to assure domestic enforcement of regime norms. In addition, domestic courts can request advisory opinions in a preliminary reference procedure similar to the EC's Article 177.

Legal Embeddedness: Who Controls Formal Implementation?

There is no monopoly on the legitimate use of force in world politics—no world state, police, or army. Therefore, even if authority to render judgments is delegated to an independent international tribunal, implementation of these judgments depends on international or domestic action by the executives, legislatures, and/or judiciaries of states. Implementation and compliance in international disputes are problematic to a far greater degree than they are in well-functioning, domestic rule-of-law systems. The political significance of delegating authority over dispute resolution therefore depends in part on the degree of control exercised by individual governments over the legal promulgation and implementation of judgments. State control is affected by formal legal arrangements along a continuum that we refer to as embeddedness.

The spectrum of domestic embeddedness, summarized in Table 3, runs from strong control over promulgation and implementation of judgments by individual national governments to very weak control. At one extreme, that of strong control, lie systems in which individual litigants can veto the promulgation of a judgment *ex post*. In the old GATT system, the decisions of dispute-resolution panels had to be affirmed by consensus, affording individual litigants an *ex post* veto. Under the less tightly controlled WTO, by contrast, disputes among member governments are resolved through quasi-judicial panels whose judgments are binding unless *reversed* by unanimous vote of the Dispute Settlement Body, which consists of one representative from each WTO member state.

Most international legal systems fall into the same category as the WTO system; namely, states are bound by international law to comply with judgments of international courts or tribunals, but no domestic legal mechanism assures legal implementation. If national executives and legislatures fail to take action because of domestic political opposition or simply inertia, states simply incur a further international legal

---

18. Advisory Opinion OC-5/85, 5 Inter-American Ct. of H.R. (ser. A) (1985), 145, cited in Henkin et al. 1999, 525.

TABLE 3. *The embeddedness continuum: Who enforces the law?*

Level of embeddedness	*Who enforces*	*International court or tribunal*
Low	Individual governments can veto implementation of legal judgment	GATT
Moderate	No veto, but no domestic legal enforcement; most human rights systems	WTO, ICJ
High	International norms enforced by domestic courts	EC, incorporated human rights norms under ECHR, national systems in which treaties are self-executing or given direct effect

obligation to repair the damage. In other words, if an international tribunal rules that state *A* has illegally intervened in state *B*'s internal affairs and orders state *A* to pay damages, but the legislature of state *A* refuses to appropriate the funds, state *B* has no recourse at international law except to seek additional damages. Alternatively, if state *A* signs a treaty obligating it to change its domestic law to reduce the level of certain pollutants it is emitting, and the executive branch is unsuccessful in passing legislation to do so, state *A* is liable to its treaty partners at international law but cannot be compelled to take the action it agreed to take in the treaty.

This is not to say that individuals and groups have no impact on compliance. Interstate bargaining takes place in the shadow of normative sanctions stemming from the international legal obligation itself. Even if governments do not ultimately comply, a negative legal judgment may increase the salience of an issue and undermine the legitimacy of the national position in the eyes of domestic constituents. And it is difficult for recalcitrant governments to get the offending international law changed. Multilateral revision is rendered almost impossible by the requirement of unanimous consent in nearly all international organizations.[19]

At the other end of the spectrum, where the control of individual governments is most constrained by the embeddedness of international norms, lie systems in which autonomous national courts can enforce international judgments against their own governments. The most striking example of this mode of enforcement is the EC legal system. Domestic courts in every member state recognize that EC law is superior to national law (supremacy) and that it grants individuals rights on the basis of which they can litigate (direct effect). When the ECJ issues advisory opinions to national courts under the Article 177 procedure described in detail in Karen Alter's article in this issue, national courts tend to respect them, even when they clash with the precedent set by higher national courts. These provisions are nowhere stated explicitly in the Treaty of Rome but have been successfully "constitutionalized" by the ECJ over

19. The EC, with qualified majority voting, is an exception. But here the unique power of proposal in the legislative process that generates most EC economic regulations is held by the Commission, which is unlikely to propose such a rollback of EC powers. Tsebelis 1994.

the past four decades.[20] The European Free Trade Association (EFTA) court system established in 1994 permits such referrals as well, though, unlike the Treaty of Rome, it neither legally obliges domestic courts to refer nor legally binds the domestic court to apply the result. Domestic courts do nonetheless appear to enforce EFTA court decisions.[21]

International legal norms may also be embedded in domestic legal systems through legal incorporation or constitutional recognition. Although the direct link between domestic and international courts found in the EC is unique among international organizations, in some situations the national government has incorporated or transposed the international document into domestic law subject to the oversight of an autonomous domestic legal system. Many governments have, for example, incorporated the European Convention into domestic law, permitting individuals to enforce its provisions before domestic courts. Despite the lack of a direct link, there is evidence that domestic courts tend to follow the jurisprudence of the ECHR in interpreting the Convention.[22] Even without explicit statutory recognition, some legal systems—such as that of the Netherlands—generally recognize international treaty obligations as equal to or supreme over constitutional provisions. In the United States, the president and federal courts have sometimes invoked international treaty obligations as "self-executing" or "directly applicable" and therefore both binding on the U.S. government and domestic actors and enforceable in domestic courts—though Congress has increasingly sought to employ its control over ratification to limit this practice explicitly.[23]

Two Ideal Types: Interstate and Transnational Dispute Resolution

The three characteristics of international dispute resolution—independence, access, and embeddedness—are closely linked. This is evident from an examination of the extent to which different international legal systems are independent, embedded, and provide access. The characteristics of the major courts in the world today are summarized in Table 4, which reveals a loose correlation across categories. Systems with higher values on one dimension have a greater probability of having higher values in the other dimensions. This finding suggests that very high values on one dimension cannot fully compensate for low values on another. Strong support for independence, access, or embeddedness without strong support for the others undermines the effectiveness of a system.

Combining these three dimensions creates two ideal-types. In one ideal-type—interstate dispute resolution—adjudicators, agenda, and enforcement are all subject

---

20. Weiler 1991.
21. Sands, Mackenzie, and Shany 1999, 148.
22. Drzemczewski 1983.
23. Although customary international law is generally viewed as self-executing in the United States, and therefore can be applied by courts as domestic law, most international treaties do not create private rights of action. U.S. courts, moreover, have been hesitant to enforce customary international law against a superseding act of the federal government. See Henkin 1996; and Jackson 1992.

TABLE 4. *Legal characteristics of international courts and tribunals*

International court or tribunals	Legal characteristics		
	Independence	Access	Embeddedness
ECJ	High	High	High[f]
ECHR, since 1999	High	High	Low to high[c]
ECHR, before 1999	Moderate to high[a]	Low to high[b]	Low to high[c]
IACHR	Moderate to high[a]	High	Moderate
WTO panels	Moderate	Low to moderate[d]	Moderate
ICJ	Moderate	Low to moderate[d]	Moderate
GATT panels	Moderate	Low to moderate[d]	Low
PCA	Low to moderate	Low[e]	Moderate
UN Security Council	Low	Low to moderate[g]	Low

Source: Sands et al. 1999.
[a]Depends on whether government recognizes optional clauses for compulsory jurisdiction of the court.
[b]Depends on whether government accepts optional clause for individual petition.
[c]Depends on whether domestic law incorporates or otherwise recognized the treaty.
[d]Depends on mobilization and domestic access rules for interest groups concerned.
[e]Both parties must consent. Recent rule changes have begun to recognize nonstate actors.
[f]Embeddedness is not a formal attribute of the regime but the result of the successful assertion of legal sovereignty.
[g]Permanent members of the Security Council can veto; nonmembers cannot.

to veto by individual national governments. Individual states decide who judges, what they judge, and how the judgment is enforced. At the other end of the spectrum, adjudicators, agenda, and enforcement are all substantially independent of individual and collective pressure from national governments. We refer to this ideal type as transnational dispute resolution.[24] In this institutional arrangement, of which the EU and ECHR are the most striking examples, judges are insulated from national governments, societal individuals and groups control the agenda, and the results are implemented by an independent national judiciary. In the remainder of this article we discuss the implications of variation along the continuum from interstate to transnational dispute resolution for the nature of, compliance with, and evolution of international jurisprudence.

In discussing this continuum, however, let us not lose sight of the fact that *values on the three dimensions move from high to low at different rates.* Table 4 reveals that high levels of independence and access appear to be more common than high levels

24. We use the term "transnational" to capture the individual to individual or individual to state nature of many of the cases in this type of dispute resolution. However, many of the tribunals in this category, such as the ECJ and the ECHR, can equally be described as "supranational" in the sense that they sit "above" the nation-state and have direct power over individuals and groups within the state. One of the authors has previously used the label "supranational" to describe these tribunals (Helfer and Slaughter 1997); no significance should be attached to the shift in terminology here.

of embeddedness, and, though the relationship is weaker, a high level of independence appears to be slightly more common than a high level of access. In other words, between those tribunals that score high or low on all three dimensions, there is a significant intermediate range comprising tribunals with high scores on independence and/or access but not on the others.[25] Among those international legal institutions that score high on independence and access but are not deeply embedded in domestic legal systems are some international human rights institutions. Among those institutions that score high on independence but not on access or embeddedness are GATT/WTO multilateral trade institutions and the ICJ.

The Politics of Litigation and Compliance: From Interstate to Judicial Politics

Declaring a process "legalized" does not abolish politics. Decisions about the degree of authority of a particular tribunal, and access to it, are themselves sites of political struggle. The sharpest struggles are likely to arise *ex ante* in the bargaining over a tribunal's establishment; but other opportunities for political intervention may emerge during the life of a tribunal, perhaps as a result of its own constitutional provisions. Form matters, however. The characteristic politics of litigation and compliance are very different under transnational dispute resolution than under interstate dispute resolution. In this section we explicate these differences and propose some tentative conjectures linking our three explanatory variables to the politics of dispute resolution.

The Interstate and Transnational Politics of Judicial Independence

What are the politics of judicial independence? As legal systems move from interstate dispute resolution toward the more independent judicial selection processes of transnational dispute resolution, we expect to observe greater judicial autonomy—defined as the willingness and ability to decide disputes against national governments. Other things being equal, the fewer opportunities national governments have to influence the selection of judges, the available information, the support or financing of the court, and the precise legal terms on which the court can decide, the weaker is their likely influence over the decisions of an international tribunal.

Political interference is common in some domestic political systems. The secretary general of the Arab Lawyers Union has described routine "intervention with the judiciary through higher decisions" and by appointment of military and special courts in much of the Arab world.[26] Judges in Central and South America have been subjected to threats and assassinations. Even in domestic systems with strong courts, political selection of judges can affect decisions. And in the United States, where federal judges serve for life, the openly politicized nature of Supreme Court appoint-

---

25. Not surprisingly, domestic legal embeddedness is less common than widespread domestic access, since the former is a prerequisite for the latter.
26. Eissa 1998.

ments is said to induce many aspiring lower federal judges to alter their decisions in anticipation of possible confirmation hearings before the Senate. The Italian and German Constitutional Courts are even more overtly politically balanced.[27] Perhaps the most infamous example of interference with the composition of a sitting court is President Franklin D. Roosevelt's effort in 1937 to "pack" the Supreme Court with additional justices of his choice. Instead, "a switch in time saved nine," as key justices suddenly changed their tune and found delegation to the plethora of new administrative agencies constitutional. In the context of de facto single-party rule in Japan, Mark Ramseyer and Frances Rosenbluth have documented the significant impact of decisions on the career trajectory of domestic judges, permitting the inference that selection processes affected judicial decisions.[28]

Evidence of government efforts to influence an international tribunal's direction through judicial selection is anecdotal. Rarely is the attempt at influence as crude as the case in September 1984, when a Swedish member of the Iran–U.S. Tribunal was assaulted by two younger and stronger Iranian judges.[29] Influence is typically more subtle. It was widely rumored, for instance, that the German government sought to rein in the ECJ by appointing a much less activist judge in the 1980s than previous German candidates, but hard evidence is virtually impossible to find. One leading ECJ judge, a long-time skeptic of the notion that the ECJ could be politicized in this way, nevertheless noted in the mid-1990s that "Things have changed. It is now 8–7 for us [that is, the supranationalists]."[30]

Restrictions on the financial resources available to tribunals may limit their independence. Such limitations have hampered efforts to transform the African Convention on Human and People's Rights into a system as effective as those found in Europe and, recently, the Americas.[31] Similarly, it has been argued that the members of the UN Security Council authorized the creation of the International Criminal Tribunal for the Former Yugoslavia to satisfy public opinion but tried to deny it sufficient resources to do its work.[32] If this strategy failed, it may have been in part because resources were ultimately provided from private sources such as foundations and wealthy individuals.[33] On the other hand, a striking difference between the ECJ and ECHR, as well as bodies such as the UN Human Rights Committee, is the relative distribution of resources, without which even an active court cannot process its caseload and make itself heard to a wider audience. Other drags include excessively cumbersome procedural rules, often designed to frustrate all but the most

27. Weiler 1998. Selection of a judge of an identifiable political stripe does not always guarantee corresponding decisions, however. Once on the bench, judges are subject to a specific set of professional norms and duties and develop their personal conception of the role they have been asked to fill in ways that can yield surprises. A paradigmatic case is President Eisenhower's appointment of Justice William Brennan, who gave little sign of the strong liberal standard-bearer he would become.

28. Ramseyer and Rosenbluth 1997.

29. Feldman 1986, 1004.

30. Lecture by Federico Mancini, Public Representation: A Democratic Deficit? Conference at Harvard University, Center for European Studies, 29–31 January 1993.

31. Welch 1992.

32. Forsythe 1994.

33. See Bass 1998; and Bassiouni 1998.

persistent individual litigants, and limits on judicial capacities, such as a court's autonomous ability to find the facts in a particular case rather than having to depend solely on the representations of litigants. Where one of the litigants is a government, the court is likely to find itself unable to challenge the government's version of events without the independent ability to call witnesses or even conduct inspections.[34]

Such potential restrictions on autonomy—along with the threat of noncompliance or treaty revision—may increase judicial solicitude for state interests. We shall return to this question in our later discussion of long-term dynamism. Broadly, however, this discussion suggests the following conjecture: The more formally independent a court, the more likely are judicial decisions to challenge national policies.

The Interstate and Transnational Politics of Access

What are the political implications of movement from low access (interstate dispute resolution) to high access (transnational dispute resolution)? Our central contention is that we are likely to observe, broadly speaking, a different politics of access as we move toward transnational dispute resolution—where individuals, groups, and courts can appeal or refer cases to international tribunals. As the actors involved become more diverse, the likelihood that cases will be referred increases, as does the likelihood that such cases will challenge national governments—in particular, the national government of the plaintiff. The link between formal access and real political power is not obvious. States might still manipulate access to judicial process regarding both interstate and transnational litigation by establishing stringent procedural rules, bringing political pressure to bear on potential or actual litigants, or simply carving out self-serving exceptions to the agreed jurisdictional scheme. Consider the evidence.

Access to classic arbitral tribunals, such as those constituted under the Permanent Court of Arbitration, requires the consent of both states. With regard to access, the Permanent Court of Arbitration is as close as we come to a pure system of interstate dispute resolution. Slightly more constraining arrangements are found in classic interstate litigation before the Permanent Court of International Justice in the 1920s and 1930s, the ICJ since 1945, and the short-lived Central American Court of Justice. In these systems, a single state decides when and how to sue, even if it is suing on behalf of an injured citizen or group of citizens. The state formally "espouses" the claim of its national(s), at which point the individual's rights terminate (unless entitled to compensation as a domestic legal or constitutional matter), as does any control over or even say in the litigation strategy. The government is thus free to prosecute the claim vigorously or not at all, or to engage in settlement negotiations for a sum far less than the individual litigant(s) might have found acceptable. Such negotiations can resemble institutionalized interstate bargaining more than a classic legal process in which the plaintiff decides whether to continue the legal struggle or to settle the case.

34. Helfer and Slaughter 1997.

Under interstate dispute resolution, political calculations inevitably enter into the decision to sue. For instance, in 1996 the United States adopted the Helms-Burton legislation, which punishes firms for doing business with Cuba. Although the EU claimed that this legislation violated WTO rules and threatened to take the case to the WTO, in the end it failed to do so: an agreement was reached essentially on U.S. terms. The forms of legalization do not, therefore, guarantee that authoritative decisions will be honored by third parties. Hence even among formally highly legalized processes, the degree of operational authority of the third-party decision makers may vary considerably. More systematic evidence comes from the EU, where governments tend to be reluctant to sue one another, preferring instead to bring their complaints to the EU Commission. The Commission, in turn, was initially—and to an extent, remains—reluctant to sue member states, due to its fear of retaliation and need to establish its own political legitimacy.[35]

Although in interstate dispute resolution states decide when and whether to sue other states, they cannot necessarily control whether they are sued. If they are sued, whether any resulting judgments can be enforced depends both on their acceptance of compulsory jurisdiction and, where the costs of complying with a judgment are high, on their willingness to obey an adverse ruling. U.S. relations with the ICJ provide an example. After pushing for the creation of the ICJ as part of the UN Charter, the United States promptly accepted the compulsory jurisdiction of the ICJ by Senate resolution.[36] The same resolution, however, included the Connally reservation, providing that U.S. acceptance "shall not apply to . . . disputes with regard to matters which are essentially within the domestic jurisdiction of the United States as determined by the United States."[37] In other words, the Senate insisted that the United States remain judge in its own case as to whether disputes were sufficiently "international" to go to the court.

To be sure, the Connally reservation has always been controversial in the United States, and the State Department has resisted invoking it when the United States has been called before the ICJ. Yet control of access does not stop there. In 1984, when the ICJ appeared to take Nicaragua's complaints against the United States seriously, the United States revoked its agreement to the ICJ's compulsory jurisdiction. The United States deposited with the secretariat of the UN a notification purporting to exclude, with immediate effect, from its acceptance of the court's compulsory jurisdiction "disputes with any Central American state" for two years.[38] It litigated the first round of the case, arguing that its revocation of jurisdiction was effective, but then simply failed to appear in the second round after the court ruled that it did indeed have jurisdiction.[39]

This sort of flagrant defiance is rarely necessary. The de facto system is one in which most states, like the United States, reserve the right to bring specific cases to

---

35. See Alter 1998b; Stein 1981; and Dashwood and White 1989.
36. S. Res. 196, 79th Cong., 2d sess., 92 *Cong. Rec.* 10706 (1946).
37. Ibid.
38. Briggs 1985, 377.
39. Schwebel 1996.

the ICJ or to be sued in specific cases as the result of an ad hoc agreement with other parties to a dispute of specific provisions in a bilateral or multilateral treaty. This system ensures direct control over access to the ICJ by either requiring all the parties to a dispute to agree both to third-party intervention and to choose the ICJ as the third party, or by allowing two or more states to craft a specific submission to the court's jurisdiction in a limited category of disputes arising from the specific subject matter of a treaty.[40] In the ICJ, procedural provisions govern time limits requiring a state to accept a tribunal's jurisdiction before a particular suit arises, time limits for filing the suit itself, the reciprocal nature of the opposing parties' acceptance of jurisdiction, and rules governing intervention by a third state whose interests may be directly affected by disposition of an ongoing suit.[41] Such procedural provisions are key weapons in the litigator's arsenal, with the result that many interstate cases, like suits between individuals, stalemate for years in procedural maneuvering. Some such provisions are promulgated by tribunals themselves, but the majority are bargained out *ex ante* among states contemplating submission to third-party dispute resolution.

More informally, potential defendants may exert political pressure on plaintiff states not to sue or to drop a suit once it has begun. When confronted by an unfavorable GATT panel judgment (in favor of Mexico) concerning U.S. legislation to protect dolphins from tuna fishing, the United States exercised its extra-institutional power to induce Mexico to drop the case before the judgment could be enforced. Another more subtle example concerns the U.S.–Nicaraguan dispute referred to earlier. Although the United States refused to participate in proceedings on the merits of the case, the ICJ ruled on 27 June 1986 that the United States' mining of Nicaraguan harbors violated provisions of customary international law, which were similar to, and should be interpreted in light of, the UN Charter.[42] The United States refused to comply with the decision, and on 27 October 1986 it vetoed a Security Council resolution, which received eleven affirmative votes, calling for it to comply with the ICJ ruling.[43] Nicaragua asked for more than $2 billion in damages, but with the electoral defeat of the Sandinistas, it requested postponement of further proceedings. In 1990 the United States asked the Nicaraguan government of President Violeta Barrios de Chamorro to abandon its claim; it was reported that the Bush administration told Nicaragua that future U.S. aid would depend on such abandonment.[44]

The preceding discussion of access suggests two conjectures:

1. The broader and less costly the access to an international court or tribunal, the greater the number of cases it will receive.

2. The broader and less expensive the access to an international court or tribunal, the more likely that complaints challenge the domestic practices of national governments—particularly the home government of the complainant.

40. Rosenne 1995.
41. Ibid.
42. ICJ, *Military and Paramilitary Activities in and Against Nicaragua.* (Nicaragua v. United States of America.) Merits, Judgment. ICJ Reports 1986, 97–99.
43. See *New York Times*, 29 October 1986, A3.
44. *See New York Times*, 30 September 1990.

TABLE 5. *Access rules and dockets of international courts and tribunals*

Level of access	International court or tribunal	Average annual number of cases since founding
Low	PCA	0.3
Medium	ICJ	1.7
	GATT	4.4
	WTO	30.5
High	Old ECHR	23.9
	EC	100.1

Source: Sands et al. 1999, 4, 24, 72, 125, 200.

We cannot thoroughly evaluate these conjectures here, but a preliminary analysis suggests their plausibility. Consider, for example, the size of an international tribunal's docket. Broadly speaking, the greater the formal access, the greater the caseload we should expect to observe. Courts cannot work without cases. They are quite literally out of business and without even a toehold to begin building their reputations and developing constituencies that will give them voice and at least a measure of independent power. Thus, for instance, if the access rules of the ECJ only gave states and the Commission the right to sue, the ECJ would—like the ICJ—probably have adjudicated relatively few cases and would play a role on the margins of European politics. The vast majority of significant cases in the history of the EU have been brought under Article 177 by individuals who request (or hope) that national courts will send them to the ECJ for adjudication. Another highly developed example is found in international human rights courts. The optional clause of the ECHR, Article 10, permitting individuals to bring complaints, has been the source of nearly all complaints before the Commission and the ECJ. Interstate complaints have been few in number, less than fifteen (all but a few involving state interest in co-nationals in other countries), compared with thousands of individual complaints.[45] The IACHR functions in a similar manner.

The comparative data summarized in Table 5 further support this conjecture. The average caseload of six prominent international courts varies as predicted, with legal systems granting low access generating the fewest number of average cases, those granting high access generating the highest number of cases, and those granting moderate access in between. The difference between categories is roughly an order of magnitude or more. While we should be cautious about imputing causality before more extensive controlled studies are performed, the data suggest the existence of a strong relationship.

Case study evidence supports the conjecture that transnational dispute-resolution systems with high levels of access tend to result in cases being brought in national

45. Moravcsik 1995.

courts against the *home* government. This is the standard method by which cases reach the ECJ. For example, the *Cassis de Dijon* case—a classic ECJ decision in 1979 establishing the principle of mutual recognition of national regulations—concerned the right to export a French liquor to Germany, yet a German importer, not the French producer, sued the German government, charging that domestic regulations on liquor purity were creating unjustified barriers to interstate trade.[46]

The Interstate and Transnational Politics of Embeddedness

Even if cases are brought before tribunals and these tribunals render judgments against states, the extent to which judgments are legally enforceable may differ. We have seen that most international legal systems create a legal obligation for governments to comply but leave enforcement to interstate bargaining. Only a few legal systems empower individuals and groups to seek enforcement of their provisions in domestic courts. However, in our ideal type of transnational dispute resolution, international commitments are embedded in domestic legal systems, meaning that governments, particularly national executives, no longer need to take positive action to ensure enforcement of international judgments. Instead, enforcement occurs directly through domestic courts and executive agents who are responsive to judicial decisions. The politics of embedded systems of dispute resolution are very different from the politics of systems that are not embedded in domestic politics.

Under interstate dispute resolution, external pressure for compliance stems ultimately from the power and interests of national governments of participating states, which back demands with threats of reciprocal denial or punishment. Reciprocity and retaliation are often effective means of enforcement, at least for powerful states whose interests are engaged. As Judith Goldstein and Lisa Martin point out in their article in this issue, governments have made little use of the escape clause in GATT, arguably because doing so would have required providing compensation at the expense of other industrial sectors. That is, reciprocity on the international level implies that gains from reneging on a given arrangement will have to be balanced by losses to some other sector; and the political protests from that sector are likely to be shrill. Using the concept of "compliance constituencies" articulated by Miles Kahler in his conclusion to this issue, it is important to recognize that even if international law is not embedded in domestic legal processes, past agreements, linked to reciprocity, may create strong political pressures for compliance. If domestic "compliance constituencies" are the key to enforcement, we should expect to see more domestic pressure for compliance in trade regimes, where concentrated, mobilized constituencies like exporters and importers tend to press for compliance with tariff liberalization. Goldstein and Martin find evidence for such pressures for compliance.

Yet despite the real successes, in some circumstances, of interstate dispute resolution, it clearly has political limitations, especially where compliance constituencies

---

46. Case 120/78, *Rewe-Zentrale AG v. Bundesmonopolverwaltung fur Branntwein* (Cassis de Dijon), 1978.

are weak. Under interstate dispute resolution, pressures for compliance have to operate through governments. The limitations of such practices are clear under arbitration, and notably with respect to the ICJ. In the case involving mining of Nicaragua's harbors, the United States did not obey the ICJ's judgment. Admittedly, the Reagan administration did not simply ignore the ICJ judgment with respect to the mining of Nicaragua's harbors, but felt obliged to withdraw its recognition of the ICJ's jurisdiction—a controversial act with significant domestic political costs for a Republican president facing a Democratic Congress. Nevertheless, in the end the United States pursued a policy contrary to the ICJ's decision. Even in trade regimes, political pressure sometimes leads to politically bargained settlements, as in the case of the U.S. Helms-Burton legislation. And a number of countries have imposed unilateral limits on the ICJ's jurisdiction.

More broadly, reciprocity does not work well when interdependence and power are highly asymmetric. Under these circumstances, reciprocal denials of policy concessions may have much more severe consequences for the more dependent party. Furthermore, powerful governments may threaten weaker targets not only with reciprocal denial of policy concessions but also with further retaliation in linked areas. The United States has, for example, used unilateral threats of sanctions under Section 301 and with respect to antidumping and countervailing duty statutes. It has also threatened numerous governments with economic and military sanctions in an effort to compel compliance with international human rights norms. Overall, interstate dispute resolution presents many opportunities for powerful states to set the agenda for a legal process, to introduce political bargaining into decision making, and to thwart implementation of adverse legal decisions.

The politics of transnational dispute resolution are quite different. By linking direct access for domestic actors to domestic legal enforcement, transnational dispute resolution opens up an additional source of political pressure for compliance, namely favorable judgments in domestic courts. This creates a new set of political imperatives. It gives international tribunals additional means to pressure or influence domestic government institutions in ways that enhance the likelihood of compliance with their judgments. It pits a recalcitrant government not simply against other governments but also against legally legitimate domestic opposition; an executive determined to violate international law must override his or her own legal system. Moreover, it thereby permits international tribunals to develop a constituency of litigants who can later pressure government institutions to comply with the international tribunal's decision.[47] Consider the language of the ECJ in its landmark 1963 decision announcing that selected provisions of the Treaty of Rome would be directly effective as rules governing individuals in national law: "The Community constitutes a new legal order . . . for the benefit of which the states have limited their sovereign rights . . . and the subjects of which comprise not only Member States but also their nationals. Independently of the legislation of the Member States, Community law therefore imposes obligations on individuals but is also intended to confer on them

47. Helfer and Slaughter 1997.

rights which become part of their legal heritage."[48] The primary individuals and groups the ECJ had in mind were importers and exporters, many of whom came to understand that they had a direct interest in helping the court hold governments to their word on scheduled tariff reductions. Individuals and groups also have incentives to bring cases in other substantive contexts, including human rights and environmental law.[49]

The politics of compliance under transnational dispute resolution tends to give courts more leverage than they enjoy under interstate dispute resolution. The result is an environment in which judicial politics (the interplay of interests, ideas, and values among judges) and intrajudicial politics (the politics of competition or cooperation among courts) are increasingly important. Judicial politics are subject to a wide range of constraints that may or may not intersect with state interests—for example, the exigencies of legal reasoning, which Thomas Franck has distilled as the legitimacy-based demands of consistency, coherence, and adherence,[50] not to mention simple logic; the texts and case law available to shape a particular decision; and the political preferences and judicial ideology of individual judges.[51] More broadly, however, the relationships between international and national courts are central to the politics of transnational dispute resolution. In the words of Joseph Weiler, "The relationship between the European Court and national courts is the most crucial element for a successful functioning of the European legal order."[52]

Transnational dispute resolution does not sweep aside traditional interstate politics, but the power of national governments has to be filtered through norms of judicial professionalism, public opinion supporting particular conceptions of the rule of law, and an enduring tension between calculations of short- and long-term interests. Individuals and groups can zero in on international court decisions as focal points around which to mobilize, creating a further intersection between transnational litigation and democratic politics.

This discussion of the politics of interstate and transnational dispute resolution suggests that the following two conjectures deserve more intensive study.

1. Other things being equal, the more firmly embedded an international commitment is in domestic law, the more likely is compliance with judgments to enforce it.

2. Liberal democracies are particularly respectful of the rule of law and most open to individual access to judicial systems; hence attempts to embed international law in domestic legal systems should be most effective among such

---

48. Case 26/62, *N. V. Algemene Transp. and Expeditie Onderneming Van Gend and Loos v. Nederslandse administratie der belastingen,* 1963 E.C.R. 1, 12.

49. This dynamic is not limited to Europe. David Wirth explains it succinctly in his analysis of compulsory third-party dispute resolution as a mechanism for enforcing international environmental law. Wirth 1994.

50. Franck 1990.

51. Mattli and Slaughter 1995.

52. Weiler 1998, 22. The ECHR has experienced considerable variation in its effectiveness, which does not seem on its face to be well explained by embeddedness. With respect to the ECHR, we believe that more research is needed to evaluate explanations that rely on embeddedness.

regimes. In relations involving nondemocracies, we should observe near total reliance on interstate dispute resolution. Even among liberal democracies, the trust placed in transnational dispute resolution may vary with the political independence of the domestic judiciary.

Although embedding international commitments does not guarantee increased compliance, we find good reason to conclude that embeddedness probably tends to make compliance more likely in the absence of a strong political counteraction. However, as Goldstein and Martin argue in this issue, by removing loopholes, legalization also takes away "safety valves" that can reduce political pressure for drastic changes in rules. As they argue with respect to the WTO, "moving too far in the direction of legalization could backfire, undermining the momentum toward liberalization that the weakly legalized procedures of GATT so effectively established." To be genuinely successful, international law needs to rest on a strong basis of collective political purpose and shared standards of legitimacy: where these conditions exist (as in the EU), embedding international law in domestic legal processes is more promising than when they are absent.

The Interstate and Transnational Dynamics of Legalization

We have considered the static politics of legalization. Yet institutions also change over time and develop distinctive dynamics. Rules are elaborated. The costs of veto, withdrawal, or exclusion from the "inner club" of an institution may increase if the benefits provided by institutionalized cooperation increase. Sunk costs create incentives to maintain existing practices rather than to begin new ones. Politicians' short time horizons can induce them to agree to institutional practices that they might not prefer in the long term, in order to gain advantages at the moment.[53]

What distinguishes legalized regimes is their potential for setting in motion a distinctive dynamic built on precedent, in which decisions on a small number of specific disputes create law that may govern by analogy a vast array of future practices. This may be true even when the first litigants in a given area do not gain satisfaction. Judges may adopt modes of reasoning that assure individual litigants that their arguments have been heard and responded to, even if they have not won the day in a particular case. Some legal scholars argue that this "casuistic" style helps urge litigants, whether states or individuals, to fight another day.[54]

Although both interstate and transnational dispute resolution have the potential to generate such a legal evolution, we maintain that transnational dispute resolution increases the potential for such dynamics of precedent. The greater independence of judges, wider access of litigants, and greater potential for legal compliance insulates judges, thereby allowing them to develop legal precedent over time without trigger-

---

53. See Keohane and Hoffmann 1991; Alter 1998a; and Pollack 1997.
54. See White 1990; Glendon 1991; and Sunstein 1996.

ing noncompliance, withdrawal, or reform by national governments. We next consider in more detail the specific reasons why.

The Dynamics of Interstate Third-party Dispute Resolution

In interstate legal systems, the potential for self-generating spillover depends on how states perform their gatekeeping roles. As we will show, where states open the gates, the results of interstate dispute resolution may to some degree resemble the results of transnational dispute resolution. However, in the two major international judicial or quasi-judicial tribunals—the Permanent Court of Arbitration and the ICJ—states have been relatively reluctant to bring cases. The great majority of arbitration cases brought before the Permanent Court of Arbitration were heard in the court's early years, shortly after the first case in 1902. The court has seen little use recently—the Iran Claims Tribunal being an isolated if notable exception.

States have been reluctant to submit to the ICJ's jurisdiction when the stakes are large.[55] Hence the ICJ has been constrained in developing a large and binding jurisprudence. Even so, it has triggered overt and effective national opposition. Before the United States revoked compulsory jurisdiction in advance of the Nicaragua case, France had previously revoked its acceptance of the ICJ's compulsory jurisdiction in response to suits brought against it by Australia and New Zealand concerning its nuclear testing in the South Pacific in the 1960s.[56] Since the USSR and China had never accepted compulsory jurisdiction, Great Britain stood alone by late 1985 as the only permanent member of the UN Security Council willing to expose itself to the risk of being brought before the ICJ on an open-ended basis. What has emerged in the ICJ is essentially a system of discretionary submission to its jurisdiction, allowing states to control access case by case. In 1945 75 percent of all states that had ratified the Statute of the Permanent Court of International Justice also accepted the ICJ's compulsory jurisdiction; as of 1995 only 31 percent of states party to statute accept compulsory jurisdiction.[57] As measured by the level of legal obligation, legalization in the ICJ has moved *backwards* over the last half-century.

Still, it is fair to note that use of the ICJ did increase substantially between the 1960s and 1990s, reaching an all-time high of nineteen cases on the docket in 1999.[58] Although this increase does not equal the exponential growth of economic and human rights jurisprudence in this period, it marks a significant shift. In part this reflects pockets of success that have resulted in expansion of both the law in a particular area and the resort to it. The ICJ has consistently had a fairly steady stream of cases concerning international boundary disputes. In these cases the litigants have typically already resorted to military conflict that has resulted in stalemate or determined that such conflict would be too costly. They thus agree to go to court. The ICJ,

55. Chayes 1965.
56. Rosenne 1995, 270 n. 17. See also *Nuclear Tests (Australia v. France)*, 1974 I.C.J. 253 (20 December); and *Nuclear Tests (New Zealand v. France)*, 1974 I.C.J. 457 (20 December).
57. Schwebel 1996.
58. Ibid.

in turn, has profited from this willingness by developing an extensive body of case law that countries and their lawyers can use to assess the strength of the case on both sides and be assured of a resolution based on generally accepted legal principles.[59]

Another factor in the expansion of the ICJ's caseload over the past two decades may have been the court's willingness to find against the United States in the Nicaragua case, thereby enhancing its legitimacy with developing countries.[60] At the same time, it has received a number of very high profile cases that seem likely to have been filed in the hope of publicizing a particular political dispute as much as securing an actual resolution. Examples include the suit brought by the United States against Iran over the 1979 taking of diplomatic hostages, Iran's suit against the United States for the destruction of oil platforms in the Persian Gulf, two suits brought by Libya against the United States and Great Britain arising out of the Lockerbie air disaster, and Bosnia's suit against Yugoslavia for the promotion of genocide. Although such cases are vigorously litigated by teams of distinguished international lawyers on both sides, the likelihood of compliance by the losing state seems dubious.

The ambiguous, even paradoxical consequences of the Nicaragua case suggest that the interaction between dispute resolution mechanisms and substantive agreement over time is complex. Not only does the nature of substantive agreement influence the probable development of legal systems over time, as we have seen, but the nature of legalization may influence the nature of substantive cooperation. In some cases legalization may even lead to more contention and conflict over the nature of the rules. This is an area where more research would be welcome.

The Dynamics of Transnational Dispute Resolution

The key to the dynamics of transnational dispute resolution is access. Transnational dispute resolution removes the ability of states to perform gatekeeping functions, both in limiting access to tribunals and in blocking implementation of their decisions. Its incentives for domestic actors to mobilize, and to increase the legitimacy of their claims, gives it a capacity for endogenous expansion. As we will see with respect to GATT and the WTO, even a formally interstate process may display similar expansionary tendencies, but continued expansion under interstate dispute resolution depends on continuing decisions by states to keep access to the dispute settlement process open. Switching to a set of formal rules nearer the ideal type of transnational dispute resolution makes it much harder for states to constrain tribunals and can give such tribunals both incentives and instruments to expand their authority by expanding their caseload. Indeed, tribunals can sometimes continue to strengthen their authority even when opposed by powerful states—particularly when the institutional status quo is favorable to tribunals and no coalition of dissatisfied states is capable of overturning the status quo.[61]

59. See, for example, Charney 1994.
60. Schwebel 1996.
61. See Alter 1998a; and Alter, this issue.

The pool of potential individual litigants is several orders of magnitude larger than that of state litigants. Independent courts have every incentive to recruit from that pool. Cases breed cases. A steady flow of cases, in turn, allows a court to become an actor on the legal and political stage, raising its profile in the elementary sense that other potential litigants become aware of its existence and in the deeper sense that its interpretation and application of a particular legal rule must be reckoned with as a part of what the law means in practice. Litigants who are likely to benefit from that interpretation will have an incentive to bring additional cases to clarify and enforce it. Further, the interpretation or application is itself likely to raise additional questions that can only be answered through subsequent cases. Finally, a court gains political capital from a growing caseload by demonstrably performing a needed function.

Transnational tribunals have the means at their disposal to target individual litigants in various ways. The most important advantage they have is the nature of the body of law they administer. Transnational litigation, whether deliberately established by states (as in the case of the ECHR) or adapted and expanded by a supranational tribunal itself (as in the case of the ECJ), only makes sense when interstate rules have dimensions that make them directly applicable to individual activity. Thus, in announcing the direct effect doctrine in *Van Gend and Loos*, the ECJ was careful to specify that only those portions of the Treaty of Rome that were formulated as clear and specific prohibitions on or mandates of member states' conduct could be regarded as directly applicable.[62] Human rights law is by definition applicable to individuals in relations with state authorities, although actual applicability will also depend on the clarity and specificity of individual human rights prohibitions and guarantees.

In this way, a transnational tribunal can present itself in its decisions as a protector of individual rights and benefits against the state, where the state itself has consented to these rights and benefits and the tribunal is simply holding it to its word. This is the clear thrust of the passage from *Van Gend and Loos* quoted earlier, in which the ECJ announced that "Community law . . . imposes obligations on individuals but is also intended to confer on them rights that become part of their legal heritage." The ECHR, for its part, has developed the "doctrine of effectiveness," which requires that the provisions of the European Human Rights Convention be interpreted and applied so as to make its safeguards "practical and effective" rather than "theoretical or illusory"[63] Indeed, one of its judges has described the ECHR in a dissenting opinion as the "last resort protector of oppressed individuals."[64] Such rhetoric is backed up by a willingness to find for the individual against the state.[65]

Ready access to a tribunal can create a virtuous circle: a steady stream of cases results in a stream of decisions that serve to raise the profile of the court and hence to

---

62. Case 26/62, *N. V. Algemene Transp. and Expeditie Onderneming Van Gend and Loos v. Nederslandse administratie der belastingen.* 1963 E.C.R. 1, 12.
63. Bernhardt 1994.
64. *Cossey v. United Kingdom,* 184 E.C.H.R., ser. A (1990).
65. Helfer and Slaughter 1997.

attract more cases. When the ECJ rules, the decision is implemented not by national governments—the recalcitrant defendants—but by national courts. Any subsequent domestic opposition is rendered far more difficult. In sum, transnational third-party dispute resolution has led to a de facto alliance between certain national courts, certain types of individual litigants, and the ECJ. This alliance has been the mechanism by which the supremacy and direct effect of EC law, as well as thousands of specific substantive questions, have been established as cornerstones of the European legal order.[66]

The significance of the alliance between domestic and supranational courts lies in part in the fact that it was an unintended consequence of European integration. There is no doubt it was unforeseen by the member states; Article 177 was an incidental provision suggested by a low-level German customs official in the Treaty of Rome negotiations. However welcome the functional benefits of ECJ jurisprudence may subsequently have been—and the fact that in recent years member states have deliberately strengthened the enforcement power of the ECJ while limiting its jurisdiction suggests that they were—the founding members of the EC intended to create something much closer to a classical interstate dispute-resolution system. Individual member states often opposed the efforts of the ECJ to transform the institutions set forth in the treaty into a functioning transnational dispute-resolution system. Nothing similar exists in the annals of interstate dispute-resolution bodies.

The assertion of the importance of the ECJ in this process—in particular, the assertion of the supremacy of European law and its direct effect in domestic legal systems—was not automatic. International tribunals with transnational jurisdiction deliberately exploit this link to deepen domestic enforcement. The role of the ECJ in encouraging the cooperation of national courts has been amply documented.[67] A new generation of scholarship has focused much more on the motives driving the national courts to ally themselves with the ECJ, noting substantial variation in the willingness both of different courts within the same country and of courts in different countries to send references to the ECJ and to abide by the resulting judgments. What is most striking about these findings is the extent to which specific national courts acted independently not only of other national courts but also of the executive and legislative branches of their respective governments.[68] A German lower financial court, for example, insisted on following an ECJ judgment in the face of strong opposition from a higher financial court as well as from the German government.[69] The French

66. See Burley and Mattli 1993; and Weiler 1991 and 1999.
67. See Stein 1981; Weiler 1991; and Burley and Mattli 1993.
68. This conclusion is not uncontroversial. Some political scientists argue that these national courts were in fact following the wishes of their respective governments, notwithstanding their governments' expressed opposition before the ECJ. The claim is that all EC member states agreed to economic integration as being in their best interests in 1959. They understood, however, that they needed a mechanism to bind one another to the obligations undertaken in the original treaty. They thus established a court to hold each state to its respective word. See Garrett 1992; Garrett and Weingast 1993; and Garrett, Kelemen, and Schulz 1998. On this view, intrajudicial politics within the EU were either anticipated by the founding states or were epiphenomenal. For a debate on precisely this point, see Garrett 1995; and Mattli and Slaughter 1995.
69. Alter 1996b.

Court of Cassation accepted the supremacy of EC law, following the dictate of the ECJ, even in the face of threats from the French legislature to strip its jurisdiction amid age-old charges of *"gouvernment par juges."*[70] British courts overturned the sacrosanct doctrine of parliamentary sovereignty and issued an injunction blocking the effect of a British law pending judicial review at the European level.[71]

The motives of these national courts are multiple. They include a desire for "empowerment,"[72] competition with other courts for relative prestige and power,[73] a particular view of the law that could be achieved by following EC precedents over national precedents,[74] recognition of the greater expertise of the ECJ in European law,[75] and the desire to advantage or at least not to disadvantage a particular constituency of litigants.[76] Similar dynamics of intracourt competition may be observed in relations between national courts and the ECHR.[77] National courts appear to have been more willing to challenge the perceived interests of other domestic authorities once the first steps had been taken by other national courts. Weiler has documented the cross-citation of foreign supreme court decisions by national supreme courts accepting the supremacy of EC law for the first time. He notes that though they may have been reluctant to restrict national autonomy in a way that would disadvantage their states relative to other states, they are more willing to impose such restrictions when they are "satisfied that they are part of a trend." An alternative explanation of this trend might be ideational; courts feel such a step is more legitimate.[78]

The incentives for expansion of a transnational docket also assume a certain familiarity and comfort with litigation as a means of dispute resolution among the potential pool of litigants. Litigants in countries with a tradition of "public interest litigation," for instance, whereby NGOs use the courts to vindicate the rights of particular minorities or otherwise disadvantaged social groups, may readily see a transnational tribunal as another weapon in their arsenal.[79] More fundamentally, litigants in any country must perceive some use in resorting to the courts at all, suggesting a correlation between the most successful transnational tribunals and those presiding over countries with at least a minimum tradition of the rule of law. Alternatively, litigants in countries with a once-functioning legal system that has been corrupted or otherwise damaged may be quicker to resort to an international tribunal as a substitute or corrective for ineffective or blatantly politicized domestic adjudication.[80]

Yet even within the EU legal system, the most studied of all transnational litigation processes, we still know "surprisingly little about the behavior and organization of

---

70. See Alter 1996b; and Plötner 1998.
71. Craig 1998.
72. See Weiler 1991; and Burley and Mattli 1993.
73. Alter 1996b, and 1998a,b.
74. Mattli and Slaughter 1998b.
75. Craig 1998.
76. Plötner 1998.
77. Jarmul 1996.
78. See Weiler 1994; and Finnemore and Sikkink 1998.
79. See Harlow and Rawlings 1992; and Alter and Vargas 2000.
80. See Helfer and Slaughter 1997; and Stone Sweet 1999.

litigators of EC law, and nothing from a comparative perspective [across EU countries]."[81] Even within apparently dynamic and expansive jurisdictions, the process is not unidirectional, varying considerably across different national courts, different issue-areas in the same court, and across countries.[82] Direct institutional links between individual litigants and an international tribunal create an internal logic of legalization that can become a powerful catalyst for growth, yet more research is required to explain precisely how this decisively important evolution unfolds.

The evolution of the ECHR has been less purely legal. In the ECHR system, as we have seen, litigants have been encouraged over time by the publicity accorded ECHR judgments and the growing willingness of national legislatures and administrative entities, as well as courts, to comply, rather than by a direct legal link on the model of Article 177 of the Treaty of Rome. The clauses in the European Human Rights Convention allowing individuals to bring cases before the Commission (Article 10) and recognizing the compulsory jurisdiction of the ECHR (Article 25) were initially optional among the members of the Council of Europe. It was three decades until individual access and recognition of the court's jurisdiction became universal. These practices were then codified in Protocol 11 to the convention, signed in 1994, whereby all parties recognized the compulsory jurisdiction of the permanent ECHR and permit individuals direct access to it in all cases. Signature of the new protocol was made a condition of admission for any new members, a simultaneous recognition of the greatly enhanced effectiveness of transnational over interstate litigation. In many cases new democracies strongly committed to a successful political transition enthusiastically embraced the clauses.[83] In other cases such willingness may have reflected the relative weakness of the candidate states relative to the members of the largely West European club they were seeking to join.

Beyond Formalism: The Dynamics of GATT and the WTO

The contrast between the two ideal types of dispute resolution we have constructed—interstate and transnational—illuminates the impact of judicial independence, differential rules of access, and variations in the domestic embeddedness of an international dispute-resolution process. The ICJ fits the interstate dispute-resolution pattern quite well; the ECJ approximates the ideal type of transnational dispute resolution. The form that legalization takes seems to matter.

Form, however, is not everything. Politics is affected by form but not determined by it. This is most evident when we seek to explain more fine-grained variations in the middle of the spectrum between the two ideal types. The evolution of the GATT, and recently the WTO, illustrates how politics can alter the effects of form. Formally, as we pointed out earlier, GATT is closer to the ideal type of interstate dispute resolution than to transnational dispute resolution. The independence of tribunals is coded

81. Stone Sweet 1998, 330. See also Harlow 1992.
82. Golub 1996.
83. Moravcsik 2000.

as moderate for both GATT and WTO. On the embeddedness criterion, GATT was low and WTO, with its mandatory procedures, is moderate (see Table 4). Most important, however, are access rules: in both the old GATT and the ITO (since 1 January 1995), states have the exclusive right to bring cases before tribunals. In formal terms, therefore, states are the gatekeepers to the GATT/WTO process.

We noted in the first section, however, that the relationships between actors in civil society and representatives of the state are very different in GATT/WTO than in the ICJ. In the GATT/WTO proceedings the principal actors from civil society are firms or industry groups, which are typically wealthy enough to afford extensive litigation and often have substantial political constituencies. Industry groups and firms have been quick to complain about allegedly unfair and discriminatory actions by their competitors abroad, and governments have often been willing to take up their complaints. Indeed, it has often been convenient for governments to do so, since the best defense against others' complaints in a system governed by reciprocity is often the threat or reality of bringing one's own case against their discriminatory measures. In a "tit-for-tat" game, it is useful to have an army of well-documented complaints "up one's sleeve" to deter others from filing complaints or as retaliatory responses to such complaints. Consequently, although states retain formal gatekeeping authority in the GATT/WTO system, they often have incentives to open the gates, letting actors in civil society set much of the agenda.

The result of this political situation is that the evolution of the GATT dispute-settlement procedure looks quite different from that of the ICJ: indeed, it seems intermediate between the ideal types of interstate and transnational dispute resolution. Dispute-resolution activity levels have increased substantially over time, as the process has become more legalized. Adjudication in the GATT of the 1950s produced vague decisions, which were nevertheless relatively effective, arguably because GATT was a "club" of like-minded trade officials.[84] Membership changes and the emergence of the EC in the 1960s led to decay in the dispute resolution mechanism, which only began to reverse in the 1970s. Diplomatic, nonlegalized attempts to resolve disputes, however, were severely criticized, leading to the appointment of a professional legal staff and the gradual legalization of the process. With legalization came better-argued decisions and the creation of a body of precedent.

Throughout this period, the formal procedures remained entirely voluntary: defendants could veto any step in the process. This "procedural flimsiness," as Robert E. Hudec refers to it, is often taken as a major weakness of GATT; but Hudec has shown that it did not prevent GATT from being quite effective. By the late 1980s, 80 percent of GATT cases were disposed of effectively—not as a result of legal embeddedness but of political decisions by states. This is a reasonably high level of compliance, though not as high as attained by the EC and ECHR. The WTO was built on the success of GATT, particularly in recent years, rather than being a response to failure.[85]

84. This paragraph and the subsequent one rely on Hudec 1999, especially 6–17.

85. The annual number of cases before the WTO has risen to almost twice the number during the last years of GATT; but Hudec argues that this change is accounted for by the new or intensified obligations of

We infer from the GATT/WTO experience that although the formal arrangements we have emphasized are important, their dynamic effects depend on the broader political context. Our ideal-type argument should not be reified into a legalistic, single-factor explanation of the dynamics of dispute resolution. Even if states control gates, they can under some conditions be induced to open them, or even to encourage actors from civil society to enter the dispute resolution arena. The real dynamics of dispute resolution typically lie in some interaction between law and politics, rather than in the operation of either law or politics alone.

The foregoing discussion of dynamics suggests that the following three conjectures deserve detailed empirical evaluation:

1. Compared with interstate dispute resolution, transnational dispute resolution offers greater potential for the widening and deepening of dispute resolution over time, for unintended consequences, and for progressive restrictions on the behavior of national governments.

2. Judges in transnational dispute-resolution systems are more likely than those in interstate dispute-resolution systems to exploit the potential for independence, access, and embeddedness to centralize political authority in international institutions, particularly dispute-resolution bodies themselves.

3. Whereas very large political differences between ideal-typical systems are well explained by formal institutional characteristics of international legal regimes, more fine-grained differences reflect differences in the ability of domestic political groups to exploit those institutional characteristics.

Conclusion

We have constructed two ideal types of legalized dispute resolution, interstate and transnational, which vary along the dimensions of independence, access, and embeddedness. When we examine international courts, we find that the distinction between the two ideal types appears to be associated with variation in the size of dockets and levels of compliance with decisions. The differences between the ICJ and the ECJ are dramatic along both dimensions. The causal connections between outcomes and correspondence with one ideal type or the other will require more research and analysis to sort out; but the differences between the ICJ and ECJ patterns cannot be denied. Their dynamics also vary greatly: the ECJ has expanded its caseload and its authority in a way that is unparalleled in the ICJ.

The GATT/WTO mechanisms do not reflect our ideal types so faithfully. States remain formal legal gatekeepers in these systems but have often refrained from tightly limiting access to dispute resolution procedures. As a result, the caseload of the GATT processes, and the effectiveness of their decisions, increased even without high formal levels of access or embeddedness. Hence, GATT and the WTO remind

---

the Uruguay Round, rather than being attributable to changes in the embeddedness of the dispute resolution mechanism. Hudec 1999, 21. Hudec acknowledges, however, that he is arguing against the conventional wisdom.

us that legal form does not necessarily determine political process. It is the interaction of law and politics, not the action of either alone, that generates decisions and determines their effectiveness.

What transnational dispute resolution does is to insulate dispute resolution to some extent from the day-to-day political demands of states. The more we move toward transnational dispute resolution, the harder it is to trace individual judicial decisions and states' responses to them back to any simple, short-term matrix of state or social preferences, power capabilities, and cross-issues. Political constraints, of course, continue to exist, but they are less closely binding than under interstate dispute resolution. Legalization imposes real constraints on state behavior; the closer we are to transnational third-party dispute resolution, the greater those constraints are likely to be. Transnational dispute-resolution systems help to mobilize and represent particular groups that benefit from regime norms. This increases the costs of reversal to national governments and domestic constituents, which can in turn make an important contribution to the enforcement and extension of international norms. For this reason, transnational dispute resolution systems have become an important source of increased legalization and a factor in both interstate and intrastate politics.

[19]

Alternative Dispute Resolution under International Law

CHRISTINE CHINKIN

1. DISPUTE RESOLUTION IN NATIONAL AND INTERNATIONAL LAW

Since about the late 1970s alternative dispute resolution (ADR) processes, and in particular forms of mediation, have become fashionable in Western jurisdictions such as the United States, Australia and Canada.[1] They are also becoming more widely known and used within the United Kingdom.[2] This popularity has manifested itself through the introduction of pilot schemes and legislative, administrative and voluntary programmes, within the formal court structures and outside them, for the resolution of disputes in many areas of domestic law.[3] ADR processes comprise forms of third party assisted negotiation (mediation and conciliation), independent expert investigation, appraisal and evaluation, and have been combined or adapted to create a range of innovative methods for the attempted resolution of disputes.

The benefits of ADR processes are regularly extolled by its advocates.[4] Among their most frequently cited advantages are cheapness, flexibility and privacy compared to litigation. The parties' freedom of choice with respect to third party facilitators allows them to draw upon appropriate technical, legal, cultural or other expertise, and even to bring together a balanced team of experts. The consensual nature of the processes is said to be empowering for disputants who can craft for themselves a mutually acceptable outcome, unfettered by the restrictions of legal procedures and remedies. The parties' retention of control over the outcome is thought likely to produce a potentially more durable, forward-looking settlement to the dispute than one imposed by a court, which will

---

[1] See H. Astor and C. Chinkin, *Dispute Resolution in Australia* (Butterworths, Sydney, 1993), especially ch. 1.

[2] See, e.g., *Modern Law Review*, "Special Issue—Dispute Resolution: Civil Justice and its Alternatives", 56 MLR (1993); Lord Woolf, *Access to Justice* (HMSO, London, 1996).

[3] In the UK, ADR processes are especially promoted for family matters and neighbourhood disputes, although there is a growing awareness of their potential in commercial disputes; for a useful summary see Resolving Disputes Without Going to Court (Lord Chancellor's Department, London, 1995).

[4] See Astor and Chinkin, n. 1 at 41.

124   *Christine Chinkin*

almost inevitably be framed in a "win/lose" formulation.[5] Further, since the dispute need not be presented in the bilateral model required by litigation, third party and collective interests can be more readily accommodated, at least in theory.

How does this trend translate into the international arena where the paradigmatic disputing parties are sovereign States? ADR processes are not new in international law, as what are more generally termed "diplomatic methods"[6] have been formally part of the framework of international dispute settlement since at least the Hague Treaties of 1899 and 1907,[7] and informally much longer.[8] An optimism that States would co-operate in international relations and seek peaceful methods of dispute resolution motivated the Hague Conferences for the Peaceful Settlement of Disputes, 1899 and 1907 and found expression in provision for third party processes of arbitration, good offices, mediation, inquiry and conciliation. Before World War II these processes were institutionalised, in both multilateral and bilateral treaties, for example through the formation of Permanent Conciliation Commissions,[9] the creation of the Permanent Court of Arbitration,[10] of the fact-finding Commission of Inquiry and of Mixed Arbitral Tribunals.[11] Despite this range of institutional options, their actual use was never extensive. Nevertheless, when the United Nations Charter prohibition on the use of force in international relations necessitated state commitment to the peaceful settlement of disputes,[12] these same processes were reiterated in Article 33 of the Charter.[13]

Despite steady restatement, for example by the revision of the General Act in 1949,[14] further General Assembly resolutions[15] and regional arrange-

---

[5] R. Fisher and W. Ury, *Getting to Yes, Negotiating Agreement Without Giving In* (Houghton Mifflin, Boston, Mass., 1981).

[6] P. Malanczuk, *Akehurst's Modern Introduction to International Law* (7th rev. edn., Routledge, London and New York, 1997), at 273–81.

[7] International Convention for the Pacific Settlement of Disputes, The Hague, 29 July 1899, 32 Stat. 1779; International Convention for the Pacific Settlement of Disputes, The Hague, 18 Oct. 1907; 3 Martens (3rd) 360, 36 Stat. 2199.

[8] J. Merrills, *International Dispute Settlement* (2nd edn., Grotius, Cambridge, 1991).

[9] *Ibid.*

[10] The Permanent Court of Arbitration was set up by the International Convention for the Pacific Settlement of Disputes, 1899, Arts. 20–9, and was only slightly amended by the International Convention for the Pacific Settlement of Disputes, 1907.

[11] Treaty of Versailles, 28 June 1919; 11 Martens (3rd) 323, Arts. 296–7, 304–5.

[12] United Nations Charter, Arts. 2(3) and (4).

[13] Art. 33(1) states: "The parties to any dispute, the continuance of which is likely to endanger the maintenance of international peace and security shall, first of all, seek a solution by negotiation, enquiry, mediation, conciliation, arbitration, judicial settlement, resort to regional agencies or arrangements, or other peaceful means of their own choice." See further *Handbook on the Peaceful Settlement of Disputes Between States* (United Nations, New York, 1992).

[14] General Act for the Pacific Settlement of International Disputes, Geneva, 26 Sept. 1928, 93 LNTS 343 revised on 28 Apr. 1949, GA Res. 268 (A III), GAOR (3rd) Pt II (A/900).

[15] E.g. Declaration on Principles of International Law Concerning Friendly Relations and Cooperation among States in Accordance with the Charter of the United Nations, GA Res. 2625, 24 Oct., 1970; Manila Declaration on the Peaceful Settlement of International Disputes, GA Res. 37/10, 1982; Declaration on the Prevention and Removal of Disputes and Situations which may Threaten International Peace and Security and on the Role of the United Nations in this Field, GA Res. 43/51, 1988.

Alternative Dispute Resolution under International Law 125

ments,[16] these processes remained institutionally under-utilised in the cold war years. Recourse tended to be on an *ad hoc* basis where advantage was taken of the inherent flexibility of negotiatory processes to mould dispute-resolution method and outcome to fit the facts, the parties and the political background of the particular dispute. Among the most frequently cited examples of recourse to international arbitration or mediation are inter-State boundary disputes such as those concerning the Rann of Kutch,[17] the Taba,[18] the English Channel,[19] the Beagle Channel[20] and territory between Qatar and Bahrain.[21] While boundary disputes may cause great political tension and be highly emotionally charged,[22] there has also been recourse to such methods in more overtly political disputes, for example the Algerian mediation of the dispute between the US and Iran over the latter's detention of American hostages in Tehran (1980),[23] and that between France and New Zealand over the sinking of the *Rainbow Warrior* in Auckland harbour (1986).[24] There were also many instances where either individual States or the Secretary-General offered their good offices to assist disputing States.[25] The Secretary-General has also exercised his good offices in conjunction with other individuals, representatives from regional organisations[26] and States.

There is currently what has been termed an "obsessive concentration"[27] upon these processes that might be compared with the enthusiasm for ADR manifest in Western domestic law.[28] This concentration can be seen in a number of forms, for example in renewed UN emphasis on the utility of specific

---

[16] E.g. the European Convention for the Peaceful Settlement of Disputes, 1957, 320 UNTS 243; the American Treaty on Pacific Settlement, 1948, 30 UNTS 55; Protocol of the Commission of Mediation and Arbitration of the Organization of African Unity, 1964, 3 ILM 1116.

[17] Indo-Pakistan Western Boundary, Rann of Kutch Award, 50 ILR 2 (1968).

[18] Arbitral Award in the Dispute Concerning Certain Boundary Pillars between the Arab Republic of Egypt and the State of Israel, 80 ILR 224 (1980).

[19] *Delimitation of the Continental Shelf (United Kingdom–France)*, 54 ILR 6 (1977).

[20] *Beagle Channel Award (Argentina v. Chile)* 52 ILR 93 (1977).

[21] The long attempts at mediation by the King of Saudi Arabia are described in the case concerning *Maritime Delimitation and Territorial Questions between Qatar and Bahrain*, Jurisdiction and Admissibility, Judgment, ICJ Reports 1994, 112; Judgment of 15 Feb., ICJ Reports 1995, 6.

[22] E.g. Chile and Argentina were on the brink of war over the Beagle Channel.

[23] See J. Greenburg, "Algerian Intervention in the Iranian Hostage Crisis", 20 *Stanford JIL* 259.

[24] *Ruling pertaining to the Differences between France and New Zealand arising from the Rainbow Warrior Affair*, 74 ILR 241 (1986).

[25] E.g. with respect to Indonesia (1947), Palestine (1956), Tunisia (1958), Cyprus (on-going); n. 13 above, at paras. 112–14; Higgins comments that the "list [of disputes where the Secretary-General has employed his good offices] is almost endless": R. Higgins, *Problems and Process International Law and How We Use It* (Clarendon Press, Oxford, 1994), at 172. See further, Merrills, n. 8 above, at 185–91.

[26] E.g. the joint effort between the Secretary-General of the UN and the Chairperson of the Organisation of African Unity with respect to both the Western Sahara and Mayotte and attempts between the Secretary-General of the UN and the Secretary-General of the Organisation of American States with respect to conflict in Central America: n. 13 above, at para. 115.

[27] M. Koskenniemi, "International Law in a Post-Realist Era", 16 *AYBIL* 1 at 2.

[28] This has been accompanied by greater use of adjudicatory methods of international dispute resolution; see C. Chinkin, "The Peaceful Settlement of Disputes: New Grounds for Optimism?" in R. St John MacDonald (ed.), *Essays in Honour of Wang Tieya* (Nijhoff, Dordrecht, 1994), at 165.

126   *Christine Chinkin*

peacemaking processes,[29] and in the proliferation of dispute-resolution clauses in treaties that require some recourse to peaceful settlement. A formula that makes compulsory some form of dispute-resolution process, while allowing parties maximum freedom to specify its form, has been adopted in some sectoral regulatory regimes.[30] Such treaties frequently contain Annexes that facilitate the operation of the chosen process, providing guidelines on such details as the method of selection of third parties, appropriate time limits, applicable procedures, preferred outcomes and third party powers.[31] Similarly, additional institutional mechanisms for dispute resolution have been introduced regionally, especially within Europe at the end of the cold war.[32]

Although there is no doubt cross-fertilisation between the domestic and international arenas, caution should be exercised in drawing comparisons. In domestic legal systems the objective has been to create effective alternatives to what are regarded as the unacceptably high costs and long delays of litigation, while in international law it has been to encourage some form of third party settlement, in the absence of compulsory adjudication.[33] Internationally, diplomatic processes were promoted as alternatives to recourse to armed force, at least in the first instance, rather than as alternatives to international adjudication. The latter was not introduced until the creation of the Permanent Court of International Justice as part of the post-World War I peace settlement.[34] Indeed in the *Great Belt* case the International Court of Justice (ICJ) affirmed that international adjudication is still an alternative to direct and friendly settlement between States,[35] the reverse of the understanding in domestic legal systems. Consequently many domestic debates about the function and efficacy of ADR processes are meaningless in the international context where all third party processes are peaceful alternatives to conflict.[36] Their common consensual basis means that they do not operate in the

[29] E.g. UN Draft Rules on Conciliation of Disputes between States, 30 ILM 231 and, more generally, *An Agenda for Peace, Preventive Diplomacy, Peacemaking and Peace-keeping: Report of the Secretary-General Pursuant to the Statement adopted by the Summit Meeting of the Security Council on 31 January 1992*, 17 June 1992, UN Doc. A/47/277, at paras. 34–45.

[30] The UN Convention on the Law of the Sea, 1982, Part XV, has become a model for this approach; see C. Chinkin, "Dispute Resolution and the Law of the Sea: Regional Problems and Prospects" in J. Crawford and D. Rothwell, *The Law of the Sea in the Asian Pacific Region* (Nijhoff, Dordrecht, 1995), at 237.

[31] Similarly Model Arbitral Rules have been widely adopted for international commercial arbitration, e.g. UN Commission on International Trade Law (UNCITRAL) Model Law on International Commercial Arbitration, 1985, 24 ILM 1302.

[32] E.g. Convention on Conciliation and Arbitration within the Conference on Security and Co-operation in Europe, 1993, 32 ILM 557; cf. the Organisation of African Unity, Mechanism for Conflict Prevention, Management and Resolution, 1993, UN Doc. A/47/558. 98 (1993).

[33] Statute of the International Court of Justice, 1945, Art. 36.

[34] Covenant of the League of Nations, Art. 14; Statute of the Permanent Court of International Justice, 16 Dec. 1920.

[35] *Passage through the Great Belt (Finland v. Denmark)*, Provisional Measures, Order of 29 July 1991, ICJ Reports 1991, 12.

[36] One example is the debate whether arbitration is properly perceived as an ADR process, or whether it has more affinity with adjudication. Arbitration by agreement between the parties has been a peaceful alternative to both conflict and diplomatic settlement since at least the UK–US Treaty of Amity, Commerce and Navigation, 1794 (the Jay Treaty).

"shadow of the law" as is the case domestically,[37] although the *Nauru*,[38] *Great Belt*[39] and *Qatar* v. *Bahrain*[40] cases might suggest a change in this respect. On the other hand international adjudication perhaps draws more from negotiatory methods of settlement than does domestic litigation.[41]

This chapter discusses three international institutional contexts where negotiatory dispute-resolution processes have been adopted and adapted for different purposes. The first is the use of similar diplomatic methods for both "compliance control"[42] and dispute resolution in what has been called "dynamic, sectoral legal systems",[43] notably institutional regimes for the regulation of the environment and the protection of human rights. The second examines the role of dispute-resolution processes in enhancing institutional good governance and democratic participation within the international financial institutions. The third looks at a more direct alternative to the use of armed force, the practice of good offices by the Secretary-General of the United Nations and the relationship between the concepts of peacemaking and peacekeeping as envisioned by the former Secretary-General.[44] These examples illustrate the potential tensions between institutional objectives and the assumptions of treaty performance, especially where the latter involve performance of obligations owed *erga omnes* and standing to assert those obligations is narrowly framed. Underlying this tension is the further strain within the international system between the private nature of negotiatory methods, institutional

[37] The expression "bargaining in the shadow of the law" has been used in domestic law to describe how parties negotiate against a backdrop of the likely consequences of litigation and their awareness of that eventuality if they cannot reach a satisfactory conclusion: e.g. R. Mnookin and L. Kornhauser, "Bargaining in the Shadow of the Law: The Case of Divorce", 88 *Yale LJ* 950.

[38] After the ICJ determined that it had jurisdiction to hear Nauru's claims against Australia, a negotiated settlement was reached between the parties and the case withdrawn from the Court: *Certain Phosphate Lands in Nauru (Nauru* v. *Australia)*, Preliminary Objections, Judgment, ICJ Reports 1992, 240; Australia–Republic of Nauru: Settlement of the Case in the International Court of Justice Concerning Certain Phosphate Lands in Nauru, 10 Aug. 1993, 32 ILM 1471.

[39] Commencement of judicial proceedings may have facilitated the negotiated agreement between Finland and Denmark: P. Magid, "The Post-Adjudicative Phase" in C. Peck and R. Lee (eds.), *Increasing Effectiveness of the International Court of Justice* (Nijhoff/UNITAR, The Hague, 1997), 325 at 343.

[40] The ICJ unusually assumed a case-management role in requiring the parties to negotiate further about submitting their full dispute to the Court: *Qatar* v. *Bahrain*, n. 21 above; *cf.* E. Lauterpacht, " 'Partial' Judgments and the Inherent Jurisdiction of the International Court of Justice", in V. Lowe and M. Fitzmaurice (eds.), *Fifty Years of the International Court of Justice* (Cambridge University Press, Cambridge, 1996), at 465.

[41] E.g. the ICJ may decide cases *ex aequo et bono*: Statute of the ICJ, Art. 38(2); it has less developed rules of evidence than domestic courts and has recourse to flexible concepts of equity in its judgments. See further T.M. Franck, *Fairness in International Law and Institutions* (Clarendon Press, Oxford, 1995), especially at 47–80 and 316–47.

[42] This expression has been labelled a current "buzz word" of international environmental law: G. Handl, "Compliance Control Mechanisms and International Environmental Obligations", 5 *Tulane Journal of International and Comparative Law* 29 at 30.

[43] T. Gehring, "International Environmental Regimes: Dynamic Sectoral Legal Systems", 1 *YBIEL* 35.

[44] An Agenda for Peace (n. 29 above); Supplement to an Agenda for Peace, 1 January 1995, UNDOC. A/50/60–S/1995/1 .

128 *Christine Chinkin*

perspectives and the interests of the wider international community in the visible commitment to the standards required through adherence to treaties.

2. INSTITUTIONAL REGIMES FOR TREATY COMPLIANCE

Innovative procedures for enhancing compliance with, and responding to, non-performance of international obligations have been included within multilateral treaties creating international regulatory regimes, especially within the area of environmental law.[45] The first such model, the Vienna Convention on the Ozone Layer, 1985,[46] and the Montreal Protocol, 1987, will be described as illustration of the major features of such procedures.[47] Article 8 of the Montreal Protocol provided the framework for a non-compliance procedure, the details of which were completed by a working party and adopted by the Fourth Meeting of the Parties to the Protocol in 1992.[48] These procedures allow a party, or the Secretariat, to raise concerns about another party's non-compliance before the Implementation Committee established for this purpose under the Protocol, making each State "a trustee" for other parties' conformity with the Convention.[49] Handl notes that party concern for compliance is not motivated solely by the desire to enhance the efficacy of international legal regulation: as the social and developmental costs of compliance with environmental standards increases, all parties have an incentive in ensuring that others are not gaining an unfair advantage through ignoring those standards.[50] The Implementation Committee considers all submissions, information and observations received with a view to securing "an amicable solution of the matter on the basis of respect for the provisions of the Protocol".

These non-compliance procedures operate through a bureaucratised body integral to the regulatory regime. This has a number of consequences both for the process and for the performance of the relevant obligations. The procedures reject the model of an independent, neutral third party expert by instead bringing together within the institutional framework those who are responsible for the articulation of the substantive norms with those who are working towards agreement as to outcome. Unlike non-institutional mediation or conciliation processes, where the parties alone are responsible for the outcome, any amicable solution must be reached in light of the provisions of the Convention. This

---

[45] Handl asserts that institutional measures for non-compliance have become an indispensable element of multilateral international environmental treaties: Handl, n. 42 above, at 32.

[46] Vienna Convention for the Protection of the Ozone Layer, 22 Mar. 1985, 26 ILM 1529.

[47] The Montreal Protocol on Substances that Deplete the Ozone Layer, with Annex A., 19 Sept. 1987, 26 ILM 1550.

[48] Report of the Fourth Meeting of the Parties to the Montreal Protocol on Substances that deplete the Ozone Layer, UNEP/OZL.Pro.4/15, 25 Nov. 1992, 3 YBIEL 819.

[49] M. Koskenniemi, "Breach of Treaty or Non-Compliance? Reflections on the Enforcement of the Montreal Protocol", 3 *YBIEL* 123. A party may also bring its own non-compliance to the attention of the Implementation Committee.

[50] Handl, n. 42 above, at 31.

model is similar to the long-established process of a conciliated friendly settlement between the government and petitioner under the European Convention on Human Rights.[51] The replacement of the European Commission on Human Rights by a single-tiered judicial process when Protocol 11 to the European Convention[52] is implemented, does not mean that settlement will no longer be attempted. The first instance Chamber of the newly constituted permanent Court can put itself at the disposal of the parties for the purposes of friendly settlement. This creates the further dilemma of conferring both negotiatory and adjudicatory powers on a single body, a blending of function that has caused disquiet in Western concepts of adjudication but is more common in other systems of law.[53]

Under the Montreal Protocol, the party whose alleged non-compliance has been raised can only submit information and comments to the Implementation Committee. It cannot participate in the elaboration and adoption of the recommendations, an exclusion that detracts both from the voluntariness of the solution and the broader understanding of diplomatic processes. Since the objective is to secure compliance, the solutions adopted tend to be forward-looking and facilitative rather than simply condemnation for failure to perform, although they may include some punitive components such as a caution or even sanctions. This blurring of negotiatory and quasi-adjudicatory function brings issues of institutional accountability and due process back into the picture. Nevertheless, preference for the compliance processes that may avert any more coercive measures is likely to influence the non-complying State's decision with respect to the proposed outcome.

The solution as to recompense or future conduct is worked out within the institutional regulatory framework, but outside the processes of general international law. The non-compliance process of the Montreal Protocol has been commended for its fostering of the dynamic development of a sectoral legal system that takes account of the expectations and understandings developed between participants to the regime, and in light of technical and bureaucratic expertise.[54] In contrast, recourse to dispute-resolution processes outside the institutional framework, such as the ICJ, *ad hoc* arbitration or conciliation would not do this. Use of binding processes (adjudication or arbitration) might be counter-productive to the on-going evolution of the regulatory regime, in that a formal ruling tends to crystallise the law in a fast-changing area, whereas the regime procedures can take into account and contribute to this

---

[51] Friendly settlement has been a primary objective of the European Commission on Human Rights upon receipt of an admissible petition: European Convention for the Protection of Fundamental Rights and Freedoms, 4 Nov. 1950, ETS No. 5, Art. 28(b); *cf.* American Convention on Human Rights, 22 Nov. 1969, OAS TS No. 36, Art. 48(f).

[52] Protocol No. 11 to the European Convention for the Protection of Fundamental Rights and Freedoms, 1994 and Explanatory Report (Council of Europe Press, 1994). Protocol 11 will come into force on 1 Nov. 1998.

[53] Astor and Chinkin, n. 1 above, at 145.

[54] Gehring, n. 43 above.

130   *Christine Chinkin*

evolution.[55] Indeed in its judgment in the *Gabčikovo-Nagymaros Project*,[56] the ICJ itself emphasised the importance of parties taking account of developing environmental norms in the performance of their institutional treaty obligations and considered that third party involvement could assist them in doing this, provided they were prepared to be flexible.

There is however another side to this analysis. A treaty is a public prescription of agreed international standards in the performance of which non-parties have an interest, as well as parties. Obligations to decrease emissions damaging to the ozone layer, or to respect human rights, are owed *erga omnes*,[57] not just to the complainant in the particular instance, or even just to other States, parties or non-parties. The concept of amicable solution or friendly settlement, reached through compromise and legitimated by the institutional framework, suggests a bilateralism that might not satisfy others' perceptions of what those obligations should entail.[58] A mediated agreement typically incorporates enough of the interests of both disputants for them to be able to accept it, that is it presents a win/win solution. However a mediated agreement may not take account of the interests of third parties, or of the international community at large.[59] An example is the agreement reached in the inter-State application brought by Denmark, France, the Netherlands, Norway and Sweden against Turkey in 1983.[60] The applicant States claimed violations of a number of Articles of the European Convention on Human Rights, including the prohibition against torture in Article 3. A friendly settlement was reached in which Turkey made general undertakings with respect to future compliance with the Convention and to lifting the state of emergency declared under Article 15. The settlement did not refer to a number of alleged violations that the Commission (which participated in the settlement) had previously found to be admissible. Robertson and Merrills have criticised this settlement on the ground that it "cannot be said to have been reached 'on the basis of respect for Human Rights' as defined in the Convention".[61] They comment further that "in a comparable case brought by an individual it is inconceivable that an arrangement so patently unsatisfactory would have been approved".[62]

---

[55] *Cf.* the development of "transnational commercial law" as described by Prof. Goode: R. Goode, "Usage and its Reception in Transnational Commercial Law", 46 *ICLQ* 1.

[56] *Gabčikovo-Nagymaros Project (Hungary/Slovakia)*, Judgment, ICJ Reports 1997, not yet reported.

[57] *Barcelona Traction, Light and Power Co. Ltd*, 2nd Phase, Judgment, ICJ Reports 1970, 3 at 32.

[58] In the case concerning the *Gabčikovo-Nagymaros Project* Vice President Weeramantry, in his separate Opinion, considered that since claims of environmental damage have *erga omnes* implications, bilateral doctrines such as estoppel might be inappropriate.

[59] The example has been given of quotas agreed by the International Whaling Commission that satisfy the parties (at least to some extent) but do nothing to save the whales: J. Dryzek and S. Hunter, "Environmental Mediation for International Problems", 31 *International Studies Quarterly* 87.

[60] Report of 7 Dec. 1985, 44 Decisions and Reports 31.

[61] A. Robertson and J. Merrills, *Human Rights in Europe* (3rd edn., Manchester University Press, Manchester, 1993), at 284.

[62] *Ibid.*

Alternative Dispute Resolution under International Law 131

While appreciating the political dilemma facing the Commission, this is brought about precisely by using private settlement processes within an institutional regulatory regime for performance of treaty obligations, including those owed *erga omnes*, and resurrects the concern about private ordering[63] that has been forcefully expressed in the context of domestic ADR.[64] While the assurance of confidentiality may be an essential factor in reaching an amicable settlement, it prevents open assessment of the parties' compliance with their treaty commitments.[65] Indeed this concern appears even more valid in a decentralised legal system where an amicable solution can generate state practice constitutive of customary international law outside the terms of the treaty. The conclusion that "[i]n inter-state cases, . . . the friendly settlement procedure should be approached with a degree of scepticism" may be equally applicable to all such compliance processes that combine state will with the institutional need for continued credibility.[66] Koskenniemi has warned of the danger that the desire to maintain the treaty and its institutions intact may allow the procedures to become ineffective for achieving their objectives and enable parties to conceal real differences while apparently dealing with them, to the detriment of upholding collective obligations[67] or individual third party interests.[68] Finally, such development can lead to the further fragmentation of the substance of international law and its structures. Views may differ on whether or not such fragmentation is desirable: on the one hand it allows for the development of specialist knowledge and expertise; on the other there is the risk of incoherence between different areas of international law. Whichever way one concludes, at the very least the potential consequences should be recognised.

The Montreal Protocol non-compliance mechanisms co-exist with, or merge into, third party dispute-resolution processes that are contained within the

---

[63] E.g. Turkey agreed to submit reports to the Commission and to participate in dialogue with it on Art. 3 and to prepare a final report on the implementation of the settlement. However all these steps were to remain confidential: *ibid.* at 292, n. 81. Similarly, confidentiality is preserved for the non-compliance procedures under the Montreal Protocol.

[64] Astor and Chinkin, n. 1 above, at 57 and 81–2.

[65] Handl, n. 42 above, at 40, notes that confidentiality may be justified because of the sensitive nature of relevant information.

[66] Similar apprehension may be felt in the context of the purported "constructive dialogue" between human rights treaty bodies and States Parties reporting to them where real concerns about non-compliance with the relevant treaty may not be adequately addressed.

[67] Koskenniemi, n. 49 above.

[68] Despite the flexibility of negotiatory processes that apparently more easily allow participation by third parties, their interests may be more effectively upheld by the more formal procedures before the ICJ. For example in *East Timor (Portugal v. Australia)*, Judgment, ICJ Reports 1995, 90 Indonesia's interests prevented the Court from deciding upon the merits of Portugal's claim and in the *Continental Shelf (Libyan Arab Jamahiriya/Malta)*, Judgment, ICJ Reports 1985, 13 Italy's claims caused the Court to limit its consideration of the maritime areas disputed by the parties, despite its earlier unsuccessful request to intervene. However the protection accorded by the indispensable third party principle is only available to third party States. At the same time, the Court may refuse to consider third party claims such as requests to intervene. See further C. Chinkin, *Third Parties in International Law* (Clarendon Press, Oxford, 1993), especially ch. 12.

132　*Christine Chinkin*

Vienna Convention on the Ozone Layer, Article 11.[69] The ICJ has held that a dispute arises when there is "a disagreement on a point of law or fact, a conflict of legal views or interests between parties".[70] The existence of a dispute may assume an allegation of breach, unsatisfactory performance or non-compliance by one party to the Convention with respect to the behaviour of another, and thus overlaps with the concerns that can trigger the non-compliance procedures. Moreover, complaints of non-compliance with the Montreal Protocol may amount to claims of breach within the terms of Article 60 of the Vienna Convention on the Law of Treaties,[71] and raise the substantive options therein specified.[72] The dispute resolution procedures to be followed in the case of claims of breach of the Vienna Convention on the Law of Treaties are those listed in Article 33 of the UN Charter, and especially conciliation.[73] The same techniques, for example consultation, independent expert investigation, seeking further information, negotiations facilitated by a third party, third party expert appraisal of the problem and the formulation of non-binding recommendations on how the issue might be resolved, underlie both compliance and the negotiatory dispute resolution processes. Indeed "amicable solution" is an appropriate description of the preferred outcome of a conciliation process, as well as the objective of the non-compliance procedures. Further, the preference of at least one of the parties in an articulated dispute may be to induce performance rather than to claim termination or redress, and the agreed outcome of conciliation may be devised to maintain the treaty relationship by including inducements for future performance.[74]

---

[69] Art. 11 allows parties to make a declaration accepting compulsory recourse to arbitration or the jurisdiction of the ICJ. If attempts at settlement through negotiation or mediation fail, and no common compulsory process has been accepted, there is compulsory conciliation that leads to a recommendatory award. These provisions follow, to some extent, the model of the UN Convention on the Law of the Sea, Part XV.

[70] *East Timor (Portugal v. Australia)*, Judgment, ICJ Reports 1995, 90 at para. 22.

[71] For full discussion of this point see Koskenniemi, n. 49 above.

[72] Vienna Convention on the Law of Treaties, 23 Mar. 19691 1155 UNTS 331, Art. 60(2) states that "material breach of a multilateral treaty by one of the parties entitles: (a) the other parties by unanimous agreement to suspend the operation of the treaty in whole or in part or to terminate it either (i) in the relations between themselves and the defaulting State or (ii) as between all parties; (b) a party specially affected by the breach to invoke it as a ground for suspending the operation of the treaty in whole or in part in the relations between itself and the defaulting state; (c) any party other than the defaulting State to invoke the breach as a ground for suspending the operation of the treaty in whole or in part with respect to itself if the treaty is of such a character that a material breach of its provisions by one party radically changes the position of every party with respect to the further performance of its obligations under the treaty". For discussion on what actions constitute material breach see the *Gabčikovo-Nagymaros Project (Hungary/Slovakia)*, Judgment, ICJ Reports, not yet reported.

[73] Vienna Convention on the Law of Treaties, Arts. 65–6 and Annex to the Convention (on conciliation procedures).

[74] The outcome may also contain some compensatory element but a win/win formula that takes account of future dealings between the parties is widely associated with non-adjudicatory dispute resolution: see Fisher and Ury, n. 5 above.

Although traditional dispute-resolution processes may not be suitable for inducing compliance,[75] the co-existence of both objectives within a single institutional regime creates a number of legal dilemmas for parties. Koskenniemi raises a number of pertinent questions. For example, can a party "specially affected" by an alleged breach of the Vienna Convention on the Ozone Layer or the Montreal Protocol claim under Article 60 of the Vienna Convention on the Law of Treaties, or must it rely upon Article 11 of the Ozone Treaty? Indeed can there be a "specially affected" State Party in the context of the Ozone Layer treaty, a question that is equally applicable to human rights treaties? Can a party to a dispute continue with the bilateral dispute resolution procedures under Article 11, although another self-designated party has commenced the institutional procedures relating to non-compliance? Standing to commence the latter is broader than that for the dispute resolution procedures. A party to a dispute may thus be pre-empted from exercising its options by the commencement of the institutional non-compliance processes by another party with what a disputing State considers a lesser interest, or even by the non-complying party itself acting deliberately to achieve such an outcome. More broadly, does the coexistence of compliance and dispute resolution procedures, both resting upon similar non-adjudicatory techniques, foster integration into, or development apart from, general international law?

Koskenniemi suggests a practical solution to the procedural dilemmas. He proposes that if a bilateral dispute resolution process progresses to conciliation (where the objective is non-binding recommendations), it should be merged with the procedures of the Implementation Committee, effectively making dispute resolution part of compliance. This does not of course address the concern about private or institutional ordering and deprives the party in dispute of its choice of conciliators and the alleged non-complying party of its active role within the process. However if the chosen dispute resolution process is arbitration or adjudication, the compliance processes should be dropped because their objectives differ and they may frustrate the adjudicatory process. The parties themselves however can always continue to seek friendly settlement. This solution would disadvantage other parties to the treaty that have only limited access to arbitration or adjudication, through the narrowly defined process of intervention,[76] but can participate in Meetings of the Parties with respect to non-compliance.

This discussion reflects the broader debate within the International Law Commission (ILC) on the relationship between state responsibility and dispute resolution.[77] In its Draft Articles on State Responsibility the ILC has extended the concept of an "injured state" in the contexts of breach of a multilateral

---

[75] Handl, n. 42 above, at 34.

[76] Statute of the ICJ, Arts. 62 and 63 (intervention before the ICJ); see Chinkin, n. 68 above, at ch. 11 for intervention in arbitral proceedings.

[77] International Law Commission, Draft Arts. on State Responsibility, provisionally adopted by the Commission on first reading, Draft Report of the ILC on the Work of its Forty-Eighth Session, UN Doc. A/CN.4/L.528/Add. 2, 16 July 1996.

134   *Christine Chinkin*

treaty[78] and of an international crime,[79] in order to encompass collective and community interests. An injured State may have recourse to counter measures to induce conforming behaviour.[80] Since the draft definition of international crimes includes a "serious breach of an international obligation of essential importance for the safeguarding and preservation of the human environment"[81] such a claim might come within an environmental treaty with a non-compliance regime. The extensive understanding of "injured" State enhances the possibility of breach being raised at the international level, but may cause friction with a directly injured State that seeks reparation in some other way, or whose interests do not coincide with those of the claimant State. Such a State might not wish to have its claim submerged with those of all other "injured" States. A further debate is whether the legality of counter measures is dependent upon a prior attempt at peaceful settlement, that is a form of compulsory dispute settlement, at least at the level of an obligation to negotiate in good faith.[82] The Draft Articles require "an injured state taking countermeasures . . . to fulfil the obligations in relation to dispute resolution arising under Part Three or any other binding dispute settlement procedure in force between the injured State and the State which has committed the internationally wrongful act".[83] There are differences of opinion in principle whether a directly injured State should be required to attempt peaceful settlement before resorting to countermeasures,[84] but in addition the relationship between the general dispute resolution provisions contained in the ILC Draft Articles and specific treaty regimes for compliance and dispute settlement remains unclear.

3. INSPECTION PANELS OF THE INTERNATIONAL FINANCIAL INSTITUTIONS

Despite the collective nature of non-compliance institutional regimes, access and participation are nevertheless restricted to treaty parties. The second example of where dispute resolution processes have been blended into innovative procedures is the Inspection Panels established by the international financial institutions, the World Bank, the Inter-American Bank and the Asian

---

[78] Draft Arts. on State Responsibility, Art. 40(e). Art. 40(f) states "if the right infringed by the act of a State arises from a multilateral treaty, any other State party to the multilateral treaty, if it is established that the right has been expressly stipulated in that treaty for the protection of the collective interests of the States parties thereto".

[79] Draft Arts. on State Responsibility, Art. 40(3).

[80] Draft Arts. on State Responsibility, Art. 47.

[81] Draft Arts. on State Responsibility, Art. 19(3)(d).

[82] The level of action required to satisfy a requirement to negotiate in good faith remains unclear. A refusal to participate in any form of negotiation could be regarded as an internationally wrongful act, but there remains the possibility of good faith disagreement within the negotiations.

[83] Draft Arts. on State Responsibility, Art. 48.

[84] E.g. B. Simma, "Counter-measures and Dispute Settlement: A Plea for a Different Balance", 5 *EJIL* 102; O. Schachter, "Dispute Settlement and Countermeasures in the International Law Commission", 88 *AJIL* 471; C. Tomuschat, "Are Countermeasures Subject to Prior Recourse to Dispute Settlement Procedures?", 5 *EJIL* 77.

Development Bank.[85] Examination of these Panels shifts the focus of the discussion in two ways: first, the complaint is against the institution itself and, secondly, the process is initiated by non-State actors, that are by definition non-parties to the institutional regime.

In 1993 the World Bank introduced the first of these panels[86] following widespread protests about certain development projects, most famously the Sardar Sarovar Dam on the Narmada river in India.[87] The Panel can be seen as an innovative method of enhancing concepts of effectiveness, good governance, transparency and accountability within international institutions where their activities directly impinge upon peoples, lives and living conditions. Creation of the Inspection Panel constitutes an acknowledgement that disputes arising out of development projects cannot be defined solely by the project State and the relevant lending agency. Thus requests for inspection of a World Bank-financed project can be made by the intended beneficiaries, that is a community, organisation or other group residing in the country in which the project is being implemented, or in an adjacent country, if the group is adversely affected, or likely to be affected, by the project. Requests may also be made by representatives residing in the same State, or in exceptional cases outside the State, if the Board consents.

A request for inspection, even if granted, does not lead to an independent evaluation of the project, nor to an assessment of its conformity with international law, but rather to an examination of the relevant Bank's compliance with its own operational policies and practices, including, for example, the policy of public disclosure adopted by the World Bank's Board in 1993. The focus is upon damage, or likely damage, especially of a social or environmental kind, flowing from non-compliance with Bank policy, not from breach of international law. The World Bank envisaged that recourse to the Panel would be limited to those "exceptional cases where the Bank's own high standards were not met".[88]

Unlike the position of the Implementation Committee described above with respect to the institutional regime for the protection of the ozone layer, the Panel is not an integral part of the World Bank, although the members of the standing panel are selected for their relevant expertise.[89] The Inspection Panel in effect

---

[85] D. Bradlow, "International Organizations and Private Complaints: The Case of the World Bank Inspection Panel", 34 *VJIL* 553; I. Shihata, *The World Bank Inspection Panel* (Clarendon Press, Oxford, 1994). For details of the operation of the Panel see *The Inspection Panel International Bank for Reconstruction and Development Report August 1, 1994 to July 31, 1996* (The World Bank, Washington, DC).

[86] The Inspection Panels each institution has developed vary in detail, so this discussion will focus on the World Bank Inspection Panel.

[87] B. Morse and T. Berger, *Report of the Independent Review, Sardar Sarovar* (Resources Futures International, Ottawa, 1992).

[88] Oxfam, *The World Bank Inspection Panel: Analysis and Recommendations for Review* (Policy Department, UK, Feb. 1996) at 1.

[89] The Inter-American Bank and the Asian Development Bank have adopted a different model, that of a roster of named experts from whom the Board may select a Panel in response to a particular request.

acts as an intermediary between the requesters, the Bank Management and Board. Its processes resemble those for dispute resolution and their flexibility allows them to be adapted to the particular circumstances. Inspection can include impartial investigation, visiting the project site, broad formal and informal consultations, for example with relevant Bank staff, local people, intended project beneficiaries (including indigenous persons), grassroots and international non-governmental organisations and local and central government agencies, appraisal of decision-making, and crafting recommendations for remedial measures. The investigation includes access to the Bank's staff and records. The Panel's findings are sent to the President and Executive Directors of the Bank who determine upon any response. Unlike either non-compliance or dispute resolution processes as such, the objective is not to reach an amicable solution between the requesters and the Bank, but rather a decision by the Board based upon informed, impartial recommendations. This decision might not conform with government aims (for example a decision not to continue financing the project), or might fail to satisfy the requesters and indeed might generate further disputes. In this sense the process is perhaps more akin to an institutional grievance procedure requiring only conformity with Bank policies, and not any re-evaluation of the project.

The bestowal of standing to commence the process upon non-State actors moves away from the traditional state orientation of international dispute resolution by broadening beneficiary participation. It acknowledges that the traditional legal and procedural exclusion of non-State actors from international dispute resolution processes disregards the reality that international decision-making impacts upon peoples' lives,[90] a position the ICJ, for example, has been reluctant to take.[91] It also directly recognises the role of financial institutions as international actors.

However there are limitations to the potential empowerment accorded by the right to request inspection. Single individuals cannot request inspection, but must be part of a community or organisation. Doubts also remain both about the ability of local groups to access the procedures and the receptiveness of the Bank to requests for inspection. Local people may be unaware of the existence and powers of the inspection panels. Even with such knowledge, they may remain unable to access information about the relevant Bank's policies and practices and the potential effects of the project, especially where there are language barriers and the government impedes the flow of information. One response is to facilitate requests from representatives, including non-local representatives, who may have greater resources. The World Bank's reason for limiting non-local representation is a reminder that non-State actors remain outside the project design and management process. The Bank seeks "to prevent

---

[90] *Cf.* "Bank funded projects have an impact upon peoples" lives that is characterised by universal upheaval and yet is uniquely experienced: Oxfam, n. 88 above, at 15.

[91] C. Chinkin, "Increasing the Use and Appeal of the Court", in C. Peck and R. Lee (eds.), n. 39 above, at 43.

well-funded western NGOs from taking up cases and politicising what some borrower governments view as domestic issues".[92] Even if such representation were more readily accorded there is need for some caution. Genuine expression of local people's views cannot be lightly assumed, and care must be taken to ensure that such representation fully encompasses local opinion, including dissenting voices. Procedural rights of the requesters once the process has commenced are poorly defined. Without, for example, the right to be heard or to have access to full documentation, the Inspection Panels may appear to offer more to affected communities than is in fact the case.

Only the World Bank Inspection Panel has to date generated a significant case-load, and by 1997 only one request had resulted in an investigation taking place, although there are others pending. After receiving the Panel's recommendations based on its investigation of the Arun III Hydroelectric project in Nepal,[93] the Board of the World Bank withdrew from the project. In other cases, the Panel has determined requests to be inadmissible or the Board has determined that other internal procedures rendered inspection untimely or otherwise inappropriate. This record has led NGOs to question the World Bank's commitment to the expressed objectives of the process,[94] but a review in 1997 has not recommended substantial change. By 1997 inspection panels had not realised their potential for opening up international institutional policy-making to beneficiary scrutiny, but the model of open access remains the greatest possibility for non-State actors to express their concerns about the impact of international decision-making upon their lives.

4. GOOD OFFICES OF THE SECRETARY-GENERAL

The third example is the institutional relationship between the peaceful settlement of disputes and other actions for the maintenance of international peace and security as exemplified in the mediatory good offices function developed by successive Secretaries-General. Although this role is not explicitly prescribed in the UN Charter,[95] its exercise is pursuant to both the peaceful settlement of disputes under Chapter Six, described in An Agenda for Peace as coming within the concept of peacemaking,[96] and Security Council powers exercised under Chapter Seven, that is peace-keeping.[97] Peace making techniques are also

[92] Oxfam, n. 88 above, at 18.

[93] The Inspection Panel Report , n. 85 above, at 14–18.

[94] Oxfam, n. 88 above.

[95] UN Charter, Art. 98 requires the Secretary-General "to perform such other functions as are entrusted to him" by the organs of the Organization and Art. 99 allows him to "bring to the attention of the Security Council any matter which in his opinion may threaten the maintenance of international peace and security".

[96] Peacemaking constitutes attempts to bring disputing parties to agreement through processes contained in Ch. 6, including Art. 33: *An Agenda for Peace*; *Supplement to An Agenda for Peace*, n. 29 above.

[97] Peace-keeping involves the deployment of UN military, police and civilian personnel in the troubled area, traditionally with the consent of all parties (*ibid.*).

138 *Christine Chinkin*

engaged in both preventive diplomacy and peace-building after conflict. Dispute resolution may therefore be attempted alongside and simultaneously with other more coercive operations, directed at other ends.

Tom Franck has argued that when the Secretary-General extends his good offices to disputing parties he deploys the authority of the international community as a whole.[98] This constructed dispute resolution role is therefore integral to the prospects of the UN itself in fulfilling effectively the requirements of peacemaking and peace-keeping in both international and internal disputes that present a threat to international peace and security.[99]

In this context too there are both institutional and process dilemmas. Entwining peacemaking with peace-keeping locates private processes for dispute resolution within the structures for global public ordering. To enhance its potential effectiveness, the exercise of good offices must appear to the parties to be fair: the concept of a mediated agreement rests upon assumptions of neutrality and impartiality between the third party facilitator and the disputants. These qualities require the Secretary-General to distance himself to some extent from the expressed policies of the UN, while working within the purposes and principles of the Charter. This position may become problematic where, for example, the behaviour of one party to the dispute has been condemned by the Security Council, where the Security Council has issued an ultimatum, or has directed that certain actions are required,[100] a situation that is occurring more frequently with the freeing up of the Security Council at the end of the cold war.[101] Franck also points to what he describes as the trend of the Security Council to limit the Secretary-General to delivering its directives to the parties. Such Security Council directives are politically inspired and are generally motivated at addressing the immediate threat to international peace and security. The responses determined upon by the Security Council may leave the Secretary-General with little room to manoeuvre as a third party facilitator, while restricting his role to that of messenger undermines his own position. However deployment of the Secretary-General's good offices might secure a mediated outcome which could better achieve long-term resolution of the issues in dispute and thus better conform with international community objectives than the preferred responses of the Security Council.

The Secretary-General may face further thorny questions: with whom should he conduct his good offices? Who are the participants in the dispute whose pres-

[98] T. Franck, "The Secretary-General's Role in Conflict Resolution: Past, Present and Pure Conjecture", 6 *EJIL* 360; for a fuller account of the successful and unsuccessful exercise of good offices see T. Franck, n. 41 above, at 173–217.

[99] Franck, n. 41 above, at 174.

[100] Franck gives the example of the tension between the authorisation given to the Secretary-General to use his good offices in Iraq after the invasion of Kuwait in Aug. 1990 and the demands made upon Iraq in SC Res. 660, 2 Aug. 1990; SC Res. 661, 6 Aug. 1990.

[101] Higgins notes that it is more usual for the Security Council to devise the proposals, and adds that "the tendency for initiatives to flow from the Security Council rather than, even informally, the Secretariat has become more pronounced since the improvement of East-West relations": Higgins, n. 25 above, at 171.

ence is indispensable to an effective process with a realistic prospect of a satis-factory outcome? This question is especially crucial when key players have not received international (UN) recognition. How much institutional support should be provided to the Secretary-General in securing, or performing, an agreement and how does this impinge upon his neutrality? Can the Secretary-General guarantee an outcome, or must he rely upon subsequent Security Council endorsement? If he is unable to offer his own assurances as to the via-bility of an agreement, the momentum of the process may be lost, but otherwise he may be embarrassed by subsequent lack of political support or by member states' failure to allocate sufficient resources to assure the outcome. Such an eventuality in turn will undermine his credibility, and that of the UN.

5. CONCLUSIONS

Since the commencement of the twentieth century, the international community has evolved a range of tools for dispute settlement that it has continuously adapted, modified and refashioned to meet the demands of new objectives, including those of inducing compliance with treaty regimes and enhancing insti-tutional transparency. These measures have become ever more technically demanding, complex, diversified and streamlined.[102] Inevitably their formula-tion and use (and projected use) have simultaneously both highlighted problems within institutional structures and contributed to the emergence of an inter-national institutional law. Non-compliance procedures, dispute-resolution processes (both negotiatory and adjudicatory) and peace-keeping measures do not take place sequentially across a continuum but may be attempted separately or simultaneously with respect to a range of different State behaviours. They may merge imperceptibly into one another. Their objectives may coincide or conflict, especially where such objectives are ambiguous, ill-defined and subject to change as the situation unfolds. Since institutional objectives will not neces-sarily coincide with those of the disputants, they may involve degrees of institu-tional coercion, even while formally identified as consensual. In addition, the private nature of such processes may disguise lack of conformity with inter-national community interests.

The vitality of international lawyers in designing innovative dispute resolution processes may also obscure real substantive conflict that continues even while the procedures are identified and agreed. It is often easier to reach consensus over the inclusion of a dispute resolution or non-compliance provi-sion in a treaty than it is to resolve the substantive issues involved. This strategy creates the illusion that something is being done to make compliance with their international obligations a high priority for States. Further, since treaty-making remains a State privilege and participation in inter-governmental institutions is

---

[102] The adjectives are Koskenniemi's. See n. 27 above, at 2.

140 *Christine Chinkin*

controlled by States, non-State interests are readily excluded or discounted. Where they are exceptionally recognised, as in the power of beneficiaries to request inspection of World Bank-financed projects, the procedures may hold out greater promise for involvement than in fact occurs. As has been the case since at least the Hague Peace Conferences nearly a century ago, the focus must be upon enhancing the political will of States to use the tools they have developed to resolve real differences between disputants, not merely to design elaborate models for their consideration. This problem is not confined to the international legal order but is prevalent within domestic systems where ADR remains more celebrated than engaged. While there are contradictory directions, what is evident is a vibrancy and innovation within the international legal system the structural, procedural and substantive consequences of which cannot yet be fully envisaged.

Name Index